SO-AJI-285

Alfred Glossbrenner's
Master Guide to Free Software for IBMs
and Compatible Computers

Praise for Alfred Glossbrenner's other books, *How to Look It Up Online* . . .

"There's a slippery ocean of online information services out there. We recommend that you hire Sir Alfred, the wisest old salt sailing on the sea of information . . . He is uncommonly trustworthy."
—*San Francisco Chronicle*

"Glossbrenner's knowledge of the online universe appears to be encyclopedic, and he presents it in enjoyable, lucid prose."
—*PC World*

"Essential to any computer owner with a modem and a business."
—New York *Newsday*

"Indispensable for ferreting out online information."
—*Byte*

"An essential guide for anyone who wants to know where and how to get information from computer databases."
—*The New York Times*

"Great reading from cover to cover."
—*Computer Book Review*

"An incredible compendium . . . I'll guarantee you'll make the book's price back during your first month of dial-up service."
—*Trenton Times*

. . . and
The Complete Handbook of Personal Computer Communications, Completely Revised and Updated

"For intelligence and thoroughness, no one else comes close."
—*The Whole Earth Software Review*

"Invaluable—and how! Highly recommended."
—*Peter A. McWilliams*

"The first truly complete book on 'connecting your computer to the world.'"

—*Esquire*

"Essential . . ."

—*Forbes*

"Definitely required reading . . ."
—*Microcomputing*

"If you're interested in computer communications, this book belongs on your shelf."
—*PC Magazine*

"Still considered by many insiders to be the best."
—UPI

"Excellent . . ."

—*Dallas Morning News*

"Definitive! This 546-page 'bible' is obviously done by a workaholic. It's worth every cent."
—John Dvorak, *InfoWorld*

"One of the best and most complete sources of information. There have probably been more words written about this book than any other serious book in the personal computer field."
—*Personal Computing*

"If any book can be described as 'the bible' on telecomputing, this is it."

—*Link-Up*

Alfred Glossbrenner's
MASTER GUIDE
to Free Software for IBMs and Compatible Computers

**ALFRED
GLOSSBRENNER**

A
Glossbrenner
Guide

St. Martin's Press   New York

ALFRED GLOSSBRENNER'S MASTER GUIDE TO FREE SOFTWARE FOR IBMS AND COMPATIBLE COMPUTERS.

Copyright © 1989 by Alfred Glossbrenner.

All rights reserved. Printed in the United States of America. No part of this book may be used or reproduced in any manner whatsoever without written permission except in the case of brief quotations embodied in critical articles or reviews. For information, address St. Martin's Press, 175 Fifth Avenue, New York, N.Y. 10010.

Library of Congress Cataloging-in-Publication Data

Glossbrenner, Alfred.
  Alfred Glossbrenner's master guide to free software for IBMs and compatible computers.
    Includes index.
    1. Free computer software. 2. IBM Personal
Computer—Programming. I. Title.
QA76.754.G536 1988   005.36′5   88–11474
ISBN 0–312–02157–7

First Edition

10 9 8 7 6 5 4 3 2 1

The author has made every effort to check information such as shipping charges, addresses, telephone numbers, and availability of updated products, but cautions the reader that these are subject to change. Readers should verify costs and product descriptions with sources before ordering.

Contents

Part III: What to Get

PART I

FREE SOFTWARE
BASICS

1

Getting Down to Business

THE INCREDIBLE SHAREWARE/
PUBLIC DOMAIN PHENOMENON

This book can save you $1000—minimum. And we're not talking about the special online system subscription discounts we've arranged, either. We are talking about top-quality, well-supported, thoroughly documented productivity programs of the sort you would pay hundreds of dollars for at your local computer retailer's. Software for word processing, information retrieval, mailing lists, and mailing labels. Software to let an inexpensive dot-matrix printer produce near *laser* quality output, as well as utility programs that will save you hundreds of hours, thousands of keystrokes, and untold moments of frustration simply by making your PC easier to use. Software, in short, for every conceivable computer-related need, whether you use a PC at work, at home, at college, or to run your own small business.

There are literally tens of thousands of programs to choose from. Most, like the works of Shakespeare or Melville, are in the public domain (PD) and can be used free of charge. Many are what has come to be called "shareware." These are full-powered, copyrighted programs, complete with on-disk manuals and documentation, that can be passed around and shared with others. If you like a shareware program and use it regularly, you are asked to send its author the registration fee he or she requests. Shareware is software on the honor system, but a clear conscience isn't the only incentive to register. The fees are modest, and many shareware authors provide professionally printed and bound manuals, free updates, site licenses, quantity discounts, and telephone support to those who register.

3

How to Save Over $1000

Now, about that thousand dollars. Let's consider just the Big Four personal computer applications—word processing, database management, electronic spreadsheets, and telecommunications. Here is what you could expect to pay at retail for each of these applications and the registration fee for comparable shareware programs:

COMMERCIAL PROGRAMS VERSUS SHAREWARE EQUIVALENTS

Commercial Applications Program	Typical List Price	Equivalent Shareware Program	Requested Registration Fee
Word Processing	$ 495	PC-Write	$ 89
Database Management	$ 250	File Express	$ 70
Spreadsheets	$ 495	As-Easy-As	$ 30
Communications	$ 200	ProComm 2.4.2	$ 50
	Total $1440		Total $239

TOTAL SAVINGS: $1201

Of course, there *are* less expensive ways to obtain commercial software. You can order programs through the mail and receive a substantial discount off the prices we've shown, but you won't receive any support. In theory, when you pay the full list price for a program from a dealer, part of what you're paying for is the privilege of calling on the dealer for help and possibly for a minimal amount of instruction in how to use the product. Unfortunately, you may find that many dealers do not fully discharge their obligations in this area.

We should also acknowledge that there are many commercial programs in the Big Four categories with list prices that are far less than those shown here. But we did not choose these particular prices to boost the total. We chose them on the basis of what you would have to pay for a program offering a certain level of capability and a particular array of features. True-blue IBMers should forgive the expression, but we made every effort to compare apples to apples. And where there was a choice, we selected the highest shareware price. For example, you can register and receive a manual for PC-Write, but no telephone support or other benefits, for as little as $35. If you don't want a printed copy of the ProComm 2.4.2 manual, you can register that program for $25. So your savings *could* be $79 more than what we have shown.

Comparable Quality

As for comparable quality, we would match these four shareware programs against anything else on the market. (We have done just that in Chapters 12 and 14 through 16.) In addition, shareware programs have the extra advantage of allowing you to "try before you buy," an offer few retailers or mail-order sources are ever likely to make. Some, such as PC-Write, even give everyone who registers a 90-day, money-back guarantee.

Our point here—indeed the main point of the entire book—is simply this: *You do not have to pay prices like these to get the software you need.* Whether you want to optimize and quickly back up your hard disk, print your spreadsheet sideways, produce stunning business graphics, *un-erase* deleted files, or do anything else your computer is capable of, commercial-quality programs in virtually every category are available for less—much, much less—once you know where to look and which programs to get. In fact, many of the most useful programs you will ever encounter are available for free.

Of course, you *will* have to pay for the disks that contain these programs, and the last time we checked, the U.S. Postal Service was still charging to deliver mail. For their part, CompuServe, GEnie, and other commercial online systems still charge for the connect time required to transmit a program to you over the phone. But these are distribution costs and have nothing to do with the software itself. After all, it costs the same to mail a blank floppy disk as it does to mail one filled with public domain or shareware programs. Fortunately, these costs are minimal, usually no more than about $6 a disk.

Definition of Terms

In the interests of simplicity, we're going to refer to the entire field as "free software," with the understanding that it contains both public domain programs, which you can alter, modify, and use without obligation and copyrighted shareware programs, for which you are expected to pay if you like and use the product. If you supply the disk, there *are* ways to obtain copies of public domain and shareware programs free of charge, but in most cases, you'll probably have to pay a small fee to cover the cost of distribution.

The IBM Shareware Phenomenon
Are These Guys Crazy or What?

Having sketched the territory and defined our terms, we're ready to get down to the real nitty-gritty. Namely, how in the world is it possible for anything of value to be available for free or for a modest registration fee? Are the people who are writing these programs crazy? Or is it just possible that the stuff simply isn't any good? The answer is a categorical "No" on both counts, but it requires a bit of explanation.

Fundamentally, the answer lies in the unique nature of computer software—any computer software—regardless of how it is marketed. In the first place, a computer program is a creative work, every bit as much as the books you read or the movies you watch on your VCR. The cost of the ink and paper or the magnetic tape and plastic cassette are important, but they have almost no bearing on the product's worth or its price. As *Business Week* (10 August 1987) put it:

> Like perfume—and unlike hardware—software prices have relied more on the perceived value of programs than on production costs. This started with mainframe and minicomputer software and continued when the first popular business program, VisiCalc, appeared in 1979. VisiCalc's authors felt around for the right price, trying $99 before settling on $250. . . . Now the top companies are using more scientific approaches to pricing. Lotus spends about $1 million a year on studies by market researchers, who try to figure out what customers will pay. . . . While the actual cost of the materials that go into a program, including several disks, a manual, and packaging, generally comes in at under $15, marketing and R&D can eat up 30% of revenues. Moreover, software companies might spend up to $20 per program on a toll-free customer service line for advice. Still, the bottom line is that with enough volume, programs selling at $400 to $700 can bring pretax margins of 20% to 40%.

Nothing Magic about Commercial Software

When you strip away the expensive office space, the marketing staff expense accounts, and the $20,000 +, four-color, full-page ads in leading computer magazines, personal computer software almost always comes down to one thing: a single individual sitting alone in front of a computer screen, laboring to turn his or her ideas into a useful product.

Nothing else can happen until the program is written. The results may be awkward and ill-conceived, or they may be elegant and thoughtfully designed. Either way, the penumbra of marketers, packaging consultants, market researchers, distributors, and retailers that surrounds a commercial program has little to do with the quality of the product. There is nothing magic about commercially sold software. You can just as easily pay top dollar for a program that turns out to be a real stinker as you can for one that will perform as advertised. Nor is purchasing a commercial product any guarantee that the company supplying it will still be around when you need its services. Commercial software publishers go out of business all the time.

The Means of Production and Reproduction

The second factor that makes computer software unique is that the means of producing it are both cheap and widely available. At this writing, a fully equipped IBM PC/XT-compatible computer with a monitor sells through the mail for about $500. Add another $250 for a printer, and a bit more for computer language programs and supplies, and for less than $1000, you can possess everything you need to write the next Lotus 1-2-3 or dBASE III. In some industries, that wouldn't buy a single drill bit or grinding wheel, let alone a complete production shop.

But with computer hardware prices so low, virtually anyone can write a program that tens of millions of IBM and compatible owners can use. The fact that the programmer—like many a novelist, artist, musician, or actor—holds down a daytime job in some other field is irrelevant. We're talking about talent. And commercial software houses have no monopoly on that.

Finally, computer software can be quickly, easily, and inexpensively reproduced. A software author doesn't need printing presses and carloads of paper or hundreds of VCRs and cartons of blank cassettes to reproduce and publish his or her work. All that's required is a magnetic disk. The same machine used to create the product can reproduce it an infinite number of times.

Distribution Alternatives

Distribution is another matter. Indeed it is the key element in the free software equation, for along with advertising, it's the only thing that costs any real money. The world's most talented programmer may be able to set up shop for less than a thousand dollars, and the costs of publishing his work may be insignificant, but if he hath not distribution, his program will be as so many tiny eight-bit symbols. Signifying, if not nothing, at least no reward for his labor.

What to do? Well, put yourself in the programmer's running shoes. Here you've got a great idea for a program, you've got the talent to execute it, and you've got the personal computer. Working nights and weekends, you'll eventually have a finished program. Now what? What are your options?

One alternative would be to form your own software company to market the product commercially. But these days it takes a million dollars or more just to get into the game. Unless you've got that kind of money lying around someplace, you're going to have to raise it from venture capitalists, banks, relatives, and friends. That's going to take a lot of time and energy, and may mean remortgaging your house and putting all of your assets at risk. And what's your family going to live on before you hit it big—if you hit it big?

Perhaps you could sell rights to the program to a commercial company instead? Many a freelance programmer has followed that route and had a lot of success. But it usually means settling for a royalty of five to ten percent on sales and surrendering all control over the product. In addition, you've got to find the right company, sell them on the idea, and hope they really can give you the distribution you need. More time. More energy. More effort put against activities you'd really rather not have to deal with. Besides, you've got your daytime job to think of.

The Shareware Option

As you can see, there's a lot more to selling a program than most people think. It is not simply a matter of building a better mousetrap, particularly not today with so many programs on the market. Whichever path you choose there will be risks and rewards, the one in inverse proportion to the other. It is for this reason that many programmers have chosen the shareware alternative. Not because they're crazy, or because their work can't hold its own against commercially sold software, but because they find the risks and rewards of shareware marketing and distribution not only acceptable but eminently appealing.

By not following the commercial route, shareware authors probably give up the opportunity to have a mega-hit, like Lotus or dBASE, that will earn them tens of millions of dollars. But a programmer can do quite well asking, say, $30 for his package. Surprisingly, perhaps, that figure is very close to the gross profit some commercial companies earn on their products.

For example, writing in *InfoWorld* (14 July 1986), W. E. Peterson of Wordperfect Corporation points out that although his company's program lists for $495,

> we receive only $173 for each copy sold to a U.S. distributor. That reflects a fairly standard discount. . . . Typically, the price to the dealer on a $495 product is somewhere between $195 and $295. . . . From the $173 we receive from the distributor, we have set a profit target of 20 percent, but we let the margin creep up toward the 25 percent level. For the first nine months of 1985, the gross profit for Wordperfect was $44 per package. Nearly half went to the U.S. government; the rest was spent on capital expenditures and added to working capital. Fortunately, our shareholders leave all of the after-tax profits in the company, so we can grow without going to the bank.

Shareware Economics

Of course, the $30 or so that you send a shareware author does not represent gross profit either. The printed manuals many authors provide must be paid for, and time (and thus money) must be spent supporting and improving the product. The most successful shareware authors also issue press releases, attend computer fairs, and publish newsletters for their registered users. But promotional expenses like these are tiny compared to an advertising schedule in a major computer magazine.

Thus, with a very good program and a firm commitment to providing user support and improving the product, someone with programming talent can do nearly as well as a shareware author as he could starting a commercial company, and much better than standard royalty agreements allow. The risks are minimal. There is no need to take a second on your house or to put all your assets on the line. There is no need to quit your daytime job, at least not until you see how things go. If things don't work out, all you really have to lose is the time you have spent writing and perfecting the program.

And if you're successful? If you're successful, you can find yourself in charge of your own small company. Jim Button, one of the original shareware authors, had sales of over $2 million in 1987. Bob Wallace, author of PC-Write, started in 1983 with sales of $17,000 for the final six months of the year. By 1986, his firm had grown to 21 employees and sales topped $1.5 million. Datastorm Technologies, Inc., the firm formed by Bruce Barkelew and Tom Smith to market their communications program, ProComm, had sales of $335,000 in 1986. By the end of 1987, the firm had more than a dozen employees, and sales had more than quintupled to $1.75 million. While these are among the most dramatic examples of shareware success, there are many, many more. Clearly, someone must be doing something right. The software must be very, very good to elicit that kind of *voluntary* response on the part of those who use the programs. After all, they've already got the product.

Shareware Channels of Distribution

All of this sounds great, but it still doesn't address the problem of distribution. Let's assume that you've got a super program, are willing to make a commitment to it, and are willing to give it away in hopes that most users will register. How can you make people aware of it? How can you get it into the hands of those who might be willing to send you the requested fee? Remember, you don't have any money to spend on advertising, and you don't have a distribution deal with a major firm.

The answer is, you tap into what we can call the "community of users." You use the channels that were established long ago by personal computing hobbyists and enthusiasts for the distribution of public domain software. What is called shareware today owes its existence to the networks, traditions, and procedures created to make free, public domain software available to anyone who wanted it. Free distribution is the key, and shareware couldn't survive without it.

Over the years, four major distribution channels have emerged. These are (1) computer user groups and clubs, (2) non-user-group mail-order sources, (3) commercial online systems, and (4) free public bulletin boards. We're going to be telling you a lot more about each of these sources in Part II of this book. Indeed, we're going to give you all the tools and techniques you need to become a *free software expert*, capable of finding any shareware or PD program for any purpose you may have in mind, with very little effort and almost no expense. But you can't operate comfortably in this environment without some idea of how it came to be, for its origins profoundly affect everything you will encounter today.

In the Beginning . . .
Computer User Groups and Clubs

Everything started with the computer clubs and user groups that themselves were the wellspring of the personal computer revolution. Like the ham radio and electronics clubs on which they were modeled, computer user groups were formed as mutual aid societies that could serve as centers for information exchange. They still fill that role today, though in the IBM world at least, you are just as likely to run into a businessman in a three-piece suit as a Pepsi-swigging hobbyist in sweatshirt and jeans.

From the beginning, these groups have had libraries of public domain programs. The programs were written by group members for fun, or to solve a particular problem, or merely as ego-gratifying tours de force. Since programs of any kind were scarce in the early days, one group would often exchange its library with another. These group-to-group relationships still exist today, and taken as a whole they form a free software network that girds the country and even circles the globe. In virtually every case, user groups make their libraries available for copying at monthly meetings, and many fill members' software orders through the mail.

BBSs, Commercial Systems, and Mail Order

As you might expect, given the ham radio and electronics background of many early members, telecommunications was always a prime interest. So it was perfectly logical for a few venturesome souls to begin exploring the possibilities of hooking a computer up to a telephone. Thanks to some crucial public domain programs, it turned out that it was possible to transmit not only messages between two personal computers but computer programs as well. This led to the formation of another channel of distribution, the free public bulletin board system (BBS). Before long, BBSs were augmented by commercial dial-up systems like the CompuServe Information Service (CIS) and The Source. One person would upload (transmit) a program for storage on these systems and others would sign on to download (receive) it.

Gradually, as the libraries of PD software grew, a third channel of distribution came into being. These were the mail-order companies, firms that in return for a small distribution fee, would send you floppy disks containing the public domain software that you wanted. In some cases, you didn't even have to buy the disks but could rent an entire library and make your own copies. For those who didn't have time to go to a user group meeting or didn't belong to a user group, mail-order PD software was an attractive alternative.

The Autumn Revolution

All of these elements were in place before the first IBM PC rolled off the assembly line and into the Boca sunshine in the fall of 1981. (Boca Raton, Florida, was the original site of IBM's Entry Systems Division, creators of the PC.) Unlike the Apple II, the PC was not a product of the user-group movement. But as hobbyists switched from the Apple II, the TRS-80 Mod I and III, and a raft of machines using the CP/M operating system, IBM PC user groups were not long in forming. Nor did it take long for a sizable quantity of PD software to develop as people enthusiastically explored the increased power offered by the new machine. Much of the early free software was "ported" to the PC from CP/M machines. ("Port" is computer talk for "translate"; it is short for "transport" and is used as both a noun and a verb.)

Public domain software is still being written for the PC. In fact, on a byte-for-byte basis, by far the majority of freely available software for IBMs and compatibles is in the public domain. As we'll see in Part III of this book, there are some PD gems that no PC user should be without. But since *How to Get FREE Software*, our first book on the subject, was written in 1983, the focus has markedly shifted. In the past, one turned to the public domain for things like games, graphics, and short, incredibly useful utility programs that simply weren't available through commercial channels. One did not normally expect to find major applications programs, though we devoted a chapter in the previous book to those few then available. It was clear at the time that shareware was a remarkable phenomenon, but few could have foreseen the role it would eventually play.

Fluegelman, Button, and Wallace: Making the Revolution
Andrew Fluegelman: PC-Talk

There have been a lot of revolutions in the PC world. The one that kicked off shareware began in March 1982, when the late Andrew Fluegelman introduced PC-Talk. Mr. Fluegelman was a practicing attorney in San Francisco when Stewart Brand asked him to edit the *Whole Earth Catalogue* in the 1960s. He edited several issues, and then formed his own book-packaging company, The Headlands Press. When he disappeared in July 1985, at the age of 41, he was editorial director of *PC World* and *MacWorld* magazines.

"I got my PC within about the first month after the machine was released," Mr. Fluegelman told us in 1983. "At the time I was working on a book with a coauthor who had a NorthStar system (CP/M), and we had this vision that we'd be able to swap files—the great promise of computer communications, you know."

Unfortunately, Mr. Fluegelman discovered that there was no communications program available at the time that would allow a PC to transfer files to a non-IBM system. He spent an evening trying to modify the programs that were available, but after looking at the code, decided that this was not the right way to go.

The next morning, I started writing a program for myself. Originally it was just for me, but once I saw that it was working, some of my friends used it and liked it and suggested that I should do something publicly with it. I think if I hadn't been in publishing for the last eight years, I would have gone ahead and taken the traditional publishing route, with advertising and marketing, and so forth.

But somehow I was either very tired of all that or very inspired by the computer vista. The local PBS station was having one of its pledge drives, and suddenly, in one of those flashes, the word "freeware" just popped into my mind. Along with the notion of sending programs out for free and encouraging people to copy them and requesting them to make donations if they liked the program. It really all kind of gelled, and from that point on it was just too unusual an idea not to pursue.

A week after posting a notice of the program's availability on The Source, Mr. Fluegelman received his first order. "I just couldn't believe it. I was making contact with a world out there that I'd only imagined existed. And very quickly I had to get a bigger post office box and hire people and replace three disk drives. The thing really mushroomed."

Jim Button: PC-File

At about the same time, "Jim Button," the nom-de-software of a former IBM employee in Bellevue, Washington, needed a program to print mailing labels for a local church congregation. He wrote the program in Applesoft BASIC but it soon evolved into a general purpose database program. "I liked what I had produced so much that the program itself became a hobby," Mr. Button says. "Something that I continued to work on and improve in my spare time."

The day after the IBM PC appeared, Mr. Button sold his Apple and bought one of the new machines. A few days later, he had successfully ported his database program to the IBM. His fellow IBMers were getting PCs as well.

I was anxious to get my comrades off to a good start. So I shared my database program with many of them. Out of a simple desire to freely share a good thing with others, PC-File was born. It didn't have a name yet (I called it "Easy File"), but it soon became a hit at the Seattle branch and throughout the Seattle area, as enthusiastic users of the free program shared copies with friends and associates.

But problems soon developed. It became increasingly expensive and time-consuming to notify the users when fixes or improvements became available. How could I identify which of the users were serious users— those who desired and required enhancements? How could I afford to send mailings to notify them of the availability of improvements?

Mr. Button decided to place a message in the program asking those who received it to voluntarily send a modest donation to help defray his costs.

The message encouraged users to continue to use and share the program with others, and to send a $10 donation only if they wanted to be included in my mailing list. The first person to receive the program with its unusual request telephoned me almost immediately. He had also received a copy of PC-Talk, a program with a similiar message.

The two original shareware programmers got together and decided to jointly refer to each other in their distribution disks. Mr. Button decided to name his program PC-File, to complement PC-Talk. Both agreed to request a voluntary payment of $25.

In May 1983, PC-File got a rave review in *PC-World* magazine.

> My family and I were vacationing in Hawaii when the magazine hit the newsstands. The response was overwhelming. Our house sitter had to cart the mail home daily in grocery sacks. When we arrived home, the grocery sacks were strewn all over the basement floor. Needless to say, life has never been the same since.

Eventually, Mr. Button left IBM, though not voluntarily. "My body forced me out," he says. "I could no longer work eight hours each day with IBM, and then come home to another four hours of work each evening. Saturday and much of Sunday were also consumed by my second job."

Today, ButtonWare, Inc. is the largest shareware company in the world, with some 18 employees, ten programs in its product line, retail distribution, and annual sales of more than $2 million.

Bob Wallace: PC-Write

Three months after the *PC-World* review of Jim Button's program appeared, Bob Wallace introduced the first version of PC-Write, and with it, the term "commission shareware." (The term "shareware" was coined by Jay Lucas and was the name of his *InfoWorld* column in the early 1980s.) To encourage people to copy and share PC-Write, Mr. Wallace's firm (Quicksoft, Inc.) pays registered users a commission when someone else registers from one of their copies. The program displays the registration number assigned to the user on the first screen. When a new user registers for the full $89 with Quicksoft, the company asks for the number shown on his or her copy. The firm then sends the owner of that number a $25 commission (unless the owner has requested not to receive commissions). New users are issued their own unique numbers when they register. According to Mr. Wallace, in 1986 the firm paid out an average of $20,000 per quarter in shareware commissions.

In 1983, Mr. Wallace told *InfoWorld* that he planned to continue his commission shareware experiment for six months and then assess its success as a marketing concept. "If I make enough money to live on," he said, "I will continue the experiment; if not, I will approach software publishers to see if they are interested in marketing a PC-Write II version of the program for me commercially."

It is difficult to determine how much of PC-Write's success is due to the commission shareware approach and how much is attributable to the fact that it is such a super program. As one of Microsoft's original ten employees and as the architect of Microsoft Pascal, Mr. Wallace could certainly have expected to garner some press attention when he introduced his own word processor. But there can be no doubt that this was magnified by his unique commission shareware concept. Quicksoft got off to a great start, and in 1986 it became one of the top 100 microcomputer software companies in the country. PC-Write is now available in at least ten foreign languages (even Icelandic!).

The Terms We Use Today

In the years since these three pioneers made the revolution, shareware has become an established marketing alternative and has increasingly been recognized as such by computer users. Trade press headlines on the subject include "Freeware Gains Respect with Corporate Users." (*InfoWorld*, 2 September 1985), "Corporate Users Back Shareware" (*InfoWorld*, 10 August 1987), and "Shareware Finds a Niche in Large Corporations" (*PC-Week*, 8 February 1988). To these could be added innumerable articles on the subject in *Personal Computing, PC, Lotus,* and other general-interest computer magazines. Even the national press has carried articles on free software, though as with most computer-related topics, they usually manage to get the details wrong.

As this marketing method has evolved, however, there has been considerable confusion over terms, and since you are sure to encounter "freeware," "shareware," and "user-supported software," as well as "public domain" and "PD" in your free software forays, it is worth spending a moment to straighten it all out. Public domain or PD software is software that is either of undetermined origin (because it isn't signed and there is no way of telling who wrote it) or software that has been placed in the public domain by its author. PD programs in this category usually carry a notice prepared by their authors attesting to their public domain status.

Freeware is a term that can legally be applied to only one program, PC-Talk. This is because Mr. Fluegelman, for reasons we have never understood, made that term a trademark of his firm, The Headlands Press. This created considerable difficulty for programmers like Jim Button and others who were using the "contribution requested" technique. As a substitute, the term "user supported" was coined and applied to all non-Freeware freeware. But that term was less than catchy and wasn't very descriptive in any case.

Shareware originally referred to programs that offered registered users the chance to earn commissions, as described earlier. However, Mr. Wallace told us he made a conscious decision not to trademark the term. As a result, shareware is the term that everyone applies these days to any program you are expected, requested, or required to pay for if you like and use the product, whether or not commissions are involved, and whether or not the author asks for an unspecified "donation" or "contribution" or a set registration fee.

Shareware and PD Software: From the User's Perspective
For Small Businesses

So far we've looked at free software primarily from the programmer's perspective. But what's in it for you, the software user? First and foremost, there is the opportunity to buy high-quality software at a very low price, or for nothing more than the cost of a floppy disk and postage or several minutes of online connect time. If you're a small businessperson (with sales of, say, $5 million a year or less), this means you can computerize your inventory and billing, automate your accounting, handle your mailing lists, and generally get in on the benefits offered by personal computers for very little money.

According to the *Wall Street Journal* (12 March 1987), for example, only 10 to 15 percent of a company's costs come from the price of the hardware needed to computerize an operation. Nearly 85 to 90 percent of the cost goes for software and training. You won't need all of the Big Four applications we've cited, at least not to start. But let's assume that you do. Total shareware cost: $239.

You're not going to need a PS/2, Macintosh, AT-clone, or laser printer, either. A "standard" XT business configuration of the sort described in Chapter 2 will offer more than enough power. At this writing, computer stores sell a complete system with a printer for between $1000 and $1200, and as the new PS/2s continue to come onstream, prices for XT-level machines are rapidly falling. In other words, your total hardware and software cost will come in at well below $1500.

It may be presumptuous of us to say so, but if you can boost productivity, offer better service, gain a better grip on your bottom line, and expand your business for an investment of less than $1500, how can you afford *not* to computerize? Do you really want to wait until competition forces you to either get into the game or get out of business?

For Large Corporations

One of the reasons commercial software prices are so high is that large corporations offer little resistance. The *Business Week* article cited earlier reports that when Computer Associates International, Inc., boosted the price of its SuperCalc spreadsheet from $395 to $495 to match the price of Lotus, company executives were surprised to find that their customers didn't even seem to notice the price change. Philippe Kahn of

Borland International, Inc., adds that for popular business programs "people just don't seem to care" about price.

The most charitable thing one can say about a large corporation that doesn't care about the price it's paying for thousands of copies of an applications program is that it simply doesn't know any better. Many companies need someone like Cheryl Currid, manager of departmental computer services at Coca-Cola Foods in Houston. Under Ms. Currid's direction, Coke has launched an aggressive program to harness shareware for its PC users.

When Ms. Currid and her staff locate an attractive program, they thoroughly test it and if it passes muster, they purchase a license from its author and distribute it throughout the company. The program's documentation is kept on file in the company's information centers. Is it worth it? According to Ms. Currid, a single free electronic mail program located by her group saved the company an estimated $300,000 in overnight mail and long-distance telephone charges. You may not want to fill Ms. Currid's role at your firm. But somebody should. And whoever does is likely to become a hero.

For Students and Parents

If you're a home user or a student, you know the frustration of having to pay top dollar for a program with more power and features than you want to deal with because there simply isn't any alternative. Even the four shareware programs cited earlier may offer more than you need, but at least you can try them before deciding to buy them. And if you do buy them, you won't feel that you're wasting hundreds of dollars on features you will never use. What's more, free software distribution channels contain many less powerful public domain programs in these categories that can be yours for the cost of a disk.

If you're a parent, you know that children can go through software faster than they go through shoes. At an average of $40 or more a program, keeping a home computer supplied with games, graphics, music, and educational software can be a real financial challenge. But the same amount of money can buy half a dozen disks full of public domain programs, and there are literally scores to choose from—everything from vocabulary builders to paint programs to very credible knockoffs of popular video arcade games.

Direct Contact with the Author

Shareware also offers something you will never find in the commercial software world—the opportunity for direct contact with the person who wrote the program. The first time we had a question about PC-Write,

we called Quicksoft and Bob Wallace himself answered the phone.
Marshall Magee, author of Automenu, one of the programs recommended in Chapter 9, reports that on numerous occasions users have
phoned his office well after East Coast business hours and have been
surprised to find him on the other end of the line. "There's always a ton
of work to do at the office," he says, "And I can't get any of my employees to work this late."

The larger shareware firms have full-time customer service representatives. "Good customer service is crucial," says Bob Wallace. "You
need someone who is both good technically and enjoys talking to people.
They're not easy to find, but it is worth the effort because the voice on
the other end of the phone *is* your company as far as many users are
concerned. That frees me to devote most of my time to programming,
which is what I really should be doing. But I'm almost always available
if the need arises."

There's more to this aspect of shareware than having your questions
answered by the man who wrote the program. Shareware authors prize
customer feedback. Most are keenly interested to know which features
you like and which new features and capabilities you would like to see in
future versions. Tom Smith, coauthor of ProComm, attributes much of
that program's amazing success to simply listening to his customers.
Consequently, when Smith and partner Bruce Barkelew sat down to
add improvements, they didn't have to guess what people would want—
they already knew.

Sometimes a shareware author will even add a feature to a program
to serve the needs of a single user. David Schulz, author of the Lotus-
compatible spreadsheet program As-Easy-As (Chapter 15), told us of
correspondence he had with a professor at a large midwestern university.

> The professor was thinking of using As-Easy-As to directly query his lab
> instruments. But to do that, he needed somehow to be able to import data
> from the PC's serial port. So I added in two macro commands for his use
> and testing.
>
> We decided to call them IOLABEL and IOVALUE. They allow you to
> send a command to the testing equipment and place the text string or
> numerical value it returns in any cell on the spreadsheet. I didn't docu-
> ment the feature because I had no way of testing it myself. But the pro-
> fessor reports that it works beautifully and it is in the program.

To which we can only add, imagine calling up Jonathan Sachs or Mitch
Kapor, the creators of Lotus 1-2-3, with a similar request.

The Free Software Problem
Who's Going to Tell You about It?

Since *How to Get FREE Software* was published in 1984, the number of computer users has grown by several millions and the availability of top-quality public domain and shareware programs has become increasingly well known. Yet at this point you may very well be asking, "If free software is so good, why haven't I heard of it before?"

The answer to that question lies in another question: Who's going to tell you about it? Certainly not your computer dealer. He makes most of his profit not on the hardware he sells you, but on the software you'll need to do productive work. Computer magazines carry occasional articles on the subject, but they'll do you no good if you never encounter such publications. Your only hope is to chance upon a piece in one of the general interest magazines, newspapers, or trade journals that you normally read, and unfortunately these rarely give you the right kind of information.

The point is that if you're like most of today's computer buyers you are simply out of the free software loop. You're not a hobbyist or a techno-whiz. You're a bright person who has decided to get a computer. So you visit the stores in your area, explain your needs to the salespeople, and do some comparison shopping. Eventually you find a deal and a store you like, and you buy the system and the commercial software packages you need. At no point in this process is there any natural way for you to hear about user groups, bulletin boards, and commercial online systems, or the vast libraries of PD and shareware programs that are waiting to save you hundreds of dollars, if only you knew of their existence.

Which Programs Should You Choose?

If you're an experienced computer user who is already aware of free software, you know how much there is to choose from and how difficult it can be to make a selection. In the commercial software business, the relative popularity of a product may or may not be a true indication of its worth. But it is certainly one of the factors that limits the number of programs appearing on your dealer's shelves. No dealer wants to tie his money up in inventory that isn't going to turn quickly, and wherever they have a choice, most dealers are inclined to stock those programs offering the highest profit margin.

In the free software world, these forces of natural selection do not exist. There is no investment in inventory, other than the cost of a magnetic disk. And there is no incentive for a user group or mail-order source to "stock" one shareware program and shun another. Since the software itself isn't being sold, there are no profit margins to compare, only a charge for distribution, and that is the same regardless of what is on a particular disk.

Consequently, PC-SIG, one of the leading mail order sources profiled in Chapter 4, has over 1000 disks containing more than 26,000 programs in its collection. The Public (software) Library, also profiled in Chapter 4, tends to be more selective, but under "Word Processing" in its catalog you will find no fewer than 38 disks containing word processing programs and text utilities. Here are just a few of these listings, shown exactly as they appear in the catalog:

1-WP-299　　Word Processing Programs #1—Dved, Eded, Fsed, RvEdit, SG3, Xed.

2-WP-510　　FREEWORD—powerful word processing program.

2-WP-624　　GALAXY 2.2— powerful, easy-to-use word processor; WordStar compatible.

2-WP-666　　NEW YORK WORD 2.2—powerful word processor, spelling chkr., key map.

2-WP-492　　PC-TYPE— powerful word processor. Spell check, mail merge.

2-WP-312　　PC-WRITE 2.7—word processing program with spelling checker.

2-WP-648　　WED 3.11—text editor for programmers.

Assume for the moment that these are the only word processing programs available. Which one would you choose? One can't fault the Public (software) Library for devoting only a single line to each disk in its catalog. Most user groups and mail-order sources do the same, because a catalog that adequately described the features of each program in the typical free software library would run to thousands of pages. Even if the libraries could afford to produce such a catalog without significantly raising their distribution fees, few people could afford to buy it.

A Free Software Consultant?

So what can you do? How can you ever hope to take advantage of all that free software has to offer?

One alternative would be to order all of the disks in a particular category and go through them one-by-one until you found an applications program that suited your needs. But printing and reading the documentation and testing each program can take an enormous amount of time. And if you're a relatively new computer user, you may not know what to look for. Besides, your time has value. If it's a question of spending 20 hours or more picking the right word processing program or spending $500 on a commercial package, you know which option you'll choose.

Of course, there is another alternative. You can hire someone to do this work for you or bring in a free software consultant. Better still, you can buy a book summarizing that person's recommendations. And that's what you have here.

How to Use This Book

The two crucial barriers that have always prevented most computer users from benefiting from free software are a lack of knowledge about *where* to get it and a lack of guidance on *what* to get. Over the years these two stumbling blocks have cost PC owners literally tens of thousands of dollars in potential savings. In this book, we hope to remedy that situation.

We begin in Chapter 2 with the background information you're going to need to immediately feel comfortable with the abbreviations and conventions of the field. We'll show you step-by-step "what to do when the disk arrives," including how to print the documentation and how to deal with "ARC" files. Logically enough, this is the place to begin, for the rest of the book generally assumes that you are familiar with this material.

Teach a Man to Fish . . .

Part II is designed to turn you into a free software expert. When you finish the chapters in this section, you will have all the tools and techniques you need to locate and obtain any PD or shareware program for any application, both now and in the years to come.

We'll look at the best computer user groups (Chapter 3), the best mail-order sources (Chapter 4), and tell you everything you need to know to obtain free software over the phone (Chapters 5 and 6). We'll also explain when it is best to get your software by telephone and when the mail-order option makes the most sense.

Next we'll look at the leading commercial and noncommercial online sources of free software, including hands-on instructions that will let you slice through the gobbledy-gook of an online system and make a beeline for the programs you want (Chapters 7 and 8). Included here as well are a variety of subscription discounts and offers of free online time. Though "downloading" programs is among the most popular of online activities, few subscribers even come close to exploiting its potential. We'll show you the ins and outs of the major systems and suggest ways for making best use of free public bulletin boards.

Ex Cathedra Recommendations

In Part III, we will quite frankly tell you which public domain and shareware programs to get for every major software application. The book emphasizes business and productivity software, but in Appendix A you will find some quick-take suggestions to get you started with education, music, graphics, and games programs.

Our goal is to give you all the information you need to locate the programs described in the libraries and catalogs available through the various free software distribution channels. Accordingly, we have used two major techniques to refer to specific programs and packages. A major package like PC-Write or ProComm typically consists of a main program file, a file containing the documentation, and a variety of support files. Because all of the files in such a package are always distributed together, either on the same disk or in an archive (.ARC) file on an online system, we have simply referred to the program by its proper name ("File Express," "As-Easy-As," and so on).

Where smaller packages and utility programs are involved, however, we have provided the filenames and filesizes (in bytes) of the main program and its ".DOC" file (if any). A program's filesize provides positive identification akin to a person's social security number. The chances of two different programs or two different versions of the same program having the same name and the same filesize are extremely remote. We have not cited any README.NOW or similar files that may accompany small packages and utilities, because they too will be on the same disk or in the same ARC file.

These opinions are based on a personal review of nearly a thousand disks and years of experience in the field. If you follow our advice, we can virtually guarantee that you will be pleased with the results. But ultimately, these are still opinions and you are welcome to disagree. Should one of the programs we have recommended not suit your needs, we hope you will use the tools provided in Part II to find one that does.

Finally, throughout the book you will find numerous "FreeTip" boxes. Some of these contain suggestions and ideas or nonvital elaborations on the subject at hand. Others provide brief explorations of side issues or numbers and names of people to contact for more information. Some are addressed to the more experienced computer user or individuals interested in certain technical information. And some offer hands-on information designed to make it as easy as possible to obtain, use, and enjoy the many free programs that will be available to you once you plug into the free software network.

FreeTip: The U.S. Navy has long been a promoter of public domain software as a way of cutting costs and providing special applications not available through normal commercial channels. One of the best sources of this software is a BBS run by NARDAC, the Navy Regional Data Automation Center in Norfolk, Virginia. The center encourages the development of PD programs by sponsoring a contest every year. One winner in the 1-2-3 template division, for example, was the Zenith Budget System. This five-disk package has saved the government hundreds of thousands of dollars by automating the Navy Air Station North Island Shore Comptrollers office in San Diego.

A contest winner likely to be of wider interest is the NEW-BAR.ARC (34,504 bytes) bar-coding utility program. There is also OPTAR, an operating target program for use with dBASE II, and something called Flight Maintenance System (CVW17-1.ARC and CVW17-2.ARC). There are two parts to the program. Both are required. A squadron of F-14A Tomcats wouldn't hurt either.

Jerry Dew, the sysop of the NARDAC RBBS-PC, has done a particularly nice job with this multiuser, networked system. The board operates round the clock. Anyone may call to download programs. Most contest winners can be found in "Directory 21" on the system. For 300/1200 bps communications, dial (804) 445-1627 (AutoVON, 565-1627); for 2400 bps communications, dial (804) 445-1121 (AutoVON, 565-1121).

Glossbrenner's Choice

For both author and reader, a book of this sort presents two major challenges. The first is the plain, hard fact that computer books tend rapidly to go out of date. The phone number, filename, or company address an author recommends may be accurate at the time a book goes to press, but can change within days of its appearance on your bookstore's shelves. That's in the nature of things. But it doesn't serve the reader, and is more than a little distressing to an author who has labored long to bring you accurate information. (Don't forget that you can obtain current phone numbers, even current "800" numbers, by dialing directory assistance. Since the phone company now charges for this service, we have no compunction about asking for the street address of the location as well.)

The second problem is free software-specific. Our goal is to make it as easy as possible for novice and computer-knowledgeable users alike to obtain the programs they need. Ideally, in addition to providing the package name or filename and filesize, we would also have been able to say that you will find such-and-such a program on a given user group disk or in a particular online library. That way, you could go right to it and not have to spend time looking for it yourself. Unfortunately, the way things change in this field, that proved to be impossible. Nor was it practical to list all of the disks in all of the various libraries that currently contain a copy of the recommended program, hoping that at least some of the information would remain accurate.

Early on it became obvious that the only way to guarantee that readers could always obtain these programs with minimal effort and expense was to distribute them ourselves. As it turned out, this approach had a number of other advantages, particularly when dealing with utility programs. As we'll see in Chapters 10 and 11, utility programs tend to be quite small, so a lot of them fit on a single disk. The problem is that when you're dealing with any particular software library, utilities are usually scattered across many different disks. Which means you have to order several disks to get all the utilities you want. Hopefully, by offering all of the small utility programs we recommend on a single disk, we'll be able to save you some money.

We have also used an archiving program to pack as much software onto a disk as it will hold. As we'll see in the next chapter, this is a technique used to save transmission time in the online world, and it normally results in space savings of 50 percent or more. Or to put it another way, it makes it possible to put nearly twice as much software on a single disk.

We have often wondered why mail-order libraries do not use this technique, but we quickly discovered the answer. Putting together a disk like this is like assembling a jigsaw puzzle. We did not always completely achieve our goal of "0 bytes free," and we cannot guarantee that new, larger versions of programs will still fit on the same disks. But we *can* guarantee that we will be here to tell you about it and keep you up-to-date. Given the continual flow of new programs and the yet-to-be exploited capabilities of IBM's PS/2 line of computers, there may even be sufficient demand to support a newsletter on the subject. In any case, all disks with compressed files contain a program for removing the files for their archives.

We have called these disks "Glossbrenner's Choice™," and in an effort to keep things as simple as possible, we will send you any disks (5¼-inch floppies) you want for $5 each. Plus $2 per order for shipping and handling. We'll pay the tax. Recognizing the growing importance of the IBM PS/2, laptops, and other systems using 3½-inch media, we will send you the same software on 3½ diskettes for $6 apiece. Please make checks payable to FireCrystal Communications. For your convenience, you might want to photocopy the order form at the back of this book. Or you can simply write to us at:

Glossbrenner's Choice
FireCrystal Communications
699 River Road
Yardley, PA 19067

Please remember that the fees cited above cover only the costs of distributing these disks. The public domain programs are yours to do with what you wish. But if you like and regularly use a shareware program, you are expected to register it by sending its author the registration fee he requests. This is something you will really want to do, however, once you see how good this software is and how much time, money, and frustration it can save you. You will find the names, addresses, and current registration terms for each shareware author under the discussion of his program.

We have done everything we can to make certain that all programs meet on a level playing field. Consequently, you should know that the copies of "commission shareware" programs found on Glossbrenner's Choice disks do not earn us commissions of any kind. Nor have we recommended a particular program because its author was willing to give you a special discount. Once we had identified what we felt was the best program in each category, we would frequently phone its creator for more information. In the course of discussing the software, some programmers volunteered to offer special discounts off the normal registration fee to readers of this book. That seemed like an excellent idea, and we have included the appropriate instructions in the relevant program discussions. Should other registration fee discounts become available, we will notify you of that fact with your order. As we have for years, we will continue to monitor the free software field, and as new applications are released we will notify you of them as well.

Let's Get Started

Although we have used them as an organizing principle throughout the book, Glossbrenner's Choice disks are only one of many options. All of the sources discussed in Part II can supply the programs we've featured and many more as well. You will probably want to get your software from many different sources. Indeed, that's part of becoming a free software expert. But before we can explore the various distribution channels, you need some basic information about how things are done in the free software world, and that's what Chapter 2 will provide.

2

Background and Basics

TAPPING THE SHAREWARE/
PD SOFTWARE GOLD MINES

It will undoubtedly come as a shock to many, but the truth is, personal computers are not easy to use. At least not until you learn how. But then, the same could be said of using an automobile. Most of us learned to use a car so long ago that we've forgotten the jerky stop-go-stop-go procedure of trying to put one in the garage without putting it through the back wall. And please, let's not discuss initial attempts at parallel parking or the hand-foot-brain coordination necessary to use a manual transmission.

None of that's a problem now. Nor is it a problem to productively use the scores of tools, appliances, and office machines that fill our lives. You don't have to know how something works if you want to use it, but you surely must know how to work it. Whether it's a car or a computer, you can't expect to get anything out of the device without first putting something into it. If you believe otherwise, we've got a bridge in a leading metropolitan statistical area you might be interested in buying.

Getting Up to Speed

You don't have to have anything even remotely resembling computer expertise to benefit from free software. Indeed, you can quite accurately look upon the major shareware packages as commercial software that is distributed by unconventional means. The only thing you may need to learn is how to print the on-disk documentation. And you may not have to do that, since if you like the program, the registration fee may bring you a printed, bound manual.

There's nothing wrong with operating at that level, of course. But if you want to really benefit from all that the free software world has to offer, you can't view your machine as a chauffeured limousine. You don't have to become an Indy expert, but you really should know how to drive it around the block. We bring this up because we know many readers are novice or new computer users, while others have yet to buy a system. Still others, of course, are old hands, or have varying degrees of experience.

The problem is that there is a certain quantum of information everyone should have to get the most out of free software. We cannot in this book tell you everything you need to know to be comfortable using a personal computer. We did that in *How to Buy Software*, a 648-page tome that devotes some 170 pages to bringing a complete novice from ground zero to true enlightenment in this area. But we have to make sure we're all playing with the same deck of cards here, and thus must present some quasi-technical explanations. In our opinion, this is the basic information that all current and prospective computer users need to have today, whether or not they plan to become heavily involved in the free software world. This is on a par with knowing that car radiators need antifreeze in winter and that windshield wiper fluid reservoirs must periodically be refilled.

We're going to make this information do double or triple duty, however. If you have yet to buy a system, it will give you the understanding you need to decipher computer ads and ask productive questions of salespeople. If you already own a system, it will give you a better idea of how to use it more effectively. And, most important for the purposes of this book, it will introduce and explain many of the terms you will encounter as you begin mining free software ore deposits. It will also give you a much clearer idea of why virtually all of the software discussed in this book will run flawlessly on any MS-DOS, IBM-compatible machine, regardless of who makes it or how it is configured or equipped.

Next, we'll present a mini DOS tutorial. We know a number of executives who are demons at Lotus but know only enough about DOS to get it to load that program. You will need to know a bit more than that, but not much. Fortunately, most of the material in the DOS manual can safely be ignored. We will direct you to the sections that really matter.

You will also need some information about how things are done in the free software world and the conventions that have evolved over the years. You need to know "what to do when the disk arrives," how to run a BASIC program, how to interpret a filename, print the documentation, remove an ARC'd file from its archive, and so on. We will handle this sequentially, describing each step you should follow after receiving a disk or signing off an online system.

Hardware/Software Compatibility
Will It Run on My System?

There *were* personal computers before IBM introduced the IBM PC. There were lots of different computers—and that was just the problem. With everyone doing his own thing, there was very little hardware or software compatibility among the various systems. At one time, for example, somewhere between 80 and 100 different, completely incompatible 5¼-inch floppy disk formats were in use. But when the PC arrived, like iron filings in the sudden presence of a large magnet, everyone oriented themselves along the IBM axis. And that was good. It is the reason why virtually all of the tens of thousands of programs available through free software channels will run on your system, regardless of its make, model, or size—as long as it is an IBM or "IBM-compatible" personal computer.

Realizing it would have to move quickly to enter the market, IBM assigned the task of developing the PC to its Entry Systems Division (ESD), an entity that at the time was an IBM Independent Business Unit or "IBU." That was important because an IBU could operate more or less as a separate company, bypassing the bureaucracy of the larger organization. As it happens, this was also crucial for consumers.

Off-the-Shelf Opened the Door

To get the product designed and out the door quickly, ESD used largely off-the-shelf parts and components, instead of following the traditional IBM practice of designing and manufacturing everything in-house. This meant that other companies could easily obtain the same parts, assemble them in the same way, and produce an IBM "clone" (a word that was at its zenith of popularity in the biological sense at the time)—or almost.

Computers can do absolutely nothing without software. They can't turn a disk drive on or put characters of text up on the screen unless someone has written instructions (software) to tell them exactly how to do it. A lot of instructions like these are required for even the simplest personal computer. The program that contains the necessary instructions is called the "operating system." Or more specifically, the "disk operating system" (DOS).

FreeTip: That term is pronounced "doss," *not* "dose" as it was mispronounced in a major 1986 television ad campaign for Epson computers. (It was an incredible gaff, but the public and press never noticed.) The word "disk" is a vestige of the days when all personal computer data was stored on punched paper tape. When disk drives finally became cheap enough for the average hacker to own, it was important to make clear that DOS was an operating system for disk-using systems. You will note that the latest operating system in the IBM world is simply called OS/2, with nary a disk in sight.

On IBM machines, the operating system is divided into two sections. One section is called the Basic Input/Output System (BIOS). The other is the actual disk operating system. Usually there is no need to make a distinction, so people refer to the whole thing as DOS. (No one ever says "the DOS.") Both parts *could* be melded together and placed on a floppy disk. But for a variety of reasons, the BIOS in IBM computers was placed in read-only memory (ROM) chips and soldered to the main system board.

Booting Up and the Phoenix BIOS

When you switch on your system, the computer's ROM BIOS chips come awake and a little program called the "bootstrap loader" begins to run. The program's job is to find DOS and load it into memory, causing the computer to in effect pull itself up by its bootstraps. If the program doesn't find DOS, either on a disk in drive A or on your hard disk, the operation will fail and you'll get an error message on the screen reading "Non-system disk" or something similar. Once the BIOS and DOS have successfully melded, however, the system will be ready to go to work.

FreeTip: The portion of the operating system that the bootstrap loader is looking for consists of two files, IBMBIO.COM and IBMDOS.COM. These programs, along with COMMAND.COM, really are the operating system. All of the other files on your DOS disk are external, utility programs. These are the three files that are transferred to a blank disk when you format it with the "system" option as described in your DOS manual. They are the only files needed to boot a system. But since they take up more than a little disk space, there's no point in putting them on every disk. The only reason to make a system disk (with the "system" format option) is if you plan to actually boot up the computer from that disk. Note that IBMBIO.COM and IBMDOS.COM are normally invisible and thus cannot be easily deleted. In Chapter 10, however, we'll show you a free program (ALTER.COM) that can reveal all hidden files (or hide visible ones).

Again, to save time, IBM didn't write its own operating system for the PC. The company ask Microsoft Corporation to supply this crucial piece of software (PC-DOS). Microsoft obliged, but reserved the right to market its own version (MS-DOS). The two operating systems are virtually identical.

Since the hardware components and DOS were readily available, the principal challenge facing the first clone makers was the BIOS, and IBM's copyright on that piece of software. Compaq Computer Corporation was the first to produce a BIOS that was functionally identical to IBM's but did not infringe on IBM's rights. Other early clone makers tried, ended up in court, and ultimately went out of business.

Then Phoenix Software Associates, Ltd., of Norwood, Massachusetts, introduced a PC-compatible BIOS that avoided copyright infringements and began selling it to would-be clone makers. Today, Tandy Radio Shack, Kaypro, Texas Instruments, NEC, HP, AT&T, Commodore, Leading Edge, GRiD, Wyse, and virtually all other IBM-compatible computers use the Phoenix BIOS. (There are other BIOS producers, but the Phoenix BIOS is generally considered the product of choice.) Compatibility, in short, is no longer much of an issue among PC/XT/AT-class machines. At this writing clones of the PS/2 line have yet to appear.

BASIC Exceptions

There are, however, two areas that can cause problems in a few cases. These are matters of screen handling and the running of programs written in BASIC. We'll have more to say about running BASIC programs in a moment. For now, you should know that BASIC is nothing more than a program called the BASIC interpreter. Its purpose happens to be that it allows you to run *other* programs—those written in the BASIC language. IBM personal computers treat the BASIC interpreter in much the same way that they treat the BIOS and DOS. That is, a portion of the interpreter program resides in a ROM chip on the main system board. The rest exists on disk. As with the BIOS and DOS, both portions of the BASIC interpreter program must meld before you can do anything with it.

If you want to run BASIC programs on an IBM compatible, you will need Microsoft's GW-BASIC ("Gee Whiz" BASIC). Unlike MS-DOS, this is not a generic product. Microsoft licenses it to major compatible manufacturers, which then customize it to their particular machines to insure that everything works properly. If you buy a clone from your local retailer, this should not be a problem. But if you are thinking of buying one through the mail, be sure to ask whether GW-BASIC is available and whether it has been customized for the machine. We should point out here that very few of the best PD and shareware programs are written in interpreted BASIC these days, so you may not need a BASIC language package.

Misbehaved Programs and Screen Handling

Screen handling is the other area where problems occasionally pop up. Think of the ROM BIOS as an adaptor plug of the sort you might use when traveling abroad or when trying to put a three-prong electrical plug into a two-prong socket. One "end" of the ROM BIOS must always be customized to fit with a clone maker's particular hardware components. The other "end," the one that MS-DOS plugs into, is uniformly the same in all machines. Because of this, MS-DOS does not have to be customized for every brand of computer. Similarly, the end of MS-DOS that an applications or utility program sees is also uniformly the same. And because of *this*, those programs normally can be run without modification on any PC-DOS or MS-DOS machine.

The BIOS and DOS thus insulate the applications program from the hardware. The applications programmer never has to write the instructions for turning on the disk drives or dumping a file to the printer, for example. All the programmer has to do is have his program tell DOS to do it, and DOS and the BIOS take care of the rest.

Most of the time this Tinker-to-Evers-to-Chance procedure works just fine. The problem is that a certain amount of time is consumed as these instructions are passed along. The delay is most noticeable when it is important to *quickly* manipulate characters on the screen. To get the speed and performance they want, some programmers incorporate screen handling routines in their code (programming) that goes around DOS and the BIOS and speaks directly to the video hardware. Such programs are not "well behaved," in the jargon of the field, though they may work just fine. The key thing is to make sure that your system is IBM-compatible in this area as well. Since most machines are these days, you will have few, if any, problems.

CGA, EGA, Hercules, and Displays

In IBM and compatible computers, the screen is controlled by an adaptor card or equivalent circuitry on the main system or "motherboard." Like all adaptor cards, the video cards plug into an "expansion slot" on the main board. The original PC offered two choices: the IBM monochrome adaptor and the color graphics adaptor (CGA). Although the text produced by the CGA is less sharp than that of the monochrome, the monochrome adaptor cannot produce the extended graphics characters described in your manuals. The CGA can be used with both a composite color monitor, a monochrome monitor, or an RGB monitor (a monitor with a separate feed for red, green, and blue signals). Some years later, Hercules Computer Technology introduced a card that would produce graphics on an IBM monochrome monitor.

These three adaptors—IBM mono, CGA, and Hercules monographics—are the least common denominators in the free software world. Some programs will ask you which type of adaptor card you have and configure themselves accordingly. Those that do not ask usually do not do any direct hardware manipulation and can be expected to run on virtually any video equipment. If a program supports the IBM EGA (Enhanced Graphics Adaptor), it will almost always be able to fall back to CGA or mono mode if necessary.

FreeTip: The traditional quick test of IBM video compatibility is whether the system can run Lotus 1-2-3 Version 1A or Microsoft's game, Flight Simulator, both of which directly manipulate the screen handling hardware. Fortunately, this is far less of a problem than it was in the past. A *PC Magazine* (14 October 1986) product comparison of cheap, mail-order IBM PC and XT clones reported that all 18 systems tested ran Lotus 1-2-3 without problems.

FreeTip: Though things could change, in the past the Hercules monographics card has not been CGA compatible. Fortunately, a number of PD and shareware programmers have written packages that allow the "Herc" card to emulate a CGA. Run one of these first, and you will be able to use Flight Simulator, PC-CAD, and other programs in their "CGA" mode.

We were not able to test them, but we have assembled three of what are said to be the best packages in this area on a Glossbrenner's Choice disk called "IBM Hercules/CGA Emulators." These are CS.ARC (not signed), SIMCGA.ARC (by Chuck Guzis), and Gary Batson's shareware HGCIBM.ARC package (version 2.01). Mr. Batson's package is quite extensive (nearly 100K in ARC form) and is apparently designed to help introduce the video driver/BIOS replacement package ATHENA.SYS ($34.95) he has designed for Hercules users. According to the documentation, this will let you do even more with the Herc card. Incidently, the HGCIBM package offers a special setting for users of the Leading Edge Model D computer. For more information, contact: Athena

Digital, 145 Green Hills Road, Athens, GA 30605; phone: (404) 354-4522.

For information on Hercules cards, call the manufacturer at: (800) 532-0600, ext. 302. In Canada call: (800) 323-0601, ext. 302. Or write to: Hercules Computer Technology, 2550 Ninth Street, Berkeley, CA 94710; sales: (415) 540-0212.

What About the PS/2?

If you've read this far, you can probably answer the question of PS/2 compatibility yourself. You can do it as a syllogism. The PS/2 line runs PC-DOS (MS-DOS.). Virtually all PD and shareware software is written to run under PC-DOS (MS-DOS). Therefore the PS/2 line can run virtually all PD and shareware software.

This is the beauty of the adaptor-plug approach used by DOS. As long as the BIOS has been customized to put something on the PS/2 screen, DOS can issue a general command to the PS/2 BIOS to do so without worrying about how the character or graphic figure actually gets there, how finely resolved it is, or anything else. Similarly, a PD or shareware program can tell DOS to put something on the screen without worrying about what DOS tells the BIOS. Thus, in its review of the IBM PS/2 Model 80, *InfoWorld* (10 August 1987) writes that "we found the Model 80 compatible with all of our usual software," including CrossTalk, Framework, Sidekick, Reflex, Windows, and Desqview.

From a practical standpoint, the only problem you are likely to have centers around the fact that the PS/2, like many laptop machines, is equipped to use only 3½-inch diskettes. Some years may be required for all free software sources to convert to this standard, though many will supply programs on 3½-inch media at your request. In the meantime, you might look into getting an add-on 5¼-inch drive, or plan to obtain most of your software online, via the telephone, though that is probably the more expensive alternative.

Processors and Clock Speeds

In the past, the chip around which a personal computer was built and the speed at which it operated were of interest only to hobbyists and technophiles. Today, thanks to the proliferation of IBM models and clones, that is no longer completely true. If you have yet to buy a computer, it is crucial to know what chip serves as its brain. If you plan to use programs that call for a lot of computation, as is the case with spreadsheets and graphics programs, you will also want to note the clock speed at which the chip operates. If you've already got a machine, it is still useful to know these things since you will see references to them as you move through the free software world.

The first thing you should know is that that PC and XT computers and clones are built around an Intel 8088 microprocessor. The microprocessor is always the brains of the operation and, in fact, it's the only computer component that does any real work. Everything else—disk drives, memory chips, printers, and peripherals—is designed to feed data to the processor, store data, or display it. Often called a "CPU" or central processing unit, it is the microprocessor that gives a machine its personality.

The Intel 8088 is part of the 8086 family. One of its cousins, for example, is the 8087 "math co-processor" that those who run statistical and other "compute-intensive" programs might want to install (provided that the program you want to use supports such a co-processor). There's even an empty slot for it on most PC/XT motherboards.

The main difference between the 8088 and the 8086 is that the former brings data into itself for processing in eight-bit chunks, while the latter is designed to work with a 16-bit data highway. IBM chose the 8088 (pronounced: "eighty-eighty-eight") for its original PC to save money, since it was much cheaper to build an eight-bit data path and everything needed to support it. Though things may have changed as you read this, the current PS/2 models 25 and 30, in contrast, are built around an 8086. Both chips can use a maximum of 640K (640,000 bytes) of random access memory.

The next step up on the ladder is the Intel 80286 processor that is at the heart of the IBM PC/AT and its clones. Usually referred to as simply a "286," this chip is used by the current PS/2 Models 50 and 60. It uses a 16-bit data path and can directly address seven (Model 50) to fifteen (Model 60) megabytes (millions of bytes) of RAM. The current top of the line is the Intel 80386, the chip that runs the PS/2 Model 80. This chip provides all the power of a multimillion-dollar 1970s-era mainframe computer. It is the chip that is required for OS/2, the new whizbang operating system that is supposed to unleash all that power. The 386 uses a 32-bit data path and can use up to 64 *trillion* bytes (64 terabytes) of RAM, while directly addressing some 16 megabytes of RAM. The Intel 80486 chip is reportedly waiting in the wings, and there are other reports of an 80586. One can only guess at the capabilities these chips will offer.

FreeTip: One thing we do not have to guess at is the downward migration of processor power to low-end PS/2 machines. In early 1988, William Lowe, the president of IBM's Entry Systems Division, indicated to industry analysts that machines currently using the 8088 would be equipped with 286 processors, while those using the 286 would have 386 CPUs. Apparently by about 1990, all PS/2s will be 386-based. There is even talk of a 386-based system from IBM selling for $1000 in the not-too-distant future. One can never be sure, but as one analyst said, Mr. Lowe "wasn't promising it but said that's the way IBM is going."

All of these chips operate at a variety of "clock speeds," a term we don't need to define here other than to say that clock speeds are measured in millions of cycles per second or megahertz (MHz). Generally, the faster the clock speed of your computer's chip, the faster it will be able to do things like recalculate a spreadsheet, adjust the text in a word-processing document to new margins, or find a customer in a database. Clock speeds in the Intel line start at 4.77 MHz for the PC/XT 8088 and run up to 20 MHz for the PS/2 Model 80. As time goes on, even that ceiling will eventually be raised.

Computer users, like everyone else, always want machines that do more, better, faster, and cheaper. From a free software perspective, that's all to the good. The only time you might experience problems is when you are using a program that depends on the system's clock speed to operate properly. A clock speed faster than 4.77 MHz could be a problem with some music programs, for example. On the other hand, most PD and shareware programmers are now accustomed to allowing for differing clock speeds and have adjusted their programs accordingly.

Printers, Plotters, Modems, and Peripherals

Because of its size and marketing clout, IBM was able to set PC operating standards virtually by fiat. Things are not quite as sharply defined, however, with peripheral equipment like printers, plotters, and modems. Fortunately, some loose de facto standards have emerged, driven primarily by whatever brand of equipment most people use. This is important because most peripherals contain small computers that must be told what to do. Before it can automatically dial the phone, for example, your modem must receive a particular command. Similarly, your printer must be told if you want it to use very small or very large type or to employ any of its other features.

You can think of these commands as a language, and with very little effort, you can imagine the chaos that would result if every brand of printer, plotter, and modem had to be spoken to in its own unique tongue. A program designed to work with this equipment would either have to be multilingual or permit you to customize the commands it sends to the relevant peripherals.

In reality, there *is* a considerable degree of chaos among peripherals and their respective command languages, due, we suspect, to corporate pride and the "not invented here" syndrome. Public domain and shareware programs approach the problem in several ways. At the highest level, programs like PC-Write ask you to specify your brand of printer and then configure themselves to match it. At the next level, programs like ProComm allow you to specify the commands they should send to a peripheral, like a modem. Your specifications are stored in a configuration file that is automatically loaded when the program is run, and they can be changed at any time. At the lowest level, some programs are written to work with specific brands and models of peripheral hardware and cannot be changed.

This last group can be divided into two categories. On the one hand, you will find programs written for many of the less popular equipment brands and models. If you happen to have a StrangeWriter printer, Model 124C41, that you want to use to produce scientific equations, you may be in luck. But if you don't have that brand and model and are chiefly interested in doing something else, these programs will be useless.

Fortunately, the second category is by far the largest. These are programs written for those who use equipment supporting the relevant de facto standard. Among dot-matrix printers, for example, the Epson command language is the standard. Any printer can be used to print text, but programs that make use of special feature print functions tend to default to Epson commands. Thus printers like those made by Citizen, IBM Graphics, Okidata (with Plug 'n' Play), Star, Gemini, the TI800 series, and many others support the Epson command language. In Chapter 13 we'll show you a program (PRINTER.COM) that lets you customize the setup codes you send to a printer and call them from a menu.

Among modems, the nod goes to the command language established by Hayes Microcomputer Products, Inc. Among plotters and to some degree, laser printers, Hewlett-Packard (HP) has set the standard. Not surprisingly, even those programs that allow you to customize peripheral commands default to the de facto standards. ProComm, for example, arrives preset to talk to a Hayes-compatible modem.

In short, as with commercially sold programs, free software closely tracks with hardware popularity. After all, it stands to reason that if there are five million Brand-X printers out there and a quarter of a million Brand-Y machines, the chances are much greater that more free programs will be produced for Brand-X units than for Brand-Y. Interestingly, however, Brand-Y programs *will* be produced and be made available on an equal footing to all who want them. Such is the nature of our free software democracy.

Software Fundamentals

The material we've just covered is really all you need to know about PC hardware to get started on the right foot. Indeed, you now know enough to confuse your friends and amaze your enemies with a few well-chosen terms. You also know enough to detect the computer nonsense most advertising and screenwriters put into the mouths of characters who are supposed to be real whizzes on the subject. Most follow the *Dallas/Riptide* school of screenwriting and simply string together a series of buzz words that may sound good but have no objective meaning or relationship to each other. One assumes this is not supposed to be funny, but it is often hilarious.

The Truth about Bugs

Now let's turn to some software fundamentals as they pertain to public domain and shareware programs. Specifically, let's talk about "bugs." This term is said to have originated in the 1940s, when computers were built of mechanical relays and other moving parts and an errant moth or other insect could give its life to gum up the works. A software bug is some unintentional, unsuspected lacuna in the code that can prevent a program for doing what it is supposed to do under certain circumstances. As any honest programmer will tell you, *all* software has bugs. Fortunately, once they have been discovered, most bugs can be fixed or (what else?) "exterminated."

The most obvious bugs can be caught by the programmer. But the only way to uncover the really subtle ones is to test a product thoroughly in real-life situations. Consequently, when a program is almost ready for release, most commercial software houses ask favored customers and others to put a product or a new version through its paces. This is called a "beta test." The beta testers note any problems and report back to the company. The bugs are then fixed and the product is shipped.

The leading shareware authors do exactly the same thing. Public domain programs do not generally undergo such a formalized procedure. But—and here's the really important point—the entire free software community serves as a tester, kibitzer, and critic for shareware and PD programs alike. As we said in Chapter 1, the two-way communication that exists between programmers and users is one of the qualities that makes the free software world so unique. Thus it is not at all uncommon for the author of a signed PD program to add features, fix bugs, and produce improved versions of his program, all at the behest of the people who are using it. After all, he has his reputation to think of. And if he doesn't do a good job, he'll hear about it on CompuServe or GEnie or some other online system the next night.

In cases where the author of a particularly good PD program is unknown, it is not uncommon for another programmer to prepare "patches" or fixes to improve the program. These patches are made available through the usual free software channels. They consist of additional programming designed to be inserted into or laid over the target program, plus instructions on how to perform this operation. In the same vein, others may write programs designed to work with or add features to popular shareware or PD programs. We will see a prime example of this in Chapter 16 when we look at programs written in support of ProComm 2.4.2.

An Equal Opportunity Arena

On the other hand, there certainly are many bug-ridden free programs. Because anyone can write a program and because there is no economic or market discipline to keep bad products out of the distribution channels, this situation is inevitable. We have seen some programs that are so failure-prone that it is incredible anyone would sign his name to them. You may encounter others that seem to work fine but about which you feel uneasy due to sloppy, incomplete documentation or the programmer's general approach. If a programmer isn't careful about preparing the instructions for using his program, is it likely that he will have been any more careful when writing the program itself?

FreeTip: One of the keys to successful programming is anticipating your user's needs and most likely responses. One indication of a programmer failing to do this concerns the use of capital letters. Over the years we have encountered many programs that present a nice-looking menu with selections A through F or something similar. We would key in an *a*, *b*, or *c* and nothing would happen. The reason was that the programmer had forgotten to allow for someone using lowercase letters instead of capitals. Worse still, he had forgotten to inform the user of the fact.

This isn't a make-or-break problem, and it occurs far less frequently today than in the past. But does raise doubts, for if the guy forgot to allow for something simple like the use of lowercase letters, what else has he forgotten?

Democracy and Marketplace

Fortunately, the very characteristics of the free software world that permit buggy programs to enter the distribution stream also provide a solution to the problem. If you don't like a program for any reason, there's always another one to try, and it will cost you virtually nothing to do so. There is also the fact that the sheer quantity of available software has set the standards for new programs very high.

Years ago, people were happy for anything that would run. But this is no longer true. Today, most of the major bases have been covered. As noted earlier, the free software field is a democracy. Anyone is welcome to contribute a program. But it is also a marketplace filled with millions of critical, demanding consumers who pay with their recognition and sometimes with their money. Any programmer who expects to be recognized for his public domain work or compensated for his shareware product has got to offer something slicker, faster, more powerful, or otherwise better than the programs people are already using. If he doesn't, the program he has labored over for so long will be quickly forgotten. It will still be available for anyone who wants to try it, but few people will. They'll be too busy testing the next new program to waste time on one that isn't up to snuff.

Brutal as it may sound, that's the approach we would recommend to any free software novitiate. Give the program you're interested in a chance, and be sure to read the documentation. But if it is needlessly difficult to use, if it seems clunky, and if it does not immediately win your confidence, forget it. There are always more where it came from.

Your Money Matters

Whenever you are considering a program designed to deal with financial matters, an even more stringent set of standards must be applied. It simply does not make good sense to commit your company's accounts or your stock portfolio to a program you have never heard of and know nothing about. Thus, in our opinion, for a serious applications program you can trust, it is almost essential to go with a shareware product. You want a professional-quality program offered by someone who will stand behind his work, not something of uncertain provenance.

Your recourse should the program prove faulty will be exactly the same as with a commercial product—which is to say you will have no recourse at all. No software product of any kind is ever warranted for anything. Though most companies will generously replace your disk should it prove defective. But as with a commercial product, you will have every reason to believe that the shareware program will do what its author says it will do.

This is not to say that public domain accounting and financial programs, Lotus templates, dBASE program files, and other business-oriented software can't be trusted. Usually they will work just fine. But if you are interested in something of this sort, in most cases you will want to review the code, the Lotus macros, and other elements yourself to make sure you know what the program is doing before you really begin to use it. This will take some work on your part, but it is much easier than trying to produce the application yourself from scratch, and it will result in a high degree of confidence in the program. Alternatively, if you know someone else who has found the program to be good or if it has a good reputation in the field, that may be assurance enough.

Utility programs are another matter. Most of these are quite short. Most are in the public domain. And with most, you will know in a second whether they work or not. Still another set of standards applies to games and recreational programs. In most cases, you either like them or you don't, and there's an end on't.

Trojan Horses, Viruses, and Logic Bombs

Okay, picture this. You're a reporter on a large metropolitan daily. Like most members of the press and the public at large, you know almost nothing about personal computers and can't be bothered to learn. All you know is that you harbor a deep distrust of computers in general, a feeling that was exacerbated some years ago when management decided to turn your newsroom into something resembling the set of the *Lou Grant* television show.

You get a tip about some poor fellow who has downloaded a "graphics improvement" program from a bulletin board only to find that it systematically erased every file on his hard disk within seconds after he ran it. To add insult to injury, the program displayed the phrase "Arf! Arf! Got you!" on the screen once it was finished.

Hot stuff! It's anticomputer, and if you put the right spin on it, possibly anti-yuppie as well. You don't know what a hard disk is, and you have only the vaguest notion of what computer bulletin boards are . . . or do . . . or whatever. But ignorance has never stopped you before. You call the fellow up, get the story, mangle it, and since it's a slow news day, it makes the front page. Not bad for a day's work.

Stories like this surface every now and then, and the general press always gives them sensational treatment. In so doing, they do everyone a great disservice. For although the facts of the individual cases are not in dispute, by focusing on just these incidents the press makes them appear to be far more significant than they really are. Few if any reporters bother to investigate the situation and tell the whole story.

As it happens, however, a major computer magazine once commissioned us to do exactly that. We spoke to leading bulletin board system operators ("sysops") and to user group software librarians. We spoke to people who had written programs to prevent such disasters from occurring. We checked the electronic networks (CompuServe, The Source, and so on). And what we found was this: Everyone we spoke to had heard of such programs, but to a person, none of them had ever encountered one of them or met anyone who had.

Obviously nasty programs of the sort described above exist. Indeed you will encounter "dirty dozen" lists of programs to avoid for just this reason. But clearly the so-called "Trojan horse" problem has been vastly overstated by the popular press.

A Trojan horse is a program that purports to be something desirable in order to get you to run it. The program cited above, for example, was called EGABTR.EXE, and supposedly would give users of EGA displays much better graphics. When you run a Trojan horse, however, it tries to distract you with some nonsense to keep you from noticing that it is busily erasing your hard disk.

Trojan horse programs are easy to write. All it takes is a devious mind and a desire to harm people you have never met. In short, any psychopath with low-level programming skills can do it. Not surprisingly, most of the nasties you will hear about are Trojan horse programs. Unfortunately, with greater programming skill, other nasties can be created. One of the worst of these is a virus or a phage program.

A virus is designed to do two things. It is designed to wreak havoc by deleting files or doing something else, but not right away. Like a "logic bomb," another computer nasty, it may be set to do its dirty work only after a disk has been accessed a certain number of times or even on a certain date. Or it may gradually eat away at your files over a period of time. It might do other unkind things as well.

The second function of a virus is to automatically replicate itself throughout the system. A virus might attach itself to your operating system and thus be loaded every time you boot the machine. If a system is thus infected, the virus might check each floppy disk put into a drive to see if it too has been infected. If not, it will promptly do so. The whole thing is rather like *The Invasion of the Body Snatchers*.

FreeTip: For a fictional treatment of computer viruses and how they can be used to bring a government to its knees, we recommend John Brunner's SF novel, *The Shockwave Rider*. The paperback was published by Del Rey/Ballantine in 1981 for $2.50.

Certainly viruses are more than a theoretical possibility. But at this writing, they have yet to surface in the IBM personal computer world, probably because they require far more skill to write than the typical Trojan horse program.

Fortunately, none of these nasties need be a problem. The only way you are ever likely to encounter a Trojan horse is if you frequent unfamiliar bulletin board systems, and even then there are ways to take precautions. Most mail-order sources, computer user groups, and the people who operate the free software sections of all commercial online systems test every program before making it available to the public. Most BBS sysops do so as well and will inform you of the fact when you sign on. The only way a Trojan horse can slip through is if the psychopath uploads it to a BBS and you download it before the sysop has tested it.

If you ever do encounter a suspect program, you can prevent it from doing any harm with Gee Wong's DPROTECT.COM or Andy Hopkins's BOMBSQAD. As discussed in Chapter 16, these programs prevent any other program from writing to (or erasing) any or all of your disk drives. Run one of them before you run the suspect program, and no Trojan horse or virus will be able to affect you.

FreeTip: It is a technical point, but you will undoubtedly hear of "interrupts" at some point in your free software career. One of the features offered by the BIOS and DOS is a collection of small programs designed to do things like writing to a disk drive, dumping the screen to the printer, or performing other services. For reasons we don't have room to explain, these subroutines are called interrupts (abbreviated as "INT"), and each has a unique number. Numbers are usually given in hexadecimal format, indicated by an upper- or lowercase *h*. Thus INT 13h (which is 19 in decimal notation) is the little program responsible for writing to a disk drive.

The interrupt subroutines are either hard-wired into read only memory (ROM) or loaded in to random access memory (RAM) during boot up. But an applications program does not need to know where they are. If a program wants to record something on disk, it need only call (tell DOS to locate and run) INT 13h. Mr. Wong's DPROTECT.COM works by intercepting any program's call for INT 13h. This prevents DOS from seeing the interrupt and running the subroutine, and thus prevents the program from recording or erasing information on a disk drive.

Style Notes

Now that you've got the hardware and software basics under your belt, it is time for us to explain the rules we have followed in this book when discussing the commands you should enter at your keyboard. We have tried to keep things as simple as possible. Accordingly, we have not used quotation marks to set off commands. Instead, we have used capital letters. These are only for emphasis and clarity. In the real world you may use either upper- or lowercase or both. We have referred to command keys by enclosing their names in angle brackets like this: <Enter>, <Esc>, <Ctrl>. If a combination key sequence is called for, we have referred to it in this way: [<Ctrl><C>], which means hold down your <Ctrl> ("control") key and hit <C>.

Finally, whenever you see the phrase "key in," you can assume that it means to type a command and *hit <Enter>*. Many brand-new computer users still forget to do this and sit at their machines puzzled over why nothing is happening. Although we will always refer to it as <Enter>, some sources refer to this key as "return," "carriage return," or "CR." This is a vestige of the days of the typewriter and teletype machine when there really was a carriage to be returned to the left margin. Today the "cursor," that little blob of blinking light on the screen, is what moves when you hit <Enter>.

A Mini DOS Tutorial

The final piece of basic information we must make certain you have concerns the operating system and how to use it to use your computer. If you're an old hand, you can safely skip this section, for it is designed to alert new users to the most crucial DOS commands. If you are a new user or someone who has never dipped into the DOS manual, please read on. We will show you which commands are truly important and give you some quick tips on how to use them. With this information you can almost ignore that boat-anchor of a manual. If you have never used DOS, we suggest that you read over this section without worrying about anything you don't understand. Then go to the manual for amplification and come back and read this again. Needless to say, we are going to assume that you are familiar with this material throughout the rest of the book.

DOS Basics

The DOS manual is intimidating, to say the least. We well remember our first encounter with version 1.0 (pronounced: "one-point-oh") and the sudden realization that the manual was little more than a dictionary that defined the command "words" but gave no hint as to how they should be used, or even which were the most important. With age comes wisdom, and we can now say with conviction that there are only a few DOS commands most people need to know.

First, you must know how to format a blank floppy disk. We're going to assume that you know what a hard disk or "Winchester" is. If you don't, Chapter 11 may be of some help. At this writing, three main types of floppy disks are in use. The standard is the 5¼-inch double-sided floppy that is capable of holding 360,000 bytes, or 360K, of information and programming. (It actually holds 362,496 bytes, and 1K is actually 1024 bytes, but the numbers are rounded off in normal conversation.) AT-class computers are equipped with one drive that can store up to 1.2 megabytes on a single, special, high-density floppy. (High-density disks look like normal floppies and can be used as such, but they have a special coating that allows them to record and hold much more data.) AT-class machines usually have a regular double-sided 360K drive as well. (Note: A 360K drive cannot read a high-density disk, though a high-density drive can read 360K disks.)

The third format is the 3½-inch "diskette," as it is currently called. The 5¼-inch disks used to be called "diskettes" as well, to distinguish them from their 8-inch predecessors. But the name never took. It probably won't with 3½-inch media either. These contain a floppy disk in a hard plastic shell, and can store 720K of data.

Formatting and Pathnames

No disk can be used until it has been formatted. Since the proper procedure is explained in the manual, we need only say that in most cases you can key in FORMAT A: and hit <Enter> to make the system format a disk in Drive A. In most cases, there is no need to worry about any of the command "switches" (/S,/V, and so on) described in the manual.

You must also know how to change your logged disk drive—that is, the drive or subdirectory that DOS is focusing on at the time. The DOS prompt when you are logged onto Drive A is: A>. To focus DOS's attention on Drive C—to log onto Drive C, in other words—you key in C: and hit <Enter> at the DOS prompt.

The best way to think of subdirectories is as separate disk drives. That's how DOS sees them and how it treats them. However, since a single floppy or hard disk can contain many subdirectories, you need to refer to them with a more detailed address. Logically enough, this address contains the letter of the disk drive and the name of the subdirectory. But if you had a subdirectory on Drive C called ACCOUNTS, you could *not* just key in ACCOUNTS the way you might key in A: or B: to

get to it. If you did, DOS would think you were telling it to run a
program or a batch file called ACCOUNTS.

Thus to log onto a different directory you key in CD ("change directory"), followed by the left-pointing backslash character—the one that
points up to eleven o'clock—followed by the name of the subdirectory.
Thus if you are on Drive C and you want to move into the ACCOUNTS
subdirectory, you key in CD\ACCOUNTS and hit <Enter>. The sequence starting with the backslash is called a "pathname" or "path."
Again, this is explained in the manual, as are the MD ("make directory") and RD ("remove directory") commands.

Copying and Getting a Directory

Next, you need to know how to copy a file or a disk. The accepted way
of referring to any file is to use the phrase "filename.ext." The "ext"
stands for "file extension." Most filenames do not *have* to have an extension, but extensions are helpful because they give you a hint as to what
kind of file it is. An extension of "TXT" indicates a text file, for example; an extension of "DOC" usually indicates a text file that contains the
documentation for a program; and so on. When speaking about files, the
period is pronounced "dot." Thus COMMAND.COM would be pronounced "COMMAND-dot-COM." We'll have more to say about PD and
shareware file extensions in a moment.

To copy a file, you enter the command COPY filename.ext A:, where
A: is the destination drive (the drive to which you want to copy fil-
ename.ext). If you like, you can use the DOS "wildcard" or "global"
characters. Thus COPY *.* would copy all files, regardless of filename
or extension. That command is pronounced "COPY star-dot-star." The
command COPY *.BAS would copy only files with the extension "BAS."
The DELETE command works the same way. To copy a disk, you may
use the DOS utility program DISKCOPY.COM. This creates an exact
duplicate of the source disk, but for reasons explained in Chapter 11,
the COPY command is usually preferable.

The next thing you need to know is how to call for a directory of files
on your disk. If you are logged onto Drive C and want to look at the list
of files on the disk in Drive A, you can do one of two things. Either log
onto Drive A and key in DIR, or key in DIR A: and hit <Enter> while
you are logged onto Drive C. The files on the disk will be listed like this:

COMMAND   COM   23791   12-30-85   12:00p

This tells you the name and extension of the file, its size in bytes, the
date it was created, and the time of day it was created. Where does the
system get the information it needs to date- and time-stamp the file?

One of two places: either from you when you boot up the system and respond to the time and date prompts, or from a battery powered clock/calendar installed on one of your expansion cards. The documentation for such a card will tell you how to make the system automatically retrieve the date and time from the onboard clock/calendar. (In Chapter 10 we'll show you how to change a file's date and time if you like.)

If you want to stop a directory from scrolling out and return to the DOS prompt, key in [<Ctrl><BREAK>]. (The <Pause> key on many keyboards is also labeled "BREAK.") The command [<Ctrl><C>] will also work. This is a good command to know in any case, for you can use it to break out of many programs and immediately return to DOS. (Be sure to see the discussion of CONFIG.SYS later in the chapter for more on the BREAK command.)

"Typing" a File

It is also important to know how to display a file on the screen. Many free programs come with files called READ.ME, README.TXT, README.NOW, or something similar. These are text files that most often contain quick-start information, cautions, suggestions, and other important information from the programmer. To quickly display such files on the screen, key in TYPE filename.ext.

What if you want to make a hard-copy printout of the file? That can be done most easily by keying in COPY filename.ext PRN to send a copy of the file to the printer.

FreeTip: Here's a nifty twist on the shareware concept likely to be of interest should you ever get stuck using DOS or just about any other program. For years Sheryl and Stephen Schuff have been providing custom programming, technical support, and training for users of IBMs and CP/M machines through their consulting firm Schuff & Associates, Inc. In July 1986, however, they decided to expand their service by offering telephone support to all callers on a shareware basis.

The service is called PC-Helpline. Most questions can be answered immediately; others, within 4 to 48 hours. And if PC-Helpline cannot answer a question, Schuff & Associates will do their best to find someone who can. After a consultation, users are sent a letter with a suggested fee. If you felt the service was worth it, you are asked to pay that amount. If not, you are asked to pay whatever you feel is fair. Fees for projects likely to cost more than $50 are quoted in advance over the phone.

The company maintains a large database of vendor information, product specifications (including the availability of updates), and hardware and software reviews. And as computer and software consultants, they own and are familiar with most of the major commercial packages (Lotus, dBASE, WordPerfect, Symphony, DisplayWrite, WordStar, and many others). Basically, you can ask the PC-Helpline just about any hardware or software question and stand an excellent chance of having it answered at a very reasonable price. The company is a member of the Independent Computer Consultants Association, the leading trade organization in the field, and operates in accordance with its guidelines. For more information, contact: Schuff & Associates, Inc., 8156 Lieber Road, Indianapolis, IN 46260; phone: (317) 259-4778.

File Types

Finally, you must know just a bit about the various types of files you will encounter. Fundamentally, there are two types: text files and machine language files. But within these two categories there are many special subdivisions. A text file contains nothing but conventional, readable text and Arabic numbers. It can thus always be displayed on the screen or printed on the printer.

As far as your computer is concerned, only three text files really matter. These are CONFIG.SYS, AUTOEXEC.BAT (and any other .BAT file), and a BASIC (.BAS) program. When your system boots up, the first thing DOS looks for after it has loaded in is a file called CONFIG.SYS. This is a file, prepared by you with a word processor, that tells the system how you want it to be configured. If DOS does not find this file, it simply uses its built-in default settings.

FreeTip: You will want to consult the chapter in your DOS manual called "Configuring Your System" for more information on the CONFIG.SYS file. However, we may be able to save you some time. If you have 512K to 640K of memory, we suggest that you move to your root hard disk directory by keying in CD.. and hitting <Enter>. Then do the following:

1. At the DOS prompt key in COPY CON:CONFIG.SYS
2. Type the following lines, hitting <Enter> after each one:

FreeTip continued

> BREAK = ON
> FILES = 20
> BUFFERS = 20
>
>
> 3. Hit <F6> and then hit <Enter>.
>
> For most people, these are the most important CONFIG.SYS settings. Again, see your DOS manual for an explanation of what they do.

Any file ending in "BAT" is seen by DOS as a batch file. That is, as a text file containing a batch of DOS commands that you want the system to execute in sequence. The file AUTOEXEC.BAT is special in that DOS looks for this specific filename in its root directory when it boots up. ("AUTOEXEC" stands for "automatic execution.) If it finds it, DOS will proceed to execute each of the commands in that file. An AUTO-EXEC.BAT file can be a great time saver, because once it is prepared you will never need to do things such as keying in the date, setting your screen colors, or doing all of the other things necessary to set the system exactly the way you want it.

> **FreeTip:** We don't have space to explain the reasons, but we strongly suggest if you have a hard disk you make one line in your AUTOEXEC.BAT file read: SET COMSPEC = C:\ COMMAND.COM. We also suggest you investigate using the PATH command in your AUTOEXEC.BAT file as explained in Chapter 10.
>
> You might also want to make the word GRAPHICS one of the lines in your AUTOEXEC.BAT file. This runs GRAPHICS.COM, a program that comes with your DOS package. The program makes it possible for you to dump a screen containing computer graphics to the printer. Graphics and text are treated differently by the PC, and if you have not loaded this DOS utility, you will not be able to print graphic images directly from the screen by hitting the <Print Screen> key, even if you have a graphics printer. You can usually ignore the DOS program GRAFTABL.COM unless you plan to be using BASIC in graphics mode (with the BASIC commands SCREEN 1 or SCREEN 2).

Any other file ending in "BAT" can be used in a similar way. Thus if you had a batch file called TEST.BAT, and if that file contained a series of DOS commands, you could tell DOS to begin executing those commands by simply keying in TEST. Batch files can be enormously powerful, as we will see in Chapter 9 when we look at the shareware program Extended Batch Language (EBL).

The third type of special text file is one containing a program written in BASIC. Like the names of many computer languages, "BASIC" is an acronym. The letters stand for "Beginner's All-purpose Symbolic Instruction Code," a phrase that is somewhat less contrived than the antecedents of most acronyms. A "BAS" file always contains the source code of a BASIC program—that is, it contains the instructions the programmer has prepared for the BASIC interpreter program. The BASIC interpreter is called BASIC.COM (or BASICA.COM), and as we'll see later you must run it before you can run a program written in the BASIC language.

A BASIC program can be prepared with a word processor, since it contains nothing but text. However, most programmers use the word processing facilities offered by the BASIC interpreter. This way they can write some lines of code, run them to see how they work, and then list them and edit or add to them, all without ever leaving the BASIC interpreter program. When they have finished, they will naturally want to save their work to disk. And here they have a choice. They can either tell BASIC to save the program as a pure "ASCII" text file (more on ASCII in Chapter 5), or they can allow BASIC to save the file in a "tokenized" format. At this point, all you need to know about tokenized BASIC is that it involves the use of both text and machine language. If you TYPE such a file to the screen, you will see some recognizable text and a lot of strange characters.

Machine Language and Compiled Programs

Although it is technically a data file (containing data for the BASIC interpreter), in at least one sense a tokenized BASIC program is a machine language file. For in the simplest possible terms, a machine language file is one that is not intended for human consumption. Like all personal computer files, it is made up of eight-bit bytes. But unlike each byte in a text file, the bytes in a machine-language file are not meant to symbolize a character of text. The video hardware will respond if you TYPE these files to the screen, but the results will be meaningless garbage. (Since you can't harm anything by doing it, try keying in TYPE COMMAND.COM and watching what appears on the screen.)

As you might imagine, machine language files are meant for the computer. Not only must a computer be told what to do each step of the way, it must be spoken to in its own special language. The main purpose of programming languages like BASIC, C, Pascal, and others is to translate human words and commands into machine language. The result is a recorded series of symbols that is to the computer what sheet music is to a musician, or what a piano roll is to a player piano.

One way or another a programmer's English commands must be translated into machine language before anything can happen. Over the years, two approaches have been developed to solve this problem. One is the approach offered by BASIC. Here, the words and phrases you enter are translated ("interpreted") each time the program is run. The other approach is the one offered by C, Pascal, and assembly language (or "assembler," as it is sometimes called). These languages require you to first write the program ("source code") and then "compile" or "assemble" it into a machine language file ("object code"). The machine language file is the one you run.

Why would a programmer choose one approach over the other? The answer is that interpreted BASIC is interactive. That is, you can write some code, run it immediately, change or correct it, run it again, and so on, as you develop a finished program. The trouble is that BASIC is slow, due to the translation process that must take place each time the program is run.

Compiled or assembled programs usually run much faster because the translation has already been done. But they can be more difficult to write, because you have to recompile the source code every time you want to test a change or correction. This is done by the appropriate language compiler program, and the process can be quite time consuming. One compromise is to buy a BASIC compiler package. This allows you to develop a program using interpreted BASIC, and when you have it the way you want it, permanently convert it to a machine language file.

Most machine language files end with "COM" or "EXE," indicating that they are "command" or "executable" files. There are technical differences between the two, but they needn't concern most people. The key thing to remember is that the COM or EXE extension means the file is a ready-to-run machine language program. All you have to do to put it into operation is key in the filename. Thus, if you see QFILER.COM on a disk, you have only to key in QFILER to run the program.

FreeTip: There are lots of things that distinguish COM and EXE files, but broadly speaking, there are two main points. The first point is that DOS is set up to look for COM files first, EXE files second, and BAT files third. Thus if you had TEST.COM, TEST.EXE, and TEST.BAT on the same disk and keyed in TEST, DOS would run TEST.COM. Second, although it is usually not noticeable, EXE files take slightly longer to load in and begin to run. This is because an EXE file is what is called "relocatable object code." It can be loaded into memory at any location, but DOS has to make some adjustments (such as telling the program where it has been loaded and re-jiggering any address values that depend on the program's location) before execution can begin. A COM file, in contrast, is designed to always load at the same memory location and thus does not require any preparation.

The programmer doesn't always have a choice about the kind of machine language file that will be created. Compiled BASIC and Pascal programs, for example, must be EXE files. Assembly language programs usually result in COM files. Sometimes an EXE file can be converted to a COM file using EXE2BIN.COM, a program that, strangely enough, is supplied with your DOS package. But that isn't something likely to be worth your time and effort to do in most cases.

What to Do When the Disk Arrives

In this section we are going to take you step-by-step through a process you may never have experienced before—receiving a disk of programs in the mail. We'll show you how to quickly evaluate a program to determine whether it will meet your needs, and we'll explain a lot of the free software jargon you may encounter as well. Needless to say, this information applies whether you get your programs on disk from a user group or mail-order source or download them from an online system.

Let's assume that you've ordered a catalog published by one of the mail-order or user group sources cited in Chapters 3 and 4. You've found a disk that sounds like it might contain the kind of program you want or need. But it's difficult to tell, since most catalogs don't have the space to provide a full description. The cost per disk is minimal, though, so you have very little to lose if the program turns out not to be satisfactory. So you place an order and a week or so later, the disk arrives. Now what?

Step 1: Make a Backup Copy

Step 1 in every case is to make a backup copy of the disk. You should always have several freshly formatted blank disks handy, but if you

don't, format several of them first. Then make your backup with COPY
. or DISKCOPY. This only takes a minute, and while making backups
is good practice in any case, it is particularly important when you are
about to run an unfamiliar program.

Step 2: Call for a Directory of the Disk

Step 2 is to put your backup copy in the disk drive and call for a directory. At this point, the key thing is to pay attention to the extension.
You will probably see COM, EXE, TXT, and DOC files, for example.
You may see BAS files and BAT files, as well as files with extensions
you do not immediately recognize. The first thing to look for is any
filename that resembles "README." This is one of the conventions of
the free software world and virtually all disks have such a file. When
you find it, TYPE it to the screen.

Step 3: Run the Program

The third step *should* be to print and read the documentation. But let's
be realistic. We all know that the next thing you're going to do is run
the program. So step 3 is to look for the COM or EXE files and key in
their filenames to run the programs. If there are batch files on the disk,
you might run them as well. But we always like to TYPE them to the
screen first to get an idea of what they're going to do. If a disk contains
several different programs and their support files, you can usually tell
which ones go together by the similarities in their filenames.

Many programs display an initial screen called the "greeting screen."
The greeting screen will usually contain the program's name, possibly a
brief discription of its purpose, and a prompt to "hit any key to continue" or something similar. If the program is shareware, the first thing
you see may be what shareware programmers call the "beg screen."
This is in effect a brief commercial, that notifies you of the program's
shareware status and urges you to register your copy. Hopefully it will
make you feel a healthy twinge of guilt if you use and like the product
but have yet to register.

The registration fee and the programmer's address are usually also
mentioned, although in most cases you will want to refer to the documentation file for details on what registration entitles you to. Policies
vary, but one benefit many shareware authors offer their registered
users is a copy of the program that does not contain a beg screen.

Step 4: Preview and Print the Documentation

Next, look for files ending in DOC, TXT, or sometimes MAN (for "manual"). These should contain the program's documentation. And since the

documentation file is likely to be more than a single screenful of text, you will undoubtedly want to print it.

Many programmers set things up so that all you have to do is key in COPY filename.ext PRN to print a neatly formatted copy of the documentation file. However, not everyone does things this way. So it is always wise to look at the documentation on the screen before printing it. You don't have to look at the whole file, just enough of it to get some sense of its format. The key thing to look for is how, or if, the documentation contains some kind of page break.

FreeTip: You can quickly preview a documentation file by keying in TYPE filename.ext and allowing the text to scroll up the screen for a page or two. To stop it and return to DOS, key in [<Ctrl><BREAK>]. An even better alternative is Vernon Buerg's invaluable program LIST.COM, discussed in Chapter 9. Among its many powers, LIST puts a text file on your screen and lets you scroll or page up and down, from top to bottom.

Ideally, a documentation file should separate pages with form-feed characters. A form-feed is a control character—an ASCII 12 or [<Ctrl><L>]—that shows up on your screen as the alchemist's symbol for female (a circle on top of a short cross). When your printer sees this character it advances the paper to the end of the current page before it continues printing. That's one of the things to look for as you preview the documentation on your screen. Some programmers separate pages with blank spaces, which usually produces satisfactory results, provided you have lined your paper up properly before you begin.

At other times you'll find that the documentation file contains no page breaks at all. If you copy a file like this to the printer, the printer will print on and over the perforations separating the paper pages. Other programmers use short pages with wide left margins in an attempt to imitate pages in an IBM-style manual, expecting everyone to use 5½ by 8½-inch continuous-form paper. Others apparently expect everyone to use the same word-processing program they use, since they include the formatting codes required by their software.

Problems like these occur most often among public domain programs. If you're a new user, we suggest that you not bother trying to produce a neat printout. Simply copy the file to the printer. If you've had a bit more computer experience, you might want to bring the file into PC-Write (Chapter 12) or your favorite word processor and clean it up to suit.

FreeTip: One quick way to print an unpaginated text is to use a
"text formatter" program like LIST.COM from System Design &
Implementation. (Yes, this program has the same name as the
completely different one by Vern Buerg.) Use John Petrey's
PRINTER.COM to set your printer to compressed print, ⅛-inch
lines, and 88 lines per page. Then use LIST.COM to print the file,
specifying two lines for the top margin (header lines) and four lines
for the bottom margin (footer lines). That will give you 82 lines of
compressed but very readable text per page. See Chapter 13 for
details on both programs.

What If There Is No Documentation File

Shareware programs almost always have documentation files, and
many of them include ready-to-print invoices as well to accommodate
corporate purchasing department requirements. Most other programs
do as well. However, it is important to be aware of two free software
conventions. The first is what might be called the "self-documenting"
program. These programs display anywhere from a single line to a single screen of instructions whenever you key in their names without any
"arguments." "Argument" is computer talk for whatever a command or
program is supposed to operate on and any specific instructions you may
wish to provide to control that operation.

Thus, although it has a documentation file, if you key in FDATE to
activate FDATE.COM (Chapter 10), you will see this on your screen:

Usage is: FDATE <filename> [mm/dd/yy] [hh:mm:ss]

The filename and the date and time information are arguments. If you
were to key in FDATE followed by one or more arguments, the above
usage information would not appear.

The second convention followed by some programmers is to put the
documentation in the source code as a series of remark or comment
statements. This is often done with assembly language and Pascal programs, and sometimes with BASIC programs. Thus if you see only, say,
CP16.EXE and CP16.ASM on your disk, but no CP16.DOC, it's a good
bet that the instructions will be in the assembly language (ASM) text
file. TYPE it to the screen or look at it with Vern Buerg's LIST.COM
to check. If the instructions are in the file, bring it into a word processing program to "clip out" the instructions and write them to a separate
file. Then simply print that file.

Version Numbers and More Extensions

As noted earlier, PD and shareware programs are frequently modified, expanded, and otherwise improved by their authors. Consequently, some method had to be developed to distinguish the latest version of a program from its predecessors. It is common practice in the field to indicate the version number in the filename. Thus CP16.EXE is version 1.6 of John Dart's CP.EXE program. LIST62A.COM is version 6.2a of Vern Buerg's LIST.COM program. And so on.

As you review your disk, you will encounter some extensions we have not yet covered. The extension HLP, for example, usually indicates a help file. This may be ready-to-print documentation, or it may be the file that the program calls when you ask it to display help information. A file ending in OVR is an overlay file and usually contains programming or data that the programmer has left on disk to save memory space. Such files are typically loaded only when you access some feature of the main program. A file ending in NDX probably contains an index of some sort, LST is usually short for "list," and BIN denotes a "binary" (machine language) file. Files ending in HEX (hexadecimal) are rare, but they are explained in Chapter 16.

How to Handle Archive (ARC) Files

You may also encounter files ending in "ARC." This means that the file is an archive file and that, in turn, means that it contains several separate files, usually in a compressed format. The ARC format was created by System Enhancement Associates (SEA) of Wayne, New Jersey. But the only thing you *really* need to know about such files is that a special utility program is required to extract and reconstitute their contents. You can think of this utility as a can opener that simultaneously opens a can of condensed soup and automatically adds the proper amount of water.

Two of the most popular archive extraction utilities are Vern Buerg and Wayne Chin's ARCE.COM and Phil Katz's PKXARC.COM. Both are small, fast, and easy to use. For example, if you have a file called TOOLCHST.ARC and you want to use either of these programs to extract its contents, you need only use TOOLCHST as your argument. You could thus key in either ARCE TOOLCHST or PKXARC TOOLCHST. Although both programs offer a range of other options, that's really all there is to it.

To make things as simple as possible, we suggest that you create a subdirectory on your hard disk called WORKAREA and copy the ARC file and your chosen extraction utility into it. Then enter the appropriate command as discussed above. If you don't have a hard disk, use a blank scratch disk instead. This will free you from having to key in pathnames and it will eliminate potential space problems. The extraction process does not affect the archive file in any way. It remains on the disk. But the files it contains can easily occupy twice the space of the archive file itself, the compression ratio is that good.

Archive files are used primarily by online sources of free software. The fact that they can contain many files means one can conveniently download an entire package in one fell swoop instead of having to download several separate files. Perhaps even more important, by compressing files, the archive format reduces the amount of time required to obtain a copy of a package, and thus helps hold down connect time and long-distances charges.

Obviously if there is a utility to extract a group of files from an archive, there must be a program to put them into archive format in the first place. In fact, there are several. The one we prefer is Phil Katz's PKXARC.COM, discussed in Chapter 16.

Also discussed in Chapter 16 are files ending in LBR ("library") and any extension with a Q (for "squeezed") as its second letter (DQC, TQT, and so on). Files with these extensions must also be processed with a utility program before they can be run. But both represent older methods of archiving and compressing files that are rarely used these days, so you may never encounter them.

Step 5: Run the Program Again

The truth of the matter is, we always run the program before looking at the documentation. Sometimes it's an enjoyable challenge to see if you can figure out how to use a program without reading the instructions. But it is more than that. In the first place, if you can indeed use the program without the written instructions, it is usually proof positive that the programmer knew what he was doing. In the second place, once you have taken a look at the program, the documentation tends to make more sense. It also helps you develop a feeling for the software, and it creates an initial set of expectations. The best programs, like the best short stories and page-turner novels, grab you in the first few moments you spend with them.

If you are seriously interested in a program, however, you will take the time to read the documentation after the initial run-through. Then you'll go back to run it again and systematically try its various features. Just as you wouldn't buy a house without looking into all of its rooms, it is important to walk through all of a program's features before settling down to make it your own. Public domain and shareware programs are no different than commercial software—the better you get to know any program, the more comfortable you will become when using it.

What If It's a BASIC Program?

Without wishing to seem snobbish, these days the best programs are not being written in interpreted BASIC. Nine times out of ten, the program you want will be a COM or an EXE file and will have been written in Turbo Pascal; in C using the Lattice, Microsoft, or Lifeboat C compiler; or in assembly language. Or it will have been written in BASIC and compiled or in Quick BASIC. All of these options produce fast-running, feature-filled programs that frankly leave good old BASIC pretty much in the dust.

Nevertheless, there are still good interpreted BASIC programs, and you are sure to encounter some you will want to run. You may even want to learn enough BASIC to be able to customize and otherwise alter them to your taste. At the very least, if you are seriously interested in programming, there is no better way to learn than by examining someone else's code.

As you know from our previous discussion of BASIC, you must first load the BASIC interpreter. Here you can choose between BASIC.COM and BASICA.COM. Both are supplied on your DOS disk. The latter is "advanced" BASIC. It takes up more memory when loaded, but memory is not usually a concern these days, and it does offer more features. Consequently, we can see no reason not to make it your BASIC of choice.

Thus, the formal way to run a BASIC program is to key in BASICA to load the interpreter. Once this is running, you are supposed to key in LOAD "filename.bas". (You actually need only the beginning quotation mark and you do not have to use the BAS extension.) Then you are supposed to key in RUN. However, you can short circuit the entire process by simply keying in: BASICA filename.bas.

When you want to stop or get out of a BASIC program, you need only enter [<Ctrl><BREAK>]. That will return you to the BASIC "OK" prompt. From there, key in SYSTEM to return to DOS. That's really all you need to know about running any BASIC program.

Naturally there are exceptions. A programmer might have disabled the [<Ctrl><BREAK>] command, in which case the quickest way out is to reboot the system. As you know, you can do this by hitting [<Ctrl><Alt><Del>]. Some compiled BASIC programs will work only if you have a program called BASRUN.EXE on your disk. This is the runtime module of the Microsoft BASIC compiler (commonly called BASCOM), and unless you have purchased that package, you will not have BASRUN.EXE. Fortunately, such programs are relatively rare.

Should you break out of a program and find that you are not back at DOS, you are probably still in the BASIC interpreter, even if you can't see a cursor or the OK prompt. Try keying in SYSTEM at this point to return to DOS. If a BASIC program leaves your screen in 40-column (wide) mode, you can key in SCREEN 0,1 and then WIDTH 80 (or string the commands together on the same line as SCREEN 0,1:WIDTH 80). The command CLS will clear the screen in BASIC as it will in DOS. The command FILES will give you a directory of the logged disk drive. The command COLOR 2,0,0 will set your screen to green text on a black background with a black screen border. The commands we have cited here are the ones likely to be most helpful when running free BASIC programs. As always, see your manual (your BASIC manual) for details.

FreeTip: By default the BASIC interpreter saves program files in tokenized format. That's good for saving disk space, but not so good if you want a printout of the program or if you want to bring it into your word processor. If you want to turn a tokenized BASIC program into a pure text file that you can print, edit with a word processor, or whatever, here's what to do:

1. Load the program as described above.
2. At the OK prompt, key in SAVE "filename.bas",A (The A stands for ASCII, and both it and the comma go after the closing quotation marks).
3. Key in SYSTEM to return to DOS, and your BAS file will be ready for formatting and printing, TYPE-ing to the screen, or whatever.

You can, of course, run a BAS file saved in ASCII format in the same way that you would one saved in tokenized form. The only difference is that it takes a little longer to load.

Tips and Techniques

It is impossible to anticipate everything you may encounter as you run free—or for that matter, commercial—programs. However, we can offer some general tips and techniques. Perhaps the best piece of advice we can offer is this: When in doubt, reboot. If a program causes your system to "hang" (freeze up and become unresponsive), think about why this may have happened for a moment or two. If no solution immediately occurs, shut the machine off, wait until the fan motor stops, then fire it back up, and try the program again. There is always a reason why something doesn't work. Although there may be a command you can enter or a key you can hit to solve the problem elegantly, it is usually much quicker to shut everything down and start over, or reboot the system.

For example, as discussed earlier, some programs have a bad habit of failing to return your screen to its former state. You might leave a program only to find that your DOS prompt is twice its normal 80-column size. You may strongly suspect that there is something you could key in that would automatically restore the screen to 80-column mode. That would be the elegant solution. But think how long it will take you to find it. It's much quicker to just reboot the system. (In these situations, the DOS utility MODE.COM usually works. Try MODE 80, for example. See your manual for other details.)

Starting from scratch can also be important when you are dealing with a "memory resident" program. You will find much more information on these kinds of programs in Chapter 10 under our discussion of the "Mark/Release" package, a program that lets you selectively *remove* "terminate and stay resident" or "TSR" programs from memory. For now, we can simply say that if a given program isn't working, think about what other programs you may have installed and consider rebooting using a plain DOS system disk. That way you'll be working with a truly clean slate.

Incidently, the reason we suggest waiting until the fan stops is to allow all of the power to drain out of the system's memory chips. That way you can be certain that you really are starting fresh. The same "turn it off and start fresh" principle applies to printers, modems, and any other peripherals that become momentarily cantankerous.

As we have mentioned several times, the [<Ctrl><BREAK>] command is often the best way to stop a process or a program and return to DOS. If that doesn't work, try hitting the <Esc> ("escape") key. If you haven't read the documentation and you are stuck, try hitting each of the "F" or "function" keys in turn and see what happens.

If numbers unaccountably begin to appear on your screen when you hit arrows or paging keys on your numeric keypad, it is because the <NumLock> key has become engaged. Break the engagement by simply hitting that key once. In Chapter 10, we'll highlight some public domain utility programs that can help you manage your <NumLock> and <CapsLock> keys.

Finally, many programs need to be configured or installed to suit your particular computer setup. This will always be covered in the documentation, but since no one reads the "doc" before running a program for the first time, you may encounter a small problem or two. The most frequent problem concerns where the program thinks it is supposed to look for its files. We usually copy a program into a hard disk subdirectory before running it, because things usually work faster from a hard disk.

Consequently every now and then, a program will need a file and Drive A will come on. When this happens, the best thing to do is to put some kind of disk in Drive A. The program will fail to find the file it's looking for and will generate an error message. At that point, it is usually best to exit the program and review the doc file for installation instructions. Usually it's a simple matter of telling the program to default to Drive C or something similar.

Glossbrenner's Guide to Low-Cost Computing

Finally, if you're a small businessperson interested in buying your first computer, if you're a parent interested in making a PC available in the home, or if you are someone who needs a second system, we may be able to save you a bit more than mere pocket change. We can also save you some money on the care and feeding of your machine.

It may be a subliminal desire to beat the system, or it may be the influence of a Scottish grandfather, but whatever the reason, tracking down the genuinely good deals in the computer world is something of a passion. So often it is simply a matter of having the right information or knowing the right place to contact.

Single-Sided Disks and Reinked Ribbons

For example, here are two tips that can save you a bundle right off the bat. First, don't buy double-sided disks—those designated DS/DD for "double-sided, double density." The only difference between a DS/DD disk and a single-sider (SS/DD) is that the former is certified to be error-free on both sides, while the latter is certified for only one side. You'd think that would make a difference, but it doesn't, for two reasons.

SS/DD and DS/DD disks are identical. The only thing "certification" means is that the company will replace the disk free of charge should it prove to be defective. That's rarely worth the bother, and besides, if a disk is really bad, it will be rejected as a result of any single-sided test the company may perform. (Some companies test every disk; others only spot test.)

Even more important, most people don't know it, but the DOS FOR-

MAT command automatically locks out any bad areas in the course of formatting the disk. That means that no data will be recorded on the "bad sectors," so you will not be in danger of losing any information when you use the disk. The only penalty is that the disk will hold perhaps 5K less data than one that is perfect. The FORMAT command will report available disk space when it is finished, and you can get a report at any time with the DOS CHKDSK.COM program.

The second tip is to reink your nylon printer ribbons. The ink in a printer ribbon gets used up or dries out long before the nylon goes. For years, computer users have been prying the tops off ribbon cartridges and giving the coiled ribbon a shot of the popular lubricant spray WD40 to revivify it. That's not a bad solution in a pinch. (Use WD40 sparingly and let the ribbon sit overnight if you decide to do this.) But it is not as effective as systematically applying fresh ink.

That's what the MAC INKER, from Computer Friends, Inc., does. The unit consists of a small aluminum table with a small motor. You place your cartridge on the table, run the ribbon around a roller, and fill the roller reservoir with ink. Let it run for about 45 minutes, and you'll have a freshly reinked ribbon for about five cents worth of ink. That compares to typical mail order prices of $5 to $10 per ribbon.

We've been using the MAC INKER for years and have nothing but praise for it. Costs range from $42 to $68.50, plus $3 shipping and handling. Over 11,000 printer models are supported. For more information, contact: Computer Friends, Inc., 14250 N.W. Science Park Drive, Portland, OR 97229; phone: (800) 547-3303.

What System Should You Buy?

Prior to 1988, this question could be answered quite simply: Get a "standard configuration" XT-class machine. That means an IBM PC XT, or clone, with 512K or 640K of RAM, probably two floppy disk drives, a 20 or 30- megabyte hard disk, a CGA or compatible video adaptor, and an Epson or IBM Graphics dot-matrix printer. The monitor could be an RGB color monitor or an inexpensive green or amber screen unit. This was not an official standard, of course, but prior to 1988 it had emerged as the workhorse of the PC world.

Systems like this are still available, but IBM doesn't make them anymore. The company has shifted its production to the PS/2 line. This represents a major change in the computer world, but it is unlike changes that have come before. The question is one of functionality and power.

Assume that a certain amount of personal computing power is needed to run your business, and assume that it remains relatively constant over the years. The machines that were available prior to the introduction of the original IBM PC in 1981 were useful, but they could not easily accommodate the demands of many firms. The PC, and the XT and AT, could and did, and more importantly, *do* offer the level of power and functionality most small businesses need. Unless your requirements are likely to change dramatically, you don't need a dramatically more powerful (and expensive) machine.

What complicates things is that, as mentioned earlier, there is every indication that IBM plans to price the new units aggressively. There is also the fact that programmers could tap the greater power of the PS/2 line to make the machines truly easy to use. Unfortunately, none of this has happened yet. Indeed, it may be some time before things settle down and a "standard" PS/2 configuration emerges.

The one thing you can be virtually certain of is that XT and AT-class machines will be around for many years to come. Tens of millions of them have been sold, and as noted, they offer more power and functionality than most people and small businesses need. They will thus continue to be available. The question is at what price?

As we said in Chapter 1, at this writing you can get a "standard" XT-class computer with all the trimmings from your local dealer for under $1500. You can do even better if you shop through the mail. That is a *very* good value. It is literally thousands of dollars less than you would have had to pay for the identically equipped machine only a few years ago. Once OS/2 begins to take hold, however, and IBM really gears up to push the PS/2, it seems entirely likely that as you read this, you will be able to get a complete XT-class system for between $600 and $800.

So, again, which system should you buy? In our opinion, everything boils down to two questions. First, ask yourself (and your computer-using friends and associates) whether you really need the additional capabilities offered by the PS/2. Second, ask yourself what you will have to pay for PS/2 power compared to the current price of an XT or AT-type machine. If you decide on the XT/AT alternative, ask yourself a third question: If I buy now, is it likely that the price will drop precipitously in the very near future?

If money were no object, we'd all buy the whatever happened to be the top-of-the-line PS/2 model at the time, plus an add-on 5¼-inch disk drive to be able to use both types of disks. But money is always an object, and in our opinion, if you are at all uncertain about personal computing, you simply cannot lose if you get an XT or AT-class computer. If a year or so after you buy it you decide to trade up, all of your data, all of your programs, and most important, all of what you have learned about running your machine, will be directly transferrable to the PS/2 line.

Buying a Computer Through the Mail

The cheapest way to obtain a new IBM clone is to purchase it through the mail, but the term caveat emptor was never more applicable than here. Some mail-order companies are companies in name only. Since all of the parts necessary to produce an IBM clone are available separately, many enterprising individuals buy the parts and assemble the machines in their garages or basement workrooms. The machines may be fine, but they usually do not come with MS-DOS or any software, and any manuals you may receive will undoubtedly have been poorly translated from Chinese or Korean. This is not the way for a novice to get into personal computing.

Consequently, we suggest that you go to the library and consult two magazines. Check *Consumer Reports*, a magazine which despite what we feel is a latent Apple/Macintosh bias does offer creditable evaluations of IBM mail-order clones. The most recent article on the subject at this writing appeared in the March 1988 issue. Second, check *PC Magazine*. This magazine has a well-earned reputation for comprehensive, in-depth examinations of various classes of hardware and software products, and it periodically turns its attention to the current crop of generic PCs.

How to Buy a Used Computer

Another option well worth investigating is purchasing a preowned computer. The wear points in a computer system are the printer and the disk drives, for they are the only electromechanical components. As a rule of thumb, if a computer's system unit works for 90 days, it will work nearly forever. (No moving parts.) Add to this the fact that there are always people who want to trade up, and you have a burgeoning used computer market.

The key point is knowing whom to call, and here we suggest that you start with the Boston Computer Exchange (BCE). BCE is the premier used computer broker. Started in 1982, BCE counts General Electric, Sun Oil, Kodak, and even the White House among its past and present customers. It maintains what is possibly the world's largest database of computers and related equipment for sale.

The process starts when someone wants to sell his or her machine. BCE handles virtually every kind of computer equipment, from modems to minicomputers. BCE adds the listing to its database free of charge. Each week BCE publishes its current list of equipment for sale. Prospective buyers can purchase this list for $10 a copy or subscribe on a weekly or monthly basis. If you are online with Delphi (Chapter 7), you can check the current BCE list at any time by moving to the Merchant's

Row section of the service. If you are a CompuServe subscriber, simply key in BCE at any main system prompt.

When you see a system you want, you contact BCE and it puts you in touch with the seller. BCE brokers will also advise you on the current range of prices for the system and guide you through the transaction. When you and the seller come to an agreement, the seller ships you the system and pays BCE ten percent for its services. As a buyer, using BCE costs you nothing. BCE can also direct you to companies that write service contracts should you wish to purchase one for your new used system. For more information, contact: Boston Computer Exchange Corporation, At Downtown Crossing, Box 1177, Boston, MA 02103; phone: (617) 542-4414.

You might also want to contact the Phoenix Computer Group. This firm charges sellers a one percent listing fee based on the asking price for the equipment. A ten percent brokerage fee, based on the final selling price, is charged when the deal is consummated. Copies of the firm's monthly list of available systems are $10 each. One of the points that makes Phoenix unique is the escrow account service it offers to buyers and sellers. In return for a $25 fee, Phoenix will serve as a middleman. You send the firm the money you have agreed to pay the seller. Once your check has cleared, Phoenix notifies the seller to ship the equipment. If you are satisfied with your purchase, you notify Phoenix to release the funds to the seller. If not, you can return the equipment to the seller. Once the equipment is back in the seller's possession, Phoenix will return your money, less the $25 fee. For more information, contact: Phoenix MultiList Systems, 2755 North Banana River Drive, Merritt Island, FL 32952; phone: (800) 843-6713; in Florida, dial: (305) 459-1555.

Finally, if you want to sell a used computer or buy one in a retail store, contact Computer Renaissance, Inc. Like Federal Express, this company grew out of its founder's university thesis-style project. The company's founder, Stephen Gold, prepared a project detailing the potential of the used computer market in 1983 as part of a course at the Carnegie-Mellon Graduate School of Industrial Administration. In 1984, Mr. Gold opened his first store in Monroeville, Pennsylvania. At this writing, the chain has grown to nearly a dozen stores. Some are franchises and some are company-owned. Needless to say, more are planned. For more information, contact: Computer Renaissance, 400 Penn Center Blvd., Suite 900, Pittsburgh, PA 15235; phone: (412) 824-5800.

FreeTip: There are advantages to using an intermediary like those we have cited. But you may prefer to make direct contact with the seller. If so, we suggest that you contact your local computer user group (Chapter 3) and review any ads members have placed in its monthly magazine. You should also take a look at the classified ad and personals sections of online services like CompuServe, GEnie, The Source, and others (Chapter 7). Both user groups and online systems can be excellent sources of good, very low cost, used equipment.

Maintenance and Repair

We have heard it said that one of the reasons to buy a PS/2 is that the machines supposedly require less maintenance and can thus pay for themselves in three to four years. At this point, that theory has yet to be proven, since the machines have only been on the market since April 1987. Though it is certainly something to investigate.

The amount of maintenance and service you will require is directly dependent on how heavily you use the machine, particularly its disk drives and printer. It is quite possible that you will never have to have the system repaired. Still, it is wise to look into your repair options before you buy.

Most computer retailers have or are associated with a repair shop. You will also find computer repair services listed in the Yellow Pages of your phone book, or in the phone book of the nearest large city. A good price at this writing is about $50 per hour with a one-hour minimum, though naturally prices vary widely. Some mail-order firms offer repair services as well, though you must usually ship the machine back to the company.

At this writing, the wide availability of maintenance and repair services is one of the advantages of buying an XT or AT-class machine. Most can be quickly repaired with off-the-shelf parts. We are told, however, that each system built around the Intel 80386 tends to use its own unique memory architecture (arrangement) and therefore cannot be as easily repaired.

FreeTip: If you like to do it yourself and are moderately handy, we recommend Hank Beechhold's *Brady Guide to Microcomputer Troubleshooting & Maintenance* (Brady Books/Prentice-Hall Press, 1987). Dr. Beechhold is chairman of the linguistics program at Trenton State College, an expert in Celtic and Irish studies, a poet, an editor, and a critic. He is also on the *InfoWorld* review board, a columnist for *Home/Office Computing* magazine, and has been involved in ham radio, computers, and electronics for more

FreeTip continued

than 30 years. Thorough, well-written, and packed with useful information for expert and novice alike, his book is invaluable to any hands-on computer user.

Conclusion

The programs highlighted in Part III of this book will be just as useful on PS/2 computers as they are on any MS-DOS machine. But as we noted earlier, free software tracks directly with hardware. You can thus bet the ranch on the fact that as the PS/2 and the OS/2 operating system become more widespread, public domain and shareware programs will be written to take advantage of their unique capabilities. The same is true of new printers, plotters, high-speed modems, voice and music synthesizers, erasable optical disks, and any other equipment you can name.

That's the beauty of free software, and it's one of the reasons why it is worth learning how to tap the free software distribution channels. Once you know the techniques, you can always keep yourself up-to-date. You will always be able to find the programs you need, regardless of the equipment you own, and in many cases, regardless of the time of day or night.

The chapters in Part II will give you all the tools and points of access you need to become a free software expert. They will show you how to glide through the free software distribution channels picking off the choicest fruit and identifying the real gold. In short: Saddle up! We are about to mount a raid on the real treasure houses of public domain and shareware software.

PART II

WHERE TO GET IT

3

Computer User Groups

FIRST-LINE SOURCES OF FREE SOFTWARE

Computer user groups are the point of origin for virtually all categories of free software. They are also the main collection points and the primary channels of distribution. Of course it's possible to get free software without going through a user group, but it is not possible to discuss the one without the other.

In this chapter we'll do exactly that. We'll look at the computer user group movement and what it means to every PC user. We'll show you how to locate a group in your area, what to expect, and how to make the most of what it offers—while making a contribution of your own. We'll also profile the Boston Computer Society (BCS), a "super group" without equal, and we'll look at what have emerged as the three leading groups for IBM and compatible users. These last three—the Capital PC User Group (Washington, D.C.), the Hal-PC User Group (Houston), and BCS's IBM PC User Group (Boston)—operate as local groups but through their monthly journals and free software libraries serve thousands of members worldwide. You'll want to join at least one of them, in addition to joining your local group.

What Is a Computer User Group?

If you've never heard of computer user groups before, you should know that first and foremost these organizations are mutual help societies that are usually staffed and run by volunteers. Dedicated to the general promotion of computer knowledge, they have a tradition that predates the advent of the personal computer by a decade or more. According to Sol Libes, professor of electronics at Union County College in New

69

Jersey, "The first computer club was founded in 1965. It was a national organization called the American Computer Society, and it had as many as 250 members. [Professor Libes should know, since he was one of them.] The first local group was the Homebrew Computer Club of Palo Alto, California, which was established in April 1975."

The Homebrewers were hobbyists. They had to be. The only micro-computer available at that time had to be soldered together by hand. The technology was new. Information was scarce. And users groups were a natural development. Today, exactly the reverse is true—there is more technology and more information than ever before. But on at least one level, the fundamental situation hasn't changed. New computer users still need help in making sense of it all, and users who are experienced in one area can benefit from the knowledge of users who are experienced in other areas.

FreeTip: That first computer was the MITS Altair 8800, and it appeared on the cover of *Popular Electronics* in January 1975. The enthusiasm that greeted this do-it-yourself kit took everyone by surprise. Created by retired Air Force engineer Ed Roberts, the Altair was a watershed machine. It was the catalyst for many of the things you will still encounter as you move through the world of personal computing and users groups. For example:

- The S-100 bus (essentially a "standard" wiring diagram for a computer's main circuit board) was introduced by the Altair and is still in use today. Though of little interest to IBM, Macintosh, and Apple users, there are still special interest groups devoted to S-100 machines today.

- Bill Gates left Harvard and joined his friend Paul Allen to create Altair BASIC, the predecessor to Microsoft BASIC, now the de facto standard in the industry. The two went on to found Microsoft, Inc., one of the two largest, most successful software firms in the country. (The other is Lotus Development, Inc.)

- David Bunnell, vice president of MITS, Inc., was the founding publisher of *Personal Computing*, *PC Magazine*, and *PC World*.

- The Homebrew Computer Club spawned by the Altair was the site chosen by Steven Jobs and Steven Wozniak to present the

Apple I, a machine they designed and built in the Jobs family garage. An original Apple I motherboard now sells for close to $20,000.

Given the tens of millions of people who now own computers, the need for mutual help has grown far beyond what even the most prescient Homebrewer could have imagined. Thus it is little wonder that by some estimates there are between 7000 and 8500 computer user *groups* in North America. What is surprising is how few computer owners are aware of them and of the many things they have to offer.

User Group Structure

Computer user groups are very much a grass-roots phenomenon. They can range from ten interested people who meet irregularly in some member's living room, to a group sponsored by your company, to a registered not-for-profit organization that regularly attracts a thousand people or more to its monthly meetings. Much depends on the group's location—groups in urban areas with a high density of computer users tend to be the largest and most active—and on the energy, imagination, and personality of the individuals involved. Consequently, it is impossible to set forth a definitive list of activities and services you can expect from each and every user group.

However, while there is no typical group, there are typical group activities, some of which you are sure to find whichever group you join. Virtually all groups, for example, hold a monthly meeting. Small organizations may meet in someone's home; large ones may take over the ballroom of a local hotel or an auditorium on a college campus. Meetings are usually held once a month on weekday evenings or on a Saturday, and after the treasurer's report, announcements, and other club business has been transacted, there will usually be a guest speaker.

Savvy hardware and software manufacturers are well aware of the word-of-mouth influence user group members wield. So at a large group's meeting it isn't uncommon for someone like Bill Gates (Microsoft), Phillipe Kahn (Borland), John Scully (Apple), Steve Jobs (Next), Rod Canion (Compaq), or other computer industry luminaries to appear. Computer columnists like John Dvorak, shareware authors like Jim Button, and computer book authors have also been featured speakers at such meetings.

Sometimes the monthly meeting will be preceded by "buying sessions." At the HAL-PC group, for example, the buying session begins an hour and a half before the main meeting, as local retailers and other vendors assemble to offer hardware, software, disks, disk boxes, printer ribbons, paper, and other supplies at discounted, user group prices. After one such session, Duane Hendricks, then president of the 6600-member group, announced as the main meeting was getting under way that 35,000 blank floppy disks had been sold, down slightly from the previous month's total.

SIGs (Special Interest Groups)

As one of the original members of an IBM user group founded five months after the PC was announced, it is easy to recall the early meetings. The PC was so new that the basic machine itself was the group's main focus. What adaptor cards should you buy? Should you get one or two (single-sided!) disk drives? What is DOS (version 1.0) all about anyhow? Will CP/M become an important alternative operating system for the PC?

That was in early 1982. The field has furcated so many times since then that no single group can address every interest or need. If you're interested in learning more about dBASE, you might find a session on local area networks a waste of time. If desktop publishing is a major interest, you don't want to sit through a session devoted to Lotus and Symphony worksheet templates. And so on.

The development of special interest groups (SIGs) within the user group structure was a natural response to this situation. Among others, for example, the Capital PC User Group has SIGs devoted to exploring APL, BASIC, CAD/CAM, educational software, Ashton-Tate's Framework, and Lotus 1-2-3, as well as SIGs devoted to applications in accounting, law, and investing. The BCS IBM group has a SIG for desktop publishing. HAL-PC has one for PC applications to the oil and gas industry. As other areas of personal computing develop, other SIGs will be formed. All that is required is a number of user group members interested in learning more about a particular PC product or application, and someone willing to serve as chairman of the SIG.

FreeTip: Do you really need to pay hefty fees to some guy or gal in a three-piece suit to train you or your employees in how to use a computer? Possibly. But before signing on the dotted line, it would behoove you to check out the computer user groups in your area. Almost every group has a "Novice," "New User," or "Beginner's" SIG, and most have SIGs devoted to the best-selling software programs as well. The annual dues for most computer user groups are usually only about $25 per person.

In fact, it would be an excellent idea to join a user group *before* you invest in a system. Group members can advise you on what to get, where to buy it, and on what really works and what doesn't. They can advise you on the best dealers in your area and on the best discount mail-order companies. They might also serve as a source of inexpensive, perfectly serviceable used equipment. As enthusiasts, many group members like to have the latest machines, whether they need them or not. But they can't afford to buy them until they sell their current equipment.

Finally, even if the SIGs can't provide the kind of training you or your employees need, you may meet someone there who can. Many SIG members are far more knowledgeable than the typical trainer or computer salesperson and some are just as communicative. Some may be willing and able to fill your training needs for considerably less money than you would have to pay a full-time trainer.

In the larger organizations, at least, most members belong both to the main group and to one or more SIGs. SIGs are typically headed by chairmen and hold regular meetings, often at someone's home one weekday evening a month. Or they may meet after the main group's monthly session. It all depends on the group.

The SIGs are a prime source of much of the free software that is available today. When you think about it for a moment, this makes perfect sense. Short of a full-time professional programmer, who is better qualified to produce a Lotus or Symphony template than someone who is interested enough to study the product and to attend monthly meetings discussing its applications? Many individuals join a SIG to learn how to use a software product to solve a particular set of business or professional problems. The result is usually a BASIC or Pascal program, a dBASE command file, a Lotus template, or some other piece of software that's been tested, debugged, and improved by its creator and other SIG members. And in the spirit of sharing and mutual assistance that characterizes the user group movement, the program is usually donated to the organization's free software library.

User Group Free Software Libraries

Free software is certainly one of the most tangible benefits of user group membership, and it has long been one of the most popular of user group services. Some groups rely on the natural fermentation process to send free programs bubbling to the surface. Others actively try to assemble a Disk of the Month (DOM) containing completely new programs or revised versions of old favorites.

One way or another, you will almost certainly find that every group has a software librarian. Some groups even have SIGs devoted to this area. The librarian's job is to collect, categorize, review, and often test programs before assembling them onto disks for distribution to group members. Some programs come from the SIGs. But the librarian and his or her assistants may also regularly scan the commercial online systems discussed in Chapter 7 and the national electronic bulletin board network discussed in Chapter 8 for new material. In addition, many shareware authors will make certain that their creations reach the librarians of major user groups. And, of course, a librarian will often swap disks with the librarian at another user group. As a result of the informal human and electronic networks that have been built up over the years, it doesn't take very long for a new program to become widely available.

Channels of Distribution

User groups distribute their free software in three major ways. Many of the larger groups maintain computer bulletin boards for members to call and download programs over the phone. (We'll have a lot more to say about bulletin boards in Chapter 8.)

A more important method is to make the group's library available at the main monthly meeting. The librarian and his or her assistants usually set up their computers in a room near the main meeting hall. Either before, after, or during the main meeting, members are free to pick up any programs they want. If you bring your own blank disks, there will usually be a copying charge of one to two dollars to help maintain the library and pay for wear and tear on the librarian's disk drives. But often a club will be able to provide you with a blank disk at a discounted price. (If you do bring your own disks, be sure to format them beforehand.) Alternatively, a librarian may have prepared copied disks that you can buy right out of inventory. At Capital PC meetings, for example, disks are available at $5.

Finally, although a small group may not offer its disks through the mail, all of the large groups do. The Capital PC mail-order price is $8 per disk ($10 for foreign orders). The BCS IBM group mail-order price for members is $5 per disk, $7 for nonmembers. In the past HAL-PC has had an arrangement with the Public (software) Library profiled in Chapter 4 to handle mail orders for its members.

Free Software Catalogs

In addition to assembling and distributing disks, software librarians and their assistants are also responsible for preparing the library catalog. The general practice here is to follow the traditional format that provides the filename, size, date, and one line of description per program. The following excerpt from the Capital PC group's catalog describing Disk 62 is a good example:

CPCUG #62 Utility IV (a two-disk set) 4/18/87

A collection of helpful DOS utilities
Selected by Tom Enrico and originally presented at
the CPCUG Education and Training Seminar on 4/18/87

Disk Number 1:

FILE NAME	SIZE	DATE	DESCRIPTION
ARCE.COM	5083	4-01-86	File de-archiver
HINSTALL.BAT	521	4-18-87	Hard disk installation procedure
HINSTX.BAT	792	4-18-87	Part 2 of hard disk installation
READ.ME	885	4-17-87	General information on installing the disks
DISPLAY.ARC	13569	4-17-87	Screen management utility programs:
BACKSCRL.DOC	12288	29 Jul 85	Save up to 28 screenfuls of a DOS session
BACKSCRL.COM	6528	29 Jul 85	
RULER.DOC	1536	23 Mar 85	A pop-up on-screen ruler
RULER.COM	2560	23 Mar 85	
SCRAT.DOC	2541	31 May 86	Change screen attributes (color, etc.) easily
SCRAT.COM	1076	19 Mar 86	
FILEMGMT.ARC	120226	1-23-87	Utility programs for managing files:
ALTER.DOC	508	23 Dec 86	Change file attributes, incl. time & date
ALTER.COM	2688	22 Dec 86	
ARC.EXE	32051	31 Jan 86	All-purpose file arcer; enter arc for instr.
ARCA.COM	3231	23 Apr 86	File archiver (i.e., add to archive)

(etc.)

Most of the files on this disk have been compressed into archives (ARC) and, as explained in Chapter 2, will have to be extracted with ARCE.COM, the first program listed above. Thus DISPLAY.ARC and FILEMGMT.ARC will appear on your screen when you call for a directory of the disk. But as the catalog shows, each of these archives contains several programs.

User group free software catalogs are usually published in several ways. One way is to produce a printed booklet or collection of photocopied sheets. These are good for browsing in your easy chair. A more common method is to put the entire catalog on a disk and offer it as part of the collection. The BCS IBM group does this, and at the Capital PC group, the software catalog is included on the introductory disk provided to all new members. Finally, almost every user group periodically runs a feature about its free software collection in its monthly newsletter. These features may cover the entire collection and include an order form, or they may be limited to new disks or programs that have been added to the library in the past month.

User Group Newsletters and Journals

As noted earlier, the three leading IBM groups are first and foremost local organizations designed to serve users who live in the Boston, Washington, or Houston area. But they serve a national and international audience as well, primarily through their monthly newsletters. Most user groups publish a newsletter of some sort, but as you might imagine, they run the gamut in quantity of pages and quality of information.

One small local group we belong to, for example, manages to produce four or five stapled, dot-matrix-printed pages a month. The newsletter is largely the creation of one man, and it always contains interesting computer-related news items he has encountered during the month, in addition to local club news and meeting schedules. A group we belong to based in Philadelphia serves as an umbrella organization for over 60 machine and topic-specific user groups. This group's newsletter runs 32 typeset pages or more each month. It contains reports from each of the user group presidents, meeting schedules, and opinion, hardware and software review, and "tips" pieces submitted by group members.

The Houston, Boston, and Washington groups, however, are at the apex of the publications pyramid. Their monthly offerings are better described as journals than newsletters. Of typeset quality, they typically run anywhere from 60 to 100 pages or more. They are highly professional publications produced by all-volunteer labor, and the useful information they contain in each issue is on a par with (and sometimes superior to) what you'll find in many commercial computer magazines.

FreeTip: Since many user groups regularly exchange newsletters, usually on disk, it isn't uncommon to find a "best of the newsletters" feature in some group publications. For example, the January 1987 issue of the *Capital PC Monitor* published a tip from Kansas Computer Society member Blaine Volz. To wit, if you

want to get rid of a subdirectory without having to key in DEL *.*
first, simply go to the directory immediately above and delete the
target subdirectory by name. If the target subdirectory is called
TEMP, for example, key in DEL TEMP. The system will ask "Are
you sure (Y/N)?" Key in Y, and then key in RD TEMP to remove
that subdirectory. You only have to do this once to appreciate the
keystrokes it saves and to make it a permanent part of your DOS
repertoire. And it only takes a tip or two like this to appreciate the
gold mine of information to be found in computer user group journals and newsletters.

The Focal Point of Group Services

The newsletter or journal is truly the focal point for all user group activities and services. If the group operates a computer bulletin board
system (BBS), for example, the newsletter will give you the number to
dial and tell you how to log on. In some cases, there will be a "best of
the BBS" column in the newsletter containing the most interesting tips
and information people have posted there during the previous month.
Some groups maintain a 24-hour information line that provides recorded
messages about meeting schedules and group activities. Those numbers
too can be found in the newsletter.

Of course, the names and phone numbers of the group's special interest group chairmen will be included. But you may also find lists of group
members who have volunteered to answer questions on specific products or topics. HAL-PC, for example, easily has over 100 members on
its Help Committee. Capital PC and the Boston group have substantial
Help Line and Dial Help (respectively) volunteers as well. The names
and phone numbers of these members are published in the journals,
categorized by topic. The number of topics covered is extensive in all
three cases. A brief sampling includes: accounting systems, AutoCAD,
astronomy, Chartmaster, Clipper, Condor, DataEase, Dataflex,
dBASE, PC Junior, PFS:Write, PostScript, RBase 5000, WordPerfect,
and WordStar. This is in addition to a topic for every major programming language, IBM-compatible computer, and best-selling piece of
hardware.

As a member, you have access to all of these people and the help and
expertise they willingly provide. Thus, whether you live close enough to
a group to benefit from its local activities or not, and regardless of
whether you plan to attend meetings, it *still pays to join* a computer
user group of some kind. Group membership always includes a subscription to a monthly newsletter or journal. The cost for most groups is

between $10 and $25 a year. Sometimes family memberships are available for an extra $5 per person. Add to this the fact that the group you choose may be incorporated as a non-profit, educational organization—which may make your membership fee tax-deductible—and you're looking at one of the bargains of the century.

How to Find a Local User Group

So if user groups are such a great deal, how come more people don't know about them? Good question. Part of the answer is that most groups don't advertise. They may operate booths at computer fairs, swapmeets, and computer flea markets, but they usually don't have the budget to place ads in local newspapers. The other part of the answer is that there is no natural point of intersection between first-time computer buyers and the user groups that could make their lives so much easier. A businessperson who's in the market for a computer goes to a computer store, gets some advice from the salesperson, and a visit or two later walks out with a system. If the businessperson has a problem, he or she phones the computer store. Hopefully the problem gets solved, and the businessperson bumps along until the next problem arises, generating another call to the store. And so on. The cycle can continue indefinitely without the businessperson ever suspecting that such a thing as a computer user group exists. Unless a first-time computer buyer hears about a group from a computer-using friend or associate, reads an article in a computer magazine, or is lucky enough to have a knowledgeable salesperson, the topic will simply never come up in the normal course of things.

Because the three leading IBM groups are so outstanding, we urge you to join at least one of them. But you will also want to join a group closer to home. To find one, start with the stores in your area that specialize in selling computers and computer equipment. If possible, try to find a store that has its own on-site service and repair facility. Then call up and ask to speak to one of the technicians. Since technicians tend to have a more passionate interest in computers than salespeople, the chances are that if anyone in the store knows about computer user groups they will. If that approach isn't possible, stop in and simply ask the first salesperson you see whether he or she knows of any computer user groups in town. If that person doesn't know, ask if he or she would mind checking with the other store personnel.

What you're looking for is a name and a phone number. You need some point of access to the user group world. Call the individual (at a reasonable hour), explain that you are interested in locating an IBM user group, and ask for the person's help. At that point, you'll be tapped into the network. You may have to make one or two more calls, but you can be certain that if there's a group in your area, you'll find it.

It's also be a good idea to ask friends or business associates who own computers for their suggestions. You might also contact someone at your local school system to see if any groups use the school's facilities for meetings. If there is a college in your area, check with the secretary of the engineering or computer science department to see if the college hosts a user group of some sort. Attending a local computer fair or swapmeet is another good way to make contact. Some groups also set up tables and booths as part of hobbyist and crafts exhibitions at local shopping malls.

FreeTip: Radio and electronics stores can also be good sources of computer contacts. Amateur and ham radio operators have been heavily involved in personal computers from the beginning. We've watched a local ham couple an interface box or two to a computer and use it to access radio-based computer bulletin boards half way around the world. (Look Ma, no phone bill!) There is thus a good chance that a member of a ham radio club will know of computer clubs in your area. It might be worth checking with an electronics store for the name of a ham radio club in your area.

FreeTip: *Computer Shopper,* a monthly tabloid-size magazine available on many newstands, runs a regular six-page list of computer user groups. The list includes not only groups in the United States but in Canada, Australia, Panama, Israel, Germany, France, and other countries as well. Only a small fraction of the world's user groups are included, but the addresses and groups on the list are virtually guaranteed to be valid. The list is maintained by FOG, an umbrella user group based in Daly City, California. If a local group does not send an update report to FOG every three months, its name is removed from the list. Since FOG and *Computer Shopper* offer a similar feature for computer bulletin board numbers, you will find more information on both in Chapter 8.

BCS: User Group Sui Generis

The Boston Computer Society, Inc. (BCS)
One Center Plaza
Boston, MA 02108
(617) 367-8080, from 9:30 A.M. to 5:30 P.M. Eastern Standard Time

Membership: 25,000

Cost of Membership

Associate (outside New England): $28

Regular: (1 year): $35;
   (2 years $65; 3 years $95)
Student (full-time): $28
Youth (under 18): $24
Senior citizen: $24

Family: $52
Overseas: $70
Sustaining: $100
Institutional: $100
Corporate: $300
Lifetime: $2500

Publications

BCS membership includes the following six publications.

- *Computer Update.* A bimonthly (six issues per year) "slick" magazine. Normally runs 50 to 60 pages and includes articles of interest to all computer users, as well as summaries of BCS's many activities.

- "Calendar." A monthly summary of meeting and event schedules. BCS and its various groups hold over 1000 meetings, events, and educational programs each year throughout the six New England states. However, since "Calendar" is not likely to be of interest to nonlocal members, it is not included in the associate membership.

- *The BCS Buying Guide.* Published in May and November, this 60-page magazine includes special offers from nearly 500 companies *nationwide* who will give you a discount on their goods and services if you are a BCS member. Discounts range from 10 to 40 percent.

- "The BCS Resource Guide." This coat-pocket-format booklet is published each year. Its 32+ pages detail "Everything you always wanted to know about BCS but weren't sure whom to ask." There are chapters on clinics, the Computer Museum, educational programs, public services/community outreach, special interest groups, and more.

- Two User Group/SIG newsletters. Many BCS user groups and SIGs publish regular newsletters and journals. A subscription to two such newsletters is included in your basic membership. Subscriptions to other newsletters are available at $4 apiece.

BCS Voice and Electronic Information Lines

For recorded information on BCS meetings and events, call the BCS InfoLine at (617) 227-0170, 24 hours a day, 7 days a week. Information is updated every Friday.

There are also BCS sections on two electronic online services. Set your system for 8/N/1 (see Chapter 5 for an explanation of communications settings), and dial CitiNet at (617) 439-5699 or Info Online at (617) 247-3048.

Machine-Specific User Groups

Apple (II through //c)
Atari (400, 800, 1200, ST)
Burroughs/Convergent
    Technologies
Commodore (64, 128, Amiga)
Compaq
CP/M computers
DEC Rainbow and VAX family
Heath/Zenith
Hewlett-Packard
IBM (PC through PS/2)
Kaypro
Laptop computers
Macintosh
MS-DOS computers
NEC
Osborne
Otrona/Attache
Sinclair/Timex
TI (99/4a and Pro Series)
TRS-80/Tandy Radio Shack
Victor
Wang

Interest Groups

Artificial Intelligence
Business
CD-ROM
Computer-Aided Publishing (CAP)
Consultants & Entrepreneurs
Databases
Disabled/Special Needs
Education/Classroom Computers
Graphics
International Users
Investment
Legal
Logo
Lotus
Medical/Dental
Music
Networking/Multi-User
Non-Profit/Public Sector
Programming Languages
Real Estate
Robotics
Science/Engineering
Social Impact
Telecommunications
Training & Documentation
Women & PCs

A Phenomenal Organization

There is nothing else like the Boston Computer Society anywhere else in the world. It was a phenomenal organization when the first edition of this book was written in 1983, and it has become even more so since—doubling its membership, piling one accomplishment upon another, with no diminuation of energy, enthusiasm, or excitement

Lots of people are responsible, of course. And certainly the proximity of Route 128, the high-tech Boston beltway that is home to so many computer hardware and software companies that it has been dubbed "Silicon Valley—East," has been an important factor. As have the many colleges and universities located in and around the Boston area. But no one doubts who's really responsible for BCS and all that it has become. The man's name is Jonathan Rotenberg ("Wrote-en-berg"), and in addition to founding BCS on February 25, 1977—when he was 13—he has continually infused it with his energy and vision, while motivating others to share his enthusiasm for the enterprise.

Mr. Rotenberg is exceptional for another reason as well. His interests have never been "computers for the sake of computers." From the beginning, Mr. Rotenberg has been dedicated to aiding the nontechnical, noncomputerist computer owner in really using and benefiting from available technology. The Boston group reflects this orientation in nearly all of its many activities.

Resource Center, Clinics, and Discounts

For example, there is the BCS Resource Center situated in the group's main office, a split-level, ten-room affair located in what used to be a bar in Boston's financial district. The Resource Center is equipped with over 20 personal computers and more than 500 software packages for on-site use by BCS members. There is also an extensive library of computer books and magazines and files of information on computers, software, applications, consultants, and training courses. The center is open Monday through Friday, 9:30 A.M. to 5:30 P.M.

At various times throughout the month BCS and its user and interest groups (U&Is) sponsor clinics, workshops, and seminars at the Resource Center and other locations. The beginners clinic, for example, is open to BCS members for $10, or $15 for nonmembers. An accounting systems clinic ($15 members, $25 nonmembers) has proved popular. Limited to 20 people, the clinic is designed to show you how to go about computerizing your accounting systems and to answer your software questions.

BCS is also affiliated with the Computer Museum, "the world's first permanent exhibition of the past, present and future of computer technology . . . 30,000 square feet of lively exhibits and hands-on demonstrations." BCS membership includes one free admission pass (worth $4) to the museum.

If you don't live near Boston, you won't be able to take advantage of these and similar activities. But you can definitely benefit from the *BCS Buying Guide*. Issued twice a year, this publication includes special offers to BCS members from nearly 500 companies nationwide. Admittedly, most of the firms offering consulting, hardware, software, training, and other services are in Massachusetts, but there are many located as far west as California and Arizona and as far south as Florida. And many serve customers nationwide, regardless of location.

One recent Buying Guide contained an offer from PC Connection, the Marlow, New Hampshire mail-order firm whose racoon-festooned double and quadruple page ads you've seen in *PC Magazine* and similar publications. "Give us your BCS member number before placing an order," the offer reads, "and we'll ship it to you free anywhere in the continental United States by UPS ground." The Hertz Corporation offers BCS members a 10 percent discount on daily car rentals with no restrictions. Book publishers, including Hayden, Howard W. Sams, Quantum Books, and MIT Press, offer 10 to 20 percent discounts to BCS members. NEBS Computer Forms offers 20 percent off on all imprinted products (such as checks, forms, labels, and stationery). And *Computer Shopper* offers BCS members a one-year subscription for $14.97 instead of the standard $21.

The U&Is and BCS Organization

BCS itself serves as a "super group" umbrella organization that is responsible for all major events and activities. Beneath that umbrella are scores of hardware-specific user groups and topic-specific interest groups. Some of the U&I groups can be quite large indeed. Over 14,000 BCS members are also members of the IBM group, for example, while the Lotus group boasts more than 3480 members.

All of the U&Is have separate meetings, and many publish their own newsletter or journal. These vary in both quality and frequency. The IBM PC journal runs to 60 pages or more and is issued monthly; the database users newsletter is typically 12 pages long and published quarterly. Both of these publications are quite good. Other group newsletters that we have received over the years are not very good at all (much depends on the energy of the person who happens to be in charge at the time).

Within the U&Is there may be any number of what BCS organizations call their Special Interest Groups. Like SIGs everywhere, these are dedicated to some aspect of the main group's interest. For example, within the Consultants and Entrepreneur's group there are SIGs focusing on marketing software, getting venture capital, accounting, business planning, and similar topics. The IBM group has SIGs devoted to communications and networking, desktop publishing, project management, Word Perfect, word processing, and PC compatibles, among other topics.

BCS Branching Out

The latest project for the group is the BCS Member Center. This will be a new location that will be designed to bring all BCS activities under one roof. "One of the major objectives of the center," according to Jonathan Rotenberg, "is to develop a much stronger package of services for non-resident members. These services will include expanded publications, national online services, improved access to BCS public domain software, a nationwide network of telephone consultants, and, eventually, kits for organizing local BCS chapters." Other plans include holding national conferences at the center on how to organize and manage a user group and turning the center into a model for similar facilities throughout the United States.

The Top Three IBM User Groups

BCS IBM PC User Group
The Boston Computer Society, Inc. (BCS)
One Center Plaza
Boston, MA 02108
(617) 367-8080

You join this group by joining BCS and indicating that you would like to receive *PC Report* as one of the two newsletter/journals you are entitled to as part of your BCS membership. As we have said, this group's journal is outstanding. In addition to features, reviews, a "best of" other user group newsletters section, and special interest group reports, each issue includes "Dial Help"—an extensive list of volunteers who stand ready to answer your questions on virtually any PC hardware or software topic or product. There is also a bulletin board you can dial up. And as a member, you can obtain public domain software disks for $5 apiece, (compared to $7 each for nonmembers). Prices include taxes, shipping, and handling and are subject to change without notice. All orders must be prepaid with checks drawn on a U.S. bank and made out to "Boston Computer Society." At this writing, there are nearly 80 disks in the library.

Capital PC User Group, Inc. (CPCUG)
51 Monroe Street
Plaza East Two
Rockville, MD 20850
(301) 762-6775, 24-hour recorded information

Membership: 4500

Cost of Membership

$25 in the United States, $40 for international members; of which $22 is
for a subscription to the *Capital PC Monitor*.

Publication

Capital PC Monitor, a monthly (except August) typeset publication
typically of 60 pages or more.

SIGs

Accounting	Framework
Advanced	Investment
APL	Leading Edge
Art/Music	Local Area Networks
Artificial Intelligence	Medical
AT&T PC 6300	Novice
BASIC	PC XT/AT
C/UNIX	Presentation Graphics
CAD/CAM	R:BASE
COBOL	Senior
Communications	Software Entrepreneurs
DataBase	Software Exchange
Desktop Publishing	Statistics
Educational Software	Word Processing
FORTRAN	1-2-3/Symphony

From its inception at a meeting of 18 people at the Washington Naval
Yard in February 1982 to the present day, the Capital PC User Group
has remained one of the best-managed, best-organized, most active
users organizations in the IBM PC world. The *Capital PC Monitor* is a
first-class monthly journal that is typically packed with hands-on tips,
bits of code, reviews of both commercial and free software programs,
and informed commentary on issues affecting PC users.

The group also sponsors several bulletin board systems for members
and offers group purchase discounts through its Buying Group. In 1986
Buying Group income and outflow were slightly under $160,000. The
Buying Group is not set up to make a profit. Members also receive dis-

counts on *PC World*, *PC*, *PC Tech Journal*, and *Software Digest* magazines. For example, as a CPCUG member you would pay $14.97 for a
one-year subscription to *PC World* instead of the regular $23.75 annual
rate. For *PC* the CPCUG price is $17.49, instead of the regular $34.97.

The group has a number of innovative programs as well. For example, there is the CPCUG Store Watch. Most issues of the *Capital PC
Monitor* contain a "Customer Evaluation Form" for members to fill out
whenever they have dealings with a computer retailer. The forms are
collated and the processed results made available to members. The
group has also published the CPCUG Bill of Rights for Software Users.
And it was the leader in the battle to establish tax exempt status for
computer user groups.

There is also the annual CPCUG Software Programming Contest. Involving six age groups and six software categories (from games to financial tools), the grand prize is $2000 in cash or a $4000 college scholarship
fund. First prizes are $100; second prizes, $50; third prizes, one year's
free membership in CPCUG. In all, a total of $9000 is awarded, with the
best of the resulting programs going into the group's free software library. The contest is open to individuals only, but you do not have to be
a CPCUG member to compete.

As a new member, you will receive the CPCUG Introductory Disk. In
addition to a summary of all CPCUG benefits, scheduled general meetings and educational training seminars, information and a tutorial on
using the various CPCUG BBSs, details on all CPCUG SIGs, and the
group's public domain software catalog, the disk contains more than 40
public domain and shareware utility programs. You will also receive the
yearly 100-page membership directory which, in addition to the addresses and phone numbers of all CPCUG members around the world,
also contains all the basic information you need on how the club and its
SIGs operate, its constitution, and the benefits available to members.

From the beginning, public domain software has been a major interest of the Capital PC group. As Rich Schinnell, the group's long-time
software librarian told us, "We had a disk of public domain programs by
the second meeting of the group. At the first meeting, we simply told
everyone that we wanted them to go home and write a program and
bring it on disk to the next meeting. That was our 'seed' disk and it was
the beginning of our software library." As we will see in Chapter 8, PC
users everywhere are indebted to the Capital PC group for fostering
the development of RBBS-PC, probably the most widely used free bulletin board package in the IBM/PC world.

At this writing, the CPCUG library contains more than 60 disks. The
disks are available only to CPCUG members, and the mail-order cost is
$8 per disk, including media, postage, disk mailer, and handling ($10 for

foreign orders). As noted, all new members receive the library catalog as part of the Introductory Disk that is included with membership.

Houston Area League of PC Users, Inc. (HAL-PC)
P.O. Box 61266
Houston, TX 77208-1266
(713) 524-8383
(713) 524-2572, interactive voice response system

Membership: 8079

Cost of Membership

$25 per year.

Publication

HAL-PC User Journal, a monthly typeset publication of about 90 pages.

SIGs

Accounting/Business	Lotus 1-2-3/Symphony
Artificial Intelligence	Medical Information Systems
Assembly Language	Microconsultants
AUTOCAD	Networking
Beginning Users	Oil & Gas
C Language	Paradox
COBOL	Paradox PAL Class
Compiled Basic	Pascal
Dataflex	PC jr
Desktop Publishing	R:BASE System V
Eagles	R:BASE Workshop
Enable	Revelation
Forth Language	Senior DOS
FORTRAN 77	Stockmarket
Framework	Systems
Graphics	Telecommunications
Heath/Zenith	Windows (Microsoft)
K-Man/Guru	Word (Microsoft)
Legal	Word Perfect

The best way to get a quick handle on HAL-PC and the high regard in which it is held is to point out that during 1986, the following personages were among the speakers at its monthly meetings: Bill Machrone, editor of *PC Magazine;* Will Fastie, editor of *PC Tech Journal;* Bob Frankston, creator of VisiCalc and now vice president of Lotus Development; Bill Gates, chairman of Microsoft; Rod Canion, chairman of

Compaq; Phillipe Kahn, chairman of Borland International; and Jim Button, one of the most successful shareware authors ever. Many of these luminaries have appeared at the Boston and Washington groups, too. But HAL-PC seems to place a somewhat greater emphasis on presenting name-brand speakers. This may be one reason why attendance at the group's monthly meeting hasn't dipped below 1000 in over a year.

Fortunately for members who don't live in the area, the *HAL-PC User Journal* faithfully summarizes all such meetings and the major points the speakers made. The publication often does the same with SIG meetings, enabling all readers of the journal to share at least part of the experience (and the benefit). You'll also find the journal's pages packed with tips and bits of code, hardware and software reviews, features on computer issues and technologies, and the Help Committee list of members you can call for assistance and advice on virtually any hardware or software product or problem. There is also a feature called DEX (disk exchange) that includes "best of" items from newsletters exchanged with other groups (on disk) around the world.

Incidentally, replacing each letter in the name HAL with the letter that follows it in the alphabet adds an extra dimension to the name shared by this group, a Lotus 1-2-3 add-in program, and a pivotal character in a certain Stanley Kubrick movie.

Making a Contribution

The computer user group movement is based on the concept of people helping people. It is powered by the time, effort, and perspiration of cheerful volunteers, not by advertising dollars or corporate funding. As we have tried to show you, user groups, both local and national, have a great deal to offer you. But as with so many things, the more you give of yourself, the more you will get out of it. User groups can pay handsome rewards for even a small investment. On the other hand, if most members are constantly on the "take" side of the equation, never giving anything back, a group and all it represents will simply cease to be.

Over the years we've corresponded with or spoken to the officers of literally hundreds of user groups across the continent. It is sad to report, but after years of devoting nearly all of their spare time to operating and maintaining their clubs, more than a few of these individuals are burned out. They are there to help, but they can't do it alone.

So what can you give? You're a new computer owner. You don't know how to program and may see no good reason to learn. You've got your hands full just trying to use your system. How can you contribute anything of value? Many of the groups we contacted said that new users can contribute by asking questions. A new computer owner often has a different perspective than someone who has been involved for several years, and can sometimes enlighten everyone by simply asking a question. Many experienced users *want* you to ask because they enjoy answering. You are, however, expected to make a good-faith effort at reading and trying to understand the manuals and instructions that came with the product.

There are many other, more substantive things you can do. As one California user group newsletter editor told us,

> I joined the group in 1979 as a novice. I am still a novice, but I put out a good magazine. Nonprogrammers can contribute, as I do, by assuming responsibility for some segment of the club's activities. I get the bulletin out, and others contribute articles. Some members take charge of our monthly raffle, others assist the membership chairman in enrolling new members. And with 50 to 60 new ones every month, that's a real job.

You could offer to help the club librarian organize and maintain the disk collection. You could volunteer to establish contact with other clubs across the country (a good use for the free word processing and mailing list programs we'll show you how to get later) and serve as liaison. You could help organize the monthly meeting, perhaps using contacts in your own business or profession to bring in interesting speakers. You might work at persuading local retailers to give club members a discount or organize a bulk purchase program to provide members with floppy disks, printer paper, and supplies at significantly reduced prices.

In short, there are *all kinds* of things you can do to lend a helping hand. Your efforts may go unpaid, but they won't go unheralded and they will always be appreciated.

4

Mail-Order Sources

THE GREAT, THE FAIR, AND THE FAIRLY AWFUL

The second major outlet for free software consists of non-user-group mail-order sources. These are companies or individuals who publish catalogs of programs and sell disks of free software through the mail. Some can afford to take display ads in *Byte*, *PC*, *PC World*, and similar computer magazines. Others typically can be found only in the classified section of *Computer Shopper*, a fat, ad-packed monthly tabloid magazine. The prices and policies of these sources vary as widely as the quality of the services they offer. With some it is difficult to prevent the word "rip-off" from forming in one's brain. Others it is difficult to praise highly enough.

In this chapter we'll introduce you to the two leading non-user-group firms: Nelson Ford's "Public (software) Library" (PsL) and Richard Petersen's PC Software Interest Group (PC-SIG). We'll also show you what to watch out for when dealing with an unknown mail-order source. But before we begin, we should say a word or two about where non-user-group mail-order sources fit in the scheme of things.

The Mail-Order Alternative

In the first place, just about all of the software offered by these firms originates in user group libraries. Indeed, for many years PsL *was* the user group library for Houston's HAL-PC user group. It may be so again in the future. For its part, PC-SIG used the library of the Silicon Valley Computer Society (SVCS) in Santa Clara, California as the basis of its collection when it started operations. Most other mail-order sources tend to duplicate the PsL and PC-SIG collections, often disk-for-disk, despite the questionable legality of this practice.

The point is that non-user-group mail order sources don't have any special access to the world of free software. There isn't a program they can supply that you can't also find in a user group collection, through one of the commercial online systems discussed in Chapter 7, or via the bulletin board systems discussed in Chapter 8. So why do such organizations exist and why might you want to deal with them?

Mail-order sources exist primarily because most computer owners don't know about computer user groups. And those who do know about user groups may not have access to one in their area. In addition, many groups simply aren't set up to handle mail-order requests from members who can't always make it to the monthly meeting. There is also the fact that not all user group libraries are created equal. The quality and comprehensiveness of any group's collection varies directly with the vigor of its software librarian. The best mail-order sources answer these needs by offering comprehensiveness and convenience, while alerting people who would never encounter or otherwise hear about computer user groups to the existence of free software.

Points of Origin

As Richard Petersen told us, he founded PC-SIG in 1982 because "Public domain programs were available all over the country, but you almost had to know somebody to find out what and where they were. There was no central place where you could look and say 'Hey, these are *all* of the things that are available.'" PC-SIG was started in hopes of establishing a national, and possibly an international, focal point for free IBM programs. Since no one was offering such a service at the time, Mr. Petersen assembled a collection based on the SVCS library and paid for a number of ads in *PC* magazine. "The only way to let people know about public domain software," he quite rightly points out, "is to advertise."

Nelson Ford and other HAL-PC members began collecting public domain software for the group in 1982. However, Ford said that

We could never find an adequate way of distributing it to the membership. We tried about a half a dozen things. We gave complete copies of the library to each one of the special interest groups. All they did was lose all the disks. Then we tried trading newsletter advertising space to a local computer rental firm, a place where you could rent computer equipment by the hour. The owner maintained a set of the library disks there, and HAL-PC members could walk in and make copies. That only worked two or three months.

One of the last things we tried was paying the guy to do nothing but take orders, make copies, and distribute the disks. He kept the proceeds. The librarians were getting nothing. Which was fine. All we wanted to do was mess with the software and let him handle the details of distribution. He did that for two or three more months and gave up on it. He said it just wasn't worth the time and effort. By that time we had exhausted every other procedure. So finally we took over what he had been doing and began offering the disks to members and others through the mail.

More Than A Volunteer Group Can Handle

In our opinion, if you don't join your local user group and one or more of the leading groups profiled in the previous chapter, you will cheat yourself out of a great deal of information and enjoyment. At the same time, however, it must be acknowledged that the free software field has grown so large and developed such momentum that no all-volunteer organization can possibly keep up on its own. The only way to assemble a comprehensive, up-to-date collection is with a paid staff and a full-time organization. As Nelson Ford told us,

> I usually put in no fewer than 90 hours a week working on the library. I used to do it part-time and found I was devoting about 50 hours a week into the library and 40 hours a week into my regular job. That was in February 1986. I was getting to the point where things were falling behind with the library, and I realized that I would have to either let my office job go or let the library go.

Mr. Ford, then a C.P.A. and microcomputer manager for a Houston firm, opted for the former. With two or three full-time employees and several part-time assistant librarians, he has devoted himself to PsL ever since. PC-SIG is also a full-time organization, with 15 to 20 people involved in almost all of its projects.

The Process of Assembling a Collection

You might not think that assembling and maintaining a free software library would be so time-consuming. But as we found in selecting the programs for Glossbrenner's Choice disks, the task consumes time and energy the way a 16-cylinder car guzzles gasoline. In the first place, you've got over 1000 disks to deal with (at this writing). Even if you've grown familiar with several hundred of them over the years, there are still hundreds more to examine.

Whether your goal is to pick the best shareware and public domain programs for a book such as this, or to decide whether a given program merits a spot in a master library like PsL's, the examination process is the same. You've got to run the program, of course. You've got to look at, and usually print out and wade through, a documentation file that normally totals scores of pages. Next, you have to test the program, often feeding it sample data you have created for the purpose or otherwise giving it something to chew on.

Naturally, you'll want to make notes on the program's performance, what it does and doesn't do, the clarity of the user interface, the clarity of the documentation, and so on. Then you must search your memory and your catalogs (both printed and disk-based) for similar programs and decide whether the one currently under consideration represents an improvement on what is already available. Often the only way to make such a judgement is to locate the older program and run a comparison test. And all of this is just for one program.

There are other details to be concerned with as well, like making sure you're dealing with the latest version of a program or making sure that all of the support files the program needs are indeed on the disk. And of course there is always the chance that some poorly written piece of software will lock up your system when you run it, forcing you to reboot, with all the waiting that entails.

Finally, whether you're writing a book or maintaining a library, it's very worthwhile to contact the authors of shareware programs directly to learn their plans for future versions and to gauge the level of support registered users are likely to receive. Your spare moments, if you have any, should be spent combing CompuServe, GEnie, and other commercial online systems, as well as periodically "working the boards" (tapping BBSs) to run down the latest PD and shareware programs.

You can have a lot of fun along the way. You'll admire one programmer's creativity while cursing another for his stupidity and lack of thoughtfulness. But nothing can change the fact that program after program after program, it's a lot of work. It is no wonder that a number of computer user groups have asked PsL to serve as their free software library. Nor is it any wonder that other groups have used the PC-SIG library as the core of their collections. And sadly, it is no wonder that what Nelson Ford refers to as "the fast-buck artists" have appropriated and marketed the PsL and PC-SIG collections without doing any of the work or adding any value of their own.

We will now take a detailed look at PsL and PC-SIG, the two leading mail-order sources.

The Public (software) Library

Nowhere will you find an individual more passionately devoted to the propagation of IBM shareware and public domain software than Houston's Nelson Ford. When he says he spends 90 hours a week working on his library, you can believe him without hesitation. For aside from being a personable, easy-going guy who isn't prone to exaggeration, the results bear him out. Ford's Public (software) Library is quite simply *the* definitive collection of public domain and shareware programs for IBM and compatible computers.

If you haven't heard of this library, you shouldn't be surprised, for as Mr. Ford says, "Advertising costs can eat your lunch!" Ford does advertise occasionally, but only occasionally, and he rarely sends out press releases. Consequently, knowledge of PsL has been limited to HAL-PC members and true free software enthusiasts for most of its existence. The organization was originally called "The Public Library," a name it shared with a regular column about free software Mr. Ford used to write for the late lamented *IBM Softalk* magazine. The "(software)" was inserted when the Houston Public (books) Library began receiving much of PsL's mail.

There are lots of things that make PsL so special, but the most outstanding feature is the meticulous care with which the library has been built and maintained. In the first place, a given program appears once and only once in the library. There are no "best of" compilations or random duplications of a program on several disks. There are pluses and minuses to this approach. Sometimes a "best of" disk can be a real convenience. But it does mean that when PsL says it has over 800 disks (at this writing), you can count on the fact that each one contains material not found on any other disk in the collection.

Second, Mr. Ford is dedicated to insuring that his library is kept scrupulously up-to-date. When a new version of a program is issued, the old version is immediately replaced in the collection. And when he or one of his assistants encounters a completely new program, perhaps on a bulletin board, PsL contacts the author to be sure of securing the latest version for the library.

Selection Standards

PsL's selection standards are also exemplary. Generally, Mr. Ford says,

> We are fairly rigid in screening out programs that have the same function if they are small programs that will go on one of our "small programs" disks. Our assumption is that you would rather get a wide variety of programs on such a disk than a dozen variations of the same program. With so many top-quality screen-blanking programs [to prevent monitor burnout] in the collection already, for example, why add more?

Every single program is tested and evaluated before being added to the library. Obviously those that do not run as they should or those with major bugs will not be accepted. Nor will any that are recognized or even suspected of being pirated versions of commercial software.

> We also reject programs in general that we can't imagine anyone other than the author having any interest in. Or that have a curiosity value that wears out after running the program once, such as "joke" programs like INSULTS or FUN_DOS. We refuse to accept programs that are offensive to a large segment of users without having any redeeming value to others, such as JIVE, X-rated picture files, or programs that use abusive language.

Programs that are tied to hardware or software that only a very small number of users are likely to have are also rejected. Nor does PsL accept "shareware programs that are severely limited in function, in the number of times they can be run, or in the length of time they will operate, or limited in other ways that do not meet the definition of shareware adopted by the Association of Shareware Professionals (ASP)." PsL did at one time have a commercial demo section consisting of programs of this sort, but it has been eliminated due to lack of time. In any case, limited or deliberately crippled programs will not be accepted as shareware.

FreeTip: The Association of Shareware Professionals (ASP) was a natural outgrowth of the PD/Shareware Convention Mr. Ford organized and HAL-PC sponsored on February 21, 1987. Most of the name authors in the field were present, and discussions begun there continued on CompuServe throughout the spring. At this writing, membership is limited to authors of nontrivial shareware programs, though associate memberships may be offered in the future. The organization has established and will enforce a set of programming standards for all members, with the goal of making ASP membership an assurance of quality for shareware customers. The organization's other major goal is to educate the public and corporate America to the quality, support, and low prices shareware affords. It is also hoped that ASP will give authors a means of taking action against those who would violate their copyrights.

The graphics and logo possibilities offered by this last goal ("Don't tread on me!", etc.) are about the only arguments in favor of retaining the current acronym. However inadvertent, the image of a small, venomous Egyptian reptile is not one likely to inspire confidence among prospective shareware users, good as the organization may be. For more information, contact Nelson Ford at the address provided later in this chapter.

Certainly PsL is open to criticism here, since any time you allow someone else to decide whether a certain program will be offered, you automatically surrender some of your freedom of choice. Who knows? There may be some small detail about one of the screen-blanking programs PsL has rejected that you would find especially appealing. It could, in fact, be just what you've been looking for.

But consider the alternative. Most of us don't have the knowledge, training, or experience to do our own legal work, so we hire an expert. Ditto for medical, dental, and major home repair jobs. Relying on the judgment and experience of Nelson Ford and assistant librarians Duane Hendricks and Baine Brimberry is no different. So much PD and shareware software is being produced that in the absence of such selection criteria the library would quickly become unwieldly and be of little use to anyone.

How to Tap PsL

The Public (software) Library makes its disks available through the mail at a cost of $5 each, plus $4 per order for shipping and handling. That's $4, regardless of the number of disks you order, a policy that in effect results in a quantity discount. The question is: How do you find out what's in the library?

PsL publishes a monthly newsletter that includes not only a complete "Listing & Description of Disks" (one line of description per disk), but also 10 to 15 pages of program reviews, commentary, bug reports, recommendations, and information on program updates prepared by Mr. Ford and his assistants. The newsletter is professionally typeset on good quality paper, but it is so packed with information that it probably will never win any awards for elegance of design. An annual subscription costs $18.

There is still more good news. When we asked Nelson Ford the best way for someone to plug into PsL for the first time, he said, "I'll tell you what. Have your readers send PsL a flat $5—no charge for shipping or handling—and we'll send them the current issue of the newsletter, plus our 'Program Descriptions' disk."

Mr. Ford went on to explain that a program is always written up in the newsletter when it is added to the library. As a review of over a year's worth of newsletters confirms, the write-ups are usually at least a paragraph in length and thus provide much more detail than the single-line library listings. The PsL Program Descriptions disk is a compilation of all of these write-ups in all of the past newsletters, arranged in an order that matches the order of the library itself. Thus for $5 you'll have a sample copy of the newsletter with its complete catalog, plus a "verbose" catalog in electronically searchable form on disk.

Library Organization and Operation

The PsL collection assumed its present form in the winter of 1983 when Ford and his assistants took on the responsibility of handling free software distribution for HAL-PC. The organization scheme has stood the test of time, and while you'll find a complete explanation in each PsL newsletter, we should touch on it briefly here.

First, every disk is assigned a number consisting of three parts in the format: n-cc-nnn. The first number is always either a 1 or a 2, and signifies that the disk consists of a large number of different "Small Programs" or contains one or two "Large Programs." A good example of a Small Program would be a 1 to 20K utility program. A Large Program is usually a major applications program like a full-featured word processor or file manager. The next two slots are alphabetic characters, and correspond to some 20 application categories (AC for accounting, DB for database, UT for utilities, and so on). The final three slots represent the number of the disk.

Since the catalog is organized by application category, this scheme makes it easy to locate all programs dealing with, say, engineering or presentation graphics. There is no need to parse the entire catalog to locate the disks you want. As an example, consider these three entries found under the Education category:

1-ED-076   MATH TUTOR—and 60+ other files. Grade school level.
2-ED-811   CANTONESE—Learn Cantonese
2-ED-082   GRADE GUIDE—a program for recording, storing, and
                      analyzing student's grades.

The second major feature to be aware of concerns the way PsL handles new small programs or updated versions of small programs currently in the library. These types of programs are added in two places. They are placed on the appropriate small program disk in the appropriate category. But they are also placed on PsL's "Monthly Additions" disks. This means that you never have to buy the same disks again just to get the latest version of a program or to get any new Small Programs that have been added since you purchased your original copies. All you have to do is get the Monthly Additions disk or disks and use the contents to update your own collection.

At this writing, there are three categories of such disks. There are the General Monthly Additions disks (always at least two, but sometimes four or more), the Lotus Additions Disk, and the Assembler Additions Disk. These may be ordered by the month at $5 each, but you can also sign up to receive them on a regular basis at a reduced rate (minimum subscription, three months). If you purchase a Large Program disk and a major revision is announced within the next two months, you may return the disk to PsL for a free upgrade.

Free Disk Copies

There are a number of conditions attached to Large Program disk upgrades policy. The offer applies only to individuals, not to anyone redistributing the programs in any form. Disks returned for updating must be received in reusable condition. Updates can only be provided as part of an order for other disks for which all fees have been paid. And there is a limit of three free updates per order.

As long as you don't abuse the privilege, PsL will go even further for you. If you buy a Large Program disk and don't like the program on it, you may return it for another program of the same type. One database program can be exchanged for another database program, for example. The purpose here is to make it as inexpensive as possible for you to select a program you like from the various alternatives. The library's catalog disks may be updated free of charge, under the above conditions, at any time. PsL produces an updated catalog disk each even month of the year. The PsL catalog disks are especially handy because they make it possible to electronically search for the programs you want.

PsL has also introduced an innovative policy under which you can receive any disk of your choice free of charge whenever you register a program with a shareware author. Most PsL disks include a file called FREEDISK.DOC, which contains a form for you to send to the shareware author with your check. The author signs the form to verify your registration and sends it back to you. You then send it to PsL with your request for the disk of your choice. Again, under the conditions set forth above.

How to Order PsL Disks

As you can tell, PsL is *serious* about free software. Its publication is of professional quality, but you shouldn't expect to find color photographs, eye-catching graphics, or nonutilitarian frills of any sort. You can order by mail or by phone, using your Visa or MasterCard. Please call during regular Central Time business hours. Checks should be made payable to The Public (software) Library. Texas residents must add eight percent sales tax on the total (disk prices plus shipping and handling) charges. Here is the contact information you need:

The Public (software) Library
P.O. Box 35705
Houston, TX 77235-5705
(713) 665-7017

The PC Software Interest Group (PC-SIG)

When we first wrote about Richard Petersen's PC-SIG, there were fewer than 200 disks in its library, each of which sold for $6, plus $4 per order for shipping and handling. The organization's published catalog was 110 pages long. Mr. Petersen handled things pretty much by himself, placing a few ads every now and then in hopes that they would generate enough interest to pay for themselves.

Things have changed tremendously since then. There are now over 1000 disks in the collection, the catalog is 424 pages long, and PC-SIG has a staff of some 15 to 20 full and part-time employees. Through it all, however, PC-SIG has held the line on prices. Disks still sell for $6, plus $4 per order for shipping and handling ($10 for foreign orders), and quantity discounts are available.

A Different Approach

The software available through PC-SIG is essentially the same as that found in the PsL library. Shareware and public domain authors gladly forward their latest creations to both organizations. Both collections are comprehensive and include virtually all of the PD and shareware programs available for IBMs and compatible computers. However, while equally valid, the PC-SIG approach is quite different from PsL's.

Here the emphasis has always been on marketing. Richard Petersen recognized early on that there were and are hundreds of thousands of PC users who would benefit enormously from shareware and public domain software if they only knew about it. But since few in this audience were likely to discover computer user groups, their chances of stumbling upon the free software gold mine were slim indeed. What was needed was a user-friendly, service-oriented approach with all the trimmings.

PC-SIG Services

For example, PC-SIG has frequently taken large ads in leading computer magazines featuring pencil sketches of leading shareware authors (Bob "PC-WRITE" Wallace, Jim "PC-FILE" Button, et. al.). They are eye-catching and their humanizing "man-behind-the-program" approach helps make the software more accessible to the average PC user. In addition, all PC-SIG disks are grey with gold hub rings and come in professionally designed custom disk envelopes. PC-SIG tee shirts bearing the same design are also available. There is a 30-day return policy for customers receiving defective, mislabeled, or blank disks, buggy programs, or the wrong disk.

Telephone orders can be placed toll-free, both inside and outside California. The hours are weekdays, from 7:00 A.M. to 6:00 P.M., Pacific Standard Time. There is also a Technical Support Hotline for customers having problems running programs on the disks. In addition, PC-SIG has built a network of some 66 domestic authorized dealers and 29 non-U.S. dealers in 17 countries. PC-SIG products and disks are available from each of them, though in spot checks we discovered that the prices they charge and the number of PC-SIG disks they have vary widely.

As noted, quantity discounts are also available. User groups can qualify to receive free copies of the PC-SIG newsletter and discounts on its published catalog. Special order forms are also available for distribution to club members. Each order form carries a club code number to enable PC-SIG to rebate a percentage of each order to the club treasury. Corporate and institutional customers ordering 100 disks or more also qualify for special discounts.

Membership Benefits

Special discounts are available to individuals as well through a membership in PC-SIG. Anyone can order from PC-SIG, but if you take out an annual membership, you receive the *PC-SIG Library* directory, a year's worth of the organization's bimonthly *Shareware* magazine, all PC-SIG directory publications printed during your membership year, the monthly "PC-SIG HotSheet," and quantity discounts on prepaid orders of ten disks or more. Members pay $5.50 per disk when ordering 10 to 24 disks, $5 per disk for 25 to 49, $4.50 per disk for 50 to 99, and $4 for 100 or more.

The cost of a one-year membership is $20 ($36 for foreign members). Note that this includes the *PC-SIG Library*, a 424-page quality paperback available in bookstores for $12.95. This is PC-SIG's master catalog. It covers Disks 1 through 705 of the 1000 disks in the collection at this writing. Since you would almost certainly want to purchase this book anyway, you're only spending an additional $7.05 for the other benefits of PC-SIG membership. This edition of the catalog, like all of the others PC-SIG has issued over the years, thoughtfully includes a section aimed at brand-new PC users. It explains how to call for a disk directory, run a BASIC program, format and copy a disk, and the significance of .COM, .EXE, .BAT, and other important file extensions.

Shareware magazine typically runs to 60 pages or more. It includes write-ups of newly added disks, reviews, program comparisons, and lists of disks that have been removed from the library because they turned out to contain commercial programs, were accidentally added to the library more than once, or because withdrawal was requested by the program's author. There's a question and answer section, regular columns that may deal with free software or whatever else happens to be on the columnist's mind, and the ever-popular PC-SIG MAN comic strip. Scattered throughout the magazine, in apparently random order, are random comments from PC-SIG customers about particular disks or programs.

The monthly "PC-SIG HotSheet" is a single long page containing the names of updated disks, paragraph descriptions of selected programs, and a standard PC-SIG order form. It is ostensibly designed to tide you over between issues of the magazine, but we suspect its real purpose is maintain your awareness of PC-SIG. On the other hand, the "HotSheet" frequently includes special limited-time, member-only discount offers, such as the opportunity to order 10 disks for $49 (that's $4.90 per disk instead of the $5.50 per disk you would normally pay on such an order, for a savings of $6).

Library Organization and the Master Catalog

Whether you're interested in a few programs or in supplying virtually all of the software needs of a small business, you will find that PC-SIG has a great deal to offer. The people are friendly. The service is good. And the collection is comprehensive.

At the same time, however, it is difficult to avoid the impression that perhaps a little too much time and energy has been expended on bringing free software to the world and not enough on the software itself. The organization of the library is a major problem. And beneath the marketing gloss there is a pervasive sloppiness that prevents PC-SIG from achieving the excellence that is within its grasp.

When the PC world was young, public domain and what we now call shareware programs were few and widely dispersed. By collecting these programs from user groups all over the country into a master "library of record," PC-SIG performed an invaluable service to computer owners everywhere. In those days, the practice was to bundle everything that came in during the month onto a disk and add the disk to the library. Thus each disk would inevitably contain a wide variety of programs whose only point in common was that they happened to come in during the same month.

This was fine at the time, for what people were most interested in was getting software—any kind of software—for their machines. Later, it became less convenient, but with 200 to 300 disks, the collection was still manageable. At worst you would have to buy two or three disks to get the programs you wanted. But at least you could locate them in the library. Today, with over 1000 disks, things are out of control.

If you don't care which program you get, if one disk's as good as another, you won't have a problem. But if you are looking for a particular program, perhaps because you read about it in a magazine or heard about it from a friend, you may be out of luck.

Buried Programs

PC-SIG has produced catalogs and catalog update booklets nearly every year of its existence. But the fourth edition, published in March 1987, represents a major departure. In the past, disks have been listed in numerical order starting with Disk 1 ("Games No. 1"), a single-sided, 160K disk dating from 1982, and continuing straight through. In *The PC-SIG Library*, however, the collection is organized by topic. There are 27 topics, ranging from artificial intelligence to home applications to screen utilities.

That's a good approach as far as it goes, and it works quite well when a single large program and its support files fill an entire disk. But it does not work with disks containing a wide variety of small programs. For example, a disk labelled "Zork Utilities" (Disk 446) contains five files for use with that famous Infocom, Inc. game. But it also contains XWING.BAS (a nifty Star Wars shoot-'em-up with overtones of Flight Simulator), QBERT.COM (a skillful imitation of a once popular video arcade game), as well as a variety of Adventure-like text games and a version of Asteroids. Or consider Disk 141 ("Programmer Utilities No. 5"). In addition to files to aid the BASIC programmer, this disk contains 123PREP.EXE (a program that lets you bring a text file into a Lotus 1-2-3 worksheet) and W20.COM (version 2.0 of the famous WASH.COM disk file management program).

Fortunately, the catalog is indexed three ways: by disk number, disk title, and subject. But unlike previous directories, it is not indexed by program name. It may be that space was the major consideration. In the previous edition of the catalog, 35 pages of small print were required for the filename index, and that was for just 306 disks.

To PC-SIG's credit, each entry gives you much more information about a given disk than ever before. Indeed, *The PC-SIG Library*, fourth edition, is the most informative catalog of shareware and public domain software available anywhere. For each entry, there is a paragraph of description that is frequently derived from the program documentation files on the disk. There are also headings for usage, system requirements, how to start, and user comments. All of this is in addition to the traditional single-line file descriptions that form the sum total of most printed catalogs.

If you're looking for a particular program you will have to spend a lot of time scanning these one-line descriptions. Because there is no index of program names, the only way to find XWING.BAS, for example, is to read through the file descriptions of all 44 disks in the games section of the catalog. Even labor of this sort would probably not be sufficient to find 123PREP.EXE and W20.COM, however. Disk 141 is in the programmer utilities section of the catalog, not in the spreadsheets and templates section or the general system utilities section.

These are only a few examples. Clearly, in the absence of a program or filename index, a system of cross-referencing, or an electronically searchable disk-based catalog, scores of useful, top-quality programs will remain buried within the current PC-SIG catalog, accessible only to the most diligent software searchers.

The Question of Quality

The problem of buried programs can be fixed rather easily. But there are other, more serious, considerations related to the quality of the PC-SIG collection as a whole. As noted earlier, the library is comprehensive. It contains virtually all of the public domain and shareware programs available anywhere. But it is important to point out that many of its disks are "best of" collections drawn from other disks. In addition, some of the disks in that total have been withdrawn for one reason or another. Others, not listed in the catalog, contain nothing but the text of old IBM user group newsletters, outdated instructions for using The Source or CompuServe, and lists of Telenet and Tymnet access numbers dating from 1983. And the justification for devoting two disks (Disks 616 and 617) to the text of a handbook on how to produce special purpose bullets for handloader hobbyists is impossible to fathom. Still other disks are crippled demos of commercial programs that will only work a certain number of times or run for a certain number of minutes.

There are other problems as well. We did not attempt to verify the promptness with which PC-SIG updates its disks or how conscientious the organization is about making sure that only the latest available versions of a program are offered. However, in going through every disk, plus years of newsletters and PC-SIG publications, we were frequently depressed by the sloppiness with which things had been done. It is one thing to misspell the adventure game Eamon as "Eaman" (Disks 296 and 297, corrected in the current catalog) or to describe the SuperStat statistics program on Disk 638 as something for "analyzing surveys and poles." And one can forgive the phrase "a virtual potpourri of programs" in describing Disk 47 (PC-SIG Sampler No. 1) when the writer was obviously reaching for *veritable* and missed.

Although errors such as these give one an uneasy feeling, they are mere peccadilloes. One cannot be so charitable about file descriptions and operating instructions that are simply dead wrong. For example, the one-line description for CATALOG.COM on Disk 478 ("Hard Disk Utilities") reads: "Make a sorted directory." But the program does nothing of the kind. It does not rearrange the list of files on your disk the way a commercial program like Peter Norton's DIRSORT.COM does. Instead, it turns out to be just another program for displaying a sorted directory on your screen.

On Disk 485, ANSI.SYS is described as a "system file." It's not, as your DOS manual will tell you. The description for Disk 567 ("DND Version 1.2") informs us that "DND is a computer fantasy role game inspired by Dungeons and Dragons, the 'granddaddy' of all computer games that was developed and played on mainframe computers back in the 60's." Not true. The game was called Adventure, and it is nothing like Dungeons & Dragons, a board game published by TSR, Inc. of Lake Geneva, Wisconsin.

And then there are examples like Disk 646. This disk contains a wonderful children's program called "Amy's First Primer." The PC-SIG-prepared instructions on the disk tell you to place the program disk in Drive B and a disk with "your BASIC in your drive A." You are then to key in a command to load BASIC from Drive A and run the program from Drive B. The only problem is that "AMY" bombs after the greeting screen appears due to a "File not found" error. Contrary to PC-SIG's instructions, "AMY" expects to find all of the files it needs not in Drive B, but in Drive A.

An experienced user could fix this program easily, but if you're a complete novice you may find it baffling. More to the point: Didn't anyone at PC-SIG review the PC-SIG instructions and run this program to make sure everything was copacetic before adding it to the collection? Apparently not. It is also apparent from the printed catalog's descriptions of FANSI Console (Disks 356 and 650), a "driver" for your CONFIG.SYS file discussed in Chapter 9, that no one at PC-SIG has a ghost of an idea of what this software does. One also wonders at the statement elsewhere in the catalog that CRC stands for "cyclic redundancy computing." It doesn't (as we'll see in Chapter 6).

These are but a few of the more easily conveyed examples of the generally sloppy approach and serious lack of personal computing knowledge and experience that characterizes much of the PC-SIG collection. You should also be aware that because they were added to the library before IBM introduced double-sided drives, most of the disks from 1 through 100, and many between 100 and 211, contain only half as many kilobytes of software as can be found on later disks.

In addition, PC-SIG has never taken advantage of the various public domain file-compression programs that have always been so popular among user group librarians. Consequently, to obtain RBBS-PC, a leading bulletin board program discussed in Chapter 8, you must purchase four PC-SIG disks. But the identical software is available from many other sources on two disks as compressed ARC files.

We called PC-SIG to ask about these problems. According to Troy Challenger of PC-SIG, the "best of" collections are due in part to the philosophy of some of PC-SIG's early librarians and in part to a desire to save customers the bother and expense of ordering several disks to get the best programs on each. "We're certainly not trying to boost the total number of disks in the library. We have plenty of material to deal with as it is."

As for the inclusion of disks containing nothing but text files, Mr. Challenger says, "We're a publisher. That's how we think of ourselves, and we're open to new approaches and ideas." Mr. Challenger also notes that offering demo versions of programs is perfectly legitimate as long as customers are aware that the disk they order is indeed a demo. "We don't want people to get the wrong impression about those few demo disks in the collection. We want to make sure they know they are demos when they order them. And of course, we'll take the disks back under our return policy if there is a problem."

Mr. Challenger acknowledges that in the past there has been a problem getting the latest versions of programs into the library in a timely fashion. "We're setting up a new procedure," he says, "with the goal of getting updates into the library within two weeks and responding to people who send us new submissions within six to seven weeks." Finally, Mr. Challenger says that there are no plans to reorganize the library: "PC-SIG is an archival library. Its contents represent a complete history of this kind of software." However, he says that plans are afoot to deal with the buried program problem. "We will either be adding an index by filename to the catalog or some kind of subclassification scheme to make it easier to locate the programs you want, regardless of the disk containing them."

The Jewel in the PC-SIG Crown

None of these criticisms are make-or-break issues, and they certainly shouldn't discourage you from taking full advantage of the many services PC-SIG has to offer. In our opinion, by coming up with the right idea at the right time, PC-SIG has found itself suddenly holding a tiger by its ears. It simply has to do a better job of managing the beast.

That PC-SIG has the ability to do this, we have no doubt, for imagination has always been one of its strengths. There is no better example of this than the speed with which it placed its entire collection on CD-ROM. As most computer users know by now, CD-ROM stands for "compact disk—read only memory." Measuring a mere 4.72 inches in diameter, a CD disk is as rigid as a piece of Formica. Although information is recorded on only one side, a single CD can store up to 600 megabytes of information. That is the equivalent of more than 1666 double-sided floppies.

The PC-SIG CD-ROM can be used with any Sony, Hitachi, or Philips laser-drive player. It contains the complete library, as well as a series of files that contain descriptions of all of the disks and the names of all of the programs with their one-line descriptions. There are also some programs to let you search these description files by the keyword of your choice or by the name of the program you seek. The entire text of the King James Bible is also on the disk, one file per chapter, and it too can be electronically searched. So capacious is a CD-ROM, that even with all of this material, the disk is barely half full.

PC-SIG offers its CD-ROM two ways. You may purchase the latest edition for $295, or you can buy a subscription for $495. The subscription gives you the current disk, plus the next three updates. Each update contains the complete library of the moment, with all the disks that have been added since the last version. At this writing, the CD-ROM is being updated every three to four months.

From one perspective, $295 is a lot of money. But if you divide that figure by the number of disks the CD contains, say 1,000, you discover that you are paying about 30¢ per disk. Since PC-SIG reports that the library is growing at about 25 disks per month, the effective CD cost per disk will be even less as you read this.

You can't beat the convenience of having over 1,000 disks at your fingertips, to say nothing of the savings on shelf space. In its floppy-disk-based version, the PC-SIG library occupies just under six feet of shelf space when stored in Flip'N'File boxes. In contrast, a CD-ROM drive takes up less space than an unabridged dictionary.

The only drawback is the cost, currently about $800 for the drive, interface card, cable, and software. Prices will certainly come down as CDs become more popular. And while an industry standard disk format has yet to emerge, virtually all of the text-based CD-ROM products you may have heard of are compatible with the type of drive the PC-SIG CD requires (High Sierra format).

FreeTip: At this writing, CD-ROM readers are available from PC-SIG for $800, plus $15 for shipping and handling. This may be your best option for now, because it is difficult to find an ad for a CD drive of any kind in a computer magazine. That certainly will change, but until it does, you might want to contact the following manufacturers for more information:

Hitachi Sales Corp. of America
1200 Wall Street West
Lyndhurst, NJ 07071
(201) 935-5300

Sony Corporation
1 Sony Drive
Park Ridge, NJ 07656
(201) 930-6104

Phillips Subsystems & Peripherals, Inc.
1111 Northshore Drive
Knoxville, TN 37919
(615) 558-5110

How to Order PC-SIG Disks

You might want to contact PC-SIG just to request more information, but you really can't lose if you purchase a one-year membership right away. The cost is $20 ($36 foreign), and as explained earlier, it includes the $12.95 book, *The PC-SIG Library*. Regardless of whether you ever order a single disk from PC-SIG, you will find this publication invaluable. Since even with the shortcomings noted above it contains more information about more programs than any other source, you can use it to decide which programs to order from user groups or which programs to download from commercial online systems of BBSs. That leaves a net cost of $7.05 for your PC-SIG membership, which includes a subscription to the newsletter and discounts on quantity orders.

Incidentaly, in its magazine ads PC-SIG has offered a special deal on memberships. For $39 (plus $4 shipping and handling), you can purchase a one-year membership and five disks of your choice. That means each disk costs you $3.80, plus shipping. It might be worth asking whether this or a similar offer is still valid when you call. Foreign orders should include payment by credit card, by an international draft in U.S. dollars, or by a check drawn on a U.S. bank. You can phone PC-SIG weekdays between the hours of 7:00 A.M. and 6:00 P.M., Pacific Time, or contact them by mail at:

PC-SIG
1030 D East Duane Avenue
Sunnyvale, CA 94086
(800) 245-6717
(800) 222-2996, in California

Visa and MasterCard accepted

FreeTip: If you live in Canada, and even if you don't, you'll be interested in Jud Newell's Canada Remote Systems (CRS). Originally called MICROCOMP, Mr. Newell's firm has grown from the four-telephone line, membership-only, RCPM bulletin board system covered in the first edition of this book into Canada's largest distributor of free software. CRS has established relationships with some 16 user groups (including the Capital PC and BCS IBM groups) focusing on every major brand of computer (IBM, Apple, Macintosh, Amiga, Commodore 64 and 128, Kaypro, DEC Rainbow, and others). It is also an authorized PC-SIG dealer and can thus supply you with any PC-SIG disk, catalog, or publication.

Software is available on disk through the mail or by modem over the phone. At this writing, CRS has 16 round-the-clock modem phone lines, three of which are accessible via Datapac and Telenet. (See Chapter 5.) CRS members are entitled to up to two one-hour downloading sessions per day, use of a technical support hotline, a bimonthly newsletter, and discounts of 20 to 30 percent on free software disks ordered through the mail.

In Canadian dollars, a full membership is $60 for the first year and $20 per year thereafter. You do *not* have to be a member to order from CRS. But if your main interest is in ordering disks, you may want to consider the CRS limited membership option. This is $35 for the first year and $20 per year thereafter. It entitles you to everything except online access to the CRS system. Corporate memberships are also available. For more information, contact:

Canada Remote Systems
4198 Dundas Street West
Toronto, Ontario M8X 1Y6
(416) 231-2383
(800) 268-2705 (NFLD, MAN, SASK, ALTA, BC)
(800) 387-1901 (NS, PEI, NB, QUE, ONT)

Other Sources

There *are* other non-user-group mail-order sources of free software, but the field is highly irregular—both in some of its business practices and in the quality of the services involved. The way to find most of these sources is to scan the classified ad section at the back of *Computer Shopper* magazine. We did exactly that and sent the identical letter to every company or individual who advertised free software in a given issue. There were 32 of them in all, and we received 19 responses.

The responses ran the gamut. At the bottom of the scale were the messy, stapled pages so dense with text as to be all but unreadable. At the top were less than a handful of professionally produced multipage catalogs. Some sources sent just a letter, but no catalog. Others scrawled a few lines across a page, while still others included personal letters explaining their policies, how they assemble and test the programs in their collections, their prices, and so on.

We found that many sources do not cite the version numbers of the major programs they offer. Others were conscientious about this, but the versions they were offering were long out of date. In paging through the materials from more than a few sources, we sensed that shareware and public domain software was not their primary interest. Indeed, considering the number of catalog pages devoted to ads for IBM clones, hard disk drives, blank disks, and computer supplies, one is tempted to conclude that free software offerings are being used as a come-on. Others are clearly more interested in developing salable mailing lists than in offering top-quality public domain software.

The programs in the catalogs were the same as those available throughout the free software world. In fact, in very many cases, the disks were identical to those of the PC-SIG library. It is our understanding that this is illegal. A book of public domain short stories, for example, is protected by a "compilation copyright" that prevents any other publisher from issuing the identical collection. Similarly, the disk-based collections of many different programs compiled by Nelson Ford and by PC-SIG cannot be offered by an unauthorized vendor.

Both Nelson Ford and PC-SIG have been victimized by unscrupulous firms. In one case, Mr. Ford discovered that a company had not only duplicated his collection but also reprinted word-for-word excerpts from his copyrighted newsletter in its catalog and ads. Both Ford and PC-SIG have successfully sued or otherwise persuaded a number of firms to cease and desist.

This is undoubtedly why some of the companies we contacted were at pains to disguise the fact that they were offering the PC-SIG library. They would give the disks different names and use a different disk numbering scheme, but to anyone with the PC-SIG catalog in one hand and their catalog in the other, the ruse would seem ridiculously thin. Worse, it makes you feel rather queasy about a company that would do such a thing.

We can't help thinking of the fable of the Little Red Hen who did all the work and the barnyard animals eager to profit from her labor. Most of these firms add no value whatsoever. And some have the unmitigated brass to charge *more* for the disks than PC-SIG does. Others charge much less. Indeed, the prices and policies of these sources vary all over the lot. Some charge less per disk but more for shipping. Some offer you the opportunity to rent disks for a week to make your own copies. There is usually a minimum rental order of anywhere from 10 to 50 to 100 disks, depending on the firm. In a surprising number of cases, it was impossible to figure out what the prices and policies of a given source were, regardless of how many times you read its order form and literature.

With all of this in mind, caveat emptor is clearly the watchword. For example, some of the firms we contacted give you only a handful of programs on each disk instead of packing it full. So even though their price per disk is very low, you must purchase more disks to get the same quantity of software. It's also worth inquiring about average delivery times. In some cases, you can wait weeks to receive your order.

Finally, it is worth asking whether a given source tests each program on each disk to make sure that it runs. This won't identify any bugs a program may have, but it will at least offer you some assurance that all of the support files a program may need are really on the disk. The only thing more aggravating than having a program stop dead because it can't find a file that is supposed to be on the disk is to discover that the instructions in the documentation file have been abruptly truncated. We have experienced both of these problems a number of times with disks ordered from sources such as these.

Now for the good guys. As we said, our letters elicited a small number of very impressive responses. Their prices range from $6 to $10 for a single disk, including shipping and handling. And their policies vary. However, on the basis of their literature, letters, and sample disks, each is obviously interested in delivering quality shareware and public domain software to customers.

They appear to be in business for the long haul. Though, of course, everything can change. So rather than summarizing the current prices and policies of each, we will simply suggest that you contact each of them yourself to request their latest information:

Disk-O-Mania/Sizzleware
P.O. Box 6429
Lake Charles, LA 70606

Public Brand Software
P.O. Box 51315
Indianapolis, IN 46251

Shareware Express
32302 Camino Capistrano,
Suite 204
P.O. Box 219
San Juan Capistrano, CA 92693-
    0219

Software Distributors
    Clearinghouse
3707 Brangus
Georgetown, TX 78628

Software Innovations
1309 E. Northern Avenue
Phoenix, AZ 85020

5

Getting Ready to Go Online

THE HARDWARE AND SOFTWARE YOU NEED

The quickest, easiest way to get free software is to get it over the phone. Unfortunately, on a cost-per-program basis, this is the most expensive method as well. Nonetheless, there's no question that the RJ-11 telephone jack on your wall—the one you bought at Sears and installed yourself one Saturday afternoon—can be a veritable faucet of free programs. And if you know how to use it effectively, it can be an economical source as well. Virtually *all* of the programs discussed in this book, and tens of thousands more besides, can be obtained instantly. Equally important, the knowledge base of a goodly portion of the community of users is yours to query at any time of day or night simply by dialing the phone. All you need is your computer, a few relatively inexpensive pieces of hardware, a communications program (available for free, of course), and the right numbers to dial.

Sending and receiving software by telephone has been standard operating procedure among computer users for a very long time, but we have always found it amazing. It's still easy to remember the joy of dialing up a distant computer system for the first time, requesting the transmission of a program, and running it moments after hanging up the phone. It was a trivial program. It did colorful things to the screen while playing the Washington Redskins fight song. But it was magic. Programs for nothing and your kicks for free.

On the more practical side, it is also easy to remember trying to edit a huge text file late at night. After struggling for a while, the realization dawned that there must surely be a PD program someplace capable of cutting such a file into more manageable pieces. We signed on to CompuServe, one of the commercial online systems discussed in Chapter 7, and within minutes had located and downloaded a nifty utility called CHOP.EXE. This program is the Sweeny Todd of text utilities: Tell it how many pieces you want and it does the rest. CHOP.EXE was exactly the program we needed at the time, and thanks to the telephone and CompuServe, it was instantly available, even at three o'clock in the morning.

FreeTip: You can do much, much more as well, once you hook your computer to a telephone. Among other things, for example, the revised and updated edition of *The Complete Handbook of Personal Computer Communications* will show you how to send and receive Telex messages with your computer, how to tap into the worldwide human/electronic network to locate an expert or find a group of friends, and how to become a telecommuter. For its part, *How to Look It Up Online* will show you how to instantly lay electronic hands on virtually any piece of information in virtually any publication you can imagine. Together, these two books cover a sizable chunk of "the electronic universe," and naturally they carry our highest recommendation. With a little luck, they might carry a few car payments as well.

An Overview of the Process

Clearly the online free software alternative has much to recommend it. It's quick. It's convenient. And it can make it easy to locate the program you want, though you'll want to watch your connect time charges and other costs rather carefully. We'll discuss these points in greater detail later in the chapter. Right now, the most important thing is to get a quick overview of the entire online process so you'll have something to use as a reference point. (Don't worry if you don't understand all of the terms. We'll explain everything in a moment.)

There are two main online sources of free software—commercial online systems and noncommercial bulletin board systems or BBSs. Commercial systems charge you by the minute of connect time you use. BBSs are usually free, though there may be long-distance telephone charges involved. Both types of system consist of some kind of computer containing free software files. In online terms, these remote computers are called "host systems." Your job is to establish a connection between your machine and a distant host.

To do this, you'll need a piece of hardware called a "communications card" or a "serial port," and a black-box telephone-connecting device called a modem (pronounced: "moe-dem"). You'll also need special software—a communications or "comm" program—to tie everything together. Once you've made contact, you will be "online" with the host system, and you'll be able to talk to it through your own keyboard. You can enlist its help in locating the program files you want, and you can tell it to send you a file over the phone. This is called "downloading," and it results in a copy of the program being recorded on your own floppy or hard disk. Once the download is over, you can tell host system that you're finished ("sign off"), hang up the phone, and begin using the program.

In this chapter, we're going to focus on the hardware and software you need to go online. In Chapter 6, we'll zero in on the process of interacting with a distant host to locate and obtain the programs you want. In Chapter 7 we'll look at six leading commercial online systems and show you exactly which commands to enter to use them most efficiently. Our suite of online chapters concludes with Chapter 8, which will show you how to plug into and tap the thousands of free BBSs that dot the continent.

Quick and Easy?

No book can be all things to all people. Our goal in this and succeeding chapters is to give you the information you need to comfortably and confidently tap the many online free software resources that are waiting for you. That means we're going to have to explain some technical points that most people in the free software wing of the community of users take for granted. We would be remiss, however, if we didn't tell you that you really do have a choice. If *your* goal is to get online and begin downloading free software as quickly as possible, and if money is no object, here's what to do.

Contact your computer dealer and tell him or her that you want a serial card, a Hayes-compatible 1200-baud external modem, a cable to connect the two, and a CompuServe Starter Kit. For software, we recommend getting a copy of ProComm, the shareware comm program discussed in Chapter 16. Besides being a super program, ProComm supports the CompuServe B protocol you will need to download files from that system. Finally, read the profile of CompuServe in Chapter 7 for instructions on which commands to enter to reach the system's IBM free software treasure houses.

That's the quick and easy approach—the one we would recommend to any good friend or relative in a hurry. You've got to take a lot of things on faith, and you'll pay top dollar for your hardware, but it *will* work. Alternatively, if you want to understand what's going on and learn how to maximize the online resources available to you, simply continue reading.

Communications Hardware

To explain what you need to know to go online, we're going to follow a bit of electronic information as it travels from your floppy or hard disk, into your system, and out again into the telephone stream. Along the way we will tell you how to choose a communications card, what to look for in a modem, how to prepare your communications software, and how to save money when calling a distant host by using the public data networks. This information applies regardless of whether you plan to call commercial systems or BBSs.

We begin with a floppy disk. When you insert one of these circles of rust-coated Mylar into a disk drive and close the hatch, a pair of read/write heads similar to the heads of a tape recorder are pressed into the plastic. It's up close and personal all the way as the disk spins and the read/write heads pick up or lay down data. It sounds silly, but think of those disk drive heads as locomotives chugging around a circular track, and imagine them using reversed cow catchers to pick up red and blue jelly beans.

The jelly beans, of course, are bits of (*bi*nary dig*its*) of computer information. Note that they are either red or blue. There are no pinks, powder blues, purples, or other shades of the two colors. There is red and blue and only red and blue. For convenience, programmers and other binary bean counters symbolize these two colors on paper as 1s and 0s. They could just as easily use exclamation points and dollar signs or some other pair of symbols. As long as each symbol is unique and as long as there are two and only two of them, the actual symbols used do not matter.

As surprising as it may seem, the simple concept of two symbols is at the very core of personal and every other kind of computing, and we will be encountering it again and again in computer communications. For example, in reality, the bits on a floppy disks are symbolized by areas of the disk track that are either magnetized or not magnetized. The disk drive heads see these areas as a pattern that they use to generate a matching series of electronic pulses that flow into the computer. The drive heads, in other words, make a copy of the pattern on the disk by translating its elements into voltage pulses. The pulses are of either a "high" voltage ("on") or a "low" voltage ("off"), with nothing in between.

The UART and the Modem: Necessary Conversions

The disk drive batches these pulses together into units of eight bits each. And as you may know, each of these units is called a *byte* (pronounced: "bite"). When they flow into the computer, they flow along eight wires in a parallel formation. If you like, you can think of them as eight red or blue jelly beans rolling down eight parallel chutes.

As long as the jelly bean bits stay within the confines of the computer, everything is fine. Where you begin to run into difficulties is when you want to make the bits flow *outside* of the machine. Yet that is exactly what must happen to send and receive information over the telephone.

In the first place, everything inside the computer is set up for the bits to roll along in parallel formation. That takes eight wires at least, which is seven more outgoing wires than you will find in most telephone systems. In the second place, things are pretty quiet inside the computer, electrically speaking. So each bit can be the electrical equivalent of a whisper and still be heard. In the big wide world of telecommunications, however, there is a lot of electronic noise and electrical resistance that would make your average computer bit inaudible.

The solution is to perform a conversion. Two conversions, in fact. First, the natural parallel paths of computer bits must be changed from eight-all-at-once to one-at-a-time. This is called a conversion from parallel to serial data communications. Second, each bit has got to be changed into a more rugged form suitable for telephone transmission. Since phone systems were designed to handle sound, that's what the bits must be changed into.

There is a piece of equipment to handle each conversion. The first conversion is done by a microchip called a UART (pronounced: "you-art"). This stands for "universal asynchronous receiver-transmitter." UARTs are the central element of components that are variously called comm, asynch (pronounced: "a-sink") or serial cards, RS-232 interfaces, or communications ports. These chips are responsible for getting each eight-bit unit lined up, adding two bits of what for now we can think of as packing material, and sending the entire ten-bit package out the door.

Fortunately, you rarely need to worry about UARTs or even be aware that they are there. What you *do* need with most PCs is a plug-in circuit board that includes "communications" as one of its features. Either that, or you need a computer with a built-in serial interface. One way or another, the UART will be in there someplace.

The second conversion, the one from electrical signals into sound, is performed by the modem. This term is a compression of the words *modulator/demo*dulator, and it refers to the device that changes outgoing computer signals into sound and incoming sound into computer signals. As noted, phone lines are designed for sound, not computer voltage levels. So the bits that began as magnetic pinpoints on a floppy disk and were converted to voltage pulses by the drive's read/write heads are transformed once again, this time into two and only two different sounds.

You can think of them as a high-pitched tone and a low-pitched tone, if you like. Though of course in reality things are more complex. You don't need to know about all that, but it is helpful to know that modems deal in two sets of paired tones or frequencies, one pair for outgoing and one for incoming information. These two sets are referred to as the modem's "originate" and "answer" modes. For communications to take place one modem must be set to originate and the other must be set to answer. In almost every case, if you are calling a distant computer, your modem should be set to "originate."

Modems are usually connected to the computer by a cable that is plugged into the "RS-232 interface" on the card containing the UART. (PS/2 machines come with RS-232 ports as standard equipment.) This is pronounced "R-S-two-thirty-two," and it stands for "Recommended Standard number 232." It's official name is RS-232, revision C, a designation you will find on some communications products as "RS-232-C." The standard was developed by the Electronic Industries Association (EIA), the Bell System, and the computer and modem industries, and it is nearly universally endorsed. It specifies that an RS-232 interface shall consist of 25 pins or sockets and it describes how each pin shall be wired, what signals it will carry, and so forth. The actual hardware is called a DB-25 connector, but you can think of it as your computer's back door, for it is through this portal that your system's bits come and go. A second cable leads from the modem to the telephone jack. Thus, the modem stands between the computer and the telephone system, modulating and demodulating sound and computer signals.

FreeTip: The computer industry has a long tradition of doing things for its own convenience and leaving the consumer to fend for himself. Thus, to celebrate the 25th anniversary of its creation of the RS-232 standard, the Electronics Industries Association in 1987 upgraded it to Revision D and changed its name. The official name is now EIA-232D. The change was made to satisfy another organization, the American National Standards Institute (ANSI), which requires that the initials of a standard's creator be part of its approved name. With three vowels in a row, "eee-eye-a two-

FreeTip continued

thirty-two dee" does not exactly roll trippingly off the tongue, and it does tend to put one in mind of a farmer named MacDonald. But neither organization allowed this fact or any potential for consumer confusion to stand in its way. Traditions must be upheld, after all.

Communications Software

You now have a complete conceptual overview of the computer communications process. Whether you tap a key on the keyboard to create a pattern of bits symbolizing a letter, or whether the pattern is stored on a floppy or hard disk, if it is to be sent over the telephone, the pattern's format must be changed. It must be transformed from the parallel arrangement used inside the computer into the serial format mandated by the existence of a single outgoing telephone wire. In addition, the bits themselves must be resymbolized by two different sounds or sound-like signals instead of the voltage levels computers use internally. The same thing happens at the other end of the connection when someone wants to send information to your computer.

The one crucial component we have not considered here is the computer software that ties everything together. We will be explaining comm programs in more detail in Chapter 16, when we look at the shareware program ProComm and the top communications-related utilities. For the moment you need only be aware that communications programs are responsible for making it easier for you to use the hardware and for organizing every aspect of the online process. For example, if you want to download a public domain program from a host, you have got to tell *your* system what name you want to give the program and which disk drive you want it to use. Your communications software will prompt you for this information and handle all of the technical details.

How to Choose a Communications Card

With this overview firmly in mind, you're ready for some hands-on information on what to look for when equipping your system for communications. When the IBM PC was introduced back in 1981, one of the options you could buy for it was a dedicated asynchronous communications card. The card plugged into one of the expansion slots, and its sole purpose was to provide you with a UART and RS-232 interface. Things have changed considerably since then.

Communications has become such an important computer activity that these days many machines come with an asynch port as standard equipment. Each of the machine's in the Personal System/2 line IBM introduced on April 2, 1987, for example, includes built-in serial, parallel, and pointing device ports. Similarly, almost all add-on memory cards for the PC line and clones include a comm port as a matter of course. Such cards may contain a battery-powered clock/calendar, a printer port, and other options, as well as sockets for you to "populate" with additional memory chips. Consequently they may be referred to as "multi-function boards" or "combo cards."

All such communications interfaces are essentially the same, so there isn't much to say on this score. However, it is important to be aware that most IBMs and compatibles can address (use) at least two communications ports, referred to as COM1 and COM2. Since it is entirely possible that you will find yourself with two or more communications ports, make sure that both you and your communications software know which is which. In many cases there will be a "jumper" on the add-on board to let you designate its RS-232 port as either COM1 or COM2 (see your combo board documentation for details).

How to Choose a Modem

Choosing a modem can be among the simplest of tasks. Indeed, if you will accept our advice, you can finish this section right here and now. Get yourself a Hayes-compatible, "1200-baud" external modem. In fact, we can be even more specific: Call one of the numbers given below and order an Avatex 1200hc modem ($120 to $130). End of story.

Hayes Compatibility

Or almost. A decent respect for the opinions of mankind requires that we set forth the reasons behind this recommendation. First, all of us owe a debt of gratitude to Hayes Microcomputer Products, Inc. of Norcross, Georgia. Because of the quality and the popularity of its products, Hayes has become the IBM of modem manufacturers. The Hayes Smartmodem has set the de facto standard that of necessity nearly everyone obeys.

Hayes was among the first manufacturers to produce an "intelligent" modem. The company did it by including a Z-8 microprocessor (a relative of the Z-80 chip of CP/M fame) on the modem's circuit board. This microprocessor is really a small computer and like the rest of the breed, it can be programmed to perform useful work, like automatically dialing the telephone for you or answering it when it rings.

The programming language Hayes developed to make this possible has become known as the Hayes AT command set. The AT is short for "ATTENTION, modem, prepare to meet your next command." Thus when you are connected to a Hayes-compatible modem and you enter ATDT 1-800-555-1212 at your keyboard, the modem knows that you want to dial the phone (D) using Touch-Tone (T), and it knows to dial the digits you have included. As soon as you hit your <Enter> key, the command will be sent to the modem and dialing will commence.

There are many other commands as well, though you'll probably never use most of them. The key thing is to get a modem that responds to the Hayes command set, for it makes life so much simpler. For example, most communications programs let you prepare and record a menu or list of frequently called numbers. Once this has been created, dialing a number is as simple as choosing a menu item. Most communications programs are set by default to send the corresponding phone numbers to the modem using the Hayes command set. Though you can change things around to match any modem, if you have a Hayes-compatible modem, this will be one less thing you'll have to worry about.

FreeTip: One of the reasons Hayes modems are so smart is that in addition to the Z8 microprocessor, they are equipped with a ROM-based 4K control program, some 16 user-setable memory registers (think of them as switches), and a RAM buffer capable of retaining up to 40 characters. Compatible modems are comparably equipped.

Thus in addition to telling the modem to dial the telephone, you can tell it to pause for a specified amount of time at any point in the dialing process. This is helpful if you have to enter one or more digits to get an outside line before dialing your target number. You can select pulse or tone dialing, at a variety of speeds, if you like. And if a number is busy, a single command can tell the modem to dial it again.

You can also put the modem into auto-answer mode, and tell it how many times to let the phone ring before picking up. This feature is more useful than you might suspect. Suppose you're in California with your laptop computer and you want to get some information from your desktop system back in New York. If your desktop PC is equipped with a Hayes-compatible modem and if it is running a program like ProComm or "host" software like RBBS-PC, you can simply dial it up, wait for the modem to pick up the phone, and log on to your New York computer as if you were logging onto People/Link or some other commercial system. (ProComm and RBBS-PC are discussed in later chapters.)

Users today take this kind of power and convenience for granted, unaware that only a few years ago one had to manually dial the phone and then flip on the modem to go online. Worse still were "acoustic couplers"—foam rubber cups that fitted over the mouth- and earpiece of the telephone handset and used microphones to send and receive their modem tones.

Why 1200 bps? Why not 2400?

Next, there's the matter of speed. Traditionally, data communications speeds have been measured in units called "bauds," named after J.M.E. Baudot, the inventor of the Baudot telegraph code. This is why you will read of 300-baud, 1200-baud, and 2400-baud modems.

Technology has outstripped terminology, however. For in reality, only 300 baud is an accurate term. A "1200-baud" modem actually communicates at 600 baud. Things get more complex from there. The misuse of the term was understandable and natural back when 300 baud was the standard speed and modems capable of four times that speed (1200 "baud") were being introduced. But with the advent of 2400 and even 9600-"baud" units, the inaccuracy is no longer acceptable.

The proper term is "bits per second" or bps and that is what we will use from now on. As long as two systems are in agreement, computer communications can take place at virtually any speed. But the most widely agreed upon levels in the personal computer world are 110, 300, 1200, 2400, 4800, 9600, and 19,200 bits per second, with most activity centering around 300, 1200, and 2400 bps.

So why recommend a 1200-bps modem? The first reason is cost. At this writing, your only other practical choices are a unit that can handle only 300 bps and one that can handle 300, 1200, and 2400 bps. There are 9600-bps modems as well, but these can cost thousands of dollars apiece, and you need a matched set. Commercial online systems and BBSs do not typically support speeds higher than 2400 bps. If you've never been online before, you're going to have to take our word for it, but 300 bits per second—which translates into 30 characters per second—is simply too slow for comfort when you are searching a database, reading your electronic mail, or doing other types of general communications. And whether you're downloading free software or something else, the process will take four times longer at 300 than at 1200 bits per second.

If you aren't sure you really want to get into computer communications, go ahead and burn $50 or so on a used 300 bps modem. But if you're even marginally serious about going online, you will be much better off spending about $100 for a 1200 bps unit—almost all of which can also handle 300 bps as well, should you ever want to use that speed.

A 2400-bps modem, on the other hand, will be considerably more expensive. At this writing, a genuine Hayes 2400-bps unit lists for around $900, though compatible units can be had for between $250 and $400. Thus, under the best of circumstances, you can expect to pay at least $150 more for a 2400-bps unit. That may or may not be significant to you, and in any case if it's in the budget, you can't really go wrong with a 2400 bps unit since almost all such units support 300 and 1200 bps as well.

You may want to use your modem for a variety of online applications, such as transferring large files from one personal computer to another, where the additional speed will be worthwhile. But from the free software perspective there are good reasons for considering such a purchase carefully, at least until the prices come down. The first reason is cost and the second is effective throughput.

Comparing the Costs

As noted earlier, ten bits are required to send a single byte or character of data—eight bits for the byte and two bits to serve as packing material. So, just as 300 bps translates as 30 characters per second, and 1200 as 120 characters, a speed of 2400 bps translates as 240 characters per second. That's far too fast for comfortable reading while you are online, so 2400 bps is only likely to be worthwhile if you are going to be doing a substantial amount of downloading and uploading (transmitting files from disk).

"Ah," you say, "but isn't that exactly what I will be doing to get my free software?" Possibly, but you may find that the most cost-effective way to use an online system is as a quick and convenient source of relatively short programs. In most cases, it's far cheaper to obtain the bulk of your software from user groups and from the mail-order sources cited in Chapters 3 and 4.

We'll show you how to figure out how much a given program will cost to download in Chapter 7. But right now let's apply a little simple arithmetic to the question of 1200 and 2400-bps modems. Not coincidentally, this comparison illustrates how the technical knowledge you have acquired so far can be profitably applied.

Let's compare the cost of downloading a single floppy disk's worth of programs at both speeds. A 5¼-inch disk can hold about 360 kilobytes of information. Each byte is equivalent to one character. Thus under optimal conditions—no interference or delays—downloading 360K at 240 characters per second (2400 bps) will take 25 minutes. Using CompuServe's lowest 1200/2400 evening rate of $12.75 an hour as an example, you will pay $5.32 for 360K worth of programs. At 1200 bps the same transfer will take 40 minutes and cost twice as much, or $10.64.

Thus, for each disk's worth of programming you download at 2400 bps you save $5.32 over what you would have to pay at 1200 bps. The question is, how many disks do you have to download to make up for the extra cost of a 2400-bps modem? Dividing a modem cost differential of $150 by $5.32 yields your answer. You must download nearly 28 disks' worth of programming before you break even.

That's a lot of software. But, if you could count on that kind of throughput every time you went online, even 28 disks might seem like a reasonable break-even point. Unfortunately, however, conditions are rarely optimal. If there are a lot of people using the same system when you are online, the system's response time will not be instantaneous, and downloads will take longer. If your telephone connection is less than perfect, electrical noise and other problems can garble your data. That means the sending system will have to retransmit portions of the file, further adding to the download time.

Garbled data can be a problem at any speed, but it is a particular problem at 2400 bps. Different signalling techniques are used to generate each communications speed, but the one constant is bits per *second*. Going from 1200 bps to 2400 bps means packing twice as many bits into the same unit of time. So naturally each bit must occupy a "smaller" portion of that time. That makes it susceptible to smaller amounts of electrical noise and interference. A short burst of static that might leave your data unfazed at 1200 bps could completely wipe out several bits at 2400. As *PC Magazine* reported in its 12 May 1988 issue: "The extra speed of 2400-bps communications can be a boon, but error-free transmission at this rate is still a long way off, as our test results of 2400-bps modems show."

We certainly don't want to discourage you from buying a 2400-bps modem. But at the same time, it is important to point out that reality can be somewhat different than the ads would lead you to believe. If you can afford it, 2400 bps is a nice capability to have. But from a free software perspective, most people will be better off buying a 1200-bps unit now and waiting for prices to come down before considering upgrading to 2400.

External Versus Internal

Finally, there's the question of physique. You can get a modem in a box that will sit next to your computer, or you can get that same modem on a card that will plug into one of your expansion slots. The choice is completely up to you and will have no effect on your ability to communicate. However, we feel there are many powerful arguments for opting for an external unit.

An external modem can be used with any computer, but a card-mounted unit can only be used in a compatible machine. An external modem does not occupy one of your system's expansion slots, doesn't get turned on until you need it, and doesn't add heat to the insides of your system. Most external units also have LED (light emitting diodode) indicator lights to tell you what they are doing and when. Internal modems have no lights, though some commercial and PD comm programs can simulate them on your screen.

As far as we can see, the only argument in favor of an internal modem is that it does not take up space on your desk. But then, if you already have a phone on your desk, you can almost always place it on top of your external modem, so that there is no net loss of desktop space. Indeed, many external modems are designed with this in mind.

FreeTip: If you have both a laptop computer and a desktop system, there's an even more important reason for opting for a standard serial port and external modem. As long as both systems have serial ports, you can cable the two together and dump information back and forth at top speed. With the phone line out of the loop and no need for a modem, you can run at the highest speed the UARTs in your two machines can handle (usually 9600 bps or 19.2 kilobits per second). Since an internal modem may not include an RS-232 interface, you may have to connect the machines modem-to-modem, in which case you will be able to go no faster than your modems will allow.

To cable two RS-232 interfaces together, you will need a "null modem" cable (sometimes also called a "crossover cable"). This cable is wired to fool both computers into thinking they are connected to modems, instead of other computers. With luck, a standard null modem cable will do the trick, particularly if you are dealing with two IBM-compatible machines. If you have problems, however, you might want to check *The Complete Handbook of Personal Computer Communications,* or better yet, contact someone at a computer user group. Your computer dealer may be able to help you as well, but unfortunately this is not something one can count on.

Where to Buy Your Modem

We entered the online world with a Hayes 300-baud Smartmodem, and once prices dropped traded up to a 1200-bps Smartmodem. Both units performed flawlessly; both came with exceptionally complete and well-written manuals; and both were housed in a snazzy extruded aluminum cases. When the 1200 began acting up some time ago, a quick phone call to the company, $80, and the old modem brought a new unit (a new circuit board in the old case) and an improved power supply. Hayes is an excellent company, with a fine product and a prompt, efficient, and courteous customer service staff.

There is just one problem. A Hayes 1200-bps external modem carries a list price of $599 at this writing. A survey of several current magazines reveals, however, that the "street price" from mail-order houses is between $350 and $390. The reason this is a problem is that there are any number of Hayes-compatible modems on the market for considerably less.

There are surely many excellent Hayes clones. Obviously we haven't tested them all. But there is one we can recommend from personal experience. This is the Avatex 1200e ($85) or the Avatex 1200hc ($99). The 1200e replaces an earlier model and now offers an internal speaker and complete Hayes compatability. It measures five by six inches and thus takes up less desk space. The 1200hc offers everything the 1200e does, plus a data/voice button, a 1200/300 speed switch, and both asynchronous and synchronous communications capabilities. When you realize that for $350 you can have either one Hayes or *three* Avatex 1200hc's, there is simply no contest.

The Avatex 1200hc comes from E + E DataComm (1230 Oakmead Parkway, Suite 310, Sunnyvale, CA 94086, phone: 408-732-1181), and it includes a CompuServe IntroPak with a free subscription and $15 worth of free online time. We should add that we have no relationship whatsoever with the firm. It's just that, attracted by the price, we bought one unit, tested it and liked it, and then began acquiring them for relatives and friends. We also deliberately tested the firm's customer service over a period of months and found it to be excellent. Finally, to locate the best sources with the best prices, we phoned the company.

According to Steve Kohn, the firm's marketing manager, E + E DataComm introduced the Avatex 1200 in April of 1986 and had sold 72,000 units by year's end. In late 1986, the company introduced the original version of its 1200hc (the "hc" stands for "Hayes compatible"). And almost immediately thereafter, the units reached their current sales rate of between 6000 and 10,000 a month, according to Mr. Kohn.

According to the company's studies, E + E DataComm had about 15% of the modem market by mid-1987.

We asked Mr. Kohn where one could get the best price on an Avatex 1200hc. Here are the names and addresses of two of the company's leading distributors:

Megatronics, Inc.
P.O. Box 3660
Logan, UT 84321

(800) 232-6342
(800) 752-2642 in Utah

Computer Software Services
2150 Executive Drive
Addison, IL 60101

Dealer locator service:
(800) 422-4912
(800) 331-7638 in Illinois

Megatronics sells directly to the public and won the 1986 and the 1987 *Computer Shopper* Best Buy in modems award for selling the Avatex 1200 at such a good price. At this writing they sell the 1200hc for $99 and may include communications software (PC-TALK, Bitcomm, or some other program). They accept Visa and MasterCard. Computer Software Services is a distributor with a special dealer locator service. If you call one of their toll-free numbers and tell them where you live, they will give you the name of the Avatex dealer nearest you. We suggest that you phone both places and go with the one offering the best price.

When you call, you might also want to ask about the Avatex 2400 (about $300 for the external unit, $250 for the internal). And, since you will need a cable to connect your computer's RS-232 port to the modem's RS-232 port, you might want to ask about that as well. Otherwise, you can obtain the cable you need from most Radio Shack, ComputerLand, or similar computer and electronics stores.

Protect Your Equipment!

As experienced computer users know, the electricity that feeds your machines isn't as pure as the driven snow. Surges, spikes, and brownout voltage reductions can play havoc with your equipment. At best they can cause a loss of data. At worst they can fry one or more internal components or cause your hard disk to crash. Consequently, for years we have recommended installing electrical surge suppressors for all computer equipment.

Power irregularities can occur at any time of day or night, regardless of the weather. But to be on the safe side, we have always avoided using a computer during an electrical storm, figuring that as long as a machine isn't switched on, nothing can hurt it. And we have always taken the safety of the telephone line for granted.

Unfortunately, we were wrong on both counts. A lightning strike that completely destroyed a telephone answering machine at five in the morning prompted an investigation. It turns out that even if a computer is off, some types of surges are powerful enough to leap the connection in the switch and damage the innards of your machine. We have also learned that a lightning flash even a mile away from a phone line that may in turn be miles from you can induce a surge on the line of a million volts or more. The lesson, then, is this: Any piece of computer equipment that uses either the electrical or the phone lines must be protected.

There are lots of surge protectors on the market. Most look like some variation of a single or multi-outlet power strip or outlet box. Ostensibly, they are supposed to intercept voltage spikes and other problems and dissipate the energy before it can get to your machine, but as you might imagine, they vary widely in their effectiveness. There are three crucial specifications to look for to be certain of getting a unit that will really do the job.

The "first stage peak clamping voltage" should be 200 volts plus or minus five percent. This is the voltage at which the unit responds, and the lower the figure, the better. Second, the response time should be five picoseconds. A picosecond is a *trillionth* of a second, or 1000 times faster than a nanosecond or billionth of a second. The faster the response, the better. Third, the unit should offer the identical protection to equipment connected to your phone line.

If you have a hard disk and live in an area prone to frequent electrical brownouts, you might also consider a unit offering "voltage dropout" protection. Such units should automatically shut everything off if the power falls to 80 volts, plus or minus five percent. The read/write head of a hard disk floats on a cushion of air created by the spinning hard disk platter. If the voltage drops and the disk spins more slowly, that cushion can disappear. The head can then plow into the platter, causing a great deal of heartache for all concerned.

Two of the leading manufacturers of surge suppressors are Dynatech and Panamax. Both offer a variety of power and phone protection units that meet the above specifications. All of the units cited here have an incoming and an outgoing phone jack. Models and prices differ with the number of electrical receptacles. We've quoted list prices here, but most units are routinely discounted.

Dynatech's DSLP model has a single power receptacle and lists for $75, while the firm's DS4LP has four receptacles and lists for $110. At this writing, neither unit includes brownout protection, though that feature is being considered. For brownout protection but no phone line, the firm offers its four-outlet Surge Sentry DSD at $120. You could thus get the DSD for your computer and peripherals and the DSLP for your phone line and modem. All of these Dynatech units come with a ten-year warranty and a one-year damaged equipment replacement plan. The company will replace any electrical equipment damaged due to the failure of the power line surge protection circuitry in its units up to a maximum of $5000.

Panamax offers a similar line. The company's TeleMAX 1 has a single power receptacle and lists for $89. The TeleMAX 4 has four outlets and lists for $129. The SuperMAX has four outlets and includes brownout protection. It lists for $149. All three units protect your phone line, and like the Dynatech units above, each plugs into the wall with a six-foot cord. Panamax products carry a five-year warranty.

Here is where to send for more information and the names of the dealers in your area carrying Dynatech or Panamax products:

Dynatech Computer Power, Inc.
5800 Butler Lane
Scotts Valley, CA 95066
(800) 638-9098
(408) 438-5760

Panamax
150 Mitchell Blvd.
San Rafael, CA 94903
(800) 472-5555
(800) 472-6262 in California
(800) 443-2391 from Canada
(415) 499-3900

The ASCII Code Set, Text, and Machine Language Files

At this point let's take just a moment to look at where we are. We've got the computer, the comm card, the modem, and telephone and electrical protection devices. And we know that a comm program will tie all of these things together. Ahead lie the public data networks (PDNs) that make it possible for you to call a distant host without paying conventional long-distance charges. That brings you to the doorway of a host system, where this chapter will end. We'll take up the matter of what happens next in the following chapter.

Right now, however, before moving on to Telenet, Tymnet, and the other PDNs, we'll take a brief intermission to discuss the ASCII code set and the types of files you will be downloading. You're going to have to know this stuff eventually, so if you don't already know the difference between a machine language file and an ASCII text file, you might as well pick it up now.

The ASCII Code Set

We can start with the ASCII (pronounced: "as-key") code set. This stands for the American Standard Code for Information Interchange, and it is as central to personal computing as microprocessors and memory chips. When you strike a key on your keyboard, an ASCII code number is sent into your system. The system looks the code up in its built-in translation table and displays the corresponding character on your screen. Similarly, should you strike the same key when you are online, the same code number goes out your serial port and over the phone lines to the remote system. Since nearly everyone agrees on the ASCII code and what the numbers mean, the remote system knows exactly what character you have sent. The same process works in reverse, of course, for your system too "speaks ASCII."

The basic ASCII code set that everyone uses contains 128 numbers, from 0 through 127. These are decimal numbers that human beings can easily use and understand. But of course they can be expressed by any type of numbering system. Thus you may encounter ASCII codes written in the hexadecimal (base 16) system or in the binary (base 2) system with its 1s and 0s.

There is an ASCII number for every capital letter, every lowercase letter, every Arabic number, and for almost every punctuation mark. But there are also numbers for things called "control codes." These are the codes that are assigned to your <Enter> (or "carriage return"), <Backspace>, and <Tab> keys, for example. They also include many other codes that are designed to control printers, modems, and other devices. There's even a code (Control-G) that will cause a computer's internal speaker to beep.

There are 26 major control codes—one for each letter of the alphabet—and they are normally entered by holding down the <Ctrl> key and striking the target letter. For example, when you are communicating with most databases, if you hold down the <Ctrl> key and hit <S>, the remote computer will temporarily stop sending you information. To tell the remote system to start up again, you have only to send it a Control-Q. On the PC, you can generate any ASCII code, "control" or otherwise, by holding down the <ALT> key and tapping in its number on the numeric keypad. (See the appendices of your BASIC manual for a complete list of codes and how the PC displays them on the screen.)

The 128 numbers in the standard ASCII code set cover just about all the bases as far as human and computer communications are concerned. Using these numbers, you can send and receive almost any readable test, whether it's "Hi Mom!" or "400 OPEN 'DATA' FOR OUTPUT AS # 1." The point to remember is that any file that exists in readable form is considered an ASCII or a text file. The term "DOS file" is also used, presumably because you can display any text file on the screen by keying in TYPE followed by the filename at the DOS prompt. It does not matter whether the text is actually Pascal, C, assembly language, or a BASIC program saved in the ASCII format (SAVE "FILE-NAME.BAS",A). It is still a text file.

"High Codes" and Machine Language

Remember the bits, bytes, and jelly beans discussed at the beginning of the chapter? We used the red and blue beans to symbolize the binary digits (on/off; high voltage/low voltage; magnetized/nonmagnetized; high modem tone/low modem tone) that are the essence of the computer's world. In the binary numbering system that computers use to make sense of all this, you can write the equivalent of a decimal 127 with just seven bits. The binary number would look like this: 1111111. But as we all know by now, computers by design have an eighth bit to work with. Adding an eighth one-bit to the above binary number adds an additional 128, bringing the total to 256 possible numbers, decimal 0 through 255 or binary 00000000 through 11111111.

As we've seen, the ASCII code set runs from 0 through 127. That's 128 slots and it provides plenty of room for all the upper and lowercase letters, control codes, and everything else. But with the eighth bit, there are now an additional 128 slots (running from 128 through 255). These are the "high codes" of the extended ASCII code set, and for hardware and software manufacturers they represent the wide open spaces. Of necessity, everyone agrees on what each of the lower 128 codes represents. But manufacturers are free to use the high code slots for anything they please.

Commercial word processing programs like WordStar and PFS:Write (also know as IBM Writing Assistant) use high codes to represent formatting commands. A soft hyphen—one that will disappear if necessary when you adjust the text to different margins—may look like a regular hyphen to you when you're using the program. But the software knows that it's not because the character has been tagged with a high ASCII code. Similarly, by default BASIC saves programs in a compressed format that includes many high codes.

The point is that if you try to display high-code files on the screen with the TYPE command, or if you try to download them as a text file, you are sure to run into problems. High codes are not meant to be seen on the screen, at least not when your system thinks it's dealing with a text file.

Binary or Machine Language Files

This leads naturally to the second major type of file: files consisting of 100 percent machine language. "Machine language" is another way of referring to the 1s and 0s we've spoken of before. But it is a more descriptive term than you might at first suspect. The high and low voltage pulses and patterns we symbolize with 1s and 0s are the only things computers can understand. They are really nothing more than the settings for an impossibly large number of impossibly small electrical switches inside the machine. Set the switches one way and the computer calculates your taxes. Set them another way, and it plays a little tune. In any case, nothing gets in or out of the box without first passing through a binary stage, for this is the only language a computer can deal with.

Machine language is called a "low-level" language because it is so close to the machine itself. And believe it or not, there are people who program using nothing but 1s and 0s. Most of us, however, prefer a higher level language, one that's closer to English (or whatever human language you happen to speak). The software that makes this possible may be called BASIC, C, Pascal, FORTRAN, COBOL, or be given some other name. Each of these languages is quite different. But all have one thing in common: Every high-level computer language is designed to translate human words into the 1s and 0s of machine language.

As discussed in Chapter 2, the translation can be done in two ways. It is either done each time the program is run, as is the case with interpreted BASIC. Or it is done once and recorded to disk, as is the case with compiled BASIC, C, Pascal, or some other language. The human-like language version of a program is called the "source code," while the compiled version is machine code. You will also hear of "assembler" or "assembly language." This is a lower level language, but the principles are the same. An assembly language programmer prepares his code as a text file and then assembles it into machine code.

Do You Really Need to Know?

Yes, this is heavy going. But we haven't told you these things merely to hear the keyboard click. You will encounter all of these terms when you go online to search for and download free software. A program in Pascal or C will do you no good, for example, if you don't own a Pascal or C compiler to turn it into machine language. You might not care to dip into assembly language, but you may find that the machine language version of a nifty-looking utility program is accompanied by its source code (as an .ASM file) but not by a documentation file. In such cases it is smart to download both files because the programmer probably put his documentation in the source code file as a series of comments, which you can print out or read with a word processor.

The most important reason for knowing the difference between a text file and a binary or machine language file, however, concerns the matter of downloading. Downloading a text file and capturing it to disk is very

straightforward. You first tell your communications program that you
want to capture incoming data, then you tell the online system to send
you the file. As the host system does so, the text of the file will appear
on your screen just as if you had typed it yourself. When the file has
been transmitted, you tell your software to stop capturing incoming
data and close the download file on disk.

Machine language files cannot be handled this way because they are
not text, and will drive your screen crazy should you try to treat them
that way. To see what we mean, get to your DOS prompt and enter the
command TYPE COMMAND.COM. Like all DOS programs and all
other files ending with either .COM ("command") or .EXE ("executable"), this is a machine language program. Most of the text characters
you see on the screen are purely accidental. They are displayed because
the hardware that controls the screen sees random bytes that happen to
correspond to ASCII codes, so it displays them. The cursor goes wild
for the same reason: The screen hardware has encountered bytes that
correspond to ASCII control codes. You'll get similar results should you
TYPE a WordStar, PFS:Write, BASIC, or other file containing bytes of
machine language.

Machine language files can only be downloaded as a direct transfer of
data from one computer to another. You won't see any portion of the file
on the screen. A thoughtfully written comm program will put something
on the screen to let you monitor the progress of the transmission, however. Often this takes the form of a pop-up window that tells you the
name of the file, how many blocks of data have been received, the
number of errors experienced, and so on.

While a download is taking place, you're pretty much out of things.
The modem's front panel lights blink incessantly as the data comes in.
The disk drive light comes on periodically as pieces of the file are recorded. And the numbers in the pop-up window change. It is strictly a
machine-to-machine conversation. Your computer will beep you when it
is finished. We'll have a lot more to say about downloading and the
software protocols (like the famous XMODEM protocol) that make error-free transfers possible in Chapter 6.

How to Set Your Communications Parameters

You don't have to spend five minutes with a computer before you begin
to suspect that there are nearly an infinite number of ways to do the
same thing. That's very much the essence of computing, as users of
electronic spreadsheet, word processing, and database programs well
know. The same is true of online communications. There are lots of
ways to send and receive data. The difference is that, because it in-

volves many different computers and many different people, communications must be highly and widely standardized. Otherwise no one could talk to anyone else.

The standard that is used for online personal computer data communications calls for sending one byte at a time, framed by what we earlier called two bits of packing material. Each byte is a binary representation of an ASCII code number. The packing material consists of a "start bit" at the beginning and a "stop bit" at the end. These bits are added by the UART as it gets everything lined up in serial fashion before booting it out the door. A single character thus enters the communications stream as a start bit, followed by the eight data bits of the byte, followed by a stop bit, for a total of ten bits in all. Remember, computers can't tell one bit from another, so you need the start bit to tell the receiving system that the next eight bits represent data, and the stop bit to mark the end of the data.

But what if you are dealing with just text—files consisting of nothing but displayable alphanumeric characters, with ASCII codes between 0 and 127, each of which can be represented with only seven data bits? Doesn't matter. Eight bits will still be sent for each character. What does matter is what the receiving computer thinks it is supposed to look for. If you tell it to pay attention to just the first seven data bits in the bytes you send, it will not count the eighth bit as data. Alternatively, if you tell it you plan to use all eight bits, then it will pay attention to all eight.

Making this decision is part of setting your "communications parameters," something you do with your communications software. There are quite a few communications parameters and many potential settings for each, but most online activity centers around only one or two configurations. In most cases, once you tell your comm program what you want, it will record your choices and use them as its default settings until you say otherwise. You can thus usually set a program once and never think about it again.

The cardinal rule of online communications is that the settings of both the calling system and the host system must match. The match points are as follows: speed, data bits (sometimes called "word length" or "character length"), parity sense, stop bits, duplex, and line feeds.

Speed is the most obvious setting. As you know from our discussion of modems, communications can take place at speeds ranging from 110 bits per second to 19.2 kilobits per second or more, though 300, 1200, or 2400 bps are the most commonly used rates. In almost every case, the speeds that a commercial system or BBS will accept will be published in one form or another. When you call them you will have to use one of those choices or you will see nothing but garbage on your screen.

Data Bits, Parity, and Stop Bits: 7/E/1 and 8/N/1

The next three settings are not obvious at all. They are the product of an industry agreement that forces all computers to perform asynchronous communication the same way. (Which is why Apples, IBMs, Macintoshes, and every other make and model of computer can easily exchange files once they are online.) Fortunately, of the dozens of possible combinations there are only two that really matter. These are referred to as "seven, even, and one" (7/E/1) and as "eight, none, and one" (8/N/1).

Translated, this means either "seven data bits, even parity, and one stop bit" or "eight data bits, no parity, and one stop bit." But you don't need to know that. (If you're curious, please see the "Optional Info" section that follows for an explanation.) For a variety of reasons these have become the most widely used comm settings, and all systems support at least one of these combinations. So when you're preparing to go online, simply tell your communications software the speed you're going to use and select one of these combinations. Your comm program documentation will tell you what commands to enter.

FreeTip: It's largely a personal preference, but whenever possible we like to use 7/E/1 when communicating with a remote system. For technical reasons explained in the optional section that follows, this setting filters out all but the standard 128 characters in the lower half of the ASCII code set. Some online systems and BBSs can be quirky, with a tendency to send strange machine language characters if you sign on at 8/N/1. This can create garbage on your screen in some cases.

On the other hand, some bulletin board operators have gotten quite fancy and offer you the option of experiencing all manner of music and graphics as you interact with their systems. Since graphics and music features use the full ASCII code set—all 256 characters—a setting of 8/N/1 is required to view or hear them.

Finally, you should be aware that signing on at 7/E/1 has no effect on your ability to download machine language programs. Both your system and the host system will automatically switch to 8/N/1 when you begin downloading a program using an error-checking protocol such as XMODEM and switch back when the transfer is complete.

Optional Info: Data, Parity, and Stop Bits

When it comes to explaining technical details there is a great tendency in the online field to pass the buck. The manuals supplied by commercial systems tell you what comm settings to use and suggest consulting your communications software documentation for more information. But most of the time such documentation is more concerned with presenting the wonderful features of the program than with explaining things like data, parity, and stop bits. This isn't a truly serious situation, for as noted above, you really don't have to know about these things to communicate effectively. But it does preserve an unnecessary air of mystery about the online process. And mystery does not build confidence. If you're curious, here are the answers you need.

As you know, when two systems are set to use seven data bits, each agrees to pay attention to only the first seven bits following the start bit in each communicated character. But the eighth bit is still there. So, people reasoned, why not take advantage of it? Why not use it as a means of verifying the accurate reception of the preceding seven bits?

That's what's behind the idea of using "parity sense" as a means of error checking. Consider a setting of even parity as an example. The sending system adds up the seven 1s and 0s of the character it is about to send: $1+0+1+1+0+1+1$, for example. If the total comes out to an odd number, the sending system makes the eighth bit a 1 so that the total of the eight 1s and 0s will be an even number. If the seven bits total an even number, the sending system makes the eighth bit a zero, which has no effect on the total of the eight bits.

To do its part, the receiving system adds up the eight bits as they come in. The receiver expects the bits of every character to add up to an even number, as per the agreement to use even parity. If the total is odd, the receiver knows that at least one of the bits has been transformed into its opposite—a 1 bit turned into a 0 bit or vice versa—during the transmission. This can happen due to electrical noise somewhere on the line, a poor connection, or a variety of other things. Whether or not the receiving system notifies the sender when it detects an error or takes some other action is a function of the software it is running.

By custom, a setting of odd parity is rarely used, but it works in exactly the same way. The only difference is that both systems agree that the bits in all characters will add up to an odd number. It also follows that if both systems agree to consider all eight bits as data bits, then no "extra" bit is available to signal parity; hence the setting 8/N/1 signifying eight data bits, no parity, and one stop bit.

Generally, parity checking is not a very good method of insuring accurate data transmission. After all, if two of the seven data bits are changed to their opposites, the oddness or evenness of the total will not be affected, and the receiving system will assume that the character is correct. But for many years it was the only real alternative.

Full and Half Duplex

The only other settings you need to worry about are duplex and line feeds. Both are easy to understand. The duplex setting concerns how the characters you type manage to appear on your screen. Most host systems, with the notable exception of General Electric's GEnie, are set up to echo characters. This means that when you type an A on your keyboard the bit pattern symbolizing a capital A in the ASCII code set whizzes out your comm port, into the modem, and down the line to the remote system. The remote system takes note of this character and then echos it back to your system. Thus the A that appears on your screen does *not* come from your keyboard—it comes from the host system. That is what is meant by "full duplex" in this instance. (The more precise term is "echoplex," for obvious reasons.)

It thus follows that if you're set for full duplex but the host system is *not* set up to echo characters, you will see nothing on your screen when you type a capital A or any other character. In such cases, you must set your system for "half duplex." This is often called enabling your "echo." When you turn on this software feature and hit a capital A, the character will go from your keyboard both to the screen and to the remote system. It also follows that if you are seeing double characters (lliikkee tthhiiss) while you are online, you are set for half duplex while the host system is set for full duplex. One copy of each character is coming from your keyboard, while the second copy is coming from the remote system. The solution is to change your setting to full duplex to match the host system.

CR/LF (Carriage Return/Line Feed)

We all know that computers are just dumb machines. You have to tell them everything, specifying your desires to the last little detail. Nothing drives this fact home more forcefully than the matter of the carriage return/line feed communications setting. When you hit the <Return> key on a typewriter, for example, two distinct things happen: the typing element or carriage zips to the left, stopping at the left margin, and the paper moves up one or more lines to give you a fresh space on which to type.

In computer parlance, the first action is called a carriage return and the second is called a line feed. Each is symbolized by a separate ASCII character control code. A carriage return is a Control-M (ASCII 13), and a line feed is a Control-J (ASCII 10). Typewriters perform both activities at the same time automatically. But if you want a computer to do this, you must give it specific instructions. Otherwise, if your machine receives only an ASCII 13 from a remote system it will move the cursor over to the far left and merrily begin overwriting whatever was there before, without advancing the display screen to a fresh line. Alternatively, if the remote system sends both a carriage return (CR) and a line feed (LF) and your own system is set to add a line feed of its own each time it sees a carriage return coming in, all text will be double-spaced due to the presence of that extra line feed.

This isn't going to ruin your ability to communicate, but obviously it's best if the two systems match. Most personal computer comm programs will let you make two settings, one for outgoing lines and one for incoming lines. In both cases you can opt to either add "LF on CR" or not. Unfortunately commercial online systems differ in their approach. On CompuServe, for example, you can set up a personal profile of user defaults within which you can choose whether you want to receive LF on CR or not. You can customize your profile on BIX as well, though that system would rather you did not send LF on CR. Except when using its mail system, Delphi doesn't care whether you send it a LF on CR or not. But since you will almost certainly be using Delphi mail, you might as well set your system to not send LF on CR when using any Delphi feature.

We don't mean to make more of this topic than it deserves, but it is something you should at least be aware of. Generally, we suggest that you set your software to send only CRs and not add a LF to incoming CRs. In other words, assume that the remote system will do all the line feed work both coming and going. If you have problems, they will be easy enough to spot and correct with a different setting.

Comm Parameter Recap

To summarize, then, you can successfully communicate with virtually any host system using the following settings:

Speed: 300, 1200, or 2400 bps, depending on the modems you and the host are using.

Data, parity, and stop bits: 7/E/1 or 8/N/1.

Duplex: Full duplex (except for the GEnie system).

Line feeds: Do not send line feeds or add them to incoming carriage returns unless you have problems.

Because there is no way for the author of a communications program to know the capabilities of your particular modem, you will almost certainly have to tell your software how fast you wish to communicate. However, since everything else is fairly standard, you may find that the program's built-in defaults match the above requirements. It doesn't hurt to check, though, and it is a good idea to see if there is a way to change your settings on the fly—that is, after you have already made your connection with the host.

Public Data Networks and Packet Switching

If you lived in California and had to place a long-distance call to Columbus, Ohio, every time you wanted to reach CompuServe, or to Cambridge, Massachusetts, every time you wanted to reach Delphi, the chances are you'd say, "Thanks, but no thanks," to online communications. It would simply be too expensive.

Fortunately, although most systems can be reached by direct dial, there's usually no need to do so, thanks to the public data networks (PDNs). The PDNs use a technology called "packet switching" that is specifically designed to allow one computer to talk to another and to do so inexpensively. As long as both locations are within the continental United States, for example, the cost of using a PDN has historically been as low as $2 an hour during nonbusiness, evening hours.

The two leading public data networks in the United States are Telenet, owned by US Sprint Communications Corporation, which in turn is owned by GTE and United Telecommunications, Inc., and Tymnet, owned by the McDonnell Douglas Corporation. In Canada, the leading network is Datapac, owned and operated by Telecom Canada. Other companies, like CompuServe and General Electric, operate networks as well, but all work in essentially the same way.

You don't need to know a great deal about the PDNs, but it's important to have a broad familiarity with them for at least two reasons. First, you will be using them virtually every time you download a piece of free software from a major commercial system. You may be able to use them for BBSs in selected cities as well. And second, it is worth knowing why PDNs can offer remote connections at such low rates.

Data Packets and the Virtual Circuit

A packet-switching network consists of hundreds of computers and thousands of modems. The computers and modems are scattered all over the country and connected to each other by high-speed (up to 56,000 bits per second or 56 Kbps) data lines. Each location on the network is called a node, and if you live near a medium to large city, the chances are that there is at least one node within your local calling area.

When you and your computer dial one of these local nodes, one of the modems at that location will answer the phone and you will immediately hear a high-pitched tone, often followed by a gravelly noise, through your modem's speaker. Your modem will sense these sounds and establish a connection with the node modem at your chosen speed. As soon as that has happened, the noise will stop. If you are using a Hayes-compatible modem, the word CONNECT will then appear on your screen.

At this point you and your computer will be in direct contact with the node computer, and after keying in some preliminary information, you will be free to tell the network node which commercial system you wish to talk to. The node computer will then patch you through to your target system using the most efficient network route available at the time. In the target system's computer room—let's say it's Rockville, Maryland, where GEnie's massive array of computers are located—the phone will ring and one of GEnie's modems will answer to complete the connection.

The word *efficient* is the key here, since the efficiencies made possible by packet-switching technology are one of the main reasons using a PDN is cheaper than placing a conventional long-distance call. When you make a voice call, an actual physical circuit must be established between your phone and the person you are calling. This requires lots of switches and a lot of wires leading to a lot of different places. But the result is a circuit that's as real and complete as any you ever assembled in seventh grade science class. And of course the circuit must remain in existence for the duration of your call, tying up all of the physical resources involved in making the connection.

Computer-to-computer calls are different. Because they communicate digitally—using the 1s and 0s we've said so much about—their transmissions can easily be chopped up into discrete units or packets. Like the counterman at a hardware store pulling lengths of rope off a spool and cutting them to a uniform size, the node computer cuts your computer's data stream into uniformly sized packets of bits, stamps them with the address of your target system and a packet sequence number, and sends them on their way.

A PDN packet contains 128 bytes and padding characters are used to round out the packet when necessary. When a packet comes into the node computer from a remote system, the computer strips off any non-relevant bits, checks the packet's address, and channels it to the correct caller. This is why a network node computer is often referred to as a packet assembler/disassembler or PAD.

A single PAD may have many incoming lines but only two or three high-speed lines connecting it to the network. However, since each packet is unique, the packets from several callers can be interleaved. What's more, they can be shot out into the network in different directions as the PAD strives for maximum efficiency in the face of ever-changing network load conditions and traffic patterns. Other node computers at various locations in the network receive the packets, check their address, and relay them to another node or to the host itself. Thanks to the address and sequence number, however, the packets are received by the correct host system in the correct order, regardless of the route each packet took to reach its destination.

The result is what's called a virtual circuit. In most cases, when you use a packet-switching network, the connection between you and a host system appears to be identical to the connection that would exist were you to dial the remote system directly, even though an unbroken, continuous physical connection between you never actually exists.

The Impact of the PDNs

So what effect does this have on a free software downloader? The first and most important effect is that a PDN's ability to interleave packets from several callers on the same line and it's ability to constantly reconfigure the path your call takes to reach a host system in response to changing load factors makes for very efficient use of the equipment. Greater efficiency means lower costs, which mean lower prices.

Second, it helps explain at least some of the delays you may experience when using a PDN and host during peak times of the day. It explains other points as well. Sometimes, for example, you may call your local node and the local node computer will tell you that no outgoing lines are available. You may also find that occasionally all incoming lines are in use, resulting in a conventional busy signal when you call. The solutions are the same in both cases: Keep trying, wait a while and try again, or simply call a different node.

Finally, there is the matter of a PDN's effect on a protocol transfer. Generally, the more "transparent" a data network is, the better. That is, once you have made the initial connection, you should not even be aware that you are actually talking to Telenet or Tymnet and that it is relaying your keystrokes to the host. Usually that's exactly the way things work, even when you're using XMODEM or some other error-checking protocol to snare a nifty free program from an online system or BBS. But there are times when this is not the case, or when the PDN itself introduces noticeable delays.

Telenet, Tymnet, and Datapac: Customer Service and Node Numbers

All of the online services we will be discussing later can be reached via Telenet, Tymnet, or both, though as noted CompuServe and GEnie can be reached via their own packet-switching networks as well. Canadian users will have to call a local Datapac node, which can then gate them into one of the U.S. networks.

Since it is in the interests of every online system to get you connected as quickly and easily as possible, you can usually count on receiving information about Telenet, Tymnet, and Datapac with your subscription package. Of course the most important piece of information is the telephone number of your local node, and usually a list of node numbers will be supplied.

However, node phone numbers can change, rendering the printed lists out of date. And while the customer service departments of most online systems can usually give you the new number, it doesn't hurt to be aware that the packet switchers operate customer service departments as well. In addition, though you probably will not need them, both Telenet and Tymnet publish "how-to" booklets that are available free of charge. Datapac publishes a small spiral-bound directory as well.

To order your copy of these booklets, report network problems, ask questions, or simply get the current number of your nearest network node, use the following addresses and phone numbers:

Telenet
U.S. Sprint, Inc.
12490 Sunrise Valley Drive
Reston, VA 22096
(703) 689-6000
(800) 835-3638

Customer Service: all states except Virginia, Alaska, and Hawaii, (800) 336-0437; outside continental U.S. (703) 689-6400

FreeTip: If you do not know your local Telenet node phone number, set your system to 7/E/1 and dial (800) 424-9494. Hit your <Enter> key three times, and then follow the prompts to key in your area code and local exchange (the first three digits of your phone number). An "at" sign (@) will appear. Key in MAIL, and respond to the prompts for username and password with PHONES in each case. The system will then give you a list of nearby Telenet node phone numbers.

Tymnet, Inc.
2710 Orchard Parkway
San Jose, CA 95134
(408) 942-5254

Customer Service (worldwide): (800) 336-0149

If you live in Canada, contact your local Postal, Telephone, and Telegraph (PTT) office to obtain the phone number of the Datapac node nearest you. For information and a copy of the enormously helpful booklet, the "Datapac Directory," contact:

Datapac Support Centre
Telecom Canada
Room 1890, 160 Elgin Street
Ottawa, Ontario K1G 3J4
(613) 567-8374

A Look Ahead

As promised, this chapter has taken you from ground zero right to the host system's door. In the next chapter we will show you what to do once you step inside, regardless of which system lies behind that door. As we will see, whether you are dealing with a commercial service or a BBS, there are seven basic steps to follow to obtain free software from any online system.

6

How to Tap Any Online System

THE SEVEN STEPS TO DOWNLOADING FREE SOFTWARE

In the previous chapter we looked at the components of online communications—the hardware and software you must have to get free programs over the telephone. In this chapter we'll focus on the process. We'll show you the technique for obtaining virtually any public domain or shareware program at virtually any time of day or night just by dialing the phone. Equally important, we'll point you in the right direction to tap the collective wisdom of the community of users for answers to your questions on the same any-time basis.

You will no doubt be pleased to learn that the entire process boils down to seven steps and that these steps are the same for every online system. Naturally, the specific commands differ with the system, and we will discuss them in the next chapter. But, to paraphrase the advertising slogan for a famous brand of Scotch, the process never varies. That process is shown below.

THE SEVEN STEPS TO DOWNLOADING FREE SOFTWARE

1. Sign on to the remote system.

2. Move to the free software treasure rooms—those sections of the system where the goodies are kept.

3. Download either a list of all the keywords used to reference the files or a list of all the filenames in the library.

4. Sign off the system and search these lists on your *own* machine, noting filenames or keywords of interest.

5. Sign on again and return to the treasure room.

6. Use your selected filenames or keywords to call up expanded descriptions of your candidate.

7. Download the programs you want using an error-checking protocol and sign off the system.

We're going to use these steps as the framework for this chapter, so don't worry if some of them are less than crystal clear at this point. You'll be hearing a lot more about them. In addition, since we're going to be covering a lot of material, you may find it helpful to use this list as a bannister or safety railing along the way. By referring to it or keeping it in mind, you will always know where you are in the process.

You won't find this seven-step procedure in any of the manuals for commercial online systems. Indeed, most officials would probably label it unconventional, and suggest that instead of doing things this way you use the search commands available on their systems to look for programs of interest while you are online.

A lot of people do just that, and a lot of them end up needlessly wasting countless connect-time dollars in the process. The online search facilities offered by all commercial systems sound good in theory. But the truth of the matter is that they are next to useless due to the erratic, wildly inconsistent nature of the databases they must search. As a consequence, you can search all day for a program you know is available on a given system and never find it. The method recommended here, in contrast, involves an extra step or two, but as years of experience have shown, it offers rifle-shot accuracy and concomitant savings in connect-time charges.

Step 1: Sign On to the Remote System

The manuals you will receive with your subscription to an online service will tell you what to do to sign on, so we won't cover the step in detail here. In most cases the process begins with a local call to a Telenet, Tymnet, or other PDN node. You'll go through a preliminary step or two to let the network match itself to your communications settings. Then you'll be prompted for the address of the system you wish to reach. Once you key in that address, the next prompt you see will ask for your account number and the one after that will request your password.

At that point you will be logged onto the host system and the connect-time meter will start running. The actual connect-time costs for each commercial system are given in Chapter 7. They will normally be billed to your Visa or MasterCard, unless you have made other arrangements. Usually the first thing you see after logging on will be a list of announcements or bulletins followed by some kind of greeting or "TOP menu." From there you'll be free to move anywhere on the system you please.

Step 2: Move to the Treasure Rooms

The SIGs Are Where It's At

You might very well wish to subscribe to more than one of the systems profiled in the next chapter. But certainly no one but a dyed-in-the-disk online aficionado or similarly crazy computer book author would be expected to subscribe to all six of them. Consequently, it's not likely that many people know how similar all online free software facilities are. It's important to be aware of these similarities, though, because once you're familiar with the general setup, you'll be able to quickly figure out how to tap any online free software facility, whether it's a commercial system, a BBS, or a part of your company's corporate system.

For our purposes here, it is helpful to compare entering an online system to strolling through the ivy-covered iron gates of a college campus—one with many separate buildings, each dedicated to a particular function. What you're looking for, if you're after free software, is Fraternity or Sorority Row. You want the computer-specific clubhouses with their information-packed bulletin boards, their meeting rooms for all night bull sessions, and their vast member-created libraries of PD or shareware programs.

In computer terms, these clubhouses are separate sections of online systems that you might think of as electronic computer user groups. CompuServe originated the concept years ago with its SIGs or special interest groups. On that system these features are now officially called "forums," although the traditional term is still widely used. The Source and Delphi follow the tradition by referring to their online groups as SIGs. GEnie uses the term "RoundTables" or RTs. PeopleLink calls such groups "clubs," and BIX uses the word "conferences." We'll refer to all such groups as SIGs unless otherwise indicated.

As with the best fraternity houses, all SIGs have a manager. This is the person whose job it is to make sure everything runs smoothly. Different systems have different official titles (forum administrator, club chairman, and so on), but almost everyone refers to SIG managers as "sysops" (pronounced "sis-op"). That's short for "system operator," and it is derived directly from the BBS world.

Running a good SIG takes a lot of time and effort, and all sysops on commercial systems are compensated for their labors. Generally they receive between two and fifteen percent of the connect-time dollars you spend using the SIGs they run. Since the online system does not charge you any more for using a SIG than for your other activities, and since compensation acts as an incentive to the sysop and his or her assistants to run a vigorous, interesting operation, this policy works out well for everyone. Indeed, some sysops earn five and six-figure incomes from their activities.

FreeTip: If being a sysop on a commercial system sounds intriguing, you should know that all of these systems are looking for people with good ideas for SIGs. You can't go into it half-heartedly, and if your main goal is the free connect time sysops receive, you might as well forget it. On the other hand, if you look at it as a business and are willing to make the large commitment of time and energy required to run a first-class SIG, it can be a very worthwhile and profitable enterprise.

You should be aware, however, that the contractual arrangements offered by each online system differ widely. On some systems, for example, you may find that you don't own the SIG or any of its files. (In other words, the SIG can continue without you should you wish to terminate your relationship.) Other systems see their role as similar to that of a landlord renting space to a retail store. Should you want to leave when the lease is up, you take everything with you and the space becomes vacant.

Clearly, as in any business deal, it pays to survey the field and the various offerings and get some professional advice before making a commitment. You can start by contacting *all* of the systems profiled in Chapter 7 and requesting copies of their system operator/SIG contracts.

An Invaluable Resource

The SIGs are where the community of users we've spoken of before hangs its electronic hat. And while they have scads of free software for you to download, they have much more to offer as well. They are the places to go for unbiased hands-on reviews of the latest hardware and software packages. You can use their facilities to locate an expert on a topic of interest. You can post questions and be nearly guaranteed a response. You can also scan their "message boards" or information exchanges for the questions and answers that others have asked and for tips, techniques, and useful technical information.

Here is a perfect example having to do with the call-waiting feature offered by many phone companies. This is the feature that makes a burp-clink noise when you're on the phone and someone else is calling your number. If you want to see who it is, you press the receiver hook once to put your current line on hold and connect with the incoming call.

Unfortunately, that burp-clink sound causes modems all kinds of problems. If you happen to be in the midst of an online session at the time, the call-waiting signal will immediately knock you offline and cause the modem to break the connection. In technical terms, the sound causes the modem to "lose carrier."

Supposedly, you can set the modem's S10 memory register to make it more tolerant of such interruptions. However, after testing many different S10 register values, we found that only once did a modem successfully ignore the call-waiting interruption.

Maybe something else had to be set as well? Is there some ideal value for the S10 register? There has to be a way. Finally we decided to tap the expertise of the community of users. We signed on to CompuServe, went to the IBM Communications SIG data library, and searched for references to CALL*. The asterisk (*) is a wildcard search character that works just as it does in DOS.

Seconds later—bingo!—a citation and brief description of a program called CW.BAS. We downloaded the program and looked at it offline. Among the BASIC remarks was the following:

> Another way that works on most call-waiting systems is to dial 1170 before any number. If the phone system returns a beep-beep-dial tone, it has received your "cancel call-waiting" request. For example, to dial 800-555-1212, send your Hayes-compatible modem 1170,800-555-1212. Call-waiting will go back into effect after the call is complete. This is a new feature of most phone systems.
>
> John de Longpre
> CompuServe 72477,636

We had checked with the phone company some months previous to this to see if there was a call-waiting disable code, and the phone company assured us that none existed. So we were a bit skeptical of Mr. de Longpre's recommendation. Naturally, we tried it immediately.

Worked like a charm. The beep-beep-dial tone was produced as advertised, and the call-waiting signal was ignored. The person calling you gets a busy signal instead of the regular ringing he or she would get if call-waiting had not been disabled. (Note that the comma after the 1170 is important, because it tells the modem to pause long enough for the beep-beep signal to be issued by the phone system.)

This information has since become public. If you look in your phone book under Tone*Block you will probably learn that the 1170 code is designed for pulse-dial phones, while Touch Tone users can enter *70 instead. But at the time, no one, not even the phone company, had the answer to our question. Only an online SIG and its community of users had what we needed.

Clearly, nothing like the SIGs has ever existed before, and you should know that their scope is far from limited to computers and related topics. There are SIGs dedicated to nearly every major interest you can think of from rock music to organic gardening. A more complete exploration will have to wait for another time. We can only suggest that any effort you invest learning to use the SIGs on your chosen system(s) will be well rewarded. Like local computer user groups, online SIGs are a little known but absolutely invaluable resource.

SIG Features: The Basic Floorplan

From the free software perspective, there are a number of important things to know about how SIGs are organized, and here the clubhouse analogy is helpful once again. As we've already noted, the clubhouse is often a free-standing building on campus. You have to cross the campus to reach it, but once you're inside you're in a separate area. An area that often has its own procedures, commands, and features.

Most SIGs use the same floorplan, based largely on the original CompuServe model. The features of this floorplan include a public message exchange that makes it possible for you to ask a question ("Does anyone know how to connect a PS/2 Model 30 to a Diablo printer?") that can be read and responded to by all SIG members. There may also be a bulletin board for members to post for sale, wanted, and other notices. There is usually a keyword-searchable membership directory to help you locate people with similar interests. There may also be some kind of CB-like conferencing facility to let you converse in real time with other SIG members or attend online lectures and question-and-answer sessions with industry notables.

Each online system does things in a slightly different way. For example, CompuServe as a whole has a large real-time conferencing facility called the CB Simulator. But each CompuServe SIG has its own real-time conferencing area for use by SIG members and guests. CompuServe SIGs also have their own public and private message exchange that is quite separate from the system's main electronic mail facility.

The Source, in contrast, offers a single electronic mail facility, accessible from within the SIGs and from the main system, for person-to-person communication. So SIG members use the PARTICIPATE conferencing feature on The Source as a SIG-specific public message exchange. Each Source SIG has a POST PLUS bulletin board, however, that is separate from the system-wide POST PLUS board.

SIG Libraries Are the Treasure Rooms

The other four systems offer similar variations on these themes. But all SIGs on all systems have libraries, and that's what we're most interested in here. SIG libraries are the data storage areas of the "club" and they can contain anything likely to be of continuing interest to SIG members. There may be files of member-written instructions on how to use the SIG or its features. There may be transcripts of real-time conferences held with industry luminaries or a particularly interesting series of comments from the public message exchange.

In a SIG for teachers, you might find essays on the significance of standardized test scores. In a SIG on culinary arts, you may find recipes for everything from blackened red fish to creme caramel. In a SIG for music lovers, you may find member-written reviews of the latest Solti or Serkin compact disk collection.

In almost every library of every SIG, however, you will find free software. Free programs may be available for downloading from other parts of a system, but it is the SIG libraries that are the real treasure rooms. And while you are likely to find relevant free programs in SIGs of every interest—teacher's grade book managing programs, recipe conversion programs, music generating programs, and so on—the richest, most robust collections can naturally be found in the computer-specific SIGs.

The Universal Four-Part Free Software Format

Fortunately, regardless of the SIG or the online system, the format used for free software files is always essentially the same. In general, each free online program will consist of four parts: a file header, a list of keywords, a descriptive paragraph, and the program itself. As an example, consider this from CompuServe:

```
[76237,316]
DBPRGC.ARC/binary    28-Aug-87 27817      Accesses: 32

Keywords: DBASE DBASEIII COLORS UTILITY PROGRAM
PROGRAMMERS
```

Utility for dBase III Plus (tm) programmer's. Allows end users of dBase
(tm) programs to select color names in plain English and, optionally,
save the selected colors for program recall. May also be used in
interactive mode to set screen colors for the current dBase (tm)
session.

The header in this case consists of two lines. The first, the one with
the numbers in brackets ([76237,316]), tells you the CompuServe account number of the person who uploaded the file. The next header line
gives you the filename (DBPRGC.ARC), reminds you that this is a machine-language, binary file, and gives you the date it was uploaded and
how many times it has been downloaded ("Accesses:") since then. The
size of the file (27,817 bytes) is also included. The keyword list is next.
Followed by a descriptive paragraph. The fourth and final portion (not
displayable) is the program itself.

There are good reasons why everyone uses this same four-part format. If it weren't for the three parts shown above (header, keywords,
and description), there would be no way to locate files of interest or
determine whether or not you want to download them once you've found
them. Thus, if you signed on to CompuServe looking for utility programs to use with Ashton-Tate's best-selling dBASE information management program, you could search for programs that had been tagged
with the keyword dBASE.

The system would rapidly scan the keyword portion of every file in
the library looking for matches. It would then put together a list of all
such files and ask you if you'd like to read the file descriptions. Which
you would almost certainly want to do since it's usually impossible to
tell exactly what a program does from its name alone. When you encountered a description that sounded interesting, you would issue a
command to download its associated program using an error-checking
protocol. Then you could either sign off or continue the process.

Shooting a Keyword into the Ether

In the best of all possible worlds, the process really can be that simple.
And when it is successful it offers a thrill that's unlike any other you
may have experienced. You sign on looking for a program that you
think *might* exist, because in your opinion something like it *should* exist. After all, with millions of computer users out there there must be
hundreds of people who have encountered the same problem or had a
need similar to yours. Surely at least one of them has written a program
to fill the bill.

But you can't be absolutely certain of that fact going in, and, of
course, you can't search for the suspected program by name because

you don't have any idea what it's called, if indeed it really does exist. All you have to work with are the elements of the search language provided by the online system and the keywords attached to each file. Those are your tools.

So like an astronomer trying to locate an invisible planet, you focus on the portion of the galaxy you reason to be the most likely location for what you seek. You fire off a keyword probe and watch for results. Sometimes you hit what you're after on your first shot. Sometimes the probe goes wide of the mark and you have to recalibrate your keywords before launching another. Sometimes several probes are required. And sometimes you come up empty.

Step 3: Get the Complete Keyword List or List of Files
The Keyword Problem

That, at any rate, is the way it is supposed to work. But your chances of success are directly proportional to your familiarity with the slang and buzz words of the free software world and the conventions that are generally followed in the particular SIG on the particular system you happen to be searching. By all means, learn the different search languages and commands on the different systems and take a crack at it if you want to. But to make the most of the online free software resources available, and to protect your pocketbook, we suggest that you follow Step 3 and give yourself an edge.

The main weakness that all free software search and retrieval systems share is the fact that the keyword lists and program descriptions are supplied by the people who upload the files. And since everyone is different, everyone has his or her own idea of what makes a good keyword list. For example, suppose you wanted to upload a favorite public domain program to one of the systems discussed here. You might do this out of the goodness of your heart. Or you might be primarily interested in the free connect time some systems offer as a bonus to anyone who uploads a program.

The system would first ask you for the name of the file. Then it would ask you to supply a list of keywords. Next, you would be asked to enter a descriptive paragraph about the program and what it does. Finally, the upload would commence. This is where the filenames, keyword lists, and file descriptions we've spoken of come from.

Conceivably your contribution would be perfect in every respect. You would have taken five or ten minutes before signing on to think about all the various terms your fellow SIG members might use to search for a program of this sort. Then you would have taken five or ten minutes more to compose a paragraph that succinctly described the program's function, any requireed hardware or software, any known incompatibilities, and so on. Then and only then would you have signed on to contribute the program to the SIG library.

But of course, your concept of a good keyword list might differ substantially from the list produced by an equally diligent SIG member. For example, if you're looking for a program to use with dBASE II or III, "dBASE" or some variation of the term will obviously be among the keywords attached to the file. But what if you're looking for a utility to help you manage your hard disk? It might be perfectly logical for you to choose "hard disk" as your search term. Yet if the person who uploaded the file you need thinks of his hard disk as a "Winchester drive" (the popular term for the first IBM hard disks) or as a "fixed disk," he might not use the term "hard disk" as one of his keywords. As a result, you could search all night on the term "hard disk" and never find the file.

In addition, while "Conscientious" might be your middle name, you can't always count on other members to share that commitment. As you will discover, some files on all systems appear to have been uploaded with a lick and a promise—just enough keywords and just enough of a descriptive paragraph to satisfy the online system and persuade it to permit the upload.

Now it is true that on many systems all uploaded files are reviewed by the sysops before being made available to the membership at large. This is done primarily to prevent possible copyright violations or guard against destructive "Trojan horse" or other booby-trapped programs. But it does offer at least the opportunity to correct deficient keyword lists and file descriptions. Yet the volume of uploaded software can be so huge that there may simply not be enough time for a sysop to bring every keyword list or file description up to par.

How to Give Yourself an Edge

This is why we suggest that instead of wasting time and money searching for terms you think *might* be in the database, you tell the system you want it to prepare a list of every keyword actually used in the SIG library you plan to search. Then sign off and print out the list. Review the list, circling the keywords that are of interest. Then sign back on and join the turkey shoot, secure in the knowledge that there is no way you can miss.

For example, here's a small part of the list of keywords used in the telecommunications library of the PC Compatibles/IBM special interest group on Delphi:

ANSWERING MACHINE (1)
ARC (3)

AREA CODES (1)
BBS LISTINGS (1)
BULLETIN BOARDS (3)
CALLWAITING (1)
COLLIE (1)
COMMUNICATIONS (19)
DOCUMENTATION (3)
DOS SHELL (1)
FIDO (1)
FIDONET (1)
HEX VERSION (1)
IBM-PC (47)
MEMORY RESIDENT (1)
PATCH (2)
PATCHES (2)
PC JR (1)
PC PURSUIT (1)
QMODEM (5)
SCRIPT (4)
SCRIPT FILE (1)
SCRIPT GENERATOR (1)
TELECOMMUNICATIONS (26)
TELIX (1)
VAX/VMS (1)
XMDEM (1)
XMODEM (18)

Don't skip over this list or merely give it a cursory glance. There is much to be learned here. Remember, every word on this list has been used as a keyword for at least one free program or other file in this library. Indeed, the numbers in parentheses next to each word indicate the number of files to which it has been applied. Therefore, it is probably not such a good idea to search on either COMMUNICATIONS, with 19 occurrences, or TELECOMMUNICATIONS, with 26, since both keywords will bring up too many files. If you are interested in lists of currently active bulletin board systems, however, BBS LISTINGS and BULLETIN BOARDS are sure bets.

Next, ask yourself how many of the words on this list would have occurred to you and whether you would have keyed them in exactly as they appear here. Would you have used a hyphen with CALLWAIT-ING? Would you have searched for PC/JR instead of PC JR? With a list like this in front of you there is no need to guess. You know *exactly* what to type in and what punctuation to use.

Finally, consider the problem of misspellings on the part of the person who assigned keywords to the file. Certainly the second to last word should be XMODEM, not XMDEM, for example. But the host computer doesn't know the difference. If someone enters XMDEM as a keyword before uploading, that is precisely what is assigned to the file. The tragedy is that unless you happened to make the same mistake and key in XMDEM when searching for an XMODEM-related program, you would never find the file. Unless you had given yourself an edge by downloading the library's complete keyword list beforehand.

What If No Keyword List Is Available?

At this writing, only Delphi and CompuServe have commands to let you download complete keyword lists, though BIX may be adding the feature in the future. Hopefully, the other systems will follow suit. In the meantime, what can you do to effectively search the software libraries on GEnie, The Source, BIX, and People/Link?

The answer is that you can download the file lists maintained by the sysops of the IBM SIGs on GEnie, The Source, and BIX. The sysops on CompuServe and Delphi do this as well. The lists are updated regularly and they are stored in files that you can download, once you are aware of their existence. Typically the lists contain one or two lines per program, like this example from GEnie:

NUMBE	NAME DESC	T	UPLOADER	ULDATE	SIZE	DOWN	LI
5885	TICKLE13.ARC Command line tickle/reminder prog.	X	L.MURRAH	870819	41580	37	3
5884	SPEECH.ARC Text to speech; Standalone & PC-VCO	X	TARTAN	870819	17640	59	6
5883	XL.COM Y/N DELETE UTILITY 96 BYTES *.* OK	X	REYCOM	870819	1260	47	5
5882	ECSRC.ARC FAST TURBO-C SCREEN SOURCE CODE	X	KEN.C.SMITH	870818	26460	51	8
5880	ASMSUB.ARC ASSEMBLY SUBROUTINES FOR R/M COBOL	X	L.FARMER	870818	10080	4	8
5878	QREV1.ARC LAN remote batch processing	X	JON.LAWRENCE	870818	7560	37	5
5876	TURBO.COM XT Clone speed selection program	X	R.SHOOP	870817	1260	49	5
5875	STARWARZ.ARC THEME SONG FROM STARWARS (MOVIE)	X	FEEBACK	870817	31500	45	7
5874	TWIZONE.ARC THEME SONG FROM TWILIGHT ZONE (.EXE)	X	FEEBACK	870817	31500	79	7
5873	DRIVERS.ARC Displays installed device drivers	X	A.E.ATWOOD	870817	10080	69	8

The list header here translates as file NUMBEr, fileNAME, Type of file (XMODEM or ASCII, which is to say binary or text), the subscriber who was the UPLOADER, the UpLoad date, SIZE, number of times it has been DOWNloaded, the LIbrary number, and the DESCription. Comparable files on the other systems provide the same kind of information.

FreeTip: One quick and easy way to identify the best programs in a SIG database is to look at the number of downloads. As we have said elsewhere, there is very definitely a free software community, and word of good (or bad) programs spreads quickly. Of course it is important to temper this information with a sense of what's normal for a given system. The norm for all files on a system like CompuServe, with over 400,000 subscribers, will naturally be higher than on a system with 50,000 or 60,000 subscribers.

It's also a good idea to compare the number with the upload date. Eighty downloads of a file that's only been on the system a month is clearly more significant than it would be for a file that is over a year old. In addition, it can be important to factor in the kind of program involved. Assembly subroutines for R/M COBOL (file 5880 above) will logically appeal to a much smaller audience than the theme from *StarWars* (file 5875), as the reported number of downloads for each file confirms.

Step 4: Sign Off and Do a Local Search

We'll tell you which files contain the library summaries in each case when we profile specific systems in the next chapter. The key thing is to download the catalog or list file and/or keyword list, record it to disk, and then immediately sign off the system. At that point you will have all the raw material you need to make the data library sing your tune.

We should warn you, however, that these SIG file lists can be quite long. The files from GEnie shown above are but the first ten on a list of over 3000 programs. The list was stored in the kind of compressed, archived file discussed in Chapter 2. But even so it took more than 20 minutes to download at 1200 bits per second. The archive file resulted in a file (LIBFILES.DBF) that was more than twice as large. At two lines per program, that's more than 90 single-spaced typewritten pages. The program lists available from other systems weigh in at a similar bulk.

Twenty minutes at GEnie's nonprime-time 300/1200-bps rate of $5.00 an hour costs $1.67. You could easily spend that much time and money searching blind on the system, firing off keyword probes that you hoped would work, and not find what you were after. But now you've got the whole database in your hands. Better yet, you've got it in your computer. There is no need to print it all out and risk damaging your eyesight parsing its pages. For if there's one thing computers are good at it's finding matches in mounds of data. What you want to do is search the data locally, *without* going online and *without* paying connect time charges.

As you will see later, the sysops and SIG members on GEnie and The Source make this exceptionally easy to do. The GEnie list, LIB-FILES.DBF, is in a form that is readily accepted by dBASE III. Simply boot dBASE, tell it to use LIBEFILES, and put one of the most powerful database programs available to work searching for the free programs you want. If you don't have dBASE, there are subscriber-contributed programs to let you work with LIBFILES.DBF on GEnie as well on the Glossbrenner's Choice GEnie Disk discussed in Chapter 16.

On The Source you'll find a file called LIBSCAN.TXT that's designed to be used with LIBSERCH.COM, a program contributed by Source subscriber Ben Bacon. LIBSERCH lets you search through the LIB-SCAN.TXT database using the same commands you would use when connected to The Source. The program is such a good mimic of The Source user interface that you will think you are really online. (These programs are online in their compressed form as LIBSCAN.ARC and LIBSERCH.ARC, respectively.)

Vern Buerg's Incredible LIST62A.COM Program

You might think that this leaves BIX and People/Link users out in the cold. BIX does have a file list (IBM__ARC.ARC) and it is possible to get a real-time listing on People/Link. But at this writing, neither system can give you a list of keywords and on neither will you find specialized local search programs like those on GEnie and The Source.

The solution for these systems—indeed the best solution for *all* systems in our opinion—is a program known as "LIST." The version current at this writing is 6.2A, or in more formal terms, LIST62A.COM. Written by a highly respected, prolific software wizard named Vernon D. Buerg, LIST is designed to let you scroll backwards, forwards, and sideways through any text file on your system.

But LIST also has a Find command that's as fast as a well-greased bullet. This command lets you search for any string of up to 31 characters, whether they are embedded in a word or represent complete words, dates, or phrases. That means, for example, that every word or portion of a word (or series of numbers) in the sample file list from GEnie shown earlier can be used as a search term. The program finds the first occurrence of the string in the file and displays the line containing it, as well as the seven lines that precede and the 15 lines that follow the target line in the file. Jumping to the next occurrence is as simple as hitting A for "again" or your <F3> key. And it is *fast*.

LIST is such a remarkable piece of programming that we recommend using it for the files on BIX, the list produced by People/Link, the files offered by the other systems, and on any text file. (Note that GEnie's LIBFILES.DBF must be converted to text first. As explained in Chapter 7, you can use SLF20.ARC, also available on GEnie, to do this.) LIST can be found in virtually all electronic and disk-based free software libraries, and it is available as one of the Core Collection programs discussed in Chapter 9. Since *list* is a common computer term, make sure that the program you get is designed to list text to the screen (not the printer) and that it is by Vern Buerg. Mr. Buerg asks a voluntary contribution of $15. His product is worth every penny.

Step 5: Sign On Again and Return to the Treasure Room

There is not much else to be said about this step.

Step 6: Call Up Expanded Descriptions of Likely Candidates

Let's suppose that your local search of either the keyword list or the catalog file has yielded ten candidates. These are indications of files that look like they may offer what you need. Or maybe they just look interesting.

There is no way at this point to know exactly which, if any, files you want to download. All you know for certain is that you probably won't want all of them and that you need more information than a simple one or two-line catalog entry can provide. It is here that the third part of the universal four-part format discussed earlier comes into play. In every case there is a command you can use to call up the descriptive paragraph attached to candidate files.

We can use CompuServe as an example, though similar commands exist on the other systems as well. If you are working only with keywords, the command to choose is the BROWSE command. You may choose this selection from a menu that will appear when you enter a SIG data library, or you may key it in as a command at the menu's prompt. Either way, the system will prompt you for a keyword. You will enter it, and the system will fetch all matching files and begin displaying the header, keyword list, and descriptive paragraph for each. After each file has been displayed, you will be given the opportunity to download it or move on to the next one on the list.

If you are working with specific filenames, you can simply enter SCAN FILENAME.EXT/DES to tell the system to fetch the description for that particular file. Should you decide to download it after reading the description, you may enter DOW FILENAME.EXT at the menu prompt and away you go. It really is that easy.

Step 7: Download the Program with an Error-Checking Protocol

With Step 7 we come to the end of the process—"end" both as in last step and as in ultimate goal. The whole point of everything we have covered in this part of the book up to now is to get to a position where we can say, "I'd like *that* program. Please wrap it up and send it to me immediately."

Now that we're here, it may seem a bit anticlimactic, because issuing that order is just about all there is to it. From that point on the machines take over. To be sure, some pretty sophisticated machine-to-machine dialogue is required to complete the process, but basically you're out of the loop until the transfer is over. The modem's front panel lights blink incessantly as the data comes in. The one thing you absolutely must do for every download, however, is pay attention to your protocols, and that's the topic we'll look at next.

A Matter of Protocol

Simple X-On/X-OFF Flow Control

There are two ways to transfer a file from a distant host to a disk in your machine. The first is what is often called the "capture buffer" approach. You tell your comm program to start recording everything that appears on the screen, storing it in a portion of your machine's RAM (random access memory). That's called opening your buffer. As the buffer fills, your comm program will periodically dump its contents to disk. To stop recording, you have only to issue a command to close the buffer.

Simple, no? Yes. And ideal for recording online instructions, menus, electronic mail, and anything else that can be displayed on the screen, including complete text files. The only protocol involved here is the simple "flow control" X-ON/X-OFF (Control-Q/Control-S) protocol that most hosts, PDNs, and comm programs implement automatically. This allows the receiving machine to tell the sender to stop sending, and it allows the receiver to take care of chores like dumping the capture buffer to disk without missing any incoming information. When the receiver is ready again, it sends the remote machine an X-ON character telling it to continue where it left off.

This is the fastest, most economical way to get your hands on a text file. No error-checking is involved, but this is not a major problem. Occasionally noise on the line will cause a few characters to be garbled in transmission. But since you're dealing with text, the errors are usually easy to spot and fix once you are offline.

The XMODEM Family of Protocols

When you're downloading a machine language program, however, nothing less than 100 percent accuracy will do. One or two bits out of place may or may not render a program completely useless, but such errors certainly create a potential for unpredictable results, which amounts to the same thing. The second approach, often called a "protocol file transfer," was developed to solve this problem.

Today there are many such protocols, but not too long ago there was only one widely used personal computer file transfer protocol. We've spoken of it before. It's called XMODEM, and it depends on an agreement between the sending and receiving systems to add up the ASCII values of the bytes and compare their results.

For example, suppose you've got a file on disk that occupies 14,000 bytes (14K) that I'd like to have. One approach might be to send the entire file, and if transmission errors occur, send the whole thing again. And again, and again, until we got it right. That doesn't make much sense. Far better to cut the file up into smaller pieces and send and check the pieces one at a time. That way if errors occur you only have to resend a small piece of the file instead of the whole thing.

So the two of us agree that you will cut it up into "blocks" of 128 bytes each and that you will assign each block a number for easy reference. As the first block leaves your system, you carefully note the ASCII value of each byte (from 0 through 255). When the first block has been sent, you add up all of the values you've noted, and send me the sum. That sum has a special meaning to me because I too am adding up the ASCII values of all the bytes in the block as they come out of the pipeline.

If the transmission has been flawless, our two sums must match. If they do, I signal your system to go ahead and send the next block. If they don't, I know that an error has occurred and I inform your system that the block must be resent. This process continues block-by-block until you have transmitted the entire file. You then send me a signal saying "That's all, folks," and both of our machines return to normal, non-XMODEM communications.

It all makes perfect sense. In fact, even the little detail we purposely left out makes sense, once you understand the reasons behind it. The total of the ASCII values you send me is called a "checksum," but in reality you don't actually send me the whole number. Suppose each of the 128 bytes in a given block was an ASCII 255. What would the checksum be? It would be 128 times 255, or 32,640. If I were to send that to you as a text number, I would need one byte for the 3, one for the 2, and so on, for a total of five bytes. Now suppose each byte in the block is an ASCII 3. The checksum in that case would be 384 and would require three bytes to transmit in text form. So how is your computer going to know that in the first case the next five bytes after the block are the checksum, but in the second case the checksum occupies only the next three bytes? Remember, to a computer, all bits and all bytes look alike.

You could create a protocol that would handle this problem, but it would be messy and require a lot more time for each file transfer. It would be much better if you could set things up so that the checksum always occupied a single eight-bit byte, regardless of the actual checksum figure. That's easy to do if you agree to let the ASCII value of the byte represent the checksum. But you've only got the numbers from 0 through 255 to work with. So after you've added up the checksum, you divide by 255. The remainder of any such division will always be less than 255 and thus expressible as a single byte. What the two systems actually compare, then, are the remainders they get after dividing 255 into their respective checksums. It is axiomatic that if the checksums are identical (no transmission errors), then the remainders will be identical as well.

What we have just described is the essence of the original (checksum) version of a protocol created by Ward Christensen in August 1977. Ward Christensen is without question the dean of public domain software, and over the years he has contributed scores of top-quality programs for the benefit of all. With characteristic modesty, Mr. Christensen has referred to XMODEM as "a quick hack" produced to fill an immediate need. But its simplicity, its high accuracy rate, and its public domain status have made it the most widely used protocol in the microcomputer world.

XMODEM began in the bulletin board community. It was officially introduced shortly after Christensen and fellow Chicagoan Randy Suess brought up the world's first bulletin board system, CBBS #1, on February 16, 1978. Members of CACHE, the Chicago Area Computer Hobbyist Exchange, needed a way to exchange messages, and CBBS #1 provided it. But Christensen included a module in the BBS software designed to work with a telecommunications program he had also written and contributed to the public domain. The program was called MODEM and the module was XMODEM. (The X stands for "transfer," as in X-ON/X-OFF or the frequently used computer abbreviation "X-fer.")

From here XMODEM spread to other PD communications and BBS programs, and from there to commercial software as well. By the time the six commercial systems considered in Chapter 7 began to get seriously interested in offering online public domain software, the protocol's popularity and status as the de facto standard left them no choice. They had to support XMODEM or give up on the idea of offering PD programs online.

One of the most fascinating aspects of public domain software is the freedom it offers programmers to build upon, expand, and sometimes (but not always) improve each other's creations. This has happened with XMODEM, of course, and while the process has produced a robust family of related protocols, it has created confusion for new users.

As we have emphasized, the main thing you have to worry about is making sure that both you and the sending system are using the same protocol. ProComm, the shareware comm program discussed in Chapter 16, makes this easy since it supports all of the protocols we're going to be discussing here (the XMODEM family, CompuServe B, Kermit, and so on). But at the same time some kind of Baedeker is bound to be helpful, so that's what we'll provide.

FreeTip: In yet another example of the gold to be mined by tapping the online user community, a user named Joe Gagnon uploaded the following to CompuServe regarding how to solve the problem of using Datapac in Canada for XMODEM transfers.

For those of us in Canada who access U.S. based information services via Datapac and would like to upload or download with the XMODEM protocol, here are the commands that Datapac requires for proper transmission via XMODEM:

```
Control-P
PROF 1 <ENTER>
SET 126:004,003:000,004:004,001:000 <ENTER>
<ENTER>
GOODBYE <ENTER>
```

Note that the spaces after PROF and SET are mandatory! That's all it takes. Happy downloading!

JLG (Joe Gagnon)

The MODEM7 Protocol

The first thing you need to know is that Ward Christensen has produced several versions of his original MODEM communications program. The XMODEM protocol was introduced in the second version, MODEM2. This was back in the days when the CP/M operating system ruled the nascent personal computer world and 64K was considered an astounding amount of memory. At that time it was not unusual for a communications program to be called a "modem program." More improvements, features, and power yielded more versions until the software reached its final iteration, MODEM7. Other programmers have added features and otherwise tweaked this program, producing subsequent versions of MODEM7, like MODEM714. But to our knowledge, no one has ever produced anything called MODEM8.

Prior to MODEM7, all versions used the same XMODEM error-checking technique. The main difference was that MODEM7 added the ability to send a batch of files and to use a wildcard character. The command SB HELLO.DOC XDIR.COM*.BAS, for example, would *Send* in *B*atch mode the first two files as well as every file in the user area ending with BAS. All that is required of the operator at the receiving computer is to key in RB (Receive Batch). The sending system automatically supplies the filenames to the receiver. This is the only real difference between the XMODEM protocol and what some call the MODEM7 protocol. Batch transfers are most useful in micro-to-micro communications when there is an operator at both machines.

XMODEM CRC-16

As we know, the original XMODEM protocol used the checksum technique of error detection. Statistically, the checksum approach will detect about 95 percent of all potential transmission errors for XMODEM's 128-byte blocks. However, different techniques can boost that percentage still further. Consequently, in later versions of XMODEM, programmers in the community of users added a "cyclic redundancy check" or "CRC-16" capability to the protocol, raising its error-detection accuracy to between 99.969 and 99.9984 percent. The CRC-16 technique is backed by some heavy-duty math, but its essence is based on the fact that if an integer is dividied by a prime number, the remainder is always unique.

Thus, if the sending computer and the receiving computer produce the same integer based on the data being transferred, and divide by the same prime number, then the remainders will always match. As with the checksum implementation, it is these remainders that are tacked onto each data block sent for comparison on the other end. They are called CRCs or BCCs (block check characters). If errors have occurred in the data, however, the two systems will produce different integers, which will *always* produce different remainders after the division takes place.

That's just common sense, right? Well, not necessarily. If the two systems were not using a prime number as their divisors—as is the case with the original checksum version—it is possible that every now and then static on the line or some other problem would transform enough bits to produce an incorrect integer on the receiving end that yielded the same remainder as the one on the sending end. Two different integers divided by the same *nonprime* number, in other words, could produce identical remainders.

For more information on how computers perform these calculations, you might want to see David Schwaderer's article on the subject in the April 1985 issue of *PC Tech Journal.* All we need to know at this point is that the remainder that serves as the CRC consists of the first 16 low-order bits (starting on the right and counting to the left) of the remainder that results from the prime number division. It is these 16 bits that are sent to the receiving computer with each XMODEM block as two 8-bit bytes, and they are the reason the technique is called CRC-16.

To summarize, XMODEM can support two types of error checking, the simple checksum of the original and the even more accurate CRC-16 method. Generally, commercial systems and BBSs support either checksum only or both checksum and CRC-16. We know of none that support only CRC-16. Some will give you a choice of methods before you begin to download. Others will let your communications software call the tune and base their response on how your program requests the first block of data.

If your comm program supports only the checksum approach, it will automatically send a NAK ("negative acknowledge") character (ASCII 21) to request the first (and every other) block. However, if your software supports both techniques, it will probably try for a CRC-16 transfer first. To signal that intent, it will send a capital C (ASCII 67) when requesting the first block instead of a NAK. Should the sending system fail to respond appropriately, your program may automatically fall back to the checksum method, issue a NAK, and proceed with the transfer.

XMODEM-1K and "Relaxed" XMODEM

You may also encounter XMODEM-1K and "relaxed" XMODEM. Designed by Chuck Forsberg, XMODEM-1K lets two systems agree to increase the normal 128-byte XMODEM block size to 1K for faster throughput. Relaxed XMODEM was designed by John Friel, author of the shareware program Qmodem. This protocol differs from conventional XMODEM implementations in that it is about ten times more tolerant of the delays introduced by PDNs and by busy mainframe hosts such as those of CompuServe. Conventional XMODEM calls for sender and receiver to talk to each other using ACK and NAK characters (ASCII 6 and ASCII 21, respectively). If the receiver wants to begin a transfer, it will send a NAK to request the first block. It will then wait ten seconds. If the sender has not responded, it will send another NAK. In computer talk, the receiver "times out" after ten seconds.

(XMODEM is designed to go through ten time outs before aborting the transfer.)

The problem is that the load factor on the mainframe host at the time of the up- or download, and the processing caused by the packet-switching networks, can introduce delays longer than ten seconds. But your system doesn't know that. All it knows is that it is supposed to send a NAK, wait ten seconds, send another NAK, and so on. If it takes the host, say, 19 seconds to respond, the host could be putting the first block into its end of the pipeline while your system is sending its second NAK. When that second NAK arrives, the host will think that it means the first block was received in error. So it will send it again. And it will get NAK'd again, and so on.

Relaxing XMODEM's normal timing requirements helps avoid these kinds of problems. The relaxation affects only your own system. As far as the mainframe knows, it is dealing with a normal XMODEM transfer.

The Forsberg YMODEM Protocol

YMODEM is a major enhancement to the XMODEM protocol designed and implemented by Chuck Forsberg. In addition to an optional batch mode similar to that described for MODEM7, YMODEM lets you use one-kilobyte blocks (1024 bytes) instead of the 128-byte blocks used by XMODEM. YMODEM is thus an example of software keeping up with hardware. Christensen used 128-byte blocks in his protocol because computer memory at the time was both limited and expensive. (In 1978 a machine with a 32K of RAM and a 70K floppy disk sold for $2315, and you had to add your own monitor and keyboard!)

With the more capacious machines of today the 1K blocks of YMODEM are easy to handle. And if the telephone connection is good, they result in faster transfers. But when a poor connection exists, YMODEM may take longer because it must retransmit more data each time an error is detected in a block. Mr. Forsberg certainly deserves the title of communications wizard. Working from his houseboat on Sauvie Island Road in Portland, Oregon, he has produced the enormously powerful (and technical) YAM communications program. The initials stand for "Yet Another Modem" [program] and they are the source of the name YMODEM. The trademarked term True YMODEM means that the protocol implements all YMODEM features, including the batch file, send/receive features. (Some YMODEM implementation do not include this feature.)

Forsberg's ZMODEM

Chuck Forsberg was commissioned by Telenet to develop a protocol that could be used on a wide variety of systems operating in a wide variety of environments (modems, time-sharing systems, satellite relays, wide-area packet-switched networks, and so on). The result was the public domain ZMODEM protocol. There is much to be said about ZMODEM, but for now we will simply note two of its most important features. One is its use of a 32-bit CRC for even greater accuracy, and the other is the fact that ZMODEM sends data continuously until the receiver interrupts to request the retransmission of garbled data. To put it another way, ZMODEM uses the entire file as its "window," a term and technique we will look at next.

WXMODEM: Windowed XMODEM

There is also a protocol called WXMODEM ("windowed XMODEM"). Under the conventional XMODEM protocol, the sending system cannot put a block into the pipeline until it hears back from the receiving system that the block it just sent is okay. If that block was not okay, XMODEM immediately tries to send it again. Under WXMODEM, the sending system can send up to four blocks without getting an acknowledgment from the receiver. In communications terms, it thus has a "window" of four blocks.

Imagine that the sender has just transmitted the fourth of 16 blocks and has just heard back that the third block was garbled. In that case, under WXMODEM, the sender would back up to the block containing the error and begin sending again. That is, it would back up, resend the third block, followed by the fourth block (which is has already sent), and so on. This is not a terribly elegant technique, but it is significantly faster than regular XMODEM. A file requiring six minutes to transmit under XMODEM, can be transmitted in as little as four minutes under WXMODEM. Useful whenever a packet-switching network is part of the connection, WXMODEM is the preferred protocol of the People/Link system. The protocol was designed by Peter Boswell (People/Link user name: TOPPER).

The Kermit Protocol
In Love with a Big Green Frog

The XMODEM family of protocols has certainly had a good run. But in micro-to-mainframe communications, at least, it seems likely that XMODEM will eventually be replaced by a protocol called Kermit. Kermit was developed at Columbia University's Center for Computing Activities, and the name is used with the permission of Henson Associates (HA!), creators of the famous green amphibian. Although not in the public domain—Columbia University holds the copyright and tries to maintain the definitive set of Kermit implementations—the protocol may be incorporated into software free of charge.

Kermit is already used widely, but like XMODEM before it, it has continued to evolve. The main purpose of the original or so-called Classic Kermit was to overcome the difficulties involved in transferring files between fundamentally incompatible systems. Some older mainframe computers can handle only seven-bit characters, for example. Others go crazy if they receive anything resembling a control code byte, even if those bytes are part of a file that is being transferred.

Classic and Super Kermit

Classic Kermit, like XMODEM, operates in what might be called a half-duplex, send-and-wait mode. It sends a packet, waits for an acknowledgment, and then either sends the next packet or resends the former packet if it turns out to have been received in error. A newer version of Kermit exists, however, and it is of special interest to free software seekers because it emphasizes throughput and speed.

The new version is informally known as Super Kermit, and it includes all of the features of its predecessor, plus "sliding windows." This means in effect that Kermit can pitch and catch at the same time. And that makes for a continuous, full-duplex transfer instead of the send-and-wait, half-duplex approach used by Classic Kermit and XMODEM.

A Packet-Oriented Protocol

Unless otherwise specified, you can assume that all references to Kermit from this point on refer to the sliding-window version. It is the sliding window that gives Kermit its speed, and the concept is not difficult to understand.

You can start with the fact that Kermit uses the same ideas employed by Telenet and Tymnet to divide a file into discrete packets. Each packet is stamped with a sequence number, the number of characters the packet contains, and possibly some other information. A checksum or CRC is then calculated and tacked onto the packet. Each packet is thus a self-contained unit, and as with Telenet and Tymnet, the order in which packets are sent doesn't really matter. The receiver has only to open the packet, read the sequence number, and slot the packet into its correct position in memory to reassemble the file.

The size of the packets is flexible and in most implementations can vary between 0 and 94 bytes. The size actually used in any given transfer is agreed upon by the two systems as part of their initial handshaking. Once the handshaking is over, each system sets up a "table," which you might visualize as a bank of pigeonholes of the sort you would find in an antique desk. There may be as few as one or as many as 31 pigeonholes in each table, depending on what the two systems agree upon.

When a transfer begins, the sending system loads up its table with packets, one per pigeonhole, and starts pitching them to the receiver. At the same time, it also starts listening to catch the receiver's response concerning the checksum or CRC of each packet. That's the full-duplex aspect of the protocol. The sender can pitch as many as 31 packets without receiving an acknowledgment of any sort. That's its "window."

Sliding the Window

Now, suppose that the sender has just transmitted packet Number 7 when the first responses begin to come in: Packet Number 1's okay? Good. Oops, a problem with Number 2 but Number 3's fine? Okay, here's the rest of packet Number 7. And now here's a retransmission of packet Number 2. Now on to Number 8.

This sounds a little daft, but you get the idea. Kermit's tables allow it to send and resend packets continuously in whatever sequence is required. When the oldest packet in a table—the packet in slot 1—is acknowledged to have been successfully received, the sender "rotates the table" or "slides the window." This means it moves the packet currently in Slot 2 into Slot 1, while the packet in Slot 3 is moved into Slot 2, and so on. Since each packet has its own sequence number, the sending system always knows where to find it, regardless of the number of the slot in the table it currently occupies.

Sliding the window leaves an empty slot at the top of the table, which the system fills with the next sequential packet in the file. The process continues until the entire file has been transmitted and the two systems have agreed that the transfer is complete.

This is only a brief sketch of how Kermit's sliding-window feature works. Kermit has many other interesting features, including a batch mode command and a "server" option, but they need not concern us here. For our purposes, the most important point is that Kermit's sliding-window approach makes for speedy file transfers—up to 50 percent faster than XMODEM in many cases.

The development of sliding windows within Kermit was funded by The Source and implemented by Capital PC User Group members Larry Jordan and Jan van der Eijk. At this writing, four of our six systems (The Source, CompuServe, Delphi, and BIX) support Kermit. But the protocol is so well-suited to micro-to-mainframe, packet-switched communications that others may offer it in the future.

FreeTip: For more detailed information on Kermit, you might want to send for the book cited below. Written by Frank da Cruz, one of the protocol's developers, it is the definitive text at this writing.

FreeTip continued

> *Kermit: A File Transfer Protocol*
> by Frank da Cruz
> Digital Press, 1987
> (379 pages; $25)
>
> You can order through your local bookseller or contact Digital Press directly by dialing (800) 343-8321 between 8:00 A.M. and 4:00 P.M. Eastern Standard Time. Visa and MasterCard phone orders are accepted. You can also order by modem by logging on to DEC's innovative Electronic Store by dialing (800) 332-3366. (To take full advantage of this system's on-screen graphics, set your software for VT-100 terminal emulation if possible.) Of course, you may also send your order by paper mail:
>
> Digital Press—Order Processing
> Digital Equipment Corporation
> 12 A Esquire Road
> Billerica, MA 01862

We've come a long way in the last two chapters. Starting with little more than a strong interest in getting free software over the phone, we've looked at the hardware you need and how to buy it, touched on the role of communications software, looked at the packet-switching networks, and explored the online process in detail. Along the way we've included information on topics that we know you're going to need or need to know about once you go online. With this information in hand, there's no reason why you can't cruise the electronic ether in comfort and style and quickly become an accomplished free software harvester.

At this point, however, the path divides. In one direction lie the BBSs, and in the other the commercial systems. The seven steps to free online software apply to both, of course, but we recommend that you begin practicing your trade on the commercial systems. BBSs are great fun, but they tend to come and go and vary widely in their quality. Because most can accommodate only about 40 callers per day, it can be next to impossible to get onto the really good ones, even if you know their numbers. That kind of frustration is not likely to enhance your first online experience.

7

Free Software from Commercial Systems

COMPUSERVE, GENIE, THE SOURCE, DELPHI, BIX, AND PEOPLE/LINK

In this chapter we'll show you how to apply what you've learned in Chapters 5 and 6 to quickly obtain the programs you want from the six leading commercial online sources of free software: CompuServe, GEnie, The Source, Delphi, BIX, and People/Link. These host systems are what might be called general-interest online systems, or "information utilities."

That term was coined by The Source in 1979. It's not wholly descriptive, but it has a nice ring to it, and at least it offers a quick-reference handle on a category of service that defies short definitions. Everyone knows what cable TV means, but how do you describe an electronic, computer-based service that offers up-to-the-minute news, weather, and sports reports, tons of investment information, facilities for electronic mail, conferencing, and real-time CB-like conversations, bulletin boards for classified ads and personals, online discount shopping, real-time games with distant, unseen opponents, and electronic banking and stock trading? You can't do the subject justice in anything less than a book, so we won't even discuss these topics. We bring the matter up to make it clear that free software represents only a fraction of what these systems have to offer. As always, for more information we commend you to *The Complete Handbook of Personal Computer Communications* and *How to Look It Up Online*. Here we will be focusing exclusively on the free software side of things, a subject that isn't always well covered by the manuals you receive with your information utility subscription.

The SIGs as Philosophers' Stone

Both The Source and the CompuServe Information Service began operations in 1979, and it is fair to say that all the other information utilities are derived from them. Broadly speaking, The Source established the norms for an information utility's interactions with its customers (subscriptions, billing procedures, manuals, and so on) and pioneered many of the now-standard online features and offerings. CompuServe invented SIGs, and in so doing hit upon the magic formula everyone was looking for.

In a world of virtually free print, television, and radio news, the opportunity to pay for the same material from an information utility has limited appeal. But the SIGs, as we've said before, are something totally unique. Once the number of computer owners reached a critical mass, SIGs simply took off. Delphi, then People/Link, *Byte* magazine's BIX (Byte Information Exchange), and General Electric's GEnie soon followed. Ironically, The Source was among the last to offer an online special interest group feature.

Before profiling the individual systems and telling you how to reach their IBM free software treasure houses, we'll look at some of the general considerations to bear in mind when choosing a system. Then we'll look at the nitty-gritty details of subscriptions, manuals, and connect-time costs, and offer some thoughts on the best way to use the free software facilities of all online systems. Finally, we'll offer some guidance on how to get started with any system, beginning with your first sign on.

Picking a System and a SIG
Which One's Right for You?

It may be that you're an experienced online communicator who already subscribes to one or more of these systems. But what if you're not? What if you've never heard of these organizations before today? Which one should you choose?

That's a tough question to answer because the system that's right for you may not be right for someone else. In the first place, each system has its own personality. You can see it in the quantity and quality of the documentation, in the connect time rates that are charged, and in the approach to customer service help lines. You can also see it in the "user interface"—the menus, commands, special features, and general way of doing things. As you know from the previous chapter, for example, you can obtain a complete keyword list on CompuServe and Delphi but not on the other systems. The Source may offer the cleanest, smoothest menus and its manual is the best by far, but at this writing its SIGs are just hitting their stride. BIX, on the other hand, has no menus to speak of, but since it is devoted primarily to conferencing, it may not need them. And so on.

Second, each SIG on each system has its own identity as well, just as all groups, organizations, and committees do. A SIG's personality is heavily influenced by the vigor of its sysop, some of whom do a better job than others. But it is also a function of the particular collection of people who use the SIG regularly and participate in its activities. Generally, for example, BIX tends to attract a higher proportion of the more technically oriented computer users. The primary orientation of People/Link, in contrast, has always been to provide a low-cost alternative for people who liked the real-time, CB-like chat features offered by other, more expensive services.

Third, like active groups everywhere, SIGs are dynamic. New features may be added and certainly, given the 20 to 25 percent annual growth rate of the online industry, new people as well. Perhaps it isn't surprising then that while few online communicators subscribe to all six services, many people have accounts on more than one system.

Oddly, the free software selections on the various SIGs may not be a major criterion. If you're looking for some highly specific or narrowly focused program—like a program to set a Gemini printer to respond properly to Epson graphics commands or some esoteric piece of assembler code—your chances of finding it will be better on the larger systems. With more subscribers to draw upon, the SIG libraries on such systems tend to have greater breadth and depth. The downside is that when a system is trying to serve a large number of subscribers simultaneously, there may be noticeable delays between the time you enter a command and the time the system responds. Downloads can take longer, too, particularly during the peak usage hours between 6:00 P.M. and midnight.

On the other hand, if your interests are broader, the size of the host system is largely irrelevant, because most SIGs carry the same PD and shareware utilities and applications programs. Programs always spread rapidly through the community of users, but among online users their propagation is particularly fast. Typically, an online enthusiast will find a new program or a new version of an old favorite on a bulletin board system, download it, run it, and, if it's good, upload it to his or her favorite SIG or SIGs. Other members will find the program in the SIG's library and repeat the process, uploading it to SIGs on other systems to which they subscribe or to their favorite BBSs.

This has been going on for years. But recently the online systems themselves have added a powerful incentive. Noting that in some cases huge numbers of subscribers spend 70 percent or more of their online time downloading files, the information utilities have realized how important it is to offer the very best collections of free software possible. Accordingly, many have established a policy of free SIG uploads, often combined with a bonus of an equivalent amount of free connect time.

Thus, purely from the perspective of free software, the main considerations are the ease with which you can locate a desired program on a given SIG on a given system and what you'll have to pay to download it. You'll find cost tables in each of the six system profiles later in this chapter, and we'll have more to say about cost comparisons and calculations later. For now, we suggest that you turn to the profiles and call the toll-free numbers for each system to request an information kit. This will give you a clearer feeling for each system and more facts upon which to base your subscription decisions.

Subscriptions, Manuals, and Connect-Time Costs

Each system may be unique, but they all do business in essentially the same way. For example, there is always an initial, one-time subscription fee to establish your account, though you may find that special deals are periodically offered in conjunction with some hardware or software manufacturer. CompuServe has long been the most aggressive in this area. In at least one case, for example, the company had free subscription kits bound into every issue of *Transactor*, a Commodore-oriented computer magazine.

If you pay for a subscription, however, you can count on receiving at least three things: an account number, a password, and some kind of manual. The account number may be called a User ID or something else, but it always serves as your public identity on the system. The password is secret and is used only when you are signing on to the system. In most cases, there will be a feature to let you change the password you are issued to one of your own choosing.

FreeTip: Keep your password completely confidential. And never key it in while you are online other than during the sign on process or while using the password-changing feature. Never. There are wolves in the electronic woods who have been known to trick unsuspecting subscribers into revealing their passwords by pretending to be customer service representatives or faking up an error message. Since your account number or User ID is public, once you give away your password you have given away the key to your bank account.

The manuals supplied by the online systems vary from the little pocket brochure offered by People/Link to the fat, slip-cased, IBM-style three-ring binder offered by The Source. Most are adequate to the systems they are designed to explain. But no printed manual (or book) in this field can remain absolutely up-to-date in every detail for very long. In most cases, you will want to supplement the manuals with printouts of the help files and new feature announcements available online. You may also receive a magazine or newsletter from the service as part of your subscription, and this too can help you stay current.

All of the services automatically bill your Visa, American Express, or MasterCard for the charges you incur. But only The Source has a monthly minimum usage requirement. Source subscribers are automatically billed $10 per month whether they have used that much connect time or not. The CompuServe Executive Service option has the same requirement, but it includes a variety of discounts and special features. For regular CompuServe subscribers there is no monthly minimum charge of any kind.

For Delphi subscribers agreeing to spend $24 a month on the system at regular rates, the Delphi Advantage program offers a prime-time discount of seven percent and a nonprime-time discount of 25 percent on all subsequent connect time. People/Link has the Frequent Plinker Club with monthly dues of $10 entitling you to 25 percent off all connect time.

When you're online, time is literally money. Some nonfree software-related features like stock and bond quotes may carry additional costs, but basically you are charged for the amount of time you are connected to the system. This may be measured to the nearest minute or fraction of a minute. There may also be a certain minimum usage requirement for each session. If you sign on to check your mail, for example, find nothing in the box and immediately sign off, you might be charged for two minutes of connect time even though the session lasted less than a minute.

The connect time charge is made up of two parts. There is the hourly rate for using the system, and there is the hourly rate for using Telenet, Tymnet, or some other packet-switching network. In the industry, the latter are often called "communications costs." The electronic and published rate cards provided by the services differ in their approach here. Some break out cost figures, showing you the components and the total. Some quote just a total hourly rate. In the profiles that follow we have reproduced the rates for calls placed from the continental United States. Rates from Alaska, Hawaii, Canada, and abroad are always higher due to higher communications costs.

Rates are lower during the evenings and all day on weekends and holidays than during prime-time business hours. And in addition to free uploads and possible bonus connect time, some systems offer special low rates for the time you spend using a SIG. There is no way to know whether this will become the industry norm, but since policies can change, be sure to check with the system before factoring connect time costs into your subscription decision.

The Best Way to Use Online Free Software Systems

Online systems and SIGs are wonderful resources. But it's important to keep them in perspective. Clearly, they are important—even crucial—tools for anyone even mildly interested in free software. But with so many cheaper alternatives available, it is foolish to use an online system as your primary source of free programs. Of course it's your money and you're free to spend as you please, but you might want to do a little arithmetic first.

Calculating the Cost

If you're looking for a little utility program like CHOP.EXE (16K), mentioned in Chapter 5, nothing could be better or more convenient than one of the SIG libraries. It'll cost you about 48¢ to download at 1200 bits per second during the evening. You'll have it on your disk in minutes and be able to begin using it instantly. But if you're interested in PC-WRITE, File Express, the As-Easy-As electronic spreadsheet, or any of the other major applications programs discussed in this book, you will be much better off obtaining them on disk through the mail. The programs themselves are quite large; they have lengthy documentation files; and often a number of substantial support files are involved as well.

We can use PC-WRITE and CompuServe as an example. The complete PC-WRITE package (version 2.71) occupies over 690K of space on two disks. It is available in CompuServe's IBM Software SIG, Data Library 1 as two files: PCW1.ARC (260K) and PCW2.ARC (237K). You will need both. Even though the files have been compressed and stored in an archive, you will still have to download a total of 497K of data.

So many variables are involved that you can never predict the exact cost of downloading a given program. However, there is a rough-and-ready formula that can give you a quick approximation. Every system will tell you how many bytes a file occupies. So divide that number by the number of characters per second to get the total seconds of transmission time. Then divide that by 60 to convert to minutes, and multiply by the applicable per-minute connect rate. As you know by now, each byte or character requires ten bits to transmit, so a speed of 300 bits per second translates to 30 characters per second (cps), 1200 bps is 120 cps, and 2400 bps is 240 cps.

The final step is to allow for the additional time added by the hardware and by your chosen error-checking protocol. Using a protocol like XMODEM, for example, adds approximately 14 percent to the time required to transfer a file. Other protocols may add less, but we can still use 14 percent to allow for various fudge factors.

We will assume that you are communicating at 1200 bps and using CompuServe's lowest rate of 22¢ per minute. Thus, 497,000 bits (497K) divided by 120 cps is 4142 seconds. Divide that by 60 and you get about 70 minutes. So at 22¢ per minute, it will cost you $15.40 to download the complete package. Add 14 percent for overhead, and your total cost will be around $17.56.

Admittedly, some commercial systems charge much less than Compu-Serve, and no knowledgeable CompuServe subscriber would use XMODEM on that system. CompuServe's own B and Quick B protocols offer much faster throughput and much lower overhead.

But even $17.56 doesn't sound like a lot to spend for the opportunity to try out a leading shareware program like PC-Write. Until you learn that you can obtain two disks containing the identical software through the mail for $9 from an organization like Software Distributors Clearinghouse (see "Other Sources" at the end of Chapter 4). And if you don't like the program, you can return the disks and SDC and other commercial mail-order sources will give you your money back, something no online service is ever likely to do.

The Up Side of Downloading

Generally, if a program is going to take you more than about 30 minutes to download (216K at 1200 bps), you'll probably be better off obtaining it through the mail. But as a quick and convenient source of relatively short programs, online systems have no equal. Among other things, they allow you to pick and choose your programs, something you cannot do with user group and mail-order sources. For example, it's conceivable that the programs you want could fit on a single disk, but because of the way the user group's collections are arranged you might have to buy three or four disks to obtain all of your target programs. In such cases it may be cheaper to use online resources to assemble your own customized collection.

Downloading also offers an easy way to overcome disk size and disk format incompatibilities. IBM Personal System 2 models and many laptop computers use 3½-inch disks. But at this writing the vast majority of free IBM/MS-DOS software is available only on 5¼-inch floppies.

This situation is bound to change, but it may take a while. In the meantime, downloading what you need is among the least expensive solutions to the problem.

FreeTip: It is perhaps a more subtle point, but the common meeting ground provided by the electronic medium lets you overcome computer and computer operating system incompatibilities as well. Apples, IBMs, and Macintoshes cannot run each other's machine-language programs or even read each other's disks. But some software manufacturers have made their programs available on all three machines. Ashton-Tate's best selling dBASE line is a good example.

Originally written for the CP/M operating system, versions of dBASE are now available for IBMs, Macintoshes, and CP/M-equipped Apples. In all three instances, users create dBASE applications by preparing *text* files using the dBASE programming language. If you can get one of these text files into your machine, you can use it with your copy of dBASE, regardless of the system the file was prepared on. The same thing is true of any applications software that includes its own programming language, and of course it is true of conventional computer languages like Microsoft BASIC. As long as the program has been saved by its creator as an ASCII file, you can download it and run it on your own machine with few if any changes.

We've already emphasized how important SIGs can be as a source of answers, tips, advice, and information. And we've suggested that you not limit yourself to the SIGs devoted to computer topics. We should say once again, however, that by exploring the libraries of such SIGs you may turn up programs that might not have made it into the main free software collections. For example, a BASIC program designed to "calculate amnioglycoside dosages from pharmacokinetic equations that consider patient characteristics and amnioglycoside serium levels" is not likely to be included in major general-interest software libraries. But you'll find it in Data Library 12 of the Medical SIG on CompuServe as DOSAGE.BAS.

First-Time Sign-On Preliminaries

The first time you sign on to an online system, it's natural to want to explore, and that's exactly what you should do. Don't let anything prevent you from enjoying the wonderful childlike sense of discovery all online systems hold for first-time users. Don't even try to figure out how the system is laid out or where everything is during your first trip. Follow the menus the system offers and let your whims carry you where they will. When in doubt, simply enter a question mark (?) or the word HELP. Such an excursion will give you the impressions and exposure that can make the system's documentation much easier to read and understand.

Top Menus, Submenus, and Command Mode

At some early point, however—possibly before your second or third session—you really should dip into the manual. When you do, there are a number of things to look for in every case. First, with the exception of BIX, all of the systems we will be considering here are menu-driven. All of them greet you with a TOP menu of initial choices each time you sign on. Each of these initial choices leads to subsidiary menus, which may lead to sub-submenus, and so on. You can get anywhere you want to go on these systems by wending your way through the menus.

This is great for new users, but menus can get tiresome after a while. As you gain more experience, you will probably want to switch each system's command mode. Command mode lets you enter a single command that will skip most intervening menus and take you directly to your desired destination. For example, keying in IBMSIG on The Source, GO IBMCOMM on CompuServe, or GROUPS PC on Delphi, will take you directly to the corresponding special interest groups.

The six profiles that follow have been written to dovetail with the manuals and documentation available from the respective systems. We will be using command mode much of the time, relying on you to refer to your system manual(s) for more detail.

Setting Your Personal Profile

Second, it's a good idea to pay particular attention to what the manual says about how you can control the way the system presents information on your screen. How many characters would you like to see on each line? How many lines on each page? The process of entering your answers to these and other questions is called setting your "system defaults" or creating your personal "profile."

The main thing to be concerned with is the number of lines per page. If your profile calls for, say, 25 lines per page, the system will pause every 25 lines while it is displaying text and prompt you to hit <Enter> or some other key before it continues. Needless to say, if you are capturing a long file of SIG instructions, bulletins, or program documentation, this can be a real nuisance. Consequently, whenever possible, it is best to set your system defaults to "0 lines" per page or whatever else is required to eliminate the pauses. (See your manual for specific instructions.)

The third point is related: Consult your comm program documentation to find out how to open and close your "capture buffer." A comm program's capture buffer is like a shunt valve in a stream. When opened, all of the water that flows by is shunted into a holding tank. When closed, the water simply flows by and disappears. Most comm programs will periodically dump the contents of their holding tanks to disk, though some require you to enter a command to do so.

Thus, by setting your profile to eliminate pauses and by opening and closing your capture buffer at appropriate points, you can display text in a continuous, uninterrupted stream, record it to disk, sign off to stop the connect time meter, and read everything at your leisure. This is unquestionably the most cost-effective way to deal with online text.

Since most computer owners upload text at 80 characters per line, a setting of "80 columns" is usually the best option for line length or width. You can always format it for 65 charcters per line later with PC-WRITE or some other word processing program.

Look for the "Scram" Command

Fourth, all systems have what can be called a universal "scram" command. This is the command you enter when you're caught in the midst of a long text display or are stuck at some other point where you do not wish to remain. Traditionally, the command has been a "BREAK." This is not an ASCII character. A true BREAK is a sustained "high" signal lasting between 200 and 600 milliseconds. Most communications programs include a command for issuing this signal.

Usually a BREAK will cause a system to stop whatever it is currently doing and return you to the nearest prompt. However, systems are inconsistent in their response, and many prefer a Control-C, a Control-Z, or some other control character. We've noted the appropriate scram commands in the profiles that follow, but it would not hurt to review relevant sections of your manual. As noted in Chapter 5, a control character is generated by holding down your <Ctrl> key and hitting a letter key. There are 26 control codes in the ASCII code set, one for each letter of the alphabet.

Issuing a scram command may not always stop a system in its tracks, but it will stop it eventually. Delays are caused by text that is already in the pipeline and by the fact that a system may have so many other people to handle at the time that it fails to notice your scram command immediately.

Sign-Off Commands and Rate Summaries

The fifth and sixth points to check are the commands for signing off a system and the commands for generating a list of the current connect time rates and charges. When you want to end a session, there is usually no need to spend time and money backing out of a SIG and returning to the top menu before signing off. In most cases you can simply enter OFF, BYE, or some other command the moment you are ready to do so, regardless of where you are. Of course, if you don't enter the proper command you'll get the equivalent of a dumb look from the online system. So avoid having to check your manual while the meter is running and locate the sign-off command before you sign on.

It's also useful to know how to check a system's current rates and charges. Is there an extra charge for 1200 or 2400-bps communication? When does the cheaper, nonprime time begin? Does the system stop the connect-time meter when you are uploading ("free uploads")? Do you receive free bonus connect time for uploading files? And so on. We've provided summaries, but since policies can change, it's a good idea to know how to check the rates yourself.

System Profiles and Directions to the Treasure Houses

We have tried to make the six profiles that follow as uniform as possible to make it easy to compare the various systems. Because most systems do not quote connect time per minute, we have divided the relevant hourly figures by 60 and rounded the result up to the next whole penny. As noted in the text, the rates given here are for users in the continental United States. Other rates (Alaska, Hawaii, Canada, and so on) are higher, and you should consult the system's customer service department for details.

Unless otherwise stated, all times refer to *your local time,* or more technically, the local time that applies to the packet-switching node you phone to make the connection. Except for routine maintenance, these systems are available round the clock. If you have questions or problems, call customer service during the hours shown here.

We have followed three conventions. Commands are presented in capital letters for emphasis only. You are free to use all upper, all lower, or mixed cases when you are actually online. Second, we have used the form FILENAME.EXT to stand for any filename. And third, when we tell you to "key in" something, you can assume this means to type the text or command and hit your <Enter> key.

CompuServe

CompuServe Information
Service, Inc.
5000 Arlington Centre Blvd.
Columbus, OH 43220
(617) 457-8600

CUSTOMER SERVICE
(800) 848-8990

In Ohio and outside the
continental U.S.:
(617) 457-8650

Customer Service Hours
(Eastern Standard Time)
Mon.–Fri.: 8:00 A.M.–midnight
Weekends: 2:00 P.M.–midnight

Initial Subscription:

There are lots of ways to subscribe to CompuServe, and all of them
include a certain amount of free time on the system. Modems, like the
Avatex models cited in Chapter 5, often include CompuServe Intro-
Paks. An IntroPak is a 45-page descriptive brochure that includes a
sealed envelope with an account number and initial password good for
perhaps $15 worth of free connect time. You might also purchase the
Radio Shack Universal Sign-Up Kit (product number 26-2224;
$19.95). Available from your local Radio Shack store, this includes
subscriptions to both CompuServe and the Dow Jones News/Re-
trieval Service, plus an hour of free connect time on each system. The
CompuServe Users Guide is not included, but you can order it once
you are online for a total postage paid cost of $12.95.

The best deal may be the CompuServe Subscription Kit. This package
includes the users guide (the main system manual) and an account
number and password good for $25 of free time. Available in com-
puter stores at a list price of $39.95, you can also order it at a dis-
count from mail-order firms. At this writing, for example, the PC
Connection [(800) 243-8088] in Marlow, New Hampshire, sells Compu-
Serve Subscription Kits for $24 plus $2 for shipping and handling.

Access:

Telenet, Tymnet, the CompuServe Network, and direct dial. Contact
CompuServe for more information concerning access via Computer
Sciences Corporation (International Access Network) and LATA net-
works.

Rates:

CompuServe has two primary rates: one for 300 bps and one for 1200 or 2400 bps communications. These rates are the same, regardless of the time of day. The cost of using CompuServe's own packet switching network remains the same as well (30¢ an hour). What changes are the rates charged by Telenet and Tymnet, the "via others" in the table that follows.

Connect time is billed in one-minute increments, with a minimum of one minute per session. Connect time rates do not include communications surcharges and product surcharges (as with stock quotes and other financial features).

COMPUSERVE CONNECT RATES

PRIME TIME
(Mon.–Fri. 8:00 A.M.–7:00 P.M.)

Speed (bps)	CompuServe connect time (per hour)	Packet-switching network charges (per hour)	TOTAL (per hour)	TOTAL (per minute)
300	$6.00	30¢ via CompuServe	$6.30	11¢
		$12 via others	$18	30¢
1200/ 2400	$12.50	30¢ via CompuServe	$12.85	22¢
		$10 via others	$24.50	41¢

NONPRIME TIME
(Mon.–Fri. 7:00 P.M.–8:00 A.M., and all day weekends and holidays)

Speed (bps)	CompuServe connect time (per hour)	Packet-switching network charges (per hour)	TOTAL (per hour)	TOTAL (per minute)
300	$6.00	30¢ via CompuServe	$6.30	11¢
		$2 via others	$8.00	14¢
1200/ 2400	$12.50	30¢ via CompuServe	$12.80	22¢
		$2 via others	$14.50	25¢

Personal Defaults:

Key in GO TERMINAL and select the item on the resulting menu that reads "View or Change Current Terminal Parameters." This produces a list of items you may change. To eliminate pauses when using most sections of CompuServe, set your "screen size" to 0 lines. In most cases, all of the other settings will be fine (Terminal type: Other, Form feeds: Simulated, etc.). However, unless you are using one of CompuServe's own VIDTEX communication software packages, you should probably turn the "inquiry for VIDTEX" setting off since it can save time by eliminating the inquiry each time you sign on.

Scram Command: Control-C or BREAK

Sign-off Command: OFF

Protocols: CompuServe B and Quick B, XMODEM, and Kermit

Special Notes:

In addition to standard service, CompuServe also offers what it calls its "Executive Option." Benefits include a 10 percent discount on all CompuServe documentation and products, additional free storage space on the system, access to certain special (largely financial) features, and access to the system's Executive News Service electronic clipping feature. There are other benefits as well.

Two costs are involved. There is an initial one-time sign up fee of $5 if you sign up when you first activate your subscription. If you want to switch later, the cost will be $10. The second cost is a minimum usage requirement of $10 a month. At 22¢ a minute, that's about 45 minutes of connect time a month or about 11 minutes a week. Since most people easily spend that much time on the system in the normal course of things, the Executive Option is worth strong consideration, even if you're not an executive.

Capsule Overview

CompuServe is enormous. With roots stretching back to 1979, it is one of the oldest general interest online systems, and with a subscribership numbering over 425,000 and a steady growth rate of between 5000 and 7000 new subscribers a month, it is unquestionably the largest. Until recently, the CompuServe Information Service was known as CIS for short. However, due to potential conflicts with the Congressional Information Service, an online database, CompuServe no longer uses the CIS

---------------------- SPECIAL DEAL ----------------------

CompuServe® subscribers who purchase this book are eligible for a $6.00 usage credit. Take advantage of this offer to explore CompuServe's electronic universe and free software treasure rooms by completing the coupon below, and mailing it to the address shown.

Instructions

1. Complete the Bonus Coupon and mail to:

   CompuServe
   Consumer Billing Department
   P.O. Box 20212
   Columbus, OH 43229

2. One coupon redemption per User ID number.

3. Coupon is not transferable.

4. No photocopies will be accepted.

5. This $6.00 usage credit offer expires December 31, 1989.

---

*Alfred Glossbrenner's Master Guide to FREE Software
for IBMs and Compatible Computers*

BONUS COUPON OFFER
$6.00 USAGE CREDIT

USER ID NUMBER: _____

NAME: ___ _____

ADDRESS: _____

CITY: _____STATE: _____ ZIP: _____

SIGNATURE: _____DATE: _____

abbreviation. Most members of the online community, though, still refer to CompuServe in that way.

Long a subsidiary of H&R Block, Inc., CompuServe has grown by accretion, starting small with a limited number of offerings and adding features and improvements in response to the needs and demands of its users. Some users complain that CompuServe responds too slowly and that by the time improvements arrive they are long overdue. But that simply isn't the company's style. All the evidence indicates that Compu-Serve likes to get a good sense of which way the wind is blowing before making any kind of change.

In recent years the wind has been blowing very strongly in the direction of the forums, CompuServe's online special interest groups or SIGs. (The terms refer to the same thing, though CompuServe prefers "forums.") Indeed, many CompuServe users think of their favorite SIG as "home" and only rarely venture out into the main system. There's nothing wrong with that, of course. And certainly everyone has benefited from the overwhelming popularity of the SIGs since it has stimulated CompuServe to install a major upgrade in the software that makes them possible. But it would be a mistake to limit all of your interactions to your favorite special interest group, for CompuServe has much more to offer.

Your *CompuServe Users Guide* and/or IntroPak booklet will give you more details on the system's many features. But the best way to get your own handle on the system is to key in GO INDEX at any exclamation (!) prompt. This will take you to a menu that will let you download a complete list of the system's features and the commands you need to reach them. While you're there, we suggest that you use the INDEX feature's search option to search on the keyword FORUM. This will produce a list of every SIG on the system. If you capture both lists to disk and print them out when you are offline, you'll find they make a handy pair of quick reference tools for getting the most out of your online sessions. Because CompuServe "page numbers" and commands can change, and because new features are always being added, it is a good idea to date your download and repeat the process every six months or so.

As you will see, there are well over 100 CompuServe forums. The actual number varies from time to time as some close down and others start up. Each focuses on a particular interest. There are the machine-specific computer SIGs, of course. And there are SIGs run by Ashton-Tate, Borland International, Autodesk, MicroPro, Microsoft, and other software producers. There are also SIGs devoted to photography, medicine, sailing, sports, education, working at home, investments, journalism, outer space, fine wine, and many other interests. All of them have tons of user-contributed information for you, and many of them have scads of free programs available for downloading as well. Fortunately, once you know how to tap one forum, you automatically know how to tap them all, for each is the creation of the same system software.

FreeTip: As part of your subscription, you will receive the monthly magazine *Online Today*. Though impressively produced (slick paper, four-color throughout), this is basically a rather bland house organ intended mainly to encourage online usage. (Still, it *is* free.) The electronic version of the magazine, available online by keying in OLT, is much better and well worth your connect time to take a look.

If free software and SIGs are your primary interest, you will definitely want to check the electronic edition's summary of newly uploaded forum files. The electronic list is updated twice a month, and it covers notable files that have been added to each SIG since the last update. Key in GO OLT-3700 to reach this feature directly. You might also want to check the current list of forum conference schedules by keying in GO-OLT-120. Most SIGs hold regular weekly online meetings in their CB-like conference areas. Sometimes a particular topic will be discussed, sometimes there will be a guest speaker, and sometimes members gather just to chew the electronic rag, disk, or whatever.

Sign On and Move to the Treasure Rooms

Rich as the other SIGs are, however, there can be no doubt where the juiciest pickings are to be had—in the IBM forums. For the IBM or compatible user, these are the real CompuServe treasure rooms. In this section, we'll show you two ways to raid these storehouses. One method is to download a complete keyword list. The other is to download a complete list of the files on the system. But first, we must show you how to reach the IBM SIGs.

When you sign on to the system you'll see either the What's New menu or CompuServe's TOP menu. What's New changes each Thursday and will appear the next three times you sign on after that. From then on, you'll be greeted by the TOP menu. Both menus end with the "Enter choice !" prompt.

Regardless of which menu appears, key in GO IBMNET at that prompt to reach the IBM forum network. Then you'll see a menu of several IBM forums. The process looks like this:

```
host: WELCOME TO COMPUSERVE NNNN

User ID: 76543,210
Password:

CompuServe Information Service
HH:MM EDT Wednesday DD-MMM-YY
           (Executive Option)
    Last access: HH:MM DD-MMM-YY


              Copyright (C) 1989
             CompuServe Incorporated
               All Rights Reserved

       1  Subscriber Assistance
       2  Find a Topic
       3  Communications/Bulletin Bds.
       4  News/Weather/Sports
       5  Travel
       6  The Electronic MALL/Shopping
       7  Money Matters/Markets
       8  Entertainment/Games
       9  Home/Health/Family
      10  Reference/Education
      11  Computers/Technology
      12  Business/Other Interests

   Enter choice number !GO IBMNET

   CompuServe              IBMNET

   The IBM Users Network

       1  IBM New Users Forum
       2  IBM Communications Forum
       3  IBM Hardware Forum
       4  IBM Junior Forum
       5  IBM Software Forum
       6  PC Vendor Support Forum
       7  Money Matters/Markets

   Enter Choice   !5
```

The focus of each of the six forums on the IBM Users Network menu is fairly evident from the forum names. With the exception of the Vendor Support Forum, each has free software and you'll have fun exploring their offerings. Start with the New Users Forum. It's a little short on software, but it includes essential information and bulletins designed to help new subscribers get the most out of the IBM network. When you select any forum for the first time, you will be ask whether you wish to join it or not. You should definitely join each one. There is no cost for joining and there are no dues of any kind. *But if you do not join you will not be permitted to download anything.*

As you can see, we've chosen the IBM Software Forum (selection 5) as our example. And since we had already joined, here is what was displayed:

```
CompuServe                    IBMSW


One moment please . . .
Welcome to IBM Software Forum, V. 4D(36)

Hello, Alfred Glossbrenner
Last visit: DD-MMM-YY   HH:MM:SS

Forum messages: 196346 to 1986441
Last message you've read: 198621

Subtopic(s) Selected:
  All Accessible
No members are in conference.

News Flash:
```

Notice the CompuServe page number IBMSW. If we had wanted to get to this forum directly from the CompuServe TOP menu, we would have keyed in GO IBMSW. As it is, we took the long way around to show you the IBM Users Network menu. All of the forums on that menu have direct access page numbers as well (IBMHW, IBMCOM, and so on). Also, notice that the last line in the above example is "News Flash:". We have not shown the short bulletins that followed, but you should be aware that most forum sysops use this feature as an opportunity to alert you to changes, new files, sources of help, and so on. Once you have seen a given news flash bulletin, it will not be displayed again the next time you enter a forum, though you can view it again by selecting "Announcements" from the forum's TOP menu. That menu will be displayed each time you enter the forum:

```
IBM Software Forum Menu

1 INSTRUCTIONS

2 MESSAGES
3 LIBRARIES (Files)
4 CONFERENCING (12 participating)
```

```
5 ANNOUNCEMENTS from sysop
6 MEMBER directory
7 OPTIONS for this forum

Enter choice !3


IBM Software Forum Libraries Menu

Libraries Available:
 0 New Uploads (S)
 1 DOS / OS (S)
 2 Txt/Word Proc. (S)
 3 Gen. Utilities (S)
 4 Programming (S)
 5 DBMS/Accounting (S)
 6 Applications (S)
 7 Compatibles (S)
 8 Misc & Demos (S)
10 Bus. Graphics (S)
11 Multitasking (S)
12 Desktop/Shells (S)

Enter Choice  !3
```

A forum's TOP menu is the menu that greets you when you enter. We have emphasized the word TOP because should you ever want to get back to the main forum menu while you are in a different part of a forum, TOP (no GO), or just T is the command to enter. If you plan to use a forum's messaging features, be sure to consult your system manual about how to set your options (selection 7 on the main forum menu). You will also want to key in SET to check or modify the number of lines per page, characters per line, and so on, the forum uses to send you text. The SET command can be used at any time, regardless of where you are in the forum. It produces an easy-to-follow menu and instructions.

FreeTip: Three tips, actually, for CIS users who have had a little experience. First, if you want the text CompuServe sends you to scroll out without pausing, you must use the SET command to turn "paging" off and to set your page line length to 0. If you don't do this, you may be prompted to hit <Enter> every 23 lines or so—a real inconvenience when you are downloading a text file from one of the libraries.

Second, you must enter your settings for *each* SIG you plan to use. Setting things up for the IBM Communications SIG has no

FreeTip continued

effect on the IBM Hardware SIG, for example. Third, the quickest
way to reach a given library is to respond to the first prompt you
see after joining or entering a forum with LIBn (where n is the
number of the SIG library you wish to enter). This saves you from
having to work through intervening menus to reach the target library. At this writing, the command DLn will also work.

As you can see, however, we opted for the forum libraries by keying
in 3. Forum libraries used to be called Data Libraries or DLs, two
terms you are virtually certain to encounter as you use the IBM SIGs.
Our menu selection produced a list of all of the libraries available in this
forum. (A given forum may have up to 18 libraries.) Next, we chose
library 3, "Gen. Utilities." The "(S)" after each library name stands for
"software" and is intended to remind you that you are using the IBM
Software forum. Note that if we had wanted to go directly to library 3
we could have done so from the forum's TOP menu by keying in LIB3.
Either way, here is what appears:

```
IBM Software Forum Library 3

- Gen. Utilities (S) -

1 BROWSE thru files
2 DIRECTORY of files

3 UPLOAD a new file
4 DOWNLOAD a file

5 LIBRARIES

Enter choice !KEY


Enter keyword (e.g. modem)
or <CR> for all:

Count:   Keyword:

1        .PIT
1        1.03
1        1.0A
3        ALLOCATION
1        ALT-KEYS
5        ANSI
1        ANSI.SYS
```

4	ASSEMBLER
9	BASIC
1	BASICA
33	BATCH
14	C
2	CAPLOCK
4	CAPS
1	CAPS-LOCK
5	CAPSLOCK
1	CAPS—LOCK
17	CLOCK
4	CPM
2	CRLF
22	DIR
5	DIRECTORIES
61	DIRECTORY
78	DISK
13	DISKETTE
115	FILE
2	FLICKER
1	FLICKERFREE
18	HEX
1	HEXADECIMAL
1	HEXASCII
1	HEXDECIMAL
1	HEXIDECIMAL
1	QU ICK-BASIC
3	QUICKBASIC
25	RESIDENT
1	SELF-EXTRACTING
1	SELF-UNPACKING
7	SPOOL
6	TROJAN
2	UNERASE
14	UNIX
1	UNIX -LIKE
1	WORDSTAR
1	XFER
4	ZIV
8	ZOO

Browsing through files, the first selection on the library menu, can be enjoyable, but using it without prior knowledge of the keywords in the database is guaranteed to burn up connect time. As your system manual explains, the BROWSE option prompts you for a keyword and displays the header, keywords, and descriptive paragraph of each relevant file. After each file's information has been displayed, you will be given the opportunity to download it or go on to the next one. The second item on the "Gen. Utilities" menu is "DIRECTORY of files." This option lets you specify a keyword if you like, but its output consists of only filenames, upload dates, and the number of accesses for each relevant file, and thus is virtually useless to an inexperienced user.

Getting a List of Keywords

All of which leads us to one of the quickest, most economical and efficient way to locate free software (or anything else) in a CompuServe SIG library—the KEY command. As you can see, entering KEY at the "Enter choice !" prompt causes the system to ask you for a particular keyword or to "hit <CR> for all." If you hit your <Enter> key at this point, you will receive a list of every keyword in the database and the number of files to which it has been attached.

The keyword list just shown has been drastically shortened to save space. The actual keyword list ran 1007 words and took less than a minute to download at 1200 bits per second. As you know from Chapter 6, getting your hands on a system's keyword list can make locating the program you want as easy as finding leaves in the fall. We will not repeat that discussion here, but we do suggest that you take a moment to peruse the above list and imagine which files you would search for if it were on your screen.

Save the keyword list to disk. Sign off the system by keying in OFF at any SIG prompt. Print out the list. Review it, circling likely candidates. Then sign back on again, reenter the SIG data library, and search for the file. Your goal at this point is to get more information about the program to which your target keywords have been attached. And the easiest way to do that is to use the BROwse command.

Key in BRO at the "Enter choice !" prompt and respond to the prompt for keywords with your chosen word. Then just hit <Enter> when you are prompted for information on the age of the file you want. We chose the keyword RESIDENT from the list, and here is what the process looked like:

```
Enter keywords (e.g. modem)
or <CR> for all: RESIDENT

Oldest files in days
or <CR> for all:

[70007,1212]
CP3.ARC/binary        19-Jul-87 15073        Accesses: 261

Keywords: CUT PASTE RESIDENT UTILITY

CutPaste version 3 is a resident utility which uses less than
6K of memory. Anything which appears on the screen may be
```

```
"cut" out and saved for later "pasting" into an application.
Includes ASM source.

Enter command, N for next file
or <CR> for disposition menu !
```

Unfortunately, the system does not tell you how many files are in the queue when you are browsing, but you already know how many "next" files there are by the "Count" number next to RESIDENT on the keyword list you've downloaded. For the purposes of this demonstration, we hit <Enter> at the prompt above to get the system to take us to the Library Disposition Menu:

```
Library Disposition Menu

1 (REA) Read this file
2 (DOW) Download this file
3 (M) Data Library Menu

Enter choice or <CR> for next ! 2

Library Protocol Menu

Transfer protocols available -

1 XMODEM (MODEM7) protocol
2 CompuServe 'B' protocol
3 CompuServe 'A' protocol
4 DC4/DC2 CAPTURE protocol
5 Kermit protocol
6 CompuServe Quick 'B' protocol

0 Abort transfer request

Enter choice !
```

If this file were a text file—with a file extension of TXT or DOC, for example—the best thing to do would be to open your comm program's capture buffer or log file and tell CompuServe you want to REAd the file. This causes the text in the file to be displayed on your screen, and it is much faster than a protocol transfer. However, since like all archived files CP3.ARC is a machine language file, we have to download it using one of the available protocols.

The best protocol to use on the CompuServe system is the CompuServe Quick B protocol. This is a windowed version of the trusty CIS B protocol that permits up to two unacknowledged packets to be outstanding. The standard CIS B protocol should be your second choice, followed by Kermit. The XMODEM protocol does not work very well on commercial systems and should be used only as a last resort. If your software supports both conventional and "relaxed" XMODEM and none of the other options, set the program for relaxed XMODEM and choose the first option on the menu above. You're not likely to find a program supporting the "A" protocol, and the DC4/DC2 CAPTURE protocol does no error checking. It is simply how CompuServe refers to an X-ON/X-OFF flow control protocol.

If you are using ProComm 2.4.2, the shareware comm program recommended in Chapter 16, downloading a copy of CP3.ARC can be as simple as choosing either CIS B protocol. ProComm 2.4.2 supports both and even lets you set up your terminal to respond to the inquiry CIS issues as part of its handshaking before starting the transfer.

FreeTip: If you would like to read the descriptions of all files tagged with the same keyword, without pausing after each one, make sure that you have used the SET command to eliminate pauses and paging. Then enter the following command at the SIG Data Library menu prompt: S/DES/KEY:FOOBAR, where "FOOBAR" is your chosen keyword.

The text that will be displayed will be the same as if you had chosen to BROwse using that keyword, but without the BROwse prompts and pauses. If you capture the text to disk, and print it out after you sign off, you can ponder your choices at leisure. Note the filenames of the programs you want, then sign back on, go to the SIG Data Library, and key in DOW FILENAME.EXT at the library prompt to download each target file.

FreeTip: Early in 1987 CompuServe began publishing "Best Of" booklets for several of its most popular forum libraries. The IBM version is 74 pages long and sells for $10.20, including shipping and handling. Files are listed alphabetically and each entry includes all of the information you would see while browsing. It is not clear what criteria were used to select the files. The booklet also includes an index derived directly from the keyword lists attached to each file.

This booklet offers a nice introduction to free software on the CompuServe IBM SIGs, and it is sure to give you hours of interesting browsing. However, it suffers from at least three drawbacks. It obviously cannot give you the latest information or include newer versions of the files it lists. It tends to narrow your focus based on undefined criteria. One has no idea whether each of the programs was run and thoroughly tested, or exactly why each has been chosen. And finally, the book is not electronic and so cannot be quickly scanned, though the inclusion of a keyword index helps remedy this problem. For more information on this publication, key in GO ORDER on the main CompuServe system.

The Summary File Approach

The KEY command and the techniques discussed here will work equally well in any other SIG on the CompuServe system. However, there is another technique that is specific to the forums in the IBM User Network, thanks to the IBM Net's sysops. All of the libraries in all of the IBM forums contain a file that lists every program in the library.

Picture it for just a minute. There are five IBM SIGs (hardware, software, communications, new user, and PC jr), and each has about ten libraries. Within each of those libraries is a text file that includes the filename, size, month and year it was uploaded, and a one-line description for each file in that particular library.

The IBM SIGs are among the best managed forums on the system, and the sysops and assistant sysops are very conscientious about keeping these files current. Each file is updated once a month. Since the filenames for these master list files follow a logical pattern, you never have to search for them. You can simply enter a forum library and request them by name. As an example, consider the following from the IBM Hardware Forum (GO IBMHW), starting with the menu of available data libraries:

IBM Hardware Forum Libraries Menu

Libraries Available:
  0 New Uploads (H)
  1 Disk/Disk Utils (H)
  2 Printers/Utils (H)
  3 Video/EGA (H)
  4 Misc. Hardware (H)
  5 PC-AT (H)
  6 Laptops (H)
  7 Compatibles (H)
  8 Village Inn (H)
  9 PS/2 (H)

Enter choice ! 7

IBM Hardware Forum Library 7

- Compatibles (H) -

1 BROWSE thru files
2 DIRECTORY of files

3 UPLOAD a new file
4 DOWNLOAD a file

5 LIBRARIES

Enter choice !REA HWDL7.DES

Notice that we have asked the system to display the file HWDL7.DES (Hardware Data Library 7—description). As previously noted, all SIG libraries used to be called Data Libraries, and that is why DL is part of this file's name. Here is a small fraction of what will appear on your screen:

Summary descriptions of files in DL7 [Compatibles (H)] of IBMHW as of September 1, 1987. Explanatory notes are at bottom of this file.

Name	Size	MY	Description
3000HL.BEN	2	17	PC Labs benchmark tests on Tandy 3000HL
6300BU.ARC	32B	37	"Tips, Tricks, and Traps" for the AT&T PC6300
AST286.ARC	20B	57	Reports on the AST Premium 286 fast AT clone
AST286.ARC	55B	67	Up-to-date thread on the AST Premium/286 computer
AT5025.ARC	1B	56	Switch AT&T monochrome display to 50 lines and back
ATT143.ARC	3B	96	Description of the latest ROM (143)
ATT2MU.TXT	2	47	Connect a NEC Multi-Sync monitor to AT&T PC6300
ATTCLK.ARC	3B	87	Set DOS system date/time from AT&T clock chip
ATTCLO.ARC	9B	47	Clock device driver for AT&T PC6300 with PC-DOS 2.xx+

We could have downloaded this file using a protocol, but since it is a text file, that isn't necessary. Just open your capture buffer and your comm program will save the text that appears on your screen. Knowing what you know now, you can probably guess at the names of the corresponding files in other libraries and SIGs. For the other IBM SIGs, the filenames to use are: SWDLn.DES, COMDLn.DES, NEWDLn.DES, and JRDLn.DES—where n stands for the number of the target "Data Library."

This is very convenient. But it gets even better. If you want to obtain a list of every file in every library in every SIG, you can either move into each library and download each DES file, or you can go to LIB0 (New Uploads) of the IBM Software Forum. Here you will find at least four files: COMSUM.ARC, HWSUM.ARC, NEWSUM.ARC, and SWSUM.ARC. These archive files contain all of the "DL DES" files for their respective forums. At this writing, downloading all four of them takes about 40 minutes at 1200 bps, but if you do it once, you may never need do it again. For the sysops also prepare separate files listing just the new additions each month. Thus SWCHG.OCT is a text file listing just the new additions for the month of October. Downloading each month's additions file can save you from having to download the master files again.

Whichever variation you choose, once you have extracted the files from their archives, you can use Vern Buerg's LIST.COM program to search them to your heart's content. As noted in the previous chapter, each word in these master list files (indeed each string of characters) becomes a keyword when LIST is at work.

FreeTip: Here's a command that can save you poring through your CompuServe manual. Suppose you have found a file that you might want to download. But before doing so, you want to read the descriptive paragraph attached to it to make sure it is what you want. To do this, go into the relevant Data Library and key in:

S FILENAME.EXT/DES

This tells the system to scan for FILENAME.EXT and display its description.

FreeTip: There isn't room to discuss the forum message exchange, though as noted earlier, this is an important part of every SIG on every system. However, we can't leave the subject of the IBM forums on CompuServe without saying a word about AUTO-SIG.EXE or "ATO" (from the Hayes modem command to go online). This program was written by Vernon Buerg, Don Watkins (a sysop in the IBMCOM forum), and many other forum members as a "joint programming hack," as they put it.

ATO is a menu-driven communications program specifically de-

FreeTip continued

signed to automate the message exchange process on CompuServe forums. It supports the CompuServe B and Quick B protocols and is remarkable both in its performance and in its origins as a multi-person volunteer project. There is a data library devoted to ATO in the IBMCOM forum, and we have arranged to make it available on the disk called Glossbrenner's Choice Comm Pack 3 discussed in Chapter 16. If you really get into the swing of things on the IBM SIGs, ATO is something you will definitely want to consider since it is designed to keep your connect time to a minimum. Similar programs (TAPCIS, ZAPCIS, and so on) have appeared, but we prefer the original.

GEnie

GEnie
GE Information Services, Dept. 02B
401 North Washington Street
Rockville, MD 20850
(301) 340-4000

CUSTOMER SERVICE
(800) 638-9636
Includes Alaska, Canada, and Hawaii

Customer Service Hours (Eastern Standard Time)

Mon.–Fri: 9:00 A.M.–midnight
Weekends and holidays:
noon–8:00 P.M.

Initial Subscription:

"GEnie" stands for the General Electric Network for Information Exchange. There is a one-time sign up charge of $29.95. There are no monthly minimums. This includes an attractively printed 200-page spiral-bound manual, a subscription to the GEnie "LiveWire" newsletter, and two free evening hours on the system (a $10 value).

All subscriptions are initiated electronically. Set your system for 300 or 1200 bps, and since GEnie prefers to operate at half duplex, enable your local echo when you call. U.S. callers should dial: (800) 638-8369. In Canada, the data numbers to dial are as follows:

Toronto (416) 858-1230
Montreal (514) 333-1117

Calgary (403) 232-6121
Vancouver (604) 437-7313

When the connection has been established, hit three or more capital H's (HHH) and <ENTER>. The U#= ("user number") prompt will then appear. Key in the user number and ID given under "Special Deal" below and hit <Enter>. You will then be welcomed to the online sign-up procedure. Have your Visa, American Express, Discover, or MasterCard, ready. You will also be asked for your home and work phone numbers and your mother's maiden name. And you will be asked to key in an electronic mail address "handle" of your choosing. The limit is 12 alphanumeric characters (K.CARLETON is the example given online). It's worth thinking about your electronic mail handle before signing on since changing it later incurs an administrative charge.

SPECIAL DEAL

We have arranged a special FREE GEnie subscription offer for readers of this book. When you call to subscribe, key in the number given below at the U#= prompt. This will entitle you to subscribe for free. GEnie has lots of online help available, so you may or may not need a copy of the manual. If you do, the cost is $12.95, plus $2 shipping and handling, for a total of $14.95. Here is the number to key in:

XJM11796,GLOSS

According to GEnie, "The very next business day, your GEnie representative will call you with your new GEnie User ID# . . . In a few days you will receive your GEnie information kit." The kit contains your manual (if you have ordered one), a pocket reference guide booklet, and other materials.

Access:

The only way to access GEnie is through the network operated by its parent, GE Information Services. There are some 650 nodes in the United States, plus the Canadian nodes cited above. Additional cities may be added in the future. Started in 1964, the GE Information Services network now reaches 90 percent of the free world. That makes GEnie particularly attractive to non-U.S. users since it keeps communications costs to a minimum. Note that the GEnie service operates best at half duplex, so you will want to toggle your local echo on. If you cannot do this, you can send the system a Control-R during sign on. This must be done after the U#= prompt appears but before keying in your user ID and password. Do not press <Enter> after the Control-R.

Rates:

GEnie rates are the same whether you are communicating at 300 or 1200 bits per second. There is a $7.50 per hour surcharge for 2400-bps service, where available. Rates from Canada, billed in Canadian dollars, are $50 per hour during prime time and $9.50 per hour during nonprime time and on weekends. No 2400-bps service is available from Canada at this writing.

The U.S. rates shown below *include* Alaska, Hawaii, and Puerto Rico. Alaska and Hawaii are considered Pacific Time and Puerto Rico is considered Eastern. A surcharge (at all hours) of $2 per hour applies to nodes in a few low-density cities, and some GEnie features carry additional charges if you use them. But all GEnie RoundTable (SIG) access is charged at the standard rates shown here. All connect time charges are billed in one-second increments.

GENIE CONNECT RATES

PRIME TIME
(Mon.–Fri. 8:00 A.M.–6:00 P.M.)

Speed (bps)	TOTAL (per hour	TOTAL (per minute)
300/1200	$20.00	34¢
2400	$42.50	71¢

NONPRIME TIME
(Mon.–Fri. 6:00 P.M.–8:00 A.M., and all day weekends and holidays)

Speed (bps)	TOTAL (per hour)	TOTAL (per minute)
300/1200	$ 5.00	9¢
2400	$12.50	21¢

Personal Defaults:

Choose the "About GEnie . . ." option from the TOP menu and select "Password & User Settings" from the subsidiary menu that will then appear. Follow the resulting menus and instructions. Alternatively, you may enter either M 905 or the word SETUP to reach the terminal setup menu directly. Note that page numbers such as page 905 are subject to change. To eliminate pauses, set your terminal page length to 0 lines per screen.

Scram Command:

A true BREAK (250 milliseconds or longer). If your comm program cannot generate a true BREAK, you may select any single ASCII character to serve as your scram command. This is done in the terminal SETUP area described under "Personal Defaults," above.

Sign-off Command: BYE

Protocols: XMODEM, XMODEM = 1K (matches ProComm's YMODEM), and YMODEM (matches ProComm's YMODEM = batch).

Special Notes:

GEnie supports both 7/E/1 and 8/N/1 comm parameters. It senses your settings through the series of capital H's (three or more separated by a pause of at least one tenth of a second) you send after you connect to the system. If you sign on 8/N/1, do not be disturbed by any garbage characters that appear next to the U# = prompt. Simply pretend they are not there. At 7/E/1, no garbage characters will appear.

If you're a real clever Jack or Jane you might be tempted to set your Hayes-compatible intelligent modem to handle the local echo by sending it (ATF0). Don't do it. XMODEM transfers require a straight shot from host to local system, without interference from a well-intentioned though misguided smart modem. Use your comm program to toggle your local echo on instead.

Capsule Overview

We haven't checked with the powers that be, but we suspect they would probably endorse the following quick handle for their system: If you like CompuServe, you'll *love* GEnie. Why? Because you can get much of what CompuServe offers and save 60 percent over CompuServe's nonprime connect-time rate (9¢ a minute versus 22¢) in the process.

That's a powerful argument. And although never stated as pointedly as this, GEnie has not exactly been shy about making it. The online community has responded enthusiastically. People haven't been deserting CompuServe in droves, but after building its subscribership to some 63,000 people in its first 18 months of operation, GEnie and its powerful parent must be the cause of at least some concern at H&R Block, the owner of CompuServe. (By the end of 1987, GEnie had 86,400 subscribers; by March 16, 1988, subscribership had topped the 100,000 mark.) GEnie officials report that the system is growing at about 1500 subscribers per month. All of which is likely to be good for consumers since competition usually leads to greater value and lower prices.

The similarities between the two systems are neither superficial nor accidental. In the first place, like CompuServe, General Electric has for many years operated a remote data processing business (GEIS) that was vastly underused during nonbusiness hours. Since such systems have to be up and running round the clock, offering a consumer-oriented service during nonbusiness hours provides a way to earn additional income with very little additional investment. GEnie is available at all hours, but a quick glance at the rate schedule above leaves no doubt as to when they would prefer to have you on the system. A differential of 25¢ per minute is a strong inducement to use the system primarily during nonbusiness hours.

The reason the similarities are not accidental is that GEnie's general manager, and one of the creative forces behind its design and implementation, is William H. Louden. Mr. Louden has been involved with online information utilities from the beginning. He was the second person to take out a CompuServe subscription back in the 1970s, and by 1980 he was working for the company. Over the next four years Bill Louden was involved in developing and marketing CompuServe's Consumer Information Service and in organizing the system's SIGs. In 1984 he joined Caribou Systems, a company that planned to set up local online services in various cities. Shortly after that, General Electric asked him to design and implement its as-yet-unnamed consumer information service.

Mr. Louden cheerfully acknowledges that in shape and substance GEnie owes a lot to CompuServe. "What we chose to concentrate on is what we knew from experience made money," he says. "I think we're five years smarter now than we were in 1980," Mr. Louden said when GEnie went live October 1, 1985. "The business is five years more mature, and we can better pinpoint the niches that are of greatest interest to consumers."

On GEnie those niches include the LiveWire CB simulator; the Business Band Real-Time Conferencing system; GE Mail, including both electronic and hard-copy delivery options; a variety of classic multiplayer games; bulletin boards; movie reviews; the Grolier encyclopedia; American Airlines EAASY (sic) SABRE travel service; financial information and stock quotes; and much more. Most important of all, however, are the RoundTables (RTs), GEnie's version of the SIG.

Sign On and Move to the Treasure Room

When you sign on to GEnie you will be greeted by several brief announcements. GEnie will then check your electronic mailbox to see if anyone has sent you a letter. GEnie does this automatically. There is no need for you to tell it to do so as part of your setup or personal profile. Whether there is mail waiting or not, you will next see GEnie's TOP menu:

```
            The Consumer Information Service
                  from General Electric
                    Copyright (C)

              You have 4 letters waiting.

    GEnie              TOP              Page      1


                  GE Information Services


     1. About GEnie . . .      2. New on GEnie

     3. GE Mail                4. LiveWire CB

     5. Computing              6. Travel

     7. Finance                8. Shopping

     9. News                  10. Games

    11. Professional          12. Leisure

    13. Reference             14. Logoff

        Enter #, <P>revious, or <H>elp? IBM
```

You might think that the first selection here, "About GEnie . . ." probably contains the typical PR department material describing what a wonderful decision you have made in becoming a system subscriber. Instead, it leads to a 12-item menu called "GEnie Help & Information" and thus is likely to be very important to first-time subscribers. Among the most important selections on that menu are the index of services, the rates, and the GEnie Online Manual. The index is particularly helpful since it can be searched by keyword. Thus, if you opt to search on the keyword ROUNDTABLE, the system will prepare a list of all available GEnie RTs for you. You can reach the system's index feature as described here, or by keying in INDEX at any system prompt.

Command words, or keywords as GEnie refers to them, are a quick way to zip around the system. As you can see, we entered the command word IBM at the TOP menu prompt instead of choosing a menu selection. This caused the following to appear:

GEnie   IBM   Page 514
IBM PC & Compatibles RoundTables

    1. IBM PC RT
    2. QMODEM RT
    3. Softronics Products RT
    4. TeleVision Products RT
    5. Microsoft Windows Developers RT
    6. DATASTORM RT

Enter #, <P>revious, or <H>elp? 1

Here we chose the main IBM PC RoundTable. The other RTs are focused mainly on product support and we will leave you to explore them on your own. The first time you enter an RT, you will be asked if you want to join. By all means do so. There is no membership charge and no difference in connect-time rates. You will be greeted by name and then you will see:

```
-----------------------------------
Welcome to the IBM PC RoundTable!
------------ Hosted by ------------
Charles Strom (GEMail STROM)
David Kozinn (GEMail D.KOZINN)
Paul Homchick (GEMail HOMCHICK)
& Dick Flanagan (GEMail WGOLD)
-----------------------------------

→ Real-Time-Conference Schedule ←
Wednesdays at 21:00 EST, PC-VCO Conference
Sundays at 21:30 Eastern, General Meeting
Be sure to bring your FACE on Wednesdays!
         *         *         *
Please refer to menu choice #12 on Page 616 if you
need help with ARC, LBR, ZOO, and sQueezed files.
         *         *         *
Refer to #5782 for file uploading guidelines.
Refer to #3522 for downloading help.
Refer to # 5993 for help with the GEnie BBS.

5 Members in Conference


GEnie          IBMPC          Page 615
IBM PC RoundTable by Charles Strom
Library: ALL Libraries
```

1. IBM PC RoundTable Bulletin Board
2. IBM PC Real-Time Conference
3. IBM Software Libraries
4. About the RoundTable
5. RoundTable News   880712
6. Feedback to Sysops

Enter #, <P>revious, or <H>elp?3

This is the RT's main menu. (See Chapter 16 and the Glossbrenner's Choice GEnie disk for the programs necessary to "bring your FACE" to a GEnie RT meeting.) As you can see, the RT's available selections follow the classic SIG floorplan.

What we want from the above menu are the IBM Software Libraries. That selection leads to the following:

GEnie   Page 616
        IBM PC Software Library
        Library: ALL Libraries

1. Description of this Library
2. Directory of files
3. Search File Directory
4. Browse through files
5. Upload a new file
6. Download a file
7. Delete a file you own
8. Set Software Library
9. Save Current Software Library
10. Instructions for Software Exchange
11. Directory of New Files
12. Explanation of Suffixes

Enter #, <P>revious, or <H>elp?

There are a number of things to notice about this menu. First, it is on "Page 616." We have taken the long way around to get here, but if you wanted to, you could have keyed in M 616 (for "move to page 616") at the TOP menu prompt and been spirited here instantly. Better still, you could have told GEnie you wanted it to take you here at the same time you were signing on. If your user ID is ABCD1234 and your password is FISHWIFE and you want to go to page 616 immediately after sign-on, you could respond to the U#= prompt by keying in: ABCD1234,FISHWIFE,616.

Second, notice the line directly beneath the menu title reading "Library: ALL Libraries." The RT classifies its programs in separate virtual libraries. You can tell the system to focus on only one of them by choosing selection 8 "Set Software Library," and responding to the subsequent menu of library names. If you do so, the system will limit its searching and browsing (selections 3 and 4 above) to that particular library. However, the option of dealing with all of a SIG's libraries at once is a major GEnie advantage, and to follow the method we are about to recommend you'll want to leave the setting at ALL.

Mounting a Surgical Strike

At this writing there is no way to obtain a complete list of keywords in the software libraries on GEnie, so the best thing to do is to obtain a list of every file in the library. You can do this by choosing 2 "Directory of files" from the menu. But that is not the best approach.

As noted in Chapter 6, the sysops of this RoundTable have prepared a master file listing every program in the library. Actually, there are currently three files of interest: LIBFILE1.ARC, LIBFILE2.ARC, and LIBFILES.ZOO. Each contains the same kind of information provided by the "Directory of files" selection, but because they have been compressed into archives, you can download them in less than half the time.

LIBFILE1.ARC contains a one-line listing for every file on the RT, except those in library 7 (games). These can be found in LIBFILE2.ARC. LIBFILES.ZOO contains *everything* in all of the RT libraries. The RT sysops decided to break things up this way because the archived files have become so large that users who don't have a hard disk would not be able to expand them onto a single floppy disk. Because policies, file numbers, and filenames can change, we suggest that you opt to search the RT using the keyword LIBFILES. You can do this by selecting item 3 from the menu shown earlier and following the resulting prompts.

Once you have downloaded your chosen file, you will need two utility programs to get to the stage where you can search the library list with Vernon Buerg's LIST.COM. First, you will need the appropriate archive extractor program. This could be ARCE.COM or PKXARC.COM for ARC files, or ZOO.EXE for ZOO files. (See Chapters 2 and 16 for more information.)

All three files extract into dBASE database file format. Thus LIBFILES.ZOO produces LIBFILES.DBF. If you have Ashton-Tate's dBASE program, you can bring this file right into it and search it that way. However, we feel the fastest, cheapest way to search this file is to convert it to a text file. To do this, you will need a program called SLF.EXE. Written by Joseph Vest, this is a program to "Search Libfiles." It is not terribly convenient to use, but it does do a nice job. Its principal value for our purposes, however, is that it has the power to convert LIBFILES.DBF into a pure text file.

Copy SLF.EXE into the same hard disk directory where LIB-FILES.DBF can be found. Then enter the command: SLF /O:LIB-FILES.TXT. The program automatically looks for LIBFILES.DBF, though you can tell it to look for something else. And, of course, you can output (/O) to any filename you choose. Once LIBFILES.TXT has been created, you're home free. This file can be searched quickly and efficiently with LIST.COM.

You can download the ZOO extractor and SLF20.ARC (the version current at this time) from GEnie, of course. But you will also find these files on the Glossbrenner's Choice GEnie disk discussed in Chapter 16. That disk also contains the complete PC-VCO package for "visual conferencing" on GEnie and other systems.

Downloading from GEnie

The LIBFILES files are updated every week, and although their assigned file numbers may change, the filename is always the same. Thus to obtain a copy, select 6 (download a file) from the library menu. That causes a prompt for the file's number or name to appear. Key in LIB-FILES.ZOO, if that is the one you want. The file description and keyword list will be displayed. You will then be given an opportunity to download it or quit:

Enter number, or name of file? LIBFILES.ZOO

****
Number: 10435 Name: LIBFILES.ZOO
Address: HOMCHICK Date: nnnnnn
Approximate # of Bytes: 264600
Number of Accesses: 63 Library: 1
****
Description:

There are many programs in Category One that will help you use this file. You DO NOT Need dBASE!!

This is a dBASE III file containing the directory of ALL files on the IBM RoundTable as of the upload date. This file is updated weekly. See # 8907 for a program to sort (7 ways), search and print this file, or #'s 9093, 5686, and 8638 for ways to turn it into ASCII and/or search it. (This file contains all R/T files through #10382). LIBFILE1.ARC contains only libraries 2, 4, 5, 6, 8 and 13, while LIBFILE1.ARC contains the directory for libraries 1, 3, 7, 9, 10, 11 and 12.
Keywords: LIBFILES.DQF,LIBFILES.DBF,LIBFILES, DIR, FILES, DBASE

File: LIBFILES.ZOO is a BINARY File.

Press <RETURN> to skip, <D>ownload, <L>ist, or <Q>uit.
?

Take a moment now to look at the file header. You'll notice that like all GEnie files, this one has been assigned a unique reference number (10435). Notice too that at over 64K this file will take a while to download. The file will result in a single LIBFILES.DBF file over 500K long. Notice too that it is "a BINARY file," which is GEnie shorthand for "You will need to use the XMODEM protocol to download this file."

Fortunately, because GEnie implements XMODEM (CRC or checksum) at the local node, transfers go very quickly. We haven't seen the benchmark test results that are said to prove that GEnie XMODEM transfers are three to four times faster than those of other systems, but qualitatively, the system certainly seems faster.

FreeTip: You need perform this massive download only once. At the same time they prepare LIBFILES.ZOO, the sysops also prepare a file called LIBNEW.ARC containing only those files added during the week. This file is typically smaller than 5K and can thus be downloaded quickly. As your DOS manual will tell you, to tack one file onto another (concatenate), you have only to key in COPY FILE-A+FILE-B FILE-AB at your DOS prompt. You might consider doing this with each week's update file and the LIB-FILES master list file.

FreeTip: If you use ProComm and you have that program set to automatically respond to a CompuServe inquiry regarding B protocol capabilities, be sure to set that feature to off before downloading from GEnie. To do this, key in [<Alt><S>] in ProComm and look at the terminal setup section. If you forget to do this, no real harm will be done. But we have found that such a setting causes a minor problem at the end of a download. GEnie fails to automatically move on to the next step at this point. So give it a push by hitting your <Enter> key.

FreeTip: GEnie IBM RT members have been generous, though not always successful, in the programs they have prepared to help fellow users make the most of LIBFILES.DBF. Some of these programs were noted in the description of LIBFILES.ARC given above. Here is a sampling, followed by our comments on what they do (or fail to do):

#5015 LFB.ARC—Pages through LIBFILES.DBF in "browse" mode. Slick windows, but no search function.

#4070 GEDBFPRN.ARC—Operative file is LIBDUMP.EXE. Prompts you with "Print all entries higher than >" then dumps the listing for each file with a higher number to the printer.

#1107 LIBMNUD8.ARC—A collection of dBASE III programs (PRG) that creates a menu to let you browse, change, delete, resequence, or print the contents of LIBFILES.DBF.

#5377 LIBMNU12.ARC—The compiled (with Clipper) version of the above collection of dBASE programs. You do not need dBASE to run this. Be warned that although you can look at files by library category, there is no search function.

Like all user-created software, these programs are bound to improve as they evolve. For a complete current list of relevant files, choose the "Search File Directory" option from the Software Library menu and use LIBRARY or LIBFILES as your keyword. You will find files to convert LIBFILES.DBF to formats usable with dBASE II, Reflex, and possibly other programs as well.

The Source

The Source
1616 Anderson Road
McLean, VA 22101
(703) 734-7500

CUSTOMER SERVICE

(800) 336-3330

In Virginia and
outside the continental
U.S.: (703) 821-8888

Customer Service Hours
(Eastern Standard Time)

Daily (except Christmas):
8:00 A.M.–1:00 A.M.

Initial Subscription:

SPECIAL DEAL

Most people who subscribe to The Source pay an initial one-time fee of $29.95, plus $3.00 to cover the shipping and handling of the manual and other documentation included in the subscription ($15.00 outside the U.S. and Canada). However, at our request, The Source has agreed to waive the entire subscription fee for readers of this book. What's more, they will give you a usage credit of $15 worth of free connect time. This special offer does *not* include The Source manual, but you can buy a copy (recommended) for $12.95, plus shipping and handling. Since the cost of the manual and the free connect time essentially offset each other, this offer is like getting a free subscription to The Source.

The offer is valid through December 31, 1989. To subscribe, call (800) 336-3366 or (703) 821-6666 during regular Eastern Standard Time business hours to order. Have your credit card number and expiration date ready. Tell the operator that you want to take advantage of the special offer associated with the following redemption number:

6450512

Monthly Minimum:

The Source has a minimum usage requirement of $10 per month. It isn't hard to use $10 in the normal course of things, but if you don't, you will still be charged $10. This charge does not include any storage space on the system. Though you probably will never need any, all storage space is extra. You may elect to pay an annual fee of $95, if you like, for a savings of $25.

Access: Telenet, SourceNet, and surcharged 800 numbers.

Rates:

As you can see from the tables that follow, in addition to the usual prime/nonprime-time rate structure, The Source also offers a special low-rate for using most sections of its SIGs. The low rate sections include the databases, the POST Plus bulletin board, the SIG member directory, online real-time chat, and the software file library. The only SIG features to which the lower rates typically do not apply are the Participate conferencing system and SourceMail, though this can vary from SIG to SIG.

SOURCE CONNECT RATES
(Packet-switching costs are *included* in the rates given below)

PRIME TIME
(Mon.—Fri. 7:00 A.M.—6:00 P.M.)

Speed (bps)	Standard Connect Time (per hour)	(per minute)	Special SIG Rate (per hour)	(per minute)
300	$21.60	36¢	$10.80	18¢
1200	$25.80	43¢	$13.80	23¢
2400	$27.60	46¢	$15.00	25¢

NONPRIME TIME
(Mon.—Fri. 6:00 P.M.—7:00 A.M., and all day weekends and holidays)

Speed (bps)	Standard Connect Time (per hour)	(per minute)	Special SIG Rate (per hour)	(per minute)
300	$ 8.40	14¢	$ 6.00	10¢
1200	$10.80	18¢	$ 7.80	13¢
2400	$12.00	20¢	$ 9.00	15¢

Personal Defaults:

At this writing, there is no way to create a permanent set of user defaults in the IBMSIG or on the main Source system. On the main Source system, the best you can do is key in a menu item number selection, followed by a space, followed by PRINT to cause a continuous scroll. It is no longer possible in most Source features to eliminate pauses by responding to the -MORE- prompt with NOCRT or NOSCROLL.

Within the SIG, keying in LEN and WID will let you set your page length and page width for the duration of the session. Keying in SCROLL ON or .SCROLL ON once will eliminate pauses for the duration of the SIG session. You must do this every time you enter the IBMSIG, however. The SET command (for permanent SIG defaults) is not supported in the IBMSIG at this time.

Scram Command: BREAK or Control-P

Sign-off: Enter Q to quit to command level and key in OFF at the arrow prompt.

Protocols:

Kermit in both traditional ("classic") and sliding-window versions (a.k.a. "Super Kermit"). Also XMODEM (checksum version only).

Capsule Overview

The Source is probably the slickest, smoothest, most user friendly of the six systems profiled in this chapter. As well it should be. Introduced at Spring COMDEX (Computer Dealers Exposition) in June 1979, a year during which personal computer sales totaled slightly more than half a million units, The Source is not only the oldest information utility, it is the system that invented the business. The Source was designed from the ground up to serve consumers, and its clean menus and helpful prompts remain as evidence of this original intent.

Although The Source in recent years has made a concerted effort to court business users—according to a 1985 survey some 25 percent of subscribers are company presidents, senior vice presidents, vice presidents, directors, or business owners—computer users of all types will find much to interest them on the system. News, weather, sports, published opinion and commentary, online stock trading and investment monitoring, games, travel, electronic shopping, probably the best electronic mail system, and unquestionably the best computerized conferencing system (Participate), are all available.

Source Telecomputing Corporation, or STC as it is often known in the online community, was started by entrepreneurs. A year later, the Reader's Digest Association, Inc. purchased a controlling interest in the firm. Then, after seven years, Reader's Digest sold the company to the venture capital firm of Welsh, Carson, Anderson and Stowe (WCAS) in April 1987. Along the way, The Source has achieved a subscribership of some 100,000 computer users worldwide.

It seems likely that the firm's subscriber base would be much larger were it not for the fact that The Source was slow to cut its initial subscription fee. At a time when CompuServe and other competitors were (and are) essentially giving away their subscriptions like safety razor companies giving away razors, The Source was charging an initial fee of $100. Combine that with the $10 monthly minimum requirement and you are in effect asking your prospective customers to spend $220 for a service most only vaguely understand, let alone feel they need. Hindsight perfects the vision, of course, but in retrospect CompuServe's original low-budget, demand-driven approach to its offerings seems positively inspired. It has netted hundreds of thousands of subscribers, most of whom would have a hard time *not* spending $10 a month just in the normal course of things.

At the same time, there can be no denying that The Source is the Cadillac of systems. The documentation supplied with each subscription is both copious and elegant. The Source New Member Kit contains a 20-page booklet listing the various services and the commands needed to access them. There is also a quick reference card covering major system commands, a large (22 by 15 inches) schematic showing the major menus and how they are connected, and other materials to get you online quickly. The Source manual is gorgeous and includes color-coded die-cut tabs for easy reference. Subscribers also receive the monthly "SourceWorld" newsletter and free user guides called "Source Quick Reference Cards" for most popular services. Toll-free customer service is available 17 hours a day, 364 days a year, and the staff are both friendly and helpful. The system itself is comfortable, even plushy, to use. In short, you really do get what you pay for with The Source.

In the past, however, like some older Cadillac models The Source has been a bit slow getting up to speed. While its competitors were raking in the long green from CB simulators and SIGs and vigorously expanding and improving these features, The Source offered only a one-on-one real-time CHAT feature. All that began to change in April 1986, however, with the introduction of the IBM SIG, the Kermit/Super Kermit and XMODEM protocols, and real-time multiperson CHAT. And while the wheel's still in spin, it is possible that STC's change of ownership will mark a return to the innovative traditions of its past.

Sign On and Move to the Treasure Room

As with all systems, The Source offers both a series of connected menus and a command mode. The two run on parallel tracks and you can hop from one to the other almost at will. It is important to point out, however, that with the exception of the SIGs, commands cannot be entered from a menu prompt on the main system. You must enter Q to "quit" the menus and get to the arrow prompt, and then enter a command, like IBMSIG. For example, here is the menu that will greet you when you sign on. Notice that we quit immediately and told the system to take us to the IBMSIG:

```
Welcome, you are connected to THE SOURCE.
Last login Wednesday, DD MMM YY HH:MM:SS.

Copyright (c) Source Telecomputing Corp. All Rights Reserved.

Now at 1200 baud.
```

```
Play Trivia in CHAT
on Tuesday at 1 pm EDT.
Type CHAT for Details.


—>

WELCOME TO THE SOURCE

1 Tutorial and Intro. <INTRO> **FREE**
2 Menu of Services <MENU>
3 Member Information <INFO> **FREE**
4 Today From The Source <TODAY>
5 News Glimpses <NEWSBITS> **FREE**

Enter item number, <H>elp or <Q>uit: Q

Have a nice day . . .
—> IBMSIG
```

There will be a brief pause while the system routes you to the computer that holds the IBM SIG. You will then see a series of SIG bulletins prepared by the sysop, followed by this menu:

```
Welcome ABC123 to the IBMSIG Main menu! <IBMSIG>

<Precede menu item names with IBMSIG at the —> prompt for direct
access.>

(* indicates special, LOW rates.)      Updated:

1  *  PC User's Databases         [USERS]
2  *  Please use POSTPLUS         [POST]
3  *  Post Messages (New Q & A)   [POSTPLUS]
4  *  Member's Directory          [MEMBERS]
5  *  On-line CHATS (Real-Time)   [CHATS]
6     PARTI Conference System     [PARTI]
7  *  IBMSIG File Library         [LIBRARY]
8     SourceMail                  [SMAIL]
9  *  PC Products/Support         [PRODUCTS]
10 *  Information about IBMSIG     [INFO]       29 Jun 1989

IBMSIG Main menu - Enter item number, <Q>uit or <H>elp: SCROLL
ON

Scroll is on.

IBMSIG Main menu - Enter item number, <Q>uit or <H>elp: 7
```

You can enter commands at the prompt level within the SIGS, and as you can see, the first command we issued was SCROLL ON. This is a good habit to develop in any case, but it is particularly important when you enter the SIG for the very first time. That's because you will be doing a lot of capture buffer downloading of SIG instructions and help files, and if you don't enter SCROLL ON, the system will pause every 24 lines or so and prompt you for an <Enter>.

The first time you use the IBM SIG, we strongly suggest that you begin with the selection called "Information about IBMSIG." This leads to a subsidiary menu with all manner of information describing the features on the main menu and how to best use them. For our purposes here, however, we're going to go directly to the treasure house, the IBMSIG File Library.

When you choose this selection, you will see several notes from the sysop designed to clue you in to some of the library's secrets. The most important secret is a file called LIBSCAN.ARC. This file contains a listing of every program in the database as of the end of the previous month. Companion files in the form LIBmmmyy.ARC contain listings of the new files uploaded each month. The file LIBMAR89.ARC, for example, would contain all of the files uploaded during March 1989. Thus, if you downloaded LIBSCAN.ARC in February, you would only have to download LIBMAR89.ARC to update your comprehensive list of the files. The sysop uploads the new LIBSCAN and LIBmmmyy files on the first or second of each month.

After the library-related bulletins have been displayed, you will see the following menu:

```
IBMSIG File Library <IBMSIG>   [LIBRARY]        Updated:

1   Search the File Library     [SEARCH]
2   Download a file by name     [DOWNLOAD]
3   Submit (Upload) a File      [SUBMIT]
4   How to . . . (Download, etc.) [INFO]        DD MMM YYYY
5   Software Disclaimer         [DISCLAIM]      DD MMM YYYY

IBMSIG File Library menu - Enter item number,
[Item name], <P>revious, <M>ain menu or <H>elp: 2

DOWNLOAD A FILE BY NAME

Please enter the name of the file/package you would like to download.
File name: LIBSCAN.ARC

Please select a protocol for download.
<KE>rmit, <XM>odem, <DI>splay: KE
```

Here, we've chosen to "Download a file by name." The reference to "package" in the resulting prompt ("Please enter the name of the file/package . . .") is confusing. It has nothing to do with the fact that an ARC file is a package of sorts. Instead, it refers to a commercial program as in "an accounting package." The word is used here because the same software that makes the SIGs possible can be used by marketers to sell software online. This is also the reason why you will encounter "PRODUCT_NAME = FILENAME.EXT" when searching the SIG, as we'll see in a moment.

After entering the filename (LIBSCAN.ARC), you are given a choice of protocols. We entered KE for Kermit. When the file is safely on your disk, you can sign off the system by entering Q at each successive prompt until you reach the main system command level. Then key in OFF. It would be nice if you could sign off without backing out of the SIG first, but at this writing, there is no way to do this. Once offline, expand the ARC file with PKXARC or ARC-E or comparable program, and search it with LIST.COM.

FreeTip: IBMSIG member Ben Bacon has written a program called LIBSERCH.ARC (38K) that is worth special mention. This program is specifically designed to work with the comprehensive and monthly LIBSCAN files. When booted, LIBSERCH looks and works exactly like the library searching feature offered by The Source. For speed and flexibility, we prefer LIST.COM as described previously, but you might want to take a look at LIBSERCH.ARC nonetheless.

Let's assume you've found a file in LIBSCAN.TXT (the main file in LIBSCAN.ARC) called ARCHIVE3.ARC. It's supposed to offer fast and efficient backups of your hard disk, but you want to know more before downloading it. So you sign on to the system, get to the IBM File Library menu, and choose the selection to "Search the File Library." You will then see the following:

```
SEARCH IBMSIG

Select by
<K>eyword, <D>ate, <U>ser id,
<FI>le name or <ALL>: FI

Enter File name: ARCHIVE3.ARC

1 item(s) found for
PRODUCT_NAME = ARCHIVE3.ARC
```

```
<N>arrow <E>xpand <REC>ap
<R>ead <SC>an <C>ancel: R
Screen 1
Item number:          1
File name:            archive3.arc
Subject:              HARD DISK BACKUP ARCHIVE 3.0A FAST
                      EFFICIENT UTILITY
User ID:              SIG004
Date:                 24 Apr 1987
File length:          20480
File type:            IMAGE
Downloaded:           19
```

Description: ARCHIVE3.ARC is a 20,480 byte archive that contains what some people have waited for for quite awhile. Its ARCHIVE 3.0A, the newest release of the excellent hard disk backup and restore utility. This version of ARCHIVE has been improved to handle more files than before. This is one of the BEST hard disk backup/restore utilities in the Public Domain . . . and it just got a little better. Unpack using Arc.exe 5.1 or equivalent.

Enter <KE>rmit, <XM>odem or <DI>splay to download, or RETURN to continue or <H>elp: KE

You key in FI to tell the system you want to specify the name of a particular file. Then you enter that name (ARCHIVE3.ARC) and the system locates the program. Since you want to know more about it, you enter R to read the description. And that is what appears next. Note that the SUBJECT field is actually a list of keywords and that IMAGE is how The Source refers to binary, machine language files. The final prompt lets you select a protocol or hit <ENTER> to return to the "Select by" prompt.

Your Source manual explains the other commands for this feature. We would only add that we have shown you the long way around. Now that you know what all of the prompts and responses are, we can tell you that you could reach the same point much faster by Quitting to command level when you sign on to The Source and entering the following batch command string:

```
IBMSIG LIBRARY SEARCH FI ARCHIVE3.ARC

1 item(s) found for
PRODUCT_NAME = ARCHIVE3.ARC

<N>arrow <E>xpand <REC>ap
<R>ead <SC>an <C>ancel: R
```

As you can see, there were no intervening menus, greetings, or bulletins to eat up connect time. Zap—enter the command and you're there.

Delphi

Delphi
General Videotex Corporation
3 Blackstone Street
Cambridge, MA 02139
(617) 491-3393

CUSTOMER SERVICE

(800) 544-4005

In Massachusetts and
outside the continental
U.S.: (617) 491-3393

Customer Service Hours
(Eastern Standard Time)

Mon.–Fri.: 8:30 A.M.–9:00 P.M.
Weekends and holidays:
    11:00 A.M.–1:00 A.M.

Initial Subscription:

SPECIAL DEAL

The standard cost for a lifetime Delphi membership is $49.95. This includes a copy of *Delphi: The Official Guide* by Michael Banks (512 pages; Brady Books, 1987). This book is Delphi's main manual and it includes a pull-out quick reference command card. It is available in bookstores for $19.95. Also included in the standard subscription are two free evening hours of connect time, a $14.40 value.

However, we can save you some money. By special arrangement with Delphi, readers of this book can subscribe for $29.95. The special subscription includes the lifetime membership, the book by Michael Banks, and one free evening hour of connect time (worth $7.20).

You may signup by calling the customer service numbers above or by calling your local Telenet or Tymnet node or (617) 576-0862 for 300/1200; (617) 576-2981 for 2400 bps. At the Telenet @ prompt enter C DELPHI. At Tymnet's "please log in:" prompt enter DELPHI. When you are prompted for "Username:" key in JOINDELPHI. When prompted to enter your password, key in

GLOSSBRENNER. Delphi has assured us that this password will remain valid indefinitely.

The online sign up option includes a free five-minute demo of the system and the opportunity to download the current rates. There is no obligation, and you can terminate the session at any time. Note that when you see the "More?" prompt, simply hitting <Enter> is the same as keying in Y or YES and <Enter>.

Access: Tymnet, Telenet, and direct dial.

Rates:

Delphi has always had an aggressive rate policy. It was the first utility to offer 2400-bps access, and the first to eliminate the extra charge for using 1200 bps instead of 300. At this writing, it is the only utility to charge the same rate for 300, 1200, *or* 2400 bps communications. The company has also traditionally offered "Summer Specials" for late night access during July and August. Delphi Advantage rates cited below are explained in the Special Notes section.

DELPHI CONNECT RATES
(Packet-switching costs are *included* in the rates given below)

PRIME ("OFFICE") TIME
(Mon.–Fri. 7:00 A.M.–6:00 P.M.)

Speed (bps)	Standard Connect Time (per hour)	(per minute)	Delphi Advantage Rate (per hour)	(per minute)
300/1200/2400	$17.40	29¢	$16.20	27¢

NONPRIME ("HOME") TIME
(Mon.–Fri. 6:00 P.M.–7:00 A.M., and all day weekends and holidays)

Speed (bps)	Standard Connect Time (per hour)	(per minute)	Delphi Advantage Rate (per hour)	(per minute)
300/1200/2400	$7.20	12¢	$5.40	9¢

Personal Defaults:

Set by modifying your "Profile." See "Sign-On and Setup" later in the chapter.

Scram Command:

BREAK signal (300 milliseconds or longer), preferred. A Control-O will also stop output and "fast-forward" you to the end of whatever is being displayed, though there will be a delay due to undisplayed text still in the pipeline.

Sign-off Command: BYE

Protocols: XMODEM (CRC and checksum), Kermit (classic), WXMODEM, YMODEM, and YMODEM batch.

Special Notes:

For frequent users, Delphi offers the Delphi Advantage. Under this plan, you pay a one-time fee of $19 and agree to use $24 worth of Delphi connect time per month, charged at the standard Delphi rates. After you have met that requirement, however, the special discounted rates cited in the rate table apply. You must be already be a Delphi subscriber to take advantage of this plan. At this writing, it is not available as an initial subscription option.

Capsule Overview

Delphi has long been the most innovative and flexible of all information utilities. It is the guerilla fighter of the industry, traveling light, moving fast, and hitting hard with new tactics and creative approaches to serving the growing online public. This way of doing things has both positive and negative aspects, however.

On the plus side, Delphi was the first system to offer 2400-bps communications. It has never charged more for 1200 bps and is currently the only system to have abolished all speed-related surcharges. It offered subscribers the opportunity to correspond electronically with people on other systems (The Source and CompuServe) years before CompuServe and MCI Mail announced their special interconnection.

At this writing Delphi is once again ahead of everyone else with a feature that lets PC users send messages to facsimile machines (and vice versa). Telex messages can also be delivered via fax, using Delphi as an intermediary. Indeed, the system has always placed its emphasis on people-to-people connections. Consequently, with a few exceptions, its information offerings are not unique as the utilities go.

There are news, weather, sports, and financial information features, brokerage services, travel information of all kinds (including the Official Airline Guide and EAASY SABRE), film reviews, online shopping via

Compustore and other merchants, an encyclopedia, and similar offerings. Among the exceptional features are an electronic gateway to DIALOG, the giant information system (350+ separate databases), the Boston Computer Exchange (BCE) with its scannable weekly catalog of used computer equipment Wanted and For Sale, the TII Translation Service (translations done from and to almost any language), and CAIN (Computerized AIDS Information Network).

Much of what makes the system unique lies behind the scenes. For example, Delphi is the only system to use the VAXCluster architecture for its hosts. This is a technical distinction, to be sure, but it means that you can move from one feature to another faster than you can on systems whose host computers are wired in a "daisychain" or rely on front-end processors. As a result, you will not see "Please wait" messages when you key in a command to enter a SIG or use some other feature. The cluster architecture also makes it easy to expand, and more importantly from Delphi's viewpoint, it makes it easy to implement *local* hosts.

One day, Delphi hopes to make it possible for you to connect with the system by placing a local call to a local host without using a packet-switching network. With appropriate connections and software, that local system will be linked with other Delphi systems around the continent in a network so seamless that you won't be able to tell whether the information you are viewing is coming from the main Delphi host in Cambridge or from a VAX acting as a file server in Phoenix. Delphi has already begun to implement this "distributed host" approach with a franchise in Buenos Aires.

A service of General Videotex Corporation (GVC), Delphi went live in February 1983. In 1986, according to the company, Delphi's user base grew at a rate of 288 percent, while revenue grew at a rate of 225 percent. Yet the management team, headed by founder J. Wesley Kussmaul (CEO), Daniel J. Bruns (President), and John Gilbert (Product Manager) remains small and as yet resistant to the bureaucracy that can stiffle innovation.

The Delphi SIGs were designed by John Gibney, after he left CompuServe to join GVC in 1984. Mr. Gibney essentially designed and wrote the computer code for the CompuServe SIGs during his four years with that organization. To no one's surprise, shortly after his arrival, Delphi introduced SIGs of its own.

Being innovative and responsive does have its downside, however. The documentation, while better than the initial offerings of the industry pioneers, has not always been up to snuff. Michael Banks's book is a great help. It is massive and clearly represents a step in the right direction. Hopefully the momentum will continue and the company will faithfully provide updates covering the features it introduces in years to come.

In addition, while Delphi's user interface is acceptable, some of its help texts need to be overhauled, and its menu selections need to be clarified. You'll see what we mean in a moment; but as a quick example, the rate information available online says nothing about the fact that the company charges the same rate regardless of communications speed. Yet that is the first question anyone who has been exposed to other systems is likely to ask. Certainly failing to anticipate user questions is endemic to the computer industry, but any service offering itself to the general public must be held to a higher standard.

Delphi is the only system that does not number its menu selections, so you must either key in the full name of the item you want or enough of the characters in the name to make your selection unique. This works fairly well if you're a good typist. And if you can remember menu and selection names you can key them in on a single batch command line to go directly to your destination. But for new users or hunt-and-peck typists, this approach is less convenient than conventional numbered menu items.

On the other hand, Delphi does give you an extraordinary amount of control in some areas. For example, if there is no activity from your keyboard for ten minutes, the system will automatically log you off and stop the meter. That's true for most online systems, but on Delphi, you can set your own "timeout" time. The parameters you can set for your terminal or your interaction with the Telenet or Tymnet PAD are mind boggling, though most subscribers need not concern themselves with these matters. Nor do most users need concern themselves with customizing the way the system handles XMODEM and Kermit file transfers, though this can be done as well. If you like, for example, you can tell the system you'd like XMODEM to re-try sending a block of data 20 times instead of stopping after the standard ten attempts. None of the other systems supports so many of the popular error-checking protocols.

Finally, as with the CHAT feature on The Source, you can page any user who is currently on the system to suggest a real-time conversation. And as on CompuServe, you can download a complete list of the keywords used in the SIG data libraries.

Sign-On and Setup

When you sign on to Delphi for the very first time, you will be put through a brief introductory session during which the system will help you set your terminal width and page length. To prevent interruptions and pauses, we suggest you set your page length to 0 lines. You may or may not want to take the five-minute tour that will be offered.

When you sign on the next time, you will see the greeting menu shown immediately below. Notice that we keyed in USING DELPHI to get to a subsidiary menu, from which we keyed in SETTINGS to get to the menu you can use to create your personal profile. You may or may not want to follow this track the first time you sign on, but you should definitely go to the SETTINGS menu before seriously tapping into the SIGs. You can do so from within the SIGs themselves or by entering PROFILE at almost any prompt. For clarity, we have used complete menu item names here, though as mentioned you may abbreviate any Delphi command to uniqueness when actually using the system.

```
Welcome to DELPHI
Copyright (c)
General Videotex Corporation

MAIN Menu:

Business & Finance          News-Weather-Sports
Conference                  People on DELPHI
DELPHI Mail                 Travel
Entertainment               Workspace
Groups and Clubs            Using DELPHI
Library                     HELP
Magazines & Books           EXIT
Merchants' Row

MAIN>What do you want to do? USING DELPHI

USING-DELPHI Menu:

Advice From DELPHI          Premium Services
Change Address              What's New On DELPHI
Credit Policy               Rates and Prices
Member Service              Settings (PROFILE)
DELPHI Advantage            Telex-Codes
Feedback                    Review Bills/Invoices
Guided Tour                 Past Bills/Invoices
Index                       Update Credit Card
Mail To SERVICE             Usage History
Manuals                     Worldwide Access Info
Membership Agreement        HELP
Network Info                EXIT

USING-DELPHI>(Please Select an Item)> SETTINGS

Some of your temporary settings are being restored to their
initialization values.

SETTINGS Menu:

BUSY-Mode                   PROMPT-Mode
DEFAULT-Menu                SET-High-bit
```

DOWNLOAD-Line-terminators   SLASH-Term-settings
ECHO-Mode   TERMINAL-Type
EDITOR   TIMEOUT
FILE-TRANSFERS   UTILITIES
KERMIT-SETTINGS   WIDTH (Columns)
LENGTH (Lines/page)   XMODEM-SETTINGS
NETWORK-PARAMETERS   HELP
PASSWORD (Change)   EXIT

SETTINGS>What would you like to set?

If you need an explanation of any of these items, key in HELP or HELP followed by the item name (HELP TERMINAL-Type, HELP BUSY-Mode, etc.). Assuming you have already set your LENGTH to 0 lines per page, the two most important options here are "DEFAULT-Menu" and "FILE-TRANSFERS." The first lets you create the equivalent of an AUTOEXE.BAT file for Delphi. That is, you can create a file that issues a series of commands to the system automatically each time you sign on. The key is to know the names of the menus and menu items that lie in the path to your destination. If you want to go directly to the PC Compatibles/IBM Special Interest Group whenever you sign on, key DEFAULT from this menu and respond to the prompt with: GROUPS PC.

The FILE-TRANSFERS option here lets you set your default method of error-checking. As we will see in a moment, after you have read the description of a given file, you will be prompted to download it or move on to the next file in the queue. If you elect to download the file, the error-checking protocol Delphi uses will be determined by this setting. Of course, you can change your chosen download method temporarily at any time (key in /FX__METHOD). But having a permanent download method preference setting is more convenient, for it saves you from having to specify a protocol each and every time you want to snare a file.

Move to the Treasure House

Keying in GROUPS at the main menu or GO GROUPS at most other prompts will take you to the groups and clubs menu. At this writing there are some 24 SIGs to choose from, including one for music (electronic and conventional), portable computers, science fiction, writers, model builders, computer artists, and game players. The two of greatest interest here, however, are the PC Compatibles/IBM SIG and the Tandy PC SIG. (The two are linked by an electronic gateway, so once you enter one you can move directly to the other and back again.)

The first time you select a SIG, you will be asked whether you wish to join. SIG membership is free, and this is something you definitely should do. When you enter the SIG, at this writing, you will see a list of newly uploaded files. This list will appear once each time it is updated. After that, you can view it by selecting the ANNOUNCEMENTS item from the main SIG menu:

PC Compatibles Menu:

Announcements	SoftSector Services
Conference	Topic Descriptions
Databases	Who's Here
Entry Log	Workspace
Forum (Messages)	Help
MAIL (Electronic)	Exit
Member Directory	Classified Ads
Poll	Questions & Feedback
Set Preferences	Tandy SIG PORTAL
PCM Services	

PC Compatibles>What do you want to do? DATABASES

As you can see, we have chosen DATABASES. We'll leave you to explore the other selections on your own. We should point out though, that among other things, the "Set Preferences" section lets you select or deselect your default topics (filing categories) for using the SIG message board ("Forum"). The normal default is for all topics; however, you can narrow the focus if you like. Once you have deselected a topic, messages in that category will not be scanned when you are searching the message base.

We bring this up because the SIG databases use the identical list of topics to categorize their contents, which makes things a bit confusing. The thing to keep in mind is that the "Set Preferences" option applies only to the forum message exchange, not to the databases. When you key in DATABASES at the above prompt, here is what you will see:

Databases Available Menu:

General Information	Utilities
Archives	Demo Programs
Business	Soft Sector Magazine ($)
Education	PCM Magazine ($)
Home & Games	Tandy Specific
Programming	Sanyo Specific
Telecommunications	IBM PC Specific

TOPIC>Which topic? UTILITIES

Despite the confusion caused by the word "topic" in the prompt, this is the menu you use to select the database you wish to tap. Here, we've chosen the UTILITIES database. And here is what will be displayed:

Utilities Menu:

Directory of Groups	Set Topic
Read (and Download)	Submit
Search (by Keyword)	Workspace
Narrow search	Help
Widen search	Exit

DBASES:Uti> (Dir, Read, Set, Exit) SEARCH

This is the menu format of every database ("topic") in the SIG. It is identical to the menu used to scan and read forum messages, which accounts for the confusing selections. The "Directory of Groups" actually generates a directory of database files (a single line per program containing the file's name, type, date of upload, and uploader's user name). "Set Topic" here actually means "select a different database," and choosing that selection will generate the list of databases ("topics") we just looked at.

Download the Keyword List

The first step here is to download the complete list of keywords for the database of interest. You do this by selecting the "Search (by Keyword)" option. The system will tell you that it is "Starting a new search." Then you will be asked "Which keyword (? for help):". At this point, enter the question mark. A brief help message will be displayed, followed by this prompt:

Which keyword (? for list) ?

Utilities Primary Keywords (Subtopics) Available:
MSDOS
Subroutines
Misc.

100 (2)
1000 (485)
8087 (1)
ACCELERATOR (3)
ACHIM (2)
ALARM (3)
ALGORITHMS (1)
ALIGNMENT (1)

When the second prompt for a keyword appears, open your capture buffer and key in a question mark (?) to get the complete list of keywords for the database. When the list has been displayed, close your buffer or otherwise write the contents to disk. Then sign off, print out the entire list, and go to work circling likely candidates.

When you have your list of candidates ready, you can speed back to the database by signing on and keying in GROUPS PC DATABASES UTILITIES (or whichever database you want to use) at the main menu. When you reach the menu for the particular database, key in SEARCH or SEARCH followed by your chosen keyword. If we assume you've chosen ACCELERATOR as your keyword, the dialogue will look like this:

```
DBASES:Uti> (Dir, Read, Set, Exit) SEARCH

Starting a new search

Which keyword (? for list): ACCELERATOR
ACCELERATOR: 3 found.

DIRECTORY, READ, WIDEN, and NARROW will now operate
on the selected items.
```

Notice the line above that indicates that READ will operate on the selected items. That's all you have to key in to read the description of the selected files. As you can see, there are three files with ACCELERATOR as a keyword, and after the description of the first one has been displayed, you'll see this prompt:

```
ACTION> (Next, Down, Xm, List):
```

The "Next" command would display the next file description in the queue. The DOWN command causes Delphi to initiate an error-checked file transfer, using the protocol that you have specified as your default. The Xm command causes the system to automatically begin an XMODEM transfer. And the LIST command will scroll the file out on your screen if it is a text file.

When you have finished downloading a file, you may read the description of the next file in the queue, or do something else, including signing off the system by keying in BYE.

BIX

BYTE Information Exchange
   (BIX)
One Phoenix Mill Lane
Peterborough, NH 03458-9990
(603) 924-9281

CUSTOMER SERVICE

From the continental U.S.
   and Canada: (800) 227-2983
In New Hampshire and
   outside the continental
   U.S.: (603) 924-7681

Customer Service Hours
(Eastern Standard Time)

Mon.–Fri. 8:30 A.M.–11:00 P.M.

Initial Subscription:

SPECIAL DEAL

The usual one-time charge for starting a BIX subscription is $39. However, we have arranged with BIX for readers of this book to sign up for $25, for a savings of $14. You can subscribe immediately by calling your local Tymnet node and keying in BIX at the "please log in:" prompt. When BIX prompts you for "Name?", key in this code word:

UG.BKGLOSS

Then simply follow the instructions that will appear. Be sure to have your Visa, American Express, or MasterCard card ready. (Invoiced or prepaid accounts are also available.) And since you will be asked to select the name you wish to use on the system at that time, it might be a good idea to think about it beforehand since all user names are permanent. For the number of your nearest Tymnet node, call (800) 336-0149.

Access: Tymnet and direct dial.

Rates:

BIX rates are the same, regardless of whether you are communicating at 300 or 1200 bits per second. At this writing, the system does not support higher speeds.

Note that if you call via direct dial, you pay BIX for connect time only (no Tymnet surcharge). Whatever long distance charges you incur are between you and your phone company. BIX calculates your charges to the nearest second, and there is no minimum charge per sign on.

BIX CONNECT RATES

PRIME TIME
(Mon.—Fri.: 6:00 A.M.—7:00 P.M.)

Speed (bps)	BIX connect time (per hour)	Tymnet charges (per hour)	TOTAL (per hour)	TOTAL (per minute)
300/1200	$12.00	$8.00	$20.00	34¢

NONPRIME TIME
(Mon.—Fri.: 7:00 P.M.—6:00 A.M., and all day weekends and holidays)

Speed (bps)	BIX connect time (per hour)	Tymnet charges (per hour)	TOTAL (per hour)	TOTAL (per minute)
300/1200	$9.00	$2.00	$11.00	19¢

Personal Defaults:

Set by modifying your "Profile." Your Profile is a recorded series of commands that are executed automatically each time you sign on, much as the batch file AUTOEXEC.BAT is executed each time you boot up your computer. Key in EDIT PROFILE at the Main area colon prompt (:). Enter L for "List," to view current settings. The system will give you a list of available commands. We recommend keying in C for "Clear" to produce a prompt for a new line (input→). Key in the items shown here:

Begin entering your text. When you are finished enter '.<CR>'.

```
input→ opt verbose
input→ edit verbose
input→ term width 80
input→ term pagelen 0
input→ Q
input→ .
```

Your BIX manual will explain the first two items. The next two, as you can guess, set your terminal width to 80 columns and your page length to 0 to eliminate pauses. The Q tells the system to quit the Options section after this portion of your Profile has been run each time. The period gets you out of input mode. The next thing you see will be "Command →," and here you should key in W to tell the system to write your new profile to disk, then Q to quit Profile editing and return to the main system.

Scram Command: Control-C or a true BREAK (no more than 350 milliseconds).

Sign-off Command: BYE

Protocols: XMODEM (checksum and CRC), YMODEM, ZMODEM, and Kermit.

Special Notes:

BIX supports full duplex settings of 7/E/1 and 8/N/1, but it does *not* want you to send a line feed on carriage return.

Capsule Overview

The byte in BIX is McGraw-Hill's *BYTE* magazine, one of the original publications of the personal computer revolution (first issue: September 1975). BIX was the brainchild of Phil Lemmons, the magazine's long-time editor-in-chief, and from its conception in 1984 through its nationwide implementation in November 1985 to the present day, the system's primary focus has always been computerized conferencing and electronic messaging. BIX is designed to promote free and vigorous interaction among *BYTE* subscribers, editors, contributors, and others who are interested in computer hardware and software, particularly in the technical aspects of these and related subjects. Not incidently, the system spins off copious material for use in the pages of the magazine.

If you've never heard of computerized conferencing, you should know that such systems are essentially collections of notes or messages from various users on a variety of subjects. That's the way to begin thinking about BIX. As with all successful computerized conferencing systems, however, there are a lot of messages on a lot of subjects—far too many to simply give each note a number and expect users to deal with the entire list each time they sign on. The challenge that BIX and all such systems face is *organizing* thousands of messages on scores of topics in a logical and convenient way.

Thus, while BIX offers an area called "Mail" for private person-to-person communications and an "Options" area for customizing your interactions with the system, the heart of BIX is the "Conferences" area.

Conferences are the first level of organization, and conference titles range from ADA (a programming language named after the world's first programmer, Ada Agusta, Countess of Lovelace) to BASIC to HAM.RADIO to UNIX. There are conferences for every major brand of computer, and often separate conferences for major models. (As the BIX manual points out, the command SHOW ALL will give you a list of all conferences currently on the system.)

The next level of organization is "topics." The IBM.PC conference thus includes such topics as SOFTWARE, HARDWARE, DRIVES, PROGRAMMING, HINTS, and CLONES. The final level consists of the messages themselves. The actual messages you will want to read are stored and numbered sequentially under the topics. Thus if you wanted to see what the BIX community of IBM PC users had to say about interleave factors on hard disk drives you would first sign on to BIX and key in JOIN IBM.PC at the main system prompt. That would take you to that conference, and after some initial announcements and bulletins had appeared, you would be presented with a list of available topics and prompted for "Topic?". (You can get a list of available conference topics at any time by keying in SHOW IBM.PC and hitting <Enter>.) Keying in DRIVES would take you to that topic and put you in position to begin reading messages. The system prompt here is "Read:". At that point you would key in SEARCH and follow the succeeding prompts to enter your keyword and retrieve and read messages that matched.

We will leave you to explore the fascinations of the BIX conferencing system on your own. However, we would strongly suggest that you make joining the USER.MANUAL conference a top priority. After you have done so, select the TABLE.OF.CONT topic and key in READ 1 at the "Read:" prompt. This will present the USER.MANUAL conference topics and the numbers of the messages under those topics you will want to read for more information on various aspects of the BIX system.

The host software for BIX is based on the CoSy ("cozy") conferencing program developed at the University of Guelph in Ontario, Canada, but much of the code is being revised and improved to accommodate BIX's growing subscriber base. (By the end of 1987, BIX had over 20,000 subscribers, up from 12,000 subscribers a year earlier.) Consequently, while the system itself will remain largely the same, some of the details are likely to change.

Sign On and Move to the Treasure Room

When you sign onto BIX, you will see the following:

```
→ BYTE COSY 3.1.9 ←
----------------------------------------------------------------
----------------------------------------------------------------
   ######  ####### ###    ###
   ### #   ###     ### ##
   ######      ###     ####      (TM)
   ###   #     ###      ## ###
   #######  ####### ####    ###
----------------------------------------------------------------
----------------------------------------------------------------
BYTE Information Exchange

McGraw-Hill Information Systems Co.
Copyright (c) by McGraw-Hill Inc.

CoSy Conferencing System, Copyright (c) 1984 University of Guelph
Written by: Alastair JW Mayer

Name? GLOSSBRENNER
Password:

You have 1 mail message(s) in your in-basket,
:You are a member of 2 conference(s)
```

That's it. There is no TOP or greeting menu on the BIX system at
this time. The Main area prompt is the colon (:), and from here you can
go to the mail subsystem, go to the options area, or JOIN (go into) a
conference. You can also enter a question mark for a brief help message, and you can enter SHOW ALL for a list of all conferences on the
system. At this writing, there are over 330 of them. You may also enter
SHOW GROUPS for a list of the dozen or so categories into which the
conferences have been classified. Since COMPUTERS is one of the
groups, keying in SHOW GROUPS COMPUTERS will give you a list of
all of the computer-related conferences on the system. At this writing,
there are some 24 of them, including conferences for Tandy, AT&T,
Compaq, HP, Zenith, laptops, and three dedicated to the IBM PC (AT,
PC, and PS).

The LISTINGS "Conference" Is the Treasure Room

The free software treasure room on BIX is the LISTINGS conference.
"Conference" is a misnomer here, for in reality, LISTINGS is more of a
separate little system within BIX. In the past, this feature was con-
sciously designed to resemble a FIDO bulletin board system. At this
writing, however, the LISTINGS feature has been completely re-
vamped and is now much easier to use.

You can reach LISTINGS by "joining" it as a separate subsystem or by going through one of the computer-specific conferences. You might key in JOIN LISTINGS, for example, or JOIN IBM.PC LISTINGS.

How LISTINGS Is Organized

The LISTINGS subsystem is organized into "File Areas." These are major categories, each of which is divided into various subcategories or "Subareas." When you are in the LISTINGS subsystem, you are always in or attached to a File Area. You can switch from one File Area to another, of course, but you can never be free floating. By default, all new subscribers are automatically attached to the FROMBYTE89 (or whatever year it happens to be) File Area. (We'll show you how to change that in a moment.)

The handling of subareas is similar but slightly different. Once you have attached yourself to a particular File Area you can choose to focus on just one of the available subareas or on all of them at the same time. This is important only if you are going to be using BIX to search for software online. For example, if you are set to focus on ALL subareas, the system will search through all of the files in all subareas to find a match. If you are set to focus on, say, just the WORDPROCESSING subarea, only files in that category will be searched.

To enter the subsystem, simply key in JOIN LISTINGS or JOIN IBM.PC LISTINGS at the Main area colon prompt (:) or at the "Read:" prompt in the Conference area. Here is what you will see:

```
:JOIN LISTINGS

File Area: FROMBYTE89   Subarea: ALL   File Description: SHORT

 1.   AREA ............. Select a file area
 2.   SUBAREA ......... Select a subarea
 3.   LIST ............. List files
 4.   BROWSE.......... Browse through files
 5.   SEND ............. Send a file to BIX
 6.   RECEIVE ......... Receive a file from BIX
 7.   TYPE............. Type a file
 8.   CHECK........... Check the contents of a file
 9.   OPTIONS......... Sct options
10.   QUIT ............. Leave the listings subsystem

Selection: 1
Area name? ?

ADA              Programs and files for the Ada programming
                 language
AMIGA            Programs for the Commodore Amiga computer
```

ASK.BIX	Tips on how to BIX, telecom files, listings
ASTRONOMY	Files and programs of interest to astronomers
BENCHMARKS	BYTE's Benchmark programs
C+UNIX	C, UNIX, XENIX, and other look-alike files
COMMODORE	Programs for Commodore computers
FORTH	Programs and files for the FORTH programming language
FROMBYTE89	Programs from BYTE articles published in 1989
FROMBYTE88	Programs from BYTE articles published in 1988
FROMBYTE87	Programs from BYTE articles published in 1987
FROMBYTE86	Programs from BYTE articles published in 1986
FROMBYTE85	Programs from BYTE articles published in 1985
FROMBYTE84	Programs from BYTE articles published in 1984
HAM.RADIO	Files for ham radio operators
IBM	IBM PC-DOS and MS-DOS programs
IBM.ARC	IBM PC-DOS and MS-DOS programs in ARC format
INDEX	An index of BYTE: January 83-December 86
LISP	Programs and files for the Lisp programming language
MEDICINE	Software for medical professionals
TANDY	Tandy/Radio Shack files
TI	Programs and files for Texas Instruments computers

Notice that the first thing we entered at the "Selection:" prompt was a 1, followed by a question mark at the "Area name?" prompt. This generates a list of the various file areas that are available. (Edited here to save space.) Notice too that we are set for the FROMBYTE89 File Area, ALL subareas, and SHORT file descriptions.

Selections 4 ("BROWSE") and 8 ("CHECK") on the above menu are worthy of special mention. If you select BROWSE, you will be taken to a submenu that allows you to search for files by name or by partial name, using a wildcard character, by date, or by keyword. The system will prompt you for details, round up all matching files, and then display their descriptions in turn. After each description has been displayed, you will be able to download the relevant file, move on to the next one on the list, or do something else.

Among other things, the CHECK command lets you review the contents—including all filenames, filesizes, and creation dates—of an ARC file before you download it. This is an invaluable feature since it can save you the trouble and expense of an unnecessary download. As you know, it is often difficult to tell from an ARC file's name, upload date, or uploader-supplied description whether it contains a newer version of a favorite program or simply a copy of a version you already have. Without the CHECK command, the only way to tell is to download the ARC file and check its contents once you are offline.

Changing Your Settings

Now let's look at how to change your File Area, Subarea, and File Description length settings. To tell the system you want to attach yourself to the IBM.ARC File Area, you would key in 1 as we did before and respond to the "Area name?" prompt this way:

Area name? IBM.ARC

File Area: IBM.ARC   Subarea: ALL   File Description: SHORT

```
 1.   AREA ............. Select a file area
 2.   SUBAREA......... Select a subarea
 3.   LIST ............. List files
 4.   BROWSE.......... Browse through files
 5.   SEND ............ Send a file to BIX
 6.   RECEIVE ......... Receive a file from BIX
 7.   TYPE............. Type a file
 8.   CHECK........... Check the contents of a file
 9.   OPTIONS......... Set options
10.   QUIT ............ Leave the listings subsystem
```

Selection: 2
Subarea name (or "ALL")? ?

APPLICATION	Non-game, non-utility programs.
DOCUMENTATION	Documentation for files in this area.
LANGUAGE	Computer language files.
LEISURE	Games and entertainment software.
OTHER	Miscellaneous programs and data files.
UTILITY	Programs that help you compute.
WORDPROCESSING	Programs and data files related to word processing.

Type RETURN to continue . . .

Notice that after setting our File Area to IBM.ARC, we decided to consider changing the Subarea setting as well. We keyed in 2 at the "Selection:" prompt and keyed in a question mark at the "Subarea name (or "ALL")?" prompt to get a list of available subareas. We decided to keep the subarea setting at ALL for the time being.

The LONG and the SHORT of File Descriptions

As with all systems, BIX follows the universal four-part format for free software files. BIX displays file descriptions in connection with the BROWSE command discussed earlier. Descriptions may be either SHORT or LONG. You specify your preference by selecting 9 "Set options" from the main LISTINGS menu and choosing "Set description length" from the submenu that will then appear. Here is an example of the LONG description for a file called ADVBAS32.ARC:

advbas32.arc   107520   Approx time (min):111 at 300 baud, 28 at
                          1200 baud

Contributed by: dmick   Date: Mon May 11 13:02:33 1987

BINARY QuickBASIC assembly utility routines . . . GREAT!! Version
3.2 of Thomas Hanlin's ADVBAS routines package. It's hard to believe
just what all this package contains. Well documented, and if you
register he'll send assembly source code for the routines. Low level
DOS functions, operations on arrays (add/subtract to all), strings
(AND mask all chars), low level file access . . . it's chock-full o' fun. Try
it!! (For an example of the low level file stuff, see
BASIC/LONG.MESSAGES.)

Keywords: UTILITY quickbasic assembly advbas dos

Download count: 27

The SHORT description, in contrast, includes just the filename, the
size of the file and the first sentence of the descriptive paragraph:

advbas32.arc   107520   BINARY QuickBASIC assembly utility
                          routines . . . GREAT!!

Setting LISTINGS Default Preferences

As we've seen, you can change File Areas and Subareas at will while
using the LISTINGS subsystem. Regardless of your settings when you
leave LISTINGS, however, your File Area and description length will
always return to your defaults the next time you enter LISTINGS—
unless you change those defaults and record them while in LISTINGS.

This is very easy to do. Simply key in 9 from the main LISTINGS
menu to "Set options." This will produce the following menu:

Setup options:

    1.   SEND . . . . Send protocol
    2.   RECEIVE . . . . Receive protocol
    3.   FORMAT . . . . Text format
    4.   DESCRIPTION . . . . . Set description length
    5.   PROMPTS . . . . Set menu/command mode
    6.   SHOW . . . . Show current settings
    7.   SAVE . . . . Save current settings
    8.   QUIT . . . . Leave the OPTIONS subsystem

Each of these selections produces a subsidiary menu of choices. All of
them are self-explanatory. However, there are two points worth noting.
First, note that there is no option on the above menu for File Area and
Subarea. To change your File Area and Subarea defaults, you must first

set them as described previously. Second, note that if you want to change your defaults you must "SAVE current settings" by choosing item 7. If you don't, your settings will remain in effect only during your current session. As you can see, you can check your current settings before saving them by choosing item 6.

The Master List File: IBM_ARC.ARC

Now that you're acclimated, getting your hands on BIX's free software offerings will be a piece of cake. The first thing you need to do is follow the instructions given earlier regarding setting your LISTINGS options. Pay particular attention to the available downloading protocols. At this writing, BIX defaults to XMODEM checksum. More than likely you will want to change that to XMODEM CRC or 1K or to YMODEM or Kermit. ProComm 2.4.2, the communications program discussed in Chapter 16, supports all of these options, but we think you'll be particularly impressed with the way YMODEM works with BIX.

Each Sunday, BIX's editors prepare a master file containing a complete directory of the IBM.ARC File Area. The file is called IBM_ARC.ARC. To get your copy, join the LISTINGS conference and get into the IBM.ARC File Area. Your subarea should be set to either ALL or to DOCUMENTATION. Then choose selection 6 "Receive a file from BIX" from the LISTINGS subsystem menu. When prompted for the filename, key in IBM_ARC.ARC. The system will acknowledge your selection and prompt you to begin the transfer. That's just about all there is to it.

The archive contains the file IBM_ARC.TXT, which weighs in at over 280K at this writing and includes the LONG descriptions for nearly 600 programs and files. Use Vern Buerg's LIST.COM program to search the file for the programs you want, and write down their filenames.

With your list of target files in hand, sign on to BIX again and return to the LISTINGS conference. Note that since IBM_ARC.TXT includes the file descriptions, there is no need to look at them again. All you have to do is download what you want. If you have set your various options and defaults as suggested here, getting public domain and shareware programs from BIX can be as easy as rolling a barrel of fish down a chute.

People/Link (PLINK)

American People/Link   CUSTOMER SERVICE
3215 N. Frontage Road, Suite
    1505   (800) 524-0100

Arlington Heights, IL
   60004-1437
   (312) 670-2666

In Illinois and outside the
   continental U.S.: (312)
   670-2666 or 670-2668

Customer Service Hours
(Central Time)
Mon.–Fri.: 9:00 A.M.–5:00 P.M.
(Weekend coverage will be
   available in the future.)

Initial Subscription:

SPECIAL DEAL

There is an initial one-time charge of $15. This normally does not include any free connect time. But by special arrangement with American People/Link, readers of this book will receive $25 worth of evening, nonprime connect time. That's approximately five free hours. To subscribe by modem, call (800) 826-8855. The modem line for Illinois residents is (312) 882-9712. When you are connected you will see a menu asking where you heard about People/Link. Respond by either keying in GLO or by entering the menu item related to this book. Have your Visa or MasterCard number ready in both cases. Regardless of how you subscribe, People/Link will send your User ID to you by paper mail. When you receive it, you can begin using your subscription.

Access: Telenet, Tymnet, direct dial, ConnNet, and Mercury (U.K.).

Rates:

Packet switching costs are *included* in the rates given below. Note that Tymnet prime time extends until 7:00 P.M. on weekdays. Telenet prime time ends at 6:00 P.M. on weekdays. Subscribers to Telenet's PC Pursuit (PCP) can use PCP to access People/Link. Key in: C PLINK,(PCP ID),(PCP PASSWORD) at the Telenet "@" prompt. You will need a PLINK subscription, of course. (For more on PCP, see Chapter 8, or dial Telenet's modem line and follow the prompts. The modem number is (800) 835-3001.

PLINK CONNECT RATES

PRIME TIME
(Mon.—Fri. 7:01 A.M.—6:00 P.M.)

Speed (bps)	Connect time (per hour)	Connect time (per minute)
300	$11.95	20¢
1200	$12.95	22¢
2400	$14.95	25¢

SUPER SAVER RATES
(Mon.—Fri. 6:01 P.M.—8:00 P.M., Sat. & Sun. 8:01 A.M.—8:00 P.M.)

Speed (bps)	Connect time (per hour)	Connect time (per minute)
300	$ 3.95	7¢
1200	$ 4.95	9¢
2400	$11.95	20¢

LEISURE RATES
(Sun.—Thurs. 8:01 P.M.—7:00 A.M. next day, Fri. & Sat. 8:01 P.M.
—8:00 A.M. next day)

Speed (bps)	Connect time (per hour)	Connect time (per minute)
300	$4.95	9¢
1200	$4.95	9¢
2400	$11.95	20¢

Calls are billed to the nearest minute, and there is a three-minute minimum per call. Direct dial calls to People/Link's Chicago nodes are always billed at Super Saver or Leisure rates.

Personal Defaults:

Key in /DEF at the People/Link Top menu and follow the resulting instructions. Note that the maximum page length available is 66 lines per page. There is thus no way to eliminate "more" prompts.

Scram Command: Control-C or BREAK

Sign-off Command: /OFF

Protocols:

PLINK will automatically try WXMODEM first. If your system indicates that it does not support WXMODEM, PLINK will fall back to
conventional XMODEM.

Special Notes:

People/Link offers special discounted rates (25 percent off) to members of the Frequent Plinker Club. Subscribers using 1200 bps would
thus pay either $9.72 or $3.72 an hour, depending on time of day.
One-time sign-up cost is $12.50. Monthly dues are $10. You may join
at any time. People/Link advises that the club is cost effective for
anyone using ten hours a month or more.

Capsule Summary

People/Link owes its existence to the popularity of CompuServe's CB
Simulator. As is the case with most mainframe and minicomputer systems, CompuServe users have always been able to chat with each other
in real time on a one-to-one basis. But when CompuServe introduced its
"multiplayer host" several years ago, it became possible for lots of people to gather and hold CB-like conversations. CompuServe used the
same facility to let groups of people battle each other in online Star-
Trek-like games.

Both features became enormously popular. What wasn't popular was
the CompuServe rate structure at the time. Merrill Millman thought he
had a better idea. He created People/Link as a low-cost alternative for
people who were primarily interested in CompuServe's communications
features. People/Link has no information, news, investments, or other
features common to the information utilities.

On Saturday December 29, 1984 the system went live at the rock-
bottom nonprime rate of $2.95 an hour for 300 bps. The prime time rate
was $8.95, and 1200-bps capability was not added until April of that
year. The rates have changed since then, but the emphasis has remained on people-to-people communications facilities.

Undoubtedly as a consequence of its low rates and communications
orientation, People/Link has not spent a great deal on documentation
and other frills. Indeed, in our opinion, the documentation is barely adequate and the system's downloading facilities are the most awkward of
the six systems considered here. At this writing the "manual" is a 14-

page pocket guide that amounts to little more than a command summary. Originally, People/Link had no SIGs. When it added them in the form of Clubs, it issued a single page of information that was about as useless as the manual it was designed to supplement. A new manual is said to be in the works. Unfortunately, given the irregular publication schedule of the system's paper newsletter, one should probably not look for an early release date.

On the other hand, People/Link is very good at what it is designed to do. It's fun, and with some 40,000 subscribers it is a popular system. Plinkers, as subscribers call themselves, hold frequent get-togethers around the country, and more than one real-life romance has blossomed online.

FreeTip: As for the lack of documentation, you should know that Scott Hoffrage ("Gamekeeper" on the system) has prepared an extensive manual for all Plinkers to download. It can be found in the GAMERS GUILD, the club for inveterate online game players. Key in /GO GAMERS at the main system menu and join the club. From the club menu, enter the library of transfer files and opt to READ on that menu. Select "Files By Title" from the READ menu that will then appear. When prompted to enter a title, key in MANUAL.

At this writing there are four files (MANUAL PART ONE, etc. through PART FOUR) totaling 215K, though one of the files contains a gargantuan appendix of nothing but Telenet, Tymnet, and ConnNet phone numbers. We suggest that you download each part of the manual, as prompted, using the ASCII option. But when the phone number list starts to appear, send the system a BREAK or Control-C to stop that particular download. Why pay for hundreds of numbers when the one you need can be gotten free of charge from People/Link customer service or one of the PDNs?

We also tried downloading some parts of the manual via WX-MODEM and discovered that for some reason they contained a passel of noxious high ASCII codes that had to be removed with a public domain utility program (FIXWS.COM) before the file could be displayed. The ASCII downloaded versions do not have this problem.

Sign On and Move to the Treasure Rooms

When you sign on to People/Link, here is the menu that will greet you:

```
Welcome to PEOPLE/LINK

-----------------------------------------------------
-----------------------------------------------------
Using over 300 baud - - Extra Value
Service - For rate info /GO 411
-----------------------------------------------------
-----------------------------------------------------


           PEOPLE/LINK Main Menu

     1   PartyLine               /PARTY
     2   Clubs & Forums          /CLUBS
     3   Mail                    /MAIL
     4   User Directory          /UD
     5   Bulletin Boards         /BB
     6   Find a Plinker          /FIND
     7   Information             /GO 411
     8   News and Publications   /GO NEWS


     Enter number, command or /HELP
     MAIN MENU>/GO IBM
```

If you'd like to see a list of all available People/Link clubs, you can choose 2 (clubs and forums). But here we've taken the express route directly to the IBM club by keying in /GO IBM. That produces a standard club menu from which you can choose "Library of Transfer Files" (selection 2). That in turn leads to this menu:

```
           CLUB DATA LIBRARY MENU

     1   Select Library Section   /SECT
     2   QuickScan File &
         Download                 /QSCAN
     3   Read About File & Dload  /READ
     4   Add File To Data Library /POST
     5   Delete File You Added    /DELETE
     6   List Library Entries

     7   Return To NOTICE Menu    /NOT
     8   Return To CLUB Menu
     9   Exit Clubs to MAIN Menu  /QUIT
    10   Info On These Options    /HELP

   Please enter number or command:
   CLUB LIBRARY>6
```

The selection you want here is "List Library Entries," and that is what we have entered. This produces a menu labeled XFERLIST LIBRARY ENTRIES MENU. Here you'll be given a choice of listing just those entries uploaded by a certain user, just those with certain keywords, and so on. The selection to pick is "All Entries in Library" (selection 1). You will then be given a choice of downloading via ASCII or via XMODEM. Choose the ASCII option, because it is faster and no error checking is required.

Here is the kind of thing you can expect to see on your screen as the incoming information is both displayed and recorded in your capture buffer:

```
DOS SHELL UTILITY; DOSAMATC SHELL UTILITY
RESIDENT                                    11/08/85 10/93      71.6
FILE VIEWING UTILITY; BROWSE TYPE UTILITY DOS  11/09/85 10/94    3.2
SEARCHES FOR FILES (PATH); PATH DOS DISK
UTILITY                                     11/09/85 10/100      6.0
A PROKEY CLONE; NEWKEY CLONE PROKEY
RESIDENT DOS                                11/09/85 10/101     36.8
ENHANCED 'MORE' FILTER; MORE DOS FILTER     11/09/85 10/104      3.8
DOS31.DOC - UNDOCUMENTED FEATURES OF
DOS 3.1; UNDOCU                             4/17/86 15/1664      4.0
BACKUP.ART - ARTICLE ON DOS BACKUP
COMMAND; ARTICLE O                          4/17/86 15/1675      2.9
V20-80.COM - RUN C/PM SOFTWARE ON MS-
DOS/V-20MPU; RUN                            4/17/86 15/1706      7.4
DOS-EDIT.BAS - CREATE DOS-EDIT.COM, PC MAG
2/11/86; CRE                                4/17/86 15/1728      3.8
```

This is the nearest thing People/Link offers at this writing to an up-to-date file list or keyword list. It is anything but elegant. The lack of a specific filename for some entries is dismaying, to say the least. The best way to make sense of it all is to look at the information from which the list is derived. Here, for example, is People/Link's version of the universal four-part free software format cited in Chapter 6:

```
IBM             Sec: 10
Name: DOSAMATC.ARC           Num: 93
By:   IBMPC       Date: 11/08/85 23:33
Bytes:   71,680   Downloads:   33
Binary!
Title:   DOS SHELL UTILITY
Keywords: DOSAMATC SHELL UTILITY RESIDENT

Program ID:    DOSAMATC.ARC
```

ARC Contents: DOSAMATC.COM
                DOSAMATC.DOC
                DOSAMATC.HLP

Description: DOSAMATC is a shell-driven system controller. It is
                touted to be a TOPVIEW look-alike. I see it as a
                1DIR/File Command type of program. However, I find
                it very useful!!!

Upload Method: XMODEM
Date Type: BINARY
XMODEM
Blocks: App 565

Notice that the first line of the all-files list corresponds to the Title
and Keywords fields in the above entry for DOSAMATC.ARC. If the
filename had been included in the entry's title field, it would have appeared on the all-files list, as indeed is the case with some files on the
list. Second, notice the second column of numbers on the all-files list.
The paired numbers in that column for the first line are 10/93 and correspond to the "Sec:" and "Num:" fields on the entry above. This stands
for library section and file number, and it means that even though the
filename is not given on the all-files list, you can still get at it directly.
The third column of numbers contains the size of the file and corresponds to the "Bytes:" field in the entry above.

The best way to tap the IBM Club free software libraries on Peo-
ple/Link is to download the all-files list as shown above using the ASCII
capture buffer option. Then sign off the system and use Vern Buerg's
LIST.COM program (described in Chapter 6) to treat the file as a list of
keywords. When you've assembled a list of likely candidates, noting the
file numbers for each, sign back on to the system. (The section number
is not relevant here since each file has a unique number, regardless of
its section.)

You can follow the menus back to the IBM Club Data Library menu if
you like, but you can get there instantly by keying in: /GO IBM;LIB at
the main menu prompt. One way or another you will see the Club Data
Library Menu again. This time, choose the selection that lets you "Read
About File & Dload /READ." This is People/Link's browse command,
and it generates the following list of options:

You May Read:

1   All File Descriptions   /ALL
2   New File Descriptions Only   /NEW
3   Old File Descriptions Only   /OLD
4   File With Certain Number   /NUM

```
 5   Files By Title                      /TITLE
 6   Files By Certain User Id            /BY
 7   Files With Certain Keywords         /KEY
 8   Files Added Since MM/DD/YY          /SINCE
 9   Files With a Certain Filename       /NAME
10   Return To Library Menu              /TOP
11   Info On Reading Lib Files           /HELP

Please Enter Number or Command:
READ FILES>4
```

Notice that we have chosen to READ "File with Certain Number," (selection 4). (The word "Descriptions" in selections 1 through 3 is misleading and we suggest that you not choose those items.) This selection leads to a prompt for the file's assigned number, and after you have entered it, a file description similar to the one for DOSAMATC.ARC will be displayed. You will then be asked whether you want to download it. You may do this or opt to return to the library menu and repeat the process with your next candidate's number.

There are two other points to make about People/Link. First, it has been our experience that when a successful download has been completed, the system takes about a minute to acknowledge the fact. The temptation here is to send a Control-C or hit <Enter> to get its attention, but it's a temptation you should resist. People/Link will get back to you.

Second, there's the matter of club sections. The IBM Club has some 15 sections, each devoted to a particular topic (Financial & Business Applications, Games & Entertainment, and so on). These are designed to be used as filters. All files, programs, and messages are assigned to a particular section when they are uploaded or created. Thus if you tell the system you want to focus on a particular section, it will scan or search or perform its other operations exclusively on the contents of that section.

8

Going By the Boards

HOW TO PLUG INTO THE WORLDWIDE
BULLETIN BOARD NETWORK

The second major online source of free software is the network of privately run bulletin board systems (BBSs) that enrobes the globe—or at least those parts of it with freely available modems and microcomputers and reliable phone service. For those three elements (modems, micros, and telephones), and the software that binds them together, are the protein building blocks of the basic BBS molecule. No packet-switching networks. No water-cooled, multimillion dollar mainframes. No subscription fees, connect-time charges, or rate tables. (No slipcased manuals and no toll-free customer service, either.)

All that's needed to catalyze these elements into action is the enthusiasm of a generous sysop (system operator; pronounced "sis-op")—someone who for 20 to 23 hours of every day, 365.25 days a year, is willing to make his machine available to all callers. (The sysop population is overwhelmingly male; hence the masculine pronoun.) Once this broth is in the beaker, there's no telling what fascinating combinations and permutations will emerge.

BBSs: The Concept

The basic idea behind a BBS is easy to understand, particularly if you've read Chapters 5 and 6. (We're going to assume you've read them. If you haven't, stop right here. Go directly to Chapter 5. Do collect $200. And put it in a safe place. You'll need it to buy your modem and modem cable.) The concept is based on the ability of a computer to accept commands and input from any "port" its owner selects. For example, with the right software, you can run a computer with a light pen, a bar code reader, a joystick, or a mouse. All of these devices communicate with the machine through a port of some kind, often the same RS-232 serial port you use to talk to your modem and through it, to the outside world.

The hardware required to set up a BBS is thus identical to the hardware required to go online. A sysop has only to switch on his modem, load some special BBS software, and wait for someone to call. Or he can go off and do something else and let his machine wait by itself. There is no need for the sysop to be there, since the computer operates automatically.

When you call a board, the sysop's modem will answer. Then the BBS host software will kick in and prompt you for your name and password (about which more in a moment). Once you're into the system, you are in effect logged on to a mini-information utility, with a message exchange and library of downloadable files. Some boards also offer real-time games, and a few multiuser systems offer real-time chats and conferences. Some are part of an international network that will automatically transmit messages to friends on distant systems and deliver messages they have sent to you, often free of charge. And if your system can support color graphics, some boards will put on a son et lumière that would shame the fuse out of a Fourth of July firecracker.

Indeed, some BBSs are so well developed that there is often no obvious way to tell whether you're connected to The Source, GEnie, CompuServe, or some guy's Taiwanese clone sitting on an orange crate in the corner of his livingroom. Further, there is no immediate way to tell whether the system you are on is an IBM PC or compatible, a Macintosh, an Apple //e, or a venerable old CP/M system of uncertain origin.

In the Beginning Was CBBS #1

There is no uncertainty about the origin of the BBS concept, however. The personal computer bulletin board was invented by Ward Christensen and Randy Suess. Their accomplishment became official on February 16, 1978 when they "brought up" (activated; the opposite of "take down") CBBS #1 (Computer Bulletin Board System Number 1) to serve members of CACHE, the Chicago Area Computer Hobbyist Exchange. Mr. Christensen was the group's assistant software librarian at the time and thus was naturally interested in promoting both group communication and the distribution of public domain software.

Christensen and Suess had been sending messages and programs between their two computers for over a year prior to the advent of CBBS #1, and at some point the idea for a bulletin board system developed. The original concept was to use a computer as the electronic equivalent of a cork and thumbtack bulletin board to allow CACHE members to exchange messages. That was the system that went on the air in February.

The board was based on a North Star computer and was ostensibly designed exclusively for messaging. There was a secret feature, however, that only a few people knew about at first. Christensen included a module in the BBS software designed to work with his MODEM communications program to allow callers to download public domain software.

CBBS #1 is still up and running today, sitting in Randy Suess's basement. As of June 1987, it had logged over 170,000 callers. Ironically, considering Ward Christensen's crucial role in developing the XMODEM protocol, the file transfer feature was removed from the board early in its history due in part to limited disk space. Discussions these days center around C and assembler, artificial intelligence, programming elegance and quick hacks, and communications. There is also a notice about subjects deemed inappropriate for the board: "Please no Atari, Adam games, C-64/VIC COCO TI TRS-80 Dr. Who etc. msgs!"

Christensen and Suess made their bulletin board software available for a nominal fee, and there are still a number of CP/M sysops who use it. Thus when you see the designation "CBBS" on a list of bulletin board phone numbers, you can assume first of all that it is running under the CP/M operating system and second that it is a wonderful place to discuss technical issues online, but it is probably not the best place to look for public domain software, even if you happen to have equipped your PC for CP/M.

The Changing Focus

To be sure, there are many, many systems in the IBM world that specialize in offering free software for callers to download. In fact, the number of megabytes of PD software a system has to offer is a mark of distinction among BBSs and sysops. Systems boasting 75 to 100 megabytes are not all that rare, though most boards probably have somewhere between 20 and 30 megabytes online. However, while there are some systems that are "download only," it seems clear that messaging is emerging as the most important BBS contribution.

FreeTip: Although we're not going to be covering them here, the message exchange features of most BBSs work just like the message exchanges offered by the special interest groups (SIGs) on commercial systems. Indeed, if you're familiar with the basic SIG floorplan, you'll have no problem finding your way around most boards. As with the SIGs, BBSs typically have a file area that is often divided into several topical libraries and a messaging area. Messages typically have TO:, FROM:, SUBJECT:, and DATE: fields, followed by the body of the message, and often you can locate items of interest by scanning one or more fields.

There are a number of reasons for this, though we should say up front that the field is so changeable that it's impossible to tell how many boards are in operation at any given time, let alone discern absolutely definitive trends. Best estimates place the number of solid, enduring boards at between 2800 and 3500 at this writing. However, hundreds and perhaps thousands of additional boards blossom and die each year due to shortages of time and money and loss of interest on the part of the sysop.

The key point to remember is that when the first boards were brought up, and for years afterwards, there *were* no commercial online systems to speak of. Those that did exist lacked the critical mass they have since achieved. Today BBSs are no longer the only alternative for someone who wants to get free software online. And, for reasons we'll discuss in a moment, they are not the better alternative for most people.

Messaging is an altogether different story. Indeed, when it comes to exchanging ideas, opinions, and unique nuggets of information—when it comes to bringing together people with shared interests—bulletin boards are nothing short of a sociological and political phenomenon. This is where their natural strength lies and where the most interesting developments will continue to take place.

Be Your Own Publisher

Imagine, for the cost of a basic personal computer system and modem, anyone can become the publisher and editor of his or her own small journal or "little" magazine. You don't have to persuade a commercial system to accept your idea. There's no capital to raise or advertising space to sell. You don't need anyone's permission. You can publish opinions, essays, news, tips, and features, or anything else that doesn't violate the law or someone's copyright (like stolen credit card numbers or pirated software). All you have to do is make the file(s) available in the board's library and post a greeting bulletin directing callers's attention to it.

You can call your board anything you like: Grendel's Lair, The Women's Room, Frank's Folly, Dew Drop Inn, The Crystal Palace, etc. And you can dedicate it to one particular topic or to all topics. Once the board is up and running, you can distribute your number through the BBS network and solicit comments and discussion of issues that concern you or your callers. After a while, and a lot of hard work on your part, the word will get around that yours is a good board to call.

Gradually you'll build up a following. There will be people all over the continent (and world, in some cases) who will call regularly to see what's going on and to put in their two cents worth. With more time and more hard work, you'll become known in the BBS community as a top sysop, and pretty soon you'll be attending BBS conventions and national sysop meetings to give lectures to admirers and newcomers on how to run a first-class board.

FreeTip: As today's thought problem, imagine yourself as the unelected leader of an authoritarian country. It is a country where, whenever a foreign company wishes to replace a photocopier with a newer model, the government's standard operating procedure is to dispatch a crew of men with hammers to smash up the old machine, lest it fall into unauthorized hands. But your country needs computers and lots of them if it is ever to emerge from the technological backwater into which it has sunk. Otherwise it will fall ever further behind in world competition. You're caught between a rock and a hard disk. Or something the "samizdat." How do you equip your people with computers without sowing the seeds of your own destruction?

A Board for Every Season

Needless to say, this is already happening. There are boards dedicated to the interests of doctors, lawyers, or engineers. There are boards to help you find the mate of your dreams by "dialing your match." As an unsystematic scan of several BBS phone lists shows, others are "dedicated to the loyal fans of 'The Young and the Restless,'" animal rights, Computers for Christ, space exploration and development, horse racing, genealogy, programs for the blind, 1960s music, emergency medical service, science fiction, and ham radio. Then there is something called "CO-VENTURING with Syd Allen . . . monthly telepath [and] readers exchange with other dimensions and entities." Plus, as you would expect, lots of boards focusing on computer-related topics.

FreeTip: If you're into computers, you'll find information on bulletin boards that is simply not available anywhere else. Several years ago, for example, a friend wanted to upgrade his PCjr (an unfairly underrated machine, in our opinion). At the time, the leading memory expansion option was the Tecmar Junior Captain sidecar, but it contained only 128K of RAM. By working the boards looking for information that might be of help, we came across several messages from callers praising a firm then called Micro-Service Company (now MSC). The messages provided the address, phone number, and details of the company's services.

We called, and learned that if you sent MSC a 128K Tecmar board, they would pull the RAM chips and replace them with chips that would boost its memory to 512K. They guaranteed a 48-hour turnaround. The friend sent the board and was very pleased with the service and his resulting 640K Junior. (At this writing, MSC supplies 512K Hotshot boards as well as 3½-inch disk drives and other components for the PCjr.)

Our point here is that this information was available nowhere else at the time. The only way to learn about MSC was by tapping the BBS network. Since that time, a file has appeared in the hardware Data Library of the PCjr forum on CompuServe called MSC.DOC. The file describes some of the services the firm offers to XT, AT, and jr owners. For example, MSC charges a flat rate for its repairs (every model from the PCjr through AT class machines) instead of charging by the hour. Depending on the system, the charges are a flat fee of between $65 and $85, plus parts. MSC replaces bad parts and chips instead of swapping boards. Since our first encounter, we have dealt with MSC a number of times and have always found them to be top-drawer. For more information, contact:

> Mr. Lou Davidson, President
> MSC
> 4764 Elison Avenue
> Baltimore, MD 21206
> (301) 325-6417

There are business applications as well. Some stockbrokers run BBSs for their clients to call in buy and sell orders at any time of day or night. Magazines, particularly computer magazines like *PC* and *PC Tech Journal*, run boards to solicit reader input and to make available the free programs they publish. (This saves readers the time and effort of keying in the code by hand, something it is hard to believe anyone in their right mind would attempt to do.) Manufacturing firms use boards to make available their current price lists and other information that can't be conveniently communicated by voice over the phone. Some companies take orders and offer customer support through boards as well. At some schools, students who are out sick can dial up the school's BBS and take tests or submit homework assignments if they have access to a home computer.

Congressmen use BBSs to communicate and solicit comments from voters in their districts. Other politicians use boards as a central information repository for their campaign workers. Even agencies of the federal government are involved. (See the special section that follows.)

―――――――――――――――― **Special Section** ――――――――――――――――

Your Tax Dollars at Work: Free Federal Bulletin Boards

Most of the federally sponsored bulletin boards listed below are free, though some do require advanced registration. Unless you live in the Washington, D.C. area, you will have to pay long distance charges to reach them. The following summary is based on information published in the May 1987 issue of *Bulletin Board Systems* (formerly "Plumb"). At this writing, the publication's status is in flux. For more information, contact: Meckler Publishing, 11 Ferry Lane West, Westport, CT 06880; (203) 226-6967.

Census Personnel Division Bulletin Board
> Job vacancies from entry level to senior management. Online 24 hours. Data line: (301) 763-4574.

State Data Center Bulletin Board
> News about new Census Bureau programs, publications, and so on. Preregistration required. Voice line: John Rowe or Larry Carbaugh at (301) 763-1580.

Population Estimates Bulletin Board
> Information and news about population and demographic projections. Online from 5:00 P.M. to 6:30 A.M., Monday through Thursday. Data line: (301) 763-5225. Key in RUN after you are connected to start. Voice line: Fred Cavanaugh at (301) 763-7722.

CMIC Electronic Bulletin Board
> Microcomputer news, software and hardware reviews, public domain software, and training programs for Census Bureau and Com-

merce Department personnel. Designed for Census Bureau personnel, but open to the public. Data line: (301) 763-4576. Hit one or two carriage returns to start. Voice line: Nevins Frankel at (301) 763-4494.

Microcomputer Electronic Information Exchange (MEI)
Operated by the Institute for Computer Sciences and Technology (ICST), National Bureau of Standards, Department of Commerce. Information on the acquisition, management, and use of small computers; also federal publications, user groups, and so on. Online 24 hours. Data line: (301) 948-5718. Hit one or two carriage returns to start. Voice line: Ted Landberg at (301) 921-3485.

Climate Assessment Bulletin Board
Operated by the Climate Analysis Center, National Weather Service. Contains daily, weekly, and monthly weather charts, heating degree days, and weekly climate bulletins. Preregistration required. For information contact Vernon Patterson at (301) 763-8071.

East Coast Marine Users Bulletin Board
Operated by the National Weather Service. Aimed at commercial fishermen. Contains mid-Atlantic marine weather and nautical information for costal waterways, tropical storm advisories, tidal information, and fishing news. Preregistration required. Voice line: Ross Laporte at (301) 899-3296.

Exporter's RBBS
Operated by the U.S. Export-Import Bank. Includes listings of Eximbank certified banks; country limitation schedules, press releases, user conferences, and more. For any individual or business interested in selling U.S. goods abroad. Data line: (202) 566-4602. Voice line: Joel Kahn or Bob Hughes at (202) 566-4690.

SRS Remote Bulletin Board Service
Operated by the Division of Science Resources Studies at the National Science Foundation. System lists federal funds for research and development, scientific and engineering expenditures, and international comparisons of science and technology data. Online 24 hours. Data line: (202) 634-1764. Voice line: Vanessa Richardson at (202) 634-4636.

OTHER FEDERALLY SPONSORED BULLETIN BOARDS

BBS Name	Organization	Data Number
Megawatts BBS	Dept. of Energy	(202) 252-1518
COE Manpower BBS	Army Corps. of Engineers	(202) 272-1514
Budget/Finance BBS	Immigration & Natural-ization Service	(202) 786-3640
Fannie Mae BBS	Federal National Mortgage Assn.	(202) 537-7475
World Bank BBS	World Bank	(202) 477-8500
NCH BBS	National Center for Health Statistics	(301) 436-6346
User Assistance BBS	Internal Revenue Service	(202) 756-6109
Info Technology BBS	Veteran's Adminis-tration	(202) 376-2184

The Problem with Bulletin Boards

We've given you the good news about bulletin boards. Now, for the bad. Speaking strictly from a free-software-seeker's perspective, the problem with BBSs is that the pipe is too narrow. The pipe we're speaking of is the single phone line serving a single bulletin board system. If you assume that a board is up 24 hours a day and that each caller is on the board for between 30 minutes and a full hour, it quickly becomes obvious that a single board can serve a maximum of 48 people a day. In reality, however, the actual number will be much lower. The board must be periodically taken down by the sysop for routine maintenance. The sysop may also need his computer to perform some non-BBS-related chores and be forced to put the board on hold. Thus most boards probably won't be available for 24 contiguous hours.

In addition, some of those 48 people would have to call during the wee hours of the morning, while others would have to call during regular business hours. That doesn't happen very often for obvious reasons. What does happen is that everyone who wants to work the boards sits down at his or her machine sometime between the hours of 5:00 P.M., when long-distance rates drop, and 11:00 P.M. or midnight, when they have to go to bed.

So you have a narrow time window combined with a narrow communications pipeline. It's a sure recipe for frustration. There you are, all set to go searching for some nifty PD program, and you can't get to first base for all the busy signals you hear through your modem's speaker. Or if it's not a busy signal, it's some telephone company recording telling you that the number you have dialed is no longer in service. BBSs tend to come and go. Obviously your list of numbers is out of date.

Before you know it, it's 1:00 in the morning. Your eyes are bleary and your fingers are tired from keying in one BBS phone number after another. But you give it one more try. You key in ATDT and the number, hit <Enter>, and the next thing you hear is the sound of a phone actually ringing for a change. At last! The next-thing you hear, however, is not the reassuring mating dance of the modems, it's some sleepy-voiced grandmother in Dubuque: "Hello? . . . Hello? . . ." Embarrassed, frustrated, and chagrined, you hang up, power down, and go to bed, resolving never to waste another evening doing *that* again. The only thing you can take comfort in is that if you had gotten through to several of the BBSs you dialed, your long-distance phone bill would probably have gone through the roof. (Inveterate BBSers routinely run up phone bills of $100, $200, $300 or more a month.)

Solutions of a Sort

These problems plague all BBSers, but they are particularly aggravating if you're trying to find a program you need. After all, if your main goal is to participate in the ongoing discussions taking place on several boards, your comments will keep. You can try again the next night. But if you *need* a program for a particular task, you don't have the luxury of waiting.

Fortunately, while there are no dead-bang solutions to these problems, there are a number of techniques that can ameliorate the situation. These include PC Pursuit, a service offered by GTE Telenet to help hold down your long-distance costs; a knowledge of where to get the most up-to-date lists of BBS phone numbers; a comm program capable of continuously cycling through a list of phone numbers until it gets an answer; and a utility program to save you from having to key in any numbers at all.

How to Save Money with PC Pursuit
Unlimited Calls for $25 a Month

As is the case with the CompuServe Information Service and GEnie, Telenet's PC Pursuit program was developed to take better advantage of under-utilized computer resources. During regular business hours, Telenet's nodes and network are abuzz with activity, but much of that activity abruptly stops after 6:00 P.M. So Telenet devised a plan that would allow PC owners to use its network to call distant bulletin boards and other systems for a flat $25 per month.

The idea is to get connected to a Telenet node in a distant city and then call a board in that city by dialing out of the Telenet node. As far as the phone company in the distant city is concerned, it's a local call. Thus to use PC Pursuit, you first call your local Telenet node. Once connected, you key in the area code of the BBS you wish to reach, followed by your PC Pursuit ID. For example, at the Telenet network prompt, someone communicating at 1200 bps who wanted to call a board in area code 206 (Seattle) would key in something like this: C DIAL 206/12, YOURID <Enter>. The network will connect you with a Telenet node in the distant city.

You will then be prompted for your password, and the system will come back with something like "DIAL206/12 CONNECTED." At that point you enter ATZ, wait for the network to send you the "OK" prompt, and then key in ATDT followed by the seven-digit phone number of the board you wish to reach. If the board is free, the sysop's modem will answer the phone, and everything will proceed as if you had dialed directly. If the board is busy, the network will display "BUSY," and you can start again with ATZ and ATDT followed by the same or a different target number. If you like, you may also tell the network that you want to switch to a different city, and it will patch you through to the appropriate node.

Codes and Nodes

You can access PC Pursuit from any location in the United States that has a Telenet node ("from hundreds of cities . . . and over 18,000 local telephone exchanges," according to the company). That's going in. Going out, things are a little more limited. At this writing, PC Pursuit can put you in contact with many of the BBSs and other data systems that can be reached as a local call from the following 25 area codes and cities, although at least ten additional cities are scheduled to be added in the near future:

404	Atlanta	617	Boston
312	Chicago	216	Cleveland

214	Dallas	303	Denver
313	Detroit	818	Glendale
713	Houston	213	Los Angeles
305	Miami	414	Milwaukee
612	Minneapolis	201	Newark
212	New York	602	Phoenix
215	Philadelphia	503	Portland
919	Research Triangle Park	801	Salt Lake City
415	San Francisco	408	San Jose
206	Seattle	813	Tampa
202	Washington, D.C.		

How to Sign Up

There is a one-time start up fee of $25 to open a PC Pursuit subscription, plus a flat fee of $25 a month. All fees are billable to your Visa or MasterCard. Your monthly fee entitles you to an unlimited number of data calls to PC Pursuit-accessible numbers during the weekday hours between 6:00 P.M. and 7:00 A.M., your local time, and all day on weekends and holidays. PC Pursuit can also be used during the daytime (7:00 A.M. to 6:00 P.M.) for a cost of between $10.50 and $14.00 an hour, depending on where you live.

PC Pursuit celebrated its third birthday in July 1988, and it has grown to be quite popular among bulletin board enthusiasts, particularly since it expanded the number of accessible cities from the original 11 and further fine-tuned its service.

FreeTip: The principal drawback to PC Pursuit is data throughput. All Telenet nodes do their own error checking on a node-to-node basis, and that combined with the delays introduced by XMODEM can cut your actual 1200 bps throughput to something closer to 600 bps. XMODEM is considered the worst offender. The best protocol to use is ZMODEM, though using WXMODEM, YMODEM, and Kermit will improve throughput as well. (We have put ZRUN.EXE, a program that lets you run ZMODEM with ProComm, on Glossbrenner's Choice IBM Disk CommPack 2; see Chapter 16.)

Bruce Barkelew, author of the shareware ProComm communications package, told us of a benchmark he ran with PC Pursuit at 1200 bps. Transmitting a given file using XMODEM between two directly wired computers (no modem or phone lines) required six minutes. Transmitting the same file using XMODEM via a PC Pursuit connection took 12 minutes. But sending the file via PC Pursuit using WXMODEM took only four minutes.

PC Pursuit Info Online

For the latest information on PC Pursuit, the area codes and cities available, and to sign up for the service, you can call the "In Pursuit Of . . ." BBS maintained by the company. Set your system to 8/N/1 and call one of these two numbers:

(800) 835-3001
(703) 689-2987

This BBS has only one line and allows only 10 minutes per session. So open your capture buffer as soon as you make the connection. Among other things, the board includes additional numbers you may wish to dial.

For information, to subscribe, and to find your closest Telenet local access number, call one of these *voice* lines weekdays between 8:00 A.M. and 5:00 P.M. Eastern Standard Time: (800) 835-3638 or (in Virginia) (703) 689-5700.

Once you become a PC Pursuit subscriber, you will have access to the Net Exchange and PC Pursuit Information BBS. This service contains complete lists of the three-digit phone exchanges accessible via PC Pursuit from each area code. There is also a message board for PC Pursuit users to exchange information, files, and so on. Subscribers can connect by dialing their local Telenet node and keying in C PURSUIT,MYID, MYPASSWORD at the main network prompt (@). There is no charge for using the Net Exchange. In Virginia, you must dial (703) 689-3561 instead of your local node.

How to Get the Best BBS Numbers
Boards Go Up, Boards Go Down

A sysop's life is not an easy one and running a good board is anything but the snap it sometimes appears. Conscientious sysops examine all of the programs people upload to make sure they don't violate someone's copyright and that they are safe to use. They also review each day's messages for stolen credit card numbers and other dicey information. And they have to answer their mail, whether it's a comment from a regular caller or a question from some new user that would never have been asked had the individual not resolutely refused to read the bulletins and helpful prompts the sysop had prepared.

There are really mundane tasks as well, such as fixing files that have become fragmented, eliminating duplicate PD programs from the library, deleting messages containing nothing but "Just testing" or similar lines, and otherwise husbanding their disk space. And of course there is the time spent tuning, tweeking, and tinkering with the hardware and software. Add to this the fact that every sysop is a target of opportunity for all the addlepated computer punks who get their jollies by trying to wreck every board they call, and it's no wonder BBSs come and go with such frequency.

FreeTip: A sysop's legal liability for the information people post on his board is not clear. (Is your local supermarket liable because someone tapes a list of stolen MasterCard numbers to its community news corkboard? Is the U.S. Park Service liable because someone staples the same list to one of its trees?) But since more than one innocent sysop has had his system confiscated by police because of something someone uploaded to his board, many tend to be more than duly diligent about preventing questionable information from slipping by.

The ephemerality of bulletin boards is a fact of online life, however, and it simply means that you must pay particular attention to the freshness of the BBS phone lists you use. Because of this, books and magazines are not usually very good sources. The lead time between the submission of the last bit of copy and the publication date can be three months to a year, and inevitably many of the numbers will be out of service by the time the book or magazine hits the stands. However, there is at least one exception, the FOG/*Computer Shopper* list.

The FOG/Computer Shopper List

Computer Shopper is a tabloid-sized magazine that regularly runs to 520 pages or more. It makes a valiant attempt at providing editorial content and articles, but people really buy it for the ads. Whether you're interested in a tiny clock crystal or a full-blown system, you can find it advertised, often at a deep discount, in *Computer Shopper*.

For our purposes here, the most important feature is the 15 to 20-page BBS directory found in each issue. The list is compiled and maintained by FOG, an leading user group based in Daly City, California. The initials used to stand for First Osborne Group, but with over 17,000 members and over 140 affiliated chapters worldwide, FOG has long been a leading group for users of all CP/M and MS-DOS computers. The group is assisted in its efforts by members of the Public Remote Access Computer Standards Association (PRACSA).

The *Computer Shopper*/FOG list is unique for a number of reasons. It is organized by state, with numbers for Canadian provinces included at the end of the list. Each BBS receives a short write-up including its city, available baud rates, operating hours, the sysop's name, and two or three sentences describing the board and what it offers. This is much more information than most BBS lists provide.

The information comes from the sysops themselves, but all of the numbers are initially verified by FOG and PRACSA members. If a number "is found to be inaccurate, it will be immediately deleted from the listing." Furthermore, "if an update report is not received every three months, the listing will also be deleted. All SysOps are responsible for forwarding accurate information to [FOG]."

You may be able to find *Computer Shopper* at your favorite newsstand, and it has recently begun to appear in the magazine racks at major bookstores. Published monthly, subscriptions are $21 a year. As a member of the Boston Computer Society (Chapter 3), you can subscribe for $14.97. For more information contact:

> Subscription Dept.
> *Computer Shopper*
> 5211 S. Washington Ave.
> Titusville, FL 32781
> (305) 269-3211
>
> Source: TCS575
> CompuServe: 70275,1023
> Delphi: CSHOPPER or SVEIT
> (Stan Veit, publisher and editor-in-chief)

The FOG RT on GEnie

The main disadvantage of this particular list is that while it is updated every month, the information you see in the magazine is always three months old due to the lead time required to prepare an issue for publication. It is still better than the lists that typically appear in other magazines, however. Other publications usually don't do any verification, and most keep reprinting a given number until some reader happens to complain that it is no longer in service.

This is why you will be happy to learn of the new FOG RoundTable on GEnie. (See Chapter 7 for a profile of the GEnie system.) You can access the FOG RT by keying in FOG at the main GEnie menu prompt. The RT will always have the most up-to-date FOG BBS list for you to download—the one that won't see print until three months later. The file to look for will have a name similar to REMSYS11.ARC, where the numbers represent the month of the year. The BBS list contains three lines per board with all the vital statistics and necessary information. To locate the current file, search the library on the keyword BBS or COM-PUTER SHOPPER. The RT offers the following list of libraries:

Novice Files

FOG-CPM Disks

FOG-DOS Disks

CPM Disk Descriptions

MS-DOS Disk Descriptions

FOG Publications

Product Reviews

New CP/M library Submissions

New MS-DOS library Submissions

Other Operating Systems

Misc Files

FOG Roundtable Archives

FOG Members Info

FreeTip: If you're a sysop who would like to be listed, send the information detailed above to:

> FOG
> Remote System Listing
> P.O. Box 3474
> Daly City, CA 94015-0474
> Voice: (415) 755-2000 (weekdays 10:00
> A.M.–6:00 P.M., Pacific Time)
> Modem: (415) 755-8315

You will also find it worthwhile to look into PRACSA. This is an association of sysops formed to "educate users and the general public in the use of remote computer systems while providing guidelines and assistance for those wishing to operate such systems in an efficient and law-abiding manner." Many of the nation's top system operators belong and will be happy to advise you in getting your system up and running. The dues are $10 a year, prorated to December 31 at 85¢ a month.

There are a number of ways to get more information. The PRACSA-preferred way is to dial up the main PRACSA board at (415) 948-2513. However, you can also contact sysop Irv Hoff via CompuServe at 76701,117 or call his voice line at (415) 948-2166. PRACSA president David McCord can be reached (voice) at (415) 948-3820 during regular business hours. Finally, you can obtain membership information and an application by contacting the address shown below (enclosing a self-addressed address label and a first-class stamp would be appreciated):

> PRACSA
> P.O. Box 1204
> San Jose, CA 95108

Lists Online: The Electronic Alternative

The main point in favor of a conscientiously prepared printed BBS list is the amount of information it provides. As noted, the *Computer Shopper*/FOG list gives you four or five descriptive sentences for each entry, so you'll have some idea of what to expect when you connect with a given board. The main disadvantage of all printed lists, aside from the problem of currency, is simply that they are printed: The numbers are on the page instead of in your computer where they belong.

Since you have a modem, however, there's an easy solution. One of the best places to look for bulletin board numbers is on other bulletin boards. Virtually every board will have at least one list of numbers in its file area. Though the richest, most varied phone number collections can be found in the SIG libraries of the commercial online systems profiled in the preceding chapter. Simply follow the same techniques we showed you for locating free programs on the system of your choice. This is one time when you can safely use the search features these systems offer, for the files you want are virtually guaranteed to be tagged with one or both of these two keywords: BBS or LIST.

For example, on October 7, 1987 we signed on to CompuServe, keyed in GO IBMCOM to get the IBM Communications SIG, and then keyed in DL0 to get to Data Library 0 (new uploads). There were no files with LIST as a keyword. But when we entered S/DES/KEY:BBS, as discussed in the previous chapter, the following files and descriptions appeared:

THELIS.V17/binary   23-Sep-87 19072

   Keywords: BBS NUMBERS TORONTO CANADA

   AN UP-TO-DATE LIST OF BBS NUMBERS AVAILABLE IN TORONTO, ONTARIO, CANADA. ORIENTED FOR IBM USERS.

CCBBS.TXT/binary   27-Sep-87 941

   Keywords: BBS RBBS COMPUCARE FREE NY

   Announcing a NEW FREE BBS in the Rochester/Buffalo/Syracuse area. Its called CompuCare BBS and is available 24 hrs a day, 7 days a week. It has just been released from beta testing an already has around 300 uploads.

IBMB10.ARC/binary   02-Oct-87 53248

   Keywords: IBM BBS FRIERSON OCTOBER 1987 BOARDS NUMBERS

October 1987 listing of over 3020 IBM/clones BBSes - drastically revised. PC-Pursuit service is noted in two manners - because of recent curtailments. Download with a protocol and unpack with ARC-E.

After this display was finished, we keyed in DL4 to move to Data Library 4 (bulletin boards). At the prompt for that library we keyed in S/DES/KEY:LIST, and here are just *some* of the files that appeared:

MEDBBS.J25   25-Jul-87 16385

   Keywords: MEDICIAL MEDICINE BBS LIST PURSUIT FIDO OPUS

   Latest Medical BBS listing. Current as of July 25, 1987. Upl/Aut Ed Del Grosso 71565,1532

PARANO.LST   09-Mar-87 768

   Keywords: PARANET BBS NETWORK PHONE NUMBER LIST

   The most current list of ParaNet BBS systems nationwide. ParaNet is a loose network of BBSs that explore and discuss the paranormal: UFOs, ESP, Channeling, etc.

AJCBR.887   09-Aug-87 14586

   Keywords: AJIS NC SC LIST TELEPHONE NUMBERS 919 803 704 BBS

   August Issue of Anonymous Jones' CAROLINA BBS REVIEW, a comprehensive list of public BBSs in NC & SC, verified monthly for carrier detect. Original is available on Anonymous Jones Information System, 3/12/2400 baud, 919-832-0034, (PC-P Node 919) (FidoNode 151/105).

CHRBBS.LST   03-Jul-87 6015

   Keywords: ICN CHRISTIAN BBS LIST

   This is an update of the ICN Christian BBS list as of //03/87. This list contains information on 68 Christian BBSs around the USA and a few in Canada. A Christian BBS review is being compiled and ICN is seeking information from SysOps of Christian BBSs.

CENT-K.BBS   09-Aug-86 3925

   Keywords: BBS KENTUCKY LIST BLUEGRASS

Master listing of the Central Kentucky Bulletin Boards - Updated 8-8-86.
Listing Provided by the BLUEGRASS TELECOMMUNICATIONS
NETWORK - An organization of local and area Sysops, whose purpose is
to enhance the BBS community through the prompt exchange of
information relating to abusive users activities, non-public domain
programming, etc.

Puzzling Out the Filenames

You will find similar files and file descriptions on *all* of the six systems
discussed in Chapter 7. And as always, it is worth taking a moment to
study the descriptions before impulsively deciding to spend time and
money downloading a file. You can learn a lot from the above information that will be helpful whenever and wherever you look for BBS lists
online.

Start with the filenames and notice how the file description usually
solves the puzzle that a filename may present. Once you know that
IBMB10.ARC is the October list of boards prepared by Meade Frierson, the "10" in the filename becomes clear. Similarly, MEDBBS.J25
becomes clear once you know it is a list of medical boards prepared on
July 25. The other filenames shown here will also yield to translation
once you read their respective descriptions.

FreeTip: The "creativity" of the filenames used for BBS listings
can drive you crazy at times. But since there's nothing you can do
about it, you might as well learn how to figure them out. This is a
particularly good skill to develop if you plan to look for your lists
on other BBSs since most systems do not permit the lengthy descriptive paragraphs found on CompuServe, GEnie, and other
commercial systems. After a while, you'll be able to guess what a
BBS listings file contains without downloading it or looking at the
description. In fact, you can start with this list of BBS phone
number files downloaded from a favorite board:

> ADULTBBS.ARC
> BBS215.TXT
> GOVTBBS.ARC
> HAWAII .ARC
> MEDBBS.J01

You should also pay attention to the dates the files were uploaded.
As we said, we conducted this search in October 1987. Some of the
files were quite fresh and some were over a year old. The size of the
file is also important, if only to get an idea of what you're in for. Even

in their compressed "ARC'd" form, some BBS listings files can be very long. (CompuServe notes the size of the file in bytes next to the date. Other systems put it someplace else.) Eventually you will want a comprehensive list, but if you're just starting, a complete list may be overwhelming.

The Darwin Systems List

As you may have noticed from the file descriptions above, some individuals have taken it upon themselves to regularly compile and maintain BBS lists. This is an invaluable service, and it represents a great deal of work. Sometimes the burden becomes too much for the list-maker who, like an exhausted sysop, will give up the ghost and cease publishing. But for some reason those rigors have not affected Peter L. Olympia, the head of Darwin Systems, Inc. in Gaithersburg, Maryland. Dr. Olympia is a chemical physicist who is also a widely acknowledged expert (and columnist) on Ashton-Tate's dBASE program. Yet twice a month for the past three and a half years he has electronically published an updated list of IBM bulletin boards.

Dr. Olympia's Darwin Systems, Inc. publishes the list, and the filename is always in the form USBBSnnc.LST. The n's are numbers; the c is a character. For example, the list current at this writing is USBBS41A.LST. Translated, this means, United States BBSs, List Number 41, revision A. That is, this is the 41st month the list has been published and the first revision for this month. In two weeks, USBBS41B.LST will be published, replacing the first revision.

We found the list on GEnie in its ARC'd form, but could not locate it on any of the other commercial systems. So we called Peter Olympia. He explained that he posts the list on his own BBS on the first day of each month, "and within about eight hours it is all over the country because other sysops call and post it on their own boards." The file spreads geometrically as sysops and BBS users alike work the boards, downloading the file from one and uploading it to another. Dr. Olympia says he doesn't post the list on the commercial systems because it is very important to him that only the most current list be available.

Unless some single individual on each commercial system takes responsibility for deleting the old list and replacing it with the newest one, there would soon be several versions in the SIG data libraries. Perhaps one day the SIG sysops will appoint someone to do this or do it themselves. In the meantime, Peter Olympia has high praise for PC MagNet, an online service run by *PC Magazine*. Apparently the sysops of that system religiously call and download the new Darwin Systems list on the first of each month. The cost for using PC MagNet is $12.50

an hour for 1200 or 2400 bps access; $6.50 an hour for 300 bps. The system is accessible from (at this writing) over 300 local phone numbers. See the free program portion of the "Productivity" section of each issue of *PC Magazine* for additional details. You can also sign on through CompuServe by keying in GO PCMAGNET.

How to Completely Automate the Dialing Process
Attack Dialing

The last two problems—redialing when you get a busy signal and laboriously keying BBS phone numbers into your system—are the easiest to solve. First, get a copy of ProComm 2.4.2, the shareware comm program discussed in Chapter 16. Like every shareware comm program since PC-TALK, ProComm has a "dialing directory" into which you may enter the phone numbers you expect to call frequently. In the version 2.4.2. of ProComm, there are 100 numbered slots in the dialing directory. If you key in a phone number for slot 5 and record it, from then on you need only enter [<Alt><D>] from ProComm's main screen to get to the dialing directory, and then hit [<5><ENTER>] to dial the corresponding number.

ProComm also has a redial feature designed to be used when the number you've called turns out to be busy. If you key in [<Alt><R>], the redial window will pop onto the screen. At that point, you can either tell the program to redial the last number dialed or you can enter a list of dialing directory entry numbers separated by a space or a comma: 5,14,37,78, and so on. ProComm gives you 40 characters of space to use for this, so at an average of three characters per entry, you can stack up about a dozen numbers.

These numbers go into ProComm's circular dialing queue. The program will dial the first one on your list, and if it's busy, move on to the second one, and so on. You do not have to remain at the console while the program is dialing. When a connection is made, ProComm will sound an alarm to tell you to put the VCR on "pause" and return to the keyboard. When that call has been completed, the number will be removed from the queue and the dialing process will pick up where it left off.

FreeTip: We won't go into it here, but if you want to, you can link each phone number to a ProComm command file that you have created to automatically handle your log on, file uploads, mail collection, and so on. Command files can take a bit of time to set up,

but once they're working, your computer need never again interrupt your careful artistic analysis of *Sally Does Sunnyvale* or similarly uplifting VCR experiences.

Computer Magic

Now for the pièce de résistance: You may never need to key in another
BBS phone number for as long as you live. We've found two dynamite
shareware programs that can take an ASCII list of BBS numbers and
automatically insert them into a ProComm dialing directory. The programs are PRCMDIR.EXE and CONVERTR.BAS. Of the two, we
prefer PRCMDIR.EXE, though both are included on the disk Glossbrenner's Choice IBM Comm Pack 2—ProComm Utilities (see Chapter
16).

PRCMDIR.EXE has the ability to parse any ASCII file in which a
BBS's phone number and name are on the same line, like this small
portion of the 885 numbers on Peter Olympia's Darwin list:

PHONE	STATE	CITY	SYSOP	T/S	Bdhrs	NAME, FEATURES
201-239-1346	NJ	Verona	Mark Rapp	BV	4	Micro-Sellar BBS,240
201-277-6522	NJ	Summit	William Pappas	V	4	Gods' RBBS, a.277-363
201-279-7048	NJ	Clifton	Frank Relotto	B	4	Dean's Office, 60M
201-290-1183	NJ	Matawan	Mike Cohen	B	4	Coneworld BBS
201-290-1349	NJ	Matawan	John Ross	D$25	4	C-Central, 133M
201-299-7914	NJ	Boontown	James Sura	B$3	4	Designed Letters
201-327-8245	NJ	Ramsey	Curt Stapleton	C		Hotel California
201-337-1327	NJ	Franklin Lks	John Dougherty	O	4,N,W	*Franklin Lk ROS
201-377-2526	NJ	Madison	Glenn Catlin	BV	4	*Stocks & Such,42M
201-396-8516	NJ	Colonia	Al Reilly		4	Software Sprmkt

When you boot the program, you will see a message from someone
known only as "Sparky." Sparky frequents a board run by the National
Electronic Service Dealers Association and the International Society of
Certified Electronic Technicians, and he's quite a programmer. He
wrote PRCMDIR.EXE in Microsoft Quick BASIC and "The Window

Machine" from Amber Systems. He offers the program as BEERware. To show your appreciation, you can either send him $15 or a case of Budweiser, though he would apparently prefer the beer. After the opening message about BEERware has appeared, you are asked for the name of the text file containing the BBS numbers and the filename you want to use for output.

The program fetches the text file and shows you the first line. Your job is to scroll through the lines at the beginning of the file until you reach one containing a BBS listing. Then you mark two areas, one for the phone number and one for the BBS name. (Using the first BBS on the above list, you would mark "210-239-1346" and "MicroSellar BBS.") Finally, you must tell the program which marked area is which. From then on, everything proceeds automatically. PCMDIR scans the file, pulling out the data corresponding to your marked areas and creating a series of files in the ProComm dialing directory format. Each dialing directory file contains 100 BBS phone numbers. If you told PRCMDIR you wanted to use BBS as your output name, the first file would be called BBS1.LST, followed by BBS2.LST, and so on.

To use one of these DIR files, you have only to rename it PRO-COMM.DIR, the filename ProComm looks for when it boots up. Since PRCMDIR does not add a 1 before a long-distance number, the only other task you must perform is to tell ProComm that you want it to send the modem the command "ATDT1," before sending each number. Once you've done that, you're all set to tell ProComm to dial a batch of BBSs.

FreeTip: If you are a PC Pursuit subscriber, you should know that PRCMDIR has the ability to check each number against the current PC Pursuit telephone exchange list. However, while it comes with EXCHLIST.PCP for this purpose, the file is more than a year out of date. You'll need to contact the Net-Exchange operated by Telenet to obtain the latest list of "Pursuitable" telephone exchanges. If you choose this option, only those numbers will be included in the resulting ProComm dialing directory files. Similarly, you can also tell the program to include just those phone numbers with a certain area code, whether or not they are "Pursuitable."

The second program, CONVERTR.BAS, was written by Meade Frierson in February 1987. We cite the date because in our opinion the current version could use some work, but a newer version may be available by the time you read this. CONVERTR.BAS does essentially the same thing that PRCMDIR.EXE does, though it is less flexible. Mr. Frierson works with Peter Olympia in handling PC Pursuit information and numbers for the Darwin list, but he also publishes a list of his own. The list "includes all free IBM boards, plus those that are too small or specialized to be included in the Darwin list."

Mr. Frierson calls his list IBMBDS.LST or IBMnnn.ARC, where nnn are digits representing the month and year of publication. (For more information, look again at the CompuServe file descriptions produced when we searched on the keyword BBS above.) CONVERTR.BAS is designed to work with either the IBMBDS.LST list or the Olympia/Darwin list, not any ASCII file. Before it begins processing, it gives you the option of having a 1 inserted in front of each number or not.

The program is a bit too clever for your own good, however. If you look back at the portion of the Darwin list shown above, you will see a column heading reading "Bdhrs." That stands for "baud rate and operating hours." As you would see if you had the code explanation that accompanies the complete list, the Darwin list uses the code 4 to stand for available communications speeds of either 300/1200/2400 or 1200/2400 bps. A 9 stands for speeds of 1200/2400/9600. Unfortunately, CONVERTR.BAS automatically sets the ProComm dialing directory entry to 2400 bits per second for each 4 it sees on the Darwin list. That's fine if you have a modem that can handle it, but very inconvenient if you have 300/1200 equipment. There are ways to get around this problem, of course, but they all require effort and that's precisely what we're trying to avoid.

How to Work the Boards

The best way to get started tapping the BBS underground is to plunge in with both feet. Don't settle for a mere handful of board numbers. Get lots of them and bring them into your dialing directory as we've just described. After all, when you're just starting, you don't care which board you reach, and having ProComm or some other program cycle through a long list will increase your chances of getting on some board somewhere. Naturally, it makes sense to limit your selections to boards within your own area code to keep costs down. In addition, while you may not have a choice, you will further increase your chances of making a connection if you call late at night or during regular weekday business hours.

Before you begin dialing, make sure there's plenty of paper in your printer, and check to see that you have plenty of room to store downloaded files and captured text on your hard disk. If you don't have a hard disk, be sure to have an ample supply of formatted floppies close at hand. Finally, it's a good idea to review the commands your software requires to open and close your capture buffer and write it to disk and the procedure for downloading a file. The comm parameter setting to use for working the boards is 8/N/1.

Initialization and Sign On

Signing on to a board is similar to signing on to a commercial system. When the distant phone rings and a modem answers, your modem will lock on and in most cases you will immediately see a question from the board appear on your screen. If the connection has been made but nothing appears, try hitting <Enter> once or twice. (The sysop may have set the board to sense your communications parameters from the first carriage return character it sees.) The board will want to know your name and in almost every case, the city and state you are calling from. Most sysops would prefer you to use your real name, and it is certainly the adult thing to do. Do not abbreviate your city, but do use your state's official two-character Postal Service abbreviation.

Depending on the board's host software, you may or may not be asked a series of questions to enable the remote system to match your computer's requirements. You may be asked whether your computer can handle upper and lower case, for example, and whether or not you need "line feeds." Though it is relatively rare any more, you may also be asked how many "nulls" you need. A null is a time-wasting signal intended primarily for callers using a teletype-like machine as a terminal. These machines have no display screen, and their printing elements tend to be rather slow. By adding one or more null codes to each line of text, the remote system can give the printing element time to return to the left margin before it must deal with the next line. A single null is 30 milliseconds, but if you are using a computer it is doubtful that you will need any.

You may also be asked for your phone number. Sysops do this for a number of reasons. Should the system go down while you are online, the sysop may want to contact you about what happened so the problem can be corrected. Requesting a phone where you can be reached also offers a nice compromise between a caller's need for anonymity and the sysop's need to protect his board from computer punks. Since the name you sign on with will automatically be appended to the messages you send on the board, if you have to be anonymous, you might want to sign on with a handle like "Sparky" or "Smokey Joe." Those names will be public information. But only the sysop will know your phone number, and you can hardly object if he wants to call to chat with you directly, since even then you don't have to give out your real name.

The Advantages of "Joining" a Board

Almost all boards keep track of each caller by using the caller's name as their reference point. This has a lot of advantages for you, the BBS user, for it means in effect that by signing on for the first time you have become a member of the board. At the end of the initial sign on process, in fact, many boards will ask you to key in a password of your choosing. From then on, the board will recognize you when you key in your name and automatically prompt you for your password to make sure you really are "Smokey Joe." You won't have to go through the initialization process or answer the same questions about your city and state after your initial sign on. What's more, again using your name or handle as a reference, many boards will automatically notify you if you have any waiting mail or messages from other board members. Note that the sysop will appreciate it if you conscientiously delete mail messages sent to you once you have read them. Only you and the sysop have the power to do this, and by taking the initiative, you will help the sysop conserve hard disk space.

Download/Upload Ratios and Time Limits

Finally, because so many people call up a board and loot its libraries, downloading everything in sight without ever uploading anything in return, many sysops have had to institute time limits and download/upload ratios. Most bulletin board software packages these days let the sysop set time limits for callers on a per-session or per-day basis. Some boards may limit you to 30 minutes per session until you upload something. Others may limit you to one hour per day, regardless of the number of sign-ons or sessions. Such policies are always announced in the board's greeting message or bulletins.

Usually, the time you spend uploading a file is not deducted from your allotment. Indeed, you may find that uploading something has the effect of instantly increasing your allotment for that session. Some sysops set their boards to immediately grant you double the time spent uploading a file. The download/upload ratio (on boards that support this feature) is also completely within the sysop's power. Most sysops set their ratios somewhere between 5/1 and 25/1. The ratios refer to events, not to time or kilobytes transferred. Thus if you have downloaded five files from a board with a 5/1 ratio, you will not be permitted to download a sixth until you have uploaded one file of your own.

FreeTip: What if you're a brand new user and you have absolutely nothing of value to upload and share with the board? When that's the case, use the message area option to send the sysop a

FreeTip continued

> private note explaining your situation. Most sysops will be sympathetic and many will loosen the board's requirements for your account, suggesting that you upload whatever you can when you can.

Bulletin Board Abusers

Of course, you can get real cute about this and upload some short, garbage file to fool the machine and satisfy the ratio. But you'll only get away with it once. The same thing goes for abusive language or objectionable behavior. If you're an abusive, deliberately offensive type of person, neither the sysop nor the other members of the board want you around. Nearly all BBS packages give the sysop a "snoop" command to monitor a caller's interaction with the board. Most include a command that lets the sysop throw a caller off the board immediately. Finally, the sysop can simply lock you out by setting the board so that you'll be summarily disconnected the next time you try to sign on.

Other sysops go even further to filter out abusive callers. Some systems grant you only enough time to key in your name and address during your first sign on. The sysop will then mail a password to the address you have provided. Only by using that password in combination with your name will you be permitted into the system. The term "instant access" in a BBS listing means that the sysop does not require such "user validation."

Still other sysops charge a small fee for membership in their boards. This not only filters out the abusive callers, it tends to insure that the people who are on his board are there because they really want to be there. Membership fees also help defray the considerable hardware and maintenance expense of running a board. And since most sysops tend to use the money to buy more disk storage, "fee systems" as such boards are called, typically have the richest selections of free software.

> **FreeTip:** Though the practice is becoming increasingly rare, you may still encounter some "ring back" systems. Most sysops these days have installed dedicated phones line for their boards. But where this isn't the case, the ring back technique allows a sysop to connect his board to his main phone line. The technique is implemented by the BBS host software, which is set to watch the phone line through the modem. If the phone rings once and stops and then rings again after more than ten seconds but less than 60 sec-

onds, the software will tell the modem to pick up the phone. Thus, if you are trying to reach a ring back system, dial the number and hang up after the first ring. Then dial back within 60 seconds, ready to go online.

Graphics and Music Options

Once you've signed on, you will probably see a bulletin announcing the board's policies, purpose and goals, major subject focus, sponsoring organization, or whatever else the sysop wishes you to see. You may also be notified that graphics and music are available and be asked whether you would like the board to use them. If your system doesn't have a CGA (color graphics adaptor) card or equivalent, you definitely don't want the board to go into graphics mode. However, if you can display graphics, then by all means opt for graphics (and music, if it is offered) on a board or two. They can be lot of fun, even spectacular, and regardless of whether the board puts on a show, graphics can make your interaction with a system more visually pleasing. But graphics displays do take time, and you may find yourself waiting for the system to finish painting the screen whenever you move to a different part of the board or return to the main menu.

Fortunately, in almost every case, you can toggle the board's graphics mode on and off. In fact, just as with the commercal systems, many boards will let you set up your own permanent user profile. When you're sampling a variety of boards, there's not much point in doing this. But once you've found a board you want to call on a regular basis, you will definitely want to set your page length to 0 or otherwise eliminate pauses and prompts to "Hit <CR> for More" while you are using the board.

The Message Area

As we said at the beginning of the chapter, using a bulletin board system is very similar to tapping a SIG on one of the commercial systems. All boards have a message base (a database of user messages) for you to scan or read, and several even let you read message "threads." This means you can follow a discussion by reading a message and then reading in sequence only those messages that are replies, or replies to replies, to that message. Here, for example, is the main menu you can expect to see once you have signed on to a board running a BBS program called RBBS-PC:

```
                  RBBS-PC     MESSAGE     SYSTEM

------ COMMUNICATIONS----  --- UTILITIES ---  -- ELSEWHERE --
 PERSONAL MAIL        SYSTEM
                      COMMANDS
E)nter a Message     A)nswer Questions H)elp           D)oors Subsystem
K)ill a Message      B)ulletins        J)oin Conferences F)iles Subsystem
P)ersonal Mail Found C)omment          V)iew Conferences G)oodbye
R)ead Messages       I)nitial Welcome  X)pert on/off    Q)uit to other Subsystems
S)can Messages       O)perator Page    ?)List Functions
T)opic of Msgs Shown W)ho else is on                    U)tilities Subsystem

MAIN command <?, A, B, C, D, E, F, G, H, I, J, K, O, P, Q, R, S, T, U, V, W, X>

57 min left
```

RBBS-PC is not only one of the most widely used BBS packages in the IBM world, it is the archetype for all IBM bulletin boards. Thus, it's worth taking just a moment to study this menu since most of the other boards you will be calling offer a similar array of features. The commands under PERSONAL MAIL are fairly obvious. The Scan command displays the TO:, FROM:, RE: fields of a message header, the number, and the time and date for each message in the message base. The Topic command shows you just the RE: field and number for each message. Thus, to locate messages about subjects of interest, toggle your printer on and enter the T command. Then toggle the printer off, open your capture buffer, and enter R for Read. You will then be asked to key in the numbers of the messages you want to see. Refer to your printout and take your pick.

The SYSTEM COMMANDS include options for answering one or more sysop-prepared questionnaires. You can also review the system bulletins, leave a private comment for the sysop, look at the initial sign-on or welcoming text again, and page the sysop for some real-time online chat. (The page causes the PC or its printer to beep for 30 seconds.) The Who command exists because up to 36 copies of RBBS-PC can be run in a shared-file, networked environment. Each copy is considered a node, and Who will tell you which users are currently signed on to any other nodes.

The UTILITIES commands let you call up help menus and information to explain how the board operates. RBBS-PC has particularly good help files, and we recommend that you open your capture buffer the first time you sign on to an RBBS system and use this command for all it's worth. When you are offline, you can edit and print out the information for future reference. (This is a good practice to follow whenever you find yourself on a type of board you have never encountered before.) Incidently, the "scram" command for RBBS systems is a Control-X or a Control-K. Conferences on RBBS are special message exchange sections devoted to specific topics. Expert mode means you will see just the command line, but no menus.

The File or Library Area

Finally, there is ELSEWHERE. If the sysop has enabled the Doors subsystem feature, you will be able to leave RBBS-PC and go into DOS on the host system. This means you can run any program the sysop will permit you to run. When you are finished, you are automatically returned to RBBS. This feature used to be called "windows"—and may still be on some older RBBS systems—but since that term has been used for so many other things, the name was changed in later versions to avoid confusion. RBBS boards consist of four main areas, called subsystems. These are Doors, Files, Messages, and Utilities. The Quit command appears on the menus for the last three subsystems to prompt you for F, M, or U, or to allow you to hang up.

The Utilities subsystem presents a menu to let you choose your preferred file transfer protocol (Kermit, XMODEM checksum or CRC, YMODEM, WXMODEM, and so on), margins, lines per page, password, and so on. This is where you would go to set your page length to 0 lines to eliminate pauses. The File subsystem, of course, is where the free software is stored. Its menu looks like this:

```
          RBBS-PC     FILE     SYSTEM

------ FILE    TRANSFER---- --- UTILITIES --- -- ELSEWHERE --
  FILE TRANSFER       FILE INFORMATION
D)ownload a file      L)ist files available H)elp      G)oodbye
U)pload a file        N)ew files listed   X)pert on/off  Q)uit to other subsystems
                      S)earch file
                        directories
                      V)iew ARC
                        Contents
                      ?)File transfer
                        tutorial


FILE command <?,D,G,H,L,N,Q,S,U,V,X>

47 min left
```

Finding the Files You Want

The Download and Upload commands work as you would expect. You will be prompted for the exact name of the file you want and asked to select a protocol if you have not included a preference in the personal profile you created in the Utilities area. But of course you must first find the files you want. The List command under FILE INFORMATION will show you a menu of all the category-specific directories—think of them as "libraries"—available to you. You can then choose one and the system will list the filename, description, and upload date for each file in the directory. The New command lets you locate files by upload date. You will be prompted for a date (enter March 24, 1989 like this: 032489) or asked if you want to focus on just those files that have been uploaded since the last time you signed on to the board. (Nice feature!). At that point you can choose to search through all available directories or limit your search to one or more specific directories.

The Search command lets you specify a string of characters for the system to find. The system scans both the filenames and the file descriptions when conducting its search, so these components are in effect the "keywords" attached to each file. Case does not matter, but there are no wildcards like the asterisks and question marks you can use in DOS. You may search any and all directories. The second to last command, View, gives you a list of the names of the files that have been packed into a specific ARC file. This is a feature we wish the commercial systems would offer.

FreeTip: Two particularly good filenames to look for on any BBS are something on the order of ALLFILES.ARC or THISBD.ARC. Files with names like these typically contain the names and descriptions of all of the files available on the board. Download them with a protocol, unpack them with the archive utility, and use the program LIST.COM to search them locally as we suggested when dealing with the commercial systems. This way you can sign back on to the board and immediately begin downloading the file(s) you want. You won't have to spend any of your alloted per-session connect time searching.

Finally, the file transfer tutorial that is displayed when you key in a question mark at this RBBS menu is quite good. It not only gives you the basic information you need, it also contains a menu that lets you call up more information on each command in this section. Among other things, for example, the tutorial will show you how to save keystrokes by stacking several commands on the same line. The same information can be gotten with the Help command.

Exiting Properly

The Goodbye command on this and the other RBBS menus is worthy of special note. Not because it is anything special in and of itself, but because you will find a similar command on every board that you access. Using it is the only proper way to leave a bulletin board. In other words, when you have finished downloading the software you want, *do not simply hang up the phone.* Instead, enter the proper command to officially sign off the system. If you merely hang up when you have taken what you want, you may prevent the host computer from resetting and preparing for the next caller.

On your way out, after you have explored a board, it's also a nice idea to leave a private message for the sysop. Don't be afraid to criticize if there are some things you think he could have done better. But do so politely and offer constructive suggestions. Don't be afraid to praise a sysop, either. If you have been particularly impressed with his system, tell him so. One of the reasons sysops go to all the trouble of putting up a board is to hear from users, even if it's a simple message on the order of, "Thanks, I liked your board."

International BBS Main Networks

There are perhaps 20 to 25 BBS software packages currently used in the IBM world. Some are public domain, some are shareware, and some are commercial products. Sysops have their own reasons for going with one program or another, but as an online free software seeker the finer points of the various host programs are likely to be of little interest. All BBSs have the same basic arrary of features, and almost all of them have files for you to download. Thus it makes no difference whether you log onto a Wildcat, ROS (Remote Operating System), PC-Board, SEA-dog, No Change, or RBBS-PC system. However, there are three types of boards that have a particular feature you should know about. They are the Fido, Opus, and Collie/Colossus systems.

In addition to supporting all standard BBS features, these boards offer you access to a national and potentially international electronic mail system. Fido was the first in the field. Then Opus (named after a certain insouciant penguin in County Bloom) came along and offered Fido compatibility with a simpler sysop interface. Then Collie evolved from a package by The Forbin Project called Colossus.

The details don't need to concern us here. All you have to know is that the creators of each of these systems have established networks consisting of various BBS nodes. Each official node has a number, and this makes it possible for you on Node 20 to send messages to a friend on Node 342, regardless of where that node is located. Ideally, you can make a local phone call to your nearest node, upload a message for Mary on Node 342, and sign off the system. That night during "mail time" (say, between 4:00 and 5:00 A.M.), all of the nodes in the network will call each other to exchange message packets. If Tom on Node 589 has sent you a note, addressing it to Node 20, it will be there for you the next time you sign on.

Some sysops charge a small fee (usually about 25¢ per message) to cover the cost of the long-distance calls that are involved, and some absorb the cost themselves. The more common practice is to ask users to put a small amount of money on deposit with the sysop to cover the long-distance costs. The computer will automatically decrement your account each time you send a message and notify you when it is getting low.

Needless to say, during mail time these systems do not accept normal BBS calls. For obvious reasons, the feature is usually referred to as "net mail." It may be offered in systems like Wildcat and SEAdog, but the three we have cited are the current leaders.

FreeTip: One of the best ways to locate the Fido board nearest you is to contact the International FidoNet Association (IFNA). Here is the necessary information:

> International FidoNet Association
> P.O. Box 41143
> St. Louis, MO 63141
> Data phone: (314) 576-2743
> (Set your modem to 1200 bps, 8/N/1)

How to Set Up Your Own Bulletin Board System

The first rule of setting up your own BBS is to think about it very carefully. The second rule is, "When in doubt, don't." As we have emphasized throughout this chapter, becoming a sysop requires a substantial investment of time and money. It is a responsibility not to be taken lightly. It can be very rewarding, however, and as long as you enter the field with no illusions, by all means, go for it.

Start by working the boards yourself as we have described here. Make notes on the features you like and dislike about the various boards you call. Then contact your local computer user group to see about getting in touch with sysops in your area so you can ask their advice. It would also be a good idea to contact PRACSA at the address given earlier in the chapter. And if you subscribe to a commercial online system, nose around there for information and contacts who may be helpful. The message base of the Telecommunications SIG on CompuServe, for example, is an excellent source of sysop and BBS information. Other systems may have similarly fruitful areas.

The Right Host Software

Bulletin board software is always a hot topic of conversation among sysops, and you will discover that each individual has his or her favorite package. As with any software product, the debate centers around features, ease of use, and performance. We've looked at many public domain and shareware BBS programs, and the one we would recommend for any aspiring sysop is RBBS-PC. It has virtually every sysop and user feature you could want and even someone with only a rudimentary knowledge of BBSs and online communications will find it easy to set up.

This program has been growing and evolving since its beginning in 1983 as a programming project of the Capital PC (CPC) Users Group, and it has a record of proven reliability that would be the envy of many a commercial software product. Much of the credit goes to Tom Mack, a CPC member who has taken responsibility for the program and shepherded it through many a major upgrade and revision. The manual for the version current at this writing (RBBS-PC, version CPC15.1B) is over 150 pages long. And the complete source code for the program is supplied.

There are only a few niggling complaints one might make. It may be that the program has *too many* features for some people. That's not a major problem, of course, and some sysops understandably revel in the complete control the program gives them over their system. But for a novice sysop, it isn't always apparent which features must be set and which can be left at their default values. Still, it's all explained in the excellent RBBS-PC manual.

The other small complaint concerns performance. Snobbishness about programming languages is as offensive as computer-brand chauvinism. But RBBS is written in BASIC (compiled) with some assembler, and from the sysop side of things it doesn't seem as snappy and responsive as other packages written in C or Turbo Pascal.

On the other hand, no other program offering so many crucial BBS features is as well documented or as easy to set up and use. If you want to start your own board, you simply can't go wrong with RBBS-PC. You'll find copies in most PC user group libraries and on most commercial systems and many BBSs. All files, including the source code, occupy nearly 940K in their ARC'd form and require nearly two and a half hours to download at 1200 bps, assuming there are no errors or delays.

The program is also available on three Glossbrenner's Choice disks: IBM RBBS-1 (program), IBM RBBS-2 (support files), and IBM RBBS-3 (source code). You do not need the source code (Glossbrenner's Choice—IBM RBBS-3), but disks 1 and 2 are essential.

For Your Personal Use

If you don't want to put up a board but would like to be able to access
your computer remotely, say, calling up your office system from home
or while you are on the road to upload or download files and run programs—we would recommend something less elaborate than RBBS. In
fact, you may not need anything more than a copy of DOS and an auto-
answer modem. Turn your modem off and set it to auto-answer on the
first ring (Switch 5 up for Hayes modems). Then disable the modem's
automatic assertion of the carrier detect signal (Switch 6 up for Hayes
modems). Make sure that the DOS programs MODE.COM and
EDLIN.COM are on your disk. Then do the following: Key in MODE
COM1:1200 <Enter>, wait for the system's response, and then key in
CTTY COM1 <Enter>.

You may now flip your modem on and leave the office for the day. As
far as the office computer is concerned, all commands and output will
now come and go through the communications port (COM1). At home,
set your comm program for 7/E/1 and call your office modem. After the
modem gives you CONNECT, the next thing you see will be the DOS
prompt from your office computer. You can now run that computer from
home just as if you were sitting at its keyboard. To download a file, key
in TYPE FILENAME.EXT. To upload a file, key in EDLIN FILE-
NAME.EXT (see your DOS manual) on the remote system. Enter I for
"Insert" on the remote (you'll see "1:*" on your screen), and transmit a
text file from your home system. When you see another number and an
asterisk, key in E to "end" the EDLIN session and write the file to
disk. There are lots of refinements you can add to this procedure. The
important thing is that it works and in a pinch will serve quite well.

Don Mankin's Minihost BBS Package

ProComm 2.4.2, the shareware communications package discussed in
Chapter 16, includes a host mode that is much easier to use. Once activated, ProComm's host mode will display a very short message of your
choosing and prompt callers for their passwords each time a connection
is made. At that point, the caller can transfer files, chat with the sysop,
or "shell out" to DOS. This last option is the equivalent of the CTTY
procedure described earlier, and it requires users to enter a second
password.

The ProComm 2.4.2 host mode is not intended as a messaging system, but it is likely to give most individuals all the power and access
they need. ProComm PLUS, the commercial version of the program,
offers a fully equipped BBS. See Chapter 16 for information on how to
take a "test drive" of this product. If you decide to use ProComm 2.4.2

as a BBS, you might consider adding a program that will automatically blank the screen after ten minutes or so of inactivity. This prevents CRT "burn in" of characters displayed in the same position for hours on end. There are a number of PD utilities to do this, but we prefer FANSI Console, a program discussed in Chapter 9.

The ProComm approach is ideal for a single user. If you want to make your machine accessible to several people—such as the members of your working group, department, or task force—we recommend a program like the Wildcat or Minihost bulletin board systems. Minihost, by Don Mankin, was written specifically to allow an individual to call his or her own system remotely to download and upload files. Mr. Mankin describes his program as "a totally secure, no-nonsense BBS, ideally suited for consultants, lawyers, and small businesses. . . . Supports up to 500 users, many xfer protocols (XMODEM, YMODEM-G, YMODEM, ASCII, SEALINK, ZMODEM, WXMODEM, and PC Kermit). . . . The ideal 'personal' BBS."

The program is offered as shareware ($25), and it is both compact (161K when ARC'd) and complete. The only drawback to Minihost is that in the current version (February 1, 1988), you must prepare a text file of commands to set up the system. Since the program comes with such a file, you need only edit it to your preferences, but this is still somewhat inconvenient. For more information, contact: Mr. Don Mankin, 3211 Crow Canyon Pl, #A296, San Ramon, CA 94583.

WILDCAT! from Mustang Software

Wildcat, by Jim Harrer with documentation by Jim Harvey, is larger (four ARC'd files totaling nearly 565K), but it is a full-blown BBS system with all of the features we've described in this chapter. (A hard disk is required.) As such, the host system displays a sysop control panel—a menu of commands and switches a sysop can toggle while running his board. It also automatically blanks the screen after a period of inactivity to prevent burn-in.

One of the program's sharpest features is its installation procedure. You have only to key in MAKEWILD to run a program that will prompt you for the way you want to set up your board: "What is the maximum allowable LOGON time in minutes?," "Should the Sysop screen PUBLIC messages before they are posted on the system [Y/N]?," "Time compensation ratio on uploads is___to 1," and so on. RBBS uses the identical technique, but Wildcat's presentation is snappier (particularly if you have a color screen) and more friendly.

Version 1.0 of Wildcat came out in March 1987, and while it was quite good, it still had a few well-concealed rough edges. Version 1.03-SW ("shareware"), the version current at this writing, was issued October

15, 1987. This version not only fixes bugs and adds features (such as more transfer protocols) but also includes a greatly expanded manual and a flexible, three-track registration policy. All indications are that Mustang Software is quite serious about its product and about staying with it, two characteristics all successful shareware authors have in common.

The "SW" version is the one that can be freely distributed. If you want to register, you have three choices. You can register for $25 and receive an acknowledgment and notices of future products and enhancements. You can pay $45 to register and receive a complete copy of the package, as well as phone support. Or you can go for the full registration package. This includes the registered user version of the program with many additional features, one year of free technical support, a coupon good for one free update, proprietary utility programs, and much else besides. For more information, contact: Mustang Software, 3125 19th Street, Suite 162, Bakersfield, CA 93301-3118; phone: (805) 395-0223.

Recommended Programs

Glossbrenner's Choice Disk Reference—Chapter 8

IBM Comm Pack 2—ProComm Utilities
Includes PRCMDIR.EXE and CONVERTR.BAS for bringing lists of BBS numbers into a ProComm dialing directory.

IBM Comm Pack 3—The Communicator's Toolchest
Includes Trojan horse prophylaxis programs. Made available for the prevention of file erasure only.

IBM RBBS-1—RBBS-PC Program Disk
The RBBS-PC bulletin board program, compiled.

IBM RBBS-2—RBBS-PC Support Files
Complete documentation file, extension programs, and required text files.

IBM RBBS-3—RBBS-PC Source Code
Nice to have, but only if you or someone you know is into BASIC. If so, you can customize and recompile the program.

IBM Minihost—Minihost BBS Package

IBM Wildcat Disk 1—Wildcat BBS Package (1 of 2)

IBM Wildcat Disk 2—Wildcat BBS Package (2 of 2)

PART III

WHAT TO GET

WHAT TO BUY

9

Core Collection

MUST-HAVE PROGRAMS FOR ALL PC USERS

Some shareware and public domain programs are so good and so essential that once you've tried them, you will simply refuse to sit down at a computer without them. Why should you have to put up with a screen that scrolls off into space? Why can't you just freeze it when necessary and scroll back through its contents the way you would rewind a player piano roll? Why can't the PC remember your past commands and let you scroll back through *them* at the DOS command line, editing and changing them as needed? Why can't you just tag the files on a disk you want to erase and delete them all with a single command?

The Core Collection

Obviously we wouldn't have led you down this path of questions if the programs we're about to consider didn't give you these capabilities and many more besides. First we'll look at FANSI-CONSOLE, a "driver" program designed to be included in your CONFIG.SYS file. FANSI (pronounced "fancy") gives you complete control over your screen and keyboard. If you have a computer anxiety reaction to anything that sounds remotely technical, please fight the urge to give in to it and read about this program. If you will but take a moment to follow our simple cookbook-like instructions for installing FANSI's scroll recall feature, you will thank your lucky stars you did as we asked.

CED, the DOS "command editor," is the next program we'll look at. With this baby installed you can use your arrow keys to scroll back through the DOS commands you have already issued and edit them at the command line as if you were using a word processor. Forget about DOS's stupid editing keys and use CED instead.

The CED description is followed by a discussion of Vern Buerg's LIST.COM program, which is crucial for displaying (and searching!) text files. Then there is PC-DeskTeam, a program that can save you from spending $50 on Sidekick, and PC-Window, for those who are mainly interested in a pop-up notepad, followed by the Professional Masterkey Utilities (PMK). With PMK on your disk, there is no need to spend another $50 or so on the Norton Utilities. PMK can not only restore erased files, it includes features not found in its commercial competition.

Next we will look at DIREDIT, a disk directory editor that lets you physically sort your directories as you please and literally "pick up" and move filenames within a directory to create a customized arrangement. QFILER is described next; this program can display two file directories or subdirectories on your screen at once, allowing you to scroll through them tagging file names for copy, delete, and other operations. In our opinion, QFILER is the best program of its type and virtually essential to all DOS users, regardless of their level of experience.

Newkey is described next, a keyboard "macroing" program that can save you from spending still another $50 or $60 on Prokey, Smartkey, Superkey, and similar commercial products. With Newkey you can load any keys or key combinations with complete strings of characters and commands. Toggle on Newkey's "learn" mode and run through your regular routine for getting into a program, and you can do it all with a single keystroke from then on.

Finally, we'll look at AutoMenu and Extended Batch Language (EBL). These two programs give experienced PC users the tools they need to make hardware and software easy for the uninitiated to use. With Automenu, you can build customized menus capable of calling other programs and returning to the home menu when finished. With EBL you can "program in DOS," using functions and commands not included in the standard DOS package.

We have used Glossbrenner's Choice disks to organize the presentation of these programs. The order of the programs is determined by which programs we could pack onto which disks and come closest to our goal of "0 bytes free," not by any order of preference. We have listed the name of the package here and not all of the files it contains. With this information, you will be able to find the featured programs in any free software collection.

Needless to say, this list of specific programs we have chosen is no accident. It is the result of many years of PC use and experience and of a continual process of searching, testing, and comparing public domain and shareware programs. Consequently, we can unequivocally state that at this writing, these are the very best programs in their class and that they are damned near essential for every PC user. Which is why we have labeled them the core collection.

Recommended Programs

Glossbrenner's Choice:

IBM Core Collection   Disk 1—FANSI Prog./CED/LIST

IBM Core Collection Disk 2—FANSI Doc./PC-DeskTeam

FANSI: The FAST ANSI Console Driver

There are so many wonderful things to say about Mark Hersey's FANSI-CONSOLE that it is difficult to know where to begin. Perhaps the most succinct way to characterize the program is to say that once you've tried it, you will refuse to use a computer without it. The program has scores of features. Indeed, one of its advantages is that it incorporates within a single framework the functions of dozens of small utility programs. But the one feature we think you will find most useful is FANSI's ability to freeze the display to let you scroll back through screens that have already been displayed.

One-Button Scroll Recall

For example, suppose you have a subdirectory containing 100 or 200 files. You key in DIR and watch as the filenames scroll by. Midway through the list you glimpse a file you don't recognize. But by the time the fact registers in your mind, the filename has scrolled off the screen. Or suppose you're online with MCI or GEnie. The electronic mail messages people have sent to you appear and scroll off into space. Only then do you realize that you've forgotten to turn on your communications program's capture buffer.

In either case, with FANSI the watchword is, "Hey, no problem." You merely hit your <Scroll Lock> key and the listing or the screen is instantly put on hold. A reverse video bar appears at the top of the screen indicating that FANSI has been invoked. Then you use your arrow and <Page Up> keys to scroll back through the information that has already been displayed. You can print the information a screen at a time with your <Print Screen> key, or using another FANSI feature

you can *clip it out and write it to a file*. When you've finished, just hit
<Scroll Lock> again to release the display, and things will continue
right where you left off.

The keystrokes, frustration, and wasted time these two FANSI features alone can save you in the course of a year make the program
invaluable. There are many other features as well. To understand them,
you must have a better idea of what FANSI is and how it works its
magic. Not coincidently, the same general explanation applies to the
ANSI.SYS driver that you received as part of your DOS package when
your purchased your PC.

The Adaptor-Plug Approach

As discussed in Chapter 2, the "adaptor plug" approach followed by
DOS is the reason both the operating system and programs written to
run under its control can work on a wide variety of systems, regardless
of the requirements of the system's hardware. The operating system
plugs into the BIOS (Basic Input Output System) and your applications
programs plug into the operating system. As we know, the BIOS is the
only one of these three software components that really knows how the
specific hardware works.

Replacing the BIOS

The downside of this approach is the trade-off between widespread compatibility and performance. All of that translating and buck passing
from applications program to DOS to BIOS takes time. So in the case of
the screen, characters don't appear as quickly as they otherwise might.
The fastest, most machine-specific way for a program to handle a PC
screen is to directly manipulate the video hardware, bypassing the operating system and the BIOS completely. The slowest, most compatible
way is tell DOS to do it or to get it done. In between is the option of
bypassing DOS and speaking to the BIOS. This offers good cross-ma-
chine compatibility and better speed than going through DOS.

It is this third approach that Mark Hersey has followed with FANSI-
CONSOLE. But he has taken it to a higher level. Instead of merely
speaking to the BIOS, which Hersey feels is still too slow, FANSI completely replaces the screen and keyboard portions of the BIOS. Thus,
any program that has been written to talk to either DOS or directly to
the BIOS will perform better with FANSI installed. Programs written
to directly address the video hardware will not be affected.

FANSI also replaces the ANSI.SYS device driver supplied with all
versions of DOS from 2.x on. (The name "FANSI" stands for "fast
ANSI" driver.) Because the DOS manuals have never done a very good
job of explaining ANSI.SYS, much confusion has grown up around what

it is and what it does. Fortunately, there is a simple answer. ANSI.SYS is a piece of software that adds a series of additional capabilities to DOS's standard screen and keyboard-handling functions. If you want DOS to have these capabilities, all you have to do is put the line DEVICE = ANSI.SYS in your CONFIG.SYS file. When the PC boots up, it always looks for CONFIG.SYS. If it finds the above line in that file, the ANSI.SYS software will be loaded and become a part of DOS. FANSI is loaded the same way, as we'll see in a moment.

FreeTip: All "device drivers" work this way. If you think about it, it is really a pretty sensible system. Just as no applications software producer can be expected to create a different version of a program for every machine, Microsoft or any other operating system producer can't be expected to create operating system software capable of handling every conceivable peripheral device. And you wouldn't want them to either, because such an operating system would gobble up ever more memory. By designing the necessary "hooks" into its software, however, a company like Microsoft makes it possible for the manufacturer of, say, a CD-ROM laser reader, barcode reader, FAX board, or specialized video board, to add an extension to the operating system by supplying you with the necessary device driver software.

Being There: "I Like to watch"

Once loaded, ANSI.SYS or FCONSOLE.DEV sit in memory watching the keyboard and the screen—the two components that make up the "console" in computer-speak. They are looking for a command intended for them, a command drawn from a specific list created by the organization known as the American National Standards Institute (ANSI).

Years ago this organization produced a set of standard commands that mainframe and minicomputers could issue to better control the screen displays of their attached terminals. A terminal, remember, is little more than a keyboard and a screen connected to a mainframe by a cable or telephone wire. Most have few, if any, "brains" at all. Before terminals, there were teletype or "TTY" printers. And before the ANSI command set was adopted most "glass TTY" terminals were limited to printer-like, one-line-at-a-time displays.

The ANSI command set (currently, ANSI X3.64—1979) as implemented with the DEC VT-100 series and other terminals, made it possible for a mainframe or a minicomputer to clear a remote terminal's screen, write text from top to bottom, and send the cursor back to the top or someplace else on the screen to request input from the user. Reverse video, intense highlighting, blinking characters or words, and separately scrolling window-like sections of the screen could also be used. There were, and are, many other features as well.

It is this set of commands and capabilities that ANSI.SYS or FCON-SOLE.DEV respond to when loaded. (FANSI, however, offers even more power and more commands than the ANSI implementation.) It is worth pointing out that by adopting a standard set of commands, Microsoft and IBM have made it possible for programmers to have a high degree of control over the screen without dealing directly with the video hardware.

Escape from the Ordinary

According to the standard, virtually all such commands begin with an ASCII decimal 27, the "escape" character, followed by a left square bracket ([, an ASCII decimal 91). That's the sequence that ANSI.SYS or FCONSOLE.DEV are waiting to see, for they know that the letters, numbers, or text strings in quotes that immediately follow represent commands for them to swing into action.

This leaves two main questions regarding extended control of your screen: What *are* the correct commands? How do I send them to ANSI/FCONSOLE? The answers to both can be found in files on the two FANSI disks. (The DOS manual gives you a hint when describing the PROMPT command, but it refers you to the *IBM DOS Technical Reference Manual* for a complete list of ANSI.SYS control codes.) Mark Hersey has included all manner of programs to make it easy to send the proper codes or to otherwise configure your system. As you will see when you remove it from its archive, the "abbreviated" on-disk documentation is over 300K long. The printed manual is even more impressive.

FreeTip: FANSI is so powerful and has so many features that it can be difficult to know where to begin. The most important thing to bear in mind is that there are two ways to tell FANSI how to configure your system. Some features can be specified only through switch settings on the DEVICE = FCONSOLE.DEV line as discussed above. Others are specified by sending or typing escape sequences to the console.

The first thing to do is to print out the manual. You're not going to have to read it from cover to cover, but you will want it for reference. Second, key in:

FANSISET filename.bat SEND

This will activate FANSISET.EXE and take you to a series of menus offering you the options of setting various FANSI features. Here's where you will want to refer to the manual. If you want FANSI to speed up your keyboard, for example, you will discover that you can use the KEYRATE setting on the FANSISET keyboard menu. The IBM/PC default is 10 (internal timer ticks), a fact that has led some software houses to offer commercial programs whose sole purpose is to speed up or otherwise give you control over this feature. A setting of 40 for this feature, however, will put just about the right amount of pep into your cursor.

Make your selection(s) and then follow the instructions for leaving the program. FANSISET will then create a batch file using whatever you have chosen as your "filename.bat" in the command above. This file will contain all of the necessary escape sequences and codes to set things up the way you want them. Each sequence will be preceded by SEND, to call the supplied SEND.EXE program responsible for transmitting them to the system. Naturally, you can incorporate these SEND sequences in your AUTO-EXEC.BAT file (use your word processor to insert the batch file FANSISET has created) so everything will happen automatically each time you boot up.

Finally, it is important to be aware of the terms SET and RE-SET. In computer talk they do not necessarily mean "on" and "off." Instead they refer to two different states. The FANSI manual uses these terms frequently, but if you keep the computer talk definition in mind, you will have no trouble understanding SET and RESET.

FANSI version 2.0, the version current at this writing, supports the PC/XT/AT line of IBMs and compatibles. It requires 32K of memory (4K when used with the EGA) and DOS 2.x or later. It does not support the PC jr, DEC Rainbow, Sanyo 550, Tandy 2000 (the 1000 and 3000 *are* supported), Tava PC, TI PC, Wang PC, or Zenith 100 (the 150 and 200 series *are* supported). And while it can be used on the PS/2 line, full compatibility won't be available until the next version.

FANSI Features

We know of at least two commercial programs (for $50 and $70) that offer just the scroll and recall feature discussed earlier. FANSI does scroll and recall with one hand tied behind its back, and this feature only scratches the surface. Among other things, for example, FANSI can:

- Automatically blank one or two screens (to prevent burn-in) after the number of minutes of inactivity you specify.

- Expand the type-ahead keyboard buffer to 255 characters.

- Make the <Caps Lock> key like that of a regular typewriter so that it unlocks when you hit a <Shift> key.

- Completely customize your keyboard, whether you want to alter the meaning of one key, swap two keys, or use the Dvorak keyboard reassignment program (included).

- Make DOS's "bell" (beep tone) as long or as short as you like.

- Generate audible key clicks. (Good for PC clones whose keyboards may not click themselves.)

- Support 43-line displays (EGA and EGD).

- Speed up your keyboard by controlling the repeat rate. (Can make a cursor zip across the screen, whether you're in DOS or using a program.)

There are other capabilities as well. Most features can be set by either adding a slash command to the FCONSOLE.DEV line in your CONFIG.SYS file or by keying a command on the fly, after you have already booted your system. To save you the trouble of digesting the manual, we have included our own explanations of the features and how to set up your CONFIG.SYS file to take advantage of them. We have also set up a series of FANSI-created batch files to give you instant access to the most frequently used features. This makes setting your keyboard's key repeat rate as easy as typing in KEYRATE 40 or KEYRATE 25 and hitting <Enter>.

You will also find a series of files related to NANSI.SYS and RAW.COM, two public domain programs. NANSI.SYS will be of interest to programmers for its C and assembler source code. RAW.COM can be used with either NANSI or FANSI to further speed up some screen displays.

The Recipe for One-Button Pause and Scroll Recall

As promised, here is a cookbook approach to implementing FANSI's scroll recall feature. First, make sure that the program FCONSOLE.DEV is on your system disk, the one you use to start your computer. Next key in COPY CON:CONFIG.SYS and hit <Enter>. The cursor will be at the left, but there will be no DOS prompt next to it. Now key in DEVICE = FCONSOLE.DEV /L = 1 and hit <Enter>. Finish up by hitting your <F6> key to end the file with a Control-Z. Now reboot your system.

As the system starts up, a one-line banner will appear at the top of the screen announcing the fact that FANSI is being loaded. From now on, each time you hit your <Scroll Lock> key, whatever the system is doing at the time will be instantly put on hold and a FANSI bar will appear at the top of the screen. Use your cursor, paging, <Home>, and <End> keys to scroll backwards and forwards through the display. When you want to resume where you left off, just hit <Scroll Lock> again. Simple, no? And absolutely invaluable!

The FANSI Console package is shareware. The registration fee is $75 for the complete package, which includes the software, a 500 + -page slipcased manual, and access to telephone technical support. Shareware registration only is $49.95 and includes a copy of the latest version on disk plus telephone support. Shipping and handling is extra in both cases (minimum charge is $4; contact the company for details). Quantity discounts and site licenses are available. Michigan residents should add sales tax. Visa, MasterCard, and American Express are accepted. Contact: Hersey Micro Consulting, Inc., P.O. Box 8276, Ann Arbor, MI 48107; phone: (313) 994-3259.

CED: The DOS Command Editor

There are a number of DOS command editors in the IBM free software world, but Chris Dunford's CED is far and away the best. If you use your computer solely to run Lotus or dBASE or some other applications program, you don't need CED. But even if you use DOS only for such simple tasks as calling for a list of files on a disk or in a subdirectory, you will not want to sit down at your machine without Chris Dunford's command editor. Fast, responsive, and thoughtfully designed, CED is absolutely essential.

Circular Command Buffer

CED has lots of functions, but there are two you will use almost constantly. The first is its ability to remember and reissue DOS commands. Once loaded, CED sets up a circular buffer in memory to record each DOS command. The buffer can be as large or as small as you like. CED defaults to 2048 bytes. PCED, the commercial version of the program, defaults to 1000 bytes. (One byte equals one character.) You can scroll backwards and forwards through this buffer at any time by hitting the up and down arrows on the numeric keypad.

Suppose, to use a simple example, you wanted a directory of files in a sub-subdirectory on Drive C. You key in DIR\FRUIT\PARES and hit <Enter>. Drive A comes on and the system gives you an error message. Obviously you thought you were on Drive C when you issued the command, but were really logged onto Drive A. With CED loaded, this is merely a minor inconvenience. You key in C to get back over to Drive C and then hit your up arrow key to scroll back through the CED command buffer until you see DIR\FRUIT\PARES appear on the command line. Then, now that you are logged onto the correct drive, you hit <Enter>.

Oops. The system gives you another error message. You hit the up arrow again to redisplay at the DOS prompt the command you just entered. Your brain has obviously been on break for you quickly see the problem. Instead of "PARES" you should have keyed in "PEARS." Here is where CED's second major feature comes into play. With DIR \FRUIT\PARES on your DOS command line, you use the left and right arrow keys to move the cursor over to the incorrect word. Then you key in your correction and hit <Enter>. The keys for insert, delete, home, and end may also be used. In short, CED lets you edit the DOS command line just as if you were using a word processing program.

We've chosen a somewhat silly example. But in real life it is very easy to make a mistake when keying in a long DOS command string or path name. Without CED, your only alternative is to start from scratch and rekey an entire command to correct a single character. But with CED, correcting such mistakes is a snap.

Define Your Own Commands

CED also lets you define command synonyms. For example, if you want the system to give you a directory every time you key in "d" (instead of DIR), you can load CED and key in "CED SYN d DIR." From then on, each time you hit an upper or lower-case *d* followed by <Enter>, the system will act as if you had keyed in DIR. Since all too frequently we find that we've keyed in "DRI" instead of "DIR," we have set CED to define "DRI" as DIR. This eliminates the "Bad command or file name" error that the incorrect command produces. It also lets you pretend that the computer really knows what you mean, even if you have not expressed yourself precisely.

Space prohibits a complete list of CED's other features. But you should know that as good as CED is, the commercial version, PCED ("professional CED") is even better. Among other things, it offers an online help command, the ability to automatically log every DOS command issued in a session to a file, a "learn" mode that lets you save the synonyms you have defined during a session to a file for reloading later, and much else besides. The documentation for the public domain version is on disk. PCED customers receive a typeset manual. In both cases, the doc is well written and complete.

Chris Dunford has generously placed CED in the public domain. PCED (version 1.01a) sells for $35, plus $3 shipping and handling (UPS in continental U.S.). Visa, MasterCard, and Choice are accepted. Maryland residents should add $1.75 sales tax. Site licenses and volume discounts are available. Contact: The Cove Software Group, P.O. Box 1072, Columbia, MD 21044; phone: (301) 992-9371.

Vernon Buerg's Famous LIST.COM Program

Vernon Buerg is an absolute wizard. He would deserve that title on the basis of LIST alone. But over the years he has made many other contributions as well, as we shall see time and again throughout the chapters of this book. All of Mr. Buerg's productions are fast, responsive, and thoughtfully programmed. All of them are of top quality. And, equally important for any successful PD or shareware programmer, all of them fill a genuine need. Clearly Vern Buerg is right up there with Ward Christensen in the pantheon of programming heroes.

You have only to take a quick look at LIST to see what we mean. The version current at this writing is 6.2a. The program started out many years ago as a tool for listing a text file to the screen. In the absence of a backscrolling feature of the sort provided by FANSI-CONSOLE, the only way to look at a text file on the screen is to TYPE it and repeatedly hit the <Pause/Break> key or load a word processing program and look at the file through it.

LIST in Action

With Mr. Buerg's program, you need only type in LIST FILE-NAME.EXT, and the first 23 lines of the file virtually flash onto the screen. The LIST "window" is framed by a line at the very top of the screen that provides the name and creation date and time of the file you are viewing, plus the current line number and right scroll offset (the number of columns to the right of the file's right margin). At the very bottom of the screen is the program "Command" prompt, followed by 31 spaces, and concluding with the list of LIST "Options" you have enabled.

You can scroll through the file a line at a time with the arrow keys, a screen at a time with the <PgUp> and <PdDn> keys, or by great leaps and bounds with the <Home> and <End> keys. And you can scroll left and right with the appropriate arrow keys. The size of the text file LIST can handle can range up to 1.6 megabytes (16 million bytes). Lines within a file may be up to 256 characters long. Lines longer than 80 characters may be viewed by scrolling right or by enabling the LIST "Wrap" option. If you have an enhanced graphics adaptor (EGA) display, LIST can show you 43 lines of text at a time. DesqView, DoubleDOS, and Apxcore are also supported.

Filters, Tabs, Line Feeds, and FIND!

LIST can also filter your files. If you want to expand tab characters, remove backspace characters (usually found as part of words that have been underlined by their creator), add line feed characters to lone carriage returns, or strip the high bits and control characters from a file created by programs such as WordStar or PFS:Write, LIST can do it in a flash. Just bring the file into LIST, set the appropriate options, and follow LIST's procedures for marking lines and dumping text to a disk file. The program includes a command to let you create a version of itself ("clone") with all of the options and colors set to your preferred defaults.

You can also freeze the top half of the display and scroll through the rest of a file in the bottom half. You can "shell" out to DOS to run another program or do something else and return to LIST with DOS's EXIT command. These and several display-related features we have not mentioned would be enough to earn LIST a place at the top of anyone's list of essential software. But LIST.COM has another feature that is pure dynamite—its FIND command.

Suppose you are using LIST to scroll through a file containing the names and one-line descriptions of literally thousands of public domain programs. It might be a file that you have downloaded from GEnie or CompuServe containing the contents of a special interest group library (see Chapter 7.) And suppose you feel like spending the evening playing an adventure game. To locate every occurrence of the word "ADVENTURE" in the file, you have only to hit <F> to generate LIST's "Find" prompt and key in ADVENTURE. LIST will search each line of the file for an exact match. (You can tell LIST to ignore or respect upper and lower case if you like.) When it finds the first occurrence, it will display the line on the screen in video highlighting or intense color. To look for the next occurrence, you have only to hit A for "again" or <F3>.

What makes this feature so remarkable is that it works so fast. LIST operates by pulling chunks of the target file into memory and conducting its search at the speed of light. If you want to create a separate file containing only the lines related to your search term, you may do that as well. Just use LIST to mark the target lines and write them to a file of your choosing. The one thing that LIST cannot do is conduct a full-scale Boolean search (AND, OR, NOT, etc.), but it is so fast that most of the time this won't matter. You can try a search word, and if you come up empty try another and still another in the time it takes just to load a commercial text-searching program.

Mr. Buerg offers LIST as shareware for the extremely modest registration fee of $15. Corporate and institutional site licensing, customization, and source code arrangements can be made by contacting the programmer: Mr. Vernon D. Buerg, 456 Lakeshire Drive, Daly City, CA 94015.

Utility in Residence: PC-DeskTeam (Formerly PC-DeskMates)

The best way to introduce this program is with the following question: Why buy Sidekick for $57 (discounted mail-order price) when you can try PC-DeskTeam for free and become a registered user for a total cost of $25? Not to mention the possibility of earning shareware commissions.

Frank Milano wrote the original version of PCDT in 1985 for his wife, who found Sidekick to be too "bytehead" for her tastes. It is written in Turbo Pascal, so it is quite snappy and responsive. It requires only 64K of memory and does virtually everything that Sidekick does. Once loaded, all PCDT features are available to you at any time, regardless of what you are doing with the PC, by keying in [<Alt><M>]. Like Sidekick, "PCDT" puts the current program on hold and pops up on top of the current screen. Its features include:

- An alarm clock that you can set to go off at a chosen time and display a chosen message, chime every hour, and display the current time in the upper right corner of your screen every 15 seconds. You can also use this feature to set the PC to automatically run a program at a specified time. Just substitute a command or the name of a batch file for the optional alarm message, preceding it with a right angle bracket character.

- A four-function, plus percentages, pop-up calculator.

- A phone dialer capable of using an unlimited number of phone books and dialing out via COM1 or COM2, so you may use two telephones. You will need at least one Hayes-compatible modem to use this feature.

- An appointment calendar for any year from 1964 through 2050. Displays any month, marked with holidays and your personal notes.

- Access to five major DOS commands from within PCDT.

- A notepad with a capacity of 2000 characters and most major word processing functions.

- A printer control menu to send special feature setup commands to your printer (compressed print, bold, double width, and so on). You may use PCDT to toggle on and off up to five printer features. The program comes with prepared printer configuration files for IBM/Epson and Okidata u92 or u93 printers with or without Plug 'N' Play. Other configuration files for other printers can be created as well.

- Typewriter mode for typing up quick notes, labels, envelopes, and the like, from your keyboard directly to your printer.

This is a very well-written, smoothly functioning program. The only important Sidekick feature that it lacks is Sidekick's ability to clip out portions of the underlying application program's screen and import it into the notepad. However, as noted earlier, you can do this with FANSI-CONSOLE. And you can do it with Newkey, a program we'll tell you about in a moment. You can also do it with the cut-and-paste function of the shareware program Homebase 2.0. This program is much more elaborate than PCDT, but it has gotten good reviews and is worth your consideration. It is available through the normal distribution channels or from Brown Bag Software, Inc. See the discussion of PC-Outline in Chapter 12 for contact information.

The company is aware of this lack, but according to Alternative Decision Support's Peggy Kalke, there hasn't been much call for it and there are no plans to add it in the future. Ms. Kalke also told us that PCDT works with Smartkey, a popular keyboard macroing program. However, it does not work with Newkey. German, Finnish, Greek, and other foreign-language versions of PC-DeskTeam are available. Call the company for details.

PC-DeskTeam is shareware, and evaluation copies are available from the company for $10. If you like the program and decide to register, the cost is $15. If you get the program from another source and decide to register, the cost is $25. Registered users receive a new PC-DeskTeam distribution disk with a unique registration number, telephone support, one free major update, and a commission of $5 on each new user who provides your registration number as a reference. (Lest you suspect we've loaded the dice, the copy of PCDT on the Glossbrenner's Choice disk does not contain a commissionable number.) You may register by phone. Visa and MasterCard are accepted. Shipping is $2.50. New York residents should add eight percent sales tax. Contact: Alternative Decision Software, Inc., P.O. Box 307, Lancaster, NY 14086; phone: (716) 684-2423.

Pop-Up Notepad: PC-Window

There's an old saw in computing stating that no matter how much random access memory (RAM) you have, it will always be one kilobyte less than you need. Even though memory is cheap today, there are so many programs available to compete for its use that it simply makes good sense to preserve as much free RAM as you can. This is one of the nice things about Borland's Sidekick: You don't have to load all the Sidekick's features if you don't want to. You can leave out the calendar, for example, or exclude the notepad. The difference between full-featured and minimal installations can be as much as 22K of RAM or more. PC-DeskTeam, in contrast, doesn't give you these options. It always occupies slightly more than 64K.

However, if your primary interest is in a pop-up notepad and if you don't really want to give up RAM for pop-up functions you may not use, then we recommend PC-Window. The program is completely compatible with FANSI and Newkey, which is a big plus in our book. And it gives you an 80-column, 12-line notepad to work with, compared to DeskTeam's 40-column, 20-line pad. Also included is a stopwatch-like timer with a "lap" or "split time" function, a settable alarm, and a pop-up ASCII table.

Once the program has been loaded, you can cause a menu containing all available features to pop up by hitting [<Alt><F10>]. Or you can look at the timer only by keying in [<Alt><1>]. This causes a colorful window to pop up, with the timer and alarm information, as well as a ticking real-time clock and the date.

You can start the timer from this point with [<Alt><2>], but you can also do so directly from DOS by keying in the same combination. The system will make a sound to acknowledge that the timer has been toggled on, but no window will be displayed. The timer offers a handy way to keep track of all sorts of things. Toggle it on at the start of an online session, for example, and off again when you finish, to get a quick estimate of how much the session cost. Similarly, you might use the alarm to remind you to hold a recreational computing session (i.e., game playing) to a certain amount of time.

The notepad [<Alt><7>] can be convenient when you're online as well. You might use it to dash off a quick reply to an electronic mail letter, for example. Or a brilliant idea—or simply yet another item for your grocery list—may occur to you while you're using dBASE or

Lotus. In fact, because PC-Window can load previously created files
into its window, you could use it to create your own pop-up screen of
crib notes for a given program. (Such files can be no longer than 960
characters.)

There is no documentation file with PC-Window, but the program's
greeting screen provides enough information to get you started. The
above paragraph should be a help as well. The payoff is that PC-Window occupies less than 20K of RAM when loaded. A savings of 44K
(over PC-DeskTeam) may not sound like much, but it is enough to accommodate a keyboard macroing program like Newkey with about 10K
to spare.

PC-Window is shareware. The registration fee is $10. The program's
source code is available for $30. Contact: Creative Freeware Unlimited,
P.O. Box 10047, Columbia, MO 65205.

Recommended Programs

Glossbrenner's Choice:

IBM Core Collection Disk 3—PMK Utilities/DIREDIT

PMK: The Professional Master Key Utilities

Like untold thousands of other PC users, over the years we have found
Peter Norton's Norton Utilities to be invaluable. The man really is a
programming genius, and a superb writer as well. Version 4.0 of the
Norton Utilities package sells for about $55 at a mail-order discount,
and while it includes many features, the one most people use most often
is its power to recover an erased file. This is possible because when
DOS "erases" a file it merely sets some software flags that free up the
space the file occupies. As long as no other file comes along to take over
that space, the "erased" data remains on the disk, something certain
national figures learned to their dismay during the Iran-Contra Hear-
ings in 1987. Recovering an "erased" file *can* be as simple as resetting
the DOS flags just mentioned.

There have been public domain programs in the past capable of doing
this, but we could find none that would work with DOS 2.x and above.
The Ultra Utilities, a package you may see in some PD catalogs, will
not work with a hard disk, and the program UNDEL.COM will work
only if you can remember the exact name of the file you wish to recover.
What we were after was something more like the Norton Utilities, and

when at last we found Reggie Gage's previous effort, the Master Key Utilites, we said "Wow!"

When Mr. Gage brought out his Professional Master Key Utilities (PMK) in November 1987, we said "Double wow and a half!" It is exactly the kind of shareware equivalent to the Norton Utilities we were looking for. In layout, design, functions, and operation it is a commercial product in every way except its price ($25). What's more, it not only recovers files, it includes features that eliminate the need for a clutch of public domain file-altering utility programs.

Undeleting Erased Files

Let's start with PMK's "undelete" feature. When the program loads in, you will see that one of its menu options lets you tell PMK which disk drive to focus on. Assume you select Drive C, your hard disk. Another option lets you tell PMK that you want to undelete files. Selecting it causes the program to display a list of all of the subdirectories, regardless of how deeply they are nested. Move the highlight bar to your target subdirectory, hit <Enter>, and a list of deleted files appears instantly on your screen. This will show you the file-creation time and date, size, and attributes of the erase file. This information can be very helpful, but it is something that the Norton Utilities package (version 3.0) does not provide.

The only difference between what you will see here and the kind of file list generated by the DOS DIR command is that the first character of each deleted filename is the Greek character sigma (the alchemist's symbol for "man"). This character was substituted for the original first letter by DOS when it "erased" the file.

Pick a file and tell PMK to undelete it. PMK will ask you to key in a character to replace the sigma. When you have done so, the program will automatically try to rebuild the file's File Allocation Table (FAT) chain using its "best guess" when necessary about where everything should go. That's the technical explanation of what we have referred to as setting certain software flags. When PMK is finished, the file will either be restored in toto or in part, or you will receive a message that file recovery cannot be accomplished for this particular file.

The Professional Master Key Utilities also let you undelete an entire subdirectory, something most commercial packages cannot do. The trick is to first recover the deleted subdirectory just as you would a deleted file. You can then tell the program to look in that newly undeleted directory for deleted files, and restore them as well if you like. This will work as long as the files you want were stored in the first cluster (a unit of disk storage space) of the subdirectory, so 100 percent success cannot be guaranteed. But some insurance is better than none at all.

Testing PMK

After successfully restoring many different files, we got just such a
message when testing PMK. (The erased file's crucial first cluster had
been appropriated by another file, but there's no need to worry about
what a cluster is.) So we asked the Norton Utilities to attempt the same
recovery. This seemed to work, and the program assured us that the file
had been restored. However, when we went to look at the newly "restored" text file, nothing but garbage appeared on the screen. That certainly doesn't amount to a benchmark test of the two programs, but it is
definitely a point of interest. In any case, whether you use the Norton
Utilities, PMK, or some other package, the sooner you attempt recovery after a file has been deleted, the greater your chances of complete
success.

Like the Norton Utilities, PMK lets you display, alter, and record
information found in disk sectors, and it lets you search for ASCII or
hexadecimal data anywhere on the disk, sector-by-sector. It will display
technical information about the disk if you like, and you can ask it to
"map" the disk or a particular file (give you a graphic representation of
space allocation) as well. But it also includes features not found in the
Norton package. Specifically, PMK lets you change the date, time, and
attributes (hidden, read only, system, or archive) of any file. Heretofore
it has been necessary to use a special small public domain utility program to perform each of these functions.

Wiping Disks and Files and Saving Hard Disks

PMK can also "zero-out" a single file or an entire disk. This means that
it can completely wipe out any traces of the data, so that even the most
clever of Congressional investigators could not restore an erased file.
Mr. Gage has also included a program to fill all free sectors of a disk
with a message of your choosing. The message would be visible only to
someone using a program like PMK to examine a disk's sectors.

Finally, the Professional Master Key Utilities package includes a program called UF (for "unformat"). This program is designed to help you
recover from accidently reformatting your hard disk. When DOS formats a floppy disk, it initializes every track on the disk and checks it for
errors. That completely wipes out all data. When a hard disk is formatted, however, only certain portions of the disk are altered (the FAT,
boot sector, and root directory). The data itself is not touched. The
PMK UF utility saves a copy of these sections to a file (on a floppy
disk), enabling you to rebuild the hard disk should disaster occur. To
benefit from the program, of course, you must periodically run it so that
the information it contains will be as current as possible.

The shareware registration fee for PMK is $25 and it includes a copy of the latest release. The 54-page manual at this writing is available only as a file on the disk. Contact: Reginald P. Gage, RPG Software Farm, P.O. Box 9221, Columbus, MS 39705-9221.

"Editing" Your Directory: DIREDIT

The only significant Norton feature the PMK package does not support at this writing is a directory sort. There are lots of programs that will *display* a disk's directory in sorted order, but few that physically sort the filenames so that, once sorted, they appear in sorted order each time you key in DIR to get a directory. Norton's commercial program DIRSORT.COM is one. Peter Fletcher's shareware DIREDIT.EXE is another.

DIREDIT lets you do the equivalent of reaching into your floppy disk directory or hard disk subdirectories to move filenames around like magnets on a refrigerator or a television executive moving weekly show around on a scheduling board. You can tell the program to do an automatic sort specifying a sort in ascending or descending order by date, filename, file extension, or file size. But you can also "pick up" a filename or subdirectory name and move it to a different location on the list, much as you might move a block of text from one part of a page to another with a word-processing program. You may also change the name and the date stamp of any file or subdirectory.

Up to 80 filenames can be displayed at a time. If you're dealing with more than 80 files or subdirectories, you can view them in 80-file chunks or windows. Simply hit the <PgDn> key to look at the next screenfull of filenames. In addition, when there are more than 80 files, the screen also divides vertically to show 40 files in the right window and 40 in the left. The two windows can be scrolled independently, if you like, meaning that the right window could be showing files 1 through 40, while the left window was showing files 121 to 160.

Unfortunately these windowing features are not very well explained in the documentation. There is no special indication on the screen to alert you that the screen has been divided vertically when there are more than 80 files, so it is necessary to experiment. The program could use a color capability (it runs in "black and white" even on a color monitor). And the screen handling could be crisper. There is a tendency for the highlight bar to run past the file you are aiming for if you use too heavy a hand on the arrow keys, for example.

DIREDIT lets you direct the program to focus on a particular subdirectory or disk when you invoke it the first time. And you can change to a different directory without leaving the program. There is also a built-in safety function that applies whenever you are using DIREDIT on a bootable floppy or hard "system" disk. The hidden DOS system files IBMBIO.COM and IBMDOS.COM will appear to DIREDIT. Since these files must always be the very first files on a bootable disk, you obviously don't want DIREDIT to sort them, and it will not do so unless you tell it to.

Online Help

Entering a question mark or hitting <F1> causes the online help text to be displayed. Because it is more than a simple sorter, DIREDIT is a little less convenient to use than Peter Norton's DIRSORT.COM if sorting is all you want to do. But it works quite well, and considering the *other* powers it offers, it is a worthy substitute for the commercial product.

Your shareware registration fee of $20 ($30 Canadian, £15 British) entitles you to "support upgrades" to get the latest version into your hands, plus help with DIREDIT-related problems (including telephone support) for a year from the date of registration. Registered users of Mr. Fletcher's HDTEST hard disk-testing program may register DIREDIT for $10. (HDTEST is the most thorough hard-disk-testing program we have ever seen. See Chapter 11 for more information.) Contact: Peter R. Fletcher, 1515 West Montgomery Avenue, Rosemont PA 19010.

Recommended Programs

Glossbrenner's Choice:

IBM Core Collection Disk 4—QFILER and Associates

Quick Filer: QFILER and Associates

The main program we will be discussing here is Kenn Flee's QFILER.COM, and it is one of those programs you just can't wait to tell someone about. The "associates" here are: FCDISK, FILECAT, LITLBOOK, LIST, ARCA, ARCE, ARCV, and FINDIT. These are programs that QFILER can call and run if you like.

QFILER is part of a long tradition of personal computer disk file-managing programs dating back to the days of CP/M. Its antecedents include such venerable programs as CLEAN, WASH (written by Michael J. Karas in 1981 for CP/M and ported to MS-DOS soon thereafter), SWEEP, CSWEEP, and VFILER ("visual filer"). Indeed, as a long-time VFILER user we were prepared not to like QFILER. But VFILER's deficiencies and Mr. Flee's wonderful programming completely won us over.

We can illustrate the primary purpose of QFILER and its relatives by asking you to imagine that you have 30 files on a disk, some of which you would like to keep and others, erase. If you use DOS to do this, you will have to key in DIR to get a list of all the names (and unless you've sorted the directory, the list will probably be arranged in random order). Then you will have to repeatedly key in "DEL filename.ext" as you work your way through the directory deleting files. There are no two ways about it, this is a *lot* of work. But DOS itself doesn't provide any alternative.

Two QFILER Windows

Now let's bring QFILER into the picture. If the disk you want to clean up is in Drive A, you have only to key in QFILER A: and hit <Enter>. The program will load and quickly divide the screen down the middle into two windows. The list of files on the disk in Drive A will be displayed in the left window. You will see the first 20 filenames on the screen and can use your cursor and paging keys to make the list scroll. At the bottom of the window, QFILER will tell you not only how much space is left on the disk but also the total number of kilobytes occupied by all of the files (this is an unexpected convenience). If you hit <F7>, the screen will blink and the list will reappear, sorted in alphabetical order. You can also sort by file extension and by date.

A bright triangle to the left of the filenames serves as your marker. Your goal is to move it through the list, stopping to mark each file that you want to delete (hit <F9>). When marked, the target filename will be displayed in highlighted text. After you have marked or tagged all of the desired files, you can enter a single command to delete all of them all at once. *Now* you're cookin'.

Let's suppose that you also want to copy some files from Drive A to Drive B. Again, scroll through the list marking the target files. Then enter a single command and respond to the QFILER prompt for destination drive and/or subdirectory. As soon as you do this, the right window will display the file list for Drive B. You can then enter a command to move your marker over to *that* window and execute commands over there. Alternatively, before copying you could tell QFILER to put some other disk or subdirectory in the right window, move over there, and delete files to make room for the files you plan to copy. You can even tell the program to display the contents of a subdirectory located within the subdirectory currently displayed in the left window (a "sub-sub-directory," as it were).

LISTing Files and Executing Programs

That's straightforward enough and certainly a convenience, but there is much more that QFILER can do. Suppose there is a text file on Drive A that you would like to look at. Move your marker to the target filename and hit <L> for "list." QFILER will then call LIST.COM and turn control of the computer over to it temporarily. You can use LIST.COM just as described earlier in this chapter. When you are finished, hit <Esc> and you will be returned to QFILER.

Perhaps even more remarkable, you can use the same technique to *execute* programs from QFILER. When the program has finished its run, you will be returned to QFILER. If you need to feed parameters to a program before running it, instead of just picking its name off a menu, QFILER has commands for that as well. QFILER also has several built-in commands to call specific programs, whether or not they are in the on-screen window at the time. One is FILECAT, another Kenn Flee program. FILECAT lets you create a database of disk and filenames, keying in keywords and descriptions for each. Once created, you can search the database for all of the files tagged with a particular keyword. FILECAT also includes a menu for setting an Epson command-compatible printer's type style and left margin. There is also FCDISK, a program designed to create an alphabetical list of files on a disk or in a subdirectory using information stored in the FILECAT database.

Mr. Flee's LITLBOOK.COM is also accessible via QFILER. Begun as a project to demonstrate the Database Toolbox from Borland International for the Madison, Wisconsin, users group, this program has evolved into a real little gem. It lets you build a database of addresses for searching and/or label printing. You can tag each address with one of up to 30 different classifications, and you can search for anything in the lines containing the address, the phone number, the comment line, or some other data item.

All three of these programs are fast and responsive, though we suspect that the main reason for linking them to QFILER is that of common authorship. The link to LIST.COM and four other programs makes more sense in our opinion.

The other four programs are Vern Buerg's ARCA, ARCE, and ARCV, and Larry McMains's FINDIT. ARCA lets you use QFILER to tag the files you want to add or place in an archive and do so with a single, simple command. ARCE lets you extract files from an archive. And ARCV displays a verbose listing of the files an ARC file contains. FINDIT is like WHEREIS (Chapter 10) and similar programs, though it appears to offer more options. Briefly, it will search for every copy of a file or every file meeting your filename search criteria on a hard or floppy disk. It delivers a list of the filenames and their locations as it proceeds.

Since QFILER is often found alone on disks and online systems, we have searched out and assembled all of the above programs onto the Core Collection Disk 4. However, it is important to point out that you do not need the additional programs to use QFILER, though you will probably want to have LIST so you can look at text files before deleting them.

The program has plenty of power all by itself, and it encompasses within it many of the functions formerly available only through a clutch of small utility programs. These include the ability to:

- Change the volume label of a disk or subdirectory.
- Rename files *and* rename subdirectories.
- Change the date and time stamp of any file.
- Change a file's attribute to hide or unhide it from the normal DIR command or protect it from erasure by changing its attribute to "read only."
- Make and remove subdirectories.
- *Move* (not just copy) files from one subdirectory to another (requires DOS 3.x)

Masterful Programming

There are other features as well. But what we feel is fundamentally impressive about QFILER is the masterful way it is programmed. There is a bounce bar you can use to select commands, for example, but the program responds to the first letters of those commands as well. Similar file-managing programs force you to use the bounce bar. There is a pop-up help screen as well, and significantly, there is no need to toggle it off before entering your chosen command. You can simply enter the command and QFILER will both take the specified action and return you to the main QFILER screen. We've looked at a lot of similar programs, and QFILER clearly tops them all. It really is a super piece of software.

Your shareware registration fee of $20 brings you a copy of the most recent version of QFILER and support programs, a printed manual, and a function key template. You will also be notified of any major upgrades and/or future enhancements. Wisconsin residents should add 5%

sales tax. Contact: Jamestown Software, 2508 Valley Forge Drive, Madison, WI 53719. For quantity purchases and site license information, phone: (608) 271-2090.

Recommended Programs

Glossbrenner's Choice:

IBM Core Collection Disk 5—Newkey 4.0 and 3.0

Configure Your Keyboard: Newkey

The essence of a personal computer is and ever shall be *infinite configurability*. Certainly you physically configure things by assembling a particular collection of hardware components, much as an audiophile assembles a sound system. But you also temporarily configure the contents of the machine's memory, its screen, its printed characters, and so on, each time you run a piece of software. A switched-off computer is like a collection of empty glass goblets waiting to be filled. Its resonance of the moment is entirely dependent on how, and with what, those goblets have been filled.

Newkey's "Learn" Mode

Frank Bell's Newkey is part of this process, for it allows you to fill individual keys (and key combinations) with whatever characters or commands you want. For example, if you wanted to make your <F1> key issue the command [DIR <Enter>] each time you hit it, you would load Newkey, enter a command to turn on its "learn" or "record" mode, hit the target key (<F1>), and key in DIR <Enter>. Then you would turn off Newkey's record mode. From that point on, each time you hit <F1> the key sequence DIR <Enter> would be sent to the system.

This general technique is called "keyboard macroing," and [DIR <Enter>] in this case is called a "macro." The term comes from the computer-talk phrase "macro expansion," and is simply another way of saying that from little acorns great oaks grow. When you hit <F1>, the program substitutes the multi-character macro you have defined for the single character <F1> normally generates.

Macros Automate Everything

Macros can be helpful in DOS, particularly when used to automate repetitive functions. But they can be even more useful when you are running an applications program. Unlike a DOS batch file, for example, Newkey can "feed" keystrokes to such programs. As far as the program is concerned the keystrokes appear to be coming directly from you via the keyboard. For example, suppose that when you boot Lotus 1-2-3 you always enter the same series of keystrokes to reach the point where you are ready to actually use the program. If you turn on Newkey's learn mode before you do this, you can load all of those keystrokes into a single key or key combination. Then turn off Newkey's learn mode, save the macro to a file, and then simply load that file to reprogram your keys each time you boot your system. (This can be done easily with your AUTOEXEC.BAT file.) Once loaded, you can reach the desired spot in Lotus by hitting a single key.

For programs that cannot respond as quickly as Newkey can issue keystrokes, you can insert any number of half-second pauses you like between keystrokes. Or you can opt for Newkey's "slow type" option. There is an option that can slow down the IBM PC/AT keyboard as desired.

Newkey goes far beyond simple macro definition. If you like you can define a macro to include one or more "fill-in-the-blanks" variables. For example, suppose you work in a senator's office and are constantly having to type the following sentences: "Thank you for your inquiry. Enclosed are the materials about (blank) that you requested. The issue of (blank) is of deep and abiding concern to the Senator." With Newkey, you need never actually type in this information again. Load Newkey, then load your word-processing program. Choose a particular key combination, like [<Alt><1>] and activate Newkey. Then key in the above sentences, using Newkey's option to leave spaces for the variables (the "blanks" above). Then turn Newkey off. From then on, each time you hit [<Alt><1>], the sentences will replay on your screen, pausing for you to key in the specific materials you are sending, and continuing after you hit <Enter>.

Saving and Reloading Newkey Macros

The Newkey package comes with a utility program to let you save the macros you have defined to a file. This utility can be called as a pop-up, appearing to let you save your macros while you are in the midst of your applications program if you like, or you can load and use it from DOS. Included in this utility is a word processor-like macro editor. With this feature you can examine and change current macros at any time or create new ones. Newkey users have even created entire files of macros for others to load when using popular programs. Newkey user Harlan Grove, for example, has prepared a complete Newkey macro file for use with Lotus 1-2-3 (included in the Newkey package).

There are many other features as well. Macros can be "nested," for example, up to eight levels. This means that you can define a given macro to include and thus "call" another macro that you have previously defined. There are date and time functions, too. With these you can define a key or key combination to automatically display the current date and time as part of its macro operation. (Newkey obtains this information from your system.)

Cut-and-Paste Screens

Newkey also has a cut-and-paste feature that can be used to clip out text, like a section of a Lotus spreadsheet or a balance sheet produced by an accounting package, and insert it into some other program, like the report you're preparing with your word processing software. To use this feature, you cause the Newkey utility program to pop up and choose "CUT" from the menu. You will then be returned to your application screen and a small help box will appear in the upper right corner. At this point you are free to move your cursor all over the screen, typing in or deleting text as you please. When you have things the way you want them, hit <Home> to start marking the text to be cut out. Hit <End> to stop marking. This will return you to the Newkey utility menu. From here you can either opt to "PASTE" the text into your current application or return to the application itself. Newkey will hold the cut text in memory until you select a place or a program into which to paste it.

There are other nonmacro-related functions, too. Newkey can automatically blank your screen after as many or as few minutes as you specify. It can sense the state of your <Caps-Lock> and <Num-Lock> keys and display a little box in the upper right corner of the screen when they are engaged. It can speed up your entire keyboard by whatever factor you choose. It can generate an audible "keyboard click" if you like. And it can extend DOS's keyboard buffer (the number of keys that can be "typed ahead").

Newkey, in short, is a *very* professional program, worth many times the $30 registration fee. It has only two drawbacks. The first is the fact that although the 92-page printed manual is good as far as it goes, one would wish that it was longer and somewhat clearer. We know from experience that if you read it and play with the program, you won't have any trouble taking advantage of Newkey's advanced features.

But if your prime interest is the basic macroing feature, you probably won't need to spend much time with the manual at all. Once Newkey is loaded, using this feature is as easy as keying in [<Alt><−>] to activate "learn" mode, following the instructions that will then pop into view, and entering [<Alt><−>] to turn it off. To save your macro file, key in NEWKEYSP and follow the menus that it will display, or enter [<Ctl></>] to cause the NEWKEYSP menu to pop onto the screen. (Note that this is a right backslash, not the backslash used with DOS pathnames.)

Resolving Conflicts

The second drawback about version 4.0 is its incompatibility with FANSI-CONSOLE, the replacement console driver discussed earlier. Newkey (version 4.0) completely deactivates FANSI's scroll recall feature, something we find intolerable because we depend upon scroll recall so much. FANSI for some reason deactivates most of the <Alt> key combinations Newkey 4.0 needs for its control commands.

Conflicts of this sort are inevitable when different programs are dealing with the machine at this level. However, we have found a solution. As it happens Newkey version 3.0 is completely compatible with FANSI. About the only major feature it does not support is the date and time macro function. If you already have version 3.0, we suggest that you turn off Newkey's screen-blanking and extended-keyboard functions since FANSI already supplies these features. Use NEW-KEYSP.EXE to do so. You might also want to turn off Newkey's fast-keyboard feature. In any case, you will find both version 4.0 and 3.0 packed onto the disk IBM Core Collection 5.

The shareware registration fee for Newkey is $30 for new users. Registered users of previous versions may obtain an upgrade for $16. Massachusetts residents should add five percent sales tax. Foreign orders should add $5 extra for shipping and handling. There is an additional handling charge of $5 for purchase orders. Registration includes an 80+-page printed manual, telephone and mail support, and a copy of the latest registered-user release. The registered-user release does not have a shareware beg screen but is otherwise indentical to the shareware product. Contact: Mr. Frank A. Bell, FAB Software, P.O. Box 336, Wayland, MA 01778.

Recommended Programs

Glossbrenner's Choice:

IBM Core Collection Disk 6—Automenu/EBL

Designer Menus: Automenu and EBL

Automenu

Some of us like our DOS straight. No fancy front ends or "shells," please. Just get me to the DOS command line and let me do my stuff.

Others, including husbands and wives, friends, business associates, superiors, and subordinates, prefer a cleverly crafted shield. And my word, but Marshall Magee's Automenu is it. We've included it as a Core Collection item because many straight DOS users are often called upon to set up systems for less enlightened users—people who don't know about DOS, don't *want* to know about DOS, and threaten not to do their share of the household chores if you ever mention it again. In short, Automenu is a program that requires almost no computer knowledge on the part of its user but more than a nodding acquaintance with hardware and software on the part of the person who sets it up.

We can summarize its features in just a few words. With Automenu you can bring any number of applications programs, DOS commands, and batch files under a single menu umbrella. You create the menu, including descriptions of the menu items and helpful comments where necessary, and assign access commands and command strings. Subsidiary menus that branch off your main menu can also be created. Then you set things up so that the person for whom the menu has been designed is automatically taken to your menu when he or she enters a simple command or turns on the computer.

When that person begins to use the menu, he or she will encounter assembly language speed, lots of online help with using Automenu itself, and very thoughtful programming. If you've done *your* job correctly, your user will never have to encounter DOS or enter any of the commands needed to summon a particular applications program. It's hard to imagine how a DOS shell program could be any better than this. Automenu is really top of its class.

Automenu is shareware. The registration fee is $50 and it provides you with a copy of the latest version, a printed manual, and technical support. Georgia residents, please add sales tax. Contact: Magee Enterprises, 6577 Peachtree Industrial Blvd., Norcross, GA 30092-3796.

Extended Batch Language (EBL): Programming in DOS

The key to understanding Frank Canova's Extended Batch Language (EBL) is the word *language*. For that's really what EBL is and what it has become since we wrote about it in the first edition of *How to Get FREE Software*. Consequently, like Automenu, it is not for the novice user. However, its power to finely control a person's interaction with the machine makes it ideal for experienced users programming for their own benefit and those charged with creating shields for DOS-shy users. As Frank Canova says, "EBL lets you put 'covers' on your programs."

Interactive Menus and Display Attribute Control

Certainly DOS itself has moved toward EBL's level over the years as Microsoft added features that were once available only through EBL. (Mr. Canova is an IBM employee who has secured permission from the firm to offer his product. He says that EBL is similar to VM/370's EXEC2.) But EBL has advanced as well. The best way to think of it is as a package that gives you complete control over a system. EBL lets you create menus, for example, or interactive programs capable of accepting and processing responses from the user. You can control the display attributes of the screen (blinking, colors, highlighting, and so on). You can concatenate strings and substrings, and you can employ as many DOS variables as you want, each of which can contain up to 127 characters.

Programming Language Commands

You can tell your EBL program to read a particular line of the screen, parse it, and take a specified action should a designated word or string appear there. You can load up the keyboard stack with commands to be fed to applications programs. As far as the applications program is concerned the commands it is receiving are coming directly from the keyboard. You can introduce pauses of any length you specify into a command string. You can open, append, write to, and read files. You can include BEEP, IF, THEN, ELSE, GOTO, RETURN, LABEL, INKEY, READ, and TRACE commands. Five function and both floating point and fractional mathematical functions can be performed. (All of Seaware Corp.'s in-house accounting programs are written in EBL.) The TYPE command offers a superior way to put text on the screen from a batch file. The list simply goes on and on.

The EBL package contains the program and a number of batch programs that demonstrate EBL's capabilities. It also includes an automated documentation/help program that presents you with a menu of topics. Choose a topic, and the program branches to a subsidiary batch program that displays text and interacts with you. This is a batch program that serves as the manual in the shareware distribution version. We have also included a number of small utility programs (ASK.COM, INPUT.COM, etc.) and batch files on the disk.

The EBL shareware registration fee is $49. This includes the latest version of the program, a comb-bound, printed manual (340+ pages), telephone support, and access to the BAT-BBS, Seaware's 24-hour bulletin board system. Registered users also receive modules for extended EBL functions (floating point and fractional math, PEEK, POKE, REBOOT, unlimited DOS variables, access to an 8087 math coprocessor, if installed, and so on) and the source code for same. In addition, the distribution disk contains all of the many batch file examples found in the printed manual, arranged for easy access and testing. Contact: Seaware Corp., P.O. Box 1656, Delray Beach, FL 33444.

Glossbrenner's Choice Core Collection Disk Reference

We've covered a lot of ground in this chapter and discussed in detail many programs whose only thematic link is that they make your system much easier to use. As noted at the beginning of the chapter, the order of presentation was determined primarily by which combination of programs would make most efficient use of the available space on the disk. Accordingly, it may be helpful here to quickly summarize what we've covered. We will not do this for every chapter, but the software discussed here is, in our opinion, so important for every PC user that a quick summary seems worthwhile.

IBM Core Collection Disk 1—FANSI Prog./CED/LIST

FANSI gives you complete control over your screen and keyboard. Included among its many features is an option to enable a one-button scroll recall feature. We've provided explanatory text that may eliminate the need to read the documentation, as well as a series of FANSI-created batch files to let you quickly pick and implement the features you want. CED is the DOS command editor that lets you scroll back through commands at the command line and edit them like a word processor. LIST is the best text-display program going, with lots of features including a super-fast find function. Included on this disk as well is LISTMOD.EXE, a program for permanently modifying LIST.COM's command key assignments and default settings.

IBM Core Collection Disk 2—FANSI Doc./PC-DeskTeam/PC-Window

The on-disk documentation for FANSI (150+ pages) and PC-DeskTeam, a top-quality substitute for Sidekick. Plus PC-Window, a pop-up notepad, timer, ASCII table, and alarm that occupies only about 20K of RAM.

IBM Core Collection Disk 3—PMK Utilities/DIREDIT

The Professional Master Key Utilities are in our opinion even more useful than the commercial Norton Utilities. Can recover erased files and much more. DIREDIT will physically resort your disk directories to your specifications, and also allows you to arrange the filename order on a file-by-file basis.

IBM Core Collection Disk 4—QFILER and Associates

QFILER is the program that can display the directories of two different disks in twin windows on your screen. You can tag files for mass deletion, copying, and ARChiving, change the disk volume label, alter the date and time stamp of files, and much more. The "associates" are the programs the QFILER is set up to call, including LIST, ARCx, FINDIT, FCDISK, and LITLBOOK. We have included LISTMOD.EXE and its associated files as well. (See Core Collection Disk 1, above.)

IBM Core Collection Disk 5—Newkey 4.0 and 3.0

Newkey is the keyboard macroing program that lets you load up any key or key combination with text, prompts, commands, and anything else you like. Useful in DOS and in getting into an applications program with a single keystroke and automating your actions once you get there. Many other features besides, including "cutting-and-pasting" display screens to move information from one program to another. Version 3.0 is for FANSI users.

IBM Core Collection Disk 6—Automenu/EBL

Both of these programs are for experienced users. Automenu is designed to make many applications, DOS functions, and so on, accessible via a single menu. Extended Batch Language (EBL) lets you program in DOS the way you might in BASIC or some other language. It adds many features and capabilities not found in standard DOS batch files.

10

Top Utilities

HAVE IT *YOUR* WAY

Traditionally, the noun *utility* has always meant one of three things: the water, gas, or electric company. Most people still think of the word in those terms. But if you're a PC user, *utility* has a completely different meaning. Usually, it refers to a compact little program that can get you out of a jam. Or at the very least, save you hours of frustration as you struggle to make the system to do what you want it to do—like changing the time and date stamp on a file or giving a hard disk subdirectory a different name.

If you're not a DOS user—that is, if you use your PC exclusively to run a single applications program like Lotus or dBASE and nothing else—these chores probably sound insignificant. But they aren't. In the absence of a utility program to handle things for you, for example, there are only two ways to get a subdirectory to both bear the name you choose and contain the files you want. You can use a highly technical program to call up the disk sector containing the subdirectory name and edit that sector on the screen. (Better brush up on the hexadecimal numbering system first, though, since that's what you'll have to use to do your editing.) Or you can make a new subdirectory using your chosen name, then log onto the old one and copy all of its files into the new, empty subdirectory. Next, go back to the old subdirectory and delete all of the files it contains, then move up to the root directory or the subdirectory above the old subdirectory and enter the DOS command to remove it.

This is can be a very time-consuming chore, particularly if there are a lot of files to be copied. It requires some knowledge of DOS and it obviously takes a *lot* of keystrokes. With a utility program like Mike

Flynn's RENDIR.COM, however, you can accomplish the same thing in just a few seconds. Key in RENDIR, respond to the prompt for the name of the old subdirectory, key in the new name you would like it to have, and hit <Enter>. That's all there is to it—once you have the right utility program.

Classic Characteristics

RENDIR.COM is typical of the classic personal computer utility program. It's tiny—a mere 640 bytes—compared to, say, major application programs like PC-Write (100,000 bytes) or ProComm (166,000 bytes). It is highly focused. Like most utilities, it was written to solve one and only one particular problem. And it is apparently in the public domain or otherwise has public domain status. There are some shareware utilites, but in many cases programmers contribute their efforts on the assumption that others with identical problems might as well benefit from the work they have done in solving those problems. Why reinvent the wheel? Small as they are, however, utilities can save you hours of time in the course of year.

Certainly not all utility programs are so tiny, but due to their intense focus on performing just one task, most don't grow much larger than nine or ten thousand bytes (9K to 10K). In other words, utilities are more on the order of short melodies and pieces of chamber music, compared to the symphonic compositions of major applications programs. This is significant for at least two reasons. First, it means that programmers who understandably shy away from the uncertain returns involved in producing a major program can still practice their craft and be appreciated for their efforts. Consequently there are *lots* of utilities.

Second, the small size and limited function of these programs tend to discourage software houses from marketing commercial equivalents. Although stranger things have happened, it is difficult to imagine a vendor mounting a million-dollar ad campaign to convince you to spend $50 on a little 1K program. The perceived value just isn't there, even though the program might actually be worth many times what it costs. Some firms have bundled small utilities and marketed them as a package. But by and large, that's not where the money is to be made in the commercial software business.

Consequently, if you want a program that will automatically park your hard disk's read-write heads safely, record a snapshot of your screen and pop it into view on command, add up the bytes occupied by all the files on a disk, in a subdirectory, or those meeting a particular criterion (like *.WKS for all Lotus worksheet files); if you want a program that will move files and subdirectories so you don't have to go back and delete them once they have been copied; in short, if you want to be able to do hundreds of *useful* things, then what you want is a utility program. And the chances are that you will not only find what you need in the public domain, but that you will find it *only* in the public domain.

Why Not the Best?

In this chapter you will find discussions of what we feel are the best general utilities. In Chapter 11, you will find the best utilities for optimizing your hard disk and otherwise tweaking your system's performance.

While running, testing, and comparing programs for these two chapters we encountered a lot of trash. But that's to be expected. There is no way to tell from a one-line catalog description or from the ad hoc paragraphs prepared by the person who uploaded the software to an online system what a given program is really like and whether it will really perform. You simply have to get your hands on the software and put it through its paces. In doing so, sometimes the bear gets you, sometimes you get the bear, and sometimes you both go hungry.

Our goal is to make it possible for you to get the bear every time. In short, the programs discussed here and in Chapter 11 are the ones to download or order from a mail order source if you want to accomplish a given task. Having said that, we must also add that we have undoubtedly managed to leave out someone's favorite program. And certainly the software we recommend can't solve every conceivable problem. But it will solve most of the problems most PC users encounter most often. It will definitely give you more power over your system. And if you need programs that are even more specialized, you can use the tools provided in Chapters 5 through 8 to locate them from an online source.

Plan of Attack

Not all of the programs recommended here fit the classic definition of a PD utility program in terms of size or status. Some are considerably larger than 1K and some are shareware instead of public domain. But each of them addresses a particular need, and taken together as a suite of programs, they cover just about all of the bases. The only exceptions are the hard disk optimizers, RAM disk, and disk cache programs we will be considering in the next chapter.

We have organized things into seven categories:

- DOS command replacements
- File operations
- File locators and catalogs

- Floppy disks

- Screen and keyboard utilities

- Memory management

- Miscellaneous nice-to-have utilities

In every case we have provided all of the information you will need to locate the programs in an online library or in a mail-order catalog. We have also packed all of this software onto three Glossbrenner's Choice disks: Top Utilities Disk 1—Quick Shots; Top Utilities Disk 2—Larger Programs; and Top Utilities Disk 3—Disk Labeling. You will find a summary of the contents of each of these disks at the end of Chapter 11.

Utility Basics

At this point you may want to review the discussion in Chapter 2 regarding how programmers handle their documentation. As noted there, some put it in their source code and some arrange for a screen of instructions to appear if you run the program without any arguments.

You should also know that occasionally such built-in documentation will save space by using terms like "afn" and "ufn." These stand for "ambiguous filename" (as in *.BAS or account?.*) and "unambiguous filename" (a specific file). Other programs use the term "filespec." Short for "file specification," this means any acceptable specific filename or file specification that includes the DOS global characters * ("any series of characters") or ? ("any single character"). Because it is more descriptive and less "bytehead" than afn or ufn, we will use filespec to refer to filenames as necessary in the text.

Mr. PATH Command

If you have a hard disk, there is also a bit of advice that falls under the rubric of "Mr. PATH Command Is Your Friend." Every file on a hard disk is located in either the root directory—the very top of the directory "tree," as it were—or in a subdirectory that branches off the root. The purpose of the PATH command is to tip DOS off as to which subdirectory to search when you enter a command.

For example, suppose you have made a subdirectory called UTILS for all of your utility programs. And suppose you are currently logged onto (located in) your hard disk's root directory. If you key in FDATE from that point, DOS would look for FDATE.COM in your current (root, in this case) directory. Not finding it, DOS would return the message "Bad command or file name."

However, if you keyed in PATH C:\UTILS at the DOS prompt and then hit <Enter> DOS wouldn't say anything. But if you *then* keyed in FDATE, DOS would first look for the program in your current directory and, not finding it, look in the subdirectory called UTILS. Of course DOS would find the program there, and it would run FDATE.

If you shut off or reboot your computer, DOS will forget the PATH command address you have given it. So, here's what we suggest. Make a subdirectory called UTILS and copy the utility programs you want into it. Then place the line PATH C:\UTILS in your AUTO-EXEC.BAT file. As discussed in Chapter 2, DOS looks for a batch file by this name in its root directory each time it loads in. If it finds it, it runs it, automatically issuing the commands you have stored there. By including this line in your AUTOEXEC.BAT file, you will make sure that DOS always knows where to look for a utility program. You will thus have access to said program at all times, regardless of the floppy disk or hard disk subdirectory you happen to be logged onto at the time.

FreeTip: If you are a brand new user, review what your DOS manual has to say about the MD ("make directory") command. Then make sure you are logged onto the root directory of your hard drive by keying in CD\and hitting <Enter>. Then key in MD UTILS to create the UTILS subdirectory. Next key in COPY CON:AUTOEXEC.BAT and hit <Enter>. Type PATH C:\ UTILS and hit <Enter>. Then hit <F6> or [<Ctrl><C>] to write AUTOEXEC.BAT to disk. Copy the utility programs you want into the UTILS subdirectory and reboot the system, and you'll be all set.

Conventions and Compatibility

Most of these programs are "well behaved," meaning they do not attempt to directly manipulate specific brands and configurations of hardware. Most use the BIOS portion of DOS, and thus should be compatible with a wide range of MS-DOS machines. If printing is involved, as with the disk labeling programs we'll be discussing, you can assume that the programs will work with IBM or Epson-command-compatible printers. If your printer is not command compatible, you may not be able to use some printing features of some programs.

We are going to assume that you are using DOS 2.x or higher, though many of these utilities will work with DOS 1.x if anyone is still using it. (We have tested all of this software using DOS 3.2.) We should also note that newer versions of DOS have at last caught up with some utilities by including commands (like ATTRIB and LABEL) that were not available in previous versions. However, utility programs tend to offer more versatility than the solutions DOS offers, and in any case your version of DOS may not have these additional commands.

Finally, for convenience we may use the terms "Drive A" and "Drive B" in describing how these programs work. But unless otherwise stated, you can assume that the software can be used with subdirectory and pathnames as well. Also, don't forget that you can almost always stop and break out of a program by keying in [<Ctrl><C>] or [<Ctrl><BREAK>].

FreeTip: As discussed in Chapter 2, in the free software world filenames often contain numbers to indicate the version of the program. CP16.EXE, for example, is Jon Dart's program CP, version 1.6. FB158.COM is Vern Buerg's file backup program, version 1.58. And so on. The version numbers are important when you are reviewing a software catalog or searching an online library, but there is no need for them on your disk. So make the programs easy to remember by renaming them. Rename CP16.EXE to CP.EXE and FB158.COM to FB.COM. Since most programs of this sort display their version numbers whenever they are run, you don't have to rely on the filename to keep track of which version you have.

DOS Command Replacements

Admittedly, many utility programs could rightly be called DOS command replacements. But since they can also be classified under other topics as well, that is where we have put them. The programs listed here, in contrast, are specifically designed to improve upon the commands DOS provides.

Recommended Programs

Glossbrenner's Choice:

IBM Top Utilities Disk 1—Quick Shots

CP16 EXE 4393
CP16 ASM 38029

This is Jon Dart's improved COPY command. You can use it like COPY, but you can also key in CP followed by a list of filenames and a destination, thus copying several files at once. Nor are you limited to filenames. You can copy entire subdirectories and all of their subdirectories as well to a given location with a single command. If the destination is a subdirectory that does not exist, CP will create the subdirectory at the destination and proceed with the copying. If you like, you can have the program make a sub-subdirectory beneath the destination subdirectory and copy the files into it. Properly used, this program can save you many keystrokes over the course of a year.

```
MV      DOC     461
MV23    EXE     4479
MV23    ASM     40793
```

Version 2.3 of Jon Dart's "move" utility, this works just like CP (described in the preceding section), including its power to create subdirectories. The big difference is that once MV has copied files or subdirectories to their destination, it goes back and erases them from the source disk or subdirectory. This saves you from doing so yourself with the DEL *.* and the RD commands.

```
NO      COM     736
NO      DOC     4608
```

Written by Charles Petzold of *PC Magazine* fame, this program *excludes* files from DOS actions. For example, as Mr. Petzold explains in his documentation, keying in NO *.BAS COPY *.* A: would copy every file at your present location to drive A *except* those ending in .BAS. You might also delete all but a specific file (ACCOUNTS.TXT) with a command like this: NO ACCOUNTS.TXT DEL *.*. The program works by temporarily setting the hidden attribute on the files you wish to exclude. That means DOS won't see them when it executes its command. NO.COM then resets the attribute to unhide the file(s).

```
NT      DOC     226
NT      EXE     10752
```

The NT here stands for "new tree," an improvement on DOS's TREE command. Shortly after keying in NT the program will give you a header screen that includes the number of unused bytes on your disk, the percentage of space that is free, and the date and time. It will then assemble a list of the subdirectories on your disk and display them in graphically pleasing decision-tree style screens. The program pauses after each screen, prompting you to hit a key to continue. Naturally, NT is most useful with a hard disk.

RENDIR   COM   640

This is Mike Flynn's program to rename subdirectories. Key in REN-DIR and respond to the prompt for the old subdirectory's name, and then respond to the prompt for the new name and hit <Enter>. Quick and easy.

RM   DOC   415
RM15   EXE   3304
RM15   ASM   22009

Rm ("remove") version 1.5, by Jon Dart, acts like the DOS DEL(ete) command, except that it can remove write-protected files and entire subdirectories (and all of *their* subdirectories) as well, if you so specify. The approved DOS alternative is to log into each subdirectory, delete all the files, move up to the subdirectory above the target, and key in the DOS RD command. The trick of keying in DEL followed by a sub-directory name that we told you about in Chapter 3 works only if the target subdirectory contains no subdirectories of its own. RM, on the other hand, doesn't care.

SDIR26   DOC   1280
SDIR26   COM   3328

"Sorted directory" programs are a public domain staple. There are doz-ens of them. This particular sorted directory program is our favorite. If you enter SDIR26 by itself, the program will display a four-column di-rectory with files sorted in alphabetical order. To permit four columns on the screen, only the filename and filesize are shown. If you opt for a six-column display by keying in SDIR26 /6, only the filenames them-selves will be shown. If you opt for two columns, you will see filenames, sizes, dates, *and* any attribute settings of the files. (See the discussion of ALTER.COM below for more on file attributes.)

You can also sort by date, size, and file extension. And you can have the program output to your printer using compressed type. SDIR26 resets the printer to regular type when it finishes. Note that sorted directory programs only sort the display of files. The actual order on the disk remains unchanged. (See DIREDIT in Chapter 9 for information on permanently changing the file order.)

File Operations

"File operations" here is a phrase of convenience, for technically almost everything you do with a computer can be considered a file operation. What we have in mind are programs that let you alter file attributes, check the free space at the destination to which you plan to copy files, compare files, and swap filenames. The line that separates these programs from DOS command replacements is somewhat hazy, but we have chosen to see it clearly. We should also point out that the Professional Master Key Utilities (PMK) package discussed in Chapter 9 can make all of the attribute and date changes that these single-function programs can. The advantage of using PMK is single-source simplicity. The advantage of using one of the utilities discussed below is speed— you don't have to wait for a large program to load in and get set up.

Recommended Programs

Glossbrenner's Choice:

IBM Top Utilities Disk 1—Quick Shots

ALTER   COM   1024
ALTER   DOC   3525

Written by Terry A. Davis, this program (which we have also seen referred to as HIDE.COM) changes the attributes of the target files. DOS's ATTRIB command can do some of the same things, but it cannot hide a file or subdirectory. QFILER (discussed in Chapter 9) can do everything that ALTER.COM can. DOS's directory entries for all files contain slots for the filename and file extension, but they also contain a single byte that you don't see. This byte holds information concerning the file's attributes. There are eight attributes, one for each bit in the byte, including attributes marking the file as read-only, system, or hidden.

A file marked read-only cannot be changed or deleted. Though they have different names and assigned bits, the system and hidden attributes amount to the same thing. When either attribute is set to on or "1," the file will be invisible to some of DOS's commands. A hidden file will *not* show up when you key in DIR and hit <Enter>, for example. Nor will it be visible to DOS's DEL(ete), RENAME, or COPY commands.

> **FreeTip:** If you have ever found it impossible to remove an apparently empty DOS subdirectory, the problem is almost always due to the presence of hidden files. These files do not appear when you key in DIR, so the subdirectory looks empty. But DOS knows they're there, and it will not let you remove a subdirectory until you first delete all of the files it contains. In most cases, the problem is caused by commercial programs that create hidden files as part of their copy-protected hard disk installation procedure. Since you can't change a hidden file's attributes if you don't know its name, use the Professional Master Key Utilities discussed in Chapter 9. Choose the "File Edit" option from the main menu, and follow the instructions to uncover the hidden file in the target subdirectory and turn off its hidden or system attributes.

If you know a hidden file's name, however, you can TYPE it to the screen. When the relevant bit is reset to off or "0," the file returns to normal. Note that in computer-talk "set" always means on or 1, and reset always means off or 0. The attributes of normal files are thus in a reset state, regardless of whether they have ever been set.

There is also an "archive" bit that is used by DOS to determine whether a file on your hard disk has changed since it was last backed up (using the DOS BACKUP command). If no changes have been made to a file, its archive bit will be in the reset state (off/0). But ALTER.COM can set the archive bit if you request it to do so.

The program can also hide subdirectories. The subdirectories will still be accessible, but only to those who know that they exist and key in the correct path.

CAT DOC 1592
CAT EXE 10177

This program by Daryll Shatz will concatenate files. That means you can give it a list of filenames and tell it to copy them all into a single file, appending the second file to the first, the third to the second, and so on. To do this with DOS would require keying in each filespec separated by a plus sign.

DISK   COM 5632
DISK   DOC 9856

This program is copyrighted by MJH Consulting, 312 Schulte NW, Albuquerque, NM 87107, with a request for a donation (amount unspecified) if you like it and find it useful. DISK has a number of options, but as its name implies, it treats entire disks (hard or floppy) and cannot be focused on individual subdirectories. If you simply key in DISK and hit <Enter>, you will be shown a complete list of all of your files in all of your subdirectories. You can also use the program as a file locator, since it will report the subdirectory location of every file meeting the file specifications you provide. Nothing terribly special there; WHEREIS.COM, considered in the next section, will do the same thing.

However, if you key in DISK/T, the program will also calculate and display subtotals of the files in each subdirectory, followed by a grand total at the end. If you key in DISK *.TXT/T, the program will do the same thing but focus exclusively on files ending in .TXT. It can thus tell you how much space is occupied by text files in each subdirectory of your hard disk. If you add another slash command, DISK will tell you both the totals of all .TXT (or any other filespec) files and the amount of free space on a floppy disk to which you would like to copy them.

There are many other options as well, including one to output to a text file. DISK's text file output is special in that there is one line per file and each file and pathname is preceded buy %1 and followed by %2. Frequent batch file users will recognize those symbols as standing for DOS variables ("replaceable parameters," as the DOS manual puts it). That means that if the DISK-created text file is called GROUP. BAT, you can copy or delete all of the files it contains with a command like GROUP COPY A:*.*. This is explained in DISK.DOC, but if you're a new user you will want to consult your DOS manual for more information on how to use batch files.

FDATE   COM   1664
FDATE   DOC   1920

This program changes the date and time stamp of a file to one of your own choosing.

FREE   COM   1024

FREE gives you a quick report on the amount of free space remaining on the floppy disk. This can be much faster than keying in DIR and waiting for DOS to announce the available free space after a long list of filenames has scrolled by.

FREE-86 COM 343
FREE-86 DOC 1152

Written by Art Merrill for *PC Magazine*, FREE-86 tells you the total capacity of the target disk, the number of bytes occupied by files, and the number of bytes that are free. It takes just a tad longer to execute than FREE.COM, but far less time than DOS's CHKDSK ("check disk") command, which is the only other way to get this information. The program is thus useful in determining whether you have enough space on a floppy disk for the files you intend to copy there (SIZE.COM and ATSIZE.COM, described later in the chapter, will calculate the byte total of a group of files).

The program can also identify unsuspected system disks (those containing the hidden files IBMBIO.COM and IBMDOS.COM), as well as blank disks with reduced capacity. (When you format a floppy disk, DOS locks out any bad or defective sectors, reducing the disk's capacity but preventing future problems.) In either case, FREE-86 will report that some of the bytes have been allocated. If no filenames appear when you call for a directory of such a disk, you know that it either contains hidden files or locked out bad sectors.

NODUPE BAT 33
NODUPE DOC 672

This is a single-line batch file to delete duplicate files on a target disk, using the subdirectory or disk drive you are currently logged onto as its reference. Copy it into a subdirectory for which you have added a "PATH" command in your AUTOEXEC.BAT file so you can call upon it regardless of your current location on the system.

PI-COMP COM 6656
PI-COMP DOC 4876

This is version 1.0 of Markus Pelt's replacement program for the DOS file compare command (COMP). It offers an excellent way to determine whether Disk A contains the identical files found on Disk B. The output is alphabetical, with the screen divided into two columns, one for each disk. There is one line per file specification, including the names and time and date stamps of matching files. Where differences exist, relevant lines are tagged with phrases like "Different size," "Missing file," or "Different date." The archive bit is checked, as are hidden and system files. Truly a superior program.

RO	DOC	355
RO11	C	1699
RO11	EXE	6144

RW	DOC	174
RW11	C	1734
RW11	EXE	6144

RO11.EXE changes a file's attribute to "ready-only." RW11.EXE changes it back to "read-write." Both are by Jon Dart, and both can deal with more than one filename at a time. You may use ambiguous filenames as well. For example, keying in Ro11 *.DOC would change all files ending in *.DOC to read-only, so that they could not be erased by DOS or altered by other users.

SIZE	COM	640
SIZE	DOC	2304
ATSIZE	COM	640

Written by Art Merrill for *PC Magazine*, SIZE.COM calculates the storage requirements of a file or group of files. ATSIZE does the same thing for AT-compatible computers. Note that the amount of disk space required to store a file is not identical to the filesize. DOS stores files in fixed-length units called "clusters." Cluster sizes vary with the type of disk being used. On a typical PC floppy disk, for example, one cluster consists of two 512-byte sectors, or a total of 1024 bytes (1K). Since DOS requires a minimum of one cluster per file, a file that is only a single byte long requires as much space as a file that is 1024 bytes (1K) long.

SWAPNAME	COM	824
SWAPNAME	DOC	1379
SWAPNAME	ASM	5496

This is Vern Buerg's program to change the name of one file to that of another and vice versa. Suppose you have ROUGH.TXT on your disk and you want to give it the name FINAL.TXT. But suppose that you also have FINAL.TXT on the same disk. DOS won't let you rename ROUGH.TXT until you first delete FINAL.TXT. With SWAPNAME, you can exchange names with a single command.

```
UPDATE1   EXE   6496
UPDATE    DOC   203
UPDATE1   C     1574
```

Finally, we have another program by Jon Dart. UPDATE1.EXE will set the date and time of one or more files to the current date and time. Make sure you have correctly set your system's date and time with the DOS DATE and TIME commands before using UPDATE1.

FreeTip: Here's one of the slickest, most useful things to come along since the WD-40 Company introduced its famous lubricant. It's the DOS batch file FOR subcommand, but you can think of it as a command loop or recursive execution. Most of the utilities discussed above are designed to handle one file at a time. But suppose you've got, say, 100 files in a subdirectory and you'd like to protect each of them by making them read-only. You could use the program RO11.EXE discussed earlier and key in "RO11 filename filename filename . . ." But that would be a real chore.

Instead, as explained under "Batch commands" in your DOS manual (assuming your version of DOS supports this feature), you could use the FOR subcommand, like this:

```
C>  FOR  %F  in  (*.*)  DO  RO11  %F
```

Sure, it looks like computer gobbledygook, and it is. But it works wonderfully well. Translated, this says, "For every filename matching the specification *.*, execute the command RO11 filename." (The "C>" is the DOS prompt, of course, and not something you key in.) The percent sign (%) could be followed by any letter. The F means nothing in and of itself. What's important is that a percent sign and a letter creates a symbol that DOS sees as a variable.

Whatever is in the parentheses is the *set* DOS is supposed to use as a source of things to substitute for the variable. In this case, the set is any filename, since that is what "*.*" (pronounced "star dot star") means. But you could just as easily protect all .DOC files by using "*.DOC" or all files beginning with SAVE by using "SAVE*.*" as your set. Once you key in the command shown above, DOS will execute RO11 (or any other program you specify) for each filename until there are no more files in the subdirectory. If you decide to turn this or any command string using a different file utility into a permanent batch (.BAT) file that you can run any time, you must use two percent signs for your variable (%%F), as your DOS manual notes.

File Locators and Catalogs

Whether your system has a hard disk or not, keeping track of your files can be a real problem. Maybe not today. Maybe not even tomorrow. But someday. And unless you do something about it, you'll always regret it.

Public domain and shareware programmers have come to the rescue with a variety of solutions. Some of their software can find a file or files meeting your filename search criteria wherever it may be on your hard disk. Others can build and search a catalog of all of the files on your floppies. Still others can locate a file containing a particular sentence or other bit of text. When you consider the alternative of logging onto each subdirectory or disk, keying in DIR, and squinting at the screen as list after list of unsorted filenames are displayed, you can see why we recommend the following programs.

<hr>

Recommended Programs

Glossbrenner's Choice:

IBM Top Utilities Disk 1—Quick Shots

WHEREIS   COM   1024
WHEREIS   DOC   2944

Based on a program originally published in *IBM Softalk* magazine (1/84), this program by Ted Eyrick will search through all of the subdirectories on your hard disk for the files you specify. You may focus the program on any drive, ask it to search for as many different files as you like at the same time, and use the DOS global or "wildcard" characters (* and ?) in your filespec. For each occurrence of a file, WHEREIS will display the relevant pathname. Compact, speedy, and effective, WHEREIS is a perfect example of a public domain utility.

LOCATE   COM   517
LOCATE   DOC   2816

Written by Steven Holzner for *PC Magazine*, this little program searches all files in the current and root directories of a drive for all occurrences of any specified sequence of characters. You may specify up to 20 case-sensitive characters and you can order the program to search all subdirectories if you choose. The program returns the path(s) and filename(s) in which the search text is found, as well as up to 20 of the characters immediately surrounding it to give you a sense of the context.

SUPER-Search   (PS.EXE et al.)

The SUPER-Search package (version 1.0) from Patri-Soft and Norman Patriquin (P.O. Box 8308, San Bernardino, CA 92412) consists of the PS.EXE program and five support files. It is a snapy, menu-driven search program that incorporates virtually every conceivable means of finding a file. You can aim it at any or all subdirectories; search for text and once found, "peek" into the target file; locate files that are older than a specified number of days or created within a particular number of days; limit the search to files whose attributes have been set or reset a certain way; pipe the program's output to a file; execute a DOS command (such as "DEL filename"); and more. If menus are not to your taste, you can operate the program directly from the command line if you so choose. This is really a very nice program, and even by shareware standards its requested $10 registration fee is a real bargain.

Recommended Programs

Glossbrenner's Choice:

IBM Top Utilities Disk 2—Larger Programs

PKFIND   COM   6821
PKFIND   DOC   8902

The "PK" in the filenames stands for "Phil Katz," the author of these and several other top-quality utility programs. Mr. Katz is best-known for his PKARC programs that speedily pack files into .ARC files, reducing the total space occupied by half or more. As discussed elsewhere, the contents of such files can be extracted using PKXARC, Vern Buerg's ARC-E, or SEA's full-blown ARC program. PKFIND is a file locator like WHEREIS and similar utilities, with an important difference: It can also search through .ARC files for the files you want. There are other helpful features as well, including an option to exclude .ARC files and one to automatically move you to the subdirectory containing the target file after it has been found. The version considered here is version 1.1. The requested shareware contribution is $20, mailed to PKWARE, Inc., 7032 Ardara Avenue, Glendale, WI 53209.

PMCAT31   DOC   29506
PMCAT31   COM   52085

There are commercial programs that let you tack notes onto your Lotus spreadsheets to remind yourself of a particular cell's contents. PmCat

lets you do the same thing with any and all files on your hard disk.
Better yet, it lets you search for files not only on the basis of their
filenames, but also on the basis of *any word you may have entered as
your comment* on the file. Competing programs like ExpanDIR let you
add short, 40-character comments, but you cannot search them on the
basis of their contents. Diskcat4, another competitor, lets you add short
comments, but the only way to search the catalogs that Diskcat4 creates
is by using the DOS FIND command.

Written in Turbo Pascal by Patrick Michaud (the "Pm" in the PmCat
name), this is a truly professional piece of software. The program works
by creating a catalog file containing the floppy disk volume numbers and
subdirectory names on your hard disk, plus the names and vital statistics for each file. (The size of the catalog is limited only by your available memory.) You may have as many catalog files as you like (possibly
one for floppies and one for your hard disk). The initial catalog file-
creation process takes only about 20 seconds or so. From then on, you
can load the catalog and update it each time you run the program.

With the desired catalog file loaded, the program will sort by filename
(or not, at your option) and display the first names on the list in a pop-
up window. (You can resort by date or size if you like.) At that point,
you can choose to add an 80-character comment line to any filename, or
search for files on the basis of their names or previously entered comments. You can edit the catalog, use your cursor, <Home>, and
<End> keys to zip through the list in the window, or "cut and paste"
your comments for duplicate files. You can set the program's defaults in
any way that you choose. (PmCat's method of guiding you thorough
setting your preferred colors should be used by every programmer.) If
you like, you can even ask for a printout of the entire catalog.

Fast, responsive, and useful, PmCat version 3.1 (the one considered
here) is a very impressive program. It is offered as shareware. A $15
contribution entitles you to a unique registration number and a $5 com-
mission on each registration that results from your copy. Or you can
forego the commission and register for $10. (Conversion to commis-
sionable registration is possible at any time for an additional $7.50.) All
registered users receive a copy of the program on disk containing their
unique registration number. Registration fees should be sent to Mr.
Michaud's partner, William C. Scott, at 4726 Everhart Road, Corpus
Christi, TX 78411.

Recommended Programs

Glossbrenner's Choice:

IBM Top Utilities Disk 3—Disk Labeling

PC-DISK COM 33408

This is a very straightforward disk cataloging program from John Friel III, author of the Qmodem communications program. We have placed it on Disk 3 only because even in its compressed (.ARC) form there was no room for it on Disk 2. Though not nearly as flexible as PmCat, PC-DISK has a number of points in its favor. It is Turbo-responsive, very simple to use (an online help feature provides its documentation), and it is designed strictly for cataloging floppy disks. Although PmCat can catalog floppies easily, in our opinion it is oriented more toward the hard disk user.

PC-DISK creates a catalog file containing the volume label and file list for each disk you ask it to read. As part of this process, you may key in up to 33 characters of comment per file as a "memo" field. Once it has loaded its catalog, the program can search for files on the basis of filename or the contents of the memo field. You an edit the memo fields and the catalog as you like, and you can give your disks any volume label you choose.

Floppy Disk Utilities

The comparative cost of personal computing falls significantly every year. But while you may not notice the changing price-to-power ratio as much in complete systems, it hits you smack in the face when you look at what hard disks are going for these days. The 20 megabyte drive we paid $2000 for (wholesale) a few years ago now sells for a mere $300 (mail order). For about $200 more, you can get a hard disk on a card that plugs right into one of your internal expansion slots. Small wonder that a "20 meg" disk is virtually standard equipment on IBM-compatible systems these days. At about $80 apiece (mail order), floppy disk drives are cheap as well. So cheap that you can probably replace one for less money than you would have to pay to have it repaired.

The 3½-inch drives IBM introduced in the spring of 1987 with its PS/2 line will undoubtedly fall in price as well. And surely the day will dawn when the 5¼-inch floppy will cease to be the standard; but from our perspective that day will be long time a-comin'. For one thing, there are millions of 5¼-inch drives installed. For another, a 3½-inch diskette in its fancy hard plastic shell will never be as cheap as a floppy disk pancake in its cardboard envelope. Consequently, the utilities that programmers have written for floppy disk use are likely to be valuable for some time to come. It is those programs that we will consider here.

Recommended Programs

Glossbrenner's Choice:

IBM Top Utilities Disk 1—Quick Shots

```
VOLSER   COM   1152
VOLSER   DOC   1408
```

Written by Terry A. Davis, this program to alter the "volume/serial number" of a floppy (or hard) disk couldn't be easier to use. Newer versions of DOS include the LABEL command to do the same thing.

```
QDR   COM   4505
QDR   DOC   6045
```

Yet another contribution from Vernon Buerg, QDR ("quick disk reformat," version 3.2b) will return a disk to its virgin, just-formatted state. It will remove subdirectories and hidden or system files, and it will do so in less than ten seconds (compared to the 50 seconds or more DOS requires to format a disk). This saves you from loading each disk and keying in DEL *.* to get rid of the visible files and going through other steps to get rid of the hidden or system files. The program can also format a disk the way DOS's FORMAT.COM program does, though as Mr. Buerg points out in his documentation, it is not much faster. The program can deal with (and format) any kind of disk used by PCs, XTs, or ATs. It marks and (optionally) reports bad clusters, and it cannot reformat your hard disk, so not to worry. At your option, it can also change the disk's volume label.

```
FASTCOPY   EXE   17620
FASTCPY2   DOC    6047
```

FastCopy 2 is a program by Jim Nech, the current president of the HAL-PC user group discussed in Chapter 3. It's purpose can best be summarized by the phrase "high-speed, production disk copying." Unlike the DOS DISKCOPY command, FastCopy 2 loads a copy of the source disk into memory and copies blank disks from there. It thus does not have to read the source disk each time a copy is to be made. Consequently, it requires a full 640K of RAM to operate. Offered as shareware, the author requests a $20 contribution. Contact: Jim Nech, 10114 Torrington, Houston, TX 77075.

Even if you do not need to copy a lot of disks, you may be interested in FastCopy's performance in formatting blank disks. You prepare the program by letting it take a complete copy of a blank, formatted disk into memory. Then you begin feeding it disks. In our tests, FastCopy required 32 seconds to format a 362K disk, compared to DOS's 50 seconds. A very impressive program. In our opinion Mr. Nech's program is better than PolyCopy, its closest shareware competitor at this writing.

DISKOVER DOC 33487
DISKVR44 COM 56576
DISKOVER COM 56503

This is DisKover by Karson W. Morrison, and if you think of it as "disk cover" you will have a good idea of what it does. We looked at version 4.4, the latest in a long series of programs starting with COVER.COM. (Version 5 is a commercial product with even more capabilities.) As the documentation points out, DisKover prints a sleeve insert for your floppy disk envelopes, and it does this seemingly simple chore with style. You can thus tell at a glance what files a given disk contains, without putting it into a drive and keying in DIR. The program works on all PC/XT/AT computers, but you will need a dot-matrix printer capable of producing condensed (17.5 characters per inch or "cpi") print or an HP LaserJet or compatible printer.

When activated, DisKover reads all of the files on a floppy (or hard) disk, sorts them by filename, and prints them out using condensed print in a box that is just under five inches on a side. The box is designed to be clipped out of the printer paper and it is sized to properly fit a 5¼-inch disk envelope. In addition to the filenames and their associated information, the program includes the volume label, number of bytes that are free on the disk, time and date the insert was created, total bytes occupied by all of the files, and an optional short comment from you.

At your option, the program will include all of the files in any .ARC or .LBR files in the listing. If there are more files than can be accommodated in a single box, the program will start a second box, allowing for a "fold line." Version 4.4 can deal with up to 650 files. The program supports the use of different print colors and up to six printer control codes for each field of data. (The commercial version lets you use up to ten control codes per field.)

Registration is $20, and all registered users automatically receive Version 5 of the program. Contact: Caleb Computing Center, RD 1, Box 531, Ringoes, NJ 08551.

Label Maker 6.10 (13 files)

LabelPrinter 3.4 (3 files)

Both of the above shareware packages are designed to produce labels that you can stick on your floppy disks. Label Maker, written by Fort Verser, will print a sorted list of the files on the disk, as well the disk's volume label, the number of bytes used and free, the current date, and several lines of comment from you. The number of comment lines the program makes available, as well as the extent of the other information it prints, is determined by the size of the label you tell it you want to use. You do not have to have the filenames printed on the label if you choose not to. The program uses a variety of enhanced printing modes in producing its labels.

Label Maker supports four label sizes, ranging from 3½ by ¹⁵⁄₁₆-inch to labels for 3½-inch diskettes. Once a label has been prepared by the program, you can print it again and again if you like. You can also look at it on the screen before printing, though of course, the expanded, double-strike, and other enhanced printing features that will be activated on the printer won't show up there. Much of the program was written in assembler, but Mr. Verser provides the BASIC source code for the print routines so you can customize certain aspects to your printer or preference.

The program is offered as shareware. The shareware version requires you to go through a set-up procedure each time the program is run. If you send the requested $25 registration fee, however, you will receive a version of the program (containing a unique serial number) that does not require you to do this. Fort's Faceting, Mr. Verser's company, can also supply you with pressure-sensitive, continuous-form labels of various sizes. Contact: Mr. Fort Verser, Fort's Faceting, P.O. Box 396, Manhattan, KS 66502.

The other program featured above is LabelPrinter version 3.4, by Paul F. Rogers. We've included this program for those who would like to create customized disk labels *without* including a list of filenames. The program began years ago as a disk label producer, though you might also use it to produce mailing labels.

Basically, this program assumes you have a dot-matrix printer and offers you three prepared label formats based on the different type sizes your printer can produce: pica (10 cpi), elite (12 cpi), and condensed (17.5 cpi). The two elements of the format are the title line and the lines of description. The number of lines and characters available vary with the typesize you choose.

Although neither the documentation nor the program prompts say so, LabelPrinter is designed to output only to 3½ by ¹⁵/₁₆-inch labels, and there are no provisions for changing the prepared formats. You can choose print modes such as draft, double-strike, emphasized, and so on, but you cannot use different modes for the disk title and the comment lines. Everything will be printed using the mode you choose.

The program is offered as shareware. A contribution of $10 is requested. Contact: Mr. Paul F. Rogers, 975 W. Tennyson Road, #203, Haywood, CA 94544.

Notes and Comments

Without question, Label Maker is the more versatile of the two programs, for it can not only put a list of files on a label but comments (or just comments) as well. LabelPrinter is limited to disk title and comments; because it does not include files on the label, however, your comments can be longer. We have looked at many different labeling programs and in our opinion these are the best at this writing.

We have included them because we know that some people need this kind of software. Most, however, do not. Unless you plan to do a large batch of disk labels at one time—at least enough to warrant the aggravation of loading your printer with continuous-form labels—you can get by quite nicely with a felt-tipped pen and the Avery or Dennison self-sticking label of your choice.

For the occasional printed label, consider using your word-processing program. PC-Write, for example, supports an exceptionally wide range of printers and can give you complete control over the special printing features you may want to incorporate in each line.

> **FreeTip:** While you're at the stationery store getting your labels, ask for a special "forms ruler" that includes scales for pica (10 pitch), elite (12 pitch), and compressed (15 pitch) type, as well as calibrations for six and eight vertical lines per inch. With this in hand, you'll be able to tell exactly how many characters and lines you have to work with in preparing a specific size label.

Screen and Keyboard Utilities

Since the screen and the keyboard are so intimately involved in a person's relationship with the machine, it's not too surprising that there are literally hundreds, if not thousands, of small utility programs that alter, customize, and otherwise tweek every conceivable aspect of these two components. Nor will it be surprising to learn that programs of this sort were among the first public domain programs to be written for the PC. Some still in use today date back to the first few months of the PC's existence.

However, time and newer software have caught up with most programs in this category. You may not mind combing through printed catalogs and online libraries for utility programs that will speed up your keyboard or customize the colors of DOS's screen. And you may not mind searching through a hard disk subdirectory containing 50 to 100 of your favorite utilities to locate the program you need when you need it. But in almost every case you will find that FANSI Console, the program discussed in Chapter 9, can give you more control and more power. The one disadvantage to FANSI is the small amount of time you have to invest to learn how to take advantage of all that it offers. To use some of the utilities discussed below, in contrast, you have only to key in their name.

Recommended Programs

Glossbrenner's Choice:

IBM Top Utilities Disk 1—Quick Shots

COLOR BAT 1152
COLOR HLP 3840

This batch file by Ed Bachmann uses the DOS PROMPT command and the ANSI escape sequences discussed in Chapter 9 to control the foreground and background colors on your screen and to set high intensity, normal, or reverse modes on any type of monitor. It is basically a long list of prepared codes and GOTO batch commands. All of which makes it possible for you to key in COLOR YELLOW BBLUE to set a blue background with yellow foreground text, or any other combination you may desire. It's simple, effective, and cleverly done.

COLOR   COM   512
COLOR   DOC   2560

Written by Terry A. Davis, this program also requires you to install ANSI.SYS in your CONFIG.SYS file as discussed in Chapter 9. The program's syntax is: COLOR N1,N2,N3, where Nx represents numbers corresponding to the desired foreground, background, and border color. You might put COLOR 2,0,0 in your AUTOEXEC.BAT file, for example, to automatically set the screen to green text on a black background with a black border each time the system booted up. The program uses the same color numbers used by the COLOR statement in BASIC, and a list of colors and corresponding numbers is included in the documentation file.

This is the program we used to use before FANSI came along. In fact we still use it today when an applications program changes the screen colors and neglects to restore them when it finishes its run. One well known commercial utility package, for example, leaves our screen's border blue when it finishes. COLOR.COM makes it easy to change back to a green foreground on a black background with a black border when that happens.

POP   COM   1280
PUSH   COM   512
PUSH-POP   DOC   5120

This pair of programs is designed to take a snapshot of your screen (PUSH) and record it to a file using the filespec *.nnn, where the asterisk can stand for any filename you care to use and the *nnn* is a number added by the program, starting with 001. You activate it with a command like PUSH A:SNAPSHOT. Once this command has been given, every time you press the [<Shift><Print Screen>] combination, a copy of the current text or graphics screen will be recorded on Drive A under the name SNAPSHOT.001, SNAPSHOT.002, and so on.

Once your snapshots have been recorded, you can bring them to the screen again with a command like POP A:SNAPSHOT.001. With a screen snapshot on the screen, you can use the function keys to customize the background colors of graphics images and the border colors of text images. You can also select background colors for individual text characters, delete text with your space bar, add additional text, and make individual characters blink. Of course, you can save your newly modified snapshot to disk.

When you get your series of snapshots in the shape you want them, you can easily write a little batch file to put on a slide show. The program requires you to hit the <Escape> key to end the display of a snapshot (and go on to the next display if you are using a batch file); however, as we will see in a moment, there is a way to completely automate the process so that the show runs by itself.

Apparently written by Larry R. Lockwood, PUSH-POP is designed for the IBM color graphics adaptor (CGA). The program reads and writes to the color display memory at the address B800H. Since it predates Hercules-compatible monochrome graphics cards and the newer color monitors, it may or may not work with your equipment. In addition, we have found that PUSH-POP does not seem to support path names, so make sure that both programs and the snapshot files are in the same subdirectory.

FAKEY   COM   3362
FAKEY   DOC   10982

FAKEY lets you prepare a batch file containing the keystrokes a program requires to accomplish your goal. The "fake" in the name comes from the fact that you are in effect faking out or fooling the target program into thinking that the input it is receiving is coming from the keyboard instead of the FAKEY file. If the name sounds vaguely familiar, it is undoubtedly because *PC Magazine* published a program called KEY-FAKE that does much the same thing. *This* program, however, was written by System Enhancement Associates (SEA), the people who introduced the original file compressing ARChive utility. In our opinion, it is better than KEY-FAKE because it allows you to build in the delays that some programs require when they are booting up.

The way to use FAKEY is to think in terms of loading the keyboard with the keystrokes a program will need before you call the program. Thus, to display one of your PUSH-POP screen snapshots for three seconds and then return to normal, you would first put this command into your batch file: FAKEY WAIT 3 \e. Then you would key in: POP

SNAPSHOT.001. The first command tells FAKEY to wait for three seconds and then issue an <Escape> from the keyboard (symbolized by slash and the lowercase *e*). As noted above, that's the command POP.COM needs to tell it to return you to DOS.

With these simple tools and a bit of imagination, you can prepare elaborate, fully automated slide shows. The one disadvantage we can see for new users is that FAKEY requires you to use hexadecimal keystroke codes in some instances, though the authors have thoughtfully provided a complete reference table. We should also point out that Newkey and Extended Batch Language (EBL), discussed in Chapter 9, can do the same thing that FAKEY does. Newkey may be the easiest of all to use, while EBL is the most complex and most powerful.

On the other hand FAKEY doesn't require nearly as much memory as Newkey. All in all, it's an excellent program that with just a little effort and experimentation can make your system do exactly what you want it to do. We looked at version 1.0, and although the software is copyrighted by SEA, it apparently is not shareware as there was no request for a registration fee in the documentation.

NL	DOC	30
NL	COM	128
NLOFF	COM	128
CAPSLOCK	COM	128
CAPSUNLK	ASM	3942
CAPSUNLK	COM	118
STATLINE	COM	409
STATLINE	DOC	2176

The above programs are so simple that we can treat them quite quickly. The NL pair turns the system's <Num Lock> state on or off. CAPSLOCK turns the <Caps Lock> key on, while CAPSUNLK unlocks it the first time you press a regular shift key and a letter key. Programs of this sort can be useful in batch files.

STATLINE, by John Socha, a well known programmer and writer, gives you a status line at the bottom of the screen indicating the state of the <Caps Lock> key with an up arrow when it is engaged, the <Num Lock> key with a hatch mark when it is engaged, and the <Scroll Lock> key with a double pointed arrow when it is engaged. The program originally appeared in *PC Magazine* and will work with IBM monochrome, CGA, and Compaq screens. Simple and clean, we prefer it to the many other utility programs that address the same problems.

Memory Management

Your system's available RAM can be a veritable battleground in some instances, thanks to the popularity of "terminate and stay resident" (TSR) programs. One of the first such programs was Rosesoft's Prokey, a keyboard macroing program that lets you load a single key or key combination with a series of keystrokes. But the trend got its major boost from Borland International's Sidekick, a package that, once it has loaded itself into memory, gives you instant access to a pop-up notepad, calendar, pocket calculator, ASCII table, and autodialer. The shareware equivalents of these programs (PC Deskteam and Newkey) discussed in Chapter 9 use the same technique, as do dozens of other commercial and shareware programs.

TSR programs are very convenient, but they can cause problems. In the first place, available RAM is always finite, and if you load yours up with a large number of TSRs, you may not have enough left to run some applications programs. Since most TSRs cannot be removed once they have been loaded, your only alternative is to reboot your system without installing your TSRs when you want to run a particularly memory-hungry application. In the second place, most TSRs watch for special signals called "interrupts," and there are only a relatively few interrupts to go around. Consequently, some TSRs cannot be used if rivals for the same interrupts are also in residence. If you have loaded TSR A, which won't work with TSR B, the only way to use TSR B is to reboot your system, making sure that TSR A is not loaded in the process, and then load TSR B.

The Mark/Release package considered below is designed to help you manage these problems. This is followed by NMI, a program to help you deal with memory parity errors, and by RAM.COM, a short program from Steve Gibson.

Recommended Programs

Glossbrenner's Choice:

IBM Top Utilities Disk 2—Larger Programs

The MARK/RELEASE Package

MARK	**COM**	**1408**
RELEASE	**COM**	**16647**

FMARK	COM	640
MAPMEM	COM	18511
RAMFREE	COM	102
EATMEM	COM	256
TEST	MRK	1030
TSR	DOC	14675

The Mark/Release package (version 2.1) from TurboPower Software helps you solve many TSR-related problems by allowing you to selectively remove TSR programs from memory at any time, without rebooting. The program does this by allowing you to insert a marker between any and all of the TSRs you want to install. For example, suppose you wanted to install PC-Deskteam and CED, two memory-resident programs discussed in Chapter 9, in such a way that you could later release the memory they occupy. You could do this by keying in the following commands at the DOS prompt:

```
MARK DESKTEAM
DESKTEAM /M
MARK CED
CED
```

We have assigned the names "Deskteam" and "CED" to the memory marks here, but you do not have to give a mark a name if you don't want to. The "/M" after DESKTEAM loads that program into memory, as its documentation explains.

You may use Deskteam and CED as per usual. But suppose you now want to release the memory occupied by CED. Keying in RELEASE CED will activate the program RELEASE.COM, causing it to release all memory from the mark called CED on. All TSRs installed after the mark called CED will be released, so Deskteam will not be affected. To release the memory occupied by both Deskteam and CED, you would key in RELEASE DESKTEAM.

To look at the current status of your TSRs and memory marks at any time, key in MAPMEM. This will show you a table containing, among other things, the name of each TSR, the number of bytes it occupies, the DOS interrupt vectors it uses, and the names and locations of your various marks. In this way you can easily see which program(s) will be removed from memory when you release a particular mark and the number of bytes that will be freed. The mark/release programs work with DOS's conventional memory, of course, but they also work with LIM EMS memory (Lotus/Intel/Microsoft Expanded Memory Stan-

dard). (See the discussion of disk caches in Chapter 11 for more on LIM
EMS.)

FMARK.COM can be used in place of MARK.COM to conserve memory, since it requires only 150 bytes to MARK's 1600 bytes.
RAMFREE quickly tells you how much RAM is available. EATMEM
lets you control the amount of memory a program thinks it has to work
with and is designed for software developers. EATMEM is a TSR and
can be marked and released with the relevant programs.

This is a really nifty package. It's only lack is the wished-for ability to
selectively release specific TSRs, regardless of the order in which they
were installed and without releasing everything loaded after the target
program. The limitation is undoubtedly due to the way DOS handles its
memory and not the fault of the programmer.

The TSR Mark/Release Utilities were written by Kim Kokkonen of
TurboPower Software, a company in the business of producing some
very neat Turbo Pascal programming tools for developers. No contribution is requested. Contact: TurboPower Software, 3109 Scotts Valley
Drive #122, Scotts Valley, CA 95066.

NMI11   COM   2304
NMI11   DOC   10342

The initials of this program stand for "nonmaskable interrupt." Should
you ever be running a program and receive an error message from DOS
in the upper left corner of the screen reading "Parity Check," you know
you've got a problem. The problem lies somewhere within the banks of
memory chips that constitute your system's RAM, but DOS won't tell
you which chip is the culprit. NMI will. Once loaded into memory, NMI
sits waiting for that special signal. (The program occupies only 1.6K of
memory.)

Should a parity check problem occur, NMI will immediately give you
the option of testing your memory to locate the 64K bank of chips and
the exact memory address that is causing the problem. DOS, in contrast, simply locks the system, forcing you to reboot.

NMI can also be run as a free-standing memory-testing program. It is
quite thorough, reading and writing each byte with five different bit
patterns and checking for parity errors each time. NMI is nondescrip-

tive (it does not wipe out the contents of the memory it tests) and it can be stopped at any time.

RAM COM 89
RAM DOC 2590

This is a short program from Steve Gibson, creator of the Gibson Light Pen and *InfoWorld*'s "Tech Talk" columnist. It does exactly what RAMFREE.COM in the "Mark/Release" package does—quickly tells you how much free RAM is available. Running either of these programs is much faster than running DOS's CHKDSK.COM, the main alternative technique for discovering the amount of free RAM currently available.

Miscellaneous Utilities

One of the joys of personal computer utilities is finding a program that supplies the predicate for the sentence beginning, "I wish there was a program that would . . ." Another is discovering a program that does something neat you hadn't thought of but now find indispensable. Both types of programs can be found in this, our miscellaneous section. The way you view this software will depend on your own needs and desires, but we think you'll find all of these programs nice to have.

Recommended Programs

Glossbrenner's Choice:

IBM Top Utilities Disk 1—Quickies

BASMENU BAS 1235

This short program is ideal when preparing a disk of BASIC programs for a child or someone who does not know much about computers. When run, it automatically creates a menu of every ".BAS" program on a disk or in a subdirectory. The user can then run programs by simply keying in a menu selection. After one program has been run, the user is returned to the menu created by BASMENU.BAS.

FreeTip: This is a beginner's hint that can save you hours of poring through your manual while making running any BASIC program much easier. The conventional way to run a BASIC (.BAS)

FreeTip continued

program is to load BASIC, then load the .BAS program (LOAD "FILENAME.BAS"), then run the .BAS program (RUN). To load BASIC, you must run either BASIC.COM or the extended version BASICA.COM programs supplied with DOS. That means keying in either BASIC or BASICA at the DOS prompt. For simplicity, we suggest that you always use BASICA and leave the nonextended version on your master DOS disk.

Many people do not know, however, that if you want to run BASMENU.BAS or any other BASIC program, you can short circuit the process by simply keying in BASICA followed by the filename (like BASICA BASMENU) and hitting <Enter>. If you don't intend to program in BASIC, the only other thing you need to know is that you can get out of any BASIC program by keying in [<Ctrl><BREAK>] or [<Ctrl><C>]. That returns you to the BASIC interpreter program, from which you need only key in SYSTEM and hit <Enter> to return to DOS.

CGCLOCK	COM	1024
CGCLOCK	DOC	3584
MONOCLK2	COM	384
MONOCLK2	DOC	1404

"Color Graphics Clock" (CGCLOCK.COM) by Dan O'Brien, requires the IBM color graphics adaptor (CGA) or compatible video card. It displays the hours, minutes, and seconds in the upper right corner of the screen and can be toggled on or off. Time is displayed in twelve-hour form, with a *p* or an *a* to indicate evening or morning, but the program can be patched to use 24-hour military time. You can also patch the program to use any color you choose, and you can patch it to beep or not beep every 15 minutes. MONOCLK2.COM by Rich Winkel offers similar capabilities to users of the IBM monochrome display adaptor.

FSPOOL	DOC	1892
FSPOOL	COM	5120

This program by Don D. Worth redirects output bound for your printer to a disk file. You can activate and deactivate the spooling action at will.

PW	EXE	16395
PW	DOC	10089
PW	PWD	8

PW.EXE lets you control access to your system and to the programs it contains. It disables the [<Ctrl><BREAK>] and [<Ctrl><C>] sequences, so neither you nor anyone else can stop (and thus get past) the program. To use PW.EXE, you create a text file containing one or more of your chosen passwords. This file can be given any name you choose (PW.PWD above is such a file), and of course you can make the file invisible by giving it a hidden or system attribute using a program like ALTER.COM or the Professional Master Key Utilities.

Once this is done, you can activate the program by keying in PW followed by the path leading to your password file. The program will check to make sure it can find your file, and then it will clear the screen and display a little box reading "Password:". The documentation includes instructions for creating CONFIG.SYS and AUTOEXEC.BAT files that will foil someone's attempt to get around PW.EXE by rebooting the system from your hard disk. The program is offered as shareware ($5) by David Scheall. Contact: MiCom Business Systems, David Scheall, 6918 Alabama Avenue, Canoga Park, CA 91303.

WAIT	COM	128
WAIT	DOC	151

WAITUNTL	COM	512
WAITUNTL	DOC	1024

These are two very convenient programs designed to be included in batch files. The command WAIT n will cause the system to pause *n* seconds before continuing. The command WAITUNTL HH:MM:SS will cause the system to wait until the time specified (hours, minutes, and seconds) arrives before continuing. Before using WAITUNTL, make sure that your system clock is properly set to the correct time (use the DOS TIME command). Also, if you plan to put the system into suspended animation for any length of time, you might want to have your screen blank to preserve its phospher. FANSI Console, discussed in Chapter 9, can handle this chore for you.

BEEP	COM	54
BEEP	EXE	768
BEEP	DOC	1669
BEEP	ASM	2200

BEEP, by Steve Leoce, produces a beep, as you can guess. It thus might be useful in batch files. However, included in the documentation are instructions for changing either or both the frequency and the duration of the beep produced.

REBEEP COM   256
REBEEP DOC   1792

This program by Mark Kelinsky, with modifications by Ken Goosens, displays the phrase "Press any key to continue" while sounding an insistent two-tone beep. Unlike BEEP.COM which beeps once and stops, REBEEP continues making noise until someone presses a key. You might use it at the end of a batch file to make the computer notify you when it has finished a task. REBEEP can thus free you to leave your machine and do other things, knowing it will summon you when it has finished.

SOUND COM   256
SOUND DOC   768

Written by Ken Goosens, this is a cute program that can add a bit of flare to your batch files. SOUND can produce three different sounds: BEEP, ALERT, and TAKEOFF. BEEP is just a beep. ALERT sounds like the warning claxon at a nuclear reactor. TAKEOFF sounds like a slide whistle.

TUNE COM   512
TUNE DOC   1024

Another cutie, programmed by Jeff Garbers, author of Crosstalk, the leading commercial communications program for PCs and compatibles. TUNE will play one of five tunes. It is activated by keying in TUNE n.x where n is a number from 1 to 5 and x is a number from 1 to 9 designating the speed at which the tune should be played. Tunes 1 through 3 are phrases from the theme song for *Close Encounters of the Third Kind*. Tune 4 is the opening phrase of the funeral march. Tune 5 consists of the opening bars of a light melody we cannot place.

SPKR SYS   1792
SPKR DOC   10112

If you want to create your own background beeps, tunes, and other noises from DOS, you will find that SPKR.SYS neatly fills the bill. Written by Chris Dunford, author of the CED and PCED programs discussed in Chapter 9, SPKR.SYS is a device driver designed to be included in your CONFIG.SYS file. Once installed, the driver turns your speaker into a device to which you can copy information, just as you copy files and information to your printer. DOS will recognize the new device as SPK (*not* SPKR).

The program lets you control both frequency and duration. Frequencies range from 20 through 30,000 cycles per second. Durations range from 1 through 65,535 PC central processing unit (CPU) clock ticks. With a CPU running at 18.2 ticks a second, a duration of 18 is about one second; a duration of 65,535 is about an hour.

You can drive the speaker by keying in information directly from the keyboard or by creating a text file containing your instructions and copying it to the SPK device. Thus if you had created a text file called DEMO.TXT containing the line 523,18 and if you keyed in COPY DEMO.TXT SPK, your speaker would produce a tone of 523 cycles per second (approximately a "middle C") for about one second (18 CPU ticks). You can send SPK a maximum of 128 frequency/duration pairs, so if you want to be really creative, you can make your speaker play short tunes of your own choosing. Mr. Dunford's excellent documentation includes a short chart showing you the frequencies for the notes A through G.

SILENCE COM 7424

Finally, there is Carl Burtner's SILENCE.COM, a program to disable/enable the PC's speaker. Keying in SILENCE ON turns the program on and silences your speaker. The command SILENCE OFF turns SILENCE.COM off and enables your speaker. Keying in SILENCE ? produces three pages of documentation.

If you tend to work late at night, perhaps in an office adjoining a room where a loved one—who has to get up to go to a real job in the morning—is sleeping, you may find this program to be especially valuable. It just may save your marriage. At the very least it will save you the trouble of cutting into one of the PC's speaker wires to install an on/off switch or permanently disable the speaker.

Please turn to the end of Chapter 11 for a summary of the disks discussed in this chapter.

11

Peak Performance

UTILITIES TO TWEAK YOUR SYSTEM

Before the word *hacker* was misappropriated by the popular press to describe adolescent system breakers and database robbers, it had a long and honorable tradition in the personal computing field. A true hacker is and always has been someone who gets to know a system so intimately that he can make it do things even its designers may never have dreamed of. Hackers explore possibilities. So perhaps it should not be too surprising that their fiddling, deep knowledge, and imaginative approaches have often yielded techniques and programs that can tweak a system to its highest level of performance. As such, they have a lot in common with the amateur mechanics and hot-rodders of the 1940s and 1950s.

In this chapter we'll highlight some of the best system-tweaking programs to emerge in recent years. We'll show you how to optimize your hard disk so that files and data can be retrieved and read faster and how to guard against potential disk disasters; how to back up all of the files on your hard disk much faster than is possible with DOS's BACKUP command; and how to make sure that your hard disk's read/write heads are parked in a safe place before moving the system.

We'll also discuss a program that lets you set up a RAM-based virtual disk drive that operates at the speed of light. Unlike the RAM disk program currently supplied with DOS, however, the size of this disk can be adjusted up and down, with no need to reboot your system. Finally, we'll suggest two disk-caching programs that can greatly speed up everything from an applications program to the time required to display a directory of the files on your disk. Along the way, we'll give you all the

350

information you need to understand what these programs do, how they work, and how to use them to best advantage.

The chapter is divided into two sections: Hard Disk Optimization and Backup, and RAM Disks and Disk Caches. All of the programs discussed are available from the usual public domain and shareware sources and on the three Glossbrenner's Choice disks discussed in Chapter 10. A summary of the contents of these disks can be found at the end of the present chapter.

Hard Disk Optimization and Backup

A hard disk's performance is at its peak when it is freshly formatted and newly loaded with programs and files. But with time and use, that performance can begin to slip. It can take noticeably longer and require a lot of disk activity to bring a file into a word processing program, for example, or to display it on the screen. The speed with which the system responds to the DIR command may be reduced. And although you may not be aware of it, the space available on your disk may be diminished over time, even without the addition of any new files. Occasionally, small portions of a disk can develop problems with their magnetic coating, creating a potential disaster should DOS eventually try to record data on those spots.

Except in very serious cases, most of these problems can be easily solved. Your disk can be returned to peak performance without the enormous inconvenience of copying its contents to a pile of floppy disks and reformatting and reloading it. Potential problems with the magnetic coating can be identified, and DOS can be prevented from ever storing a file at such locations. Should DOS have already put a file in a spot that has become defective, there's a good chance that most of the file can be saved. All it takes in any of these cases is the right software. Commercial programs are available for this purpose, and you may want to consider them. But you may very well find that the shareware programs discussed here offer the same degree of sophistication at a much lower price.

DOS and the Disk: Tracks, Cylinders, Clusters, and Sectors

To understand how these programs work, you have to know a thing or two about how files are stored on a disk. We don't have room for a full-blown explanation, but we can briefly tell you what you need to know. We begin with a circular piece of magnetic material that's as blank as a piece of fresh audio or video tape. To store information on this disk, DOS must first build a framework of reference points. It must magnet-ically divide the disk up into a series of slots, each of which can store the same amount of information, and each of which is assigned a unique reference number. That's why you must always format a blank disk before using it, for it is during the formatting process that DOS lays out this magnetic structure. The read/write heads of your drive do the actual work, but DOS tells them where to go.

The magnetic structure or framework consists of concentric circles called "tracks" on a floppy disk and "cylinders" on a hard disk. Tracks and cylinders are subdivided into "sectors." A sector is an arc—a piece of the circumference of a circle. Thus if the clock on the wall reads 12:10 and you draw a line along both the big and little hands to the clock's rim, the portion of the rim between the 12 and the 2 would be a sector of the clock's circumference.

A sector is the smallest unit of disk space, and technically its size in bytes depends on the disk format. The actual size of a sector *could* vary from 128 bytes to 1K if IBM or some other party so desired. The programming necessary to support these formats already exists in the PC's Basic Input/Output System. However, at this writing, DOS has always used 512-byte sectors, regardless of the type of disk. The higher-capacity disks that DOS supports simply have more sectors.

The Logical Structure: FAT and File Directory

That's basically all there is to the physical division of a disk. The rest concerns how the sectors are used, or in computer talk, the "logical structure" of the disk. DOS uses some sectors to store the disk's table of contents or its "file directory." The term is confusing because the same words are used separately to refer to other things as well. The file directory is actually a separate file that only DOS can read, and thinking of it like that can help you avoid confusion. DOS has another private file as well. It's called the "file allocation table" (FAT) and it contains the map of where all the pieces of a file are located.

The remaining sectors on the disk—those in the "data area"—are used to store the files themselves. And here is where the first bit of complexity raises its ugly head. DOS does not "think" of sectors as sectors when it is storing files. It thinks in terms of "clusters." Clusters always consist of sectors, but the number of sectors involved varies with the disk format. For example, on a single-sided floppy disk, one cluster contains one sector. On double-sided floppies, a cluster is two contiguous sectors. On our 30-megabyte hard disk, there are four contiguous sectors per cluster.

This variability is one of the reasons why you will encounter such intentionally nonspecific terms as "file allocation unit" or "block" in your DOS manual and in the documentation for some of the programs discussed here. Generally, the actual number of bytes in a given sector or sectors in a given cluster need not concern either us or the programs we run. DOS knows in every case, and usually that's all that matters.

As we said, DOS deals in clusters, and there is a minimum of one cluster per file. So when you create a file, like a letter or a financial report, DOS checks its inventory of available clusters and begins storing your file in the first one available. Often a file will require more than one cluster, and following the "first one available" principle, DOS will work its way through the disk until the entire file has been stored.

To make sure that it can reassemble the file again when asked to do so, DOS keeps notes on where each piece of the file is. These notes are put in the file allocation table (FAT) and consist of instructions that say, in effect, "Okay, start with cluster 10 . . . now go to cluster 27 to get the next piece of the file, then go to cluster 48," and so on. These notes are called the "space allocation chain," for obvious reasons.

Going on a Scavenger Hunt

Finally, DOS makes an entry in its file directory that includes the name of the file, its date and time stamp, size, attributes, and most important, the starting entry for the file in the FAT. For DOS, rebuilding the file is rather like going on an old-fashioned scavenger hunt. First it goes to the disk's directory, where it picks up the starting address in the FAT. It then goes to that address in the FAT and discovers the location of the first cluster. It gets the first cluster's data, goes back to the FAT for the location of the second, and so on until it comes to the end of the chain.

Now, here's the payoff for taking the time to learn a bit about file storage. When your hard disk is freshly formatted and you load it up with files, all of those files are stored in *contiguous* clusters. So the read/write heads of your drive don't have to fly hither and yon to assemble all of the pieces of a file. As time goes on and you create and erase more files, or add more information to existing files, the files on your disk become fragmented.

The Fragmenting of a File

Remember, DOS goes by the "first available cluster" rule. So if you start with a freshly formatted hard disk on Monday and create a report, all the pieces of that report will be stored in contiguous clusters. Tuesday comes along and you write a letter, and its pieces get stored in the first available clusters after Monday's report. On Wednesday you get the report back from your manager and decide to add some more material. The new material gets stored in the next free clusters following Tuesday's letter. So your report file is no longer contiguous. Your read/write head will have to move to at least two different locations to assemble the complete report for you, whereas on Monday it had to go to only one location to scoop up all the data.

Multiply this simple example by many days and many files, and you can begin to see how the performance of your drive can deteriorate over time. You can use DOS's CHKDSK command to locate fragmented files in a given subdirectory. For example, to check all files in a subdirectory on Drive C called WORKING, key in: CHKDSK C:\WORKING*.*.

Stupidly, the DOS manual does not make clear the fact that you must do this for every subdirectory. You cannot tell CHKDSK to do the entire disk in a single command. (The LISTFRAG program in the PACK-DISK Utilities discussed later in the chapter, however, can easily handle the entire disk.) Even more stupidly, the DOS manual tells you how to identify the problem of fragmented files but says nary a word about how to correct it.

Fortunately, the answer is simple. Just use the COPY command to copy each fragmented file to a different filename or location. Then use COPY again to copy it back to its original location. In the copying process, DOS assembles all the pieces of a file and lays them down at their destination as contiguous clusters. (The DOS DISKCOPY command that you use with two floppy disks, in contrast, simply makes a carbon copy of the source disk, fragmented files and all.)

This is a quick and easy fix if you have but a handful of fragmented files. If you have a lot of them, however, PACKDISK and SST (discussed below) offer a better way to accomplish the same thing. Two other programs, SCAVEN23 and HDTEST, will alert you to any clusters on your disk that have gone bad since the disk was formatted and help you take either preventative or restorative action as needed. The FBR programs by Vernon Buerg will help you deal with the onerous but essential chore of backing up your hard disk. We have arranged the programs below in the order in which you should use them as you set about optimizing your hard disk.

FreeTip: Should you ever find that portions of a file appear to be missing, it may be because some of the clusters used to store it have gotten lost by somehow becoming detached from their space allocation chain. To solve the problem, run CHKDSK against the subdirectory containing the problem file(s), only this time use the command: CHKDSK /F. The /F tells the program that you want to be able to fix any problems it finds.

If CHKDSK finds any lost clusters, it won't have any way of knowing where they belong, but it can help you save the information they contain by copying their contents to a file. Once you give your permission for the program to do this, it will copy the data as described and free up the clusters that held it. You can then look at the file(s) CHKDSK has created and try to repair the damage to the files from which the information came.

Glossbrenner's Choice:

IBM Top Utilities Disk 2—Larger Programs

FB158	COM	3110
FBR158	DOC	17210
FR152	COM	2744
FS150	COM	1717

Admonishments to back up your hard disk are rather like your mother telling you to bundle up before you go out to play some sunny March day. It was a pain then and it is a pain now, with one important difference: As an adult you recognize the wisdom of the practice, even if the nuisance hasn't diminished with time.

Backing up a hard disk is similar to copying all of the files in a specified subdirectory to a floppy disk with the COPY *.* command. But there are two elements that set the procedure apart. First, when you are using a backup program you basically say, "Please back up this particular subdirectory or my entire hard disk," and the program salutes smartly and begins putting files onto floppies. You don't have to worry about how many files will fit on a floppy or whether part of a file ends up on one floppy and part on another. When one disk has been filled, the program will prompt you to insert another. The COPY command, in contrast, will just quit when the first floppy is filled, telling you that there is no more free space on the destination disk.

The second thing that backup programs do is monitor the status of the archive bit discussed in Chapter 10. The existence of this bit makes it possible for a program to tell whether or not a file on your source disk has been changed since it was last backed up. If it has, the backup program will back it up again; if it hasn't, the program will not back it up again but instead move on to the next file on the source drive list. The archive bit will be off ("reset") if a file hasn't changed since it was last backed up; it will be on ("set") if changes have been made.

Unfortunately, the DOS BACKUP command doesn't operate much faster than a regular copy command, so it can take quite a while to backup a given subdirectory and a very long time indeed to back up even a half-filled hard disk. Accordingly, a number of companies have produced programs that encode and compress files and use other techniques to greatly increase backup speed. Fast Back ($80) is probably the best known of these, and it is quite impressive.

Mr. Buerg's FBR (File Backup/Restore) package is impressive as well. It is not as fast as a program like Fast Back, and the version current at this writing (version 1.58) can only deal with one subdirectory at a time. (According to Mr. Buerg, future versions will be able to handle all subdirectories in the current directory with a single command.) However, FBR operates about twice as fast as DOS's BACKUP command and has the added advantage of being able to alternate between Drive A and Drive B when filling floppies. It's also free. Mr. Buerg holds the copyright, but he offers the package for your personal use with no requested contribution.

The FB, FR, and FS stand for "file backup," "file restore," and "file status," respectively. FB backs up the files from a subdirectory into one large file per floppy disk. FR restores the files from the floppy onto the hard disk. And FS can look at the single large floppy file and tell you the names of all the individual files it contains:

On Disk 1—Quick Shots:

```
SCAV23   COM   18176
SCAV23   DOC     768
```

On Disk 2—Larger Programs:

```
HDTEST   EXE   32546
HDTEST   TXT   42588
HDCHEK   EXE   25456
```

The next step in the hard disk optimization process is to test your disk for any bad clusters. Hard disks consist of coated metal platters spinning—usually at 3600 rpm, or ten times faster than a floppy disk—in a hermetically sealed compartment. It is not at all unusual for a hard disk to come fresh from the factory bearing a sticker noting that certain cylinders tested as bad. IBM's specifications allow for this and in any case, such problems don't cheat you out of the space you're paying for. Because hard disks are designed to hold more than their nominal rating, a drive rated at 20 megabytes will hold 20 megabytes, bad cylinders notwithstanding.

FreeTip: A technician whose advice we respect suggests that if you order your hard drive from a mail-order source you send back any drive that comes from the factory with 10 to 15 bad cylinders, since this may be an indication of other problems. If you buy your system from a dealer, it wouldn't hurt to ask your salesperson to remove the computer's cover and show you the hard drive unit. The drive should bear a sticker telling you which, if any, cylinders tested as bad at the factory. Again, if the number is between 10 and 15, you are within your rights to ask that the drive be replaced before purchasing the machine.

DOS's FORMAT program automatically detects and locks out any bad areas on a disk. The program makes an entry in the FAT to prevent DOS from later trying to store data at those locations. Over time, however, anomalies in the metal oxide coating or other problems can sometimes cause portions of a disk to go bad. Since this happens after the initial formatting process, DOS doesn't know that defects have developed, and eventually it will try to store a file at that location. It may be able to do so successfully, but if the condition worsens, DOS may not be able to get the data back out again. Clusters that were perfectly good when the disk was new and now contain data can also go bad, leading to the same situation.

The two programs listed above, SCAV23 ("scavenge") on IBM Top Utilities Disk 1 and HDTEST ("hard disk test") on Disk 2, are designed to identify and lock out clusters that have gone bad since a disk was formatted. The "23" in SCAV23 apparently refers to the fact that this program is for DOS versions 2.x and 3.x, not to a version of the program itself. Written by Tom Jennings, the man who created the FIDO bulletin board package as well as LU86.COM, a leading file compression utility in years past, SCAVENGE is similar to the DiskTest (DT) program that is one of the commercially available Norton Utilities. SCAVENGE reads all the clusters on a disk and "marks unused bad ones in the FAT so that DOS will not use them later. It will not touch files with bad blocks." But it does identify them and as Mr. Jennings suggests, you should copy them to another location, delete the original, and run SCAVENGE again "to map out the bad blocks" that file occupied so they won't be used again.

The HDTEST (version 2.73) package is offered as shareware by Peter R. Fletcher of 220 Ballard Drive, West Hartford, CT 06119. The registration fee is $30 ($40 Canadian, according to the documentation). "As a bonus, registered users will get a copy of V3.00 of HDTEST, which includes a number of significant enhancements over V2.73, and will be entitled to support and help with HDTEST-related problems (including telephone support) for a year from the date of registration. . . . I will return your registration fee if I cannot support your system." HDTEST is one of the most thorough hard-disk-testing programs available today. The program writes 20 different test patterns to every cluster on the disk and checks that each pattern can be read back correctly, while preserving the contents of the clusters that already contain data. "As long as HDTEST can read the data from a flaky cluster correctly once (and it tries quite hard), it will be able to save the file of which that cluster is a part intact, while marking the cluster so that DOS does not try to use it again."

Most of the hard-disk-testing programs we looked at merely identify the defective areas they find without doing anything to solve the problem. HDTEST, in contrast, automatically "remaps" bad clusters by reading the data they contain, writing it to a good cluster, and marking the bad cluster as bad.

Depending on the size of your disk, HDTEST can take between two and five hours to complete its work. Consequently, we suggest that you use SCAVENGE first. If SCAVENGE identifies any bad data-containing clusters, you can then either try to save them yourself or if you are not successful, run HDTEST and let it try. Finally, if bad cluster problems show up regularly, you should probably have your disk professionally checked or consider replacing it.

The PACKDISK Utilities:

PACKDISK	COM	4549
LISTFRAG	COM	2798
DELDIR	COM	3110
MANUAL		23415
NAMEDIR	COM	2909
PARK	COM	372
TRANSDIR	COM	3821

The Seek Stopper:

SST	COM	45399
SST	DOC	9425

Now at last we're ready to optimize the disk. We had to make sure that there are no bad clusters first, since both of the above programs will abort if they find any on your disk. Also, these programs are designed for single-user hard disk drives and will not work in a network configuration. If you have installed copy-protected programs on your drive, be sure to "deinstall" them before running either PACKDISK or SST, and then reinstall them when they are finished.

As you can see, the PACKDISK Utilities consist of several programs, including utilities to delete entire subdirectories with a single command, rename them, transfer them to a different location, and a program to park a hard disk's read/write heads in a safe portion of the disk.

LISTFRAG, as noted earlier, will list every fragmented file on the drive with a single command. In addition, it will not only list all fragmented files (noncontiguous clusters) but will also list all fragmented DOS file directories for a disk or subdirectory, and all noncontiguous chains.

FreeTip: You can get a graphic representation of the current state of your drive or any given file on it with either the Norton Utilities or the Professional Master Key Utilities discussed in Chapter 9. Select the options that allow you to look at a visual map of disk or file space. This is not a bad thing to do before and after running one of these programs since it dramatically illustrates what has been accomplished.

The main event, however, is PACKDISK. This program eliminates file fragmentation by copying files to contiguous clusters, but it does other things as well. For example, it will free up lost clusters that CHKDSK may be unable to touch because they are located too far down the subdirectory "tree."

It will also pack the file directories, a point that requires a word of explanation. As you know, DOS uses a file directory ("table of contents") and a FAT to keep track of and locate files on a floppy disk and for each hard disk subdirectory. Every time a file is created, DOS makes an entry in its file directory, appropriating clusters as necessary to accommodate the new entries. What most people don't know, however, is that once a cluster has been assigned to a file directory, it is never released, even after the file to which an entry refers has been erased. PACKDISK fixes this by making all file directory entries contiguous and freeing any clusters that are no longer needed as a result. The amount of space freed in this way will depend upon how actively you create and delete files. In our experience, the program usually frees up between 2K and 6K of space.

The PACKDISK Utilities are offered as shareware ($30). Contact: Soft-Patch, P.O. Box 11455, San Francisco, CA 94101. Registration includes technical support and notices of updates and new products.

The Seek Stopper (SST) by Alfred J. Heyman also packs file directories and makes the data areas of your files contiguous. But there is one obvious and one subtle difference between SST and PACKDISK. PACKDISK "buffers data to disk," meaning that as it is picking up data from fragmented clusters with one hand, it is almost simultaneously recording the data in contiguous clusters with the other. PACKDISK thus requires a certain amount of free space on a disk to use as a work area.

SST, in contrast, buffers data in memory. This allows it to operate much faster than PACKDISK and it means that you can use it on a disk containing no free space at all. However, it also means that should there be a power failure while SST is working, you will probably have to reformat and reload your entire disk. SST can optimize any standard DOS disk, up to 32 megabytes (DOS's current official limit). The amount of memory required varies with the size of the disk. For a 32-megabyte disk, at least 512K is required. For smaller drives, the memory requirements are much lower.

SST will pack DOS file directories the way PACKDISK does, but SST will not free up the clusters in those directories that are no longer needed because the files they referenced have been erased. However, SST does something subtle that PACKDISK does not, a fact we discovered when we called Alfred Heyman. After PACKDISK reported that all of the files on our disk were contiguous, we ran SST and were surprised to find that the program felt some 7000 clusters had to be moved. Puzzled, we phoned Mr. Heyman and learned that his program takes a slightly different approach concerning the location of DOS's file directories.

DOS always puts the FAT and the file directory for the root directory (the one at the very top of the "tree") in specific locations on the disk (in the outermost track or cylinder). The file directories for the subdirectories that branch off the root directory (the terminology's awful, isn't it?) may be stored all over the disk. Most disk-optimizing programs make

DOS's file directories contiguous, as explained, and most store them out near the root directory and FAT. Mr. Heyman's program, in contrast, stores the file directories next to the actual files they refer to. Which is why SST wanted to move 7000 clusters on our disk, even though all files were already contiguous.

Is it worth it? Apparently it is, for Mr. Heyman didn't do this on a whim. His benchmark tests reveal a measurable improvement in the performance of hard disks that are optimized this way. What's more, on the basis of SST, a well-known software company hired Mr. Heyman to produce a commercial disk optimizer of the same design. The commercial version sells for much more than the $10 Mr. Heyman asks for his shareware product. Mr. Heyman is a principal of Heyman/Hirsh, a software house specializing in CAD/CAM vertical markets. His address is Alfred J. Heyman, Room 101, P.O. Box 172101, Memphis, TN 38187.

NEWPARK:

```
PARK   COM    663
PARK   DOC    1660
PARK   ASM    14284
```

The read/write heads of a hard disk never actually touch the surface of the spinning platters when they are in operation. Instead, they float directly above the surface on a thin cushion of air. If the heads ever do touch the portion of the disk used to store data, that data may be wiped out. This is why you're supposed to "park" your heads before moving the machine. When properly parked, the heads are located over portions of the disk that are never used to store data. So if they get jostled, they won't do any damage to recorded information. This is more than just theory, as we discovered to our dismay during a recent move. After doing the penance of reformatting and reloading the disk, we have gotten religion and will never move the system anywhere again without first parking the heads.

IBM provides a head-parking program on the IBM Diagnostics disk, and you will encounter a number of programs in free software channels. Most, unfortunately, have the same name. You may find this one referred to as "NEWPARK," though the actual names are those given above. Written by Carl Hayes, this program is especially attractive for two reasons. First, unlike many parking programs it can park the heads of both hard drives, should you have two of them in your system. And second, it does not automatically move the heads to a specific cylinder.

Instead, the program tries ever higher cylinder numbers until it finds a cylinder to which the heads cannot move. The process takes less than half a second in this version of the program (the version number is not given, so you must go by the size in bytes), and it assures that regardless of the make, model, or size of your drive, the heads will always be parked in a safe place.

FreeTip: Many hard disk manufacturers supply head-parking utilities with their equipment. Since the safe parking zone on a disk can vary with the make and model, however, the program supplied by manufacturer A will not necessarily safely park the heads of a disk made by manufacturer B. Thus before using a friend's parking utility, be sure to consult the documentation to make sure that its parking zone corresponds to a safe area on your own disk. When in doubt, you can always phone the manufacturer of your drive.

RAM Disks and Disk Caches

Recommended Programs

Glossbrenner's Choice:

IBM Top Utilities Disk 2—Larger Programs

The Adjustable RAM Disk (ADJRAM.EXE, et al.)

Gary Cramblitt's Adjustable RAM Disk package (version 3.1) contains ADJRAM.EXE and five support and source code files. A RAM disk is simply an area of memory that has been configured to fool DOS into thinking it is a disk drive. It is also referred to as a "virtual disk," as is the case with the VDISK.SYS device driver that now comes with the DOS package you received when you purchased your computer. The chief advantage of a RAM disk is speed. Once copied into a RAM disk, programs load and files appear on the screen nearly at the speed of light, with no wait for a floppy disk to get up to speed or for a hard disk's read/write heads to find the desired file. RAM disks are particularly helpful with programs that use "overlays"—files, online help information, or pieces of a program that are kept out on disk until the user requests them.

RAM disks are a valuable tool, but they are not without their disadvantages, as we'll see when we look at disk-caching programs in a moment. The disadvantage we want to focus on here, however, concerns the fact that you must usually specify how large you want the disk to be when you boot up or initially load in the RAM-disk-creating program. Should you later find that you need the memory allocated to your RAM disk to run a particularly memory-hungry applications program, you must reboot your computer without the RAM-disk-creating program or specify a smaller size.

ADJRAM, in contrast, lets you vary the size of your RAM disk *without* rebooting and without losing any data already stored there. You can adjust the disk size up and down in multiples of 64K at any time. The program offers limited support of the LIM EMS version 3.2 (Lotus/Intel/Microsoft Expanded Memory Standard), should you want to use that memory instead of your system's regular memory.

There is an online help facility should you forget the commands, and the manual is extensive and well written. Mr. Cramblitt expressly states that "You are not expected to make a donation to the author for using this program. Enjoy—and try to do the same for others some day." Truly an outstanding piece of software.

Recommended Programs

Glossbrenner's Choice:

IBM Top Utilities Disk 1—Quick Shots

CACHE

CACHE3	**COM**	1043
CACHE3	**ASM**	26467
CACHE3	**DOC**	6709

Expanded Memory Cache:

EMC110	**COM**	2948
EMC110	**DOC**	14808

As noted, RAM disks do have some drawbacks. The first is that you must copy files into them before you can use those files at RAM-disk speed. The second, and most important, is that you must always remember to dump any file that you have changed or created on a RAM disk back onto a real disk before turning off the system. If you don't, that wonderful opening chapter you've just written for your great American novel will evaporate into thin air once the power is off.

Disk-cache programs such as those featured above represent yet another way to speed up your system's disk-related activities. Though the speed improvement offered is not as dramatic as that of a RAM disk, you do not have to copy files into a disk cache or remember to dump their contents to a real disk before powering down. You can thus think of caches as marginally intelligent RAM disks. When installed, a cache program sets aside a certain amount of memory as a temporary holding area. Then it inserts itself between DOS and you or your applications program. From this position, it can act as a filter and a shunt. Thus, when you or a program order DOS to go out to disk and bring in a file for processing, the cache program intercepts the information DOS has read off the disk and puts a copy of it into its holding area before passing it along to you or the requesting program.

That in itself doesn't save any time. The savings take place the *next* time DOS is told to go out to disk. When that happens, the cache program intercepts the call and checks its holding area to see if the material you want is already there. If it is, the cache program responds by supplying the material (at RAM-disk speed), and DOS is never told to turn on the disk drive. If the requested material isn't in the cache, the program passes the request to DOS and the information is retrieved from disk as per usual, with a copy automatically being added to the cache once it has been retrieved. Eventually, of course, the cache will fill up. At this point, most cache programs make room for new information by getting rid of the least recently accessed material.

Cache programs also typically read in and maintain copies of a disk or subdirectory's FAT and file directory. (Please see the previous discussion of disk optimizers for more on the FAT and the file directory.) This in itself speeds up your system's operation, since it means that DOS does not have to search for this information on disk when you want to locate a file. According to Barry Simon writing in the *Capital PC Monitor* (March 1987), "A cache can avoid anywhere from one third to two thirds of your disk accesses."

A good cache program handles write (as opposed to read) requests by passing the information to DOS directly so that a copy will always be recorded on disk. Such programs are referred to as "write-through caches." At the same time, the cache program should update its own copy of the changed file if it has one in storage. This means that you do not have to worry about text or data evaporating when you shut off the power.

At this point, we should point out that DOS comes with a disk cache of its own. These are what the DOS manual refers to as disk buffers and they are used in exactly the same way that a cache program is, except that DOS often does not write its buffer contents to disk immediately. Mr. Simon refers to the practice as "keeping dirty buffers." DOS's buffer cache size is set in units of 512 bytes. The default setting for PCs and XTs is two buffers; for ATs it is three. If you do not use a caching program, Barry Simon and most other authorities advise changing these defaults by inserting a line like BUFFERS = 20 in your CONFIG.SYS file. For technical reasons, the optimum number of buffers lies somewhere between 15 and 20 on most systems. If you do use a caching program, you will probably be better off allowing DOS to use its minimal default settings since the cache will do a better job than DOS's buffers.

We have looked at many shareware and public domain caching programs, and in our opinion CACHE3 and EMMCACHE are the best. There is a shareware version of Multisoft's PC-Kwik (SHARE-PCK.ARC) that works quite well. But we cannot recommend it, for its makers have seen fit to cripple it such that it automatically gobbles up all available memory over 360K. At this writing, only Multisoft's commercial versions allow you to adjust your cache size, and they cost between $40 and $80.

CACHE3 was written by Quick and Dirty Software, Inc., based on logic supplied by Steven Holzner in *PC Magazine* (6 August 1985, "How to Realize Cache Savings," pp. 207–211). Designed for use on PCs, XTs, and compatibles, CACHE3 lets you specify the size of the cache(s) you wish to create and the drive(s) to which you wish them to pertain. CACHE3 stores sectors only if they are read in singly. This means that CACHE3's storage space will not be overwhelmed by lots of large programs, and it means that programs and data files that occupy more than one sector (512 bytes) will not be affected. CACHE3 keeps the FAT and disk directory permanently in its storage area.

According to Mr. Holzner, "I've tested CACHE with a program that first reads a sector on one track, then reads a sector from a different track and repeats the whole process 50 times. Before caching, the program took a full 25 seconds to run; after caching, it took about 1."

EMC version 1.10 (also known as EMMCACHE) by Frank Lozier of the Department of Mathematics at Cleveland State University is for use on computers with Lotus/Intel/Microsoft (LIM) expanded memory. In the DOS world (as opposed to the brave new world of OS/2), conventional memory is the one megabyte of RAM and ROM most IBM-compatible computers are designed to use as their work, storage, and system area. Of this, a maximum of 640K is typically available for you and your programs to use.

Beyond conventional memory is extended memory, ranging above the one megabyte limit to as many as 16 megabytes. You need an AT or some other machine using the Intel 80286 microprocessor to access all of this memory, but if you add a special board to your XT or AT, you can get at a part of it. This part is the lower half and it is called expanded memory. Expanded memory ranges from the one megabyte limit up to eight megabytes, and it is here that EMC puts its disk cache.

EMC caches only hard disk drives and will not work on systems using hard disks that exceed DOS's current 32-megabyte size limit through the use of special device drivers and larger sector sizes. There are some other limitations as well, all clearly explained in the supplied documentation. If you have a standard system, however, you will find the program can boost your hard disk's data-transfer rate by about 400 percent and nearly triple the drive's overall performance, based on tests we performed with CORE International, Inc.'s CORETEST program.

Finally, we should point out that disk caches and RAM drives are not mutually exclusive. If you use only a few programs without lots of data files, a RAM disk is probably all you need, assuming you have enough memory to create one large enough for your programs. If your main computer usage centers around database programs and others with extensive data files, a cache program may serve you better. If your usage is somewhere in between, you may want to install both a RAM disk and a disk cache.

Ultimately, if you have the time, the best approach is to experiment with both types of software. Leave the technical benchmarks aside. Based on the particular way you use your system, if a RAM disk or disk cache does not produce a *noticeable* improvement, then there is little point in installing it. We think you'll be pleasantly surprised, however, at how a RAM disk, disk cache, and periodic hard disk optimization will boost your system's performance—all courtesy of public domain and modestly priced shareware software.

Glossbrenner's Choice Disk Reference—Chapters 10 and 11

IBM Top Utilities Disk 1—Quick Shots

DOS Command Replacements

CP16.EXE—Improved COPY command. Can copy several files and/or subdirectories at once.

MV23.EXE—*Moves* files and subdirectories. Eliminates the need to go back and delete something from its source location after copying it to a new destination.

NO.COM—Makes specified files invisible to DOS commands. Lets you copy or delete everything *except* the files you specify, for example.

NT.EXE—Nifty "newTREE" command. Much better than DOS's.

RENDIR.COM—Renames subdirectories.

RM15.EXE—*Removes* subdirectories without deleting files and using the DOS RD command.

SDIR26.COM—The best "sorted directory" program. Sorts the display, not the disk. See DIREDIT in Chapter 9 (the Core Collection) for that function.

File Operations

ALTER.COM—Can alter any and all file attributes, including attributes to hide files and subdirectories.

CAT.EXE—Improved file conCATenation. Will work from a prepared list of files if you like.

DISK.COM—Key in DISK /T and the program will calculate and display subtotals of the files in each subdirectory. Can be made more specific with * and ? global characters and file extensions (.BAS, .TXT, .WKS, and so on).

FDATE.COM—Changes the date and time stamp on any file.

FREE.COM—Instantly reports the amount of free space on a disk.

FREE-86.COM—Instantly gives you disk information otherwise available only from DOS's CHKDSK command.

NODUPE.BAT—Batch file to delete duplicate files between the source and target disks or subdirectories.

PI-COMP.COM—Much improved alternative to DOS's COMP command. Tells you *how* compared files differ, instead of just reporting that a difference exists.

RO11.EXE/RW11.EXE—Quickly makes files read-only so they cannot be changed or erased, or returns them to normal read/write status.

SIZE.COM/ATSIZE.COM—Calculates the floppy disk storage requirements for a specified group of files.

SWAPNAME.COM—Swaps the names of two files.

UPDATE1.EXE—Gives specified files today's date and time. Make sure you have correctly set your system's TIME and DATE with the DOS commands of those names.

File Locators and Catalogs

WHEREIS.COM—Reports the subdirectory(s) containing the filename you specify.

LOCATE.COM—Searches through every file for the text string you specify.

PS.EXE—The SUPER-Search package. Lets you search for files and for text within files by virtually every conceivable means.

(See also PKFIND and PMCAT on Disk 2 and PC-DISK on Disk 3.)

Floppy Disk Utilities

VOLSER.COM—Changes the volume label ("title") of a disk.

QDR.COM—Quick disk format. Ten seconds per disk, compared to 50 seconds for DOS's FORMAT command. Returns a data disk to just-formatted condition.

(See also "DisKover" on Disk 3, "FastCopy" on Disk 2, and the disk-labeling programs on Disk 3.)

Screen and Keyboard Utilities

COLOR.BAT—Lets you set foreground, background, and border colors in DOS by keying in color names.

COLOR.COM—Does the same as COLOR.BAT, but faster. Requires the keying of numbers for each color, however.

PUSH.COM/POP.COM—PUSH takes a snapshot of any screen and records it to disk. Activate with [<Shift><Print Screen>]. POP will redisplay recorded snapshots. Requires CGA-compatible graphics adaptor.

FAKEY.COM—Feeds keystrokes to your programs. Better than Key-Fake, a similar program, because you can introduce pauses. Can be used with POP for a slide show, for example.

NL.COM/NLOFF.COM—Turns <NumLock> on or off.

CAPSLOCK.COM/CAPSUNLK.COM—Ditto for <CapsLock>.

STATLINE.COM—Tells you on the screen when <NumLock>, <CapsLock>, or <Scroll Lock> are engaged.

Memory Management

NMI11.COM—Tests memory and identifies the defective chip should you ever get a nonmaskable interrupt due to a parity (memory) check error.

RAM.COM—Quickly tells you how much RAM is free.

(See also the Mark/Release package on Disk 2.)

Miscellaneous Utilities

BASMENU.BAS—Automatically prepares a menu containing the names of any BASIC (.BAS) program on your disk. Users need only key in a menu item to run a given program. Returns user to the BASMENU when the chosen program has finished.

CGCLOCK.COM/MONOCLK2.COM—Displays clock in upper right corner of screen on CGA or monochrome screens.

FSPOOL.COM—Redirects output bound for the printer to a disk file.

PW.EXE—Prevents anyone from using your system without first keying in an acceptable password.

WAIT.COM/WAITUNTL.COM—Designed for batch file use. Makes the system wait a specified number of seconds or until a specified time before continuing.

BEEP.COM/REBEEP.COM—Another batch file-oriented set. BEEP issues a single beep when run. REBEEP keeps beeping until someone presses a key.

SOUND.COM/TUNE.COM/SPKR.SYS—Various programs to generate or allow you to create sounds on your speaker.

SILENCE.COM—Disables/enables the speaker.

Hard Disk Utilities and Disk Caches

FB158.COM/FR152.COM/FS150.COM—File backup and restore package. Twice as fast as DOS's BACKUP command.

SCAV23.COM—Locates and locks out defective clusters on your hard disk so DOS won't use them.

CACHE3—Conventional memory disk cache for PCs/XTs/ATs.

EMC110—Also known as EMMCACHE. Disk cache for machines with expanded memory.

IBM Top Utilities Disk 2—Larger Programs

ADJRAM.EXE—Sets up a dynamically adjustable RAM drive or "virtual disk." Change the size on the fly at any time.

FASTCOPY.EXE—High-speed, production disk copying. Takes only 32 seconds per disk.

HDTEST.EXE—The most thorough hard-disk-testing program we've ever seen. Does more than test. Will attempt to recover portions of files found to be stored in defective clusters. Then it will lock the bad clusters out so they won't be used again.

PARK.COM—"NewPARK" analyzes your particular disk and parks the heads in a safe place. Similar programs don't take your brand of hard disk into account.

PACKDISK.COM/SST.COM—Both PACKDISK and Seek Stopper (SST) are "disk-optimizer" programs. If your files are fragmented (which happens in the normal course of things), they can make the files contiguous. That speeds up disk access and often frees up several thousand bytes of space formerly occupied by trailing directory clusters or orphaned clusters.

MARK.COM/RELEASE.COM—This is the TSR: Mark/Release package. Lets you remove terminate and stay-resident programs—such as Sidekick, SmartKey, and lots of others—from memory without rebooting.

PKFIND.COM—Can search ARC files for names and text, as well as conventional file searches.

PMCAT2.COM—Lets you tack 80-character notes to the filenames in your directories.

IBM Top Utilities Disk 3—Disk Labeling

DISKOVER44.COM—DisKover, version 4.4. Produces covers designed to be inserted and folded over floppy envelopes. Cover contains list of all files, free space, date, and so on in attractive format and compressed print.

PC-DISK.COM—One of the best floppy disk cataloging programs. Searches on the basis of filename or attached memos.

Label Maker 6.10—Capable of producing four different sizes of disk labels containing a sorted list of files on the disk, a short comment from you, and other information. Can uses a variety of enhanced printing features.

LabelPrinter 3.4—Prints labels measuring 3½ by $^{15}/_{16}$ inches. Includes title line and comments (no file list). Can use a variety of enhanced printing features.

12

Word Processing, Outlining, Typing, and Text Utilities
THE SUPERCONDUCTORS OF THOUGHT

Word processing has always offered the ideal conceptual bridge for explaining personal computers and the impact they can have on your work and on your life. Everyone, after all, knows what a typewriter is and does, and with that as a reference point it is relatively easy to discuss text creation on a computer. Without a doubt, word processing is the single most widely used personal computer application, so it is only fitting that we make it the focus of the first of our chapters on free or shareware productivity programs.

But of course, word processing isn't the only text and idea-oriented type of software. In this chapter we'll also discuss a passel of utility programs designed to operate on text files. We'll look at a program that will help you create an index of a book or a report, a program to help you evaluate your writing style, an "idea-processing" or outlining program on a par with Thinktank and Ready, and a program to help you master or improve your touch-typing skills.

Word Processing

According to *Webster's Ninth Collegiate Dictionary*, the term "word processor" came into being around 1977. And the very fact that it is listed in that book is proof enough that one can expect to find the phrase used in general parlance. In short, most people today have at least a broad idea of what word processing is all about.

You may never have actually tried word processing, however. And perhaps you really shouldn't. For once you start, you will find it addictive. Imagine being able to merely think a thought and have it appear on the screen. Imagine being able to soar and pirouette and dive, free of the surly bonds of ink, paper, and pen. If you do any kind of writing at all, it can be a heady experience. Though for best results, you must be able to type.

If you are more inclined to purely practical matters, consider the potential savings of installing a PC and word processing software in your office. Suppose you're an executive who has just dictated a letter to an important customer. The letter runs two pages, and you've got a top-flight secretary, so when the letter is returned to you for signature it is perfect. On reading the letter, however, you discover that you have left out a key fact or feel you don't come across in quite the right way, or whatever. As happens tens of thousands of times a day, the letter must be revised and returned to the secretary for retyping.

Let's assume that retyping the letter will require half an hour. Now, you know what you're paying that top-flight secretary. With wages, vacation, and benefits it could easily work out to $16 an hour or more. So, in effect, retyping that letter will cost you and your firm about $8. If your secretary had a word-processing computer, in contrast, generating a fresh, fully revised, perfect copy of the same letter might require a mere ten minutes. That's about $2.67 worth of your secretary's time, for a productivity-induced savings of more than $5. For *one* business letter.

Certainly there are many other variables to be factored into the equation. Computers and printers are cheap, but they're not free. And you will have to pay your secretary for the time spent learning to use the equipment effectively. By the same token, however, if a modest investment in equipment and training results in one secretary becoming so productive that you don't need to hire a second person to handle the workload, then your savings will be even greater than we have suggested.

Recommended Programs

Glossbrenner's Choice:

> IBM PC-Write Disk 1—Program Disk
> (Contains main editing and printing programs,
> tutorial, and Quick Guide manual)

> IBM PC-Write Disk 2—Utilities Disk
> (Contains "Printer Picker" program and 50,000-word
> spelling checker)

Word processors and text editors are among the most numerous of public domain and shareware creations. There are scores of them. And as is always the case, when you're thumbing through a printed catalog of programs, they all look more or less the same. Unfortunately, computer magazine reviews often add to the confusion by failing to give readers the kind of guidance they need. Such publications prefer to keep everybody happy, and since there is usually at least something good one can say about any competently written piece of software, their reviews tend to conclude by firmly straddling the issue: "You might like program A or you might like program B or you may prefer program C. Ultimately it's up to you."

One can sympathize, and certainly it can be argued that it is a magazine's role to inform, not necessarily to make judgments. But that doesn't help the reader, who must obtain and then spend hours testing programs A, B, and C before making up his or her mind. Happily, in this book we can tell it like it is: PC-Write by Bob Wallace is hands-down the best word processing program for the IBM PC, PS/2, and compatibles—including programs available as public domain, shareware, and commercial products.

Of course we realize that those who are currently using a different program may disagree. But that's fine. The most important thing about a word-processing program is that you be very comfortable with it. If your current program offers everything you want in a word processor—if it acts as a superconductor of thought—by all means stick with it. But if you're just starting out, we think we can make a powerful case for choosing to learn PC-Write.

Rather than present a "mego" ("my eyes glaze over") list of program features, we will simply say that there are three reasons why we recommend PC-Write so strongly. The first, of course, is the program itself. In addition to virtually every feature you can imagine, some 45 instantly available help screens, a spelling checker (50,000 words, to start), and specialized support for some 300 printers, PC-Write offers you unparalleled speed.

According to *InfoWorld* (22 December 1986, p. 45),

We searched for the word *the* in a 32K byte ASCII text file and replaced it with *xxx*. Word Perfect 4.1 took nine seconds to perform 296 replacements, Xywrite III 3.09 took 53 seconds, and PC-Write 2.7 took only seven seconds. . . . We used a 60K ASCII text file to evaluate scrolling speed. The first time Word Perfect took 14 seconds to move from the top of the file to the end, then six to eight seconds in subsequent moves up or down. Xywrite III hesitated briefly and then popped to the other end of the file. PC-Write moved instantly.

The reason PC-Write is so fast is that it does everything in memory. And as a conversation with Bob Wallace confirmed, this is one of the reasons why PC-Write's file size has always been limited to 60K (about 30 double-spaced pages). In technical terms, the Intel 8088 chip that is at the heart of the PC is designed to deal with 64K data segments, and while one could use multiple segments, Mr. Wallace has chosen not to do so. The program overcomes this limitation by allowing you to break a file into smaller chunks and link them at print time.

Version 3.0

This limitation on file size is about to be removed, however. The version current at this writing is 2.71, but as you read this, version 3.0 should be available. According to Mr. Wallace, in version 3.0 file size will be limited only by available memory. Mr. Wallace notes that while the new version will work well with DOS, it is especially suitable to OS/2 with its "virtual data segments" capability. (Under OS/2, in a process that is completely "transparent" to the applications program, any data segment can be swapped out to disk if the program needs the physical memory that data currently occupies.) Version 3.0 will also incorporate a column move feature. This refers to the ability to box and move a column of text from one location to another without affecting other text on the same lines. It has always been possible to move paragraph-like blocks of text with PC-Write.

Finally, version 3.0 will offer an interactive way of entering many of PC-Write's special font and "dot commands." For example, if you want a word to be printed in boldface, you will be able to place the cursor on the word and hit a key to call up a menu. Choosing the boldface option from the menu will cause the program to automatically insert the necessary font codes at the cursor location. In version 2.71, you must key in [<Alt><B>] at the locations you wish boldface printing to begin and end. Other fonts are specified in a similar manner.

Unparalleled Value

The second reason for recommending PC-Write so highly is the remarkable sense of value offered by Quicksoft, Inc., Mr. Wallace's company. We have watched Quicksoft grow from a one-person shop in 1983 to a 20-person organization, and it has always taken a "you approach" in its operations. For example, at this writing the mail order discount prices for commercial word-processing software range from $250 for Multimate 3.3 to $200 for PFS:ProWrite to $110 for WordPerfect 4.2, and paying those prices are your only options.

Quicksoft, in contrast, offers an entire range of product and service configurations. At the top is the full Registered Package ($89). This includes the two PC-Write disks, a hardbound copy of the User's Guide (360 typeset, illustrated pages with an excellent index), a 32-page Quick Guide booklet, a quick reference command card, one year's worth of Full Support, and the opportunity to earn a shareware commission of $25 on each package registered by someone using your copy. At the bottom is a simple $10 fee for a copy of the program disk or $16 for both the program disk and the utilities disk. Note that the program disk contains a 17-page tutorial and the 44-page Quick Guide. The utilities disk contains a program that automatically creates a printer definition file that lets PC-Write use your printer's special features. The word list that the program's spelling checker uses to identify misspelled words is also on the second disk. Note that you may add words to this list as you please.

If the Registered Package does not appeal, you can simply order the manual ($35 for softcover; $45 for hardbound). If you want just the Basic Support service (questions answered by phone or by mail, a subscription to the quarterly *Quick Notes* newsletter, and the right to earn commissions), it is available for $20 a year. Full Support is the Basic Support Service plus two reply cards good for updated disk sets. It too is sold separately at $35 a year. The program's source code is available as well, should you want to make alterations. There are also quantity discounts ranging from 20 to 40 percent. You can even order labels and brochures to spruce up the disks you provide to others (in hopes of earning shareware commissions). And to top it all off, if you are not satisfied with any Quicksoft product you may return it within 90 days for a full refund.

A Programming Genius

The third and final reason for recommending PC-Write is Bob Wallace himself. Mr. Wallace began designing text processors in 1969 while a student at Brown University. He holds a master's degree in computer science, and in 1978 he was one of the first dozen people to join a little Bellevue, Washington, firm called Microsoft. While at Microsoft, Wallace designed the language and architecture, wrote the compiler front end, and wrote much of the runtime for Microsoft's MS-Pascal. As discussed at the beginning of this book, influenced by Freeware originator Andrew Fluegelman (PC-Talk) and Jim Button (PC-File), Bob Wallace invented the concept of shareware when he introduced the first version of PC-Write in August 1983. The term has since come to be applied to any contribution-requested program, whether or not commissions are involved.

Mr. Wallace's commitment to his product is obvious for, as with all successful shareware authors, he is constantly updating and improving it. But the only way to experience his artistry is to try the program. You can order directly from Quicksoft by calling (800) 888-8088 between the hours of 7 A.M. and 5 P.M. Pacific Time (Visa and MasterCard accepted), or by writing to: Quicksoft, Inc., 219 First North #224, Seattle, WA 98109. As noted, the two-disk package is $16. The price for 3½-inch disk users is the same. Or we can send you the software as Glossbrenner's Choice disks. (Lest anyone think we've stacked the deck here, these disks do not contain a commissionable registration number.) One way or another, once you're tried PC-Write we think you'll agree that, as good as other word-processing programs may be, there simply isn't any point in fooling around with anything else.

─────────────── **Special Deal Coupon** ───────────────

Readers of this book can receive a special $15 discount off the regular price ($89) of PC-Write's Full Registration package. Simply photocopy this coupon, fill it out, and mail it with your check for $74 or your credit card information to:

> Glossbrenner Book Offer
> Quicksoft, Inc.
> 219 First North #224
> Seattle, WA 98109

This coupon is valid through December 1989. Washington state residents, please add 7.9 percent sales tax. This offer is valid for U.S. and Canadian shipments only and may not be combined with other coupons or discounts. This discount can only be honored on mail orders received with a copy of this coupon.

Circle Disk Size: 5.25" or 3.5"

Name: _____

Company: _____ Day Phone: _____

Address: _____

City, State, ZIP: _____

Visa/MC Number: _____Expires: _____

Signature: _____

PC-Write Quick-Start Guide

The criticism of PC-Write one encounters most often is that the program is too powerful for the novice user. Since we know how easy it is to get started with PC-Write, we've always found that puzzling. Still, if you are a complete novice, here are the main commands you need to know to get started immediately. After you have made a backup copy of your disk:

- Key in ED filename.ext to start.

- When the program says the file does not exist and asks whether it should create filename.ext, follow the prompt and hit <F9> to create it.

- You will now be into the program and should hit <F2> to display the margin line at the top of the page. Then hit your down arrow key once to get into the composition area.

- Finally, hit <F1> to display the F-key commands across the top of the screen. Hitting <F1> again will take you to the program's help facility.

- When you are finishing writing, hit <F3> to save your work to disk and hit <F2> to exit the program, as the command line at the top of the screen tells you.

Naturally, you will want to properly install the program before you begin to really get down to brass tacks, and the batch files on the distribution disks make this easy. But if you're in a hurry, just follow the steps given here. If you have a moment or two more, you can change margins by moving up into the margin line and adding or deleting spaces. Then move back down and begin to write. To adjust a paragraph of text to new margins, hit <F7>.

As you can see, virtually any computer user can begin creating text immediately with PC-Write. If you need only a simple word processor, there is no law requiring you to learn PC-Write's other features. The commands outlined above will be fine. Simply learn to use the features you need as you need them.

Mr. Wallace is aware of the complexity criticism, of course, and while he agreed with the "use what you need and forget the rest" approach, he said,

> But people are funny. On an emotional basis they just don't like to have all of those features there. They don't like seeing them on the menus and

help screens, and they worry that they will accidently hit a key combination that will do something unexpected.

So after going to a lot of computer shows and listening to a lot of people, I've finally figured out that really they want something that at least *looks* simple.

Accordingly, Mr. Wallace plans to do a version of the program that will mask all but the most basic features. As things stand now, he envisions such a version as being equipped with an "add-a-feature feature." You would start with a bare-bones program and add features as needed by calling up the "add-a-feature" menu. Once a feature was added, the appropriate selections would appear on the program menus and help screens, and the keys to activate it would be enabled.

Mr. Wallace is already at work on this kind of program, but he does not know when it will be released. In the meantime, we feel that it still makes much more sense to focus on one fully powered word-processing program and learn it well over a period of years than it does to start with a "simple" program that you may soon outgrow.

Text Utilities

A machine-language file can't really be changed, but a text file is almost like clay. There are all kinds of things you can to do shape it, filter it, or otherwise prepare it for your special needs. The programs discussed in this section are among the best text shapers and treaters of their kind. Most are quite small and quick, and all of them are available from bulletin boards, online systems, and most other free software sources.

Recommended Programs

Glossbrenner's Choice:

IBM Text Treaters Disk 1—Utilities/Indexing/Style

CHOP3	EXE	36400	HEAD	EXE	2698
CHOP3	DOC	10985	INVERT	COM	15348
CRLF	DOC	1792	INVERT	DOC	783
CRLF	COM	12227	LOCK	DOC	2304
DWASC	EXE	22144	LOCK	COM	340
FECHO	COM	128	LOWER	COM	384
FECHO	DOC	696	SNGLSPC	COM	768
FEED	COM	384	SNGLSPC	DOC	205
FEED	DOC	714	SORTF225	COM	3005
FILTERS	DOC	3852	SORTF225	DOC	9052
HEAD	DOC	1831	STAT	EXE	15393

STAT	DOC	2045		TRUNC	DOC	1041
STRIPLF	DOC	2308		TRUNC	COM	128
STRIPLF	EXE	5674		TRANSLIT	DOC	3456
TABS19	ASM	15910		TRANSLIT	EXE	7168
TABS19	DOC	3038		UNIQUE	COM	640
TABS19	COM	2047		UNIQUE	DOC	363
TAIL	DOC	1124		UNLOCK	COM	340
TAIL	EXE	2917		UNWS	DOC	493
TEXT21	DOC	1280		UNWS	EXE	2816
TEXT21	COM	16896		UP-LOW	DOC	715
TRANSLAT	DOC	522		UPPER	COM	384
TRANSLAT	COM	256				

CHOP3, by W. J. Kennamer, will cut a text file into as many smaller text files as you specify. CRLF, by Rahul Dhesi, the creator of the ZOO method of file packing, makes sure that every line in a text file ends with a carriage return and a line feed so that it can be displayed and edited properly. This program is likely to be most useful when you are dealing with text files that you have downloaded from an online system. If the file was created on an Apple computer, for example, there's a good chance that each line will end in a carriage return but be missing the line feed character. If the text was created on a mainframe, each line may end in two carriage returns or two line feeds. Unlike similar programs, CRLF is smart. It will add or remove whatever characters are necessary to ensure that each line ends in one carriage return and one line feed. STRIPLF by David Kozinn removes the line feed from a carriage return/line feed pair.

One of the nice things about PC-Write is that it creates pure ASCII text files. Other word processors take a different approach and insert high ASCII codes (codes above 127) into the text. As long as you use the file with the word processor that created it, you will not see these codes and will have no problems. But should you try to TYPE the file to the screen in DOS, you will see many "garbage" characters mixed in with the text. And while you can upload the file to an online system successfully, no one else will be able to read it.

Since PC-Write automatically strips out high codes, one way to clean up a file is to simply bring it into that program and then save it to disk. Another way is to use a text-cleaning utility. DWASC ("Displaywrite to ASCII"), for example, is designed to convert .PRN text files created by IBM's Displaywrite word-processing package into pure ASCII text. UNWS ("un-WordStar"), a speedy program by Gene Plantz (one of the leading BBS sysops in the IBM world), will do the same thing for text files created by WordStar.

FECHO and FEED by Joi Ellis make it easier to use any DOS filter or pipe, as explained in FILTERS.DOC and your DOS manual. HEAD by Jon Dart will display the first n lines of a text file. For example, the command HEAD -25 FILTERS.DOC would display the first 25 lines of FILTERS.DOC. Mr. Dart's TAIL program will do the same thing for the last n lines in a file. INVERT will accept a stream of text from one file and output it to the screen or to another file in reverse order. The program can handle files up to 65,000 lines long.

LOCK and UNLOCK by Steven Holzner offer quick encryption of a text file. The syntax is LOCK TEXTFILE.EXT LOCKEDFILE.EXT, so your original file (TEXTFILE.EXT) remains unchanged. The LOCK program will prompt you for a password (up to 64 characters long), which it will use as the basis for encoding the text into LOCKED-FILE.EXT. UNLOCK works the same way. The program is limited to a maximum file size of 62K. For longer files, and an even greater degree of security, see the discussion of file encryption programs later in the chapter. LOWER and UPPER by Joi Ellis will convert every character in a text file to lower or upper case. SINGLSPC by the same author removes all blank lines from a file.

SORTF225 is the latest version (at this writing) of Vern Buerg's famous file sorting program. The easiest way to understand this program is to visualize a file containing several columns of numbers. You can tell the program to sort the file (outputting to a different file) on the basis of what it finds in any of those columns. You can also use multiple sort keys, telling the program to sort first on the basis of the contents of one column and then sort on the basis of a different column, and so on. You can even tell it to create an output file containing only the data in the sort keys you have specified.

As with all of Mr. Buerg's efforts, this is a superb piece of programming. Files as large as 40,000 records or 16 megabytes can be sorted, and the sort order can be based on as many as 16 key fields. Needless to say, this is much better than DOS's SORT filter.

STAT by Daryll Shatz offers a nifty way to get a file's vital statistics. It will quickly tell you, for example, the total number of lines, words, and characters a file contains (as well as the total number of printable, control, alphabetic, and numerical characters). It will also tell you the average number of words per line and average number of characters per line, as well as the maximum used in each case. You can also ask STAT to tell you how many times a particular single character or code appears in the file.

Vern Buerg scores again with TABS19. The program will replace a series of blanks with a single tab character (ASCII 9) or expand the tab characters it finds in a file into spaces. The program is set up for tab columns at 9, 17, 25, and so on, advancing eight spaces each time.

TEXT21 by Walter Kennamer lets you remove all leading white space on each line of a file. This is helpful when you are dealing with a file created by someone who set his left margin at, say, ten, and you want each line of the file to begin at column one. At your option, TEXT21 will also delete all white space or all trailing white space on each line, and it can convert all white space (series of blanks) into a single blank space. The program can also convert a file to all upper or lower case.

TRANSLAT will put every word of a file on its own line. TRUNC will scan a file for the character you specify. Each time it finds that character it will truncate the balance of the line containing it. Both programs are by Joi Ellis, as is UNIQUE, a program that will search for and remove any identical lines it finds in a file.

Finally, TRANSLIT, by Michael Hanson, will scan a file for every occurrence of a specified character or range of characters (such as A-F or 1-7) and translate it into a different character or range of characters or delete it. If you wanted to translate every *a* to *A* in the file TEST.TXT, for example, you would enter this command: TRANSLIT a A < TEST.TXT > CAP-A.TXT. Your original file would remain untouched, but in the filtered version (CAP-A.TXT) all lowercase *a*'s would now be in uppercase. Mr. Hanson's program makes it especially easy to translate or delete control characters like form feeds, back spaces, tabs, spaces, and carriage returns. You simply specify a backslash and an *f* to designate the form feed control character, for example. For more elaborate translations or to search for and replace entire words, use PC-Write.

Indexing and Style Analysis

Recommended Programs

Glossbrenner's Choice:

IBM Text Treaters Disk 1—Utilities/Indexing/Style

Peter Norton's Index Preparation Program:

INDEX	DOC	4896
BUILD	EXE	29696
INPUT	EXE	29696
MERGE	EXE	30464
SORT	EXE	36096

(plus .BAT and Pascal source code files)

Once you've prepared a lengthy report, piece of computer documentation, or even a book, you may want to use the PC to prepare an index. Generally, public domain and shareware programs follow one of two approaches. Some programs ask you to print your file to disk in paginated form and then request a prepared list of the words you want them to look for. Such programs then scan the file, keeping track of the pages by counting the page breaks, and create a separate text file containing your index.

The other approach is the one followed by Peter Norton, and as you might expect from a programmer of his caliber, it is much cleaner and more logical. Basically, Mr. Norton has created a highly specialized text-entering program. With a printed, paginated draft at your side, you key in ENTER and the program prompts you for index entries. The leftmost columns of each entry line are occupied by a page number. The program starts with "000001:=", followed by a blank line of about 50 spaces. You read page one of your typescript, keying in each word you want to appear in the index for that page. When you turn to the second page, you merely hit <F2> to increment the program's page counter. The <F1> key lets you set the counter to a completely different page number at will. That means you can easily go back and add words after you have finished with a particular page. Page numbers do not have to be numeric.

This process results in a data file of index entries and page numbers. You can place additional entries in the data file at any time and in any order. When you are finished, a separate program will sort the data and create the actual index text file. Review this file for errors, print it out, and you're done.

Mr. Norton's index preparation program works quite well and will unquestionably take much of the drudgery out of creating an index. However, it is important to note that there is more to indexing than simply preparing a list of key words and page numbers. Producing an index worthy of the name almost always requires the services of a professional. We have always felt that a top-quality index is a sine qua non, particularly in a computer book. And in the wee hours of the morning, while looking for a particular fact or figure, we have silently cursed many an author for refusing to pay for a really good one. Certainly most people can index long reports and similar material, but for a book-length work, you really need a pro. Either way, though, whether you use the software yourself or pass it to the indexer you hire, Mr. Norton's program makes the process much easier.

Recommended Program

Glossbrenner's Choice:

IBM Text Treaters Disk 1—Utilities/Indexing/Style

PC-Style   (12 files)

The Fog Finder   (2 files)

A computer's text-scanning capability can also be used to analyze what you have written on the basis of several predefined algorithms, such as average sentence length and average word length. The Fog Finder uses the Gunning Fog Index as promulgated by Robert Gunning in his 1964 book *Take the Fog Out of Writing* (Dartnell Press, Chicago). According to the documentation, the index measures writing "complexity as an average grade level (elementary, high school, college) at which the text could be easily read. For instance, a Fog Index of 9 means 9th grade reading level." The Fog Finder scans your file, produces a reference chart, and reports the Fog Index of the file. The safest index number apparently is 6, the level of *People* magazine and *TV Guide*, according to the reference chart.

PC-Style is a more elaborate program. It reports readability level, but it also reports the number of sentences, words, and syllables per word, as well as the percentage of long words, personal words, and action verbs. It also presents a series of graphic scales measuring readability, personal tone, and action. Perhaps most important of all, given the decline in reading skills over the past decade, PC-Style lets you modify its defaults and add to or alter the lists of personal words (he, her, I, me, yours, and so on) and action verbs (bear, cast, hold, keep, strike, and the like) that it scans for.

These are interesting tools, but we cannot help but be troubled by the fact that the Fog Finder reported a Fog Index of 8.0 and PC-Style reported a readability level of 9.2 for the identical text file. So you might want to take their results cum granis salis.

Both programs are offered as shareware. The Fog Finder was written by Joey Robichaux (1036 Brookhollow Drive, Baton Rouge, LA 70810), requested contribution: $15. PC-Style is offered by Buttonware (P.O. Box 5786, Bellevue, WA 98006), registration fee: $34.95.

Thought Processing with PC-Outline

Recommended Program

Glossbrenner's Choice:

IBM Idea Processing Disk 1—PC-Outline

As noted earlier, one of the great things about a word processor is the ease with which you can rearrange text in any order that you please. Thus if you wanted to create a "to-do" list with a word processing program, you could start by keying in the things you want to accomplish as they occur to you. Once everything is on the screen, you can use the program's powers to organize items by their relative priority, moving text about as needed.

If your to-do lists, project plans, and business reports are of modest length and complexity, that's exactly how you should handle them. For as readers of *How to Buy Software* will recall, one of Glossbrenner's "Secrets for Software Success" is to learn as few programs as possible. So do it with your word processor, whenever you can.

However, if you find that making lists and outlines with your word-processing programs requires too many keystrokes or feels too cumbersome, you're probably ready for an "idea-processing" or outlining program. The category was created several years ago by Living Videotext, Inc. when it introduced Thinktank (suggested retail price $195). It flared briefly, as all new software categories do, and then settled down to a steady state.

Written by John Friend and marketed by Brown Bag Software, PC-Outline is, in our opinion, the top shareware product in this category. What's more, it is so smooth, so well thought out, and so professionally produced that it may well be the best idea processor of all. This is the program we will be referring to as we explain what an idea processor is and does. We will be referring to version 3.34. As you read this, version 4.0 will be available.

An idea processing program is essentially word processing software that has been optimized for the creation and easy alteration of outlines. For example, if you were to use PC-Outline to create a to-do list containing six items, you might start by keying them in as separate outline elements, designated Roman numerals I through VI.

Let's assume that the first element is: "I. Get car inspected." As you are reviewing your list of elements, you realize that there are some subsidiary tasks you should perform as part of that first element. The tasks might include checking the oil, calling the garage for an appointment, and checking the tread of your left rear tire. Those tasks could be entered under element I as items A through C, and they would be indented on the screen, just the way Miss Hawkens taught you back in sixth grade.

At this point, you might go to one of the elements II through VI and add subsidiary points to some of them as well. Looking again at element I, however, you realize that you want to be sure to check the price of 10-W-40 oil at the local discount store before taking the car in, so you add a sub-subelement under "A. Check oil." It reads "1.) Check oil prices at K-Mart." We could go even further, but you get the idea.

Now, let's suppose that something happens to force you to reorder your priorities. Perhaps getting the car inspected should now be fourth on your to-do list. With PC-Outline, moving element I—and all of its subsidiary elements or "children"—to a different position is a snap. The program will automatically adjust the outline's numbering scheme to match. But where PC-Outline's real magic comes into play is in promoting or demoting outline elements.

It's a silly example, but imagine that you've got all of the elements associated with getting your car inspected in their proper place when you suddenly realize that you don't own a car. Obviously, "Buy a car" will have to precede "IV. Get car inspected." Again, with PC-Outline, this is not a problem. You can easily enter "IV. Buy a car" and "Get car inspected" will *automatically* be demoted from element IV to element A under IV. All of the associated children will be similarly demoted.

To translate this into a more productive example, imagine that you're preparing a complex report. You've studied hard and know your subject cold, but the moment you begin writing, everything starts flowing together at once. Again, PC-Outline makes it easy to get a handle on your organization. You can write a paragraph about subject A and then a paragraph about subject C. 1.) i.), then subject IV, and so on. You can easily rearrange the order of individual paragraphs or entire families of paragraphs as you please. Then, when you've keyed in all of the information you want to include, you can bring the resulting file into a word processing program to stitch the paragraphs together and give the report a final polish. Or you can use PC-Outline's word processing features to do the job.

We don't have space to tell you about PC-Outline's pull-down menus, macro creation, overlaying windows to let you view up to nine different outlines, cut-and-paste capability, or a host of other thoughtful features. We can only suggest that if you're interested in idea-processing software you would be foolish not to give PC-Outline a try.

The shareware package comes with the 23-page "Getting Started" portion of the actual PC-Outline manual. This, along with the many sample outlines provided on the disk, is more than enough to let you actually begin using the program to produce useful work. But of course the abbreviated manual doesn't explain all of the program's features.

Registration is $94.95 ($89.95 plus $5 shipping and handling) and includes the most recent version of the program, a copy of the complete typeset manual, and toll-free technical support five days a week between the hours of 9 A.M. and 5 P.M., Pacific Time. You also receive automatic notices when new versions are released and have the right to purchase upgrades for $29.95 plus $5 shipping and handling.

For more information, contact Brown Bag Software at Suite 114, 2155 South Bascom Avenue, Campbell, CA 95008; phone: (800) 523-0764; in California: (408) 559-4545. Visa, MasterCard and American Express are accepted. California residents, add 7% sales tax.

Learning to Type with PC-FASTYPE

Recommended Program

Glossbrenner's Choice:

IBM Typing Disk 1—PC-FASTYPE

The American public—and parents in particular—have been sold a bill of goods. The single most important thing little Johnny and Janey need to insure their success in an increasingly computerized world is *not* a knowledge of programming. It is, plain and simple, an ability to type. Nascent voice recognition technology notwithstanding, the way all people communicate with all computers is through the keyboard. Typewriting is the universal computer language, and the more easily you can "speak" it the more easily you will be able to use any computer or computer program. Go west if you want to, young man, but first learn to type.

As it happens, computers are not only designed to accept typewritten input, they are also superbly suited to teaching typing skills. We learned touch typing at night school some 25 years ago and then as now, most of a student's time is spent in drills. The instructor clicks a stop watch and everyone begins typing from a page of text. When the stop watch is clicked again, students count up the number of words they have typed and the number of errors and thus calculate their accuracy and speed in words per minute.

None of this is fun, but it can be much less onerous if you let your computer handle everything but the typing itself. For a computer, presenting you with text to type and comparing the keys you hit to that text, timing the entire process, and calculating your accuracy and words per minute is child's play. This is undoubtedly one of the reasons why there are lots of typing instruction programs on the market, most of them selling for about $50.

We haven't looked at all of them, of course, but in our opinion you'd have to go a long way to beat PC-FASTYPE (version 3.01). Written by William J. Letendre, the original version of this program was called FAS-TYPE. Mr. Letendre says that that version "languished for about two years before things started to pick up and the respectability of shareware as a source of good, high quality software came into its own. The registrations started coming in, giving me the impetus to upgrade the program."

PC-FASTYPE requires a 256K IBM or close compatible with graphics display (CGA, EGA, or equivalents). You may also use a Hercules Monographics Card, thanks to the Hercules CGA emulator program (SIMCGA.COM) included on the disk. (See Chapter 2 for more on this and other Herc card CGA emulators.)

PC-FASTYPE will work properly regardless of the clock speed of your computer (4.7 to 20 megahertz). The program does not interfere with the system clock, and it can be used with either the original-style PC keyboard or the new IBM Enhanced Keyboard distributed with the PS/2 line, XTs, ATs, and so on. (If you have twelve function keys across the top of your keyboard, you have the enhanced version.) There is also special support for the keyboard used on all Tandy Radio Shack MS-DOS machines.

PC-FASTYPE's operating theater is a detailed color graphics picture of your particular model of keyboard that occupies about two thirds of the screen. The top third of the screen contains a timer, the name of the drill you have chosen, and the characters or words you are supposed to type. A typing rhythm sound beeps in the background as the character you are to type next changes color and blinks on the keyboard. If you hit the wrong letter, an X briefly appears over the incorrect letter and a video game-like sound is issued. There are other details, depending on whether you select the beginner, intermediate, or advanced levels.

When the drill is over, the top portion of the screen instantly presents your raw speed, the number of errors, and your computed speed, a figure that is calculated by subtracting a penalty for each error from your raw speed. The number of characters in the drill, number of keystrokes entered, and percentage accuracy are also given. After you have completed your first drill, a figure for your "best WPM so far" also appears, making it easy to gauge your performance on the drill you have just completed.

There are other nifty features as well. You can turn the metronome and all other sounds on or off, request that no letters be shown on the key tops, and specify how many characters (from 10 to 99) you want the program to present in each beginner's drill. You can opt to work on numbers, special characters, capital letters, words, three or four-letter groups, phrases, or create your own drills and record them to disk. You can opt to concentrate on just the "home" keys, and you can ask the program to outline the keys that should be hit with each finger.

The program includes lots of help screens and easy-to-use menus, and there is a well-written 43-page manual on the disk. Only two things are lacking in version 3.01 in our opinion. The first is an option to permanently record the settings you have entered (like toggling off the sound) so that you do not have to repeat the process each time the program is run. And the second is a basic beginner's explanation of the "home" keys in touch typing and the letters each finger is responsible for hitting. This information is supplied in the program's help section, but we wonder how many beginners will know to look there. The setup/toggle question isn't really a problem. If necessary you could use a program like Extended Batch Language (Chapter 9) or FAKEY (Chapter 10) to automatically issue the requisite commands. An inexpensive book on touch typing can fill the other need.

We wrote Mr. Letendre about these points and received a helpful letter in reply. "Please don't worry about being a 'busybody' and making suggestions about improving the package—that's what shareware is all about, and that's how our products get better—we listen to the end user and make changes accordingly. Saving setup specs is a good idea; I've added that to my list of forthcoming improvements." We also learned that Mr. Letendre is thinking of adding a feature for advanced users to allow them to replace the display of the keyboard with more typing drill text. "Making the explanation of which fingers should strike which keys part of the printed documentation is a good idea too and will be implemented in the next release."

The registration fee for PC-FASTYPE is $20, and it entitles you to a copy of the program without the shareware beg screen, a copy of a commercially published typing and keyboarding book written especially for the PC, and free telephone and mail support. Site licenses for educational institutions ($200) and corporations ($295) are available. For more information, contact: Mr. William J. Letendre, President, TRENDTECH Corporation, 14 Ella Lane, Wayne, NJ 07470; phone (201) 694-8622.

File Encryption and Security

Glossbrenner's Choice:

IBM Encryption Disk 1—PC-CODE3/4 and The Confidant

Our cryptographic expertise got arrested at an early age when a fellow ten-year-old cracked a code we had invented based on assigning a number to each letter of the alphabet. From then on our attention turned to writing with lemon juice and trying to perfect an invisible ink. That didn't pan out either. Eventually we discovered personal computing, and it proved to be ideal. It is one place, though sadly not the only one, where plain English can be as indecipherable as the most secure DES (Data Encryption Standard) code.

However, in an age when lasers can reproduce conversations by monitoring the vibrations of distant windowpanes and supersensitive receivers can raid your computer by picking up the minute emissions of its central processing chip, data security is serious business. Either or both of the programs cited here can help.

Written by Richard Nolen Colvard, PC-CODE 3 (version 6.1) and PC-CODE4 (version 6.2) are designed to encode/decode text and binary files, respectively. A variety of coding options are offered in both cases, including something called "super-encipherment" in which "each character of plain text is both scrambled (transposed) as well as substituted for some random 'other' character." Or, as the documentation for an earlier version puts it when describing how thoroughly coded your results will be, "visualize a safe with 25 dials, each with graduations between 1 and 21,476,483,646. A typical combination office safe might have 4 numbers each between 1 and 100."

Coding of this sort is beyond our expertise, but we were impressed by the sense of authority in Mr. Colvard's documentation. He certainly seems to know what he's talking about, though we would wish for a more complete explanation of coding techniques and the way his programs implement them. On the other hand, by following the examples and using the sample files provided, we had no problem turning a text file into complete gibberish and back into text again.

We should also note that Mr. Colvard has released these programs into the public domain, reserving only the commercial rights. He has provided the Microsoft FORTRAN-77 version 3.30 source code, should you want to make modifications. The object code (also provided) is compatible with both MS-DOS and Microsoft Xenix. They need only be linked to their respective libraries should you need to transport them to a non-PC computer.

The Confidant by Stan W. Merrill is a polished, well-presented encrypting program that's a snap to use. When the program comes up, you key in the name of the file you want to encrypt in one box, the name of the destination (encrypted) file in a second box, and your chosen password in a third. At that point you have two options. You can either opt to have the file encoded using the nearly unbreakable Bureau of National Standards Date Encryption Standard (DES) algorithm, or you can choose the quicker and somewhat less secure "privacy" coding option. Based on our tests, the program will successfully encode and decode both binary and text files.

The Confidant is so easy to use that for most purposes it would be our program of choice. However, there are a few small problems to be aware of. First, if you try to decrypt a file using the wrong password, the program will not notify you of your error. Instead it will proceed as normal, using the incorrect password to produce a completely garbled "decrypted" file. Because the decoding process can take a while with a large file, you will not discover your error until much later. Second, one of the menu options permits you to erase a file, but as the Professional Master Key Utilities (PMK) discussed in Chapter 9 reveal, the file can easily be recovered. For safety's sake, you should use PMK's ZEROFILE utility to completely wipe out a file. Finally, the documentation, although copious, is largely presented as a "casebook" short story that you may find long on wind and short on operational details.

Still, The Confidant does work quite well and it is easy to use. The program is offered as shareware with a requested contribution of $10. For more information, contact: Data Sage, Yale Station 2902, New Haven, CT 06520.

A Look Ahead

The printing module that is part of PC-Write can handle all of your word processing-related printing needs. However, computer users do not live by word processors alone. There are many other times when you need to use your printer, and the programs we'll look at in the next chapter can help you do so with far less effort than you may currently be expending. There is also some printer magic to be done—some of the programs we'll look at can give you 24-pin printer quality output with a garden variety eight-pin Epson printer. Others can print text in columns or redirect printer output to a disk file or free you to run another program while the printing is being done. You will even be able to design your own special logo, monogram, or a complete typeface, with every letter and number just the way you want it.

13

Printer Programs

LASER QUALITY, CUSTOM FONTS, AND CONVENIENT UTILITIES

Few devices on God's green earth have been the cause of more heartache, frustration, and neural burnout than computer printers. They can be enormously capable, to be sure, with options for compressed, italic, emphasized, double-strike, underline, and other varieties of print, plus super- and subscripts, scientific and foreign-language characters, and more. But sometimes just getting one to print a simple declarative sentence in a standard vanilla typeface can be a chore—while trying to use a printer's extended capabilities can absorb the better part of an afternoon.

A working knowledge of English as written by someone for whom it is a third or fourth language will help you decipher the "manuals" that accompany many printers, of course. But you'll probably be better off plugging into the public domain shortly after plugging in your printer, since there are hundreds of free programs that can instantly get you up, running, and printing in any style your printer can produce with just a few simple keystrokes from you.

For example, a program called COMPRSON.COM is only 19 bytes long, but when you type in the word COMPRSON and hit <Enter>, your Epson, IBM Graphics, or compatible printer will be set for compressed print. From then on, everything you send to the printer will be printed at 17.16 characters per inch (132 characters per line on eight-inch paper), instead of the normal ten characters per inch (80 characters per line on eight inch paper). A companion program, COMPRSOF.COM, turns off the compressed print feature. You simply can't beat that for simplicity, unless you rename the file to something like CO ("compressed on") to save even more keystrokes.

This program is often found in the company of other programs to select and deselect other Epson modes (double-width, emphasized, italics, and so on). Indeed, because printers are nearly as common as computers and available in nearly as many varieties, the free software distribution channels are rich in printer programs and utilities of every sort. We'll consider many of the best printer-related programs in this chapter. But before we do, a bit of background information may be helpful.

Printer Basics

Generally, there are four main types of computer printers: daisywheel, dot matrix, ink jet, and laser. Daisywheel printers use essentially the same printing technique used by typewriters. They press a preformed metal or plastic letter into an inked or carbon ribbon that stands between the letter and the paper. These fully formed letters are cast or molded and then attached to the "petals" of a "daisy" that snaps into the printing element. When a letter is to be printed, the machine rotates the daisy into position and a small hammer smacks the tip of the petal from behind, forcing it into the ribbon to make the image on the paper. Changing the typestyle on a daisywheel printer is literally a snap. You have only to remove the current daisywheel and snap in another with a different style of type on its petals.

However, aside from using a vertical line character to draw boxes, most daisywheel printers cannot reproduce computer graphics. They do produce exceptionally crisp characters, though, characters that are indistinguishable from those produced by a typewriter.

The printing element ("printhead") of a dot-matrix printer is quite different. It consists of the tips of anywhere from 5 to 24 wires arranged one on top of the other like the lenses of an impossibly long traffic light. Each wire can be moved forward and back so that it either protrudes or returns to its recessed position. Individual letters are created by pushing some of the wires into the ribbon, causing them to make dots on the paper.

With the possible exception of the exclamation point, which consists of a single vertical column of dots, all characters produced by this type of printer consist of a *matrix* of dots. Thus to create the letter O, a dot matrix printer would begin by firing the middle portion of its pins to create the left side of the O. Then it would move ever so slightly to the right and simultaneously fire its uppermost and lowermost pins to create the top and bottom of the O. It might then move once again and fire the same middle portion of pins with which it began to create the right side of the O.

In reality, even the cheapest dot-matrix printer would probably make at least five moves left to right to create a single character. Some might make as many as ten moves or more. Our point here is that every character is created using a uniformly sized matrix of dots and spaces—hence the name "dot matrix."

Although each character produced by a dot-matrix printer may consist of a pattern of unconnected dots, when we look at the results we see a discrete letter because our minds fill in the blanks. The same phenomenon occurs when we look at a photograph in a magazine. As a good magnifying glass will reveal, published black and white or color photos consist of nothing but tiny dots. And in both photos and computer printers, the smaller the dots and the greater their number, the better the resolution or crispness of the image.

Most dot-matrix printers operate in "draft mode" by default. That is, unless you tell them otherwise, they produce characters quite rapidly, using as few dots as possible. But since each character is created on an ad hoc basis, these printers have enormous flexibility. You're not locked into whatever characters happen to be on the petals of a daisywheel. By pushing some pins forward and holding others back, you can produce letters of many different sizes, as well as all manner of graphic elements. And by telling the printhead to shift itself slightly up or down and go back and reprint a line, you can produce more dots per character, for an even crisper image. In some cases, it is even possible to produce "letter-quality" printouts on a dot-matrix printer. This means the text will look as though it was produced by a typewriter (or daisywheel printer) and will be of such a quality that you wouldn't be ashamed to use it for a business letter to your best customer or client.

There are also ink-jet and laser printers to consider. An ink-jet printer creates its images without a ribbon. Instead, it literally sprays dots onto the page to create its characters. A laser printer works by using a laser to reproduce images on a revolving drum or belt of the sort you would find in most photocopiers. Indeed, once the image has been transferred to the drum, the reproduction process is virtually identical to that of a photocopier. Laser printers offer the greatest flexibility of all since they can create a nearly infinite range of images, characters, lines, and tones.

Focusing on Dot Matrix

There are public domain programs that can make it easier for you to use virtually every type of printer. Such programs do tend to be brand and model-specific, however, and as is always the case, the public domain here is a direct reflection of the market. The more popular a given brand of printer, the more PD programs you will find to support it.

Since Epson and Epson-compatible dot matrix printers are probably the most popular of all, that's what we'll focus on here.

FreeTip: If you have a different type of printer, the quickest, easiest way to locate PD programs for it is to sign on to one of the online services discussed in Chapter 7 and do a search using the brand or model as your keyword. On CompuServe, for example, you'll find that printer programs are stored in Data Library 2 of the IBM Hardware Forum (GO IBMHW).

At this writing, there are programs to make it easier to control printers and models made by Canon, C. Itoh, Gemini, Hewlett-Packard, Juki, NEC, Okidata, Toshiba, Royal, and many others. As laser printers come into wider use in the IBM world, there will undoubtedly be files of downloadable fonts (typefaces) as well.

The Printer As Computer

We tend to think of printers more as computer peripherals than as computers in and of themselves, but that's really what they are. They may not contain an actual CPU processor-type chip—although the trend toward truly "smart" printers is growing—but most do contain both ROM and RAM chips. The RAM chips are used to temporarily store characters between the time they are received from the computer and the time they can be printed. That's what's meant by a "print buffer." The ROM chips have programming permanently burned into them to control the printer's actions. "Graphics" printers contain an additional set of ROM chips that hold the instructions needed to create sets of graphic (nonalphanumeric) characters. We'll have more to say about this later.

Though it need not concern us here, dot-matrix printers are normally connected to the main computer using either a serial (one-bit-at-a-time) or a parallel (eight-bits-all-at-once) interface and cable. The important point is that the two units communicate, sending signals back and forth, one "computer" to another.

Programming the Printer

Dot-matrix printers usually come from the factory set up to print in their fastest or "draft" mode by default. If you want them to do any of their fancy stuff, like compressed or boldface printing, you've got to program them. Many of the newer models are equipped with buttons or switches on their front panels that make it easy to select or deselect a particular mode of printing. And certainly one can argue that this is the way things should have been done from the start.

But, undoubtedly for reasons of cost, things were not done this way and as a result, regardless of when you bought your printer, there's a good chance that it must be programmed in the traditional way—by sending it special codes from the main computer.

Unfortunately, the manuals that come with most printers do not make this easy. Should you ever plunge into your printer manual, for example, there's a good chance that you'll encounter something like this: "SI Shift In (Compressed); Changes the printer to the Compressed Character print mode; Example: LPRINT CHR$(15)."

This is absolutely outrageous. Here you've plunked down anywhere from $250 to $700 for a printer capable of all sorts of magical tricks and the above sentences are the sum total of what the manual tells you about how to get the printer to do compressed printing. The information on the other print modes and printer functions is likely to be equally skimpy.

Even if you knew enough BASIC to recognize the LPRINT command ("print to the line printer") and the CHR$ ("C-H-R-dollar") function ("use the ASCII character symbolized by the number in parens"), you'd sitll have to write a separate one-line BASIC program to select and deselect each printer feature. Then you'd have to load BASIC and run the blessed thing every time you wanted to change printing modes. Surely there must be a better way.

There is, of course. Thanks to public domain and shareware software. In this chapter we will start with programs designed to make it easy for you to send the necessary codes to your Epson-compatible printer to enable or disable its special features. We will also cover the following topics:

- Print spoolers—to let you use your system while one or more files are being printed.

- Printer redirection programs—to let you redirect output bound for the printer to a disk file.

- Text formatters—to let you quickly tell the system how many lines you want per page, whether you want a header or footer, and so on when you want to print a plain ASCII text file.

- Print packers—to let you fit more—many more—characters on a page.

- Print enhancers and custom fonts—to let you produce 24-pin quality output on an inexpensive nine-pin printer and design your own characters, monograms, or whatever.

Printer Setup Programs

Recommended Programs

Glossbrenner's Choice:

IBM Printer Pack Disk 1—Printer Utilities

COMPRSOF	COM	19	EMPHASON	COM	19
COMPRSON	COM	19	ITALICOF	COM	19
DBLHITOF	COM	19	ITALICON	COM	19
DBLHITON	COM	19	RESET	COM	19
DBLWDEOF	COM	19	UNDERLOF	COM	19
DBLWDEON	COM	19	UNDERLON	COM	19
EMPHASOF	COM	19			

The programs listed above will enable or disable the following Epson/IBM printer features: compressed printing, double height characters, double width characters, emphasized printing, italics, and underlining. The program RESET.COM will clear the printer's memory and reset it to its default power-up state. All of these programs were created by writing a single-line BASIC program like LPRINT CHR$(15), compiling it into an EXE file, and converting that into a COM file. (If you do not understand these terms, please see Chapter 2.) Anyone could do it—provided they had purchased the Microsoft/IBM BASIC compiler software package (about $150) and used it to perform a one-time translation from BASIC into machine language. Undoubtedly the programmer prepared these programs for his or her own convenience, but in the true spirit of public domain software, made the work available for others to use. The free software distribution channels have similar programs for many other leading brands and models of printers. There are also more elaborate, menu-driven programs that let you set several printer features at once. The commercial equivalent of such programs would cost you about $30. (*Facelift* from Companion Software sells for $29.95, for example.)

All such programs are convenient to use. But each usually suffers from the same limitation. Each tends to be printer-specific and usually printer-model-specific. If you happen to own the printer they were prepared for, then fine. But if you don't, you're out of luck since it is virtually impossible to customize or change a program once it has been compiled into machine language.

```
PRINTER   COM    1152
PRINTER   DOC   10240
PRINTER   DAT    512
```

That's what makes PRINTER.COM by John Petrey unique. This is a menu-driven program that is specifically designed to be customized for any brand or model of printer. The one drawback for the complete computer novice is the need to initially set up the program's menu. But with the information we will provide here and your manual, this should not be a major problem. More experienced computer users will have no difficulty at all.

Computers usually communicate with their printers in the same code they use to communicate with modems and other computers. As discussed in Chapter 5, the code is called ASCII ("as-key") and it includes a number for every upper and lower-case letter of the alphabet, the major punctuation marks, and the digits from 0 through 9. The "extended" ASCII code set includes all of these characters, plus 128 "high codes" that can be used to represent virtually anything a computer manufacturer chooses. On IBM computers the high codes are used to represent international language characters, mathematical and scientific notation, and character graphics.

Most important for our discussion here, however, the ASCII code sets also include 32 "control codes." These are the codes from 0 through 32, and many of them have traditionally been used to control printers of one sort or another. By general agreement, most printers respond the same way to an ASCII 13 ("carriage return") and an ASCII 12 ("form feed"). But nearly every printer requires its own set of control codes to get it to produce different print styles or to enable other features. Thus, your first step should be to consult your printer manual for the codes you need.

How to Use PRINTER.COM

The next step is to look at PRINTER.COM and its doc file. As you will see, the program consists of two major parts. The main program displays a menu and lets you use it to send control codes to the printer. PRINTER.DAT is the data file that contains the menu item information and the control codes that correspond to them. For example, were you to key in PRINTER on our computer, you would see the following:

```
Printer (1.1) - Special Print Functions
0   -   Compressed Print
1   -   ⅛th Inch Spacing
2   -   Lines/page Prep
3   -   —to 88 lines
4   -   Emphasized Print
5   -   Double WIDTH on
6   -   Double Strike Print
7   -   UNDERLINE Prep
8   -   —Underline ON
9   -   —Underline OFF
Esc   -   Exit
Your Choice __
```

And were you to key in TYPE PRINTER.DAT on our system, you would see this:

```
Compressed Print$015000
⅛th Inch Spacing$027048
Lines/page Prep$027067
—to 88 lines$088000
Emphasized Print$027069
Double WIDTH on$014000
Double Strike Print$027071
UNDERLINE Prep$027045
—Undlerline ON$001000
—Underline OFF$0000000&
```

If you take a moment to compare these two lists, you will notice that the words in PRINTER.DAT correspond exactly to the menu items displayed by PRINTER.COM. What you don't see on the menu are the dollar signs and the ASCII code numbers to their right.

John Petrey's documentation file (PRINTER.DOC) is excellent, and as it explains, all you have to do to customize the program's menu and capabilities to your own needs is to create your own PRINTER.DAT file. Use a word processor like PC-Write (Chapter 12) to key in both the menu item text you want to appear and the ASCII codes your printer requires for each feature. The dollar sign tells the program where the ASCII codes begin and the ampersand at the very end of the file tells it that this is indeed the end.

Altogether, you can have ten menu items, each of which can send up to two ASCII codes to your printer. Should your printer require three codes to enable a particular mode, simply use one menu item as a "prep" command to send the first two codes and a second menu item to send the last code. This is what we did with the UNDERLINE (On and Off) codes above, for example.

Two final points. First, if your manual uses the "LPRINT CHR$ (n)" convention to describe the necessary ASCII codes, use the number n in parentheses in your PRINTER.DAT file. As the program's documentation explains, two-digit numbers like 27 (the "Escape" code) should be entered as 027. Second, you may have as many PRINTER.DAT files as you wish. The program will look for its PRINTER.DAT file on the default drive, but you can tell it to look on a different drive by entering PRINTER followed by the drive letter when you activate the program.

FreeTip: There *are* other ways to get the necessary control codes into your printer. They are not as elegant, but they are quick and quite easy. The general concept is to create a file on disk containing the necessary control codes and then just copy it to your printer when you want to force it into a different mode.

If you know what codes are required, you can do this in less than 30 seconds from the DOS prompt. For example, assume the code required to activate compressed printing is an ASCII 15. Get to your DOS prompt and key in COPY CON:COMPRESS, then hit <Enter>. This tells the system that you want to create a file called COMPRESS from the console (the keyboard).

Next hold down your <Alt> key and key in 15 on your numeric keypad. That will produce a carat and a capital O on your screen, the symbol for a "Control-O." Hit <Enter> and then hit F6 to generate a "Control-Z." This tells your system that the file ends here. Hit <Enter> again and your computer will write the file COMPRESS to disk.

Now key in COPY COMPRESS PRN to send the file you have just created to your printer. Nothing will appear to have happened. However, should you then hit your <Print Screen> key, or [<Shift><PrtSc>] on older PC keyboards, you will find that your printer produces compressed print. It will continue to do so until you either shut the printer off to clear its memory or, as your Epson or IBM manual points out, send it an ASCII 18.

Should you need to use an "escape" code (ASCII 27) in your code series, you will have to use a slightly different technique. We suggest using PC-WRITE to create the file to be copied to the printer in such cases. For example, the Epson requires an ASCII 27 followed by an ASCII 45 followed by an ASCII 1 to activate its underline mode. You can create such a file easily in PC-WRITE using the <Alt> key and the numeric keypad. Simply key in ED UNDER to tell PC-WRITE that you want to create a file called UNDER. Hold down the <Alt> key and key in the numbers above. Do not hit <Enter>. Use PC-WRITE's F3 command to write the file to disk. Then get out of the program and return to DOS. Finally, key in COPY UNDER PRN to send the file containing these codes to your printer.

You can use PC-WRITE to create any kind of printer control file, not just those that include the escape character. And, of course, you can fully automate the printer set up process by putting several COPY FILENAME PRN commands into a .BAT (batch) file.

LPTPORT	DOC	2048
LPTPORT	COM	20
PRSWAP	DOC	1152
PRSWAP	COM	256
FASTPRT	COM	366
FASTPRT	DOC	5856

These three programs aren't exactly printer setup utilities, but they are valuable and at least marginally related to that theme. LPTPORT and PRSWAP are both by John Dickinson. The first allows you to use two parallel printers with software that normally supports only one. The program makes the switch from one printer port to another in software, freeing you from the need to do so by physically exchanging the plugs or purchasing an A-B switch. PRSWAP converts on-screen graphics into suitable characters so that the images can be printed on a nongraphics printer.

FASTPRT by J. Craig Hill is shareware. The program allows you to bring a print screen operation to an instant halt. It also speeds up the operation in many instances because it clips any trailing blanks (blank characters between the end of a line and the screen's 80-column right margin) so the printer never sees them. Mr. Hill suggests a contribution of $10 "or 10 cents for every minute the program will save you over the next 5 years, whichever is lower." Contact: Sunbelt Computing, 1274 N. Emory Place, NE, Atlanta, GA 30306.

Print Spoolers

As you know, printers and computers do not operate at the same speed. It takes much longer to print a character on paper than to display the same character on the screen. Add to that the fact that most computers are set up to print a file and do nothing else until the process has been completed, and you will quickly see the need for a type of utility called a "print spooler" to free both you and your computer to do other things while a file is being printed.

Normally, if you copy a file to the printer or tell your word-processing software to print a file, the computer takes the file into its memory and begins doling out characters to the printer. The RAM-chip print buffers built into most printers are not very capacious. Most can hold only about a line or two of text at a time. When that buffer has filled, the printer signals the computer to tell it to temporarily stop sending characters. As the printer removes characters from its buffer to print them on the page, buffer space is freed up and the printer signals the computer to send more characters. This process continues until the entire file has been printed, at which time the printer signals the computer that the job is complete. Then and only then does the computer become free to respond to your next command.

Print spooler programs solve this problem by setting aside a certain amount of your computer's memory as an extended print buffer. Once a spooler program has been activated, it sits in memory waiting for the next print command. From then on, whenever you tell your computer to print something, the spooler quickly absorbs the text the computer thinks it's sending to the printer and issues the "job complete" signal. At that point, as far as your computer is concerned, the file has been printed and it is free to go about your other business.

The spooler meantime begins sending the text to the printer in the traditional way. The result is that you can tell your system to print a report that might normally tie up your machine for ten minutes to half an hour—but be free to load and run Lotus or complete some other task just seconds after issuing the print command. In other words, printing will continue while you use the computer for something else.

Spooler Trade-offs

There are two drawbacks to print spoolers. First, they do cordon off a portion of your available RAM when they are operating. That leaves less memory for other tasks. Second, more time will be required to print a given quantity of text than would otherwise be the case. This is because printing is done during your computer's off moments, instead of as a continuous process. As you may know, the heart of any computer is its central processing unit (CPU), the microchip that is the brains of the whole operation. Nothing can happen without its involvement, including the sending of text to a printer.

Statistically, most CPUs are idle most of the time. For to a microchip even the fractions of a second between two keystrokes entered by a very fast typist can be an eternity. Print spoolers take advantage of this fact by grabbing up every spare microsecond the CPU has available. Thus, when you are sitting contemplating the figures on a spreadsheet or the text of a business letter, the CPU is completely idle and printing can continue at the fastest rate. But if you call on the CPU to recalculate a spreadsheet, adjust the text in a word-processing program, or simply generate a directory of the disk in drive A, less CPU time will (temporarily) be available for the print spooler program, and printing will slow down or temporarily stop. Thus, the more demands you make on your CPU during a print spooling operation, the more time will be required to print a given quantity of text.

Recommended Programs

Glossbrenner's Choice:

IBM Printer Pack Disk 1—Printer Utilities

MSPOOL2 COM 1020
MSPOOL2 DOC 7914

Rich Winkel's MSPOOL2.COM ("Multi-Spooler Version 2") is without a doubt one of the best of the many print spooling programs in the public domain. In addition to its smooth operation, it is especially noteworthy because of the flexibility designed into the program. MSPOOL2 lets you spool up to four printers simultaneously, supports both parallel and serial printers in any combination, and best of all, lets you determine the size of the print buffer you want to use, up to 63K.

This last point is particularly important because many other PD print spoolers are preset to seize a certain amount of RAM, and there is nothing you can do about it. With MSPOOL2, in contrast, you can set aside anywhere from 7K to 63K of RAM (in 7K increments) as your buffer each time you activate the program. The command "MSPOOL2 1 2," for example, tells the program that you want to spool LPT1 (line printer 1; see your DOS manual for more information on "standard output devices" if you do not understand this) and use (2 × 7K) or 14K of RAM as its buffer. Once activated, everything you or an applications program sends to the spooled printer will be intercepted and put into the MSPOOL2 buffer.

Should you wish to deactivate the program at a later time, you can key in "MSPOOL2 1" and respond to the resulting prompt to purge the buffer, disable, or reenable the program. Note that the utility PRINT.COM that comes with DOS is similar to MSPOOL2 in that both are print spooling programs. The difference is that with PRINT.COM you must specify exactly which files you wish to spool, while MSPOOL2 spools everything you send to the printer once it has been activated.

Redirecting the Printer

"Have you ever wanted to get some data from your screen into a program?" asks Mark DiVecchio in the documentation for his program LPTX.COM. "Have you ever wanted to grab onto some printer data and put it into a disk file. . . ?" Our answer is "Often!" to both questions. The two programs discussed below will show you how to do it.

Recommended Programs

Glossbrenner's Choice:

IBM Printer Pack Disk 1—Printer Utilities

LPTX6	ASM	46824
LPTX6	COM	18019
LPTX6	DOC	8521
FSPOOL	DOC	1892
FSPOOL	COM	5120

Imagine, for example, that you're writing a book about public domain and shareware software and you want to "clip out" the on-screen menu presented by a program like PRINTER.COM. You really don't want to type the menu from scratch, but unless you can get it recorded as a file on disk, you will have no choice.

LPTX6 to the rescue. By keying in LPTX B:TEMP.TXT, you tell the program to redirect everything that would normally go to the printer to a file called TEMP.TXT on Drive B. Then you activate the program you plan to write about. The menu appears and you hit your <Print Screen> key. But because LPTX has been activated, your system prints the screen to disk instead of to the printer. Finally, you check your work by logging onto Drive B and keying in TYPE TEMP.TXT and, voilà, there's a perfect copy of the screen you plan to integrate into your manuscript.

LPTX can also be a help whenever you are using a program that does all of its formatting at print time. PC-WRITE, for example, gives you the option of printing a formatted copy of your document to disk, with all the page breaks, headers, and footnotes in place. But many other word processors do not. That can be a problem if want to check the formatting of a long document or if you want to create a copy of a properly formatted document on disk to give to someone else.

LPTX uses about 7K of memory for its resident data buffers, and it is very simple to operate. Since it includes a built-in help menu, you may be able to begin using it before reading the documentation. For example, keying in LPTX ? will produce the following:

```
LPTx - Line Printer Redirection Program - V6.00
   Copyright 1987 Mark C. DiVecchio
Calling sequence :
LPTX −p −f <[d:][\pathname\pathname]filename>
   where p = printer number : 1, 2, or 3
         f = function : o for open a print file
                        c for close a print file

         drive letter & pathname are optional
   defaults : p = 1
              f = o
LPTx Status :
lpt1:   redirected to disk file b:\TEMP.TXT
lpt2:   not redirected
lpt3:   not redirected
```

As you can see, LPTX6 is capable of redirecting up to three printers simultaneously, though of course you must enter a separate command line for each one. If you don't specify a printer, it assumes LPT1. Similarly, if you do not specify a function (open or close a print file) it assumes you want to open one. Thus as noted earlier, things can be as simple as keying in LPTX6 B:TEMP.TXT to start printer redirection. Stopping redirection can be as easy as keying in LPTX6 − c to close the open file.

Finally, there are two caveats to be aware of. First, as Mr. DiVecchio points out in his documentation, LPTX6.COM intercepts the standard BIOS printer I/O interrupt 17(hex). That's the same interrupt utilized

by print spooling programs. Consequently, if you are likely to be using
both, it is best to load your print spooler first and then run LPTX6.

Second, LPTX will capture graphics screens, but when you TYPE the
disk file you will probably see garbage on your screen (depending on the
type of graphics used). We tested this with the PC-PICTURE GRAPH-
ICS program discussed in Appendix A and found that while garbage
appears on the screen, when the file is copied to the graphics printer,
the original graphic image is produced.

We located the program FSPOOL.COM ("file spool") because an earlier
version of LPTX did not work with DOS 3.1 or 3.2. Since LPTX6 *does*
work with those DOS versions, you may not need FSPOOL. It is a
much simpler, less capable program, but it does work quite well.

Text Formatters

As you cruise through the free software world, you will encounter many
programs classified under the general rubric of "text formatter." These
programs are intended to make it easy for you to produce a neat
printout of a text file that does not contain the formatting codes one
would normally insert with a word processor. Two good examples of
such files would be material you download from BIX, GEnie, The
Source, or some other online system; and lengthy programs you have
written in some computer language. Though not intended to compete
with word-processing software, text-formatting programs offer a quick
solution to the problem of producing a neatly formatted printout.

Recommended Programs
_____

Glossbrenner's Choice:

IBM Printer Pack Disk 1—Printer Utilities

LIST   COM   45353
LIST   DOC   26287
LINSTALL   COM   121919

Of all the text formatters we have looked at, we feel that LIST.COM is
at this writing the very best. (Note: This is *not* the Vernon Buerg
LIST.COM discussed in Chapter 9.) As you can see from Figure 13.1,
the program presents you with a full-screen menu of formatting choices.
You can specify several files in several locations, separating each with a

space. You can even use the global or wildcard symbol (*). In addition you can set lines per page, line width, left margin, and line spacing. And you can key in any text you would like the program to use as a header, a footer, or both.

Figure 13.1 The LIST.COM Menu.

```
DAY MONTH DATE YEAR                               Directory: C:\PRINTER\LIST

File(s) to Print [                                                    ]
Print to          [LPT                    ]

Lines per page   [  65]
Line length      [  80]
# Header lines   [   2]
Heading          [                                                    ]
# Footer lines   [   2]
Footing          [                                                    ]
Line spacing     [   1]
Left margin      [   0]

Document begins with page  [    1]
Start printing with page   [    1]
Stop printing with page    [    0]  (NOTE: Enter 0 to print to END of document.)

Number pages?             [y]
Date and Time stamp?      [y]
Pause between pages?      [n]
Tab width setting         [8]

F1-path   F2-dir   Alt+D - DOS   ↑, ↓, ←┘-select fields   Esc-exit   End-print
```

As we have said, this is a very good program. But you should be aware that you can do exactly the same thing with PC-WRITE's printing option. There is no need to bring a file into PC-WRITE before printing it. You can simply enter the command PR FILENAME.EXT to be taken to the printer set up menu. However, you may find that for a quick printout using a simple format LIST.COM is the easier way to go.

It is also worth noting that while LIST.COM does not have an option for setting your printer to compressed type, there's nothing to stop you from activating PRINTER.COM as discussed above to set your printer to that mode before activating LIST.COM. Indeed, you may find it convenient to put your standard setup commands into a batch file to automate the entire process. You can use either Extended Batch Language (Chapter 9) or FAKEY (Chapter 10) to do this since both can feed commands to programs as if they were coming from the keyboard.

The shareware registration fee for LIST.COM is $10. Contact: System
Design and Implementation, 2331 Cheshire Way, Redwood City, CA
94061.

PR   COM   1819
PR   DOC   1152

This is another program by John Dickenson. PR.COM formats a text
file into 80 columns, expands ASCII tab characters, and adds a seven-
line header and a blank footer. The program automatically prints 55
lines of text on each 66-line page. The header contains the name of the
file, the page number, and the file's date stamp information.

Obviously PR.COM is nowhere near as flexible as LIST.COM, but it is
quick and easy and it does produce nice printouts. You will especially
appreciate the header giving you the name of the file. This is the program *PC Magazine* uses to produce the source code listings you will see
in those feature that include ready-to-key programs.

FreeTip: Here's an example of the kind of software synergy that
is possible in the free software world. When you write books on
personal computer communications, you naturally do a lot of downloading from online systems. None of the stuff is formatted for
printing, of course, and keying in text formatting commands,
header text, and dates can get quite old quite fast. The introduction of Frank Canova's Extended Batch Language made things a
lot easier. Without going into detail, it is possible to write a batch
file called, say, PC.BAT ("print compressed") that can completely
automate the printing and formatting process. Thus to print a file
called SOURCE.TXT, using compressed print, with a header
reading "Download from The Source" and page numbers on every
page, all we have to key in is this: PC SOURCE.TXT Download
from The Source.
   The EBL batch file calls PRINTER.COM and issues the necessary commands to set the printer for compressed print, ⅛-inch line
spacing, and 88 lines per page. Then it calls the PC-WRITE page
printer program. Since EBL sees "SOURCE.TXT," "Download,"
"from," "The," and "Source" as discrete variables, it can feed this
information to the printer program, telling it which file to print
and what words to use as a header. With a little work, you can do
the same thing with LIST.COM or any other text-formatting program if you like. But it goes without saying that none of us could

do any of these things were it not for public domain and shareware software.

Incidently, as noted in Chapter 2, you may find that using compressed print and ⅛-inch line spaces with an 88-line page works best if you leave a top margin of two lines and a bottom margin of four. That gives you 82 lines of text per page, and it certainly saves paper.

Print Packers

If you do a lot of printing and are irritated by needless waste, or if you're interested in saving money or trees or both, then the next three programs will be of special interest. As actor Richard Anderson used to say at the beginning of every episode of *The Six Million Dollar Man:* "We have the technology." Or in this case, the public domain and shareware programs to do the job.

Recommended Programs

Glossbrenner's Choice:

IBM Printer Pack Disk 1—Printer Utilities

MP COM 3035
MP DOC 9169

Kenneth Whitney's "MicroPrint" package requires an IBM/Epson or compatible dot-matrix printer, though custom versions are available by contacting the program's author: Mr. Kenneth D. Whitney, 1325 S. West Street, Arlington, TX 76010. The program is likely to be especially useful to anyone who must print large quantities of text because it can put up to 120 lines on a single letter-size page.

MP.COM is designed to automatically print text files at 17 characters per inch and 120 lines per page. To do this it uses the compressed Epson superscript and subscript modes, automatically toggling between one and the other with each line to "promote the even use of the printhead pins and to prolong ribbon life." The program automatically prints page headers containing the name of the file at the left and the page number at the right. On the first page the current date is automatically inserted instead of the page number. (Remember, you can set your computer's time and date with the DOS TIME and DATE commands.)

The headers can be suppressed, if you like. You can also set the program to print on both sides of the page. If you have activated this feature, the program will print all odd-numbered pages and then pause for you to change the paper to the other side. The even-numbered pages will then be printed in ascending sequence. It is also possible to set the page length to 90 lines (about seven inches) should you want to trim the pages to fit six by nine-inch binders.

This is an altogether well thought-out and smooth running program. The type it produces is quite small, but it is quite clear and readable. As the documentation points out, Mr. Whitney retains the copyright but allows the program to be freely distributed. Mr. Whitney has also written MicroDial, a RAM-resident autodialer (Hayes "AT-command-compatible" modem, required). The cost is $19.95 plus $2 shipping and handling. We haven't seen it, but if it is as well done as MP.COM it is likely to be very good indeed. For more information, or to place an order, contact Mr. Whitney at the address given above.

TL	COM	13615
TL	DOC	4327
TL	PAS	4919

TinyList (version 2.0) is one of the niftiest print packers we've ever seen. The program has the ability to fit nearly 20K of text—or about 2,800 words—on a single 8½ × 11-inch page. To work its magic, TinyList uses superscripted and condensed print and line spacing of 15/216 inch. This allows 150 lines per page, plus top and bottom margins. The program also automatically formats text into two columns, each of which is 66 characters wide. Lines that are longer than 66 characters are automatically wrapped around within the column. The columns read like a newspaper, with the top of column two picking up where the end of column one left off.

Text files that are not long enough to require two columns (like TL.DOC) are printed in a single column. If you do not want the program to wrap words, you can toggle this feature on and off by inserting Control-Q characters in the text. Thus if there were several lines in the file running 80 characters or more that you wanted printed as separate lines, you could insert a Control-Q at the beginning and end of that section. The first 66 characters of the first line would be printed, followed by the remaining 14 characters on the next line down. (The program does not break words, so the printed lines may contain less than 66 characters and more than 14 characters.) Then the program would space down and print the first 66 characters of the second 80-character line, and so on. When it encountered the second Control-Q, word wrap would be toggled back on, and all succeeding lines would be run together as per usual.

As provided, TinyList is set up for Epson-compatible dot-matrix printers. However as the documentation points out, you can modify the Pascal source code to support other machines, though of course, you will need a Pascal compiler. Written by Mike Binnard, TinyList is shareware ($10). Contact: Peninsula Software, 28510 Blythewood, Palos Verdes, CA 90274.

Print Enhancement: Letter Quality and Variable Fonts

Scientists say that human beings use only about five percent of their available brain capacity. Much the same could be said of the typical nine-pin or nine-wire dot matrix printer. These are by far the most common PC printers in use today, and models are made by NEC, Panasonic, Star, Okidata, and of course, Epson.

The original 1981-model IBM/Epson dot matrix printer sold for about $750 (list). The equivalent models today go for around $240 (mail order discount). They tend to be faster, around 100 to 120 characters per second (CPS) versus the original speed of 80 CPS, and they have additional features. But while they are fine for printing quick drafts or doing screen dumps, you wouldn't exactly be proud to have your name at the bottom of a business letter they had produced. Even in emphasized or double-strike mode, the print quality just isn't there with a nine-pin printer.

The latest 24-pin printers are a different story. Developed in Japan to print that country's complex kanji characters (kanji is sort of a modernized version of traditional Japanese pictograms.), 24-pin printer quality is outstanding. But so too is the price. At this writing, the cost is around $500 per machine.

Well have we got a surprise for you: Print quality from an inexpensive nine-pin dot matrix printer so good that you will absolutely not believe your eyes. Crisp character definition, a wide variety of fonts (type styles), and special print features so impressive that the correspondence produced by your inexpensive nine-pin dot-matrix printer need never take a backseat ever again.

Text Mode and Character Sets in ROM

The secret, as is always the case with computers, is in the software—although in this case the hardware plays a major role as well. Most nine-pin printers can be operated in two ways: text mode and bit-image graphics mode. The difference is not too difficult to understand if you think back to our explanation of how a dot-matrix printer works. Remember the printhead with its wires arranged like a nine-light traffic signal, and remember the stop-fire-stop-fire-stop-fire (and so on) sequence used to produce the letter O. With Epson/IBM nine-pin printers there are five pin-firing positions per character, so the number of pins involved could be anywhere from 45 (5×9) to one. A capital W, for example, requires 20 dots, while an apostrophe (') requires only two.

Now, if the printer had to figure out how to move the printhead and which pins to fire at each position for each character every time you wanted to print something, it would take far too long to print even a one-page business letter. Printer manufacturers have solved this problem by putting all of the information required to create every character of the alphabet into one or more ROM chips inside the printer. ROM chips can be thought of as programming frozen in silicon.

Thus, when the printer is operating in text mode, the computer has only to send it a single ASCII code number for each character to be printed. To cause a capital W to be printed, for example, the computer sends the number 87 to the printer. For technical reasons, this number can be symbolized using just seven bits. Indeed all the numbers from 0 through 127 can be symbolized with seven bits.

When the printer receives this code, it channels it directly to its character-generating ROM chip. Since the ROM chip "knows" exactly how the printhead should be moved and how the pins should be fired to create a W, that's just about all there is to it. Next case, next character, please.

Bit-Image Graphics Mode

When a printer is operating in bit-image graphics mode, however, the ROM chip is completely out of the loop. Here the computer controls the movement of the printhead and the action of each individual printhead pin. Each pin is controlled by a single bit. The computer in effect says, "Okay, kiddo, you're in graphics mode. Now, move the printhead here and fire pins 1, 3, and 7. Move the printhead there and fire pins 4, 6, 7, and 8. Move the printhead here and . . ."

Clearly, more bits are going to have to flow from the computer to the printer to create even a single character. A lot more. Let's use a capital W as an example again. As we said, that character requires 20 dots on the typical nine-pin printer, so at least 20 bits will be required just to fire the pins on the printhead, should you want to duplicate the text-mode type style in bit-image graphics mode. In text mode, remember, only seven bits had to be sent from the computer, thanks to the hard-wired translation tables burned into the ROM chip.

Needless to say, printing characters in bit-image graphics mode is going to take much more time. But the benefits are considerable. In the first place, direct control over the printhead frees you from the limitations imposed by the character set in the printer's ROM. Unless you have leafed through a book of fonts and type styles of the sort found in most commercial printshops, you may not fully appreciate the fact that there are a virtually infinite number of ways to produce the same character. But if you compare capital W's from a newspaper, several magazines, and this book, you will immediately see what we're getting at. The character is always recognizable, but the actual design of the image may vary considerably.

The 20-dot, text-mode capital W we've been using as an example may be burned into an Epson printer's ROM, but it is not graven in stone. Someone at the design stage made the decision that this is how a capital W will be produced for this printer. But there are *many* other ways to do it. By offering your computer complete control over the printhead and its pins, bit-image graphics mode in effect puts a blank page and a pen into your hands. You (or the software you are running) can create entire alphabets of different typestyles or fonts.

The second advantage of using bit-image graphics mode is that you can pass the printhead over the same line of text more than once. This of course is what happens in text mode when you do double-strike or emphasized printing. But the characters that are being double-struck or emphasized are those of the printer's ROM. In bit-image graphics mode, you can make one pass with one configuration of dots and a second and third pass with slightly different configurations as you build up a line of characters.

In graphics mode only eight of the nine printhead pins are used, and so the arithmetic becomes quite simple indeed. As Mark Harris, the author of the LQ.COM program recommended below, told us, "Three passes with eight pins per pass means you can create the same kind of print quality found on a 24-pin printer. It just takes you three passes instead of one to do it."

Software-Created Fonts and Type Styles

Once you understand the hardware component of the process, the software component falls into place easily. Commercial programs, including Adapta-Print ($65), Fancy Font ($180), NicePrint ($95), and Printworks

($69.95), basically consist of complete software font sets and a translation program. These programs and their public domain or user-supported equivalents insert themselves between the computer and the printer. Thus when the computer sends an ASCII 87 to the printer to print a capital W, the software intercepts this information, translates it into a series of bit-image graphic instructions, and sends them instead. The reference table the program uses to perform the translation from an ASCII 87 into a stream of bits is called the font or character set.

Some PD programs offer only one font; others offer a selection of fonts, any one of which can be used at one time. The best offer an entire series of fonts that can be intermixed within the same document, plus a clutch of print modes (emphasized, expanded characters, underline, and so on) that can also be intermixed.

We've looked at many of these programs, and the two that stand head and shoulders above the rest are LQ.COM ("Letter Quality") and ImagePrint (IMP80.COM and IMP136.COM). Each is slightly different. Indeed, until recently the authors had never heard of each other or seen the others' programs. But both are of such high quality that it is impossible to recommend one above the other. We would only point out that you can make the contributions requested by both authors and *still* pay less than you would for a single equivalent commercial program. You may receive more total capability as well.

Recommended Programs

Glossbrenner's Choice:

IBM Printer Pack Disk 2—Letter Quality/ImagePrint

The Harris Letter Quality (LQ.COM) Package

Mark Harris, the author of the shareware LQ.COM Letter Quality package, is a mathematics and computer science professor at Appalachian State University. He has written many commercial educational packages, including ARBPLOT (coauthor), The Slide Projector, and GraphChallenge for the Apple and one called GraphCalc for the IBM. Most of his programming is done during the summer, which is how he came to call his company Granny's Old-Fashioned Software.

> I do a lot of bicycling, and in the summer one of my favorite activities is to go off with some program ideas on a bike ride, think about them as I'm pedaling, and stop at Granny's Old-Fashioned Doughnuts when things have crystalized. I usually sit down with a cup of coffee and a doughnut

and get out the scratch paper and start programming. All my major ideas come when I'm out on a bicycle or in the garden.

As is so often the case with public domain and shareware software, Mr. Harris wrote LQ.COM for himself. In his words,

The easiest way to summarize what LQ does is that it makes 9-pin dot matrix printers look pretty close to 24-pin dot matrix printers. It is designed to spruce up business letters, not produce artwork.

I have an Epson MX-80. It's a 1981 printer, and I did LQ when I was faced with the decision to buy a new printer or not. I knew I needed a better quality of print for correspondence. The dot matrix emphasized mode was reasonably acceptable about five years ago, and I tried very hard to convince myself that it was all I needed. But it wasn't. It just didn't measure up.

I think what made me do it was the fact that when the 24-pin printers came out it was easy to see that by making three passes with eight pins you could get the same effect as one pass with 24 pins. And that's what LQ does. So, if you could put up with the longer printing time, there was no reason not to do it.

LQ.COM (version 2.26) comes with 20 different fonts, including two versions of Courier, Greek, two versions of Helvetica, two versions of Roman, Palatino, and two versions of Sanserif. There are italicized versions of most fonts as well. Finally, there is a computeresque font, and two IBM fonts that include all of the high code graphics and international language characters in the IBM code set. Figure 13.2 shows nine of the 20 fonts included with LQ.COM at this writing. Most have italic versions, and all can be reproduced using your printer's double-width, boldface, underline, subscript, superscript, and other modes. LQ includes a command to enable proportional spacing, and one to print triple-high letters as well.

If you load LQ into memory, you can call a pop-up menu at any time to select one of four preloaded fonts. (You can make these default fonts anything you want to using the LQ install program.) The menu also lets you activate or deactivate LQ. When active, the program will print all text sent to the printer in the font you have set. By default, the program installs a print spooler to keep from tying up your system while it is printing. When deactivated, LQ will have no effect at all.

You can also use LQ in file mode, whether or not you have loaded it into memory. In this mode, you tell the program which file you wish to print and which of the 20 fonts you want it to use. You can also embed special LQ control sequences in a document to mix up to two fonts at print time. And you can take full advantage of your printer's compressed, emphasized, proportional, double-width, superscript, subscript, and other special modes using LQ fonts.

Figure 13.2. Selected LQ.COM Fonts.

COURIER
!"#$%&'()*+,-./0123456789:;<=>?@ABCDEFGHIJKLMNO
PQRSTUVWXYZ[\]^_`abcdefghijklmnopqrstuvwxyz{|}~

GREEK
!"#$%&'()*+,-./0123456789:;<=>?@ΑΒΓΔΕΦΓΗΙΘΚΛΜΝΟ
ΡΞΡΣΤΥΥΩΧΨΖ[\]^_`αβγδεω ηιθκλμνοπΕρστυνωψγζ{|}~

HELV2
!"#$%&'()*+,-./0123456789:;<=>?@ABCDEFGHIJKLMNO
PQRSTUVWXYZ[\]^_`abcdefghijklmnopqrstuvwxyz{|}~

MAIN
!"#$%&'()*+,-./0123456789:;<=>?@ABCDEFGHIJKLMNO
PQRSTUVWXYZ[\]^_`abcdefghijklmnopqrstuvwxyz{|}~

MAINITAL
!"#$%&'()*+,-./0123456789:;<=>?@ABCDEFGHIJKLMNO
PQRSTUVWXYZ[\]^_`abcdefghijklmnopqrstuvwxyz{/}~

ROMAN
!"#$%&'()*+,-./0123456789:;<=>?@ABCDEFGHIJKLMNO
PQRSTUVWXYZ[\]^_`abcdefghijklmnopqrstuvwxyz{|}~

SANS2ITA
!"#$%&'()*+,-./0123456789:;<=>?@ABCDEFGHIJKLMNO
PQRSTUVWXYZ[\]^_`abcdefghijklmnopqrstuvwxyz{|}~

IBM1

IBM2

By default, LQ.COM is configured for the Epson command set, including Epson's Escape-3, -A, and -J control sequences. However, the package includes configuration files for several other popular printers as well (Imageprinter, IBM Proprinter, C. Itoh, Star, and so forth). If your printer is not among them, the manual explains how to create the configuration file you need. Note that you do not need a "graphics printer," equipped with a special grapics ROM chip, to use LQ. As long as your printer offers a bit-image graphics mode, you can take full advantage of the program.

You can use LQ with any word processor or text editor, but there is special support for MultiMate, WordPerfect, Microsoft Word (with or without a mouse), and proportional spacing and microjustification with PC-Write. The version current at this writing (version 2.26) also includes a special graphics editor program to create high-resolution designs (measuring one inch by one inch) suitable for letterheads and other purposes. There is also a program called BIGPRINT that will produce a poster or banner using any of the LQ typestyles.

The Harris Letter Quality package is commission shareware. The registration fee is $35, and it entitles you to the current version of the program including all available fonts, a mail-in card for a future version of LQ, a printed manual, and telephone support for your technical questions. In addition, you will earn a $10 commission each time someone registers from one of your copies of the program. (No commissions are earned on the copy of LQ.COM on the Glossbrenner's Choice disk.) Naturally you don't have to have a copy of the program to register. You can simply call or write to Mr. Harris at: Granny's Old-Fashioned Software, Route 4, Box 216, Boone, NC 28607; phone: (704) 264-6906. Visa and MasterCard phone or mail orders are accepted.

Everything Included

However you obtain the program, you will find that the LQ package includes the entire manual on disk, plus the complete program with all available fonts.

> I spoke to Bob Wallace, author of PC-WRITE, [Mr. Harris says,] and I mentioned that withholding fonts would be one way to encourage people to register the program. But Bob talked me out of it. He said, "Give it your best shot. Don't hold anything back. The way to get that user support is not by teasing the public but by showing them what you've got." Fortunately I took his advice, and I've been very happy with the results.

In addition to the extra features and programs cited above, Mr. Harris's best shot also includes a nifty program called EDCHAR.COM. This program lets you quickly and easily create your own characters, symbols, or entire fonts. You might, for example, replace a seldom-used character like the tilde (˜) with a monogram of your own design. Or you might create other characters for special applications. We don't have space to go into it, but this is really a super program in and of itself.

One final point to save you some confusion. PC-SIG Disk 283 contains a program also called LQ.COM. However, this is not the same program. It carries the copyright of Image Memory Products, Inc. In recent years the program has been renamed LQ-Print and the company has changed its name to Centar Technology (Sunnyvale, CA). Ironically,

Mark Harris reports, PC-SIG ignored his submission of LQ.COM several times, apparently because the organization thought it already had the program in its library. Fortunately, this has all been straightened out.

The McVicar ImagePrint Package

It is fascinating to see how two creative programmers can tackle the same problem and come up with two different but equally valid solutions. LQ.COM loads itself and four fonts into memory and includes an automatic print spooler and a pop-up window. ImagePrint (IMP80.EXE et al.), a package written by Christopher McVicar, operates in command line mode. That is, you activate it by entering IMP80 at the DOS prompt, followed by the name of the file you wish to print, followed by one or more backslash commands to set its various modes. But where LQ.COM can mix two fonts per document, ImagePrint can mix six or more, even to the point of using different fonts for individual letters. Font mixing is done on the basis of the commands you embed in the text file. And while no spooler is included, we tested it with MSPOOL2 and found that it worked just fine.

The available fonts differ as well. With ImagePrint, for example, Orator, OCRA, and a font of letters in outline are available. But at this writing, ImagePrint has no Greek. Or helvetica. On the other hand, it includes a utility called NATIONAL.COM to let you use international characters, and it offers a "six pass laser quality" bold printing option. It also includes support for the Epson JX-80 color printer.

Figure 13.3.   ImagePrint Fonts Demonstration.

```
                  IMAGEPRINT FONTS DEMONSTRATION

FONT1 is CUBIC. It is included on the ImagePrint distribution
diskette.

FONT6 is SMALL. This font is good for footnotes. It looks best when proportionally spaced,
but can be used at 12 characters per inch and 10 characters per inch.

FONT7 is HOLLOW. Really stands out when expanded:

   SOMETHING VERY IMPORTANT

FONT8 is PICA. It is like Courier without embellishments.
This is printed in 6 PASS LASER QUALITY.

FONT9 is BLOCK. Thick and dark; excellent as a heading.

FONT10 is TIMES2. Stylishly bold. Good at 10 cpi.
```

Figure 13.3 shows several of the fonts and printing modes available through ImagePrint. As noted, FONT1 (cubic) comes with the distribution disk. The other fonts shown are provided when you become a registered user.

As we have said before, it is simply impossible to choose one program over the other. Both have considerable virtues. Both have made a special point of working with and otherwise meshing with PC-Write. Both have extensive, well-written manuals. So instead of trying to compare the two point-for-point, we've tried to make it as easy as possible for you to test them yourself by putting both programs on the same Glossbrenner's Choice Disk 2. After you've tried LQ.COM and ImagePrint, you will feel so good about the programs that you will really want to become a registered user. They are simply superb.

We should point out that the two programmers have also taken somewhat different marketing approaches as well. Christopher McVicar and Image Computer Systems have chosen to offer only one font (cubic) on the distribution disk. This is eminently useful and may be all you need. But if you register ($20), you will receive Roman, outline, small, pica, and block fonts as well. Additional fonts (courier, elite, italic, orator, typewriter, OCRA, and OCRB) are available at $5 each. The distribution disk includes a demonstration program to show you what all available fonts look like. The output is much more complete than the fonts demonstration shown in Figure 13.3.

A CP/M version (if you have to ask, you don't need to know) of ImagePrint is also available for $30, including six fonts. The list of supported disk formats is long, though at this writing it does not include Apple. The company also offers a program called MetaText ($89). This program is very similar to LQ.COM in its operation. It loads itself and three chosen fonts into memory and automatically intercepts output destined for the printer. It includes a "puck," described as "a small, flat device which sits on your desktop," and is "attached to your printer port by a flexible cable. Turning over the puck is all that you need to do to switch between quality typeface and regular printer operation." The seven fonts listed above (courier, elite, and so on) are included with the package. MetaText and ImagePrint (for a total of 13 fonts) are available as a package for $99.

The company has also developed a circuit board controller for Okidata 192 and 193 printers that allows them to produce "high quality bar code and large character printing." According to the ImagePrint manual, all of the "complex real-time bar code generation algorithms are contained in the Image controller." Also, "large characters can be up to eight inches high by eight inches wide," including five shading options. The product sells for $300 in single quantities. Additional information and print samples are available.

The shareware registration fee for ImagePrint is $20. This includes the latest version of IMP80.EXE, plus IMP136.EXE for wide printers, six fonts, and telephone support. Site licensing and quantity discounts are available. Contact: Image Computer Systems, P.O. Box 647, Avon, CT 06001; phone: (203) 678-8771, 8:30 A.M. to 5:30 P.M. weekdays. Visa and MasterCard phone or mail orders are accepted.

Finally, Image Computer Systems is one of a growing number of shareware software firms with an international connection. The ImagePrint distribution disk sells for nine pounds in Great Britain, plus 15 percent value added tax. All other products are available as well. For more information, contact: Image Computer Systems, 27 Cobham Road, Wimborne, Dorset, England; phone: (0202) 876064.

FreeTip: Image Computer Systems offers one other product at this writing that is likely to be of special interest to BASIC programmers, particularly those wishing to emulate the seemingly omnipresent pop-up windows of Turbo Pascal. The program is called the BASIC Windowing Toolbox or B-WINDOW. It is available from most free software sources, as well from Image Computer Systems. The toolbox gives you what you need to easily add multicolored, overlaid, variable-sized, independently scrolling windows to your BASIC programs. The tools work with both Quick-BASIC and the Microsoft compiler, as well as in interpreted mode. Registered users ($20) receive additional files and expanded capabilities, though the distribution version works quite well as it is.

Conclusion

Word processing and printing are arguably the most widely used computer applications. Filing, information sorting and retrieval, and other *database* applications are probably next. For many users, however, *accounting*, electronic *spreadsheet*-based "what if?" scenarios, and other number-crunching activities run a close second.

In the next chapter we'll look at database applications and suggest some ways to get a handle on your inventory (household or business), billing, videotape collection, mailing lists, and anything else that involves organizing and manipulating many disparate pieces of information. In Chapter 15, we'll turn on the number crunchers. In both cases, you will find that these are tasks your PC does exceptionally well. The programs we will be recommending will make it easy for you to take full advantage of the power resting at your fingertips.

14

Database, dBASE, Filing, and Free Text Searching

INFORMATION ON DEMAND

Personal computers are not good at everything. But if there is one task at which they excel, it is the task of information retrieval and manipulation. For example, suppose you're a businessperson with 10,000 parts in inventory, and you want to call up a screen of information about a particular part. The screen could contain information on the part's name, its physical location in the storeroom, its unit cost, selling price, supplier, current number of units on hand, the last time a unit was sold or taken out of inventory, color, size, shape, part number, and any other relevant information you wish to have about the parts in your inventory.

What's more, you could search for and locate that screen of information on the basis of any of the items we've just described. If you can't remember the part number, for example, but do remember that it came from the Ajax Tool and Die Company, you could search for the target part on the basis of the supplier's name. But suppose the Ajax Tool and Die Company supplies nearly 100 parts to your firm. Very well; perhaps you also remember that the part in question costs under $30. In that case, you could say to the computer, "Give me a list of all parts supplied by Ajax that cost less than $30." In seconds you might have a list of, say, ten parts meeting those criteria. From there, finding the target part would be a simple matter of paging through no more than ten screens of information.

Now suppose that you want to produce a report listing all parts supplied to your firm by the Zephyr Manufacturing Corporation, sorted by part number. But you also want the report to tell you how much money you have tied up in your inventory of Zephyr products. You'd like a subtotal by part number and a grand total at the end of the report.

One way to do this would be to tell your computer to find every part listing Zephyr Manufacturing as its supplier and copy the information for all of those parts into a separate file. You could then tell the machine to sort that file by part number. Finally, you could ask for a printed report that includes a place for the dollar amount that results from multiplying the number of units on hand by the cost per unit in each case. There will also be a spot at the end of the report for the computer to insert the grand total of those dollar figures.

None of this is difficult to do, for as we said, computers are simply aces when it comes to locating and manipulating information. As you will have guessed, however, the one component you need to make it all possible is a database management (or simply "database") program. That is one of two types of software we'll be considering in this chapter; the other type is free-text-searching software. We will also point you in the right direction to obtain files that can help you use Ashton-Tate's best-selling dBASE programs and other commercial database software of all kinds.

Database Management Software

As we've already seen, a database management program gives you virtually complete control over almost any kind of information. This type of software can keep track of things, calculate and issue invoices, and produce custom reports to give you a snapshot of your data and the situation it represents. Database programs are also ideally suited to producing mailing lists.

Consequently, next to word processing software, a good database management program is probably the most essential kind of software for any business to have. After all, regardless of the products we manufacture or the services we provide, ultimately most of us are really in the business of managing information. Of course, as with all software, there are home and personal applications for database management programs as well. Just remember that however you use this kind of software, none of it will do you any good until you sit down and key in the data you want it to manage. Furthermore, once you've created a database, you must keep it up to date if you expect it to give you the correct answers to the questions you ask.

Database Basics

If you've never used a database or information retrieval program before, there are some basic things you need to know. The most important of these is the difference between a free-text-searching program and a traditional database management program. Computers locate information by scanning a file for a match between the characters or words you have specified and the contents of the target file. This is true regardless of the type of information management software being used. The difference between free-text-searching software—or a "free form database" as it is sometimes called—and a conventional database program is one of structure.

Vernon Buerg's LIST program is a good example of a free-text-searching program. As we saw in Chapters 6 and 9, you can use this program to locate any string of characters in any text file. ("String" is computer talk for any series of characters that are viewed as text, be they characters, words, phrases, ZIP codes, phone numbers, or something else.) You don't have to prepare the file in any way before starting to search, and the program could not care less how the text is organized. If the file contains an exact match of the character string you have specified, LIST will find it and display it, surrounded by about a dozen of the lines that come before and come after it.

However, while you could use LIST to locate a particular name in a file containing several hundred addresses, you cannot use it to print mailing labels for everyone in, say, the state of Maine. Nor can you use LIST to do "Boolean searches" (those involving AND/OR/NOT specifications) or greater than/less than parameters. There are free-form databases that can perform Boolean searches, as we'll see in a moment, but you must allow them to process the target text file first.

To accomplish the kind of work described in our parts inventory example above, you need the structure of a database management program. This structure can be succinctly described as "file, record, and field." That phrase is the mantra of database management. You will hear it constantly, and the sooner you understand what it means, the sooner you'll be able to fully tap your PC's information management power.

File, Record, and Field

Let's use a common Rolodex address file as an example. The entire collection of Rolodex cards taken as a whole is a *file*. Each individual card is a *record*. And each bit of information on each card—name, street address, city, state, ZIP code, area code, phone number—is a *field*.

Alternatively, you can think of the white pages of a phone book as a file, each one-line entry as a record, and each component of an entry as a field. Or you can think of your collection of last year's cancelled checks as a file. Each individual check is a record, and each separate piece of information on a check (check number, date, payee, numerical amount, signature) is a field. As you can see, "file, record, and field" are all around you.

This structure allows database programs to particle-ize your information. And that's their secret, for once a block of information has been broken up into separate particles, a computer can do all kinds of things with it. It can find records by focusing on a particular slot containing a particular kind of particle. It can sort records by comparing the particles in the same slot in each record. Or it can print reports containing only those information particles from each record that you specify.

Using a Database Management Program

With that as background, let's look briefly at how a database management program works. Here it is worth remembering that no applications program is monolithic. Each is designed to perform certain functions, and to perform those functions, each requires you as the user to take certain steps. Examining the way each program of a given class handles these steps and combining that information with the program's capacities and performance offers an excellent way to compare similar programs. Nowhere are the steps you must follow more clearly defined than in the area of database management.

The first step in all database management programs is to define the structure of your database. You have to tell the program the names of the fields you want to include in each record, how long each field should be, and whether its contents will be text, numbers, or something else. Thus, if you're preparing a database of addresses, you must decide whether you want a single field called "NAME," or one field for a person's first name ("FNAME") and one for his last name ("LNAME"). Should there be a field for a person's company? For her title? You have to decide.

The next step is to actually begin entering data. During this phase, the program usually presents you with a blank record—a record containing the field names you have chosen, often with some indication of the space you have allocated for each one, but nothing more. Entering data is like filling in the blanks on a paper form. When you are finished with one record, you hit a key to save it to disk, and the program automatically presents you with another blank record screen.

During this phase some database programs force you to do things their way. They offer only a left-justified column of field names. Others, like those we'll be discussing in a moment, let you lay out the data entry form any way you like, positioning fields all over the screen. This can be especially helpful since it allows you to make the screen closely match the paper forms you or your staff may be accustomed to using.

When the last record has been entered, you will have a complete database and be ready to go to work. At this point, you can search for records on the basis of the contents of some field or the contents of more than one field. You might want the program to give you "all addresses in which STATE = MAINE OR VERMONT AND PRICE is < \$30," for example. Or you can sort the database by the contents of a particular field: alphabetically by last name, by ZIP code, by part number, or whatever. In most programs you sort on multiple fields, as you might if you wanted your addresses sorted first by ZIP code and within each ZIP code, sorted alphabetically by the name of the addressee. Of course you can also add, modify, or delete records at any time.

In addition to letting you design the database structure, enter data, and the sort and search functions, all database management programs will let you output data in a variety of ways. In computer talk, this is called "printing reports," and it is the last major step in the process. A report can contain any of the information you have put into your database, and in most cases you can specify where on the page you would like each piece of information to appear. In one instance, a report could be a run of mailing labels. In another, it could be a summary of each salesperson's activities for the month, including calculations for total goods sold, sales tax, and sliding sales commission. Both reports could come from the same file of information. As with the structure of the database, the format of a given report—its title, column headings, fields of data, and any calculations or formulas—is something you must decide.

"But All I Want to Do Is Labels"

As is always the case with computer software, there is a trade-off between simplicity and power in information retrieval and management programs. If you want to quickly locate every occurrence of a particular string of characters in a text file, the program of choice is Vernon Buerg's LIST. Within seconds after keying in LIST filename.ext and hitting <Enter> you can have your answer. But if you have a document on disk and you want to find, say, "Madison" wherever it occurs within 100 words of "Marshall" in that document—but no place else—then you need a free-form, free-text-searching program. Before you can use such a program, however, you must allow it to parse the target file to build the index that it will use in executing your searches. Finally, as we have seen, if you want to be able to do the kind of retrieval and manipulations discussed in our parts inventory example, you need a conventional, structured database program. In short, the complexity rachets up with the power a program makes available.

But what if you merely want a program that will produce mailing labels for the customers of your small business or members of your social club or bowling league? What should you do then? There *are* shareware and public domain mailing label programs, but in our opinion, you will be better off using a conventional database program instead. In the first place, mailing label programs are really just database programs that have been optimized for producing labels. They free you of some of the work needed to get a database up and running, but by no means all of it. And, of course, they aren't nearly as flexible or as powerful. In the second place, many programs, including those discussed below, offer features specifically designed to make it easy to produce mailing labels from your data.

Finally, we have long maintained that one of the keys to software success is to learn as few programs as possible, and as a corollary, to make sure that the programs you choose to master offer the features and power you may need in the future. Thus, if you are going to invest time building a database of addresses and producing mailing labels, you will receive a much better return if you make your investment in a full-featured program. You may not need or want a particular feature today, but who knows about tomorrow? Database management programs aren't much more difficult to learn than programs designed to produce only mailing labels, but they can pay big dividends for the extra few hours you may have to spend learning to use them.

Recommended Programs

Glossbrenner's Choice:

IBM File Express Disk 1—Program Disk

IBM File Express Disk 2—Users Guide and Supplemental Programs

IBM ExpressGraph Disk 1—Business Graphics

There are scores of public domain and shareware database programs for IBMs and compatible computers, but two of them stand head and shoulders above the rest. These are Jim Button's PC-File + and David Berdan's File Express. PC-File + is the latest edition of one of the two programs that began the shareware revolution. (The other was the late

Andrew Fluegelman's PC-Talk.) PC-File was introduced in 1982. The first edition of File Express came along in 1984, and as a consequence is less well known.

Both are very capable, top-quality programs, easily on a par with commercial products listing for $250 or more. Both have long and successful track records punctuated by regular updates and improvements. Both are well supported by their authors, and both carry shareware registration fees of $69.95. It isn't easy to choose between them. Yet after a great deal of consideration, we must come down on the side of File Express.

We have two main reasons for recommending File Express (FE) over PC-File (PCF). The first is packaging and presentation, and the second is comparative capacity and capability. File Express has always had a slicker, more friendly user interface than PC-File. Its screen layout and use of line graphics and color give the program a very commercial feel. (You don't need color capability to run FE, but as with any program, it's nice to have.) PCF's menus, in contrast, are perfectly servicable but rather spare. They do not offer much in the way of visual aids or design.

Naturally enough, perhaps, the distinction carries over to the documentation you receive when you register. The File Express manual is 300 pages long, typeset, illustrated, and indexed. It arrives in a three-ring binder measuring a little over nine inches on a side. That means it lies flat for easy reference when you are actually using the program. At some 234 pages, the PC-File manual is quite extensive as well, and it too is typeset, illustrated, and indexed. But the documentation is supplied as a 5½ by 8½-inch perfect-bound paperback book. Short of nailing it to the desk or breaking its spine, there is no way to get it to stay open.

Though very important, especially for new users, packaging and presentation are meaningless if a program is not up to snuff in its operation. If that were the case with FE and PCF, we would have no hesitation about recommending the latter, bare bones screens or not. But at this writing, quite the reverse is true. Both File Express, version 4.15, and PC-File+, version 2.0, were released at approximately the same time (late 1987 to early 1988), so it isn't a question of comparing an older to a newer program or vice versa.

Capacity Comparison

Every software of every type has limits. The limits may or may not impinge on your use of a given program, but they are always there and it is very important to be aware of them. Thus, the first thing to do when examining any program is to ask "How many?" and "How long?" at every possible opportunity. With database management software, for example, you should always ask questions like: How many records may I have per file? And how long can each field be? The literature supplied by both program authors makes it easy to summarize the answers to such questions in the following table.

	FE v. 4.15	PCF+ v. 2.0
Maximum number of . . .		
Records per database	16.7 million	65,533
Characters per record	3000	3000
Fields per record	120	70
Characters per field	250	200
Simultaneously sorted fields	10	10

Naturally, comparisons of this sort don't tell the whole story. Realistically, you'll probably never need anything close to 65,000 records per database, let alone 16.7 million. The popular commercial program PFS:Professional File (version 1.01), for example, does quite well offering a maximum of 29,500 records per database. If you figure an average of seven characters per word, a limit of 3000 characters per record gives you the equivalent of about 425 words to work with. That's a little more than one and a half double-spaced typewritten pages (46 lines of text at 65 characters per line). Again, plenty of room for most applications. For all practical purposes, then, in records per database and characters per record, the two programs are equal.

Actually Usable Fields

The maximum number of fields per record, however, requires a bit of elaboration. In PC-File, you may have 70 fields, but you must somehow fit them on a single screen measuring 21 lines (rows) by 80 columns. You cannot continue your record on a second or third screen. Clearly that's not going to be practical in most instances, so the *effective* number of fields per record with PCF will usually be less than 70. With File Express, however, a single record can occupy up to six screens. Since each screen measures 21 lines, you have a maximum of 6 × 21 = 126 lines to work with. Both programs have a "paint" function that allows you to design your own data-entry screen by positioning your fields wherever you want and adding custom text and graphics elements.

You should also know that PC-File will allow you to create a single "superfield" in a database that can be as long as 1665 characters, depending on the total number of fields the database contains. You might use this for memos, notes, comments, and miscellaneous details pertaining to the data in a particular record. You can retrieve records on the basis of what the superfield contains, with one important limitation. The program will look for matches in the superfield, but it will only consider the first 65 characters. If the detail you are looking for is deeper in the field than that, the program will not be able to find the record containing it.

Formula Follows Functions

Another measure of a database program's capabilities concerns the functions it offers for calculating the contents of fields or items on a report. When designing a database to track your company's sales, for example, you might have a field for units sold and one for price-per-unit. You could then create a third field for the total sale amount and tell the program to automatically enter the required data on the basis of a formula you specify. In this case, the formula would be a simple multiplication of whatever you put in the units sold field by the price-per-unit field. As soon as you key in the number of units sold, the program will do the calculation and automatically insert the correct figure in the total sales field.

Both PC-File and File Express offer the four basic mathematical functions, plus percentage, exponents, and remainders. But FE also offers trigonometric functions (sine, cosine, tangent, and arctangent), plus integer, square root, natural log, and absolute value. There is also a File Express ROUND function to round calculated results to a specified number of decimal places, and an AGE function to compute the number of days, weeks, months, or years between two dates. Virtually all of the string functions familiar to BASIC users are available as well (LEFT, RIGHT, MID, CHR, INSTR, and so on).

The Utility of Functions

We don't have room to explain each function, but since it can be difficult for new users to appreciate how useful functions can be, we can use AGE as a quick example. Suppose you're a car dealer and you have a database with a record for each car on the lot or in the showroom. And suppose that each record contains a field labeled PURCH-DATE for the date on which you purchased the car from the factory. If you wanted File Express to produce a report containing the number of days each car has been on the lot, you could tell the program to include a heading called something like "Days in Inventory" on the report. When you do this, File Express will ask you to key in a formula for it to use in calculating the information to be printed under that heading. You would respond with something like this: AGE(PURCH-DATE). The program will then use today's date (the system date that was set when you booted up your computer) and the information in each PURCH-DATE field to perform its calculations and print the result under your "Days in Inventory" heading.

Logical Operations and Natural Language

File Express can also perform IF/THEN/ELSE logical operations. If you wanted to use a sales-tracking database to print invoices, for example, you could use this capability to automatically add the applicable sales tax, based on the state to which the order is being shipped. Assuming you have a series of address-related fields, one of which is named STATE, you could create a field called SALES TAX and attach a formula to it reading something like this: IF STATE IS TX THEN USE .08 ELSE USE 0. This would ensure that only orders shipped to Texas addresses would be charged sales tax. You could allow for additional states and tax rates by appending other IF/THEN/ELSE strings to this formula.

That formula illustrates something else as well—File Express's "natural language," English-like capabilities. You could write the same formula like this: IF STATE = TX THEN .08 ELSE 0, and File Express would not care. But being able to substitute "is" for " = " and insert "use" makes the command more like everyday speech.

You can get even more conversational if you like. If you wanted to tag each customer's record with a rating to make it easier to quickly identify your best customers, you might create a field in each record called GRADE and enter a formula like this: IF PURCH IS GREATER THAN 90 THEN A ELSE IF PURCH IS GREATER THAN 80 THEN B ELSE IF PURCH IS GREATER THAN 70 THEN C. This would assign a grade of A to every customer who had purchased more than 90 units (or spent more than $90 or whatever), a grade of B to customers in the 80 to 90 range, and a grade of C to customers between 70 and 80.

Mail Merge and "Personalized" Form Letters

Both PC-File and File Express make it easy to produce "mail merge files." These are the kinds of files you need to generate "personalized," individually typed form letters. You might, for example, want to send one letter to all of your A customers and a different letter to all of your B and C customers. If you have created a field for customer grade as described above, your database program can easily prepare the appropriate mail merge address lists in each case.

You will also need a master form letter or "template file." The master form letter is usually created with your word processing software. It contains all of the text that will be printed, but wherever the letter refers to a specific person, place, or thing, the template actually contains a specially labeled slot called a variable. The salutation of such a letter might literally read "Dear [FNAME]," for example. During the merging process, the specific information in the mail merge file is substituted for the variables in the template file to produce and print the actual, customized letter. Thus if the first record in your mail merge file had a field for an individual's first name ("FNAME") and if the first person on your list were Bob Anderson, the first merged letter produced would begin "Dear Bob," instead of "Dear [FNAME]."

The manual for PC-Write, the word-processing program recommended in Chapter 12, devotes an entire chapter to the creation of templates and mail merge files. Indeed, we should point out that you do not need a database program to create a mail merge file. You can do it all with your word processor. But if you've already keyed in a database of customers, clients, suppliers, or others to whom you would like to send a letter, it's only smart to use your database program to produce the necessary file of addresses and other information.

Both PC-File and File Express will work hand-in-glove with PC-Write (and most other word processors) to produce the letters you need. Note that it is the word processor that does the actual merging. The database programs simply supply the information you want to incorporate in your letters in a format that your word processor can use to perform its substitutions.

The Import/Export Business

There are no two ways about it—keying data into any program is sheer drudgery. A certain amount of data entry is necessary, of course, but whenever possible it is almost always worth looking for ways to avoid keying the same information into two different programs. For example, suppose one of your databases contains your company's weekly sales totals and related information that you would like to bring into a spreadsheet program. Doing so would let you analyze the data in different ways. As we will see in Chapter 15, an electronic spreadsheet will instantly give you the answers to questions like "What if each salesperson increased his or her weekly sales by two percent?" The problem is that neither you nor your secretary has time to extract the necessary information from the database and rekey it into a spreadsheet program.

If you have never used a database program, however, you're in for a very pleasant surprise. As noted earlier, the secret to this kind of software's success is that it particle-izes information. That means you can in effect tell such a program to "Take particle A and write it to a different file. Now add a comma immediately after it. Then take particle B and add it to that file. Add another comma . . ." and so on. When you're finished, you'll have a separate file containing the information in the fields you have chosen, separated by a comma, quotation mark, set number of blank spaces, or some other character. You will have *exported* information in your database into a separate, specially formatted file.

There is no need to discuss the actual specifications of possible formats. All you need know at this point is that there are several widely agreed upon file formats that make it possible to quickly and easily move data from one program to another. Most spreadsheet programs, for example, have an *import* function that allows them to read one or more of these data file formats. Most database programs have an import function as well, so you can usually develop information in your spreadsheet and export it in a format that your database program can read. The mail merge files discussed earlier are merely another example of this process. You export addresses and other information to a mail merge file, which your word processor then imports and uses to produce customized form letters.

If you wanted to, you could use the report printing facilities of either PC-File or File Express to export information in any format you choose. You need only enter your report specifications and tell the programs to print to disk instead of to a printer or the screen. But in most instances this won't be necessary, since both programs can automatically export data in a number of different formats. You need only tell the program which format you want to use. The same is true for importing files created by other programs.

"Relational" Capabilities

At this writing, PC-File + offers two major features not found in File Express. One is a table look-up feature styled after a relational database and the other is the ability to produce business graphs. Technically speaking, both PC-File and File Express, like PFS:Professional File, Q&A, Rapidfile, Reflex, and other commercial products, are "flat file" database programs. This means that the data in a given database file exists independently of any other database file. Thus, if you have one database of customers and one database of best customers, and if Anderson is the first name on both lists, the characters needed to spell the name Anderson are actually present in *both* files.

In a truly relational database, like dBASE III + or Paradox, this would not be the case. The characters needed to spell Anderson might be physically present in your master customer file, while the best customer file would contain only a "pointer" telling the program where to find the characters for Anderson in the master file. When you are actually using them, both files will appear to be completely independent. But in reality, they are closely related. What's more, your best customer file could have a similar relationship with a third file that in itself has no relationship with the master customer file. From there, things really become complex.

The relational feature in PC-File + is similar to the relational feature in the discontinued commercial ButtonWare product, PC-File/R. Basically, you can specify a field and attach a formula to it that tells the program to go out to another PC-File database, locate a particular field, and bring the data it finds there into the database with which you are currently working. That data then becomes a physical part of the current database, just as if you had keyed it in yourself.

Business Graphics

In the past, ButtonWare has offered a shareware program called PC-Graph for those who wanted to be able to produce business graphs from PC-File (and PC-Calc) data. PC-Graph is now offered by a different company. But anyone with a CGA, EGA, VGA monitor or Hercules monochrome card can now produce horizontal bar, vertical bar, line, scatter plot, and pie charts without ever leaving the PC-File + program.

Although relational database-style table look-ups and business graphs are not a part of the current File Express release, David Berdan reports that his firm is already well along toward adding these capabilities. File Express is also being rewritten in C to give it even more snap and speed. (PC-File + has already made the transition to C.) Mr. Berdan also reports major work on upgrading ExpressGraph, his shareware business graphics program (registration: $49). Scatter plots, horizontal bars, and stockmarket-style high-low graphs, for example, will be added to the vertical bar, line, and pie charts ExpressGraph currently produces. Pen plotters will also be supported. Data can be loaded into ExpressGraph from most spreadsheet and database programs, including, of course, File Express.

The Certainty of Updates

As we said earlier, both PC-File + and File Express have a long and distinguished history marked by regular updates. We have presented a comparison of the two programs as they exist at this writing. But given the track records of Messrs. Button and Berdan, there is no question but that both products will be further improved and enhanced in the future. Ultimately, you can't go far wrong with either PC-File + or File Express, though for the reasons we have cited, we recommend the latter.

For more information on PC-File + and other ButtonWare products, contact: ButtonWare, Inc., Box 5786, Bellevue, WA 98006; Phone: (206) 454-0479.

File Express Registration

The registration fee for File Express is $69.95 plus $3.50 shipping and handling. (Washington state residents should add 8.1 percent sales tax; non-U.S. orders should add an additional $10.) In return, you receive a registered copy of the latest version of the program (a two-disk set), a professionally printed manual in a three-ring binder, and one year of free telephone support. In addition, you receive a free subscription to "ExpressNews," a quarterly newsletter containing news about Expressware products and tips and tricks for using Expressware programs. You also receive discounts on new versions of the program as they are released. Special arrangements and discounts are available to educational institutions. Contact Expressware for details.

SPECIAL DEAL

A special discount of $20 off the regular File Express registration fee is also available to readers of this book. When you call or write to register your copy of the program, mention the word GLOSS-BRENNER or print it on your check and you can register for $49.95, plus $3.50 shipping and handling. We have no relationship whatsoever with Expressware. When we called to verify details of the program, they suggested this special offer, and we are happy to oblige. To register or place an order, contact: Expressware, Inc., P.O. Box 230, Redmond, WA 98073; phone: (206) 788-0932. Visa and MasterCard are accepted.

Free-Text-Searching Software

The nice thing about a string-matching search program like LIST is speed. As we saw in Chapter 6, within seconds of downloading a list of public domain and shareware programs from a system like Compu-Serve, you can be offline and searching it with the LIST program. The one drawback is that the program will only find exact matches. If you were searching a file of movies, their directors, and their stars for "John Wayne," LIST would locate and display every reference to John Wayne, starting with the first one in the file. You could not use LIST to find *only* those films starring both John Wayne and Maureen O'Hara, though they would of course be among those that LIST found.

You could use a database management program like File Express to conduct such a search. Indeed, you could locate every film that starred John Wayne, was directed by John Ford, and was made after 1955. Just feed File Express the search formula and it will go right to the matching record. The problem is that before you can start searching you've got to also feed File Express the data. And that means setting up fields for a movie's title, stars, director, date, and so on, and keying in all of the information.

Free-text-searching programs offer you a middle path. They give you more powerful search functions than string-matching programs, but they do not require you to prepare a conventional database. If you have a text file on disk, you can use this kind of software to search it in fairly sophisticated ways. The one catch is that before you can begin searching, you must allow the program to prepare a separate index of the target file, and even with commercial free-text-searching programs, that can take some time.

Recommended Program

Glossbrenner's Choice:

IBM AnyWord—Free-Text-Searching Software

Free-text-searching software is relatively new as software categories go, and perhaps because of this and because such programs can be quite challenging to write, you probably won't encounter very many of them. One such program, Instant Recall by Michael Fremont, has recently become a commercial product. Mr. Fremont told us that it is now being marketed by Broderbund Software, Inc. as Memory Mate ($69.95).

Interestingly, at about the same time, AnyWord by Eric Balkan moved from the commercial realm into the realm of shareware. Mr. Balkan formerly marketed the product as Total Recall ($49.50), but recently sold that trademark to another party and decided to offer the program as shareware under the AnyWord name. Mr. Balkan has long made his living as a contract programmer and consultant for companies and government agencies, but he has an irrepressible entrepreneurial urge. With experience as one of CompuServe's first SIG sysops and as president of his own small publishing company, offering a powerful shareware program was an obvious next step.

AnyWord has a great deal to offer to anyone who needs free-text-searching capabilities at a very low price. As a commercial product it was purchased by attorneys, college professors, librarians, and businesspeople. According to Mr. Balkan, a writer in Connecticut has put all of Conan Doyle's Sherlock Holmes stories on disk (25 of them!) and uses AnyWord (née Total Recall) to access the data. In Arizona, a college professor has incorporated the program into his bulletin board system to let callers search his database of First Amendment cases.

Mr. Balkan maintains that at a registration fee of $35, AnyWord is "probably the most cost-effective way of rapidly retrieving text." And he may be right. Commercial free-text-searching programs sell anywhere from $70 (Memory Mate) to $700 (ZyIndex) to $1000 (Textbank). It is important to point out, however, that while AnyWord does work as advertised, in its current version it has a few rough edges. Most of these could be smoothed out with a few cosmetic changes and the expansion of one or two points in the 40-page on-disk manual. In addition, AnyWord creates its index of the target text file at a rate of about one double-spaced typewritten page (2K) per minute on a standard PC/XT 4.77 MHz machine. If your computer runs faster, less time will be required, but AnyWord may still be somewhat slower at indexing than many commercial programs. When searching, however, it can keep up with the best of them.

Mr. Balkan acknowledges these problems, noting that a *Washington Post* reviewer said that the program was as user-friendly as a wet cat, but that he was using it profitably after a couple of hours. Mr. Balkan is working on the rough spots, but until they have been corrected, the program's README.1ST file alerts users to expect to spend one to two hours before being able to do any useful work.

That's the bad news. The good news is that in return for your time investment you will have a program that can search your text files with much of the sophistication offered by commercial online information systems like DIALOG, BRS, and the Dow Jones News/Retrieval Service's //TEXT feature. (For a full explanation of such services, see *How to Look It Up Online*.) Indeed, if you have ever used DIALOG's Knowledge Index, you will have an excellent idea of how to use AnyWord since Mr. Balkan patterned the program after that product.

Space prohibits a complete explanation of AnyWord's features. However, you should know that after a text file has been indexed by the program, you can search using wildcards (searching for "comput?" will retrieve computer, computing, computation, and so on); the Boolean operators AND/OR/NOT; and proximity searches (finding one search term within a specified number of characters of another search term).

As with commercial online information systems, you can also use search sets. For example, if your first search request was for "JOHN WAYNE AND MAUREEN O'HARA," the results of that search would be Set 1. If on your next search you wanted to look for every movie in Set 1 that also contained the year 1952, you could enter: -1 AND 1952. The program will notify you of the number of occurrences ("hits" in information retrieval talk) it has found for each search term individually and for all of the terms in your search taken as a whole. You can review your sets and their search results at any time. And, when you are ready to look at a result, you have only to hit <D> for "Display" and tell the program which set and hit you want to see.

You can also extract the text you have found and store a copy of it in a different file. You can look at an alphabetical list of indexed words at any time (as you can on DIALOG with the EXPAND command). You can "shell out" to run a DOS command or call another program, and be automatically returned to AnyWord when you are finished. And you can control the default number of characters or lines that can separate two search terms.

You can control virtually everything else about the program as well, including the "stop words" you do not want it to include in its index. Indeed it is in setting these parameters that most of the complexity arises. The program itself is not difficult to use, particularly if you have ever used an online information system. Fortunately, Mr. Balkan supplies a file containing all of the parameters the program needs, as well as a preindexed demonstration file.

FreeTip: About all you really need to do to point AnyWord at one of your own files is to rename the supplied PROFILE.MOV to something else (like TEST.PRO) and bring it into your word processing program. Look for the line reading FILES=. Replace whatever is to the right of the equals sign with the file you want to index. Save TEST.PRO to disk, and key in INDEXER TEST.PRO. That will set the indexing program to work indexing the file you have specified in TEST.PRO. When the indexing program is finished, key in FINDER TEST.PRO to start the main AnyWord program, and search away. Note that the entire manual is available via menus when you are using the program.

Scheduled enhancements include the ability to index and append new text to previously indexed files and the ability to deal with files larger than one megabyte. Such features may already have been incorporated as you read this. The registration fee is $35, and it entitles you to free telephone support, news of updates, and special discounts. A printed manual is available for $10. Contact: Eric Balkan, Packet Press, 14704 Seneca Castle Ct., Gaithersburg, MD 20878.

FreeTip: Packet Press also offers at least three on-disk databases. The Movie Database is a two-disk package ($10) that contains basic information about more than 4000 films, including title, release date, director, screenwriter, MPAA rating, and major cast members. A package called *386 World: A Buying Guide* is a database of hardware, software, books, and other products designed to help you make the most of machines built around Intel's 80386 processor. There is also a database of some 400 PC publications and writers ($79). All three databases have been indexed and are ready for immediate searching with AnyWord. Mr. Balkan has also begun to publish book excerpts on disk through a shareware-style product line he calls "BookScan."

---

dBASE and Other Commercial Programs

Flat file databases are enormously capable, but for the ultimate in PC database power, one must turn to a commercial relational database management system (DBMS). According to *InfoWorld* (24 August 1987),

> dBASE III Plus is currently the most popular relational database on the PC market. Even though a number of competing programs offer more speed, power, and ease of use—sometimes at a lower price—dBASE III Plus has been able to hold on to its preeminent position. . . . Many unseasoned computer users aren't even aware that any other package is available. We've seen it purchased time and again by very small organizations that simply want to produce mailing labels—a criminal act of overkill.

The program lists for $695 in its single-user version; dBASE IV has been announced but has not been released at this writing.

We cannot advise you on whether you need a full-blown DBMS program or not. If you're in doubt, contact your local computer user group, as discussed in Chapter 3. We can virtually guarantee that someone there will be able to help you, for it was to answer such questions that user groups were created in the first place.

If you do decide you need a commercial relational database program,

however, you should know that public domain and shareware libraries
are filled with files that can help you get the most out this kind of software. This is because most commercial DBMS packages include a programming language that allows you to create your own applications.
Such languages are to their parent programs what the BASIC language
is to BASIC.COM, the BASIC interpreter that comes with your DOS
package. Consequently, public domain and shareware programmers
have created billing and accounting packages, menu-driven inventory
tracking programs, mailing list programs, tax preparation packages,
and many other applications in various DBMS languages. There are also
hundreds of short utility routines designed to be incorporated in your
own DBMS programs.

Not surprisingly, this kind of software is available from the same
sources discussed in Part II of this book. Nelson Ford's Public (software) Library offers over nine disks of programs and utilities for users
of dBASE II and III, for example. Both the Boston Computer Society
and the Capital PC Users Group have separate SIGs devoted to database-related subjects. And the HAL-PC group has separate SIGs for
Dataflex, dBASE, Paradox, R:BASE System V, and Revelation.

In the online world, you'll find that at this writing at least four of the
six commercial systems discussed in Chapter 7 have special database-
related SIGs. CompuServe and The Source offer SIGs sponsored by
Ashton-Tate, publisher of dBASE, Framework, MultiMate, Rapidfile,
and other products. The Source also offers a SIG sponsored by Nan-
tucket Corporation, publisher of the Clipper dBASE language compiler.
A similar Nantucket-sponsored conference can be found on BIX. There
is also a Source SIG sponsored by Data Based Solutions, Inc., publisher
of *Data Based Advisor* magazine. GEnie offers a RoundTable sponsored
by the same firm, and on BIX you'll find a conference called DBMS.

The online database-related SIGs can be especially useful. You can
use their membership rosters to locate consultants or simply other users
with similar problems. The conferencing and electronic mail facilities
can be used to discuss those problems or ask questions of the membership. And in the library sections you will find not only downloadable
programs and utilities for your particular DBMS package but magazine
articles devoted to various DBMS topics. The SIGs sponsored by Data
Based Solutions contain many articles and programs originally published in the firm's magazine. The Ashton-Tate SIGs contain articles
that originally appeared in the company's monthly *TechNotes* magazine.
The Ashton-Tate SIGs also give you a direct electronic mail pipeline to
the company's customer service department.

For more information on print subscriptions to *TechNotes*, contact:
Ashton-Tate, 20101 Hamilton Avenue, Torrance, CA 90502; phone:

(800) 828-2514 or (213) 329-9989. For more information about *Data Based Advisor*, contact: Data Based Solutions, Inc., 1975 Fifth Avenue, San Diego, CA 92101; phone: (619) 236-1182.

A Look Ahead

No single type of software has done more to promote the use of personal computers than the electronic spreadsheet. Adopted by businesspeople because of its incredible ability to quickly answer "What if. . . ?" questions, the spreadsheet has remained the mainstay of "serious" applications software. Unfortunately, the price of most commercial spreadsheet products has remained as lofty as their powers. Which is why you will be happy to know that not only have we found a shareware spreadsheet, but it is a spreadsheet that bears a striking resemblance to the leading commercial program in the field. As we'll see in the next chapter, it is a program that's as easy as, er, 1-2-3.

15

Spreadsheets, Lotus 1-2-3, and Accounting

NUMBER CRUNCHERS

Electronic spreadsheet software made the PC revolution. The two Steves (Jobs and Wozniak) may have designed and marketed the first commercial personal computer, but it was the two Dans (Bricklin and Flystra) and a Bob (Frankston) who forced the Steves out of the Jobs family garage and into new quarters capable of keeping up with the demand for Apple II computers. It wasn't until Bricklin, Frankston, and Flystra began selling a little 20K program called "VisiCalc" that corporate America realized a personal computer was something it could not live without. For a time, Apple computers were actually referred to as "VisiCalc machines," all of which validates once again the primacy of software over hardware.

VisiCalc, for those who tuned in late, was the first electronic spreadsheet program and the first commercial program of real significance in the microcomputer era. Introduced in April 1979, its principal benefit was to allow corporate planners, executives, and anyone else accustomed to preparing paper-based spreadsheets to ask "What if . . ." questions of their data: What if the prime rate rises by a quarter of a point? How will that affect the cost of completing this project? What if we add another store? What will its monthly sales have to average over the first year to pay for our initial investment? And so on.

A Taxing Example

If the term "spreadsheet" is unfamiliar, you need only recall the last tax return you filed to immediately grasp its meaning. If you filed the long form, you know that most of the figures on your Form 1040 came from somewhere else. Namely Schedules A, B, and if you run your own business, C and SE. Plus whatever other special schedules you must file. Each schedule guides you through a series of calculations (for business expenses, charitable contributions, and so on). The results of these calculations are then transferred to Form 1040, meaning that most of the numbers on Form 1040 depend on other numbers and other calculations done on other forms.

To appreciate the value of spreadsheet software and the impact it made on American business, imagine that you're sealing your tax return envelope one April 14th and suddenly realize that you forgot to include a major deduction. After your stomach returns to normal, you remove the completed forms from the envelope and set to work recalculating everything. By hand.

Hell hath no drudgery like redoing a tax return in the middle of an April night. We apologize for bringing up such an unpleasant thought, but we did it to make a point. And the point is this: If your tax return had been prepared with an electronic spreadsheet program, you could change any single figure on any schedule, and all of the figures that depended upon it would *automatically* change accordingly.

That is the essential power of spreadsheet software. And it is the reason why a corporate executive can key in a change in the marginal tax rate or the inflation factor or anything else and immediately see the effect on his or her bottom line. It is also the reason why a sales clerk can key in the number of units sold and have the computer automatically issue an invoice with all of the correct calculations, or why the payroll department can key in the number of hours worked by a given employee and have the computer automatically calculate his or her pay, withholding, and deductions. In short, as with database management software, an electronic spreadsheet can be a powerful engine capable of driving applications ranging from cash flow analysis and income statements to loan analysis and payroll.

Layout and Operations

Personal computer spreadsheets are essentially a grid. They consist of rows numbered along the left side of the screen, from top to bottom, and columns designated by letters running across the top of the screen from left to right. Each intersection of a row and a column forms a cell. Just as the lines of latitude and longitude on a map let you precisely locate any point, the numbering and lettering scheme of a spreadsheet lets you refer to each cell with a unique address (A1, C37, DD128, or whatever). This setup is what gives you so much control over your data, for it provides an easy way to refer to each individual piece of information when you want the program to do something.

Thus if you've got gross profit in cell A1 and expenses in cell B1, you can tell the program that it should subtract B1 from A1 and put the results in C1—or DZ173 or wherever else you like. What's more, you can permanently attach those instructions to the target cell by assigning it a formula. From then on, whenever you change the data in cells A1 or B1, the program will automatically execute the formula and change the contents of C1 to match.

The Advent of Lotus

VisiCorp, the company formed to market VisiCalc, was wildly successful. To capitalize more fully on that success, the firm decided that it needed a graphics and statistics package to complement its primary product. It soon contracted with Mitchell Kapor, a former Yale student, teacher of transcendental meditation, and disc jockey (the vinyl kind), who held a masters degree in psychology and had written a statistics and graphing program called Tiny Troll.

In 1980, Kapor delivered VisiPlot and VisiTrend. The programs were introduced in April 1981, and after the first six months had earned him nearly half a million dollars in royalties, thanks to a contract that paid him a 33 percent royalty. (Today's software publishers have a much better understanding of the market and royalty contracts are more on the order of 10 to 15 percent.) VisiCorp was happy to buy Mr. Kapor's rights to the programs for $1.2 million in 1982.

Mr. Kapor wanted to create additional products for VisiCorp or some other company to distribute. But things did not work out that way, and with $400,000 of his royalty money he started Lotus Development, Inc. One year and about $2.6 million in venture capital later, the company formally introduced its first product at the December 1982 COMDEX (Computer Dealer's Exposition) in Las Vegas. The product was Lotus 1-2-3, and personal computer software has never been the same since.

Lotus took the basic VisiCalc model to a higher power. Written in assembly language by Jonathan Sachs and largely designed by Kapor, the program offered a much larger spreadsheet (524,288 cells to Visi-Calc's 16,000) with a dozen more functions. Lotus also added a database manager and a business graphics program. All three applications were integrated into a single package, which is why the product is called 1-2-3. (The name Lotus undoubtedly has its roots in Mitchell Kapor's past as a teacher of TM.) The integration made it easy to share data among the various modules, so you could work up a spreadsheet, hit a few keys, and immediately display the results as a graph.

Shareware Spreadsheets

Lotus 1-2-3 was clearly the right product at the right time, and it not only made pots of money for everyone originally associated with it, it set the standards for an entire category of software. Those standards not only include performance but also the way you interact with a spreadsheet program and the various features it offers.

When we wrote *How to Get FREE Software* in 1983, we looked long and hard for a spreadsheet that we could recommend. At the time, the only viable shareware spreadsheet program was PC-Calc. Written by Bill Willis, the program then offered 36 columns and 255 rows and was patterned after SuperCalc, an early Lotus competitor. The latest version offers 256 columns and 64 rows, as well as many sophisticated financial and statistical functions, though a newer edition (PC-Calc+) should be available as you read this. Still shareware, it is offered by ButtonWare as PC-Calc and by Expressware as ExpressCalc. Mr. Willis is a partner with David Berdan in Expressware (Chapter 14), and it is our understanding that the principal difference between the two products is that PC-Calc can import data only from PC-File databases, while ExpressCalc is more catholic in its tastes. PC-Calc/ExpressCalc remains what *PC Magazine* praised as "A SuperCalc, Version 1, knock-off with a good manual and a shareware price ($49)."

In the intervening years, PC-Calc has been joined by spreadsheets like FreeCalc, QubeCalc and its memory-resident version, InstaCalc, as well as several others. All of them are fine programs, but it is our feeling that if you're going to learn a spreadsheet you should get as close as you can to the Lotus 1-2-3 standard without paying retail. At the very least, this will allow you to effortlessly exchange worksheet files with 1-2-3 users. But equally important, it will give you access to the enormous number of public domain and shareware support files and programs designed to work with 1-2-3. It also means that you can use virtually any book written about how to make the most of Lotus. At this writing, there is only one program that meets that criterion, and it is so good that it will knock your socks off. The shareware registration fee is a mere $30, compared to $495 (list) for Lotus 1-2-3 release 2.01.

Recommended Program

Glossbrenner's Choice:

IBM Spreadsheet Disk 1—As-Easy-As

Written by David A. Schulz, As-Easy-As version 3.0 is packed with features and power. But to tell you about them we have to "talk spreadsheet" and use a number of terms that may be unfamiliar to you. Consequently, if you have never used spreadsheet software before, you may want to buy or borrow a book about Lotus 1-2-3 and how to use it before reading the following section.

The most useful way to present As-Easy-As is to follow *PC Magazine's* lead and organize things more or less as a chart highlighting major features. *PC* and *InfoWorld* do excellent, in-depth product comparisons of hardware and software products, usually focusing on a particular application each issue. The framework we will be following is based on the spreadsheet chart that appeared in the February 16, 1988 issue, though *PC* will certainly have cycled back to spreadsheets again as you read this.

In addition to commercial products like Lotus 1-2-3, PFS:First Choice, and Microsoft Works, that issue also considered the shareware programs FreeCalc, ExpressCalc, and Qube- and InstaCalc. Unfortunately, As-Easy-As was not reviewed, but that omission will be corrected here. The information comes from the program's author, the printed manual all registered users receive, and our own testing of the product. To offer a frame of reference, we have also included information on Lotus 1-2-3, release 2.01, the latest version of the classic release 1A on which As-Easy-As is modeled.

AS-EASY-AS vs. LOTUS 1-2-3

Size	As-Easy-As	Lotus 1-2-3
Maximum columns and rows	256 × 1024	256 × 8192
Range of column widths	0 to 72	1 to 240
Database can be larger than spreadsheet	No	No

By setting an As-Easy-As column to 0, you can make it disappear. You will always know that there is still data in the column because each time you move the cursor to a cell within it, the cursor shrinks from its normal fat, highlight bar to a small blinking bar of the sort you see in DOS.

The As-Easy-As database is limited by the amount of free memory you have to work with. Hypothetically, you could have as many as 1024 rows by 256 columns, but realistically, if you tried to fill up every single cell you would very quickly run out of memory.

Lotus operates the same way, though there are integrated programs with databases limited only by available disk space. Unfortunately, this tends to slow down response time since the program must go out to disk to get the required information.

Enhancing Performance	As-Easy-As	Lotus 1-2-3
Sparse memory matrix	Yes	Yes
Uses expanded memory	No	Yes
Uses math coprocessor	No	Yes

The term "sparse memory matrix" means that when you put data into a cell, the program allocates only the memory needed to store that data. Other spreadsheet programs, notably Lotus release 1A, allocate memory for entire blocks of the spreadsheet, even if you are entering a single cell of data. Thus if you start with an empty spreadsheet and enter a number in, say, column H, row 75, they will allocate memory for all of the cells in the rectangular block that starts at A1 in the upper left, and runs down to A75 and then across all rows to column H.

As-Easy-As in written in Turbo Pascal using an overlay technique that gets around the current version of that compiler's 64K code size limit. This gives you the option of either leaving the overlay information out on disk or allowing them to load in with the program. If you leave them on disk (by starting the program with the command ASEASY /O), you will have an additional 70K of memory to work with. (You will need a minimum of 256K in your system to run As-Easy-As.) The overlays contain primarily menu information and are brought in only when a menu is activated. On a floppy-based system you will notice a small delay, but the delay is negligible if you run with a hard disk. We tried the program on a hard disk both with and without the overlays loaded into memory and could detect no difference.

Mr. Shulz reports that math coprocessor support could easily be added to the program, but that this would make it incompatible with any machine not equipped with an 8087 chip. Rather than have two versions of the same program in shareware channels, he opted not to do this.

Functions and Formulas	As-Easy-As	Lotus 1-2-3
Number of . . .		
Math functions	16	17
Logical functions	3	7
Financial functions	5	11
Date and time functions	5	11
Statistical functions	7	14
String functions	None	11
Logical and arithmetic operators	14	15

As we said earlier, a spreadsheet's power is rooted in the fact that you can attach formulas to cells instructing the program to perform some kind of automatic calculation using data entered in other cells. A *function* is like a prepackaged formula. Thus if you put @SQRT(A46) in a cell, the program would automatically calculate the square root of whatever happened to be in cell A46 and put it in the cell you have chosen. The "at" sign (@) is the first character of all functions in both programs. Math functions include things such as square root, pi, log, arc, sine, tangent, and so on. The only Lotus math function As-Easy-As does not offer is @ATAN2(x,y), the function for a four-quadrant arc tangent.

Logical functions deal with true and false tests. As-Easy-As offers @TRUE, @FALSE, and @IF(condition, x, y). The last function causes the program to look at a specified condition or test argument. If it is "true," then x is the value that will be used in whatever comes next. If not, then the value y will be used. Thus if you put @IF(F15>20,100,50) in a cell, you would be telling the program: "If the value in cell F15 is greater than 20, put 100 in this cell. If not, use 50." Logical functions can be used with other types of functions, of course, and you can couple them with logical operators such as greater-than (>) and less than or equal to(<=), as well as operators such as #AND# and #OR#. In As-Easy-As, "not" is handled by a function (@NOT).

Financial, date, and statistical functions are those such as @IRR (internal rate of return), @NPV (net present value), @MONTH, @TODAY, @COUNT(list), @STD (list), and @VAR(list). These last three examples will count the number of items and give you the standard deviation or the variance of all items in a specified list.

Macro Capabilities	As-Easy-As	Lotus 1-2-3
Macros reside in worksheet	Yes	Yes
Macros reside in library	No	No

The term "macro" is short for "macro expansion," and as we know from the discussion of New Key in Chapter 9, this refers to the ability to load a single key with a series of keystrokes that will be executed whenever that one key is struck. Spreadsheet macros work in much the same way. However, they can do much more than simply duplicate keystrokes. This is because there are special macro commands that, considered as a whole, form a very powerful programming language. You can thus use macros to create customized applications, complete with menus, help screens, special prompts, and all the trimmings that will run in 1-2-3 or As-Easy-As the way a BASIC program runs in BASIC. The person who uses the application need never be aware that he or she is actually using a spreadsheet. The macros in both cases can be placed in any cell on the spreadsheet.

As we'll see at the end of this chapter, the availability of a "Lotus programming language" has stimulated the creation of hundreds of public domain spreadsheet templates and applications—everything from price-volume analysis to budgets and line-of-credit trackers. The majority of these were written for use with Lotus release 1A, and because the *functions* offered by 1A and As-Easy-As are virtually identical, you will be able to use them immediately.

However, the *macro language* used by As-Easy-As is not completely Lotus-compatible. Because macros duplicate keystrokes, the menu structures and commands used by the two programs would have to be absolutely identical to guarantee that a given macro could be used in both. As it happens, however, all of the "/X" macro commands offered by release 1A *will* work. Other 1A commands are recognized as well, though when you are programming a macro in As-Easy-As you will probably want to use its own name for the command. Where Lotus uses /XM to take you to a menu, for example, As-Easy-As uses MENUCALL. As-Easy-As also has at least two undocumented macro commands capable of reading data from the serial port (IOLABEL and IOVALUE). These were added at the request of a user who wanted to directly incorporate data produced (as ASCII characters) from his laboratory instruments.

FreeTip: Many spreadsheet users never feel the need to get into macro programming, and David Schulz reports that those of his registered users who do, start from scratch so that they can create a highly customized application. Sometimes that really is the easiest way to go. However, one of the benefits of public domain software is the opportunity it provides for adapting someone else's code to your own needs. If someone else has already worked out the programming logic and created an application you find appealing, you can save yourself a lot of work by modifying his or her code to suit your needs or incorporating pieces of it in your own program. Whether you're translating a public domain macro or building your own in As-Easy-As, you will find that books like David Paul Ewing's *1-2-3 Macro Library* (Que Corporation, 1985) can be a big help.

Worksheet Commands and Features	As-Easy-As	Lotus 1-2-3
Can do named range	Yes	Yes
Cursor keys enter cell data	Yes	Yes
Hides columns	Yes	Yes
Hides rows	No	No
Hides individual cell components	Yes	Yes
Has cell protection	Yes	Yes
Number of split screens	2	2
Split screens scroll independently	Yes	Yes
Split screens format independently	Yes	Yes
Can back-step through previous commands	Yes	Yes

continued

Warns against file overwrite	Yes	Yes
Does recalculation in logical order	Yes	Yes
Formats cells to display numbers as words	Yes	No
Has context-sensitive help	No	Yes

Both programs let you split the screen into two separately scrolling windows. You can think of this as folding the spreadsheet so you can look at two separate areas on the same screen. When you split the screen horizontally, a duplicate row of alphabetical designators appears at the boundary. When vertical windows are used, a duplicate column of row numbers appears. The windows can scroll independently or in sync. Both programs also offer a feature that allows you to freeze several rows and columns so that they remain on the screen as the spreadsheet scrolls. Lotus calls these devices "titles." In As-Easy-As they are called "headings."

As-Easy-As uses an "intelligent" or "natural" recalculation technique that lets the spreadsheet recalculate only those cells affected by whatever data you have entered. It does not blindly recalculate everything. And it does not process one formula until it has processed all of the other formulas upon which it depends. This technique makes the program quite fast at recalculating and allows you to recalculate row-wise or column-wise if you like.

Formatting cells to display numbers as words with As-Easy-As's [/*R*ange *F*ormat *T*ext] command lets you tell the program to display the actual formula attached to a cell within the cell itself, instead of displaying the numerical results of that formula.

As-Easy-As has a nice help function, but it is not "context-sensitive." That is, you cannot call for pop-up information about the task you are performing as you are performing it. Instead, you must back out to the "Ready" mode and hit <F1>. The help area offers 36 screens of information, accessible by topic menu or by paging. Since full-sized screens of text are used, each screen can contain a lot of information. Taken together, they form a mini-manual on how to use the program.

Data Exchange	As-Easy-As	Lotus 1-2-3
Merges contents of spreadsheets	Yes	Yes
Imports .WKS files	Yes	Yes
Exports .WKS files	Yes	Yes
Imports .WK1 files	Yes	Yes
Exports .WK1 files	No	Yes
Imports ASCII files	Yes	Yes
Exports ASCII files	Yes	Yes
Imports .DIF files	No	No
Exports .DIF files	No	No

Worksheet files ending in .WKS are in the format created by Lotus 1-2-3, release 1A. Files ending in .WK1 are created by release 2.01. The naming convention doesn't make much sense from the user's standpoint. It would have been a friendly gesture to have made the newer program produce files ending in .WK2 to match its release number. Fortunately, however, the two formats are very similar, and this allows As-Easy-As to read (import) either one of them. The similarity of file structure also allows the program to read .WRK files created by Symphony, another Lotus product, as well as worksheets created by commercial Lotus clone programs. When As-Easy-As saves information (exports), however, it uses the .WKS format.

Plain or delimited (with commas or spaces) ASCII text can be brought in as well. This means that you can develop data in File Express (Chapter 14) or some other database program, export it to an ASCII file, and bring it into As-Easy-As for further analysis.

Lotus does have a translation facility that lets you convert files to and from different formats, including the Data Interchange Format (.DIF) introduced by the creators of VisiCalc. But Lotus cannot import or export in these formats from within the main Lotus program. The DIF file format was invented by the creators of VisiCalc. Its main advantage is that it saves both text and data, automatically distinguishing between the two. A genuine DIF file contains words such as TABLE, VECTORS, and TUPLES to specify the order of the text and data.

You can tell As-Easy-As to bring numbers in as numbers so they can be used in calculations, or you can have the program treat numbers as text. Interestingly, we found that if you use the As-Easy-As /File Import Values (/FIV) command, you can bring a text file into the spreadsheet with all text intact and all numbers treated as numbers *without* first enclosing each line of text in quotation marks. If you want to achieve this same result with Lotus 1A and 2.01, you must go through the file and add quote marks to each line that is to be treated as text.

FreeTip: The one thing to remember about the As-Easy-As /FIV command is that each word in a line will be placed in its own column, so several spaces will separate each word. We would argue that this is not a problem considering the convenience the /FIV command affords. The command makes it easy, for example, to sign on to a remote database and download stock quotes or other labeled numerical information in whatever tabular format the database uses. You can then bring this information directly into your As-Easy-As spreadsheet for instant analysis. No need to run it through a word processor first to add the necessary quotes.

Printing	As-Easy-As	Lotus 1-2-3
Prints spreadsheets larger than 80 columns on a single page	Yes	Yes
Prints user-defined area	Yes	Yes

As-Easy-As lets you send setup commands to your printer from within the program, so you can tell your printer to use compressed type to fit more columns on a page. Next, you tell As-Easy-As what you want it to use as your right margin. If necessary, the program will print the spreadsheet in multiple pages, automatically breaking it at the correct margin boundary. You can then tape the two or more pages together along their vertical edges to view the entire spreadsheet.

FreeTip: To be sure, taping two halves of a spreadsheet together does not make for a particularly elegant presentation. One way

FreeTip continued

around this problem for those using an 80-column printer is Side-Ways, a program from Funk Software ($69.95). The program converts the characters in a .PRN file (a worksheet that has been printed to disk) into graphics images that it then sends to printer. The result is a sideways-printed spreadsheet. The program does a very nice job, but if your needs are not great, you may find that one of two public domain and shareware programs will serve just as well. These are PDSW ("public domain SideWays") by Donovan Kuhn and Side Writer by Robert W. Dea. PDSW can print *any* text file sideways, up to a maximum of 48 lines and 1024 columns, on an Epson or compatible printer, like the IBM Graphics Printer. Side Writer (shareware: $15) will work with Epson printers, HP ThinkJets, and compatibles, up to a maximum of 999 lines and 255 columns. We have included both on Glossbrenner's Choice IBM Spreadsheet Disk 1.

Graphics	**As-Easy-As**	**Lotus 1-2-3**
Number of graph types	4	5

The four graph types As-Easy-As offers are line, bar, pie chart, and XY. Lotus offers the same, but adds a fifth type: stacked bar graphs. Due no doubt to Mr. Schulz's training as a professional engineer, his program also offers log scales for either horizontal or vertical axes. Graphs can be instantly printed out in a choice of heights and widths, defined in pixels (picture elements) and in either high or low density. (See the FreeTip on The Draftsman at the end of this chapter if you want to generate even more elaborate business graphs from your spreadsheet data.)

Other Points of Interest

As you can see, As-Easy-As compares extremely favorably with Lotus 1-2-3 release 2.01. There even some features that are exclusive to the shareware program. You can choose to use the program with either the classic Lotus horizontal bounce-bar style menus or with pop-up vertical panel-style menus. The pop-ups can be set to appear anywhere you like on the screen. There is also a macro command to produce tones on the speaker [TONE freq., duration], which means you can incorporate a variety of sounds and even complete tunes in your spreadsheet. (A sample worksheet MUSIC.WKS demonstrating this capacity comes with the package.) You can also easily control the color of everything that appears on your screen. As-Easy-As automatically senses the kind of graphics board you are using and will work with the CGA, EGA, Hercules, and AT&T screen adaptors. It also works on the IBM's PS/2 computers. Mr. Shulz reports that the program has been successfully tested on the Heath/Zenith Z-152, IBM PCs with the monochrome adaptor, Compaqs, and the IMB PCjr.

The registration fee for As-Easy-As is $30. This includes a copy of the latest revision of the program, a 150-page paperback manual, a quick-reference command sheet that displays all menus and their interconnections, and telephone support from the program's author. The manual is also available separately, priced on a sliding scale. For 1 to 10 copies, the cost is $30 each. For 11 to 50 copies, the cost is $27 each. For 51 to 100 copies, the cost is $24 each, and so on. Site licenses are also available ($500), and there is a special site licensee discount on copies of the manual. Mr. Schulz says that quite a few corporations and educational institutions have registered under this plan.

For more information, contact: Mr. David Schulz, TRIUS Inc., 15 Atkinson Street, Lynn, MA 01905; phone: (617) 596-1594. Incidently, nearly half of the registration card you are supposed to fill in and return to put your name on file with TRIUS, Inc. is devoted to space for user comments and suggestions. Mr. Schulz is quite serious about this. Good as As-Easy-As is, he says, "I'm obsessed with making it even better. I'm always working with it." One enhancement scheduled for the very near future is a boost in the program's already impressive recalculation speed. "The new compiler (Turbo Pascal version 4.0) is just a fantastic environment," Schulz says. "With just preliminary coding, with no optimization, it increases As-Easy-As's recalc speed by 100 percent. So the big boys are really going to have to watch out!"

Accounting: GL, AP, AR, and PR

Double-entry bookkeeping hasn't changed much since the Florentines invented the practice shortly before Columbus discovered America. We no longer sit on high stools making journal entries with quill pens, but for most of us, doing the books is still a laborious chore. Perversely, putting everything on the computer can just make things worse. Often it is more trouble than it's worth, particularly if yours is a small business doing, say, less than $5 million a year.

But it doesn't have to be this way, if you can find the right program. Whether you go the commercial or the PD/shareware route, there are basically three alternatives. You can use a database program like one of

Ashton-Tate's dBASE products, you can use a spreadsheet like Lotus 1-2-3, or you can use a program specifically written as an accounting package. The advantage of the first two alternatives is that whether you start from scratch or modify a public domain file, you can create a highly customized package. The disadvantages are that you must be fluent in either the dBASE or Lotus language and already own or buy one of those commercial products.

You can steer a middle course and buy a set of commercial templates designed to run on Lotus. CPA Plus ($199) and Ready to Run Accounting ($199) fall into this category. But as *InfoWorld* noted in one of its product comparisons (16 November 1987),

> Lotus 1-2-3 simply wasn't designed as an accounting system. Accounting systems are specialized financial databases chock-full of information designed to be stored on disk. . . . Although an accounting solution based on 1-2-3 does work, it reminds us of using a screwdriver to hammer a nail to the wall. It does the job, but it's not the right tool.

Most businesses follow the third route and use a dedicated accounting program, or set of programs including general ledger (GL), accounts payable (AP), accounts receivable (AR), and payroll (PR). And here there are lots of commercial, public domain, and shareware programs to choose from. The problem with many commercial packages is that they are overpriced and overly complex. The problem with the free alternative is that much of what is available simply isn't up to the job. Many have a clunky feeling to them. Others lack polish and essential features. Even more important, many lack some indication of who wrote the program and how it was created. It is one thing to take a chance on a public domain game or printer utility and quite another to entrust your company's finances to an unsupported program of uncertain origin.

Recommended Program

Glossbrenner's Choice:

IBM Accounting Disk 1—
Jerry Medlin's Shareware Accounting Programs:
GL/AP/AR/PR

Fortunately, a number of excellent shareware accounting programs are available as well, and the PC-GL, PC-AP, PC-AR, and PC-PR programs written and supported by Jerry Medlin are among the very best. These programs are aimed squarely at small businesses and companies that want the benefits of commercial quality accounting software without being required to pay for modules they will never use. "The typical small business writes perhaps 100 to 150 checks per month," Mr. Medlin says, "and most have many, many fewer general ledger accounts than the 4000 that the PC-GL module allows for. Most of my registered users typically find that they need and use only one or two modules." (Registration is $35 per module.)

Mr. Medlin started his career as an industrial engineer. "But I got tired of following people around with a stopwatch to eliminate their jobs." Mr. Medlin left that position and became involved with a franchised mobile bookkeeping service. "That didn't last," he told us with a chuckle, "but it did get me interested in accounting. I now teach accounting courses at a nearby junior college and do some contract work for small businesses. But my main activity is supporting the programs and generally trying to take care of my registered users."

Jerry Medlin told us that his first computer was a Tandy Model 1 with 16K of memory and a BASIC interpreter. "They told me I couldn't write an accounting package on it, but I did, for my own uses." All of the current modules are written in Turbo Pascal, and because they do everything in memory, each has a fast, responsive feel. (The Turbo Pascal source code is available for between $95 and $125 depending on the module, should you want to customize or modify the program.) The Accounts Payable and Accounts Receivable modules require a minimum of 256K each, while the other two can run with 128K each. But in every case, you will need 512K of memory to use a module's maximum number of accounts, transactions, employees, and so on.

As we have said before, the most crucial questions to ask of a program are very often "How many?" and "How long?" We'll be doing just that in a moment as we look at each module. But before getting into specifics, we should note that with all four modules you can add, change, and delete data on a single screen, use the 10-key pad to both scroll and enter data without disengaging the <NumLock> key, and print reports at any time in any order to the screen, a file, or to the printer. A printer capable of printing 96 columns is required to make full use of the Payroll module, but all the others are designed to print in 80 columns. Also, historical data are always saved for later review in every case.

PC-GL Double-Entry General Ledger Program

Since general ledger is the one accounting function almost everyone uses, we'll spend a bit more time with it than with the other modules. We should say at the beginning that none of Mr. Medlin's programs is designed to teach you double-entry bookkeeping and accounting, though if you've had some experience in these areas you will know immediately how everything works. (The documentation includes instructions for using PC-GL as a simple single-entry system for keeping track of your income and expenses.) However, PC-GL does come with a file containing the standard chart of accounts commonly used by professional accountants. There are accounts for inventory, cash on hand, leasehold improvements, and so on. You can delete or modify these in any way or you can simply start from scratch.

You can tell the program to use any length of accounting period you choose, and as noted, you can print reports to the printer, a file, or the screen at any time. The one exception is the general ledger report. This report *must* be printed on the printer before the program will save historical data and allow you to begin a new accounting period. This is in keeping with the Generally Accepted Accounting Principles (G.A.A.P.) published by the Accounting Standards Board, for it forces the creation of a paper audit trail. The program will save up to 12 accounting periods. In addition, once an amount has been posted to an account, the only way to modify the account balance is to post an offsetting transaction to the same account. This, too, helps ensure the creation of an audit trail.

Account numbers can be three digits long (000–999), but the maximum number of items on the chart of accounts is 800. This offers most people plenty of room to group similar or related accounts into the same subrange of account numbers. When you are entering data you will be prompted for the account number, but should you forget which one you want to use, you can simply enter 999. This allows you to immediately scroll through all of the names you have assigned to your various accounts until you find the one you want. There is no need to leave the data-entry screen.

Account codes are two-digit numbers, the first of which determines the account type (assets, income, net profit, and so on). The second digit specifies the totaling level (what totals and subtotals will appear on reports). You may enter up to five digits to serve as a check or reference number, and there is a feature to automatically increment the number when you are entering sequentially numbered checks. The account description may be up to 27 alphanumeric characters long. The data-entry field is ten digits, so the maximum transaction amount you can enter is $99,999,999.99—one penny less than $10 million—should the occasion ever arise.

Every entry is verified instantly, and a maximum of 4000 transactions are permitted per accounting period (assuming you have 512K of memory or more). The program can print the following reports: chart of accounts, transactions, general ledger, income statement, balance sheet (three-columns), and account summary. The account summary is a summary of the transactions in any one account, and you can request that the program give you a report for any or all prior accounting periods, up to a maximum of 12 periods.

When you register your copy of PC-GL, in addition to the latest version you will receive a program to permanently configure certain PC-GL features. These include color selection, laser printer support, number of months to save (you can change the program's default of 12 to any number between 1 and 30), default data drive or path, income statement heading, balance sheet heading, and footers (short comments to be inserted at the end of a report) for the income statement and balance sheet. Registered users also receive a program (ANNUAL.COM) that will enable PC-GL to print a single general ledger report for an entire year.

PC-AP Accounts Payable Program

When we asked Mr. Medlin whether his programs were integrated he said, "No, they aren't, and deliberately so. Generally it takes far too much time for a PC to transfer all of the postings from one module into another. It really slows things down. Instead, I advise users to take, say, the sales total from AR and put it into GL as a single entry. This can usually be done in less than five minutes."

Mr. Medlin pointed out that there is one exception regarding module integration, however. The Accounts Payable module *is* integrated with the GL module. Thus, as the documentation notes, "You must have PC-GL in order to use the Accounts Payable program."

PC-AP will post checks to PC-GL (cash basis) and invoices for accrual-basis accounting. Vendors are automatically sorted in alphabetical order. Invoices can be sorted by due date. Checks are printed on standard check forms. The documentation even gives you the NEBS (New England Business Systems) form number, should you wish to use that supplier. (The configuration program supplied to registered users lets you choose an alternate check form, with the stub on the bottom of the check.) The check listing is printed in check number order, and PC-AP can handle up to 1500 vendors and invoices per month.

The PC-AP main menu contains the following selections:

```
Enter or Change Vendors
Enter, Change or Select Invoices
Print Checks For Invoices Selected
Print Check Listing
Print Vendor Activity Report
Print Mailing Labels
Print Vendor Listing
Start a New Accounting Period
Export Vendor Data to ASCII File
Save Data and End
```

PC-AR Accounts Receivable Program

This module offers 30, 60, and 90-day aging, and lets you summarize sales by sales codes, and access different late charges for different customers. The program can handle a maximum of 2000 customers and 2500 charges per accounting period. Customers are automatically sorted by customer code. Either numeric or alphanumeric customer codes (to a maximum of 10 characters) may be used. You may also have invoice numbers of up to five alphanumeric characters. Statements and mailing labels are sorted automatically by ZIP code. (Most elements of the customer address can be up to 31 characters long.) Statements are printed only for customers with ending balances for the period. You can also automatically post fixed amounts for each customer.

The PC-AR main menu includes the following items:

> Enter or Change Sales Codes
> Enter or Change Customers
> Enter or Change Charges and Payments
> Print Mailing Labels
> Print Charges & Payments Listing
> Print Accounts Receivable Ledger
> Print Statements
> Print Sales Summary
> Print Customer Activity Report
> Apply Charges & Payments
> Print Customer Listing
> Export Customer Data
> Save Data and End

In addition to being an accounts receivable program, PC-AR is also a sales analysis tool. Each charge or payment is posted to a sales code, and you may have up to 80 of them. Each code can be up to three alphanumeric characters long; each description, up to 21 characters. When you request a sales summary report, charges and payments are thus listed by sales code and description. In addition, customer data can be exported to a .PRN file, which you can then import into programs like Lotus 1-2-3, Reflex, or As-Easy-As to analyze your sales with a spreadsheet's power, including displaying things graphically.

As distributed, PC-AR prints customer statements on a common statement form. (The names and toll-free numbers of several forms vendors, along with the corresponding item number of the statement form you will need, are given in the documentation.) Among other things, the configuration program supplied to all registered users allows you to print statements on plain paper, customize the statement header, and add a custom message as a footer.

PC-PR Payroll Writing Program

PC-PR can generate checks for a maximum of 500 employees, paying each up to twice (1000 checks) per pay period. Before running the program, you must first key in your employer data, including the name of your firm and your federal and state identification numbers. You may also specify up to six payroll deductions. The first deduction is always federal income tax withholding (the current federal tax tables are built into the program), but you can specify the rest, including the current applicable FICA (Social Security) percentage and cutoff amount. The California state income tax tables are also built into the program and are available for use as a deduction if you so choose. You may specify an annual limit for each deduction, except federal income tax.

Next you must prepare a screen of data for each employee. Employee name and street address may be up to 25 characters long each. A total of 25 characters is alloted to city, state, and ZIP code. There are also blanks for Social Security number, marital status, number of allowances claimed, hourly wage rate, and department number. For salaried employees, the hourly rate can be set to the entire pay period amount. You would then specify one hour of pay when actually preparing the check. Also, if the employee is exempt from federal tax, you may enter "E" for allowances. Or you may enter "S" if you want to enter the federal tax from the keyboard.

You can go back and make changes at any time, of course, but once you have these components set up, you're ready to begin issuing checks. The program prints checks on a common form with the check stub on the bottom of the check. A list of check suppliers and item numbers is provided in the documentation. The configuration program supplied to all registered users lets you choose a different format if you like.

There are blanks on the employee record for date, check number (up to four characters), total hours, overtime hours, other income, and non-taxable payments. To prepare a check, you merely call up an employee's screen and fill in the necessary blanks. The program will then automatically perform all calculations and ask if you want to print the check. If so, the check will be printed then and there. If not, you can abort, make changes, or move onto the next employee, and no data will be saved.

As the documentation notes, the program is not recommended for any payroll applications that require FICA wages to be different from taxable wages. "This includes companies that deduct for pension and deferred compensation plans, supplemental unemployment compensation plans, and students working for private schools. . . . If you have different payroll periods for different employees, the program won't work for you." There are also some situations in which you must enter amounts manually. The program can automatically handle state income taxes that are a fixed percentage of income or a fixed percentage of federal tax, but other than the state tax for California, "I am unable to support state withholding. Most users have found that it doesn't slow them down too much to manually enter this amount."

In addition to receiving a configuration program, registered users receive a separate program for printing W-2 forms at the end of the year. Finally, here is the PC-PR menu:

> Enter or Change Employee Data
> Enter or Change Payroll Checks
> Print Employee Listing
> Print Payroll Check Listing
> Print Payroll Ledger
> Zero Employee Balances
> Enter or Change Employer Data
> Export Employee Data
> End Processing

Registration and Support

Each module comes with an on-disk manual that runs 15 to 25 pages. As noted earlier, neither the programs nor their manuals will teach you the finer points of accounting. But if you've been doing your books by hand, you don't really need that kind of instruction. If you've never run an accounting program before, you'll find that accounting is largely a matter of good common sense and the manuals are written from that perspective. In our opinion, Mr. Medlin's programs and on-disk manuals are so well done that even complete novices can tap their power with very little trouble.

Registration is $35 per module, and it entitles you to a disk with a copy of the module and the appropriate configuration program to let you change the module's default settings. It also entitles you to telephone support from Mr. Medlin. For more information, contact: Mr. Jerry Medlin, 310 S. Jefferson Street, Napa, CA 94559.

Lotus 1-2-3 Programs, Templates, and Utilities

Finally, as you would expect given the power and versatility of the Lotus programming language, there is a great deal of public domain software and shareware that takes advantage of it. (A somewhat smaller number of files is available for Lotus Development Corporation's Symphony product.) There are literally hundreds of macros, spreadsheet templates, complete applications programs, and utilities designed to work with Lotus 1-2-3's Add-In Manager, for you to use or adapt to your own purposes. The topics covered include many of the financial, investment, and analytical applications traditionally associated with Lotus. But we know of at least one template that lets you use Lotus to spec type—you choose one of 30 popular type styles, enter the character count, point size, leading, and line length, and the program will calculate the length of the typeset copy in lines and picas. (The author is Mark Schaeffer; CompuServe: 72457,1442.)

A shareware 1-2-3 add-in by Gerald Lerman (CompuServe: 73557,1453) will simplify the task of editing formulas with the <F2> key by causing the program to display formulas with range names instead of cell coordinates. Thus instead of editing @INDEX (G11..K23,0,D14), you can edit @INDEX(VALUES,0,COUNT). As we have said, the list goes on and on.

The distribution channels for Lotus-related public domain and shareware software are the same as those discussed in Part II of this book. All three of the user groups profiled in Chapter 3 have Lotus/Symphony SIGs. The Boston Computer Society (BCS) has a SIG called Lotus/Boston. However, judging from several years' worth of its newsletter, this 3500-member group could be more dynamic. At this writing, there are only about 14 Lotus disks and seven Symphony disks in its library, each of which sells for $7. We may be judging the group unfairly—its monthly meetings may be dynamite for all we know—but if you don't live in the Boston area, there is little benefit to selecting "Lotus/Boston" as one of the two SIG newsletter subscriptions that come with your BCS membership.

HAL-PC and the Capital PC user groups are a different story. The newsletters published by both groups contain regular columns for Lotus or Symphony users. You may want to join these groups just to have access to this information, particularly the "Lotus Questions and Answers" column Betty Brooks has long done for the *HAL-PC User Journal*. Serious Lotus users will also want a subscription to the company's monthly *Lotus* magazine ($18 per year). Contact: Lotus Publishing Corporation, P.O. Box 9123, Cambridge, MA 02139-9123; phone (617) 494-1192.

The best mail order source of Lotus files is unquestionably Nelson Ford's Public (software) Library (PsL). At last count, there were over 38 "small program" and over 20 "large program" disks of Lotus and Symphony utilities, macros, templates, and add-ins. Indeed, there are so many Lotus and Symphony-related programs that Mr. Ford has prepared a dedicated Lotus catalog disk (PsL Disk #992). The disk contains one-line descriptions for each of the files available on the more than 58 Lotus disks in the PsL library. The disk contains the PsL Lotus catalog as a text file, which you can easily search with Vernon Buerg's

LIST program. But it also contains the index as a Lotus and as a Symphony file, so you can use one of those programs to do your searching.

The Lotus catalog disk is $5 plus $1.50 shipping and handling. But PsL also offers a monthly Lotus Additions Disk that lists the new Lotus/Symphony files that have been added to the library. The cost is $5 per month, including shipping and handling. The minimum subscription is three months ($15). For contact information, please see Chapter 4.

Finally, if you have a modem, you should definitely know about "The World of Lotus" (GO LOTUS) on CompuServe. This is a feature sponsored by Lotus Development Corporation, and it is an excellent place to get "straight from the horse's mouth" information on Lotus products as well as public domain and shareware software. The feature consists of two CompuServe forums, one for Lotus 1-2-3 integrated products (GO LOTUSA) and one for Lotus stand-alone products (GO LOTUSB) like Manuscript, Metro, and Express. Here is a summary of the data libraries available in each forum:

AVAILABLE DATA LIBRARIES

Lotus Integrated	Lotus Stand-Alone
1 New uploads	1 New uploads
2 General Lotus information	2 General Lotus information
3 Peripherals/drivers	3 Peripherals/drivers
4 1-2-3 Utilities	4 Graphics products
5 HAL utilities	5 Manuscript
6 Symphony utilities	6 Metro/ Express
7 Jazz utilities	7 Signal/One Source
8 Business applications	8 Other products
9 Science/engineering applications	
10 Statistics applications	
11 Personal finance	
12 Communication utilities	

At this writing, the librarians of the Lotus Integrated forum follow a practice similar to that of the IBM Forum libraries (Chapter 7). They include in LIB1 New Uploads a file called DLSUM.ARC containing short, one-line descriptions of the files in libraries 2 through 12. This file is updated every month, usually on the first. A second file, DLCHGS.DOC, summarizes the changes and additions made to the libraries during the month. Thus, if you download DLSUM.ARC once, you can stay current by downloading DLCHGS.DOC every month from then on. Each library also contains a file in the form DLxxSUM.DOC (where xx is the single or double-digit DL number, like DL6SUM.DOC or DL12SUM.DOC). These files summarize the contents of their respective libraries.

You might try to download these files using the names given here, but should the names have changed, you should be able to locate them by keying in S/DES/KEY:INDEX (scan on the keyword INDEX and display the filename and description) at the library function menu prompt. Or simply use the BROwse command to search for files with INDEX as one of their keywords. (We were unable to find similar files in the Lotus Stand-Alone libraries, but they may have been added as you read this.) Once the target file has been downloaded and removed from its ARChive, you can use LIST.COM as discussed in Chapter 6 to search it offline.

FreeTip: Ever since Lotus 1-2-3 arrived on the scene, spreadsheets and business graphics have gone hand-in-hand. But while Lotus and As-Easy-As graphics are quick and convenient, neither program gives you the power and flexibility of a dedicated business graphics package. ExpressGraph, the program cited in Chapter 14, is very good. And since it will accept DIF and other file formats as its input, you can avoid the chore of keying your spreadsheet data in by hand. But The Draftsman, a program by Jan Gombert, is so good that we simply cannot allow it to go unremarked. We have placed it on the Glossbrenner's Choice disk called IBM Business Graphics Disk 2—The Draftsman.

Mr. Gombert is one of the creative forces behind the popular commercial program, Dr. Halo. He wrote The Draftsman while employed by Starware, a company owned by David Stang. The program was licensed by Plantronics for use with that firm's graphics card, and many copies were sold commercially at $200 each. Now it is shareware, with a registration fee of $25.

Space prohibits a complete list of its features, but among other things it can produce regular and exploded pie charts, stacked and clustered bar graphs, line graphs, and scatter plots. Graphs can be sized and moved, and you may have several on the screen at the same time. A graphics display adaptor (CGA, Hercules, and so on) is required, and you may use up to three foreground and one background color per screen.

The Draftsman can import data from DIF files, from comma or space-delimited text files (such as those you can produce with dBASE and many other programs), as well as from a plain text file. Three data files may be active per session, and you can edit

FreeTip continued

> graphs, legends, footnotes, titles, and so on, dynamically. Graphs
> can be embellished with arrows, circles, ovals, lines, and rec-
> tangles. You can even add logos, signatures, and other freehand
> drawings. (The section of The Draftsman that makes this possible
> can also be used as a drawing program.) There is also a built-in
> "slide show" feature to let you organize and display graphs in se-
> quence.
>
> The Draftsman supports Epson MX-80 and compatible printers
> and offers a complete menu of options for controlling HP-7470 pen
> plotters. There are context-sensitive help screens and a 50-page,
> indexed, on-disk manual. For more information, contact: Mr.
> David Stang, Hire Education, 3631 Jenifer Street, N.W., Wash-
> ington, D.C. 20015.

And speaking of communications . . . well, that's exactly what we're
going to be doing in the next chapter as we look at what is certainly one
of the most professionally produced products in the shareware pantheon—ProComm from DataStorm Technologies, Inc. We'll also look at
a clutch of ProComm utilities produced by other parties and at several
special programs for CompuServe and GEnie users.

16

Communications and Related Programs

GOING ONLINE WITH THE WORLD

Communications programs organize the process of going online discussed in Chapter 5. They speak to the UART and the modem, handle the inflow and outflow of data, and make it possible to upload (transmit) and download (capture) files. In our opinion, a good comm program is an essential part of any computer owner's software arsenal. A personal computer without communications capabilities is like a car with a nonfiring cylinder—it runs, but you will never be able to take advantage of its full potential. Of course, we may have a certain bias, having made a speciality of online communications over the years.

Nevertheless, it is a fact that more and more PCs—including all IBM PS/2 models—are arriving from the factory equipped with a built-in serial port. Add an inexpensive modem and an even less expensive comm program, and you're ready to go online with the world. That means sending and receiving electronic mail, Telex messages, and even photographs. It means accessing your company's mainframe or local area network from home or from a distant hotel room. It means instant access to a major chunk of mankind's collected knowledge—everything from the *Congressional Record* or the Library of Congress to local and regional newspapers to priceless corporate, investment, and marketing intelligence.

It also means instant access to thousands of public domain and shareware applications programs and utilities. And having covered the aforementioned online subjects in other books, here we'll confine ourselves to telling you which comm program to get, discuss the add-on programs

469

various PD/shareware authors have written to extend its power, and identify the most important general communications utilities. We'll also touch briefly on two specialized programs designed to help you get the most out of a CompuServe forum or a GEnie RT.

Making Life a Little Easier

Whether your main interest is downloading free software or searching a remote database for every article on artificial sweeteners published in the last 15 years, a really good communications program will make your online life much easier. For example, if you have a Hayes-compatible or other intelligent modem, you can set many comm programs to automatically dial the phone, redial if a number is busy, or try the next number on a given list. This is especially helpful if you plan to tap remote bulletin board systems, as described in Chapter 8. In addition, many comm programs these days have the ability to follow prepared scripts, making it possible for them to conduct entire online sessions automatically, whether you're there or not. Once the script has been prepared, you have only to issue a single command or arrange for your computer to do so for you at a preset time.

Too Many Choices

For a variety of reasons, telecommunications and free software have been closely intertwined from the beginning. One of the first and most famous public domain programs, MODEM7 by Ward Christensen, was a comm program. So too was the late Andrew Fluegelman's PC-TALK, the program that introduced the idea of Freeware and user-supported software. And as you know, people have been making their efforts available on bulletin board systems and other data networks for years.

It is undoubtedly because of this that so many PD programmers have tried their hands at communications software. Indeed, today there are probably as many public domain and shareware comm programs as there are text editors and word processors. We have looked at most of them, and we're happy to report that most are quite good. But at this writing there is really only one comm program of choice: ProComm by Bruce Barkelew and Tom Smith. The program is so good that it blows everything else, including most of its commercial counterparts, completely out of the pond. With ProComm and the key communications utilities discussed later in this chapter, you will be superbly equipped for any online task.

Recommended Programs

Glossbrenner's Choice:

IBM CommPack 1—ProComm 2.4.2

IBM CommPack 4—ProComm PLUS Test Drive

It is impossible to say enough about ProComm. It is well thought out. It's quick. It's responsive. It simply *feels* good. In fact, it feels like a BMW. But at the same time, because of its thoughtful design, it is well-suited to online communicators of all levels of experience. If you're new to the online world, you will discover that ProComm will smoothly handle all of the basic online chores without forcing you to learn about its other features. If you are an experienced user or if you will be communicating in a corporate environment, you will find that ProComm has all the power and capabilities you are likely to need. It is simply a super program. Small wonder that ProComm Version 2.4.2 has been a *PC Magazine* "Editor's Choice" two years in a row, or that it was voted the communications Product of the Year (1986) by *InfoWorld* readers. Reporting on the results of a reader survey, *Personal Computing* magazine (November 1987) noted that "not only did it make the top 10 list of communications programs, it topped the list, with 21 percent of the respondents using it."

At this writing, there are two major versions of the program. Version 2.4.2 is the shareware version. PLUS is an even more powerful and feature-filled version that is the centerpiece of a complete commercial package. The shareware version contains a manual on the disk and can be registered for $25. This is the license fee for the use of the program. For $50, you can register and receive a printed, bound copy of the manual for version 2.4.2. The full PLUS package sells for $75 (list) and includes two disks containing the PLUS program and a series of support and script files, a 340-page, bound and indexed manual and tutorial, and 90 days of telephone support. (Additional support can be purchased separately.) Also included are free subscriptions to CompuServe (including a $15 usage credit), the Official Airline Guide—Electronic Edition (the normal subscription is $50), and GEnie, the system on which you will find the ProComm RoundTable. This support and information exchange forum is open to anyone.

According to Tom Smith, coauthor of the program,

There are actually two different versions of PLUS. There is ProComm PLUS and there is what we're calling ProComm PLUS Test Drive. Test

Drive is the version that is available for shareware distribution. ProComm PLUS is the registered version, and it carries the standard software license permitting duplication only for backup purposes.

The differences between the two are essentially just cosmetic. The registered version has a different logo and does not have the shareware "beg screen" asking that you register. Test Drive does not come with an external program that allows the keyboard remapping you might want to do when emulating a particular mainframe terminal. Because the manual has tripled in size compared to 2.4.2, Test Drive does not include it on the disk, but it does include the same 40K context-sensitive, online help file found with PLUS.

Version 2.4.2 will still be sold and supported. But people who register it will be notified of PLUS and be given an option to upgrade. Users who paid $25 for 2.4.2 can upgrade for $50, and those who paid $50 for the complete 2.4.2 package can upgrade to PLUS for $25. We're not going to force anyone to buy two separate products.

How ProComm Came to Be

ProComm is the brainchild of Bruce Barkelew, who began writing it at the end of 1984. When we spoke to him, version 2.4.2 was the most current, though ProComm PLUS was nearing completion. He told us that "Right before I finished ProComm, QMODEM came out, and with its pop-up menus it had a very similar look, which was kind of surprising. I guess John [Friel, author of QMODEM] kind of beat me to the draw on that." (QMODEM SST by John Friel is a shareware program, $30, that would be our next choice after ProComm.)

I was a computer science student at the University of Missouri at the time, and I got tired of waiting in line to use the limited number of terminals available on campus. I finally bought an IBM-PC to use from home. But I couldn't find a commercial comm program that provided the complete terminal emulation I needed.

I wanted to learn the architecture of the PC, and I also wanted to learn C, which the university didn't offer then because there was no C compiler for the System 370 [mainframe] at the time. So I decided to combine all three goals into a single project, and it just grew into what it is today.

We asked Mr. Barkelew about the significance of writing ProComm in C.

C lets you get at the low-level guts of the machine, but the code you write remains portable. Normally, the only other way to do that and get that kind of performance would be to write in assembler, which results in very machine-specific code.

At the appropriate time, we may bring it over to other machines, and of course we've looked closely at Unix and Xenix environments. In the meantime, the next version [ProComm Plus] will include support for the new high-speed 9600 bps and 19.2 kilobit self-correcting modems, and we have two or three related products planned.

After school, at the suggestion of classmate Tom Smith, Mr. Barkelew applied for a programming job at the San Francisco engineering firm where Smith worked. The two programmers decided to improve upon Mr. Barkelew's program and eventually released it as shareware. The program was such a success that they quit the engineering firm, moved back to Missouri, and began devoting full time to what became Datastorm Technologies. Today, ProComm is used by many government agencies and *Fortune* 500 companies. According to Marvin Bryan, writing in *Personal Computing* magazine (November 1987), ProComm even played a role in the Iran/Contra affair, being the program of choice of a certain military figure who was central to that controversy.

ProComm PLUS and ProComm 2.4.2 Specifications

As a group, communications programs probably have more features per square byte, as it were, than any other class of software. There are some features that you will almost certainly never use, while there are others that you don't think you'll use but are awfully glad to have when the need arises. And there are some, of course, that are absolutely essential.

We'll try to give you a fully rounded picture of the capabilities and capacities of both ProComm PLUS and ProComm 2.4.2. But there is so much ground to cover that to do so, we're going to have to switch to terse mode. For a more detailed discussion of what the features cited below can mean to you, please see Chapter 5 of this book and *The Complete Handbook of Personal Computer Communications*.

Communications Speeds, Ports, and Parameters

Version 2.4.2 supports speeds ranging from 300 bits per second (bps) through 19.2 kilobits per second. Parity can be odd, even, none, mark, or space. Data bits are 1 to 7; stop bits are 1 to 2. Communications ports supported are COM1 through COM4. The program also offers a user-settable upload throttle, a true BREAK signal with adjustable duration, and a translation table for stripping or converting incoming characters. ProComm PLUS offers all of the above, plus speeds of 38.4, 57.6, and 115.2 kilobits per second, and a total of eight "COM" ports. All communications parameters can be changed on the fly.

Terminal Emulation and Error-Checking Protocols

You can talk to any mainframe or other non-personal computer with virtually any communications program. But your interaction with the system will be one-line-at-a-time in most cases because the mainframe will see you as a teletype ("TTY") system. This is the lowest common denominator, and it is fine for most online tasks. However, it is also possible to emulate a specific mainframe terminal equipped with many special functions. We won't go into all the functions that terminal emulation makes available. We will simply say that for most people, the most striking difference between TTY communications and terminal emulation is that with the latter you can move your cursor all over the screen, just as you would with a word processing program.

ProComm 2.4.2 can be quickly set to emulate any of the following terminals: ANSI, ADDS Viewpoint, DEC VT-52, VT-100, and VT-102, IBM 3101, TeleVideo 910/920 and 925/950, Lear Sieglar ADM 3/5 series, Heath/Zenith 19, and the Wyse 100. ProComm PLUS supports all of these, plus the IBM 3270 (asynchronous) and the Wyse 50 and 100. More emulations may be added in the future.

The ProComm 2.4.2 manual includes the keyboard translation tables you will need to know for which IBM keys to hit for the desired function for each terminal. But, as Bruce Barkelew told us before PLUS was released, many users reassign keys with Newkey, the keyboard macroing program discussed in Chapter 9. Registered users of ProComm PLUS receive an external program that will handle this function for them. Both versions of ProComm offer a keyboard macro function that lets you load keys with frequently used commands, like the user name or password you use when signing onto a remote system. The macros are stored in files, so you can have as many macros as you like and load the same keys with different information for different systems.

As you know from Chapters 5 through 7, error-checking protocols are essential for uploading and downloading machine language programs. You can use any protocol you like, as long as it matches the one used by the remote system. ProComm 2.4.2 gives you lots of options, including XMODEM (CRC, checksum, and "relaxed"), MODEM7, YMODEM and YMODEM Batch, Telelink (often used on FIDO BBSs), Kermit and Super Kermit ("sliding window"), WXMODEM, ASCII, and CompuServe B, which also supports the CompuServe Quick-B protocol. ProComm PLUS also supports SEALink, IMODEM, and YMODEM-G. SEALink is a full-duplex derivative of the XMODEM protocol promulgated by System Enhancement Associates, creators of the original ARChive program. IMODEM and YMODEM-G are specially designed streaming protocols for use with high-speed error-correcting modems.

PLUS also has provisions for up to three user-callable protocols. (See the discussion of ZRUN.COM later in this chapter for more on how you might call an external protocol.)

FreeTip: As noted in Chapter 7, the CompuServe B protocol is the ideal one to use on that system. The "Quick B" version of this protocol was introduced in 1987. The Quick B protocol is a full-duplex, windowed version of the plain B protocol. This means that the CompuServe system can send up to two 1K packets before receiving an acknowledgment from the downloader. Plain B, in contrast, requires an acknowledgment of the first packet before it will send the second.

ProComm 2.4.2 has always been wonderfully well suited to using the CompuServe B protocol. But until speaking with Tom Smith, we had no idea that 2.4.2 would support Quick B as well.

ProComm 2.4.2 has always supported Quick B on our side. In other words, it was able to handle the packets coming through. Sometimes it hiccups on the first block, but after that it takes off. The implementation of Quick B in PLUS is pretty much the same as that in 2.4.2, though we will be supporting Compu-Serve's B Plus protocol whenever it is released, either internally or in an external, callable module.

To tell CompuServe you want to use Quick B when downloading a file, key in DOW FILENAME.EXT/PROTO:QB at the Data Library prompt. According to CompuServe Customer Service, if you do this or key in DOW/PROTO:QB (no filename) once, the system will use Quick B for the duration of your session *in that forum.* If you leave and come back again or go to a different forum, you will have to specify QB again the next time you download a file.

Auto-Dialing and Script Language

Andrew Fluegelman's PC-Talk was not only the first shareware (Free-ware) program, it was also one of the first PC comm programs of any kind. In it, Mr. Fluegelman effectively defined the major components of all personal computer communications software. One of these features is a "dialing directory" or phone book that lets you record the phone numbers of packet-switching nodes, bulletin boards, and other systems you expect to access on a regular basis. The dialing directory acts as a menu from which you can quickly select the number you wish the program to dial. Virtually all PC comm programs since PC-Talk, and certainly all of the PD and shareware comm programs, have incorporated this feature.

The dialing directory in ProComm 2.4.2 has room for 100 numbers, including a descriptive name, any long-distance or other dialing prefix codes, and the name of a script file containing the commands you want to have executed once the connection has been made. (You do not have to specify a script file if you don't want to.) Should the number you've chosen be busy, you can tell ProComm to automatically redial it, pausing a specified interval before making each attempt. ProComm PLUS expands the directory to 200 entries and can be set to automatically redial a number if it is busy. It will also auto-dial several numbers, cycling through a list until it gets an answer and picking up where it left off after you hang up. PLUS also allows you to specify the terminal emulation and/or protocol you wish to enable for each number. It will also keep track of the date of your last call and the total number of calls for each entry. It will also keep a log of the calls you make and their date and duration to make it easier to reconcile your phone bill.

ProComm 2.4.2 includes a very powerful command file script language that makes it possible to automate many of your online sessions. But ASPECT, the programming language in PLUS, goes this several times better. There are conditionals (IF/THEN/ELSE and SWITCH/ CASE), advanced screen handling, file I/O, mathematical functions, looping, memory variables, subroutines, and much more. Fortunately, scripts prepared for 2.4.2 are compatible with PLUS, which was not the case when 2.4.2 replaced an earlier version. PLUS also includes a "RECORD" mode that allows it to "learn" log-on sequences and other tasks by recording system prompts and your responses to disk. The program will then generate a script file that you can use to automate these tasks in the future.

Many Other Features

Both ProComm versions offer a HOST MODE that allows you to access your system remotely, as if it were a bulletin board. You can also "shell" out to DOS or otherwise run programs remotely, and you can assign user IDs, passwords, and security levels to others whom you may want to allow to access your system. ProComm PLUS (Test Drive and registered copies) includes a context-sensitive help facility. This means that the help text that appears when you key in Alt-Z is always relevant to whatever you happen to be doing at the time. PLUS also offers two "hot keys" to run external programs with a single keystroke from within ProComm PLUS itself. PLUS users can choose to operate with either pop-up menus or a Lotus-style bounce bar.

Both versions let you call for a disk directory, view a text file, or call your favorite word processing program. There is a pop-up elapsed time window to show you the date, time, and elapsed time of your current or last phone call. There is also a split-screen chat mode that you will find especially useful in real-time conferences, CB conversations, and the like on GEnie, CompuServe, and other systems. Incoming text is displayed in the top half of the screen, while the text you type is displayed in the lower half.

Finally, two ProComm features we have always found especially useful are the scroll-recall buffer and screen dump features. Generally, it's not a bad idea to set a comm program to capture all incoming text and write it to a disk file. If nothing you want to save comes across the screen, you can always delete the file at the end of the session with no harm done. If you do see something you want to extract, simply bring the file into PC-Write and clip out the material.

If you have forgotten to set the program to capture to disk, you will almost always become aware of the fact just as something really interesting is scrolling off your screen and into the ether. With both 2.4.2 and PLUS, however, you can hit a key to put the session on hold and tell the program to redisplay the last 125 lines (10,000 characters) that have come in. If then you want to save any of this information, you can hit another key combination and the program will dump the screen to disk. Since ProComm appends each succeeding screen dump to the file, you can easily recapture a great deal of material in this way.

System Requirements and Registration

ProComm 2.4.2 and ProComm PLUS run on the IBM-PC family and compatibles under DOS 2.0 or higher. (Be sure that the CONFIG.SYS file on your DOS disk contains the line FILES = 20 or some number higher than 20.) The programs can be used in several multitasking environments, including Microsoft Windows, DESQview, TopView, Multi-Link, and Double DOS. You can use them in direct connections (two computers joined by a null modem cable) or with virtually all kinds of modems.

As noted earlier, registration for ProComm 2.4.2 is $25, while for $50 you can register and receive the typeset, bound version of the on-disk manual. The ProComm PLUS package sells for $75 and includes the program disk and a disk of support files (including one to remap the keyboard likely to be especially useful when emulating a mainframe terminal), a 340-page bound manual and tutorial, 90 days of telephone support, and free subscriptions to CompuServe, GEnie and the OAG-Electronic Edition. Additional telephone support may be purchased separately. General support is available to everyone via the ProComm RoundTable on GEnie. Site licenses and quantity discounts are available. For more information, contact: Datastorm Technologies, Inc., P. O. Box 1471, Columbia, MO 65205; phone: (314) 449-7012. For Visa and MasterCard telephone orders, call: (800) 626-2723 (orders only, please). The company pays all shipping and handling. Missouri residents should add 6.475 percent sales tax. Subject to certain restrictions, purchase orders are also accepted. Contact Datastorm for details.

FreeTip: Tom Smith, vice president of Datastorm, told us that the company's sales totaled $325,000 in calendar 1986 and topped $1.75 million in calendar 1987. At this writing, the firm has nearly a score of full-time employees. Indeed, their number seems to double every time we call. Several of the new hires are programmers who are at work on two or three additional communications-related products. Clearly ProComm and Datastorm Technologies are a shareware success story of the first order.

Why?

I think first of all, we have a super product. I've always thought that. Others seem to think so, too, since we consistently get rave reviews. But there's something else. And that's the fact that we listen to our users and let them tell us what they want. That's part of the shareware process. Without question, one of the biggest strengths of shareware publishing is the closeness and the openness of the feedback channels between the users and the authors of a program.

You have to remember that both Bruce and I have technical degrees. We didn't have a business education. (Though we're getting one as we go.) So we probably have a slightly different approach to things like product development.

Thanks to the way ProComm had evolved through shareware user feedback, when we sat down to do PLUS we knew we had a very full-featured program to build on. It was full of the features not that we thought people would like but that we *knew* they would like because they told us.

With the success of ProComm and PLUS—and the other products we're working on—Bruce and I are very busy these days. But you can bet we'll always pay close attention to what our users say. We simply don't know how to do business any other way.

ProComm 2.4.2 Utilities

In the best shareware tradition, ProComm 2.4.2 has stimulated programmers and hobbyists to create a variety of utilities and script files to work with the product. We'll look at some of the best of these in a moment. Before we do, you should know that the ProComm 2.4.2 package *includes* several utilities and script files. If you already have ProComm 2.4.2 and you see these files on a bulletin board or SIG library, downloading them will probably be a waste of money since you almost certainly already have them:

CMDCNVT.EXE	Converts .CMD (ProComm command scripts) files created for previous versions to 2.4.2. format.
COMPUSRV.CMD FIDO.CMD PCP-MENU.CMD RBBS.CMD SOURCE.CMD	A series of simple script files to automate dialing and log-ons to CompuServe, FIDO and RBBS bulletin boards, Telenet's PC Pursuit system, and The Source. PCP-MENU.CMD shows you how to create menus and branches in your script files.
PRCMSORT.EXE	Utility to sort ProComm dialing directories.
README.TEF TEF.EXE	ProComm's Timed Execution Facility and brief documentation. Just key in TEF file.CMD HH:MM to tell the program when you want it to execute the specified .CMD file.

Recommended Programs

Glossbrenner's Choice

IBM CommPack 2—ProComm Utilities

CVTFON	**COM**	**259500**
CVTFON	**DOC**	**110320**

Written by Steven Linhart, CvtFon converts the phone directories used by one comm program into a format that can be used by a different comm program. This version supports ProComm, PibTerm, Qmodem 1.x/2.x, PC-Talk III (input only), and Termulator. The doc file will give you all the instructions you need.

DLX	**CMD**	**43990**
DLX	**DOC**	**46910**

DLX is a ProComm command or script file that will let you automatically download up to four files from any single CompuServe forum data library (DL). The DLX script uses the CompuServe B protocol offered as one of ProComm's options, and it will log you off when it is finished. The documentation will tell you everything you need to know *except* how to get a complete list of files found in the IBM SIG libraries (see Chapter 7). Note that while you may set DLX to prompt for additional four-file lists, ProCommDL, also on this disk, lets you prepare an unlimited list of files for downloading from over a dozen types of BBSs and commercial systems, including CIS (see below).

PHELP   COM   21504

There is no doc file with this, but you really don't need one. The program provides RAM-resident, pop-up help for creating ProComm script files. Load it by keying in PHELP and hitting <Enter>. Then go into your favorite word processing program and start creating your ProComm script. When you need help remembering or using 2.4.2 commands, hold down the <Ctrl> key and hit F10. PHELP will pop onto the screen with a menu leading to items of help information. This is very well done.

EXCHLIST	**PCP**	**25494**
PCP	**BAT**	**185**
PRCMDIR	**DOC**	**12105**
PRCMDIR	**EXE**	**105370**
TELENET	**CMD**	**54**
USBBS40A	**LST**	**69490**

PRCMDIR may be one of the neatest ProComm utilities ever. With this program on your disk, you'll never again need to key another BBS or other phone number into your ProComm dialing directory. The file USBBS40A.LST (or its current equivalent) is Peter Olympia's master list of IBM-oriented BBSs. EXCHLIST.PCP is a list of PC Pursuit telephone exchanges, which you will have to update when you subscribe to that service. For more information on these and a demonstration of PRCMDIR.EXE, please turn to Chapter 8. Note that ProComm PLUS comes with a utility to convert 2.4.2 dialing directories into its own format. That means you can use PRCMDIR to automatically bring BBS numbers into 2.4.2 format, and then convert the resulting file for use with PLUS.

PROCOMDL	**COM**	**29985**
PROCOMDL	**TXT**	**8225**

ProCommDL will create ProComm scripts to download (that's what the "DL" stands for here) the files you specify from more than a dozen systems. There are bulletin boards ranging from FIDO to NoChange and three commercial systems (The Source IBMSIG, People/Link, and CompuServe). The program is not likely to be of interest if you normally download only one file at a time. But if you have a long list of files, you can in effect hand the list to ProCommDL, sign on to your chosen system, put the ProCommDL command file into operation, and walk away. This, as opposed to checking back every few minutes to see if one download is over so you can start the next one. You can have the command file automatically log you out after the downloading is over, so you really don't have to return to your machine at all. "Set it and forget it," as the TV commercial says.

```
PROCMD   COM   53769
PROCMD   DOC   13382
PROCMD   FRM    2189
```

The ProComm CMD Editor package is quite snappy looking and very cleverly done. Its purpose is to let you create ProComm command files, and to do so it maintains a list of all available ProComm commands on the screen. As you move the cursor to any of them, a brief explanation of what the command does is displayed above the list. Below the reference list is your workspace. Use it as you would a word processor to create a command file.

As noted, this is a very nice program. The one caveat is that you really have to have at least some familiarity with how to write a computer program to use it effectively. And a familiarity with ProComm and its script language would be even more helpful. In short, the ProComm CMD Editor won't write your scripts for you. But it does make the process easier.

CONVERTR   BAS   7723

This is a program by Meade Frierson designed to do essentially what PRCMDI (above) does. It is considerably less flexible, however, since it will work only with Peter Olympia's Darwin Systems list or with Mr. Frierson's own IBMBDS.LST, not any ASCII text file. Mr. Frierson's list is available on CompuServe as IBMnnn.ARC, where the nnn stands for the month and year of publication. Check Data Library 0 (New Uploads) in the IBMCOMM SIG for the latest copy.

PRC24 CMD   9450

This is a full-blown ProComm command file designed to serve as a model for anyone, but particularly for those using CompuServe. It isn't likely that you'll really want to automate all of the functions PRC24.CMD provides for, but it offers an excellent template for creating a version customized to your needs.

ZRUN   COM   11892
README   ZR   1594

This program gives ProComm the ability to handle the ZMODEM protocol created by Chuck Forsberg, author of YMODEM and many of the most important XMODEM mods. As the doc file explains, you add this to ProComm 2.4.2 by substituting ZRUN.COM for your editor/word processor. That is, you change the ProComm setup such that it calls ZRUN when you key in Alt-A instead of a text editor. You should also be able to use this with PLUS by designating it as one of three callable external protocols. It remains to be seen whether ZMODEM will become the dominant protocol. But it has a better than even chance, given the fact that Forsberg is a communications genius and ZMODEM is in the public domain, thanks to Telenet, the firm that commissioned him to write it.

Essential Utilities and System-Specific Programs

All you need for most online activities is a good communications program. But sometimes, particularly if you're interested in downloading PD and shareware programs, a comm program alone isn't enough. Virtually all programs available from bulletin boards and commercial systems these days have been compressed and stored in archive files. As noted in Chapter 2, ARC-ing a package in this way eliminates the inconvenience of having to download a program and its documentation and support files individually. And it saves connect time and long-distance dollars as well since the amount of data that must be transmitted is often cut by half or more.

Before you can use a program or read its documentation, however, you must first extract it from its archive, and that requires a special utility. Other methods of compressing and grouping files may also be used, and you'll need a utility for each of them. There are some other short programs you may find convenient as well, and we'll look at them in a moment.

We should also say a word or two about what might be called "system-specific" programs. These are programs that people have written for use on a particular online system. AutoSIG and the various color graphics display programs discussed later in the chapter, for example, are specifically for CompuServe users. SLF20.ZOO is specifically for GEnie users, and while PC-VCO and ZOO.EXE are used on all systems, they are particularly popular among members of the GEnie IBM RoundTable.

Recommended Programs

Glossbrenner's Choice:

IBM CommPack 6—The AutoSIG Package

ATO560	**ARC**	**130896**
ATODOC	**ARC**	**68301**

This is the current version (version 5.60 at this writing) of AutoSIG, a joint programming project that has been growing and evolving over the years among CompuServe IBM Forum users. The principal authors are Vernon D. Buerg, Jim McKeown, and Don Watkins, with help, suggestions, and bits of code from many others. The documentation runs nearly 70 pages, including its index.

You can use AutoSIG to talk to any system, but it is specifically designed to automate your interactions with CompuServe SIGs and that system's EasyPlex electronic mail feature. You can set it up to automatically dial the phone, sign on, go into the SIGs of your choice, and download all messages addressed to you. It will then automatically sign off and thus stop the connect-time meter.

Once you are offline, you can read and compose replies to the messages you have downloaded with the built-in editor, and then use ATO to sign on again and upload your replies to the appropriate places. If more messages have arrived for you in the meantime, ATO will pick them up as well. By automating your online sessions in this way, ATO can save the dedicated CompuServe user a great deal of money, compared to the cost of composing replies and keying in commands while you are online.

AutoSIG can also be used interactively as you would any comm program. And since it supports CompuServe's Quick B protocol it can save you money when downloading files from SIG libraries. Speaking of which, you can always find the latest version of AutoSIG in DL1 (Auto-

SIG) of the IBMCOMM forum. Download the file COMDL1.DES for one-line descriptions of the library's contents. If you really get into using AutoSIG, you will also want to download a program called ACLS.ARC. This program will keep a continuous log of your Compu-Serve usage and calculate the total cost of each session. To use ACLS, you must use AutoSIG.

A commercial knockoff of AutoSIG, TAPCIS from OMNI Information Resources, incorporates usage and session-logging functions within the main program. But, although you will find evaluation copies of TAPCIS in various CompuServe SIGs, as its greeting screen makes plain, after a 21-day evaluation period users are to send them $79 for a printed manual and software license.

FreeTip: AutoSIG brings on a certain nostalgia for "the good old days" of personal computing. In the early 1980s things were just as crazy as they are now, but everything was new to everyone. There was a sense of joint exploration and experimentation, of using the new tools to do something that had never been done before. AutoSIG is a perfect example of this spirit. Its authors used the new medium (systems like CompuServe) to exchange information and write a program that would in turn help others use that medium more effectively. It is a virtual certainty that Auto-SIG's authors would never have encountered each other, let alone worked together, without such a common electronic meeting ground.

AutoSIG also recalls the original spirit that has generated so much top-quality free software. As Don Watkins says in the most recent edition of the documentation.

> ATO is to my thinking a community hack in the true sense of the word. That is, lots of people contributing time and effort just for the sheer joy of programming and throwing their modems online for testing. Why is this inspiring? Since day one ATO has been free. The only motive of the authors is that you enjoy it.

IBM CommPack 3—The Communicator's Toolchest

DISPHR	EXE	11008
FBI	RLE	9585
FBI	TXT	2486

"DISPHR" stands for "display high resolution graphics." (A color graphics screen is required.) To use this program, you simply key in DISPHR FILENAME.RLE. "RLE" stands for "run-length encoded" graphics, the technique CompuServe uses to transmit graphs of historical stock data from its TREND feature, its Radar Weather Maps, and mug shots from the FBI's Ten Most Wanted list. Users of Compu-Serve's CB Simulator have also stored pictures of themselves online in CBSIG (CompuServe will scan a subscriber's photo and upload it as an RLE file for a small fee), and there are scores of RLE files of movie stars and celebrities to be found in the Hollywood Hotline feature.

To obtain an RLE file from CompuServe, download the file on the system as a text file. Do not worry that the system will warn you that the file may not be visible. This prompt appears whenever you do a download like this and are not using one of CompuServe's own VIDTEX comm programs. (The system queries your PC to see if you are running VIDTEX shortly after you sign on.) The same thing applies to the system's TREND or Radar Weather Maps.

What you're after in all cases is a text file. So when the download is over, use your word processor to delete all the junk up to the point where you see an Escape character, usually followed by a GH. This is the beginning of the RLE code sequences and it is where your file should start when you are finished editing it. Don't worry about any garbage at the end of the file. The RLE file will be one long string of characters occupying a single line and stretching out to the far right. There should be no carriage returns or line feeds in it.

Note that your system may display the Escape character (ASCII 27) differently; however, in PC-WRITE it shows up as a little left-pointing arrow. You can generate it by holding down your <Alt> key and keying in 27 on the numeric keypad. FBI.RLE is an example that can be used with DISPHR.EXE. FBI.TXT describes the heinous crimes the man on the screen committed and how he was caught.

RLETRAP2 COM 1228
RLETRAP DOC 3656

Written by Don Shoff, this program is designed to be used with Pro-Comm. If you install it before you boot ProComm, you will see RLE images while you are online, as they are being transmitted. This is the way CompuServe's VIDTEX programs handle things. However, you will still want to capture the RLE files to disk so you can view them later with DISPHR.

PK36 EXE   118784

Many years ago we can remember collecting breakfast cereal boxtops to be mailed in to the company for a collection of magic pills. If you dropped the pills in water and waited, strange things began to happen. Very shortly a warrior or a monster or some other latter-day "action figure" began to take shape and grow as the pill absorbed water. PK36.EXE works something like that.

When you key in PK36 and hit <Enter>, the program begins to unfold itself as it creates Phil Katz's complete PKARC package. The files that spring into being in this way are:

PKARC.COM, PKARC.DOC, to put files into an archive. Version 3.6.

PKXARC.COM, PKXARC.DOC, to "X-tract" files from archive. Version 3.5.

PKXARCJR.COM, to remove files from archive if you have limited memory. Only 74K free memory is required for this version. The "JR" has nothing to do with the IBM PCjr, though these programs will run on that machine.

MAKESFX.COM, used to build a file called PKSFX.PGM, which lets you create your *own* self-extracting ARC'd files. PKSFX.DOC, a file explaining just how to do this, also appears.

When PK36 finishes, you can almost hear the program say, "Ta-da!" And in truth, it is a boffo entrance for an all together remarkable package of programs.

As you know from Chapter 2, this is one of at least three available packages for compressing one or more files and storing them in a single archive file. But it is the one we like best. According to Mr. Katz, his utilities work faster and result in smaller archive files than comparable programs. (The programs are written in C and include several highly optimized assembly language routines.) We haven't done a benchmark, but Mr. Katz's programs certainly *seem* faster. And we have found nothing to dispute his claim of compression ratios of between 40 and 60 percent. The programs are also very well documented.

We also admire the fact that PKARC will automatically choose the best compression method for a given file. There is no need to get into the technical details, but you should know that one of these techniques is called "squashing." PKARC's introduction of this technique caused some controversy for a while because other archiving programs did not support it.

The problem was that because all archiving programs produce archive files ending in .ARC, there was no way to tell which program created it and whether it might contain any squashed files. If the extraction program you happened to be using did not support squashing, there was the chance that you would not be able to reconstitute all of the files. A small squashing-related bug was also discovered in the original release of PKARC Version 35A, but that has now been corrected. In addition, the file extraction program by Wayne Chin and Vernon Buerg (ARCE.COM) began supporting squashed files with version 3.lb (September 16, 1987). Also, it is possible to configure PKARC such that it will *not* squash files. Alternatively, you can apply a patch to permanently disable this feature. (To obtain the necessary patch, see DL3—General Utilities of the IBMSW forum on CompuServe.)

The PKARC utilities are shareware. If you like them and use them, you are asked to register by sending $20; for $45 you "will be registered to receive a diskette with the next version of PKARC and PKXARC when available." Site licenses are also available. Contact: PKWARE, Inc., 7032 Ardara Avenue, Glendale, WI 53209.

```
LUE220   COM   2988
LUE220   DOC   4815
```

The name of this file stands for "Library Utility—Extraction, version 2.20." The librarying technique is the direct antecedent of today's archive files. The concept was developed by Gary Novosielski years ago to get around the limitations CP/M imposed on the number of files you could store on a single disk. When it was brought to the IBM world, file compression techniques were added. Various versions of the library utility have been created, including LU86, written in 1984 by Tom Jennings and Paul Homchick. (Mr. Jennings is also the author of the FIDO BBS system; Mr. Homchick at this writing is the chairman of the IBM RT on GEnie.)

LUE220 was written by Vern Buerg (April 28, 1986), and its sole purpose is to extract the contents of a library file (.LBR or .LAR). Occasionally you will still find a .LBR file on an online system and thus will need this utility. These days, however, almost everything is ARC'd.

USQLC10   COM   12288
USQ   DOC   3597

This is the latest version of the UNSQUEEZE utility. "Squeezing" is a technique that predates the librarying technique, but it too has its roots in CP/M. The technique is based on the "Huffman algorithm" as proposed by D. A. Huffman in 1952. Richard Greenlaw is the programmer who first implemented squeezing for personal computers. Squeezing is still used by ARC programs when this particular approach will yield the best results for a given file. Any time you see a filename with an extension like .DQC (".DOC") you know that the file has been squeezed and must be unsqueezed before you can read or use it. The LUE220 program above will automatically unsqueeze any files that have been squeezed before being placed in the library, but it cannot deal with plain "squeezed" files. Note that "squeezing," "squashing," "crunching," and so on, all refer to different and specific file compression techniques.

HC   COM   3456
HC   DOC   2456

With this file and the technique it represents we go back even further into personal computer history. The "HC" here stands for "hex converter," and this particular program is an exceptionally good one.

Years ago, when XMODEM, Kermit, and other error-checking binary file transfer protocols were not as widespread, one technique that was used to send and receive binary (machine language) files, like those ending in .COM or .EXE, was to convert them into the Intel hexadecimal format and send them as text. (Hexadecimal numbers consist solely of the digits 0 through 9 and the letters A through F.) The number of bytes doubles when you do this, since each machine language byte is converted into two hexadecimal bytes. And no error-checking was involved. But at least you could get the file from point A to point B.

Once downloaded, the receiver had to convert the file back into machine language. This program goes both ways. You may never need it, but it is not quite an artifact, for even today we find ".HEX" files on BBSs and other online systems.

COMSTA   COM   17280

Written by T. H. Housh, Jr., "Communications Statistics" will tell you how many XMODEM blocks and how many minutes will be required to transmit one or more files at 300, 1200, and 2400 bits per second. When you key in the program name, the instructions will appear.

DPROTECT	**COM**	793
DPROTECT	**DOC**	4026

BOMBSQAD	**COM**	3072
BOMBSQAD	**DOC**	5209

"Drive(s) Protect" lets you tell the system to forbid any writing of any kind to one or more drives. Written by Gee M. Wong, this program will prevent "Trojan horse" programs and other nasties from wiping out files or from infecting your system with a virus or phage. None of these things can happen if the booby-trapped program can't get to your disk drives, and that is precisely what DPROTECT prevents.

Andy Hopkins's BOMBSQAD is a more sophisticated program. It can be set to monitor any or all disk activity (read, write, erase, format). When a request for disk access is made by a program, BOMBSQAD puts the system on hold and displays a window informing you of what the program has asked for. You can then either grant or deny permission. In our opinion, the entire Trojan horse problem has been overblown by the popular press, but should you ever have reason to be uncertain of a program you have downloaded from an unknown bulletin board, run DPROTECT or BOMBSQAD before running the suspect software.

CGCLOCK	**COM**	1648
FIXWS	**COM**	1536
MONOCLK2	**COM**	384
WAIT	**COM**	128
WAITUNTL	**COM**	512

These programs are described elsewhere in this book. We have included them here because they can be useful for communications sessions. When you are online, it can be nice to have a clock on the screen to remind you of the time you're spending, for example (CGCLOCK and MONOCLK2). You may also need a utility to remove high ASCII codes from documentation and other files you download that were created with WordStar (FIXWS). And, if you're not using ProComm's TEF program for automatic, timed execution of an online session, you may find that WAIT and WAITUNTIL can offer you similar features if incorporated in a batch file. Please note, however, that at this writing there are "0 bytes free" on the Communicator's Toolchest disk. Consequently, the five programs above may have to be removed to make room for other comm-related tools as they become available.

Recommended Programs

Glossbrenner's Choice:

IBM CommPack 5—GEnie Utilities and ZOO.EXE

ZOO150   EXE   46976
SEZ230   ZOO   7424

Just as an archive file extraction utility like PKXARC or ARCE is a sine qua non for bulletin boards and other commercial systems, a ZOO file extraction utility is essential to GEnie users. Written by Rahul Dhesi, ZOO.EXE simply offers another way of compressing and archiving files. From time to time there are online debates about which archiving approach is most effective, but we don't have to get into that here. All you need to know is that like files ending in .ARC on other systems, files ending in .ZOO in the GEnie IBM RT must be processed with the proper extraction facility before you will have anything to run or read. You will also find many .ARC files on GEnie, but ZOO is the RT's declared archiver of choice, and it has more ZOO files than any other system.

ZOO150.EXE is a self-extracting program. When you key in the program name and hit <Enter>, it will create five files, including the main ZOO program and its manual. SEZ230.ZOO contains the "self-extracting ZOO" program SEZ.EXE and its documentation. With this program, you can create your own self-extracting files like ZOO150.EXE.

XMODHLP   ZOO   3542

This archive contains the text file XMODEM.HLP. Written by Paul J. Homchick, host of the GEnie IBM RT, it offers some excellent tips for anyone having difficulty downloading files from GEnie using the XMODEM protocol.

G-PCFLE   ZOO   1731
GENICDF   ZOO   1498

These two ZOO archives contain files for importing the GEnie IBM RT's master lists of files into PC-FILE and File Express, respectively. (See the profile of GEnie in Chapter 7 for more information.) G-PCFILE contains everything you need, including a nice set of instructions, for bringing LIBFILES.DBF into Jim Button's shareware PC-File database program. PC-File has the ability to import databases created by dBASE III (.DBF).

File Express can import a variety of formats, but at this writing the dBASE III format is not one of them. Consequently there is no way to get LIBFILES.DBF into File Express without going through an intermediary program. However, it is the RT's policy to upload and store files summarizing the new programs that are added to the library each week. These files are always called LIBNEW.ARC, and they are in a "comma-delimited format" (CDF), and they *can* be imported into File-Express. GENICDF.ZOO contains the header, index, and other files File Express will need.

The main reason for bringing this information into a database program is to be able to use the program's search commands to locate programs meeting several criteria. We still feel, however, that converting the information to a straight text file and searching it with Vernon Buerg's LIST.COM is the fastest, most efficient approach.

SLF20   ZOO   35821

The name of this program translates as "search LIBFILES," but we feel the main benefit it offers is its ability to convert LIBFILES.DBF into a pure text file, in preparation for searching with LIST.COM. There are other programs on the system specifically designed to do this. But at this writing each puts the names and descriptions of each file in the library on a single, very long line, forcing you to constantly scroll from left to right when you are viewing the file with LIST.COM. The command to use with SLF20 is SLF /O:LIBFILES.TXT. The program will automatically look for LIBFILES.DBF on your disk, though you can also tell it to look for a different filename.

PC-VCO20   ZOO   223900

Usually when you move to the IBM RT on GEnie, something like this will appear as part of the greeting announcements:

```
------------------------------------------------------------------
          →Real-Time-Conference Schedule←
        Wednesdays at 21:00 EST, PC-VCO Conference
        Sundays at 21:30 EST, General Meeting
        Be sure to bring your FACE on Wednesdays!
```

The program PC-VCO.EXE and several support files are what you will need to "bring your FACE" to the meeting. Written by R. Scott McGinnis (TARTAN on GEnie and PeopleLink), PC-VCO is the "PC Visual COnferencing" system. The package contains a module that lets you draw up to nine versions of your "face" (happy, sad, bored, and so on) and store them in a special file. You then upload that file to GEnie or some other system and tell your friends that it is there. Other subscribers can download your face file and save it in their own VCO library. Faces are keyed to a person's conferencing or CB handle or user name, and you must be using the special PC-VCO communications module for them to appear. You must also have a color graphics adaptor or compatible.

But appear they do, should you ever be in a conference with someone whose face you have on file. All real-time conferencing systems automatically display your handle each time you enter a comment. As soon as PC-VCO sees one of these handles, it searches its library and displays the corresponding face on your screen. If the person wishes to change the expression of his or her face on the screens of all other PC-VCO users—usually in reaction to what is being said in conference—he issues a special command. Your system sees that command and automatically fetches the appropriate face from the nine expressions of his face available in your face library.

The graphics aren't great on the PC, but certainly PC-VCO makes real-time conferencing more exciting. You can also send and receive sounds (horn blasts, buzzers, or chirps, for example), and you can hook up a voice synthesizer if you like. You can even exchange faces with Macintosh users.

There are VCO enthusiasts on all systems, but they tend to be quite active on GEnie. PC-VCO is shareware with a requested contribution of $35. For more information, contact: CABER Software, R. Scott McGinnis, P.O. Box 3607, Merchandise Mart, Chicago, IL 60654-0607.

Conclusion

In 1982, searching for a compact way to refer to the online world, we came up with the term "the electronic universe." It certainly is compact, and it is vague enough to stand for anything you say it stands for, an ideal situation for a writer. At this point you know about the electronic side, and you know about the multitude of PD and shareware programs that are available online. But you have only glimpsed the universe.

Most computer users don't have any idea of the power resting in their own fingertips. Imagine being able to obtain the information you need about any subject at any time of day from any location on the face of the earth simply by dialing the phone. Imagine meeting, conversing, and sharing ideas, problems, solutions, and friendship with scores of people all over the country and all over the world, people you may never see in person but would never have met any other way. Imagine being able to send and receive national and international Telex and TWX messages from your PC, or being able to put a paper copy of a letter on someone's desk within four hours of its creation, regardless of your respective locations, without using a facsimile machine. Or for that matter, imagine using your PC as a FAX machine.

All of these things can be and are being done today, thanks to personal computer communications. But you'll never find out about them, let alone benefit from all they have to offer, if you don't go online. Buy someone else's books if you like, but do it. We promise you, your life will be the richer for it.

APPENDIX A

GAMES, GRAPHICS, MUSIC, AND
EDUCATIONAL SOFTWARE

Free software is truly a never-ending story. There are excellent shareware programs and programs in the public domain for virtually every personal computer application. However, one must draw the line somewhere. In this book we have chosen to concentrate primarily on productivity software, since that is what most PC users most need. Yet we would be remiss if we didn't also show you the lighter side.

As we said at the very beginning of the book, a computer program is a creative work. So it isn't surprising that some programmers choose to express their creativity and inventiveness in programs whose sole purpose is your pleasure. Nor is it surprising that others have chosen to produce graphics and music programs designed to serve as tools for freeing your own creative impulses. Still others have combined programming and pedagogic skills to produce software designed to delight and instruct.

In this appendix we will identify and introduce you to what we feel are the best games, graphics, music, and education-related programs. As with all of the software featured in this book, these programs are readily available from many public-domain and shareware sources, as well as on Glossbrenner's Choice disks.

Tips and Tricks

As you cruise the oceans of free software, you will find that many of the available games, music, and educational programs are written in

BASIC. You certainly don't have to know BASIC yourself to run these programs, but there are a few tips and tricks that can make things easier. For example, although both BASIC.COM and BASICA.COM are supplied with your DOS package, there is no reason to use the former. Consequently, you will probably want to leave BASICA.COM on your working disk but remove BASIC.COM. You may want to rename BASICA.COM BASIC.COM or even B.COM for added convenience.

You should also be aware that you can run any BASIC program directly from DOS by keying in: BASIC FILENAME. You do not need to run BASIC, LOAD filename.bas, and RUN it. Nor do you need to key in the .BAS filename extension. You can stop almost any BASIC program by keying in [<Crtl><BREAK>]. This will return you to the BASIC interpreter, from which you can return to DOS by keying in SYSTEM.

There are several other key commands as well, and each of them is explained in more detail in your BASIC manual:

- SCREEN 0—This command will return the screen to text mode from medium or high-resolution graphics mode. If you return to DOS and find that the screen is in 40-column, large-character mode, make sure that the DOS program MODE.COM is available, then key in MODE 80 to restore an 80-column display.

- COLOR n,n,n—Use this command when you are in the BASIC interpreter to restore the screen's color to your preferred foreground, background, and border colors. COLOR 2,0,0, for example, sets the screen to a green foreground with black background and foreground. If you find that a program puts you into DOS without restoring your default colors, use COLOR.COM, one of the utilities discussed in Chapter 10 to restore DOS screen colors without rebooting or returning to BASIC.

- FILES—This is BASIC's equivalent of DOS's DIR command.

- RUN "filename—Note that no closing quotation mark is needed. Use this command to load and run a program with a single command. You might also want to use BASMENU.BAS, a program discussed in Chapter 10, to run all BASIC programs on a disk or in a subdirectory from a master menu.

- SAVE "filename.ext",A—Saves a BASIC program in ASCII (text) format, as discussed in Chapter 2. This is useful should you ever want to print or edit a program with a word processor.

Some programs, particularly some game programs, require the lines BUFFERS = 10 and FILES = 10 to be in your CONFIG.SYS file. The numbers in both cases can be higher if you like. The important thing is that you have a CONFIG.SYS file on your boot disk or in your root directory containing lines like these. See your DOS manual for details.

Finally, many game and music programs are written to run at 4.77 megahertz, the speed of a standard PC or PC/XT. If you are using a PC/AT or compatible or some other machine that runs faster than 4.77 megahertz, you may find that some game and music programs are unusable unless you clock down to 4.77. If your particular computer does not have an actual switch to do this, you may want to use one of the speed adjusting programs on Glossbrenner's Choice IBM Games Disk 8 to accomplish the same thing.

Games

Recommended Programs

Glossbrenner's Choice:

IBM Games Disk 1—Adventure/Cavequest/Castle

Adventure

Adventure is both the quintessence and the progenitor of all personal computer games. Created in the mid-1970s by Will Crowther of MIT and Don Woods of the Stanford Artificial Intelligence Laboratory (SAIL), the program originally ran on a DEC PDP-10, a popular minicomputer of the era. It quickly spread through the computer underground, and when personal computers were invented, it quite naturally spread to them as well. Indeed, one of the very first programs Microsoft made available in 1981 for the new IBM/PC was Adventure.

The game is text-based and, as one might expect given the artificial intelligence background of its creators, it consists of a dialogue between you and your machine. Like a good radio drama, the action and images occur in your head, not on the screen. Thematically, the game has its roots deep in Tolkien's Middle Earth. (Rooms at SAIL were named after Middle Earth locations, and the lab's printer reportedly was equipped to handle three different Elven typefaces.) There are dwarves and trolls and treasure, plus all manner of interesting, useful, and sometimes magical items to be encountered as you explore the Colossal Cave.

However, save for a single long paragraph that appears whenever you key in HELP, there are *no* instructions. This is deliberate, for part of the fun of Adventure is the joy of discovery. We have located and included on the disk a file of Adventure hints and solutions, but we urge you not to look at it unless you really get stuck.

It is easy to remember playing Adventure for the first time in 1981. Shortly after the game began, the computer reported, "You are in a 20-foot depression floored with bare dirt. Set into the dirt is a strong steel grate mounted in concrete. . . . The grate is locked." On a whim we keyed in, "ABRACADABRA." Without missing a beat, the PC came back with, "Good try, but that is an old, worn-out magic word." From that moment on, we were hooked.

Widely available through free software channels, the version of Adventure on this disk is the full implementation of the original game. The C source code was provided by J. R. Jaeger, with UNIX standardization by Jerry D. Pohl.

Cavequest

This shareware program requires a color graphics adaptor. Said to be similar to the commercial program Temple of Apshai, Cavequest is a fantasy and role-playing game in the tradition of Dungeons & Dragons (D&D). You start by creating your character, specifying the attributes you wish to have and stocking up on weapons, armor, and magic items. When you are ready to play, your character appears on the screen, and you move him or her through a partially revealed maze, using both commands and command keys to pursue your quest. A status screen listing your current state of restedness, potions, arrows, treasures, and so on appears on the right.

Castle

This shareware program uses character graphics and so can be played on either a CGA or monochrome system. The program can best be described as Adventure with graphics. You use your cursor keys to move your character through the rooms of a deserted castle, picking up treasures, fighting off ogres and other monsters, and escaping, you hope, with your booty. As you move from one room to the next, the computer displays text describing the room's location, contents, creatures (if any), and so on. You may also key in one- and two-word commands as you would in Adventure.

Recommended Programs

Glossbrenner's Choice:

IBM Games Disk 2—Bridge/Backgammon/Gin/Casino Games

Bridge

We have found two very good bridge programs. Turbo Bridge (TBRIDGE.COM, 63872 bytes) is a snappy contract bridge program written in Turbo Pascal. Bridge 3.1 (BRIDGE.BAS, 13260 bytes) offers both contract and duplicate bridge. Both support color, but since they use character graphics to display the cards, you can use a monochrome system as well.

Turbo Bridge is particularly impressive. You choose your position (north, south, east, or west) and opt to see both your opponents' and partner's cards or not. When the time comes to play, you can opt to play manually or let the computer go into "auto-play." The computer keeps track of the bids and handles the scorecard.

Though not designed as instructional programs (both assume you already know how to play bridge), TBRIDGE.COM and BRIDGE.BAS could be used as such if accompanied by a popular book on the subject.

Backgammon

This is SC-BACKGAMMON, version 2, a shareware program from Software Creations. There is no documentation file, but there is extensive online help describing how to play the game. The program supports color, but uses character graphics and so can be played on a monochrome system.

Gin

Written by J.B. Pontefract, GIN.EXE (19584 bytes) is certainly one of the best gin rummy games ever. Color and monochrome are both supported. There is an online help function, and a nice documentation file. You can opt to play Hollywood or Oklahoma versions of the game. Either way, you indicate the cards you want to play by moving your cursor and tell the system what you want to do with your function keys. This is very nicely done.

Casino Games

This is the heading under which we have placed the best blackjack (color and black-and-white versions), craps, poker, and solitaire games. All of these games are in BASIC and thus can be modified to suit, should the need arise. We particularly like Michael E. Lind's "Buck Mann's Poker for One" and Patrick Leabo's blackjack games, both for their execution and the humorous comments made by the computer-dealer. The poker game will even send you to a loan shark should you run out of money, and it keeps track of your account so you can pick up where you left off the next time you play.

Recommended Programs

Glossbrenner's Choice:

IBM Games Disk 3—Chess/Sleuth/Norland Hangman

Chess

EPCHESS (CGA required; shareware) by Mike Carpino is enormously impressive. You can play against the computer or against another player and can save up to twenty-six partially completed games to disk for later play. A complete history of all or part of any saved game is also available for review. In addition, you can set the board up to reflect any chess situation and start from that point. There are four levels of play, which you can change in the midst of a game if you like, as well as a four-move look-ahead feature. Castling, en passant, draw, stalemate, and pawn promotion are all supported. If you happen to have a joystick, the program will automatically recognize the fact and allow you to use it to move your pieces, thus saving you from having to key in FROM and TO coordinates. Timers for both players are displayed near the bottom of the screen. The documentation file, which we have cleaned up for easy printing, runs some eighteen pages.

Also on the disk is a program called CHESS88.EXE (9472 bytes) by Don Berg. This is a much more limited game, but its large CGA graphic pieces and the fact that you can move them with the cursor keys make it ideal for introducing a youngster to the game, or for playing a quick game yourself.

Sleuth and Norland Hangman

We have grouped our discussion of these two programs together, because both are shareware from Eric N. Miller of Norland Software. Both are absolutely top-drawer. Sleuth is rather like a combination of the board game Clue, Adventure, and Castle (see above). "It is a dark and stormy night . . . and a murder has been committed," Sleuth begins. A schematic of the mansion in which the evil deed was done then appears. Your job is to move through the mansion with your cursor keys, examining evidence, questioning suspects, and searching for the murder weapon. When you think you have the answer, you assemble all of the suspects in a single room and reveal your solution. If you like, you can opt to give the characters the names of your close friends and relatives, or call them Colonel Mustard, Mr. Green, or whatever. The game is different every time you play.

Mr. Miller's hangman game is now officially called "Hangman for the Superintelligent." That is not perhaps the most felicitous of titles, but one can sympathize with the author's need to distinguish his product. There are scores, if not hundreds, of versions of this old standby in the free software channels, and their quality varies widely. Mr. Miller's program is the best we have ever seen, and as he has added even more improvements and variations, it has remained at the top of the list for years.

As the program begins, you are given the option of choosing one of several hangman games. Under the standard ("basic") option, the computer selects words for you to guess. Under the educational option, the computer gives you the definition of a word and asks you to guess it. "Literate Hangman" offers you a quotation and requires you to guess its author. "Personalized Hangman" lets you pick your own words and play with up to nine other players. In all cases you can opt for amateur or expert levels of play, and you can opt to make time a criterion or not in playing the game. The program's music and sound features can be toggled on or off.

French and Spanish versions are available from Norland Software, as is Customized Hangman to allow you to create your own lists of words and phrases. The Customized version supports English and most European languages. The registration fee/purchase price for each Norland hangman game is only $15. All of the Norland games support color, but none requires a graphics card.

Recommended Programs

Glossbrenner's Choice:

IBM Games Disk 4—"Trivial" Programs

"Trivial" Programs

There are three trivia type programs on this disk. One of the slickest is the Trivia Machine by Bob Perez. This shareware program supports both color and monochrome adaptors, automatically sensing which one you have when it loads in. It offers music, limited animation, a timer, and lots of interesting questions.

Tune Trivia by Jan Eglen and Bill Lanke (shareware) is also very professional. This program supports both video adaptors and can be played by up to six players. The program will play a song and give you up to 20 seconds to identify it. (Hit a key to stop the music and key in your guess.) The program will also, at your option, quiz you on popular music trivia and allow you to earn extra points for correct answers. (We had no idea that John Denver wrote the Peter, Paul and Mary hit "Leaving on a Jet Plane," for example.) The program stores its music in text files as BASIC PLAY data, and there is an entire module to guide you through adding your own songs (in BASIC) and trivia questions.

Finally, a program called "The Trivia Game" (TRIVIA.EXE, 24414 bytes) will display questions and monitor your answers for up to seven categories. The package comes with questions for astronomy, grab bag, science, Star Trek, Star Wars, television shows, and words. But you can add your own categories and questions as you please. The display is rather pedestrian, but the questions are tough and the option to customize the categories means you could use this game as an educational tool.

Recommended Programs

Glossbrenner's Choice:

IBM Games Disk 5—Hack/Spacewar

Hack

PC HACK (V. 3.6 at this writing) by Don Kneller is a display-oriented dungeons and dragons game similar in style to ROGUE, a game popular on UNIX systems. The original UNIX version was written by Jay Fenlason. This program is the full implementation, and it is designed to run on any MS-DOS system with the ANSI.SYS screen driver (supplied with DOS). By all accounts, HACK is as addictive as Adventure and has a substantial following in the computing community. Though you don't have to be a computer nut to play it, brand new users will need some help setting up the program and configuring its options.

Spacewar

Written by Bill Seiler, this shareware package includes versions for the CGA, the Hercules card, AT&T personal computers, and the PC jr. It is a nifty one- or two-person shoot 'em up and thus should properly be called an arcade game. (There wasn't room for it on the Arcade disk.) You can play against the computer, against a fellow human, or request that the computer control both space ships. The goal, of course, is to destroy your opponent's ship using photon torpedos. There are phasers, a cloaking device, variable speed impulse engines, hyper space, black holes, and planets to contend with. Parents will be pleased to note that there is an option to turn off the sound during play. The first time you encounter this game, we suggest that you activate the two robots by selecting <F3> and <F4>, then hit <F2> to watch the two ships battle it out automatically.

Glossbrenner's Choice:

IBM Games Disk 6—Eamon/DND

Eamon

Eamon is a text-based Adventure-like game with two important differences. First, the characters, monsters, orcs, elves, and other personalities, tend to talk to you directly. And second, you can design and implement your own adventures with the Eamon dungeon designer module and other files. All Eamon files are either BASIC or text files, so they are easy to modify or customize to your liking.

Eamon was originally written by Donald Brown for the Apple II, and it has gained quite a following in the Apple world. (There are scores of user-created Eamon adventures for Apple owners.) This version was converted from Applesoft BASIC into Microsoft BASIC by Jon Walker.

DND

This shareware package from R.O. Software (DND version 1.2:1 at this writing) is a fast-moving combination character graphic and text dungeon and dragons-style adventure. The graphics and screen presentation are not as good as those found in Cavequest—the program moves the dungeon pathways around your character as you "move" instead of actually moving the character—but then DND doesn't require a CGA either. In addition, DND seems to move a bit faster as a game. There are monsters, obstacles, and treasures to deal with at nearly every turn. At your option, you can enter The Cavern, Lamorte, Shvenk's Lair, Telengard, or The Warren.

Glossbrenner's Choice:

IBM Games Disk 7—Phrase Craze ('Wheel of Fortune')

Phrase Craze

This shareware program from Excelsior Systems is quite simply the best implementation of the TV game "Wheel of Fortune" available anywhere. It's got everything but Vanna White, which may actually be a plus by some lights. Up to five people may play the game, and you can use a monochrome, CGA, or PC jr system, since Phrase Craze automatically senses the kind of monitor connected to the computer. There is an option to add your own phrases if you like. Registered users can order an enhanced version of the program with even more power, flexibility, and phrases. One feature we particularly like is that the program tells you where the phrase came from and reproduces the quotation from which it was taken, if applicable.

Recommended Programs

Glossbrenner's Choice:

IBM Games Disk 8—Arcade/Pinball/Kids/Tools

ARCADE.ARC

This is an archive file containing what in our opinion are the very best arcade-style PC games at this writing. These include: BRICKS, a colorful, fast-moving "Break Out"-like game by Vincent Bly; JUMPJOE2, a five-level "Donkey Kong"-like game programmed by Kevin Bales, who also wrote Castle; SPACEVAD, a good version of "Space Invaders;" and FROGGER. We searched out the source code for FROGGER.EXE (HOPPER.BAS) and have included it as well, should you want to modify this popular game. Also included are "Target," a relatively simple but satisfying game that involves moving crosshairs around the screen and firing phasers to shoot down a fast-moving image of (gasp!) the starship *Enterprise*, and "Bouncing Babies," a game in which you move a fireman's net to catch diaper-clad babies jumping out of a burning building. Guaranteed to break the ice at parties.

In PARATROOPER, a very professional game by Greg Kuperberg, your job is to manipulate and fire a stationary anti-aircraft gun to shoot down planes and parachuting commandos. In SEAWOLF you are a submarine commander trying to torpedo a variety of ships. In METEOR you dodge falling meteors. "Bert and the Snake" by Bill Piazza is a very high-quality "Qbert"-like game in which you move a character up, down, and across a 3-D pyramid of blocks.

Finally, POKE MAN by Al J. Jimenez has got to be the best Pac-Man–style game in the free software world. It can be played on any style screen, and you can choose among three available speeds of play. The program does not support a joystick, but with your right hand nestled into the numeric keypad, you won't need one. The only drawback is that there is no file explaining how to play the game. That may not have been necessary at the height of Pac-Man fever, when the game was created, but even now it is difficult to recall the significance of all those little dots, energy pellets, and ghosts.

Kids and Pinball

These are two archive files containing an assortment of games for the young and young at heart. PINBALL includes two compiled programs created with Bill Budge's Pinball Construction Set (CGA required). The games are MASTER BLASTER and RAIN, and both can be played by more than one player. You may use a joystick or simply use the two <Shift> keys on your keyboard to work the flippers and launch balls. Use the <Esc> key to exit.

In the KIDS archive we have placed 3-D Tic-Tac-Toe, Grinch, Match, and Tick. The first program lets you play Tic-Tac-Toe in three dimensions. In Grinch, the object is to find the Grinch hiding in the beanfield. After each guess the Grinch chirps, and the length of the chirp tells you how close you are. Match is a PC version of the television show "Concentration." And TICK.BAS will turn your PC into a very expensive large-letter digital alarm clock. It ticks away the seconds and plays the Westminster chimes on the hour, but you can turn off the sound if you like.

TOOLS.ARC

This is an archive file containing a collection of programs we think you will find especially helpful when playing games, or music for that matter. One of the most useful is BASMENU.BAS, a program that will automatically scan the disk or subdirectory in which it is located for every file ending in .BAS. It will then present these files to you on a menu, allowing you to run them by keying in a single selection number.

We have often used BASMENU to prepare a package of BASIC files for new users. The trick is to include a line in each of the .BAS files reading CHAIN "BASMENU." This way, when the user exits a given program, he or she is automatically returned to the BASMENU menu.

SAVEBASE.COM, UN-NEW.DOC, UNPROT.DOC, and UN.P are likely to be of greatest interest to new BASIC programmers. The first file will recover a BASIC program that you forgot to save before returning to the system. The second will show you how to recover a BASIC program after you have keyed in NEW. And the third and fourth files are for use in unprotecting a BASIC program that has been saved with the P option.

Also included are SILENCE.COM and COLOR.COM and .DOC, two of the top utilities discussed in Chapter 10. SILENCE.COM will keep the speaker quiet when you (or your kids) are playing games. COLOR.COM can be used to restore the screen to your preferred colors, should a program fail to do so.

Finally, if your computer runs faster than 4.77 megahertz, you will be interested in VARISLOW.COM and DELAY.COM. Written by Ray Usher, VARISLOW is the better of the two. The assembler source code for both is included, should you wish to make modifications. When you load VARISLOW, you are informed that pressing the left shift key slows the system down, while pressing the right shift key speeds it up. Pressing both simultaneously restores the system to its normal default speed. The more times you press the left shift key, the slower the system runs.

We suggest that you experiment with a pinball or other speed-sensitive game. Then use FAKEY, the keystroke-issuing program discussed in Chapter 10, and a batch file to load and adjust VARISLOW and load and run your chosen game automatically.

Recommended Programs

Glossbrenner's Choice:

IBM Games Disk 9—The Best 'Star Trek' Games

Like Adventure, Star Trek began as an underground mainframe computer game, the kind of program you load into memory and play only when you're sure the boss isn't around. "Trek" quickly made the transition to the micro world when PCs became available, and today there are scores of versions. All follow essentially the same scenario: You are captain of a Federation starship charged with destroying Klingons and the occasional Romulan, should one chance to venture across the Neutral Zone. Shields, phasers, photon torpedoes, warp speed, and impulse power all come into play as you cruise from quadrant to quadrant daring boldly to split infinitives no man has split before.

We have run dozens of Trek-like games and the four that can be found on this disk are, in our opinion, the very best. The program that is most faithful to the original version is Larry Jordan's Galaxy Trek (version 2.1), also referred to as "TREKRUN."

The left quarter of the top half of the screen in Galaxy Trek contains a short range scan of your position. The second quarter contains a compass rose showing directions as numerical coordinates and a status readout containing information on your current sector and quadrant coordinates, photon torpedoes, force field (shields), and available energy units. At the very bottom of the screen is a horizontal list of available commands (at lower levels of difficulty). Your ship, Klingons, starbases, and other items are represented by character graphics in the short-range scan screen. When you enter a navigational command, the elements of the screen are rearranged to reflect your new position.

PC-TREK, a shareware BASIC program by Birk Binnard devotes two-thirds of the screen to the "Star Sector Scanner." The left third of the screen shows, via horizontal bars, the current status of your phasers, impulse, warp engine, and other characteristics. This program uses character graphics too, but here the elements automatically move around the screen, as does the "E" representing the *Enterprise* when you boost it into action. PC-TREK thus uses "movies" where Galaxy Trek presents a series of snapshots.

Graphics

Recommended Programs

Glossbrenner's Choice:

IBM Graphics Disk 1—PC-Key Draw/PC-Foil

PC-KEY DRAW (PCKD)

Written by Edward H. Kidera IV, PC-KEY DRAW is a commercial quality drawing, graphics editing, and computer-aided design (CAD) program of amazing power. In addition to drawing a specified geometrical shape automatically, once you give it the necessary points on the screen, the program supports shading, spray painting, smears, replication, variable-size paint brushes, object and full-screen bidirectional zooms, rotation by color or by object, grid points at any spacing, isometric mode, and calculations. There is also a slide-show feature to create continuously running presentations of your images. Indeed, the demonstration slide show Mr. Kidera includes with his package must be seen to be believed. You'll think you're running a color Macintosh. There is much, much more to the program than we can go into here. Suffice it to say that Mr. Kidera is an engineer and his wife is an architect and artist, and both regularly use PCKD in their professional work. You'll need a CGA for this shareware program. And, despite its name, the program includes support for a mouse.

PC-FOIL by Don Logan and Wally Anderson is a shareware program for producing overhead transparencies ("foils"). The program must be used with a dot matrix graphics printer and is capable of producing letters of seven different sizes, ranging from very small to half-inch-tall letters. The program also draws boxes and supports emphasized print and underlining. As the documentation points out, PC-FOIL can also be used to produce computer documentation, manuals, and other publications requiring large headlines, boxed text, and other fancy printing features.

<hr>

Recommended Programs

Glossbrenner's Choice:

IBM Graphics Disk 2—PC Picture Graphics/PC-Present/Designs

PC Picture Graphics (PCPG)

PC Picture Graphics is a shareware program (CGA required) from Eugene Ying. Like PC KEY DRAW, PCPG is a completely professional program with extensive capabilities. However, while both programs can be used for business or for pleasure, in our opinion, it is somewhat easier to get started with PCPG, and the program is instantly fun to use. Consequently PCPG is the program we would recommend for someone who wants quickly to get his or her feet wet drawing on a PC's screen.

Without question, one of the features that allows PCPG to offer immediate gratification is the collection of more than 200 images Mr. Ying has prepared and included in his package. These range from all manner of birds, fish, and other animals to everyday items and images like a screwdriver, an airplane, a caduceus, the signs of the zodiac, and so on. These pictures can be combined and moved about on the screen, colored, enhanced with text, and reduced or expanded to one of three sizes. And of course, you can create your own images and add them to the libraries on the disk.

PC-Present

This program from SML Services of Atlanta, Georgia, is a shareware product (CGA required) that can best be described as a faithful clone of the commercial PC Storyboard package ($275 list). PC-Present is designed to put on a super slide show. You can create your images using PCKD, PCPG, or some other graphics program and save them in the BASIC BSAVE format. Or you can use the program's "camera" mode to take a snapshot of any screen created by any program. You can then edit your slides (change colors, invert graphic images, and so on) and assemble your "slide tray."

The next step is to prepare a script designating the slide, the length of time it should remain on the screen, and one of twelve types of dissolves (replace, fade in, pull down, sweep, etc.). You may choose to have the slides displayed in automatic, self-repeating mode, or you may choose to operate the machine like a conventional slide projector, clicking forward and backward through the "tray" at will. The package includes a nifty demonstration program that will show you PC-PRESENT's very impressive capabilities.

Designs

DESIGNS.BAS was coded by Marty Smith, based on routines that originally appeared in *80-Micro* magazine. A CGA board or compatible is required. The program presents you with a menu of over twenty patterns or designs, including spirals, moiré patterns, rotating squares, and a four-leaf rose. All of these designs are based on geometric formulas. You can control color selection and intensity, and you can put the program on automatic pilot so that it will continuously draw and display different patterns.

Recommended Programs

Glossbrenner's Choice:

IBM Graphics Disk 3—HI-res Rainbow

HI-res Rainbow

This is a full-featured shareware paint package from Orlando and David Rivera. The program includes pull-down windows, icons, multiple device inputs (joysticks, mice, keyboards, drawing tablets), rays, zooms, spray paint, smear, and screen swap. Perhaps most remarkable of all, the program offers 640-by-200 pixel high resolution with four colors, plus twelve color combination patterns that create the impression of additional colors. Just as color printing uses only four colors of ink but varies the size and mixture of the tiny dots of ink that appear on the page, Hi-res Rainbow uses four pixel colors but varies their apparent size and mixture to create the impression of more colors than your CGA card is capable of producing. Indeed, the authors of the program bill their package as "the first software alternative to the EGA (Enhanced Graphics Adaptor) card."

In our opinion this package could use a little more polish and more and better documentation. However, HI-res Rainbow is not difficult to use and it is an awful lot of fun. Its authors have told us that they are working to smooth out the few remaining rough edges.

Music

Recommended Programs
_____

Glossbrenner's Choice:

IBM Music Disk 1—Neil Rubenking's PIANOMAN Package

IBM Music Disk 2—The Best Ready-to-Play Music Selections

Pianoman

There are several music composition programs in the free software world, but Neil Rubenking's Pianoman is head and shoulders above the rest. This shareware program turns your PC into an electronic piano keyboard. You can change octaves, toggle legato on and off, control pitch, adjust tempo, transcribe, compose, record, and edit music till your ear's content. The version current at this writing (version 4.0) requires a machine that is compatible enough to run IBM PC-DOS. The author reports that it runs on some PS/2 systems, but not all configurations.

Ready-to-Play Music

Mr. Rubenking's package includes a program to convert Pianoman .MUS files into .COM programs that can be run directly from DOS. This program is called Player Piano, and many free software contributors have taken advantage of this fact to create and make available scores of tunes for you to play. Others have transcribed programs into BASIC and either compiled the results into .EXE files or simply provided BASIC programs for you to run.

The results are truly amazing. Some music programs are so good that it is difficult to believe IBM PCs and compatibles really have only one "voice" and can play only one note at a time. Selections range from Bach to Happy Birthday, from Brahms to Gilbert and Sullivan. There are also a number of Christmas carol packages designed to play continuously several favorite songs of the season. We've collected what we feel are the very best ready-to-play musical offerings in the public domain and packed them onto Glossbrenner's Choice IBM Music Disk 2. You may want to incorporate some of these compositions into your own programs or you may simply want to sit back and listen. Either way, in this case at least, hearing is believing.

Education

Glossbrenner's Choice:

IBM Education Disk 1—Amy/Alphabet/Animals/Teachtot/WPK

Amy's First Primer

Amy's First Primer is probably the most remarkable shareware education program ever created for the PC. As the Introduction to the documentation points out

> Programs for young children are hard to find. They must be extremely simple to use, very colorful and attractive, and they need to be fun and free of negative rewards. Our own five-year-old, Amy, wouldn't spend five minutes with the programs her older brothers enjoyed. She didn't like the idea of destroying things or being destroyed. In addition to being frustrated with the family computer, Amy's birthday came on September 8, forcing her to wait almost a year longer than some of her friends before going to kindergarten.

> Amy's First Primer was written by her father and brothers to help her work on the things her kindergarten friends were doing. After much testing and reprogramming, the programs finally met Amy's full approval. We think your child will approve, too.

The authors, Rob, Garth, and John Robinson of Orange City, Iowa, have provided six truly delightful programs designed to give a child a head start with the alphabet, numbers, counting, shapes, matching, problem solving, and pattern recognition. Amy's First Primer is worth many times the requested $10 shareware registration fee. This disk also includes a version of the program designed for PC jr users.

Alphabet, Animals, Teachtot, and WPK

Alphabet makes clever use of music and graphics to teach the alphabet to young children. Animals teaches simple counting, number sequences, addition, and subtraction using nicely detailed animal drawings and music. Teachtot uses music and guessing games to teach numbers, letters, and shapes. WPK stands for "Word Processing for Kids," a shareware program by Sidney D. Nolte. WPK uses very large letters and command icons to make word processing both fun and accessible to a young audience.

Recommended Programs

Glossbrenner's Choice:

IBM Education Disk 2—Math Tutor/Funnels/Flash Cards/Polyglot

Math Tutor is designed to drill and test students on the math skills needed to attain a passing level in grades 1 through 6. You are asked to specify your grade at the start of the program. Everything from simple addition to mixed fractions and ratios is covered.

Funnels is an enjoyable time-sensitive game designed to drill on arithmetic questions. An equation falls from the top of the screen, and you must key in your answer before it hits the bucket at the bottom to earn points. The Flash Card Maker lets you create, edit, and drill with your own on-screen flash cards. You can opt to have the program use either side of the card as the test question.

Polyglot, a shareware learning tool by Harrison P. Lantz, is a highly adaptable program that can be used to create multiple-choice quizzes on virtually any subject. As supplied, the program includes a variety of vocabulary drills as well as a "fill in the blanks" quiz. There are no instructions on how to create your own quizzes, but the technique is easy to figure out. You need only use one of the supplied quiz files as a template and key in your own questions and answers with a word processor. The disk also includes a program to print a calendar for any month of any year and one to teach a child how to tell time.

Recommended Programs

Glossbrenner's Choice:

IBM Education Disk 3—The Language Teacher
(French, German, Italian, and Spanish)

The Language Teacher was originally sold commercially by Acorn Software Products, Inc. For each language (French, German, Italian, and Spanish), the program offers drills and tests in vocabulary (typically 800 or more words), phrase translation (150 to 200 phrases), and verb conjugation (1600 to 2000 verb conjugations). You can opt for language-to-

English or vice versa (which means non-English speakers can use it to learn English), select either multiple-choice or fill-in tests (and ask to be retested on your misses), print out such tests for distribution to a class, and more.

This is an excellent program to sharpen your skills and expand your foreign-language vocabulary. Though not specifically designed for customization, there is no reason why a user could not create his or her own drills, since all the data is stored in text files.

Appendix B

ORDER FORM
GLOSSBRENNER'S CHOICE DISKS

Glossbrenner's Choice Disks

Name: _____

Address: _____

_____

City: _____ State: _____ ZIP: _____

[Please PRINT.]

Number of disks		Totals
_____	5.25-inch floppies × $5 =	_____
_____	3.5-inch diskettes × $6 =	_____
	Shipping and handling:	$2.00
	TOTAL Enclosed:	_____

Instructions:

1. Photocopy the order form.

2. *Print* your address information above.

3. Check off the disks you want on the list below.

513

4. Total the checkmarks and multiply by $5 for 5.25-inch floppies, or by $6 for 3.5-inch diskettes. Add $2 for shipping.

5. Make check payable to FireCrystal Communications and mail to:

> Glossbrenner's Choice
> FireCrystal Communications
> 699 River Road
> Yardley, PA 19067

Note: If you like and regularly use a shareware program, please be sure to send its author the requested registration fee. Prices and contents of disk are subject to change without notice. All orders must be *pre-paid* with U.S. funds drawn on a U.S. bank.

(Chapter 2)
_____ IBM Hercules/CGA Emulators

(Chapter 8—Bulletin Board Software)
_____ IBM RBBS-1—RBBS-PC Program Disk
_____ IBM RBBS-2—RBBS-PC Support Files
_____ IBM RBBS-3—RBBS-PC Source Code
_____ IBM Wildcat Disk 1—Wildcat BBS Package (1 of 2)
_____ IBM Wildcat Disk 2—Wildcat BBS Package (2 of 2)
_____ IBM Minihost—Minihost BBS Package

(Chapter 9—The Core Collection)
_____ IBM Core Collection Disk 1—FANSI Prog./CED/LIST
_____ IBM Core Collection Disk 2—FANSI Doc./PC-DeskTeam/PC-Window
_____ IBM Core Collection Disk 3—PMK Utilities/DIREDIT
_____ IBM Core Collection Disk 4—QFILER and Associates
_____ IBM Core Collection Disk 5—Newkey 4.0 and 3.0
_____ IBM Core Collection Disk 6—Automenu/EBL

(Chapters 10 and 11—Top Utilities and System Tweakers)
_____ IBM Top Utilities Disk 1—Quick Shots
_____ IBM Top Utilities Disk 2—Larger Programs
_____ IBM Top Utilities Disk 3—Disk Labeling

(Chapter 12—Word Processing and Text Utilities)

_____IBM PC-Write Disk 1—Program Disk (1 of 2)

_____IBM PC-Write Disk 2—Utilities Disk (2 of 2)

_____IBM Text Treaters Disk 1—Utilities/Indexing/Style

_____IBM Idea Processing Disk 1—PC-Outline

_____IBM Typing Disk 1—PC-FASTYPE

_____IBM Encryption Disk 1—PC-CODE3/4 and The Confidant

(Chapter 13—Printer Programs)

_____IBM Printer Pack Disk 1—Printer Utilities

_____IBM Printer Pack Disk 2—Letter Quality/ImagePrint

_____IBM Printer Pack Disk 4—On-Side (sideways printing)

(Chapter 14—Database and Filing)

_____IBM File Express Disk 1—Program Disk (1 of 2)

_____IBM File Express Disk 2—Users Guide and Supplemental Programs (2 of 2)

_____IBM Business Graphics Disk 1—ExpressGraph

_____IBM Free Text Search Disk 1—AnyWord

(Chapter 15—Spreadsheets and Accounting)

_____IBM Spreadsheet Disk 1—As-Easy-As

_____IBM Accounting Disk 1—Jerry Medlin's Shareware Accounting Programs: GL/AP/AR/PR

_____IBM Business Graphics Disk 2—The Draftsman

(Chapter 16—Communications)

_____IBM CommPack 1—ProComm 2.4.2

_____IBM CommPack 2—ProComm Utilities

_____IBM CommPack 3—The Communicator's Toolchest

_____IBM CommPack 4—ProComm PLUS Test Drive

_____IBM CommPack 5—GEnie Utilities and ZOO.EXE

_____IBM CommPack 6—The AutoSIG Package

(Appendix A—Games, Graphics, Music, and Education)

Games

_____IBM Games Disk 1—Adventure/Cavequest/Castle

_____IBM Games Disk 2—Bridge/Backgammon/Gin/Casino Games

_____IBM Games Disk 3—Chess/Sleuth/Norland Hangman

_____IBM Games Disk 4—"Trivial" Programs

_____IBM Games Disk 5—Hack/Spacewar

_____IBM Games Disk 6—Eamon/DND

_____IBM Games Disk 7—Phrase Craze ('Wheel of Fortune')

_____IBM Games Disk 8—Arcade/Pinball/Kids/Tools

_____IBM Games Disk 9—The Best 'Star Trek' Games

_____IBM Games Disk 10—Empire et al.

Graphics

_____IBM Graphics Disk 1—PC-KEY DRAW/PC-Foil

_____IBM Graphics Disk 2—PC Picture Graphics/PC-Present

_____IBM Graphics Disk 3—HI-res Rainbow

Music

_____IBM Music Disk 1—Neil Rubenking's PIANOMAN Package

_____IBM Music Disk 2—The Best Ready-to-Play Music Selections

Education

_____IBM Education Disk 1—Amy/Alphabet/Animals/Teachtot/WPK

_____IBM Education Disk 2—Math Tutor/Funnels/Flash Cards

_____IBM Education Disk 3—The Language Teacher

ABOUT THE AUTHOR

Alfred Glossbrenner has been called "the Isaac Asimov of personal computing," a sobriquet that, while flattering, probably shouldn't be taken too seriously considering the disparity in the two writers' output: fourteen books of Glossbrenner's to the Good Doctor's hundreds (and still counting). Nevertheless, it is Mr. Glossbrenner's intent to build a foundation for the understanding of all things computer and to, in some small way, help bridge the gap between "the two cultures" of science and the humanities first identified by C. P. Snow in 1959.

Few images are more repellent than an eternity of human subservience to inhuman machines. Yet few scenarios are so easy to avoid, for nothing about computer hardware, online databases, telecommunications, or software (free or otherwise) is difficult to understand—once it has been explained properly. From there it is but a short step to making the machines work for *you* as you begin to sample the incredible power they place in your hands.

Mr. Glossbrenner preaches the gospel of computer power through computer understanding from a variety of pulpits, including articles and columns in leading computer magazines, lectures, books, and consulting projects for associations, Fortune 500 firms, and small businesses. Mr. Glossbrenner lives with his wife (and his computers) in a 1790s farmhouse on the Delaware River in Bucks County, Pennsylvania. His electronic mailboxes include 70065,745 on CompuServe and AGLOSSBRENNER on MCI Mail.

Index

519

Other bestsellers from Alfred Glossbrenner . . .

HOW TO LOOK IT UP ONLINE
496 pages, Appendices, Index.
$14.95 Paperback
• A Main Selection of the Macmillan
   Small Computer Book Club
• An Alternate Selection of the Library
   of Computer and Information Sciences

"A valuable handbook for professional information seekers or amateurs desiring to increase their knowledge of the vast online world."
                                        —*Booklist*

"Bravo!"

                                        —*ScholarNotes*

"Alfred Glossbrenner has done it again."
                                        —*Online Today*

"As Karl Malden might say: 'Don't go online without it.'"
                                        —*Louisville Courier-Journal*

"Readers familiar with Glossbrenner's erudite style will welcome his newest addition . . . The wealth of material is insightful . . . Great reading from cover to cover."
                                        —*Computer Book Review*

THE COMPLETE HANDBOOK TO PERSONAL COMPUTER
COMMUNICATIONS (Revised Edition)
546 pages, Resources, Glossary, Index.
$14.95 paperback

• A Main Selection of the Macmillan Small
   Computer Book Club
• A Book-of-the-Month Club/Science and Quality
   Paperback Book Club Alternate Selection

"An enjoyable book. Invaluable."

> —Bert I. Helfenstein,
> president and C.E.O.,
> *Source Telecomputing*
> *Corporation (The Source)*

"Alfred Glossbrenner is a master explainer. He really *does* deliver 'Everything You Need to Go Online with the World.'"

> —Ardell Taylor Flesson,
> *Graphnet, Inc.*

"Fills an enormous void. Personal computer users are really hungry for this kind of information."

> —Thomas B. Cross, director,
> *Cross Information*
> *Company*

"Clear, well-written, packed with useful information—it's an absolute must for computer owners everywhere."

> —Gary G. Reibsamen,
> vice-president and general
> manager,
> *NewsNet, Inc.*

"Not only is Glossbrenner's the best book to use with a personal computer, it may be the best reason to *buy* one."

> —David Elias, Inc.,
> *newsletter to investors*

"Unequivocally the most informative and best-written I have ever seen."

> —Norman Burnell, president,
> *Electronic Safety Products,*
> *Inc.*

To order these books, please use the coupon below.

Books are available in quantity for promotional or premium use. Write to Director of Special Sales, Patti Hughes, St. Martin's Press, 175 Fifth Avenue, New York, NY 10010, for information on discounts and terms, or call toll-free (800) 221-7945. In New York, call (212) 674-5151.

ST. MARTIN'S PRESS, INC.   CASH SALES DEPARTMENT
175 FIFTH AVE., NEW YORK NY 10010

Please send me: ____copy(ies) of HOW TO LOOK IT UP ONLINE by
       Alfred Glossbrenner @ $14.95 each*
     ____copy(ies) of THE COMPLETE HANDBOOK OF
       PERSONAL COMPUTER COMMUNICATIONS
       by Alfred Glossbrenner @ $14.95 each*
     ____copy(ies) of ALFRED GLOSSBRENNER'S
       MASTER GUIDE TO FREE SOFTWARE FOR
       IBMs AND COMPATIBLE COMPUTERS
       @ $18.95 each*

     *Plus $1.50 postage and handling for the first book and
     50¢ per copy for each additional book. I enclose a check
     or money order for $ _____

_____ Return coupon with check to:

Name (please print)

               St. Martin's Press
_____ Cash Sales Department
               175 Fifth Avenue
Address   New York NY 10010

_____

City   State   Zip